IET TELECOMMUNICATIONS SERIES 59

Dynamic Ad Hoc Networks

Other volumes in this series:

Dynamic Ad Hoc Networks

Edited by
Habib F. Rashvand and Han-Chieh Chao

The Institution of Engineering and Technology

Published by The Institution of Engineering and Technology, London, United Kingdom

The Institution of Engineering and Technology is registered as a Charity in England & Wales (no. 211014) and Scotland (no. SC038698).

© The Institution of Engineering and Technology 2013

First published 2013

The Institution of Engineering and Technology
Michael Faraday House
Six Hills Way, Stevenage
Herts, SG1 2AY, United Kingdom

www.theiet.org

British Library Cataloguing in Publication Data
A catalogue record for this product is available from the British Library

ISBN 978-1-84919-647-5 (hardback)
ISBN 978-1-84919-648-2 (PDF)

Typeset in India by MPS Limited
Printed in the UK by CPI Group (UK) Ltd, Croydon

Contents

List of figures

List of tables

Editors biography

 **Habib F. Rashvand** is a Chartered Engineer with a distinguished career working with a number of industries and academic institutions including Racal, Vodafone, Nokia and Cable & Wireless and Universities of Tehran, Zambia, Southampton, Reading, Portsmouth, Coventry, Magdeburg, Warwick and the Open University. His interests include innovation, engineering management, wireless sensor systems and distributed systems. He is the author of over 100 publications including two books: *Distributed Sensor Systems: Practice and Applications* (Wiley, 2012) and *Using Cross-Layer Techniques for Communication Systems: Techniques and Applications* (IGI Global, 2012).

 **Han-Chieh Chao** is a Professor at the Department Computer Science & Information Engineering and Electronic Engineering of National Ilan University, I-Lan, Taiwan (NIU). His research interests include high-speed networks, wireless networks, IPv6-based networks, digital creative arts, e-government and the digital divide. He has authored or co-authored four books and has published about 400 refereed professional research papers. He has completed more than 100 MSEE thesis students and four PhD students. Dr. Chao is the Editor-in-Chief for IET Networks, Journal of Internet Technology, International Journal of Internet Protocol Technology and International Journal of Ad hoc and Ubiquitous Computing. He is an IEEE senior member and a Fellow of IET.

Authors biography

Ivan Andonovic, an ITI Techmedia Professor of broadband networks, joined the Electronic and Electrical Engineering Department at the University of Strathclyde in 1985, following a three-year period as a Research Scientist at Barr & Stroud, responsible for the design, manufacture and test of guided wave devices for a variety of applications. His main interests centre on optical networks, photonic switching and routing, optical code division multiple access, wireless sensor networks and wireless ad hoc networking. He has edited two books and authored/co-authored five chapters in books and over 200 journal and conference papers. Presently, he holds the ITI Techmedia Sponsored Chair in Broadband Networks facilitating the interaction between fundamental research in communications technologies and digital media, and precompetitive development of technologies that will form the input to commercialization activities in Scotland. Professor Andonovic is a Fellow of the IET and holds Senior Member status in the IEEE.

V. S. Anitha received her Master's degree in Computer Science and Engineering from Indian Institute of Technology, Madras, in 1997 and PhD degree from National Institute of Technology Calicut in 2011. She is a Professor in the Department of Computer Science and Engineering, Govt. Engineering College, Wayanad, Kerala. Her research interests include ad hoc and sensor networks, network security, design and implementation of mobile ad hoc routing protocols, cloud computing and QoS management.

Mohammad Inayatullah Khan Babar received Master and Doctoral degrees from School of Engineering, George Washington University, Washington DC, USA, in 2001 and 2005. His primary doctoral research was based on issues in information retrieval and computer networks with special emphasis on mobile ad hoc networking. He completed his BSc Electrical Engineering from UET Peshawar in 1997. Due to his excellent academic credentials, he received Highest Educational Achievement National Award in 2000 from the President of Pakistan. With more than 40 publications in engineering and computing conferences and journals of international repute, he is also a member of ACM USA and IEEE USA and had the honour to chair a conference session at the

International ACM Conference in the US in 2004. Currently, he is working as Professor and Head of Department in the Department of Electrical Engineering, and also as a Director Operations of Information Service Centre, UET Peshawar, Pakistan.

Michael Taynnan de Albuquerque Olivera Barros was born in Campina Grande - PB, 1990. He has MSc in Computer Science at Federal University of Campina Grande and BTech in Telematics at the Federal Institute of Education, Science and Technology of Paraiba (IFPB) Campina Grande Campus. Lately, he joined the Telecommunications Software and System Group (TSSG) at Waterford Institute of Technology (WIT) as a PhD student. His experience concentrates on dynamic optical networks, vehicular ad hoc networks, routing, IP Traffic Classification and QoS-DiffServ Aware Networks. He is interested in nano networks, molecular communications and bio-inspired techniques.

Kai-Di Chang received his Master's degree from the Institute of Computer Science and Information Engineering at National I-Lan University, Taiwan, R.O.C. He is currently pursuing his PhD degree in Electrical Engineering at National Taiwan University of Science and Technology. His research interests include VoIP, IP multimedia subsystem, Internet of Things and network security.

Tsung-Hui Chang received a BS degree in Electrical Engineering and a PhD degree in Communications Engineering from the National Tsing Hua University (NTHU), Hsinchu, Taiwan, in 2003 and 2008. Since September 2012, he has been with the Department of Electronic and Computer Engineering, National Taiwan University of Science and Technology (NTUST), Taipei, Taiwan, as an Assistant Professor. Before joining NTUST, he held research positions with NTHU (2008–2011), and University of California, Davis, CA (2011–2012). He was also a visiting scholar of the University of Minnesota, Minneapolis, MN, USA, and the Chinese University of Hong Kong, Hong Kong. His research interests are in signal processing problems in wireless communications and smart grid, and convex optimisation methods and its applications.

Chi-Yuan Chen received his MS degree in Electrical Engineering from National Dong Hwa University, Hualien, Taiwan, in 2007. He is currently working towards a PhD degree in Electrical Engineering at National Dong Hwa University. He is a member of IEEE and ACM. His research interests include next generation networks, network security and quantum computing.

Chi-Tsun Cheng received a BEng and MSc degrees from the University of Hong Kong, Hong Kong, in 2004 and 2005, and a PhD degree from the Hong Kong Polytechnic University, Hong Kong, in 2009. He was a recipient of the Sir Edward Youde Memorial Fellowship during his studies. From 2009 to 2011, he was a Post-Doctoral Fellow with the Department of Electrical and Computer Engineering, the University of Calgary, Canada. He was involved in a GEOIDE project, which is supported by the Government of Canada through the Networks of Centers of Excellence Programs. From January 2012 to August 2012, he was a Post-Doctoral Fellow with the Department of Electronic and Information Engineering at the Hong Kong Polytechnic University, Hong Kong. Currently, he is a Research Assistant Professor at the same department. His research interests include wireless sensor networks, bio-inspired computing and meta-heuristic algorithms.

Chong-Yung Chi received a PhD degree in Electrical Engineering from the University of Southern California, Los Angeles, California, in 1983. He has served as a Technical Program Committee member for many IEEE sponsored and co-sponsored workshops, symposiums and conferences on signal processing and wireless communications, e.g., General Co-chairman of 2001 IEEE Workshop on Signal Processing Advances in Wireless Communications (SPAWC), and Co-chair of Signal Processing for Communications (SPC) Symposium, ChinaCOM 2008 & Lead Co-chair of SPC Symposium, ChinaCOM 2009. He is currently a Professor at National Tsing Hua University, Taiwan. He has published more than 200 technical papers, including more than 70 journal papers (mostly in *IEEE Transaction on Signal Processing*), two book chapters and more than 130 peer-reviewed conference papers, as well as a graduate-level textbook, *Blind Equalization and System Identification*, Springer-Verlag, 2006. His current research interests include signal processing for wireless communications, convex analysis and optimization for blind source separation, biomedical and hyperspectral image analysis.

Shan Chu received BS and MS degrees in Telecommunications Engineering from Zhejiang University, Hangzhou, China, and a PhD degree in Electrical Engineering from Stony Brook University, Stony Brook, New York. She is currently with Motorola Solutions, Holtsville, New York, USA. Her current research interests include MIMO and cooperative communications, ad hoc networks and cross-layer design.

Anderson Fabiano Batista Ferreira da Costa graduated in Telematics from the Federal Institute of Education, Science and Technology in 2004, and achieved Master and Doctor degrees from the Federal University of Pernambuco in 2005 and 2011. He is now a Professor at the Federal Institute of Education, Science and Technology of Paraiba. He has experience in computer science, with emphasis in computer networks, acting in the following themes: optical and vehicular networks, clustering methods and symbolic data analysis.

Jaafar Elmirghani is a Fellow of the IET and Fellow of the Institute of Physics. He is the Director of the Institute of Integrated Information Systems and Professor of Communication Networks and Systems within the School of Electronic and Electrical Engineering, University of Leeds, UK. He joined Leeds in 2007 having been chair in Optical Communications at the University of Wales Swansea, 2000–2007. He has published over 350 technical papers, co-edited *Photonic Switching Technology – Systems and Networks*, IEEE Press 1998, leads a number of research projects and has research interests in communication networks, wireless and optical communication systems.

Mahmood Fathy is an Associate Professor at the School of Computer Engineering, Iran University of Science and Technology. He received his BSc from Iran University of Science and Technology, Tehran, Iran, MSc from Bradford, UK, and PhD from UMIST, UK, in 1985, 1988 and 1991. Dr. Fathy's main research interests are wire/wireless networks, quality of service, computer architecture, image processing and intelligent transportation systems (ITS).

Wei Feng received his Bachelor degree from Nankai University in Tianjin in 2002, received his Master degree from University of Swansea in the UK in 2006, and received his PhD degree from University of Leeds in the UK in 2010. He worked as a post-doctor in Tsinghua University between 2010 and 2012, and he is currently working in China Center of Information and Industry Development (CCID). His current research is focused on sensor networks, ad hoc networks, energy efficiency and cyber security.

Hossein Ghaffarian is a PhD student at the School of Computer Engineering, Iran University of Science and Technology. He received his BSc from Shahid-Bahonar University of Kerman, Kerman, Iran, and his MSc from Iran University of Science and Technology, Tehran, Iran, in 2003 and 2007. Mr. Ghaffarian's main research interests are: wired and wireless networks, switching, quality of service, fuzzy controllers and intelligent transportation systems (ITS). In his PhD thesis, Mr. Ghaffarian works on VANET, traffic, mobility models and ITS.

Reinaldo Cézar de Morais Gomes graduated in Telematics at the Federal Institute of Education, Science and Technology of Paraiba in 2004, and achieved Master and Doctor degrees at Federal University of Pernambuco in 2005 and 2010. He is a researcher at Federal University of Pernambuco and Professor at Federal University of Campina Grande. He has experience in computer science, with emphasis in computer networks and distributed systems. He acts in the following themes: negotiation, self-configuration, dynamic networks, policies and inter-domain communication.

E. Hemmati was born in Semnan, Iran, in 1984. He received a BS degree in Electrical Engineering from Iran University of Science and Technology, Tehran, Iran, in 2007 and MS degree in Electrical Engineering from Islamic Azad University, Tehran, Iran, in 2010. He is currently a PhD student at Iran University of Science and Technology, Tehran, Iran. His research interests include communication and computer networks, intelligent systems and neural networks. He has published more than 10 papers in journals and international conferences.

Rutvij H. Jhaveri completed his Master's degree in Computer Engineering from Saradar Vallabhbhai National Institute of Technology, Surat, and Bachelor of Engineering from Birla Vishvakarma Mahavidyalaya, V.V. Nagar, India. Since 2002, he has worked as an Assistant Professor in SVM Institute of Technology, affiliated to Gujarat Technological University in India. He has numerous publications including those in IEEE Xplore, Springer digital library and renowned international journals. He is also a member of ISTE, IJACT and other technical organizations. His research interests include security issues in wireless networks and information technology management.

Shih-Wen Hsu received his MS degree in Electrical Engineering from National Dong Hwa University in 2011. He is currently pursuing his PhD degree in Computer Science at National Tsing Hua University. His research interests include IP multimedia subsystem, cognitive networks and cloud computing.

P. Venkata Krishna is Professor at School of Computing Science and Engineering, VIT University, Vellore, India. He received his BTech in Electronics and Communication Engineering from Sri Venkateswara University, Tirupathi, India, MTech in Computer Science & Engineering from REC, Calicut, India and his PhD from VIT University, Vellore, India. Dr. Krishna has several years of experience working in academia, research, teaching, consultancy, academic administration and project management roles. His current research interests include mobile and wireless systems, cross layer wireless network design, QoS and grid computing. He is the recipient of several academic and research awards such as the Cognizant Best Faculty Award for the year 2009–2010 and VIT Most Active Researcher Award for the year 2009–2010.

Francis C. M. Lau is a Professor and an Associate Head of the Department of Electronic and Information Engineering, The Hong Kong Polytechnic University, Hong Kong. He is a Fellow of IET and a Senior Member of IEEE. He is a co-author of *Chaos-Based Digital Communication Systems* and *Digital Communications with Chaos: Multiple Access Techniques and Performance Evaluation.* He is co-holder of three US patents, and one pending US patent. He has published over 230 research papers. His main research interests include channel coding, cooperative networks, wireless sensor networks, chaos-based digital communications, applications of complex-network theories and wireless communications. He has served as an associate editor for various international journals including *IEEE Transactions on Circuits and Systems I & II*, *IEEE Circuits and Systems Magazine*, *International Journal and Bifurcation and Chaos*. He is currently serving as the Chair of Technical Committee on Nonlinear Circuits and Systems, IEEE Circuits and Systems Society.

Ali Mahani received his PhD in Electrical Engineering from Iran University of Science and Technology (IUST) in 2009. Since then he has been with the Department of Electrical and Electronic Engineering of Shahid-Bahonar University, where he is currently an Assistant Professor. His interests focus on wireless networks, fault tolerant systems and testable design, and performance evaluation.

Sahibzada Ali Mahmud did his BSc in Electrical Engineering at the University of Engineering and Technology Peshawar. He was awarded a PhD scholarship and is associated with the Wireless Networks and Communications Centre at Brunel University, London, UK. He did his PhD in Wireless Communications and Networks in January 2010, and since worked as an Assistant Professor in Electrical Engineering Department of UET Peshawar. He is founder and Project Director of Centre for Intelligent Systems and Networks Research at UET Peshawar. His research interests include scheduling for real-time traffic, wireless sensor networks, intelligent transportation systems, smart grids communication, M2M communication and short-range wireless networks. He served as a TPC member for conferences like IEEE ICC, IEEE PIMRC and IEEE WCNC on several occasions, reviewing for IET Communications and IEEE Communication Letters. He has worked on various funded projects, and has published in various reputed journals and conferences.

Abbas Mohammadi received his BSc degree in Electrical Engineering from Tehran University, Iran, in 1988, and his MSc and PhD degrees in Electrical Engineering from the University of Saskatchewan, Canada, in 1995 and 1999. Since March 2000, he has been with the Electrical Engineering Department of Amirkabir University of Technology, Tehran, Iran, where he is currently a Professor. Abbas Mohammadi has been an ICORE visiting Professor in Electrical and Computer Engineering Department of the University of Calgary, Canada. He has published over 60 journal and 120 conference papers and holds three US patents. He has co-authored, *Six-port Technique with Microwave and Wireless Applications* (Artech House, 2009) and *RF Transceiver Design for MIMO Wireless Communications* (Springer, 2012). His current research interests include broadband wireless communications, adaptive modulation, MIMO systems, mesh and ad hoc networks, microwave and wireless subsystems, software design radio and direct conversion transceivers.

A. R. Naseer is Principal and Professor of Computer Science and Engineering at JITS and is affiliated to JNTU Hyderabad, India. He received his PhD in Computer Science and Engineering from IIT Delhi (1996) and MTech in Industrial Electronics from NITK Surathkal, India (1985). He has served as Chairman and as a member of several university boards and committees in India and abroad. He is recipient of IEEE Best Student Paper Award, Distinguished Teacher Award, Life-Time Achievement Award for Education, Asia Pacific International Award for Education Excellence at Tashkent, Indo-Nepal Unity Award, Gold Star Asia International Award for Education Excellence at Kathmandu Nepal, Bharat Shiksha Ratan Award, Mother Teresa Excellence Award, Rajiv Gandhi Excellence Award, Indira Gandhi Shiksha Shiromani Award and was included in Marquis Who's Who in the World 2013, USA. He is a member of IEEE Computer Society, Communications Society, USA, and life member of ISTE, CSI and VSI. His areas of research interests include security in WSN and MANET, data mining and warehousing, cryptography and network security, multi-core architectures, design automation and FPGA-based synthesis.

Roya E. Rezagah received BSc in Electrical Engineering from Sharif University of Technology, Tehran, Iran, in 2002, and MSc and PhD in Communications Systems from Amirkabir University of Technology in 2006 and 2011. She has joined several industrial projects as a researcher and system designer. Her research interests include wireless communications, ad hoc networks and next generation of cellular networks. Since 2011 she has been a researcher in the Electrical Engineering Department, Tokyo Institute of Technology, Tokyo, Japan, where she has been working on coordinated multipoint (CoMP) in cellular networks in close collaboration with mobile service providers.

Professor V. Saritha is with School of Computing Science and Engineering, VIT University, Vellore, India. She received her BTech in Electronics and Communication Engineering from Andhra University, Visakhapatnam, India and MTech in Computer Science and Engineering from VIT University, India. Her research interests include mobile and wireless systems and databases.

M. P. Sebastian received his Masters and PhD degrees in Computer Science from the Indian Institute of Science, Bangalore. His career includes service as a Scientist at Space Applications Centre (ISRO), Ahmedabad, at Bharat Electronics Ltd, Bangalore, and as Professor and Head of Computer Science at National Institute of Technology Calicut. His areas of teaching/research interests include enterprise cloud computing, enterprise resource computing, information security management, IT strategy, networks management and software project management.

Faisal K. Shaikh is an Associate Professor in the Department of Telecommunication Engineering, Mehran University of Engineering & Technology, Jamshoro, Pakistan. He received PhD in Computer Science from the Technische Universitât Darmstadt, Germany. Dr. Shaikh is investigating energy efficient communication protocols in wireless sensor networks (WSN) for mobile, ubiquitous and pervasive applications. He is interested in environmental monitoring, vehicular ad hoc networks, smart homes, telehealth (body area networks) and Internet of Things. He has published over 30-refereed journal, conference and workshop papers. His research is financially supported by grants and contracts including MUETRnD, ICTRnD and PSF. He is a member of PEC, IEEE and ACM.

M. Sheikhan was born in Tehran, Iran, in 1966. He received a BS degree in Electronic Engineering from Ferdowsi University, Meshed, Iran, in 1988 and MS and PhD degrees in Communication Engineering from Islamic Azad University, Tehran, Iran, in 1991 and 1997. He is currently an Associate Professor in Electrical Engineering Department of Islamic Azad University-South Tehran Branch. His research interests include computer and communication networks, intelligent systems, speech processing and neural networks. Dr. Sheikhan has published over 70 journal papers and about 60 conference papers. He has also published two books and was selected as the outstanding researcher of IAU in 2003, 2008, 2010 and 2011.

Farhan Siddiqui received a BE degree in Computer Science from Osmania University, India, in 2000, and MS and PhD degrees in Computer Science from Wayne State University, MI, USA, in 2003 and 2007. She was a full-time faculty member at

Bradley University, IL, USA during Fall 2008. Since March 2009, she has been a faculty member in the School of Information Systems and Technology at Walden University, MN, USA. Her research interests are in mobile and ubiquitous computing, home networking, voice over IP, security, quality of service and cloud computing.

Mohsen Soryani is an Assistant Professor at School of Computer Engineering, Iran University of Science and Technology. He received his BSc from Iran University of Science and Technology, Tehran, Iran, MSc from Heriot-Watt University, Edinburgh, Scotland, and PhD from Heriot-Watt University, Edinburgh, Scotland, in 1980, 1986 and 1989. Dr. Soryani's main research interests are computer architecture, image processing and intelligent transportation systems (ITS).

Yin Sun received a BEng degree and PhD degree in Electrical Engineering from Tsinghua University, Beijing, China, in 2006 and 2011. He received the Tsinghua University Outstanding Doctoral Dissertation Award. He is currently a Post-doctoral Researcher at the Ohio State University. His research interests include probability theory, optimisation, information theory and wireless communication.

Jesús Téllez is a System Engineer who graduated from the Central Technological University (UNITEC), Venezuela. He received his doctorate in Telematics Engineering from the Universitat Polit'ecnica de Catalunya, Spain. He is an Associate Professor at the Computer Science Department of the University of Carabobo, Venezuela. He has been serving as a Technical Program Committee member in some international conferences and his research interests include Internet security, performance evaluation of systems, mobile computing, mobile payment systems and vehicular ad hoc networks.

Alicia Triviño-Cabrera is Assistant Professor at the University of Málaga (Spain). Her thesis, which was defended in 2007, focused on mobile ad hoc networks connected to the Internet. An important workload of the thesis concerned the mathematical modelling of MANETs and the consequent optimization techniques to improve the integration of MANETs into the Internet. She has published several papers in prestigious journals and books concerning this subject. She has also an extensive experience on the review of research works on MANETs in international conferences and journals.

Chi K. Tse is a Chair Professor of Electronic Engineering at the Hong Kong Polytechnic University, Hong Kong. His research interests include nonlinear circuits and systems, power electronics, complex networks and communication systems. He serves and has served as Editor and Associate Editor for a number of international journals. He is a Fellow of the IEEE and a Fellow of the Institution of Engineers, Australia.

Fan-Hsun Tseng received his Master's degree from Institute of Computer Science and Information Engineering at National I-Lan University, Taiwan, R.O.C. He is currently pursuing his PhD degree in Computer Science & Information Engineering at National Central University. His research interests include network planning and cloud computing.

G. Varaprasad was born in Kamalapadu village (16 km from Guntaka, Andhra Pradesh, India) and obtained BTech degree in Computer Science and Engineering from Sri Venkateswara University, Tirupati, in 1999. He received MTech degree in Computer Science and Engineering from Visvesvaraya Technological University, Belgaum, in 2001, and then obtained PhD degree in Computer Science and Engineering from Anna University, Chennai, in 2004 under guidance of Dr. R. S. D. Wahidabanu. His PhD work was supported by University Grants Commission, New Delhi, India. In 2004, he joined Protocol Engineering Technology (PET) Lab, Department of Electrical Communication Engineering, Indian Institute of Science, Bangalore, as a Postdoctoral Fellow. Since 2005, he has been with B.M.S. College of Engineering, Bangalore, in Department of Computer Science and Engineering, where he is now Associate Professor under PG studies. In his credit, he has 50 journal publications, 41 conference publications and has two patents/copyrights (and five applied). He has authored three textbooks, is carrying four external funded R&D projects and has received seven awards.

Jing Wang received BS and MS degrees in Electronic Engineering from Tsinghua University, Beijing, China, in 1983 and 1986, respectively. He has been on the faculty of Tsinghua University since 1986. He currently is a Professor and the Vice Dean of the Tsinghua National Laboratory for Information Science and Technology. His research interests are in the area of wireless digital communications, including modulation, channel coding, multi-user detection and 2D RAKE receivers. He has published more than 100 conference and journal papers. He is a member of the Technical Group of China 3G Mobile Communication R&D Project. He serves as an expert of communication technology in the National 863 Program. He is also a member of the Radio Communication Committee of Chinese Institute of Communications and a senior member of the Chinese Institute of Electronics.

Xin Wang received a BS and MS degrees in Telecommunications Engineering and Wireless Communications Engineering from Beijing University of Posts and Telecommunications, Beijing, China, and a PhD degree in Electrical and Computer Engineering from Columbia University, New York. She is currently an Associate Professor in the Department of Electrical and Computer Engineering of the State University of New York at Stony Brook, New York. Her research interests include analysis and architecture design in wireless networks and communications, mobile and distributed computing, infrastructure design and performance enhancement across network layers, applications and heterogeneous networks, network and mobility management, QoS, signalling and control, as well as support for advanced network services and applications.

Yuanyuan Yang received a BEng and MS degrees in Computer Science and Engineering from Tsinghua University, Beijing, China, and the MSE and PhD degrees in Computer Science from Johns Hopkins University, Baltimore, Maryland. She is a Professor of Computer Engineering and Computer Science at Stony Brook University, New York, and the Director of Communications and Devices Division at New York State Center of Excellence in Wireless and Information Technology. Her research interests include wireless networks, optical networks, high-speed networks and parallel and distributed computing systems. She has published over 240 papers in major journals, refereed conference proceedings and holds six US patents. She is a Fellow of the IEEE and the IEEE Computer Society. More information about her and her research can be found at http://www.ece.sunysb.edu/~yang.

A. J. Yuste received his MSc degree in Telecommunication Engineering from the University of Malaga (Spain) in 1994, and his PhD degree in Telecommunication Engineering in 2012. Since 2003, he has been an Associate Professor with the Telecommunication Engineering department in Jaén University in Jaén (Spain). His current research interests include routing in ad hoc networks, grid computing and trace analysis of computer networks. He is also involved in research projects of the Spanish Ministry of Science and Education and projects involving private companies.

Mohammad Haseeb Zafar received a BSc degree (with Honours) in Electrical Engineering from the University of Engineering and Technology, Peshawar, Pakistan, in 1996, a MS degree in Telecommunications and Computers from the George Washington University, Washington DC, USA, in 2003 and a PhD degree in Wireless Mobile ad hoc Networks from the University of Strathclyde, Glasgow, UK, in 2009. From 2011 to 2012, he was a postdoctoral researcher at the University of Strathclyde, Glasgow, UK. He has more than 16 years of teaching, research and industrial experience and is currently an

Associate Professor in the Department of Computer Systems Engineering at the University of Engineering and Technology, Peshawar, Pakistan. His research interests include data communications, computer networks, wireless communications and mobile ad hoc, sensor and mesh networks. He has authored and co-authored many research papers in journals of international repute and has presented his research works at various international conferences.

 **Sherali Zeadally** is an Associate Professor in the Department of Computer Science and Information Technology at the University of the District of Columbia, Washington DC, USA. He received his Bachelor's degree and doctorate, both in Computer Science, from the University of Cambridge, UK and the University of Buckingham, UK, respectively. He is a Fellow of the British Computer Society and a Fellow of the Institution of Engineering and Technology, UK. His research interests include computer networks including wired and wireless networks, network and system security, mobile computing, ubiquitous computing, RFID, performance evaluation of systems and networks.

 **Lin Zhang** received all his degrees from Tsinghua University in Beijing (BSc '98, MSc '01, PhD '06) and is currently an Associate Professor at Tsinghua University and a Visiting Associate Professor at Stanford University. His current research focuses on wireless sensor networks, distributed data processing and information theory. He is a co-author of more than 40 peer-reviewed technical papers and has five US and Chinese patents applications. Lin and his team were also the winners of IEEE/ACM SenSys 2010 Best Demo Awards.

 **Xiaofeng Zhong** received his PhD degree in Information and Communication System from Tsinghua University in 2005. He has been the Assistant Professor in Dept. of Electronic Engineering of Tsinghua University, where he focuses on the MAC and Network protocol design and resource management optimisation for wireless ad hoc network, cooperation network and cognitive radio network. Dr. Zhong has published more than 30 papers and owns seven patents.

 **Shidong Zhou** is a Professor at Tsinghua University, China. He received his PhD degree in Communication and Information Systems from Tsinghua University in 1998. His BS and MS degrees in Wireless Communications were received from Southeast University, Nanjing, in 1991 and 1994. From 1999 to 2001 he was in charge of several projects in the China 3G Mobile Communication R&D Project. He is now a member of the China FuTURE Project. His research interests are in the area of wireless and mobile communications.

Preface

Some 50 years ago when the electrical communication systems were using truly unreliable links for their connections, the idea of ad hoc style networking would have been considered unthinkable. However, with the 1970s, new trends in interconnecting large computers and progressing towards a fully digitalized era put a heavy demand on developing centralized controllers and network management systems. In order to solve the emerging complexity problems of centralized systems, coincided with the rapidly expanding mass production of low-power high-speed programmable integratable devices, the idea of using distributed systems and open systems interconnected seemed the best solution. This approach resolved the critical problem of the ever-growing centralized controller from becoming too bulky, too risky and too complex. To that effect, employing a number of agile and high-performing functional nodes in distributed fashion will be helping with the growth as well as enabling the upcoming systems to have smoother service whilst being controlled for greater speed, accuracy and precision in support.

Generally speaking ad hoc networking indicates application-based unstructured communication configuration in two forms: (a) without using any underlying networking or making use of a highly flexible predetermined structure and (b) using a specially designed dynamic mechanism so that the application network is kept free from any dominating infrastructure's bottlenecks, normally imposed by the rigid disciplines set by underlying infrastructure. The latter group, if designed properly with minimum imposed interference, will give sufficient freedom to help the application systems benefit from effective features enabled by the underlying infrastructure.

Basically the most natural features of ad hoc networking is built upon its inherent dynamic connectivity, where some simple and relax routing or interconnecting mechanism frees application networking from any possible firm and rigid dominating networking complexities. That is, when we weaken the network from its traditional 'strong structure', as a result we have loosened up the control elements in the system. This can remove some of infrastructural dependencies over the required connectivity, which in turn enables the ad hoc networking to freely use its own reliable strategies to regain any lost controls due to the disappearance of intensive embedded controlling elements in the system. The firm-control has always been in the nature of traditional systems imposed by the centralized network management.

Under the ad hoc–based distributed systems, we can vision a whole new emerging distributed style of features that we have never experienced before. Features such as distributed intelligence, distributed security, distributed control and many more new and superior distributed application technologies can emerge that require a better understanding and pass over onto our new and younger researchers to take on board for future technological innovations. With the ever-growing capabilities of the information-communication technologies (ICT), there are always more choices and even more selectivity capabilities to develop new embedded superior applications in new forms of smart nodes at the user and service ends for more reliable and dependable connections, where many superior new scenario-based applications can be established using localized self-controlled agent-style processes than ever before. They can be used for controlling and monitoring systems using superlight, reliable and simple intelligent micro-controllers to maintain many sophisticated operations including effective inter-connections, reliable routings, fault-tolerant networking while maintaining the required quality, security and efficiency of the systems. The most interesting concept coming along with ad hoc networking is its strong networking association with emerging technologies in a very wide range of cases. These cases spreading all the way from lesser complex but very intelligent surveillance systems such as an intergalactic computer networking all the way up to massively distributed systems like cloud computing and heavily busy city road traffic control systems. In more complex systems the protocols, routing and other networking features can be easily split and then integrated into the application scenarios for higher performance. Among the leading technologies using ad hoc networking are new wireless-based systems where extensive gains can be achieved mostly due to the unique natural features of the wireless technology.

Although both ad hoc and dynamic processes, as a new concept, have been known to the engineering communities for a very long time. In practice, we should seek their real impacts emerging along with the dawn of mobile and wireless technologies in the 1990s. Typical examples are providing a dynamic style clustering of the mobile cells using ad hoc networking approach or devising Dynamic Source Routing in ad hoc style and using relaying-style Cluster-based Dynamic Source Routing in Wireless ad hoc Packet Radio Networks. With the turn of the century, we saw some earlier work that used ad hoc style relay-rich-networking technologies to develop towards the smart sensor application areas, called Wireless Sensor Networking (WSN).

Further developments towards enabling lightweight ad hoc in support of application-oriented interconnections using dependable unstructured overlay net-working started to arrive in the latter part of 2010. To mention a few research and development examples we have: mobile agents topology control, ant-based routing, urban vehicular networking, internationally spread P2P networking, mobile cloud computing, fault-tolerant and failure detection, delay-tolerant networking, adaptive and dynamic nodes selection, automatic topology update mechanisms, tracking in dynamic anchorless wireless networks, dynamic location management, building up the trust in mobile ad hoc and much more to improve various features of ad hoc networking for higher reliability, security, energy efficiency and application-specific optimized performance to bring in new approaches.

Now as many new applications of distributed systems such as networked sensors, cloud computing and intelligent agent technologies are arising into their deployment stage we see a new life in the ad hoc networking technology. Many experts are now realizing that the real growths require practical ad hoc networking under the dynamic ad hoc networking (DANET). To shed a light on ideas for the future research upon ad hoc associated applications, we call upon the need for lightweight networking. This includes lightweight routing, lightweight relaying, lightweight distributed sensing and overlay technologies within the networking disciplines, which may extend to application-based research and optimization for deployment of the systems including controllability, fault-tolerance, lightweight management, trust and dependability, security, and ubiquitous accessibility. Throughout the research both the energy and complexity should be reduced through a better use of intelligence and smarter networking nodes by exploiting the features of DANET for long-awaited applications for sensing, monitoring, health industries, automatic production, robotics, vehicular and transportation, aerospace, at the lower complexity range to the cloud computing, social networking and e-government at the higher.

This book is a compilation of sample chapters along with selective contributions from the experts and researchers in various areas of ad hoc networking who have already proven their in-depth understanding of the technical expertise areas authorships of the IET/IEE and the IEEE journals and conference research papers. Here we have 19 chapters organized in four inter-related parts: 'Concepts and Principles', 'Networking Techniques', 'Ad hoc Network Management' and 'Applications of ad hoc Networking'.

Part I comes with five chapters. Chapter 1 is a survey contribution from well-known experts in the field who discuss the critical issues of security techniques for DANET, addressing the dynamic area of ad hoc for the key management and associated schemes. Chapter 2 also provides a collection of recent developments in energy-efficient routing methods used in various ad hoc networks, including Mobile ad hoc Networks (MANET), ad hoc Mesh Networks and Cognitive Radio Networks, where their features are discussed and compared highlighting their operational benefits and strategies. Chapter 3 addresses one of the emerging and security sensitive application areas of ad hoc networking, where the intelligent transportation systems and security-enabled Vehicular ad hoc Networking (VANET) have been explained for improved road safety and a wide variety of secure value-added services. Chapter 4 discusses a growing application area for the ad hoc technology under the title of 'internet-gateway discovery in mobile ad hoc networks', where the discovery process is enabled through controlling the propagation of the gateway messages in the network. The dynamics of the application network are controlled via two propagation parameters of the gateway messages. Chapter 5 expands recent research work on the capacity of wireless ad hoc networks where a new definition for the total capacity of ad hoc network is formulated as a function of the cumulative distribution function (CDF) of the received signal to interference power ratio (SIR). This statistical model is explained mathematically and exemplified for analysis and as how to set the outage threshold for maximized capacity.

Part II includes six chapters, chapters 6 through 11. Chapter 6 explains authors' new method to be used for a specialized communication discipline supported by the vehicles. Vehicular Dynamic ad hoc Networks (VANET) represents a state of art of routing using new protocols. In this system the vehicles connect themselves supporting the infrastructure at roadsides and street corners whilst allowing users applications such as driver assistance, location of gas stations and automated toll collection to help the driver to have full control over common and emergency information resources. The next chapter under the title of 'Exploiting Cooperative Relays in MIMO ad hoc Networks' is a relaying system that takes the system further in using Multiple-Input Multiple-Output (MIMO) technology for improved throughput in all application scenarios enhanced with descriptions of the variation of node density, link failure ratio, packet-arrival rate and using the retransmission threshold. The authors also formulate their cooperative relay packet scheduling under MIMO ad hoc networking for both centralized and distributed controlled relay transmissions. The authors of Chapter 8 explain their research work for the dynamic use of ad hoc networking in real-time applications such as voice and video. They show how using single and multi-path routing of MANET could fully benefit from dynamic features of the ad hoc networking. This chapter discusses challenges of ad hoc routing for mobility of nodes, rapid changes of topology, limited capacity, hidden and exposed terminal problems and limited battery power. Then, Chapter 9 explores their research work using the ant-based routing protocols for MANET. They make use of swarm intelligence and link disjoint multipath routing in their dynamic routing system, where their ant colony inspired routing for mobile ad hoc networks is fully explained. Their mathematical model uses a path preference probability to overcome multiple paths of the QoS constraints. Chapter 10 makes use of intelligent algorithms to enhance the reliability of routing in MANET by employing the Hopfield neural network with optimized parameters. The use of a swarm optimization algorithm improves the learning iterations performance in terms of reliability and system complexity. The MANET based dominating set clustering protocols of Chapter 11 complete Part II of the book using a self-configuring, dynamic, multi-hop network for mobile nodes that operate without a need of an infrastructure. It uses stable, scalable and adaptive clusters for highly performed MANETs using the minimal overhead for fast convergence rates. Their proposed scenario-based clustering algorithm uses a greedy algorithm for selecting a dominating set enhanced to a distributed election mechanism for a higher reliability in selecting an optimum cluster-head and adaptive variable diameter clusters.

Part III, ad hoc Network Management, then comes with four chapters, 12 to 15. Obviously, network management function in ad hoc is more of a service management, significantly less structured and much less complex than the structured networks. For example, Chapter 12 can be regarded as network security where a break-down of the network in a harsh operational condition such as a disaster, flood, cyclone, earthquake or an emergency operation can get disintegrated and lose its control where normally a temporary network forms up through interconnecting some mobile nodes, which usually suffer from weakness like Black and Gray holes that opens up the network to vulnerability and insecurity issues such as denial of service attacks. Authors explain how their On-demand Distance Vector route discovery method can secure a MANET from these attacks without loss of performance. Chapter 13 uses a MAC-based distributed channel reservation method to make use of DANET features to overcome the performance problem caused by the negotiation overheads. The author explains how to use medium access control's distributed coordination function to resolve persistent problems of wireless local area networks such as hidden terminals, mixed up control and data traffic bottlenecks. Then under 'Energy efficient local forwarding schemes', Chapter 14 is upon the geographic routing algorithms and uses two energy efficient local forwarding schemes for a two-dimensional ad hoc wireless network for a reduced energy consumption scheme and balances the residual node energy to enhance the network lifetime and less energy cost using network performance metrics. Finally, under 'Dynamic spectrum sharing between cooperative relay and ad hoc networks: towards real-time optimal control', Chapter 15 takes on ad hoc into a dynamic spectrum sharing scheme for real-time applications, where cooperative relay networks access the spectral band of a dynamic ad hoc network whilst avoiding collisions with the ad hoc traffic. Dynamic ad hoc requires an optimal spectrum-access strategy to be applied within a short time.

In the last part of the book, under 'Applications and Uses of ad hoc Networking', we present four remaining chapters, 16 to 19. Chapter 16 explains the provision of quality of service controlled multimedia service applications over the mobile ad hoc network. A variety of algorithms have been discussed in this chapter, where efficient resource allocation using the weighted fair queue system ensures provision of required QoS in the MANET environment. An interesting application of dynamic ad hoc networking comes from Chapter 17 under 'Road traffic management: traffic controllers, mobility and VANET'. Following a brief review of five main road traffic components the authors present some mobility models explaining the intelligent transport system in conjunction with the architectures macroscopic and microscopic traffic controllers and practical issues for collaboration between VANET and traffic controllers. Chapter 18 looks into sensor networking application of DANET and discusses the interesting trust features of these networks under 'Energy efficient trust-aware routing for WSN'. In this chapter the author explains how to reduce the nodal monitoring activities whilst holding on to the required performance for a desirable level of trust. Finally Chapter 19 provides an insight into 'Bio-inspired scheduling schemes for wireless ad hoc sensor networks', where two bio-inspired scheduling schemes for wireless sensor nodes dynamically operating in different modes are analysed and discussed. It is shown that the scheme can operate in a fully decentralized manner and stay highly adaptive to changes in network densities.

Editors
H. F. Rashvand and H.-C. Chao
05 February 2013

Acknowledgement

We would like to thank the IET Book Publishing Department, associated staff members and MPS Ltd for provision of the professional index. We thank all our expert authors for providing us with the fundamental constituents of this volume. The editors wish to acknowledge acquiring extensive help from Dr. Chi-Yuan Chen (Justin) who has generously given his time to analyse the chapters, providing valuable comments and the lists. We also acknowledge the time and effort put in from Advanced Communication Systems Ltd staff, helping us at the later stages of the editorial process with communicating with the authors, checking quality, amendments and finalizing the contents.

Finally, Habib dedicates this work to his family, especially Liz, Joan, Cyrus, Leila, James and baby Madeleine.

Josh dedicates this work to Vivian Chiang, Vivian Chao, Brian Chao and Annie Chao.

We hope you will enjoy reading these great selective chapters on DANET.

Editors
H. F. Rashvand
University of Warwick, UK
H.-C. Chao
National Ilan University, I-Lan, Taiwan

List of acronyms

3G	Third Generation Mobile Communications Technology
4G	Fourth Generation Mobile Communications Technology

A

A-STAR	Anchor-based Street Traffic-Aware Routing
AGPS	Assisted Global Positioning System
AID	Agreement Indicator
AMC	Adaptive Modulation Coding
ANN	Artificial Neural Network
AODV	Ad hoc On-demand Distance Vector
AODV-BR	Ad hoc On-demand Distance Vector Backup Routing
AOMDV	Ad hoc On-demand Multipath Distance Vector
AOTDV	Ad hoc On-demand Trusted-path Distance Vector
AP	Access Point
AR	Access Router
ASCENT	Adaptive Self-Configuring Sensor Network Topology
ATSR	Ambient Trust Sensor Routing
AU	Application Unit

B

BAMPS	Battery-Aware MIMO-mesh-network Power Scheduling
BANT	Backward ANT
BER	Bit Error Rate
BFS	Breadth First Search
BLUETOOTH	Wireless Technology Standard for Exchanging Data Over Short Distance
BPS	Backup Path-set Selection
BPSK	Binary Phase Shift Keying
BS	Base Station
BWA	Broadband Wireless Access

C

CA	Certificate Authorities
CAM	Cluster-head Advertisement Memo

CAP	Contention Access Period
CAR	Connectivity-Aware Routing
CBR	Constant Bit Rate
CBRP	Cluster Based Routing Protocol
CCC	Common Control Channel
CCH	Control Channel
CCI	Co-Channel Interference
CDF	Cumulative Distribution Function
CEDAR	Core Extraction Distributed ad hoc Routing
CFP	Contention Free Period
CH	Cluster Head
CHA	Cluster Head Advertisement
CI	Computational Intelligence
CKN	Connected K-Neighbourhood
CLD	Cross Layer Design
CM-AODV	Cross-layered Multipath AODV
CO-OP	Cooperative
CONFIDANT	Cooperation of Nodes Fairness in Dynamic ad hoc Network
CORE	Collaborative Reputation Mechanism
CPU	Central Processing Unit
CR	Cognitive Radio
CRAHN	Cognitive Radio ad hoc Network
CRATER	Cautious Rating for Trust-Aware Routing
CRF	Channel Reservation Function
CRN	Cooperative Relay Network
CSMA/CA	Carrier Sense Multiple Access with Collision Avoidance
CTMC	Continuous Time Markov Chain
CTS	Clear to Send

D

DANET	Dynamic ad hoc Network
DCF	Distributed Coordination Function
DD	Detection Delay
DEAR	Device and Energy-Aware Routing
DESAR	Delay and Energy-based Spectrum-Aware Routing
DF	Decode and Forward
DGR	Direction Guided Routing
DoD	Department of Defense
DoS	Denial of Service
DQ	Distributed Queue
DQDC	Distributed Queue Dual Channel
DRBTS	Distributed Reputation-based Beacon Trust System
DS	Dominating Set
DS-CDMA	Direct Sequence Code Division Multiple Access

DSA	Dynamic Sub-channel Assignment
DSCAM	Distributed SCAM
DSDV	Destination Sequenced Distance Vector
DSR	Dynamic Source Routing
DSRC	Dedicated Short Range Communications
DTN	Delay Tolerant Network
DYMO	Dynamic MANET On-demand

E

E-HEALTH	Electronic Health
E2IRP	Energy Efficient Integrated Routing Protocol
E2R	Energy Efficient Routing
EARA	Energy-Aware Routing Algorithm
EASR	Energy-Aware Source Routing
ECD	Energy Consumption Distribution
ECPP	Efficient Conditional Privacy Preservation
ECSD	Energy Consumption Per Successful Detection
ED	Export Data
EDCA	Enhanced Distributed Channel Access
EDCF	Enhanced Distributed Coordination Function
EEAODR	Energy Efficient On-Demand Routing
EECARP	Energy-Efficient Congestion-Aware Routing Protocol
EELAR	Energy Efficient Location Aided Routing
EEPAR	Energy Efficient Power-Aware Routing
EMPIRE	Efficient Monitoring Procedure in Reputation System
ENDMR	Energy-aware Node Disjoint Multipath Routing
EPP	Energy-Proportional Principle
EPS	Evolved Packet System
ETC	Electronic Toll Collection
ETR	Energy and Throughput-aware Routing

F

FANT	Forward ANT
FBP	Full Beacon Piggyback
FCC	Federal Communication Commission
FDMA	Frequency Division Multiple Access
FHI	First Hand Information
FHSS	Frequency Hopping Spread Spectrum
FTP	File Transfer Protocol

G

G-MMDSR	Game-theoretic Multipath Multimedia Dynamic Source Routing
GBR	Greedy-based Backup Routing

GEANDMRA	Grid-based Energy-Aware Node Disjoint Multipath Routing Algorithm
GEAR	Geographic and Energy-Aware Routing
GETAR	Geographic, Energy and Trust-Aware Routing
GLAP	Group-based Lightweight Authentication Protocol
GloMo	Global Mobile, Information System
GPRS	General Packet Radio Service
GPS	Global Positioning System
GPSR	Greedy Perimeter Stateless Routing
GR	Geographic Routing
GREP	Graph Reply
GREQ	Graph Request
GRSSN	Gaussian Reputation System for wireless Sensor Network
GS	Group Signature
GSIS	Group Signature and Identity-based Signature
GSM	Global System for Mobile Communications
GSR	Global State Routing
GSR	Geographic Source Routing
GVDSR	Generic Vehicular Dynamic Source Routing

H

HM	Hello Message
HNN	Hopfield Neural Network
HSDPA	High-Speed Downlink Packet Access
HSR	Hierarchical State Routing
HT	Wireless Hotspot

I

ID	Identification
IEEE	Institute of Electrical and Electronics Engineers
IETF	Internet Engineering Task Force
ILP	Intelligent Loss Prevention
IP	Internet Protocol
IRPCE	Intelligent Routing Protocol for City Environment
ITS	Intelligent Transportation System

J

JTRS	Joint Tactical Radio System

L

LAMOR	Lifetime-Aware Multipath Optimized Routing
LAN	Local Area Network
LAR	Location Aided Routing

LARS	Locally Aware Reputation System
LASM	Logical Application Stream Model
LBF	Load Balancing Factor
LBPC	Location Based Power Conservation
LC	Logical Constraints
LET	Link Expiration Time
LP	Locked-up Packet
LQF-MWM	Longest Queue First-Maximal Weight Matching
LRoS	Logical Realization of Service
LS	Logical Service
LTE	Long Term Evolution
LUoW	Logical Units of Work

M

MAC	Medium Access Control
MANET	Mobile ad hoc Network
MCRF	Multi-channel CRF
MCU	Micro-Controller Unit
MDM	Misbehaver Detection Metric
MDQDC	Mesh DQDC
MDSR	Multipath Dynamic Source Routing
MFR	Most Forward within Radius
MHC	Multi-Hop Communication
MIMO	Multiple Input Multiple Output
MISO	Multiple Input Single Output
MMRNS	Multipath Multicast using Reliable Neighbour Selection
MOVE	Mobile-networking for Vehicular Environment
MP	Mesh Point
MP-OLSR	Multipath-Optimised Link State Routing
MPR	Multipoint Relay
MRA	Modified Router Advertisement
MRS	Modified Router Solicitation
MSR	Multipath Source Routing
MTRTP	Minimum Total Reliable Transmission Power
MTXOPACK	Mesh Transmission Acknowledgment
MTXOPREQ	Mesh Transmission Opportunity Request
MTXOPRSP	Mesh Transmission Opportunity Response
MURU	Multi-hop-routing-protocol for Urban

N

NBBTE	Node Behavioural-strategies Banding Belief for Trust Evaluation
NBP	No-activity Behaviour Period
NDMR	Node Disjoint Multipath Routing

NFP	Nearest Forward Progress
NHA	Next Hop Availability
Ni	Neighbour List of i
NL	Nomination List
NMA	Nodal Monitoring Activity
NP-C	Nondeterministic Polynomial-time Complete
NS	Network Simulator
NSI	Network State Information
NTDR	Near Term Digital Radio
NTVE	Nonlinear Time-Varying Evolution

O

OBU	On-Board Units
OCEAN	Observation-based Cooperation Enforcement for ad hoc Networks
OFDM	Orthogonal Frequency Division Multiple-access
OFEB	Optimal Forward with Energy Balance algorithm
OLSR	Optimized Link State Routing
ORF	Optimal Range Forward
OSCA	Optimal Sniffer Channel Assignment
OSI	Open Systems Interconnect
OSPF	Open Shortest-Path First
OTCL	Object oriented Tool Command Language, NS-2

P

PAN	Personal Area Network
PAR	Power-Aware Routing
PC	Personal Computer
PDA	Personal Digital Assistant
PDF	Probability Density Function
PEAS	Probing Environment and Adaptive Sleeping
PESM	Power Efficient Scheduling Method
PGB	Preferred Group Broadcasting
PGP	Pretty Good Privacy
PHY	Physical
PKCS	Public Key Cryptography System
PLUS	Parameterized and Localised Trust-management Scheme
POP	Payload Only Piggyback
PPAA	Peer-to-Peer Anonymous Authentication
PPMA	Probabilistic Predictive Multicast Algorithm
PRNet	Packet Radio Networks
PSD	Power Spectral Density
PSM	Power Save Mechanism
PSO	Particle Swarm Optimisation

PU	Primary User
PVN	Plausibility Validation Network

Q

QAM	Quadrature Amplitude Modulation
QAMR	Quality-of-service-enabled Ant-colony-based Multipath Routing
QoS	Quality of Service

R

RA	Router Advertisement
RBFNN	Radial Basis Function Neural Network
RBTMWSN	Recursive Bayesian-approach to Trust Management for WSN
RelEE	Reliable and Energy-Efficient
RERR	Route Error
RFC	*Request For Comment*
RFP	Route Finalized Packet
RFSN	Reputation-based Framework for High Integrity Sensor Networks
RIP	Routing Information Protocol
RLS	Reactive Location Service
RMD	Route Metric Discovery
RMREP	Route Metric Reply
RN	Relay Nodes
ROAM	Routing on-demand Acyclic Multipath
ROMSGP	Receive on Most Stable Group Path
RPG	Reference Point Group
RQ	Research Question
RR	Resource Reservation
RRD	Random Receiver Identifier
RREP	Route Reply
RREQ	Route Request
RSD	Random Source Identifier
RSU	Road-side Unit
RTS	Request to Send
RTSN	Real Time Session

S

SCAM	Scenario-based Clustering Algorithm for Mobile ad hoc Network
SCH	Service Channel
SDMR	Spatially Disjoint Multipath Routing
SDR	Software Defined Radio
SER	Spectrum and Energy-aware Routing

SHI	Second Hand Information
SI	Service Interval
SI	Swarm Intelligence
SI^{2}BTC	Simple Intelligent ILP-Based Traffic Controller
SIMO	Single Input Multi Output
SINR	Signal-to-Interference-plus-Noise Ratio
SIR	Signal-to-Interference Ratio
SISO	Single Input Single Output
SMORT	Scalable Multipath On-demand Routing
SMR	Split Multipath Routing
SMS	Shortest Multipath Source
SNARE	Sensor Node Attached Reputation Evaluator
SNR	Signal-to-Noise Ratio
SOP	Spectrum Opportunities
STRAW	Street Random Waypoint
SU	Secondary User
SURAN	Survivable Radio Networks
SVD	Singular Value Decomposition

T

TARF	Trust-Aware Routing Framework
TBRPF	Topology-dissemination Based Reverse-Path Forwarding
TCC	Traffic Control Centre
TCNN	Transient Chaotic Neural Network
TCP	Transmission Control Protocol
TDMA	Time Division Multiple Access
THR	Target Hit Rate
TOPO	Two-phase-routing Protocol
TORA	Temporally Ordered Routing Algorithm
ToS	Type of Service
TTL	Time to Live
TIBFIT	Trust Index Based Fault in Tolerance
TTP	Trusted Third Party

U

UDP	User Datagram Protocol
UMTS	Universal Mobile Telecommunications System
UoW	Unit of Work
UWB	Ultra-Wideband

V

V2I	Vehicles to Infrastructure
V2R	Vehicle-to-Road Side Unit Communication

V2V	Vehicle-to-Vehicle Communication
VANET	Vehicular ad hoc Network
VC	Vehicular communication
VIPER	Vehicle-to-Infrastructure-communication Privacy Enforcement Protocol
VLR	Verifier-Local Revocation
VPKI	Vehicular Public Key Infrastructure

W

WAVE	Wireless Access in Vehicular Environment
WFQ	Waited Fair Queue
Wi-Fi	Wireless Fidelity
WiMAX	Worldwide Interoperability for Microwave Access
WLAN	*Wireless Local Area Network*
WPAN	Wireless Personal Area Network
WRP	Wireless Routing Protocol
WSN	Wireless Sensor Network
WUSB	Wireless USB

Z

| ZIGBEE | Open WPAN Standard based on the IEEE 802.15.4 Protocol |

Part I

Concepts and principles

Chapter 1*

Dynamic ad hoc networks and associated key management

*Chi-Yuan Chen[a], Kai-Di Chang[b], Fan-Hsun Tseng[c],
Shih-Wen Hsu[d] and Han-Chieh Chao[a,e]*

Abstract

Dynamic ad hoc networks (DANETs) are similar to mobile ad hoc networks (MANETs), but the network density and mobility change significantly over time and space. Many researchers have proposed types of key management schemes for ad hoc networks. In this chapter, we provide a timely survey of the existing solutions and describe the state-of-the-art techniques for DANETs security key management, where we particularly consider those more suitable for DANET. Following a brief discussion on the limitations and challenges of key management in DANET, we introduce the main and desirable features and evaluation metrics of key management. Then a categorization of existing key management systems is presented. Finally, we conclude this chapter with a summary of further developments.

1.1 Introduction

Due to technological advances and innovation, more and more people communicate and access different services via broadband wireless access (BWA) technology. With wireless technology, users can use Internet services at any time and almost anywhere. When users try to establish connections with other network devices, they are directly connected to the wired LAN or through wireless infrastructures, such as a base station (BS) or an access point (AP). However, early wireless technologies

*H. F. Rashvand and H.-C. Chao (Eds.), *Dynamic Ad Hoc Networks*, The IET Book Publishing Department, 2013, ISBN 978-1-84919-647-5, eISBN 978-1-84919-648-2
[a]Department of Electrical Engineering, National Dong Hwa University, Taiwan, ROC
[b]Department of Electrical Engineering, National Taiwan University of Science and Technology, Taiwan, ROC
[c]Department of Computer Science & Information Engineering, National Central University, Taiwan, ROC
[d]Department of Computer Science, National Tsing Hua University, Taiwan, ROC
[e]Institute of Computer Science and Information Engineering, National Ilan University, Taiwan, ROC

were limited by these infrastructures because of the fixed transmission range in both BS and AP [1], and users would experience disconnections when the wireless network devices exceeded the cover range. Therefore, the wireless ad hoc networks attracted the attention of researchers. Wireless ad hoc networks are connected by all working nodes without infrastructure or centralized management. All working nodes, as well as BSs, APs, routers, etc., have a routing mechanism and they are able to take the initiative to discover the route and maintain their own routing information.

Wireless ad hoc networks are suitable for disaster detection, emergency rescues, military applications, information collection, and so on. Many researchers have extended the original wireless ad hoc network with dynamic characteristics. DANETs are focused on rapid network changes over time and space. However, DANETs have inherited the traditional security problems of the original wireless ad hoc network because of its decentralized nature and ever-changing network density and mobility.

In traditional networks and early wireless networks, the network connection was based on a hierarchical architecture to construct a stable topology. The static infrastructure provided a series of security mechanisms and strategies, such as encryption, authentication, access control and rights management, firewalls, etc. Ad hoc networks still apply basic security requirements, such as confidentiality, integrity, availability and authenticity; nevertheless, they cannot sacrifice a lot of power for complex calculations considering the energy consumption of wireless transmission and radio spectrum resources. In addition, limited by the node's hardware resources, a robust security protection mechanism was difficult to achieve. As ad hoc network resources were so limited, many traditional network security policies and strategies could not be directly applied, so numerous modifications to the existing security methods and strategies were required. Moreover, the ad hoc network nodes act both as routers and as communication end points are easy victims of passive eavesdropping, active message insertions, denial of service and battery-exhaustion attacks [1]. In dealing with multiple threats to network environments, the use of cryptographic keys has been one trustworthy solution [2]. Specific key management strategies are required to maintain ad hoc network robustness.

In this chapter, existing key management methods and state-of-the-art techniques are investigated, with the focus on those most suitable for DANETs.

1.1.1 Dynamic ad hoc networks

The characteristic of 'dynamic' in ad hoc networks has a considerable impact on network robustness. For example, different velocity vehicles compose a communication network called a vehicular ad hoc network (VANET). Each car is equipped with communication equipment, which conducts interactions without APs. Velocity differences cause unstable topologies and complexity of message transmission routes. In metropolitan areas, mobile devices carried by people can also form an ad hoc network. Due to the high density of the nodes in the network, the network environment can vary rapidly from time to time [3]. In DANETs, links between two nodes can change frequently and cause possible disconnection.

1.1.2   Challenges of key management

Security issues of the most concern in DANETs are the same as those in a traditional Internet framework; they include: (1) confidentiality, (2) integrity, (3) availability, (4) authorization, (5) dependability and reliability and (6) accountability [4]. In fact, designing security protocols for DANETs is more difficult than designing security protocols for wired networks or wireless infrastructure-based networks. Dynamic environments require additional caution under unstable network conditions. Attackers are intent on damaging any layer of the network's protocol stack. Spread-spectrum techniques, frequency hopping and interleaving are often used for the lowest layer's defence mechanism. For protection from threats to the higher layers, the essential methods involve cryptographic techniques. A key management scheme must have secure and efficient cryptographic mechanisms for ad hoc network security. This can be defined as establishing and maintaining the key relationships between authorized parties with cryptographic techniques and procedures [5]. A key management scheme includes: (1) public or private key pairs, (2) secret keys and (3) initialization parameters.

There are several challenges for key management in DANETs. The most important problem is how to identify which routing information can be trusted. Ensuring that all working nodes in the network are legitimate members is also necessary. These legal nodes are equipped with the keys for conducting safety communication while complying with other transmission strategies. Many researchers have proposed cryptographically signed routing messages, but without the necessary details for key management. Robust authentication mechanisms have also been proposed to achieve security goals [6]. The network can use something known to be associated with an identity to realize authentication. Authentication depends on the context of usage. For critical or privacy information transmission, complete authentication mechanisms are essential [7].

Another challenge in key management is how to provide keys for the network layer. In the application layer, the key management scheme can be regarded as an already running network service. However, in the network layer, some trust-based protocols should be in place before conducting communication. Most of these protocols are for secure routing, which calculate trust values based on the char-acteristics of the nodes. Thus, key management schemes for the network layer require proper planning in order to prevent malicious attacks and to construct a secured network.

In short, key management in DANETs integrates techniques and procedures for nodes to establish a service in a secured environment. It should be initialized at the beginning when constructing a network, while the keying materials'generate, distribute, install and control methods are imposed. Once the network circumstances change, the keying materials' update, revoke and destruct methods should be completed.

1.2   Background

In this section, the desirable features of DANETs and the evaluation metrics of key management are stated and discussed. A DANET is changeable when the network features frequently alter over time and space. Therefore, the network characteristics and evaluation metrics are somewhat different from conventional ad hoc networks.

1.2.1   Desirable features for DANETs

The original ad hoc network was composed of static nodes that communicated with each other without infrastructure and within its transmission range [8]. These nodes played the role of a source node as well as a destination node in self-organized networks [9]. In other words, these nodes were equipped with transceiver ability. Unlike a normal ad hoc network, mobile nodes change their geographical position with varied velocity in MANETs. In MANETs, mobile nodes can be portable devices and handsets. The network density is based on the population density and the network variation is determined by the user's mobility.

The nodes in ad hoc networks can be vehicles in VANETs [10]. In a VANET, the node density is determined by the number of vehicles and changes based on the mobility speed of the vehicles included. The sensor nodes communicate with each other as in ad hoc wireless sensor networks (WSNs) [11], and they can be firmly deployed. The nodes are responsible for detecting new environments and monitoring variable situations, but they are battery powered and have energy limitations. The military networks are another example of ad hoc networks, such as the Joint Tactical Radio System (JTRS) program of the U.S. Department of Defense (DoD). The armies acquire infrastructure-less voice, data and video communications through wideband spectrum accessing, and the same concept is applied to those offering relief in the disaster area.

According to their various applications, ad hoc networks have been widely used and investigated [5, 12]. In this subsection, the network features of DANETs are discussed, such as network structure, network formation, resource limitation, node mobility and security issues.

1.2.1.1   Infrastructure-less and distributed architecture

In the third generation (3G) or fourth generation (4G) of cell phone mobile communications, users use mobile devices to communicate through the base station. Whether in Worldwide Interoperability for Microwave Access (WiMAX) or Long-Term Evolution (LTE) networks, the infrastructures must be deployed before commercial services are commenced. Not only the construction costs are high the network scalability is also low. Unlike telecommunication networks, in MANETs, the mobile nodes exchange data packets and routing information with each other without any predefined infrastructure. The mobile nodes self-organize an ad hoc network within their transmission range and impersonate not only the source node in a route but also the destination node in another route. According to the above characteristic, the multi-hop relay phenomenon occurs.

An infrastructure-based network implies that communication is centralized and that the prevention of anonymous attacks is relatively easy to achieve. In MANETs, all of the mobile nodes are responsible for maintaining network functionality, but there is no central prevention of malicious behaviour. The infrastructure-less framework can cause loopholes in the security, as it is hard to detect malicious nodes due to the distributed architecture. Therefore, a novel architecture via a mixed ad hoc network was proposed, which combined the features of an infrastructural network and a multi-hop relay network.

1.2.1.2 Network topology and density

In normal MANETs, there is no explicit definition for network density. Liu and Wu [13] suggested that the DANETs resembled a dense ad hoc network. In a dense ad hoc network, critical problems can occur due to the sparse distribution of the mobile nodes. For example, the network density may influence the number of participating nodes in many routing protocols, or it may limit the performance of many existing algorithms and mechanisms. Another example is that many secured routing protocols are conducted by grouping nodes; hence, the network density can affect security. Moreover, network density also has an influence on computing complexity because of the different joined nodes during the routing selection.

Because the ad hoc network is self-organized by the mobile nodes, node mobility varies frequently. The network topology of a DANET is changeable and the network's stability and link connectivity are unstable and easy to be interrupted. This problem also has a negative impact on the robustness of security due to the dynamic network topology. Security sustainability must be ensured, and the protection of communications should always be available among all mobile nodes.

1.2.1.3 Network formation

The network formation of a self-organized ad hoc network is recreated instantaneously and unexpectedly. As time passes, the node information becomes unstable and the network formation is alterable, such as the node locations, neighbour nodes, node mobility and next-hop selection. In cognitive radio ad hoc networks, a secondary user attempts to access the spectrum hole without interfering with the primary user and other secondary users. The dynamic network members influence the occupied channels; hence, channel management is complicated in the distributed network formation. The same situation applies in VANETs, with vehicles cooperating to gather the computing resources together. However, the dynamic network formation makes cooperation even more sophisticated. Furthermore, malicious attacks are hard to avoid due to the decentralized control nature. The online trust model [14] is more effective than conventional offline trust models; hence, the hybrid architecture that integrates the infrastructure prototype with the distributed network formation could be an effective solution for DANETs.

1.2.1.4 Resource limitations

The resource limitations of DANETs present a critical problem for researchers investigating this field. The resources are restricted within the essence of the mobile nodes, such as the portable devices in MANETs, vehicles or on-board units (OBUs) in VANETs, wireless transceivers in military networks, and so on. The conventional resource limitations are computation capability of the mobile nodes, main memory of equipment, energy resource of battery and transmission bandwidth. For example, numerous researchers have focused on minimizing power consumption in WSNs. The sensor nodes, being battery powered, have energy limitations. Most mobile nodes are small and thin, such as the Personal Digital Assistant (PDA), smart phone and tiny sensor nodes, i.e., user equipment that cannot afford the power for high computing tasks. The trade-off between computing performance and energy saving is well known. Although the OBU of a vehicle may not limit the energy resource, it still works with the transmission bandwidth due to the high mobility of vehicles.

1.2.1.5   Node mobility

In conventional MANETs, the nodes are regarded as the mobile nodes, such as vehicles and movable user equipment. In DANETs, the mobile nodes are provided with high mobility and changeable velocity. Therefore, many researchers have investigated different node mobility issues [15]. For example, Shila and Cheng [16] studied the mobility, capacity and delay in ad hoc wireless networks. The authors investigated the effect on capacity and delay in the restricted mobility model and showed that the average end-to-end of the hybrid network was smaller than the pure mobile ad hoc network. Especially in VANETs, researchers have focused on investigating the mobility model, such as References 17 and 18.

1.2.1.6   Inherent security problems

The security leaks in the above-mentioned features have resulted in many security issues in DANETs. Many researchers have surveyed the security issues for wireless ad hoc networks over the last ten years, such as References 19 and 20. Malicious attacks in ad hoc networks can be classified into the following types: intrusion detection, centralized and distributed denial of service (dos) attacks, blackhole [21], grayhole attacks, wormhole attacks, replay attacks and counterfeit routing information.

Some of the vulnerability is generated from the insufficient capability of mobile nodes and some is inherent in ad hoc networks due to their infrastructureless architecture. Given the lack of both centralized administration and encryption ability, mobile nodes can be exploited to compromise other mobile nodes; therefore, some distributed security schemes for wireless ad hoc networks have been proposed. However, robustness and scalability natures have remained the major obstacles for these distributed security mechanisms. For example, Gao and Li [22] proposed the cluster-based security architecture and used a distributed authority among the cluster members. The authors claimed that the proposed scheme was more flexible and scalable for key management in ad hoc networks.

1.2.2   Evaluation metrics of key management

In a community, finances and status are often used to assess a person's importance and value. However, the narrowness of these criteria hardly allows for an accurate representation of a human being's actual worth. The implication is that a different decision metric for the judgment would lead to a two-sided result. Similarly, for a better understanding of evaluation metrics in DANET we introduce and discuss the performance metrics of key management in MANET.

The desirable features of key management schemes in DANETs [2] include applicability, complexity, robustness, scalability and security. Applicability represents the practicability of the key management schemes. For example, whether the assumptions and conditions of schemes can be applied from a centralized single domain to decentralized multiple domains or not, and whether the designed network environments are sensible and acceptable or not. Complexity denotes the computing and operating complexity of the designed key management schemes, which influence the scalability due to the number of participating nodes. Moreover, the scarce bandwidth also restricts the scalability when the management traffic occupies the available bandwidth. Finally, robustness and security are used to ensure the strength of the key management schemes. For instance, the key management scheme should maintain high detection accuracy, even if there are attacks from compromised nodes. Furthermore, the key management scheme should provide great security under different attacks. The fundamental evaluation metrics for key management schemes are introduced within the above features, such as trust level, route selection scheme, transmission delay, packet dropping rate, detection accuracy, overhead, throughput and energy consumption.

1.2.2.1 Applicability

Applicability is equal to the practicability of the key management schemes, which implies a suitable scenario and range. The assumptions of key management schemes affect the applicability, such as the network architecture, network size, group members and node mobility. If the network architecture of the key management scheme is centralized, it may decrease the trust level in a distributed scenario due to the different number of administrators. Moreover, the different key exchange method can also cause increased computing complexity and control overhead, such as a pairwise symmetric key or a group symmetric key.

The participative mobile node of a key exchange operation works on a different trust level, route usage, detection accuracy, control overhead and energy consumption. In general, the more group key members with a higher trust level and detection accuracy, the higher the control overhead and energy consumption. Therefore, a higher trust level with lower control overhead is encouraged. Finally, the node mobility may influence the packet dropping rate and goodput.

1.2.2.2 Complexity

Complexity is the most familiar evaluation metric in key management. According to the operating procedure of a key management scheme, complexity can be generated by communication and computation. When the cooperative nodes generate a group key in both contributory and distributive schemes, the generation belongs to a computation complexity that wastes transmission time and energy. When the key is shared and updated among mobile nodes, the communication overhead leads to communication complexity and exhausts the network throughput.

In order to synchronize the nodes to prevent false information attack, the synchronous broadcast method is often used. Nevertheless, the synchronous process also increases the inessential control and communication overheads. The distributive schemes update and redistribute the key frequently; hence, the distributive key distribution schemes have higher communication and computation complexity.

1.2.2.3   Robustness

The robustness metric is used to estimate the correctness when there are faulty nodes or malicious nodes in the DANETs. The rationalities of assumptions are also used to judge if a key management scheme is robust or weak. A case in point is the familiar synchronization broadcast system in key management schemes. Researchers often assume that there is a synchronous broadcast system in distributive key schemes. However, a robust key management scheme should not be limited to the synchronization problem.

A robust key management scheme should work well even if there are some compromised nodes or attackers. Few schemes present high detection accuracy after a key exchange from false information and most schemes fail in the packet-dropping rate. In conclusion, key management schemes need fault-tolerant capability.

1.2.2.4   Scalability

The scalability metric of key management schemes is critical and significant. Because the mobile nodes and network density are hard to predict and easily altered, the key exchange operation should be executed as soon as possible; otherwise, the schemes fail to precisely select the primary route. Another aspect of scalability is decided from the control overhead, which consumes the available network bandwidth and limited energy. A perfect key management scheme should be completed in an acceptable and timely manner and minimize the management traffic during the operation of the key agreement or distribution.

1.2.2.5   Security

There are many topics in the security metric, such as the authentication method, intrusion detection ability, trust level maintenance and probable vulnerabilities. The security metric is the most important metric in the key management scheme. A secure key management scheme should overcome malicious attacks and prevent exposure of the private key to unauthenticated nodes.

Authentication methods are mainly classified into on-line and off-line authentications, with the on-line authentication being more suitable for DANETs but harder to achieve. The intrusion detection ability is utilized to excavate the attackers. For example, false information and malicious behaviour can be recognized from an incorrect time stamp and user identity. Moreover, the trust level may be influenced frequently. The centralized authority is efficient in certification but with low scalability. However, the distributed authority should be able to withstand anonymous attacks. Finally, no matter what kind of key management scheme is applied, vulnerabilities in the DANET can exist. The appropriate key length encryption methods reduce the vulnerability. Furthermore, the key distribution and update method can limit the different probabilities that compromise the scheme.

1.3   Categories of key management schemes

There are many methods for classifying key management schemes. These schemes are primarily related to DANETs, and the major categories of key management schemes are contributory key management and distributive key management. The classification of key management schemes used in this chapter is shown in the Figure 1.1.

In contributory schemes, the key is acquired through the cooperation of many nodes, while distributive schemes can be neither centralized nor distributed. The nodes generate their key and distribute it to other nodes. The distributive category can be further classified into symmetric and public key schemes. Traditional certificate-based schemes and identity-based schemes are considered public key schemes, while symmetric schemes can be divided into MANET schemes or WSN schemes. WSN stands for a new class of ad hoc network with more constrained nodes than traditional MANETs. The feature of contributory schemes is that there is no trusted third party who works on key generation and distribution. However, the communication pairs cooperate with each other to establish a secret symmetric key. The distributive schemes are related to one or more than one trust node(s), which include the public key system and symmetric system. Real ad hoc networks need trusted nodes to accomplish the impromptu requests when the network is initialized.

1.3.1   Contributory key management schemes

In this section, the representative contributory schemes in DANETs are discussed and the major implications and limitations of each scheme are detailed.

Survivable Group-Based Public Key Management (SG-PKM): The concept of initiator groups (IGs) was proposed in SG-PKM [23]. IGs consist of nodes whose owners or users have a good/friendly relationship. There are no cluster heads in IGs

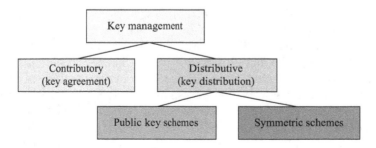

Figure 1.1   Classification of key management schemes

as all nodes in each group are essential for a new node joining the system, getting a certificate and updating/renewing keys. In SG-PKM, the maintenance of IGs is not essential because IGs have the ability to self-adjust to changes, minimize the computational cost in group maintenance and reduce network overhead.

A Group-Based Key Management Protocol for MANET (AGKP): AGKP [24] is a new key management protocol that utilizes certificate graphs and distributed certificate authorities (CAs). Each user shows the trust relationship with his neighbours by a certificate graph. Then, the CAs are selected through the maximum clique of the certificate graph. The basic assumption in AGKP is that the initial certificate graph construction is secure. Each user in the graph is good and has many friends, while bad ones have fewer; thus, a reliable group can be constructed. Finally, it is most important that the most trusted subset of good users, whose clique is the highest, be elected as the governor of the group. The node with the highest clique takes the responsibility of CA.

1.3.2   Distributive key management schemes

Hao *et al.* proposed a Distributed Key Management Framework (DKMF) [25], which was based on a group signature to provide privacy for users or nodes. This scheme can be adapted to both DANETs and VANETs. Unlike traditional centralized key management with existing group signature schemes, distributed key management is expected to overcome the revocation of malicious vehicles/compromised nodes, thus achieving better system maintenance and security policies for heterogeneous environments. The roadside unit (RSU) plays the role of key distributer in the DKMF framework. In this case, the semi-trusted RSUs could be compromised. In order to overcome this, Hao *et al.* developed security protocols capable of detecting compromised RSUs and their colluding malicious vehicles. They also discussed the issue of huge computation overhead due to implementing the group signature. In order to reduce the verification overhead, a practical cooperative message authentication protocol was proposed, with vehicles just needing to verify a small number of messages in the protocol. Possible attacks and the corresponding solutions were also analysed, resulting in the development of a medium access control (MAC) layer model. In this section, a survey of the public key and symmetric key management schemes for DANETs is discussed.

1.3.2.1   Public key schemes

Pretty Good Privacy-Like (PL) Scheme [26] is a fully distributed self-organizing public key management infrastructure for handling the public key management problem. PL is based on the PGP (Pretty Good Privacy) functions. Nodes in PL have to create their public and private keys pairs. Unlike PGP, all the certificates are saved and kept in centralized certificate repositories; certificates in PL are stored, distributed and managed by the nodes in a fully self-organized technique. In the PL system, the chains of public key certificates are used to perform key authentication. A node creates its public and private keys and the public-key certificates are generated based on trust relationships. PGP-like defines a mechanism with periodic exchanges of certificates between neighbour nodes. This mechanism is used to distribute the certificates and enhance the efficiency of finding a chain of public-key certificates. Furthermore, this mechanism prevents conflicts through updating and revoking keys. The PGP-like also handles misbehaviour in nodes, such as operations to crosscheck the keys in certificates and detect inconsistencies. When two or more are related to the same user, the certificates are inconsistent. However, the different keys or related the same public key to different users are presented in this research.

Ubiquitous and Robust Access Control (URSA) Scheme [27] is a ubiquitous, decentralized, self-controlled and robust access control solution for MANETs. In URSA, no single node monopolizes the access decision or is assumed to be completely trustworthy. Furthermore, most nodes jointly monitor a local node and certify/revoke its ticket. Conspiracy Tickets are used to perform conventional digital certification, with expiration time, personal public key of the node, signature and identifier; they are certified and updated in order to prevent attacks by many anomalous nodes or misbehaving nodes. In addition, the certifications are based on the RSA cryptosystem and on a threshold cryptography-based signature to enhance security. URSA can handle a localized group trust model. The node in-group is considered trustworthy if it can be trusted by majority of related nodes. A certain interval of valid ticket time is used to determine the trust relationship. In this model, the trusted nodes can give tickets with a signature for other nodes in the group, even to the whole network. These nodes observe and monitor other nodes that could prevent misbehaving nodes from appearing in the network. If there were one anomalous node or misbehaving node in the network, the ticket would be revoked and the attack on the network is prevented. Furthermore, in order to enhance network security, all tickets are renewed periodically, which improves the resilience of the system. Other researchers have investigated ideas similar to URSA and applied the threshold approach to deal with the public management problem to make the management more decentralized and robust.

Securing Cluster-based (SC) Scheme [28] is a mechanism proposed to address key management in cluster-based MANETs. The most important challenge has been the lack of centralized management, which has made it difficult to implement key management schemes in this kind of network. In order to overcome this issue, Li *et al.* propose an ID-based fully distributed multiple-secret key management scheme (IMKM). The SC key management scheme was implemented with a combination of ID-based multiple secrets and threshold cryptography. Furthermore, the SC key management scheme eliminated the requirement for certificate-based authenticated public key distribution and provided an efficient mechanism for key update and key revocation. These features made SC key management scheme a suitable, economically viable, adaptable, scalable and autonomous key management for DANETs.

Hierarchical Identity-Based (HI) Scheme [29] is especially suited to military applications where the organization of network architecture is already hierarchical in nature. Most key management schemes concentrate on network architecture and key allocation algorithms instead of considering the attributes of nodes. A security benefit could be attained when the node states are considered in the process of generating a private key due to the distributed and dynamic nature of MANETs. Richard *et al.* proposed a distributed hierarchical key management scheme in which nodes' keys were updated from their parent nodes or a threshold of sibling nodes. This scheme finds the best node from all nodes by considering their security and power status, and this node then takes on the role of private key generator. Finally, the proposed scheme was able to decrease the probability of the network being compromised and to extend network lifetime.

Scalable method of cryptographic key management (SMOCK): He *et al.* propose SMOCK [30], which is a self-contained public key-management scheme. It is also a scalable method of cryptographic key management and achieves almost a zero communication overhead for authentication, and the service availability is high and stable. In this scheme, just a few cryptographic keys are stored off-line inside nodes before they are deployed in the network. To achieve and provide good scalability for nodes and storage space, a combinatorial design of public–private key pairs is considered in this scheme, which means nodes combine more than one key pair to encrypt and decrypt messages. Finally, SMOCK provides controllable resilience capability when anomalous or malicious nodes compromise a limited number of nodes before key revocation and updating.

Markov Chain Trust Model (MCTM): The Markov Chain Trust Model (MCTM) [31] adopts the public key infrastructure based on the RSA encryption algorithm; then, the trust relationships among mobile nodes can be established. In other words, a multicast MANET with some critical chances could result in being intruded. Examples are nodes joining, members leaving, CA/BCA competitions, session key distribution and key regeneration. Thus, Chang *et al.* proposed a model to provide secure trust procedures to prevent intrusion in multicast MANETs. The six phases included in this procedure are: (1) group initial phase; (2) node-joining phase; (3) member-leaving phase; (4) CA-leaving phase; (5) BCA-leaving phase and (6) group-leader-leaving phase.

1.3.2.2   Symmetric schemes

Joshi's approach (JA) [32]: Joshi *et al.* proposed a fully distributed certificate authority scheme based on secret sharing and redundancy. The private key of the certificate authority (CA) is divided into different parts in this secret sharing mechanism, and the different parts of the secret are distributed among the nodes in the network. In order to communicate with other nodes, nodes have to create their own key. From the total number of key sharing, the certificate authority (CA) key can be updated or recreated by the combination from the key sharing. There is one critical situation when a number of nodes asks for or requires the key to be recreated, but the key cannot be found in the communication area. If the node cooperates with other nodes to incorporate redundancy into the network, the number of key sharing per node would be more than one. The number of nodes required to recreate the CA key can then be reduced since the nodes can store more than one key sharing, which would increase the changes of legal nodes needed to recreate the CA key. In other words, the redundancy results in a challenge because of the chances of an intruder entering in the network and increases the number of CA keys. When an intruder attacks the network and compromises one node, the intruder becomes a valid/good node in the network. To overcome this problem and avoid this situation, an intrusion detection system (IDS) is used. Finally, the misbehaving nodes or compromised nodes can be identified and removed from the network.

Distributed node selection for threshold (DNST) [33] is a distributed key management scheme that selects nodes dynamically with master key sharing to achieve the private key generation (PKG) service. Yu *et al.* considered security and energy states in selecting a node process to accomplish a private key generator (PKG) with the best nodes, and the stochastic optimization problem was used to formulate the node selection process. In addition, the authors modelled the intrusion detection system (IDS) as noisy sensors to observe the system's security situations in their scenario.

Distributed hierarchical key management (DHKM) [34] let nodes obtain the needed keys and update them from the optimally selected nodes. Wang *et al.* formulated the key management problem as a stochastic system and proposed DHSM in order to find the best nodes from all available nodes based on each one's security conditions.

1.4   Further developments

The research issues and directions for DANETs can be categorized as follows:

1. *Routing*: With rapid changes in network topology, an efficient routing protocol is a key element in DANETs. An effective routing between the sender and the receiver involves finding an optimal path for communication and information delivery.
2. *Multicasting/Broadcasting*: Simultaneous transmissions can cause packet collisions and contention problems. Broadcasting can communicate with all users, but it results in redundant rebroadcasts and can produce broadcast storms.
3. *Location service*: A node's location information uses the Global Positioning System (GPS), Assisted Global Positioning System (AGPS) or a geographical technique to obtain the physical position and transmission destination.
4. *Clustering*: The clustering method is practical for ad hoc networks. A node can be a cluster head, a gateway or simply a member. Using a clustering method to partition the nodes into several clusters is convenient for network management.
5. *Mobility management*: In the ad hoc network environment, mobility causes route changes, and sometimes the link time between two nodes is in the range of seconds. Mobility management handles the node information, message transmission and topology maintenance to help network configuration.
6. *TCP/UDP*: In DANETs, nodes usually use TCP and UDP conduct according to the data application. They are easy to use in wired networks and wireless

infrastructure-based networks, but hard to implement in ad hoc networks. Determining how to use these protocols in a dynamic environment is a daunting task.

7. *IP address*: Setting up an IP address for each node is important in ad hoc networks because nodes do not have pre-assigned static addresses. In addition, auto-configuration schemes for ad hoc networks have been proposed to strengthen network connectivity. For information transmission in some specific applications, the destination is not a particular node, but rather a group of nodes, and additional strategies are needed to prevent unnecessary network overhead in message delivery.

8. *Multiple accesses*: Ad hoc networks need an efficient medium-access control (MAC) protocol for multiple-access and multi-hop routes. Network throughput and spectral reuse can be optimized through MAC schemes.

9. *Radio interface*: Radio interface is associated with the physical layer. Many researchers have developed different radio modulations and antenna techniques to make a node's transmission more robust.

10. *Bandwidth management*: Bandwidth is a limited resource in wireless networks. Thus, bandwidth management is a major problem in ad hoc networks as it significantly affects the node's traffic ability and network utility.

11. *Power management*: Some nodes in ad hoc networks rely on battery power. Thus, an efficient power management scheme can help to reduce power consumption and extend the lifetime of the entire network.

12. *Security and privacy* [35–37]: Due to their unique features, DANETs are more vulnerable than wired networks and wireless infrastructure-based networks. Malicious node detection and attack avoidance is necessary for operating security-sensitive applications, such as financial transactions, military operations and personal data transmission.

Furthermore, TCP/IP of the traditional seven-layer open system interconnect (OSI) model has been used for several decades, but a traditional TCP/IP might not be able to solve all potential problems because of the strict boundaries enforced between the layers. Using cross-layer optimization [38, 39] is considered one way of solving problems across multiple layers. Especially in security problems as mentioned above, security is no longer built into a single network layer, as is the case with mobility, QoS, etc. Using a Cross Layer Design (CLD) [40] to create global strategies from the multi-layer point of view will make it possible to solve these problems while providing more efficient network resource allocation methods and services over DANETs.

1.5 Conclusion

The issue of 'dynamics' has rarely been discussed in ad hoc networks, but network density and mobility have changed significantly over time and space, thus increasing the challenge of devising key management strategies for DANETs. In this chapter, the existing key management schemes in DANETs with multiple perspectives have been surveyed and discussed. The design metrics and proposed schemes were also introduced. From our survey results, it was impossible to select one strategy as superior to the others. Some challenges for secure and efficient key revocation remain to be overcome. In addition, the ability to face new threats in dynamic network environments, devise novel techniques and come up with comprehensive schemes for DANETs is the challenge facing future research.

References

1. Marcelo G. R., Igor M. M., Miguel E. M. C., Luis H. M. K. C., Otto C. M. B. D. 'A Survey on Wireless Ad Hoc Networks', in Guy P. (ed.). *Mobile and Wireless Communication Networks*. Boston, MA: Springer; 2006. pp. 1–33
2. Anne M. H., Eli W., Stig F. M., Chunming R., Oivind K., Pal S. 'A Survey of Key Management in Ad Hoc Networks'. *IEEE Communications Surveys & Tutorials*, 2006;8(3):48–66
3. Xiong L., Libman L., Mao G. 'Uncoordinated Cooperative Communications in Highly Dynamic Wireless Networks'. *IEEE Journal on Selected Areas in Communications*, 2012;30(2):280–288
4. Dow C. R., Lin P. J., Chen S. C., Lin J. H., Hwang S. F. 'A Study of Recent Research Trends and Experimental Guidelines in Mobile Ad-Hoc Networks'. *Proceedings of the 19th International Conference on Advanced Information Networking and Applications (AINA 2005)*; Taipei, Taiwan, March 2005 (IEEE, 2005), pp. 72–77
5. Johann V. D. M., Dawoud D., Stephen M. 'A Survey on Peer-to-Peer Key Management for Mobile Ad Hoc Networks'. *ACM Computing Surveys*, 2007;39(1):1–45
6. Dirk B. S., Dirk B., Smetters D. K., Paul S., Wong H. C. 'Talking to Strangers: Authentication in Ad-Hoc Wireless Networks'. Presented at 2002 Network and Distributed Systems Security Symposium (NDSS'02); San Diego, CA, 2002
7. Nguyen D. T., Soh B. 'Key Management for Lightweight Ad-Hoc Routing Authentication'. *Proceedings of the 4th International Symposium on Wireless Pervasive Computing (ISWPC 2009)*; Melbourne, Australia, February 2009 (IEEE, 2009), pp. 1–7
8. Liao X., Liu K., Liu Y., Xu W. 'Distributed Coverage in Wireless Ad Hoc and Sensor Networks by Topological Graph Approaches'. *IEEE Transactions on Computers*, 2012;61(10):1417–1428
9. Galluccio L., Morabito G., Palazzo S. 'Analytical Evaluation of a Tradeoff between Energy Efficiency and Responsiveness of Neighbor Discovery in Self-Organizing Ad Hoc Networks'. *IEEE Journal on Selected Areas in Communications*, 2004;22(17):1167–1182
10. Jeremy J. B., Azim E., Lance J. H. 'Challenges of Intervehicle Ad Hoc Networks'. *IEEE Transactions on Intelligent Transportation Systems*, 2004;5(4):347–351
11. Jennifer Y., Biswanath M., Dipak G. 'Wireless Sensor Network Survey'. *Computer Networks*, 2008;52(12):2292–2330

12. Michele N. L., Aldri L. d. S., Guy P. 'A Survey of Survivability in Mobile Ad Hoc Networks'. *IEEE Communications Surveys & Tutorials*, 2009;11 (1):66–77

13. Liu C., Wu J. 'Adaptive Routing in Dynamic Ad Hoc Networks'. Presented at The 2009 IEEE Wireless Communications and Networking Conference (IEEE WCNC 2009), Budapest, Hungary, 2009

14. Cho J.-H., Swami A., Chen I.-R. 'A Survey on Trust Management for Mobile Ad Hoc Networks'. *IEEE Communications Surveys & Tutorials*, 2011;13 (4):562–583

15. Tracy C., Jeff B., Vanessa D. 'A Survey of Mobility Models for Ad Hoc Network Research'. *Wireless Communications and Mobile Computing*, 2002;2(5):482–502

16. Devu M. S., Cheng Y. 'Ad Hoc Wireless Networks Meet the Infrastructure: Mobility, Capacity and Delay'. Presented at The 31th IEEE International Conference on Computer Communications (IEEE INFOCOM 2012), Florida, USA, 2012

17. Jerome H., Fethi F., Christian B. 'Mobility Models for Vehicular Ad Hoc Networks: A Survey and Taxonomy'. *IEEE Communications & Surveys*, 2009;11(4):19–41

18. Karnadi F. K., Mo Z. H., Lan K.-C. 'Rapid Generation of Realistic Mobility Models for VANET'. Presented at The 2007 IEEE Wireless Communications and Networking Conference (IEEE WCNC 2007), Hong Kong, China, 2007

19. Zhou L., Zygmunt J. H. 'Securing Ad Hoc Networks'. *IEEE Network*, 1999;13(6):24–30

20. Jean-Pierre H., Levente B., Srdan C. 'The Quest for Security in Mobile Ad-Hoc Networks'. Presented at The 2nd ACM International Symposium on Mobile Ad Hoc Networking & Computing (MobiHoc 2001), California, USA, 2001

21. Tseng F.-H., Chou L.-D., Chao H.-C. 'A Survey of Black Hole Attacks in Wireless Mobile Ad Hoc Networks'. *Human-Centric Computing and Information Sciences*, 2011;1(4):1–16

22. Gao F., Li G. 'Key Management for Large Ad Hoc Networks'. Presented at The 7th International Conference on Wireless Communications, Networking and Mobile Computing (WiCOM 2011), Wuhan, China, 2011

23. Nogueira M., Silva E., Santos A., Albini L. C. P. 'Survivable Key Management on WANETs,' *IEEE Wireless Communications*, 2011;18(6):82–88

24. Chen Q., Lin X., Shen S., Hashimoto K., Kato N. 'A Group-Based Key Management Protocol for Mobile Ad Hoc Networks'. Presented at IEEE Global Telecommunications Conference (GLOBECOM 2009), Hawaii, USA, 2009

25. Hao Y., Cheng Y., Zhou C., Song W. 'A Distributed Key Management Framework with Cooperative Message Authentication in VANETs'. *IEEE Journal on Selected Areas in Communications*, 2011;29(3):616–629

26. Capkun S., Buttyan L., Hubaux J.-P. 'Self-Organized Public-Key Management for Mobile Ad Hoc Networks'. *IEEE Transactions on Mobile Computing*, 2003;2(1):52–64

27. Stallings W. *Cryptography and Network Security*, 4th edn. New Jersey, NJ: Prentice Hall; 2005. p. 592

28. Li L.-C., Liu R.-S. 'Securing Cluster-Based Ad Hoc Networks with Distributed Authorities'. *IEEE Transactions on Wireless Communications*, 2010;9(10):3072–3081

29. Yu F. R., Tang H., Mason P. C., Wang F. 'A Hierarchical Identity-Based Key Management Scheme in Tactical Mobile Ad Hoc Networks'. *IEEE Transactions on Network and Service Management*, 2010;7(4):258–267

30. He W., Huang Y., Sathyam R., Nahrstedt K., Lee W. C. 'SMOCK: A Scalable Method of Cryptographic Key Management for Mission-Critical Wireless Ad-Hoc Networks'. *IEEE Transactions on Information Forensics and Security*, 2009;4(1):140–150

31. Chang B.-J., Kuo S.-L. 'Markov Chain Trust Model for Trust-Value Analysis and Key Management in Distributed Multicast MANETs'. *IEEE Transactions on Vehicular Technology*, 2009;58(4):1846–1863

32. Joshi D., Namuduri K., Pendse R. 'Secure, Redundant, and Fully Distributed Key Management Scheme for Mobile Ad Hoc Networks: An Analysis'. *EURASIP Journal on Wireless Communications and Networking*, 2005;2005 (4):579–589

33. Yu F. R., Tang H., Fei W., Leung V. C. M. 'Distributed Node Selection for Threshold Key Management with Intrusion Detection in Mobile Ad Hoc Networks'. Presented at International Conference on Computational Science and Engineering, Vancouver, Canada, 2009

34. Fei W., Yu F. R., Srinivasan A. 'Distributed Hierarchical Key Management Scheme in Mobile Ad Hoc Networks'. Presented at IEEE Global Telecommunications Conference (GLOBECOM 2009), Hawaii, USA, 2009

35. Rong B., Chen H.-H., Qian Y., Lu K., Hu R. Q., Guizani S. 'A Pyramidal Security Model for Large-Scale Group-Oriented Computing in Mobile Ad Hoc Networks: The Key Management Study'. *IEEE Transactions on Vehicular Technology*, 2009;58(1):398–408

36. Lu R., Lin X., Liang X., Shen X. S. 'A Dynamic Privacy-Preserving Key Management Scheme for Location-Based Services in VANETs'. *IEEE Transactions on Intelligent Transportation Systems*, 2012;13(1):127–139

37. Chen C.-Y., Chao H.-C. 'A Survey of Key Distribution in Wireless Sensor Networks'. *Security and Communication Networks* [online], 2011. Available from http://onlinelibrary.wiley.com/doi/10.1002/sec.354/abstract [Accessed 15 Jan 2013]

38. Vineet S., Mehul M. 'Cross-Layer Design: A Survey and the Road Ahead'. *IEEE Communications Magazine*, 2005;43(12):112–119

39. Sanjay S., Theodore S. R., Peter C. K. 'Cross-Layer Design for Wireless Networks'. *IEEE Communications Magazine*, 2003;41(10):74–80

40. Chen C.-Y., Chao H.-C. 'Cross-Layer Design for Network Security Enhancement' in Habib F. R., Yousef S. K. (eds.). Using Cross-Layer Techniques for Communication Systems. IGI Global; 2012. pp. 138–151

*Chapter 2**

Energy-efficient routing protocols in ad hoc networks

Farhan Siddiqui[a], Sherali Zeadally[b] and Faisal Karim Shaikh[c]

Abstract

Wireless ad hoc networks consist of a collection of mobile nodes that dynamically form a network without the use of any existing network infrastructure. In such networks, each mobile node can serve as a router. Packet delivery is achieved through a single-hop transmission if the communicating nodes are neighbours, otherwise packets can be routed through multiple intermediate nodes. Energy efficiency is important issue in ad hoc networks, where mobile nodes are powered by batteries and it may not be possible to recharge them during a session. The limited battery lifetime can cause one or more links in the network to fail and affect the operation of the network. To maximize the network lifetime, traffic should be routed such that the energy consumption is minimized. We present a survey of energy-efficient routing approaches that have been proposed for various types of ad hoc networks, including mobile ad hoc networks (MANETs), ad hoc mesh networks, and cognitive radio networks. We discuss the main features of each approach and analyse their benefits and operation strategies.

2.1 Introduction

An ad hoc network is a collection of wireless, mobile communication devices that wish to communicate, but have no fixed infrastructure available, and have no pre-determined organization of available links. Individual nodes are responsible for

*H. F. Rashvand and H.-C. Chao (Eds.), *Dynamic Ad Hoc Networks*, The IET Book Publishing Department, 2013, ISBN 978-1-84919-647-5, eISBN 978-1-84919-648-2
[a]School of Information Systems and Technology, Walden University, Minneapolis, MN, USA
[b]Department of Computer Science and Information Technology, University of the District of Columbia, Washington DC, USA
[c]Department of Telecommunication Engineering, Mehran University of Engineering and Technology, Jamshoro, Pakistan

dynamically discovering which other nodes they can directly communicate with. A key assumption is that not all nodes can directly communicate with each other, so nodes are required to relay packets on behalf of other nodes in order to deliver data across the network. A significant feature of ad hoc networks is that rapid changes in connectivity and link characteristics are introduced due to node mobility and power control practices. Ad hoc networks can be built using any wireless technology. These networks are suited for use in situations where infrastructure is either not available, not trusted, or should not be relied on in times of emergency. Ad hoc networks may be deployed in war for military soldiers in the field, in conferences for establishing dynamic connectivity, in space exploration, undersea operations, etc. [1].

The rest of this chapter is organized as follows. In Section 2.2, we describe various types of ad hoc networks. Section 2.3 discusses the need for designing energy-efficient routing protocols for ad hoc networks. In Section 2.4, we present various energy-efficient routing approaches for mobile ad hoc networks. Sections 2.5 and Sections and 2.6 describe the energy-efficient routing protocols for ad hoc Mesh and Cognitive ad hoc networks, respectively. Finally, in Section 2.7, we conclude the chapter.

2.2 Types of wireless ad hoc networks

Wireless ad hoc networks do not have a pre-defined network topology. The topology is created through dynamic network connectivity. Wireless ad hoc networks may be of different types including mobile ad hoc networks (MANETs), ad hoc mesh networks, and cognitive radio networks.

A MANET (as shown in Figure 2.1) is a collection of wireless mobile terminals, which are able to form dynamically a temporary network without any support from a fixed infrastructure or centralized administration. MANETs are strongly affected by the mobility of its nodes. A path in a MANET may break due to node mobility, and leads to the re-routing operations and the degradation of network performance. To reduce routing operations, path reliability is an important factor in selecting optimal paths in MANETs. The reliability of a path depends on the reliability or availability of each link of this path [2].

A wireless ad hoc mesh network (shown in Figure 2.2) [31] consists of a set of mobile or static end-user nodes with the capability of receiving, transmitting, and performing routing to form a mesh topology. The mesh topology can provide end-to-end routes to every other node in the network through multiple hops [3].

A cognitive radio (CR) is intelligent radio that senses the environment and adapts its transmission parameters to efficiently utilize the scarce radio spectrum. Cognitive Radio ad hoc Networks (CRAHNs) [4] , as shown in Figure 2.3 are distributed multi-hop architectures where licensed (primary) and unlicensed (secondary) users co-exist. Primary users (PUs) have high priority in the utilization of

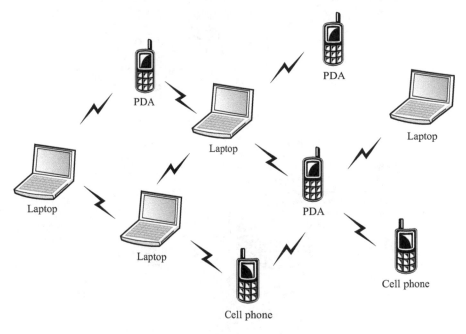

Figure 2.1   Mobile ad hoc network

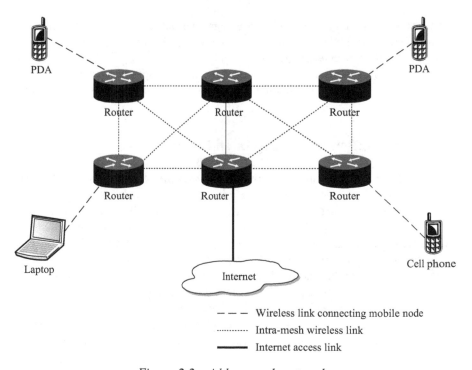

Figure 2.2   Ad hoc mesh network

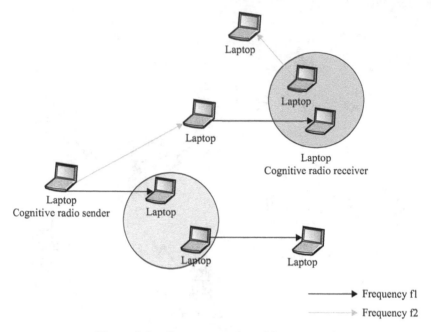

Figure 2.3   Cognitive radio ad hoc network

the spectrum; secondary users (SUs) are cognitive devices able to sense the spectrum and detect available spectrum opportunities (SOP) for transmitting. SOPs are defined as a set of frequency bands currently unoccupied by PUs and, therefore, available for SUs. An SU can opportunistically access a spectrum band not used by a licensed PU and it has to immediately vacate this spectrum when the PU becomes active [5]

2.3   Energy-efficient routing in ad hoc networks

To facilitate communication within the ad hoc network, a routing protocol is used to discover routes between nodes. The primary goal of such an ad hoc network routing protocol is correct and efficient route establishment between a pair of nodes so that messages may be delivered in a timely manner. Route construction should be done with a minimum of overhead and bandwidth consumption [1].

At the same time, mobility and limited battery capacity of the nodes can be critical issue in an ad hoc network because wireless devices are not connected to any constant source of energy [6]. This implies that data packets have to be relayed via energy-constrained nodes. The nodes have limited initial amounts of energy that is consumed at different rates [7]. Mobility of nodes results in continuously evolving new topologies and the routing algorithms have to adapt the routes according to these changes. The limited battery capacity poses a challenge for the routing algorithms: to distribute the packets on multiple paths in such a manner that the battery of different nodes deplete at an equal rate so that, the lifetime of the network could be increased. Thus, ad hoc routing protocols need to be not only energy-efficient but also to provide the same performance as that of the existing state-of-the-art routing algorithms [8].

Battery power of nodes is primarily consumed while transmitting packets (in addition to performing the processing in the nodes). ad hoc networks may be multi-hop and a node may be involved in data transfer regardless whether it is a target or a source. The routing algorithm decides which of the nodes need to be selected in a particular communication. Thus, routing algorithms play an important role in saving the energy of a communication system and the life of the nodes and ultimately the energy of the whole network. Traditional routing algorithms such as Dynamic Source Routing (DSR) and ad hoc On-Demand Distance Vector Routing (AODV [9]) do not take into consideration the energy of nodes in determining a route. This leads to an imbalance of energy level in the network. Some nodes die out soon as they are used in most of the packet transmission paths and at the same time, some nodes may not be used even once. This energy imbalance affects the reliability of the system [10].

Thus, routing protocols for ad hoc networks are required to minimize the energy consumption and maximize the battery life of nodes. This will ensure a longer network lifetime of the ad hoc network, thereby increasing reliable packet delivery.

2.4 Energy-efficient routing approaches in MANETs

A MANET [11] consists of autonomous, self-organizing and self-operating nodes characterized by links with lower bandwidth, nodes with constrained resources such as energy, memory, and processing power. In MANETs, communication between nodes out of transmission range greatly relies on intermediate nodes. It is possible that certain intermediate nodes will eventually run out of battery and eventually start dropping packets as they try to save their battery power. Therefore, it is a challenging problem to find a routing approach that can minimize energy usage and reliably deliver data packets in the network.

In this section, we focus on various energy-efficient routing approaches that have been proposed for routing in MANETs.

2.4.1 *Reliable and energy-efficient routing (RelEE)*

RelEE [12] is a reliable and energy-efficient routing approach that considers both, the reliability of data packet transmission and the energy utilization. RelEE defines a new cost function based on residual battery level to avoid a path with malicious nodes. This method can adjust route selection to preserve energy consumption and keep the ratio of successfully delivered packets over a threshold (γ).

The RelEE approach assumes that malicious nodes in MANETs will simply drop received data packets. Hence, residual battery level of malicious nodes will remain high. On the other hand, a good and cooperative node will forward data packets to its neighbouring nodes and consume energy for every transmitted packet. Thus, the battery level of cooperative nodes will be decreased and will be lower than the malicious nodes' residual battery level. Thus, the residual battery level is incorporated in the route selection algorithm to avoid malicious nodes. Based on the assumption that the battery level of malicious nodes will remain high after joining in the network for a period, a route having malicious nodes tends to have a higher cost following the maximum battery level in the cost function. A new cost function based on residual battery level of each node along the potential path is incorporated in the RelEE approach as follows. For each path l, the 'maximum battery node' is determined by:

$$B'_l = \max_{\forall i \in l} \{B(i)\} \text{ (where } B_i \text{ is the battery of node } i)$$

In order to avoid malicious nodes and select the potential path with a minimum cost, $C'_l = (P_l)^1 (B'_l)^1 (B_{init})^{-1}$

P_l = energy consumption along the path
B'_l = maximum battery node
B_{init} = initial battery of the node

In the RelEE algorithm, the Mincost and Reputation route selection approaches are also adopted to minimize energy consumption and increase network lifetime as well as provide reliable data transmission. In the Reputation algorithm, the reputation is defined as a ratio of the number of packets received to the total number of packets forwarded. Hence the path selection algorithm based on reputation will select a path with the highest reputation value for reliable data transmission to achieve a high ratio of successfully delivered packets. The Mincost routing algorithm combines both energy consumption and battery level in a cost function used in route selection. Suppose that some source and destination nodes are connected by a set of multiple paths, L. For each path $l \in L$, the energy consumption along the path can be determined by:

$$P_l = \sum_{\forall i \in l} E(i) \quad E(i) \text{ is the energy consumption of node } i$$

The algorithm can adjust the route selection process based on network changes using the ratio of successfully delivered packets. The ratio of successfully delivered packets (R_{pkt}) is defined as:

$$R_{pkt} = \frac{\#\text{of times packets are succesfully received}}{\#\text{of times packets are sent}}$$

The threshold value (γ) is calculated from the average ratio of successfully delivered packets (R_{pkt}) after a number of initial data packet transmissions.

$$\gamma = \sum_{k=1}^{K} \frac{Rpkt}{K}$$

where, K is the number of transmissions. The RelEE algorithm initially calculates the threshold value (γ) based on the Mincost scheme for the first K number of packet transmissions.

The RelEE approach can have a high ratio of successfully delivered packets using low average energy consumed per delivered packets as well as uphold the network lifetime.

2.4.2 Energy-Efficient On-Demand Routing Algorithm (EEAODR)

The EEAODR algorithm [10] considers the power level of each node while calculating the route, in order to increase the network lifetime. Whenever a node is involved in any transaction, it loses some amount of energy whose value depends on factors such as the nature of packets, their size and the distance between the nodes. EEAODR defines an optimization function that considers all these factors and decides which one, among all the discovered paths, should be selected for an energy-efficient transmission. The algorithm reduces the probability of repetitively selecting a particular node, which can lead to early exhaustion of the node, thereby affecting the network connectivity. The algorithm, however, considers individual battery power in deciding the path: if there is a path with a node having a very low energy level, then the optimization function does not choose that path, irrespective of whether that path is time efficient. Additional criteria that are considered in the optimization function include the number of hops and the time needed to reach the destination. The number of hops is an important criterion because as large number of hops will help in reducing the range of power transmission and, thus, saving energy. The transmission time is also a criterion because the lower the time, the shorter will be the path, and the lower will be the total amount of energy consumed.

In the EEAODR scheme, when a source node wants to transmit data to a destination, it first looks whether there is any existing valid path in the routing table. If it exists, the node uses that path. Otherwise, it sends Route Requests (RREQs) to its neighbour nodes. When a node (either destination or intermediate) receives a RREQ, it ensures that the received RREQ is not a duplicate RREQ, in order to prevent looping paths. If the neighbour node is the destination, it sends a route reply (RREP). Otherwise, the neighbour nodes see whether they have any valid path in their tables. If they do, they forward RREQs to that path. Otherwise, they send new RREQs to all their neighbour nodes to find the destination. When the destination gets the first RREQ, it waits for some time and collects all other RREQs coming in this time interval. After the time interval expires, the destination node calls the optimization function to determine the best path to select and sends a RREP. It also stores some other relatively inferior paths as backup paths, which may be used if there is some network failure, thereby avoiding energy and time wastage in recalculating the path. When the source gets the RREP, it sends the data packets.

The EEAODR algorithm performs better than the popular conventional on-demand routing algorithm (such as AODV) with respect to the network lifetime and energy consumption. This is due to the fact that network lifetime increased by distributing the network load and selecting paths containing nodes with higher power levels.

2.4.3   Energy-Efficient Congestion-Aware Routing Protocol (EECARP)

EECARP [13] is an on-demand routing protocol that aims to create congestion-free routes by making use of information gathered from the MAC layer. EECARP employs a combined weight metric in its standard cost function to take into consideration network congestions. To establish multiple disjoint paths, EECARP uses the idea from the ad hoc On-Demand Multipath Distance Vector Routing (AOMDV) [14]. AOMDV computes multiple paths between the source and destination nodes. Each of these paths is guaranteed to be disjoint and loop-free. In EECARP, multiple paths are computed during the route discovery phase. Then the node weight (NW) metric is calculated, which assigns a cost to each link in the network. The NW combines the link quality (L_q), MAC overhead (OH_{MAC}), effective data rate (D_{rate}), residual energy (RE) and the average delay D_{avg}, to select maximum throughput paths, avoiding the most congested links. The application requirements are also matched closely to the route selection process. The Quality-of-Service (QoS) requirements are different for various types of applications. Applications can pass their individual requirements to the EECARP protocol. For example, a video conferencing application requires high bandwidth and is also delay sensitive. In this case, EECARP parameters for a video conferencing application will be configured as follows: $c_1 = 0.5$, $c_2 = 0.4$ and $c_3 = 0.1$, where c_1 corresponds to the Link quality, c_2 corresponds to the effective data rate and c_3 corresponds to the residual energy. The EECARP protocol uses the information given by applications in the form of c_1, c_2 and c_3 to calculate the link-weight for selecting a route using the equation shown below:

For an intermediate node i with established transmission with several of its neighbours, the NW for the link from node i to a particular neighbouring node is given by: $(c_1. L_q * c_2.D_{rate} * c_3.RE) (OH_{MAC} *D_{avg})$.

EECARP achieves high throughput and packet delivery ratio by reducing the energy consumption, packet drop and delay.

2.4.4   Progressive Energy-Efficient Routing (PEER)

PEER [15] is a cost-based energy efficient routing protocol. In a cost-based routing protocol, the total cost of all the links on each available path between the source node and the destination node is calculated, and a minimum cost path (meeting certain criteria) is be selected. As link cost is very important in the cost-based energy efficient routing protocols, PEER attempts to derive an accurate link cost metric to obtain an optimal path. The PEER protocol includes a quick and low overhead path discovery scheme and an efficient path maintenance scheme for reducing energy consumption especially in mobile environments. PEER searches for the energy-efficient path quickly during the route discovery process, and maintains the route actively so that it can respond to topology and channel changes quickly. The basic searching algorithm in PEER includes: (1) search for all shortest (fewest hops) paths, and (2) selecting the minimum energy path(s) among the shortest paths in (1). To implement this algorithm, the RREQ packet carries two pieces of information: one is the hop count. The other is the energy consumption. The source node first broadcasts the RREQ packet with both hop count and energy consumption set to 0. Once an intermediate node receives a RREQ packet, it first updates the hop count (increased by 1, and energy consumption information in the RREQ packet. Then, it rebroadcasts such a packet only if one of the following conditions holds:

1. The node has not received such a packet before or the packet comes from a shorter (smaller number of hops) path.
2. The packet comes from a path with the same number of hops as the best path so far, but the energy consumption is lower.

The first condition ensures that the shortest path is selected, while the second condition selects the minimum energy path from all the shortest paths. The route obtained in the path discovery phase is sub-optimal and may still lead to higher end-to-end energy consumption than that of the minimum energy path. In addition, the network environment can change dramatically due to node movements and dynamic channel conditions, and the previous energy-efficient route may no longer be efficient over time. Therefore, the route maintenance phase is critical for energy-efficient routing protocols. As extra signalling messages consume more energy, the route maintenance scheme of PEER does not use additional periodic messages. Instead, an observing node passively monitors data packets exchanged in its neighbourhood and collaborates with its neighbours to look for a more energy-efficient path. Each node can estimate the necessary transmission power and the link cost to a neighbouring node once it receives a Request to Send (RTS), Clear to Send (CTS) or a broadcast packet from the neighbouring node. In PEER, each forwarding node inserts the link cost into the IP header of the packet targeted for its next-hop receiver as an IP option, and every node monitors the data packets exchanged in its neighbourhood to intercept the corresponding link costs and use these link costs to estimate the cost of a path segment. For each data packet transmitted, received or overheard by a node, the node records the following information into a link cost table: (a) sender, (b) receiver, (c) link cost between the sender and the receiver, (d) source, (e) destination, (f) IP header ID and (g) current time. Among these parameters, (a) and (b) can be obtained from the MAC header, while (c)–(g) can be obtained from the IP header. The information for a link is kept only for a short time for accurate information and minimizes storage overheads. Based on the informa-tion recorded in its link cost table, a node can help reduce the cost of a local path segment and hence the cost of the end-to-end path between a source and a desti-nation with the use of the following three operations: remove, replace and insert.

The PEER protocol uses an accurate link cost, and can search for a more energy-efficient path. PEER protocol can adapt the path to the environment change quickly, and better maintain an energy-efficient path. The PEER protocol reduces about 2/3 routing overhead and path setup delay as compared to a conventional energy-efficient routing protocol, and is highly adaptive to environmental changes.

PEER protocol performs much better than normal energy-efficient routing protocol such as Minimum Total Reliable Transmission Power (MTRTP) for both static and mobile scenarios, and under all circumstances in terms of node mobility, network density and load.

2.4.5   Energy Efficient Power Aware Routing (EEPAR) algorithm

The EEPAR routing algorithm [16] aims to increase the lifetime of the network with minimal overheads while achieving the desired features of MANET's routing protocols. EEPAR selects optimal paths using power aware metrics and optimizes the power consumption and bandwidth utilization while keeping overheads low. It supports reliability by providing nodes disjoint paths and it provides stability (i.e., increased node lifetime) by distributing the burden of routing and congestion control between all nodes in the network.

EEPAR uses the following four main mechanisms: route selection, route discovery, maximization of network lifetime with congestion control and route maintenance.

2.4.6   Route selection based on cost function

EEPAR's route selection involves the selection of optimal paths to prolong a network's lifetime and it is based on a cost function. The main objective of the cost function is to give more weight or cost to nodes with less energy and thereby prolong their lifetime.

2.4.7   Route discovery

EEPAR makes modifications to the Dynamic Source Routing (DSR) protocol to enable the discovery of energy aware node disjoint paths.

2.4.8   Modifications of control packets

In EEPAR, the format of RREQ packet and RREP packet of the DSR are modified. The RREQ of the DSR is extended to RREQ of the EEPAR by adding two extra fields (the cost field and the max-cost field). The RREQ in EEPAR therefore contains the type source address, destination address, unique identification number (ID), hop count, max-cost field, cost (cumulative cost) field and the path field.

2.4.9   Modifications at the source node

In the case of DSR, when a source node wants to send data to a destination, it looks up its route cache to determine if it already contains a route to the destination. If it finds that an unexpired route to the destination exists, then it uses this route to send the data. But if the source node does not have such a route, then it initiates the route discovery process by broadcasting a RREQ packet. In the EERP, the functions of the source node are similar, but source node maintains energy aware node disjoint multipath to a destination and it chooses the optimal path to send the data.

2.4.10 Modifications at the intermediate node

In DSR, when an intermediate node receives a RREQ packet, it checks whether its own address is already listed in the route record of the received RREQ packet. If its address is not found, then it appends its address to the route record of the received RREQ packet and it is broadcasted to all its neighbours. Otherwise the received RREQ packet is dropped. Later, if an intermediate node receives duplicate RREQ packets (whose source address and ID are same as the source address and the ID of the currently received RREQ packet) from other paths, then those duplicate RREQ packets are dropped. The pair (source address, ID) is used to distinguish packets.

2.4.11 Modifications at the destination node

In DSR, when the destination receives the RREQ packet, its address is appended to it and it generates the route reply by inserting the path information into it. In DSR, the destination sends single route reply. Later, duplicate RREQ packets are dropped and the destination node does not send any reply. In the case of EERP, the destination generates several replies and sends them to the source. When multiple RREQ packets reach the destination, the destination appends its address and adds total cost to each RREQ. At this point, each RREQ contains a path from source to destination. In the conventional on demand multipath routing protocols, the source node computes optimal path(s) from multiple paths that were supplied by the destination in the route reply. In EERP, the computation of optimal paths is assigned to the destination instead of the source to reduce the overhead.

2.4.12 Maximization of network lifetime and congestion control

A node cannot operate after its battery power is exhausted. To maximize the lifetime of the network, each node maintains a minimum energy level, also called the threshold or cut-off value that is always greater than one. During the transmission of data, each node checks whether its energy has reached this threshold. If its energy reaches this threshold then node sends a choke packet to the source node along the reverse path. After receiving the choke packets, the source node stops the data transmission on the selected path and it uses the alternate path if available. If an alternative path is not available, it initiates a discovery process to continue the data transmission. Choke packets are also used when there is network congestion along the network path (from the source to the destination).

EEPAR significantly reduces the total number of route request packets which result in: an increased packet delivery ratio, a decrease in the end-to-end delays for the data packets, lower control overhead, fewer packet collisions, increased reliability and a decrease in the power consumption.

2.4.13 Energy Aware Routing Algorithm (EARA)

The EARA algorithm [17] assumes that the devices operating in the MANET have dual channels, i.e., a channel and a control channel. The data channel is used for the transmission of data packets and the control channel is for medium access, i.e., Request to Send (RTS) or Clear to Send (CTS), and for wake-up calls in the end-to-end path. However, power consumption is more during data transmission when compared to transmitting control signals. When a MANET node joins the network, its data channel is switched off to save battery resources. Only the control channel is kept active and is ready to transmit. The device is now in partial active state. At the beginning, all the nodes have their data channels closed. When a node needs to send some data packet, it issues a wakeup call over its control channel. As it is a high-power signal the receiving nodes simply forward it to their neighbours. Effectively, this is a broadcast using multiple hops. The nodes receiving this wakeup signal not only forward it to their neighbours but also open their data channels. In this state, the device is said to be in a fully active state. The initiating node will broadcast Graph Request Packets (GREQs,) over the data channel. The GREQs are used to generate the graph corresponding to the MANET and to get the residual battery power of each node in the network. When a node receives a GREQ packet, it responds with a Graph REply Packet (GREP) with its identity and power values. EARA uses Breadth First Search (BFS) for collecting the global topology information.

After obtaining the global topology with the residual battery power at every node using BFS, the cost of each node is calculated as follows:

$$A = (100 - P_{down})/S$$
$$B = (P_n - P_{down})$$
$$Cost = S - (B/A)$$

Where P_{down} is set to 10% of 5%, i.e., the residual battery power when a device switches off or hibernates. At this point a node is said to be isolated from the MANET or is dead.

P_n is the power value of the node that is received in the GREP reply.

S is the scaling factor. S is taken as the next higher power of 10 of the number of nodes in the network.

Each node calculates this cost before replying to GREQs. The cost values are updated using an adjacency list for route computations.

After collecting the global topology information and the cost associated with each node, the Dijkstra's shortest path algorithm is used to find out the least cost path to the desired destination. This gives the path to the destination and the information about the nodes participating in the data transfer. These nodes are known as the pool of active nodes. At this point, a Route Finalized Packet (RFP) is sent with the end-to-end path information to tell the pool of active nodes not to shut their data channels on hearing the next 'SLEEP' control signal. If the sender node receives an ACK signal, it initiates the 'SLEEP' signal over the control channel. All nodes, except the pool of active nodes, switch off their data channels keeping their control channels alive. However, when the data channels of the nodes are off, a sender can acquire the medium using RTS/CTS signals over the control channels. Now that an energy aware path is available, the source and destination can exchange data packets using the data channel in the usual way. To minimize the variance in the energy of nodes in the network, the concept of 'refresh intervals' is used. By recalculating the path at refresh intervals, the variance of the network can be taken into consideration. If a large amount of data is transmitted over the same nodes, the battery of these nodes will get used up faster. The use of refresh interval ensures that the same nodes do not get used quite often thereby saving their battery resources.

EARA introduces a method for computing the cost function for maximizing the average residual energy of the network, minimizing the variance of the power of the nodes in a MANET, while reducing the transmission cost for each packet over the mobile network. EARA works fairly well when deployed in multimedia application environments where a large amount of data is typically streamed between the source and destination nodes.

2.4.14 *Energy Efficient Integrated Routing Protocol (E2IRP)*

The E2IRP algorithm [18] is an integrated MAC and routing layer protocol designed for applications such as remote surveillance systems, precision agriculture etc., where mobility is rare.

As shown in Figure 2.4, in a typical E2IRP network, the nodes are distributed around the gateway, each node has a communication range of R. E2IRP is based on the assumption that an event can be triggered at any point in the region, and that only one node detects and reports the event. E2IRP operates in two phases: the

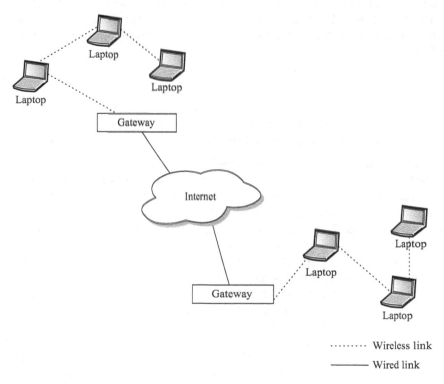

Figure 2.4   E2IRP network

configuration phase and the active phase. The actual communication between the source and the sink can take place only after the configuration phase is completed and hence this phase needs to be completed just after the deployment of the nodes.

2.4.14.1   E2IRP configuration phase

The purpose of the configuration phase is to organize the nodes into tiers around the gateway. The width of each tier depends on the communication range of the nodes. There are two ways of organizing the network into tiers. In the first method the gateway initiates the configuration phase by sending out a TIER message. All the nodes within the communication range of the gateway and the nodes that receive this message organize themselves into TIER 1. These nodes in turn forward the TIER message after incrementing the TIER number. Thus, a node receiving a TIER message with TIER_ID 'N' organizes itself in TIER 'N' if it is not already organized into lower tier. Alternatively, the gateway sends out the TIER message at varying power, and nodes receiving the message organize themselves accordingly, corresponding to the communication range R. The shape of the tiers may depend on the variation in the nodes' waking time or the radio reachability of the nodes.

2.4.14.2   E2IRP active phase

The actual event handling takes place only during the active phase. The normal route reply is sent by unicast with the MAC address. However, E2IRP uses Short Random Identifiers (RSD and RRD) that are used as unique identifiers in a RREQ packet instead of a MAC address. In E2IRP, the following issues have to be considered:

- The node should identify itself with the random identifier rather than the MAC address.
- The random identifier should be unique in the sense that no two nodes should be identified by the same identifier.
- The random identifier generated should be communicated to other nodes.

In order for the node to identify itself using the random identifier rather than the MAC address, it has to maintain the random identifier till the event is dealt with. The second issue deals with the duplication in the random identifiers. This condition may arise when two events are detected at the same time and more than one node generates the same identifier. Duplication of random identifiers must be avoided as it may lead to ambiguity during the reply phase. Nodes receiving the same random identifier should notify the source node, to resend the message with a new random identifier. In traditional routing protocols, as in AODV, the retrieval of MAC address is handled by the Address Resolution Protocol (ARP) protocol. When a packet has to be unicast, an ARP request is broadcast with the IP address as its parameter. The node with the corresponding IP address replies with the MAC address in the reply packet. The node, which requested for the MAC address can now unicast the reply packet. In E2IRP, the source sends the unique random identifier along with the route request. So, the nodes receiving the request can update their ARP table without the need of ARP request and reply. This in turn reduces the battery power required for the construction and processing of these packets. The event detected at a node is communicated to the sink by the method of any cast. In other words, if the packet originated in tier number 'N', only the nodes in tier number '$N - 1$' receive the request and respond to it. If the event is detected at TIER 'N', a route is established from the source to the sink. In response to the route request packet received the node stake one of the following steps:

- If the node is in tier ID '$N + 1$' or 'N', the packet is dropped. This prevents uncontrolled flooding of the packet in the network.
- If the node is in tier ID '$N - 1$' and the node is not the destination, the packet is forwarded.
- If the node is the intended destination, the gateway, then a route reply is sent along the path from which the route request was obtained.

The use of RSD in RREQ establishes route as follows:

1. When a node in tier ID 'N' sends out a route request, it creates a RSD that is unique for the particular node and particular event.
2. When a node in tier ID '$N - 1$' receives this packet the ARP table is updated to reflect the random identifier of the node, which sent the request.
3. Finally when the destination, the gateway, receives the request, it already knows the reverse route to the source of the event.

This method of route establishment avoids the transmission of ARP request packets to update the ARP table. The removal of ARP requests and replies tremendously improves the performance of the network. This is because when the data packets are ready to be transmitted, the route has to be established first. The route request packet is broadcast, but the route reply should be unicast, in the sense that, the hardware address of the receiver node should be known. In normal protocols this is done by ARP requests and reply. But, in the case of this integrated MAC and routing protocol, the hardware address (in this case, the random identifier) is transmitted at the time of the route request itself. This eliminates the requirement of these requests and replies. Moreover, the MAC address in RTS and CTS is replaced with the random identifiers RSD and RRD. The advantage of including the random identifier is that even if the node gets displaced the routing is not disturbed. The size of the random identifier is also far smaller than the MAC identifier thus reducing the overhead of transmitting and receiving the packets and also in processing of the packets.

2.4.15 *Power-aware Routing Protocol (PAR)*

The PAR protocol [19] maximizes the network lifespan and minimizes the energy utilization by selecting less congested and more stable routes during the source to destination route establishment process. The three parameters focused by PAR protocol are: accumulated energy of a path, status of battery lifetime and the type of data to be transmitted. These core metrics are the focus of PAR during the route selection time. Hence, less congested and more stable routes for data delivery are considered. Thus, the network lifetime is increased if different routes for different types of data transfer are provided. PAR outperforms related protocols such as DSR and AODV with respect to diverse energy-related performance metrics for high-mobility scenarios. Nevertheless, PAR incurs increased latency during data transfers, but the discovered route lasts for a long time, and enormous energy saving is achieved.

2.4.16   *Energy Efficient Location Aided Routing (EELAR)*

The EELAR protocol [20] was proposed to make significant reduction in the energy consumption of the mobile node's power by limiting new route discovery to a smaller zone. This assisted the network to have significantly reduced control packet overheads. The basic algorithm for this proposal is Location Aided Routing (LAR). EELAR uses a reference wireless base station while the network's circular area centred at the base station is divided into six equal sub-areas. Packets are only flooded to the sub-area of the destination nodes instead of flooding control packets to the whole network area during route discovery. Hence, the base station stores locations of the mobile nodes in a position table. The EELAR protocol minimizes the control packet overhead and improves the packet delivery ratio compared to AODV, Location Aided Routing and DSR protocols.

2.4.17   *Location-based Power Conservation (LBPC) Scheme for MANETs*

The LBPC scheme [21] uses the location information provided by an inbuilt Global Positioning System (GPS) to extract information such as average distance of the first hop neighbours and the random distance between the nearest and furthest first hop neighbours to adjust the transmission range. LBPC provides power conservation in the range of 10%–50%. This significant amount of energy conservation is achieved by various adjustments done to the network transmission range. However, the energy conservation process results in lower throughput and end-to-end delay. The LBPC protocol finds the Euclid distance (r) between a node and all other nodes within the network. LBPC only works well without extra overheads being added in MANET that uses Location Aware Routing (LAR) algorithms where each node's location is already known without necessarily computing the Euclid distance of other nodes within the network. Simulation results obtained with LPBC were encouraging especially when the node density increases because this also improves node connectivity and a reduction in transmission range. Nevertheless, the limitation imposed by the computational complexities of the non-LAR compatible algorithm limits the benefits of the LBPC scheme.

The Location-based Power Conservation (LBPC) scheme utilizes the location information to reduce the power consumption during route discovery in MANETs. In this scheme, it is assumed that each node is aware of the location of all other nodes within the network and the nodes' location that is used may be provided by a built-in GPS. The LBPC scheme works as follows:

Each node searches for all first-hop neighbours:

1. The Euclid distance (r) between the node and all other nodes within the network is calculated.
2. The Euclid distance r is compared with the maximum radio transmission range (R_{max}) of the node. If $r \leq R_{max}$, then this node is a first-hop neighbours, otherwise it is not.

The Radio Transmission Range (R) is adjusted according to one of the following criteria:

1. Maximum distance (r_{max}), which means the transmission will reach the farthest first-hop neighbour, i.e., R is set to r_{max}
2. Average distance (r_{avg}) and its associated standard deviation (σ), i.e., R is set to $r_{avg \mp \sigma}$
3. Random distance (r_{ran}) lies between the nearest and farthest nodes, calculated as:

$r_{ran} = r_{min} + (r_{max} - r_{min})\xi$, where r_{min} and r_{max} are the distances of the nearest and farthest nodes, respectively and ξ is a random number between zero and one ($0 \leq \xi \leq 1$), i.e., set $R = r_{ran}$

The criterion that is used for adjusting the transmission range may affect other network parameters, such as the number of retransmissions, average duplicate reception, and reachability. The efficiency of the proposed scheme is defined in terms of a power conservation ratio (P_c), which is calculated as:

$$P_c = (1 - (n^{\wedge}R^2 / n'R^2_{max})) * 100$$

where $n^{\wedge}$ and n' are the number of retransmission with and without implementing the power conservation scheme, respectively; R and R_{max} are the adjusted and maximum radio transmission range, respectively.

For MANETs that use the LAR algorithm, each node is already aware of the location of other nodes within the network. Therefore, this scheme can be implemented in such networks with little overheads. In a network that uses other routing algorithms and in order to minimize communication overheads, nodes can be configured to exchange their location information with their first-hop neighbours only.

LBPC achieves a power conservation ratio of 10%–50% depending on the network environment. However, power conservation may reduce as node density or the transmission range increases.

2.4.18 Cluster-based routing protocol (CBRP)

CBRP [22] is a robust and scalable routing protocol for MANETs. CBRP has a low overhead and high throughput compared to the AODV protocol. This routing protocol is designed for medium to large MANETs. This protocol divides the nodes of the ad hoc network into several overlapping or disjoint 2-hop diameter clusters in a distributed manner. Each cluster chooses a head to retain cluster membership information. The node with a lowest ID among its neighbours is elected as the Cluster Head (CH). Each node maintains a Neighbour Table (NT) and a Cluster Adjacency Table. The NT is a conceptual data structure that holds link status sensing and cluster information. The Cluster Adjacency Table keeps information about adjacent clusters for Adjacent Cluster Discovery. These tables updated periodically by Hello Messages (HM).

CBRP is based on the concept of source routing. The cluster structure is exploited to minimize the flooding traffic during the route discovery phase. Based on the cluster membership and information kept at each CH, inter-cluster routes are dynamically discovered. During the Route Discovery process, only cluster heads are flooded with RREQ packets while searching for a source route. Each CH node forwards an RREQ packet only once and it never forwards it to a node that has already appeared in the recorded route. It proactively acquires its intra-cluster topology information through the exchange of HELLO messages.

In CBRP the nodes are organized in a hierarchy. The CH coordinates the data transmission between clusters. The advantage of CBRP is that only CHs exchange routing information, therefore the amount of control overhead transmitted through the network is far less than with traditional flooding methods. However, as with many other hierarchical routing protocols, there are overheads associated with cluster formation and maintenance. This is because some nodes may carry inconsistent topology information due to long propagation delays. A NT in every node of CBRP keeps the information about link states and the state of its neighbours. A CH keeps information of its neighbouring clusters in addition to the information on all members in its cluster. Such information includes the CHs of neighbouring clusters and the gateway nodes connecting it to the neighbouring clusters.

To save energy, all member nodes (except the gateway node) go into sleep mode when they are idle. In this method, only CHs and gateway nodes are reactive for any communication with the backbone of the network.

We present a summary of the various energy-efficient routing approaches presented above in Table 2.1.

2.5 Energy-efficient routing approaches in ad hoc mesh networks

A wireless mesh network is composed of access points, mesh routers and mesh clients. The fixed access points are wired to connect to the Internet to provide high-bandwidth connections to the Internet backbone. The meshing among wireless routers and access points creates a wireless backhaul communication system. The backhaul provides each mobile client with a limited number of entry points connected to the Internet. These entry points, along with the access points, are usually referred to as Hot Spots. Mesh clients may be devices such as laptops, tablet PCs, PDAs, IP phones, Radio Frequency Identification (RFID) readers, etc.

Table 2.1 Summary of energy-efficient routing protocols for mobile ad hoc networks

Protocol	Approach	Metrics for route selection	Advantages
RelEE	Cost-based. Also use Mincost and Reputation Route Selection	Energy consumption, battery level	High ratio of successfully delivered packets, low energy consumption per packet
EEAODR	Network life increased by distributing the network load and selecting paths containing nodes with higher power levels	Battery power in node, number of hops, time to reach destination	Performs better than conventional AODV protocol
EECARP	Based on modifications made to the AOMDV protocol	Link quality, MAC overhead, residual energy, average delay	High throughput and packet delivery ratio, low energy consumption, packet drop and delay
PEER	Optimal routing path based on link cost metric. Path chosen is the shortest path with least energy requirement	Number of hops, minimum energy path	50% reduction in energy consumption compared to MTRTP
EEPAR	Based on modifications to the DSR protocol	Battery capacity in node	Reduced end-to-end delay, low control overhead, fewer packet collisions
EARA	Routing decision based on cost function that maximises residual energy of the network	Residual battery, number of hops	Well suited for multimedia application environments
E2IRP	Nodes organized in to tiers. Improves network performance by avoiding the transmission of ARP request packets to update the ARP table	Location of node and energy consumption	Reduced packet transmission and processing overhead
PAR	Maximizes network lifespan by selecting less congested and more stable routes	Accumulated energy of a path, status of battery lifetime, and type of data	Outperforms AODV and DSR in high mobility scenarios
EELAR	Based on modifications made to the LAR protocol	Position of the node and expected energy consumption	Improves control packet overhead and delivery ration compared to AODV, LAR, and DSR protocols
LBPC	Uses location information to reduce power consumption during route discovery	Euclid distance	Power conservation ratio of 10%–50%
CBRP	Based on the concept of source routing. Energy saving implemented using sleep mode in wireless devices	Energy consumption of node	Powerful, scalable, low overhead and high throughput compared to AODV, provides high energy savings in an ad hoc network, thereby maximizing network lifetime, stability and connectivity

Mesh routers have sufficient power supply from the backbone Internet. However, mesh clients (forming an ad hoc network) are limited in their battery capacity. Therefore, it is essential to design efficient routing schemes that can be used for mesh clients in order to minimize their power consumption and improve their network lifetime. Below, we discuss some of the most recent routing protocols that have been designed to implement energy-efficient routing in ad hoc mesh networks.

2.5.1   Energy and throughput-aware routing

Energy and throughput-aware routing (ETR) [23] is a routing algorithm for 802.11 based wireless mesh networks. The design objectives of ETR are to provide flows with throughput guarantees, and to minimize the overall energy consumption in the mesh network. ETR's network model is based on the notions of link and link group. A link exists between two interfaces if these two interfaces operate on the same channel and can establish direct communication. A link group is a set of interfaces that operate on the same channel and can directly communicate with each other.

ETR assumes that the channels of the wireless mesh networks are carefully assigned in order to avoid undesired interferences. This is typical in planned networks (e.g., an operator-owned network where channels are centrally assigned in such a way so that the overall interference in the network is minimized). Following the above target scenario, ETR assumes that the channel assignment algorithm results in the following: all the interfaces that belong to the same link group are assigned to the same channel and are in the transmission (and collision) range of each other. The stations that do not belong to the same link group do not cause transmission errors to each other, either because they are assigned to different non-overlapping channels or because (although using an overlapping channels) they are physically located far enough from each other. Following the above assumption, a transmission from an interface will be successful as long as it does not interfere with any transmission from the same link group, independently of whether the interfaces that belong to other link groups transmit or not.

In ETR, the mesh network is deployed with careful channel assignment. In addition to channel assignment, link adaptation techniques support the use of modulation schemes that prevent external interference from causing transmission errors. To minimize energy consumption, ETR uses a simplified model that requires devices to consume a constant power when switched on while neglecting the energy dedicated to individual transmissions. This model follows the 'on–off' energy profile. Following the 'on–off' model, the ETR approach implements the switching off as many devices as possible in order to minimize the overall energy consumed by the wireless mesh network.

2.5.2   Battery aware multiple input multiple output (MIMO) mesh network power scheduling (BAMPS)

The key idea of battery awareness in mesh networks is to dynamically schedule mesh radio transceivers for network coverage and backhaul network routing.

Neighbouring routers can collaboratively adjust their transceiver radii and alternatively recover their batteries. For example, if a network has two routers A and B and the distance between them is $L = 10$ m. Each router has a battery with $1.8 \times 10\,4$ mA minimum capacity. A and B collaboratively cover mobile clients on the line between them. The two routers alternatively use radii R and r, ($L = R + r$ and $R = R/r$), each for a period of time. In the first period, B uses a shorter radius and has a battery that is currently lower than A, and it recovers its battery during this first period. In the next period, A adopts a shorter radius to recover its battery. In this way A and B together can minimize the total battery discharging loss and maximize their lifetime. A and B can alternatively choose R and $L - R$ as their radii for a period of 20 minutes. In this case, the maximum power consumption occurs when A and B adopt an equal radius of 5 m. This is because none of the two routers have a chance to recover their battery discharging loss in this schedule. In this example, the network achieves minimum power dissipation by letting A and B alternatively adopts radii of 3 m and 7 m, respectively. This example shows that network performance can be effectively enhanced by taking advantage of the battery behaviour [24].

The BAMPS [24] scheme consists of two parts: the coverage algorithm and the backhaul routing algorithm for mesh client coverage and backhaul routing, respectively.

The idea of the coverage algorithm is that each mesh router periodically calculates its battery discharging loss, and broadcasts it to its one-hop neighbours. After obtaining all neighbours' discharging loss values, a router calculates a feasible radius according to the transceiver model and the router's battery status. To ensure that the entire network area is covered, each router chooses the distance between itself and its farthest neighbour for the radius calculation. For example, if a network consists of routers A, B and C, in period 1, C adopts a short radius that leads to the battery recovery for C. In the next period, A has the opportunity to recover its battery, and so on. This is a distributed algorithm, and each mesh router only needs to communicate with at most n neighbours. In backhaul routing, mesh backhaul nodes communicate through directional radios. Whenever there is a need to transmit data packets to or from Access Points (APs) and neighbour routers, a directional connection is set up from the sender to the receiver. The idea of the backhaul routing algorithm is to relay data packets through different neighbours. Thus it can recover batteries on those routers not currently in use. Since the data traffic transmitted among mesh backhaul nodes is generally quite heavy, relaying data packets through a specific router would soon use up its battery without letting it recover the over-charged power. The BAMS routing algorithm lets the sender periodically poll the battery status of its relay routers and assign the relay route on the best-recovered routers.

2.5.3   Energy Efficient Routing (E2R)

E2R [25] is a scalable, opportunistic, and energy efficient routing protocol that utilizes an opportunistic forwarding scheme to deliver control messages and data packets. E2R is designed to increase end-to-end performance by reducing the control message overhead caused by the maintenance of forwarding paths and forwarder lists. E2R also utilizes spatial diversity (broadcast nature of wireless communications) by introducing an implicit probabilistic multipath routing mechanism that reduces the probability of route discovery and local route repair due to link failures.

In E2R, the source node does not specify any particular paths. Both route metric discovery packets and data packets are delivered through broadcast. Nodes that have better opportunities to deliver the packets are automatically selected to forward the control packets and data packets. E2R operates in two phases: route metric discovery and data delivery.

2.5.3.1   E2R route metric discovery phase

In this phase, route metric discovery packets are delivered via broadcast. E2R addresses two challenges in this phase. The first challenge concerns how to prevent the repeated flooding of route metric discovery packets when the network is first constructed. At the early stage of network construction, Route Metric Discovery (RMD) packets must be delivered to every node inside the network because the source node and intermediate nodes do not know the direction of the destination node. Controlled flooding schemes (e.g., each node always forwards the newly received RMD packet once or multiple times) may be applied. However flooding schemes can cause many unnecessary rebroadcasts of RMD packets especially when the network density is high. To address this challenge, E2R utilizes the greedy forwarding algorithm in the distribution of RMD packets. The current forwarding node's covered neighbour list is embedded into the control packets. A node is declared as 'covered' if it has already received the packet. Whenever a node receives the packet it marks whether its neighbours have already been covered based on the covered neighbour list in the packet. Then the node sets a waiting (back off) time based on the number of its neighbours that have not been covered. A node with more uncovered neighbours should have higher priority to forward the packet. Therefore, if a node has a large number of uncovered neighbours, its waiting time is shorter.

E2R also addresses the need to reduce redundant transmissions of the Route Metric Reply (RMREP) packet. After the destination node receives the RMD packets, the destination node tries to deliver the RMREP packet back to the source node. This challenge differs from the first one because the destination node and the intermediate nodes already know the direction of the source node since they have received the RMD packet initiated from the source node. Therefore, the challenge is to utilize this knowledge to further reduce redundant transmissions. To address this challenge, E2R introduces an efficient self-suppression scheme which suppresses the forwarding of the route metric reply (RMREP) packet based on the route metric.

2.5.3.2   Data delivery phase

After the route metric discovery phase is executed, the source node obtains a route metric for the new destination. The source node now needs to deliver data packets to the destination node. The challenge is how to utilize spatial diversity to improve end-to-end performance and reduce energy consumption (by reducing the total number of packet transmissions inside the networks). To address this design challenge, a forwarder self-selection scheme is deployed. The source node attaches the obtained route metric to data packets and broadcasts the data packets without designating forwarding nodes. Upon receiving the data packets, the nodes that have smaller route metric value than the attached route metric value are eligible to further forward the data packets. Before these nodes forward the received data packet, they wait for a small amount of time to do a back-off based on their own route metric values for the destination. For example, the node with a smaller route metric value will have shorter back-off time and selects itself to forward the received data packets. During the back-off time interval, these nodes listen to the channel and suppress the forwarding of received data packets if they overhear data packets forwarded by a node with a smaller route metric value. When the back-off timer expires, the node updates the route metric value in the data packets by attaching its own route metric and forwards the data packets.

2.6   Energy-efficient routing approaches in Cognitive Radio ad hoc Networks (CRAHNs)

With the introduction of Dynamic Spectrum Access (DSA), unlicensed users may use licensed spectrum bands opportunistically in a dynamic and non-interfering manner. Implementation of DSA is possible via Software Defined Radios (SDRs) which allow the development of spectrum-agile devices that can be programmed to operate on a wide spectrum range and tuned to any frequency band in that range with limited delay. Cognitive Radio (CR) transceivers have the capability of completely changing their transmitter parameters (operating spectrum, modulation, transmission power, and communication technology) based on interactions with the surrounding spectral environment. They can sense a wide spectrum range, dynamically identify currently unused spectrum blocks for data communications, and intelligently access the unoccupied spectrum, also called (SOP) [26].

Devices with cognitive capabilities can be networked to create Cognitive Radio Networks (CRNs), which have recently attracted a lot of attention as viable architectural solutions to address the limited spectrum availability and the inefficiency in the spectrum usage.

2.6.1   *MANETs versus Cognitive Radio ad hoc Networks*

CRAHNs and MANETs are both ad hoc networks. But the opportunistic spectrum policy mainly differentiates MANETs from CRAHNs. CRAHNs and MANETs share the following similar characteristics: (1) dynamic topologies, (2) energy constrained operation and (3) relay assisted routing. However, CRAHNs and MANETS also have different characteristics: (1) opportunistic transmission spectrum and (2) multi-hop/multi-spectrum transmission. These unique characteristics of CRAHNs make the routing protocol design more complex, and make it challenging to apply energy-efficient routing approaches developed for MANETs to CRAHNs [27].

2.6.2   *Spectrum and Energy Aware Routing (SER) protocol*

In SER protocol, whenever the source CR user has packets to send to the destination CR user, the source CR initiates a route discovery process by broadcasting a spectrum aware RREQ message on the Common Control Channel (CCC) to all of its neighbours [30]. The fields of RREQ are shown in Table 2.2.

SER selects an energy efficient path by using the following metrics: residual energy in a node and the hop count. Initially, at the source CR user, the value of minimum residual nodal energy, mE_{res} is equal to the initial battery energy. To avoid CR users having very poor energy in a route; intermediate CR users should have a threshold energy, E_{th}.

In SER, an intermediate CR user v starts a timer whenever it receives the first RREQ. For each RREQ received from a neighbour CR user u before the timer expires, CR user v determines if communication along the link $l = (u, v)$ is possible. If it fails to find a feasible assignment, it drops the corresponding RREQ. If v successfully determines a communication segment, it attaches itself to the current partial path, includes *SSeg* in the header, updates the other information and rebroadcasts it by appending its own information to *route_seq* and *FSeg*. Consequently, the CR user increases the value of hop count (*HC*) and decreases the value of time to live (*TTL*). Similarly, the destination CR user sets up a timer to collect multiple RREQs for a connection request.

After receiving the first RREQ packet, destination CR user waits for a time period to get more RREQs before it makes RREP. After the completion of a predefined time period, the destination CR user then replies to the source CR user with a RREP packet through the CCC. Accordingly, the communication segment selected for each link along the path is reserved for data transmission. While RREP is forwarded towards source CR user, intermediate CR users reserve the communication segments in accordance with the information in the RREP packet. However, if the communication segments that have been tentatively selected during route discovery phase may be reserved by another RREP during the reservation phase. Finally, after receiving the RREP packet by the source CR user, the data transmission begins.

Table 2.2   RREQ packet fields in SER

req_id	Unique route request sequence number determined by the source CR user
src_id	Address of the source CR user
dst_id	Address of the destination CR user
mEres	Minimum residual nodal energy in a route
route_seq	List of the address of CR users from the source to the current traversed user
Fseg	List of free communication segments (channel-timeslot) of each user from the source to the current traversed user
Sseg	List of the selected communication segment of each user from the source to the current traversed user
HC	Hop count
TTL	The limitation of hop-length of the search path

2.6.3 Delay and Energy-based Spectrum Aware Routing (DESAR) protocol

DESAR [28] is a reactive protocol that selects paths for routing by considering both energy and delays (caused by switching, backoff, and queuing) of the nodes. To cope with the heterogeneity characteristic of CRAHNs, the DESAR protocol selects both, the route and spectrum band jointly. In the DESAR protocol, a single radio is used for both data and control messages.

DESAR performs a spectrum-aware route discovery procedure. The route discovery procedure is based on AODV with some modifications. When a sender S wants to communicate with destination D, the sender broadcasts a RREQ message to its neighbouring nodes to forward them to other nodes. Each node maintains a list of locally available channels currently not occupied by the PUs. Unlike AODV, the proposed protocol allows multiple paths to propagate to the destination. The RREQ message also contains the information about available channels of all the nodes along the path to the destination. Each RREQ message is uniquely identified by the source and destination IP addresses. When an intermediate or relaying node receives a RREQ message it determines if it is the destination node. If it is not then the intermediate node attaches its identifier, energy status, delay status and its available channel list with the RREQ message and rebroadcast the message. In DESAR, the RREQ message (Table 2.3) contains the following fields:

During the route discovery procedure, there are multiple RREQ messages forwarded along different paths towards the destination. Each RREQ message has a full path from the source. When a destination node receives the first RREQ message for a given flow, the destination starts a timer (T_r) and collects all the RREQ messages as long as the timer T_r has not expired. When the timer expires, all the subsequent RREQ messages are discarded. The destination node knows about the SOP's distribution information of all nodes along the path when it receives the RREQ messages. The route is selected by the destination on the basis of proposed cumulative metric (that includes both delay and energy). After selecting the best path, the destination sends a unicast RREP message back to the source that encapsulates the appropriate assigned frequency band. The intermediate nodes assign the frequency band with the help of RREP message and path information

Table 2.3   RREQ packet fields in DESAR

Field	Description
rreq_id	Unique route request sequence number
src_id	Address of the source CR user
des_id	Address of destination CR user
node_id	Node unique id
sop_list	List of available spectrum band free from PU activity
d_status	Delay caused by switching, backoff and queueing
P_energy	Energy of the path which is combination of residual energy of the each intermediate node

from the previous RREQ message. Finally, after receiving the RREP message the source CR user begins the data transmission.

The DESAR protocol has two main features: first, its handles spectrum heterogeneity by selecting the spectrum band and route jointly. Second, DESAR selects an efficient path based on the cumulative metric that considers delay and energy together.

2.7   Conclusion

The establishment of efficient, reliable routes is an important design issue in MANETs. However, a more challenging goal is to provide energy-efficient routes because mobile nodes' operation time is the most critical limiting factor. In this chapter, we have presented a survey of several routing protocols designed to implement energy-efficiency in various types of ad hoc networks, namely MANETS, Mesh and Cognitive Radio networks. Most of these energy-efficient protocols base their routing decisions on a cost function, which is formulated using a combination of different parameters such as energy consumption, residual battery power in the node, number of hops, position of the node, Euclidean distance, etc. The cost function is a weighted function that assigns various weights to its parameters depending on the design of the protocol. Numerous energy-efficient protocols have been developed for MANETs. However, it remains a significant challenge to develop effective energy-conserving routing schemes for ad hoc mesh and cognitive radio networks.

Acknowledgements

We thank the reviewers for their constructive feedback that helped us to improve the presentation of this chapter. Sherali Zeadally was partially supported by a District of Columbia NASA Space Grant and an NSF TIP grant (Award Number 1036293) during the course of this work. Faisal K. Shaikh was partially supported by Mehran University of Engineering and Technology, Jamshoro, Pakistan and National ICT R&D Fund, Ministry of Information Technology, Pakistan under National Grassroots ICT Research Initiative. We would also like to thank the editors Professor Rashvand and Professor Chao for their encouragements and support throughout the preparation of this chapter.

References

1. Ramanathan R., Redi J., 'A Brief Overview of Ad Hoc Networks: Challenges and Directions', *IEEE Communications Magazine*, 40(5), 20–22, 2002
2. Ali N., Ahmed R., Aljunid S., 'Link Availability Estimation for Routing Metrics in MANETs: An Overview', IEEE International Conference on Electronic Design, Malaysia, pp. 1–3, 2008

3. AbolHasan A., Wang J., Franklin D., 'On Indoor Multi-hopping Capacity of Wireless Ad Hoc Mesh Networks', IEEE International Conference on Mobile, Ad Hoc, and Sensor Systems', Pisa, Italy, pp. 1–6, 2007
4. Talay A., Altilar D., 'POPCORN: Routing Protocol for Cognitive Radio Ad Hoc Networks', IEEE International Conference on Ultra-Modern Telecommunications and Workshops, St. Petersburg, Russia, pp. 1–6, 2009
5. Abbagnale A., Cuomo F., 'Gymkhana: A Connectivity-based Routing Scheme for Cognitive Radio Ad Hoc Networks', IEEE Infocom Conference on Computer Communications, San Diego, CA, USA, pp. 1–5, 2010
6. Tran M., Simon V., 'Altruism for Energy Efficiency in Ad Hoc Networks', 73rd IEEE Vehicular Technology Conference, Budapest, Hungary, pp. 1–5, 2011
7. Mahimkar P., Shyamasundar R., 'S-MECRA: A Secure Energy-Efficient Routing Protocol for Wireless Ad Hoc Networks', 60th IEEE Vehicular Technology Conference, vol. 4, pp. 2739–2743, 2004
8. Wedde H., Farooq M., Pannenbaecker T., Vogel B., Mueller C., Meth J., Jeruschkat R., 'BeeAdHoc: An Energy Efficient Routing Algorithm for Mobile Ad Hoc Networks', in proceedings of The Genetic and Evolutionary Computation Conference Washington D.C., USA, pp. 153–160, 2005
9. Yen Y.-S., Chang H.-C., Chang R.-S., Chao H.-C., 'Routing with Adaptive Path and Limited Flooding for Mobile Ad Hoc Networks', *Computers & Electrical Engineering*, 36(2), 280–290, March 2010
10. Dhurandher S., Misra S., Obaidat M., Bansal V., Singh P., Punia V., 'An Energy-Efficient On-demand Routing Algorithm for Mobile Ad-hoc Networks', 15th IEEE International Conference on Electronics, Circuits, and Systems, St. Julian's, Malta, pp. 958–961, 2008
11. Yen Y.-S., Chan Y.-K., Chao H.-C., Park J.H., 'A Genetic Algorithm for Energy-Efficient Based Multicast Routing on MANETs', *Computer Communications*, 31(4), 858–869, March 2008
12. Naruephiphat W., Charnsripinyo C., 'Reliable and Energy-Efficient Routing in Mobile Ad Hoc Networks', IEEE International Conference on Information Networking, Chiang Mai, Thailand, pp. 1–3, 2009
13. Santhosh B., Narasimhan B., 'An Energy-Efficient Congestion-Aware Routing Protocol for Heterogeneous Mobile ad hoc Networks', IEEE International Conference on Advances in Computing, Control, & Telecommunication, Kerela, India, pp. 344–350, 2009
14. Loscri V., De Rango F., Marano S., 'Performance Evaluation of On-Demand Multipath Distance Vector Routing Protocol over Two MAC Layers in Mobile Ad Hoc Networks', IEEE International Symposium on Wireless Communication Systems, Trondheim, Norway, pp. 413–417, 2004
15. Zhu J., 'Model and Protocol for Energy Efficient Routing over Mobile Ad Hoc Networks', *IEEE Transactions on Mobile Computing*, 10(11), 1546–1557, 2011
16. Ajina A., Saktidharan R., Miskin K., 'Study of Energy Efficient, Power Aware Routing Algorithm and their Applications', IEEE Second International

Conference on Machine Learning and Computing, Bangalore, India, pp. 288–291, 2010

17. Murali P., Rakesh K., Hota C., Yla-Jaski A., 'Energy-Aware Routing in Mobile ad hoc Networks', IEEE 1st IFIP Conference on Wireless Days, United Arab Emirates, pp. 1–5, 2008

18. Kathiravan K., Divya V., Selvi S., 'Energy Efficient Integrated Routing Protocol for MANETs', IEEE International Conference on Mobile Ad Hoc, and Sensor Networks, Wu Yi Mountain, China, pp. 340–346, 2009

19. Rishiwal V., Yadav M., Verma S., Bajapai S.K., 'Power Aware Routing in Ad HocWireless Networks', *Journal of Computer Science and Technology*, 9(2), 101–109, Oct. pp. 59–66, 2009

20. Mohammed M., 'Energy Efficient Location Aided Routing Protocol for Wireless MANETs', *International Journal of Computer Science and Information Security*, 4(1, 2), pp. 59–66, 2009

21. Kaabneh K., Halasa A., Al-Bahadili H., 'An Effective Location-based Power Conservation Scheme for Mobile Ad Hoc Networks', *American Journal of Applied Sciences* 6(9), 1708–1713, 2009

22. Hosseini S., Wan T., Budiarto R., 'Energy Efficient Cluster Based Routing Protocol for MANETs', International Conference on Computer Engineering and Applications, Haikou, China, pp. 380–384, 2011

23. Oivia A., Branchs A., Serrano A., 'Throughput and Energy-Aware Routing for 802.11-based Mesh Networks', *Computer Communications Journal*, 35(12), pp. 1433–1446

24. Ma C., Ma M., Yang Y., 'A Battery Aware Scheme for Energy Efficient Coverage and Routing in Wireless MIMO Mesh Networks', IEEE Conference on Wireless Communications and Networking, Hong Kong, pp. 3603–3608, 2007

25. Zhu T., Don T., 'E2R: Energy Efficient Routing for Multi-hop Green Wireless Networks', IEEE International Conference on Computer Communications Workshop, Shanghai, China, pp. 265–270, 2011

26. Cesana M., Cuomo F., Ekici E., 'Routing in Cognitive Radio Networks: Challenges and Solutions', *Ad Hoc Networks*, 9(3), 228–248, 2011

27. Hou L., Yeung H., Wong K., 'A Vision of Energy-Efficient Routing for Cognitive Radio Ad Hoc Networks', 6th IEEE International Symposium on Wireless and Pervasive Computing, Hong Kong, pp. 1–4, 2011

28. Asif R., Muhammad S., Muhammed K., 'Efficient Delay and Energy-based Routing in Cognitive Radio Ad Hoc Networks', IEEE International Conference on Emerging Technologies, Islamabad, Pakistan, pp. 1–5, 2012

29. Kamruzzaman S., Kim E., Jeong D., 'Spectrum and Energy Aware Routing Protocol for Cognitive Radio Ad Hoc Networks', IEEE International Conference on Communications, Xidian, China, pp. 1–5, 2011

30. Layuan L., Xinwei Z., Zhingqiu X., 'Maximizing Network Lifetime in Wireless Mesh Networks', 4th IEEE International Conference on Wireless Communications, Networking and Mobile Computing, Shanghai, China, pp. 1–4, 2008

Chapter 3*

Security in vehicular ad hoc networks

Jesús Téllez[a] and Sherali Zeadally[b]

Abstract

In the last few years, Vehicular ad hoc Networks (VANETs) have attracted a lot of attention and have triggered the development of many new attractive applications. They have become a fundamental component of many intelligent transportation systems and VANETs are being used to improve road safety and enable a wide variety of value-added services. Nevertheless, VANET applications have stringent security requirements because they affect road traffic safety. Several security threats and different types of attacks against VANETs have emerged recently that attempt to compromise the security of such networks. These attacks can cause catastrophic results such as the loss of lives or the loss of revenue for those value-added services. Therefore, making VANETs secure has become a key objective for VANET designers. Since traditional security mechanisms are not always suitable to some unique features in VANETs (e.g., high mobility of nodes), industry and academia have been focusing on improving VANET security. We present threats and attacks that can be launched on VANETs and we identify the security solutions to mitigate them. We also highlight VANET security challenges that still need to be addressed to enable robust, scalable, cost-effective secure solutions for VANETs.

3.1 Introduction

Nowadays, there is a revolutionary change in the way information is being handled due to the proliferation of mobile devices (cell phones, personal digital assistants (PDA), laptops and other handheld digital devices), and the exponential growth in the wireless sector in the past decade. Today, users carry mobile devices that run

H. F. Rashvand and H.-C. Chao (Eds.), Dynamic Ad Hoc Networks, The IET Book Publishing Department, 2013, ISBN 978-1-84919-647-5, eISBN 978-1-84919-648-2

[a]Universidad de Carabobo, Computer Science Department (Facyt) Av. Universidad, Sector Bárbula, Valencia, Venezuela

[b]University of the District of Columbia, Department of Computer Science and Information Technology, Washington DC, USA

applications and access network services, among which data services are the most demanded by users. Currently most of these connections between mobile devices are infrastructure based. For example, two or more laptops communicate with each other using a wireless access point; cell phones are connected via cell phone towers [1, 2].

However, the high cost to set up an infrastructure for mobile device communications along with the number of mobile devices in use that have only short range wireless capability, have triggered the development of an alternative way for mobile device communication in which each mobile device (node) communicates with each other over wireless links without the support of an infrastructure, forming a Mobile ad hoc Network (MANET).

The growing need to improve safety and traffic efficiency in vehicles has prompted various research efforts around the world by government, academia and industry to integrate computing and communication technologies into vehicles to address the above issues, which has resulted in the development of the Intelligent Transportation System (ITS). Vehicular communication (VC) is an important component of ITS where vehicles communicate with other vehicles and/or roadside infrastructure, analyse and process received information, and makes decisions based on the analysis [1].

VANETs is a special type of MANET and forms the basis of ITS. VANET was developed with a view to enable real-time communication between mobile nodes (either vehicles or roadside infrastructures) over wireless links to improve road traffic safety and efficiency.

Driver behaviour, mobility constraints and high speeds create unique characteristics of VANETs that have important implications when designing and implementing these networks. Moreover, performance and security are two important requirements that contribute to make VANET safety applications challenging unlike other wireless applications. Authenticating a message sender, verifying the validity of a message (such as vehicle's position), providing node privacy with non-repudiation, certificate revocation and availability are security issues that should be addressed and supported to make VANETs secure.

The application space for *vehicle-to-vehicle* and *vehicle-to-roadside* communications opens up tremendous business opportunities and research challenges with *security* as of the most important ones. Thus, VANETs are envisioned to support the development of a wide range of applications that can be broadly classified into two major categories (see Figure 3.1) [1, 3–7]:

1. *Safety applications:* Applications in this category share a common characteristic: the relevance to life-critical situations, where a lack of a service may cause life-threatening accidents. Security for this applications category is mandatory. Examples of applications in this category include collision avoidance, cooperative driving, traffic optimization, lane-changing assistance, traffic signs violations warning and road conditions warnings. These can be further categorised as safety-critical and safety-related applications [1]:

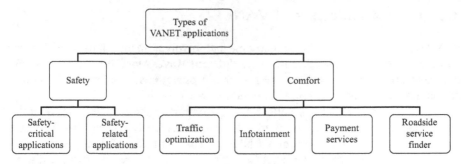

Figure 3.1   Types of VANET applications

(a) *Safety-critical:* These are used in the case of hazardous situations (such as like collisions), which include the situations where the danger is high or the danger is imminent. Therefore, such applications have the highest priority in accessing the communication channel and involve communication between vehicles (V2V) or between vehicles and the infrastructure (V2I) or between the infrastructure and vehicles (I2V).

(b) *Safety-related:* This category includes safety applications where the danger is either low (curve speed warning) or elevated (work zone warning). Safety-related predictable applications can be V2V or V2I/I2V.

2. *Comfort applications:* This class of applications improves passenger comfort and traffic efficiency and/or optimizes the route to a given destination. Some of these applications will be free, while others would require a service subscription or a one-time payment [8]. Moreover, security is also required in this application category, especially in the case of payment services.

Comfort applications mostly involve V2I or I2V communications and have access to the channels in the communication system, except the control channels. Examples of applications in the category include:

(a) *Traffic optimization:* Traffic information and recommendations, enhanced route guidance, etc.

(b) *Infotainment:* Internet access, instant messaging, media downloading, etc.

(c) *Payment services:* Electronic toll collection, parking management, etc.

(d) *Roadside service finder:* Finding closest fuel station, restaurants, etc. This involves communication of vehicles with road side infrastructure and the associated databases.

In the last couple of years industry and academia have much of their research efforts on safety-related applications because this is an important area of the automotive domain. Nevertheless, since comfort applications also offer great business opportunities, it is expected that research in this area will continue to attract attention of researchers and designers to develop a wide range of non-safety applications [4].

3.2   Basic architecture of VANET

A VANET is a self-organized network that involves many entities, which can communicate with each other in many different ways. Most of them are vehicles but there are other entities that perform basic operations such as reliable storage and computation for cars, communication between vehicle-to-vehicle and vehicle-to-roadside communications, collecting information on the vehicle's status and its environment, communications with an infrastructure network, etc. in these networks. A system architecture for VANETs consists of different domains and many individual components as depicted in Figure 3.2. The figure shows three distinct domains of in-vehicle, ad hoc and infrastructure, and individual components as application unit, on-board unit (OBU), and roadside unit [1, 9, 10].

3.2.1   In-vehicle domain

The in-vehicle domain refers to a network logically composed of an OBU and one or more Applications Units (AU) inside a vehicle. An AU is typically a dedicated device that executes a single or a set of applications and utilizes the OBU's communication capabilities. An AU can be integrated as part of a vehicle and be permanently connected to an OBU or it could be a portable device such as a PDA, a mobile phone or a gaming device that can dynamically attach to and detach from an OBU. An OBU is equipped with at least a (short range) wireless communication

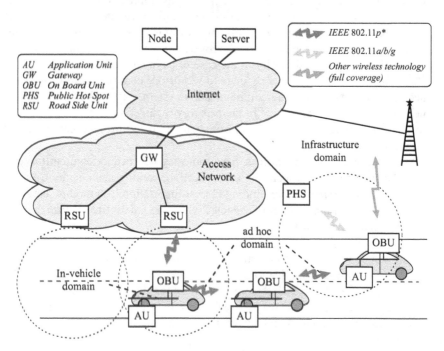

Figure 3.2   VANET system architecture [9]

device dedicated for road safety, and potentially with other optional communication devices (for safety and non-safety communications). AU and OBU are usually connected with wired connection, but the connection can also be wireless, such as using IEEE 802.15.1 (Bluetooth), IEEE 802.15.3 (ultrawide band (UWB)), IEEE 802.15.4 (Zigbee) and wireless USB (WUSB). The distinction between AU and OBU is logical; they can also reside in a single physical unit [1, 9, 11].

3.2.2 Ad hoc domain

The ad hoc domain, or VANET, is composed of vehicles equipped with OBUs, a set of sensors and a Trusted Platform Module (TPM) and stationary units along the road, termed Roadside Units (RSUs). OBUs form a mobile ad hoc network which allows vehicle-to-vehicle (V2V) and vehicle-to-infrastructure (V2I, I2V) communications in a fully distributed manner without the need for a centralized coordinating entity. OBUs directly communicate if wireless connectivity exists among them. In case of no direct connectivity, dedicated routing protocols allow multi-hop communications, where data is forwarded from one OBU to another, until it reaches the destination [1, 9, 12].

3.2.3 Infrastructure domain

The infrastructure consists of RSUs and wireless hotspots (HT) that vehicles access for safety and non-safety applications. The RSUs are typically set up for Internet access by road administrators or other public authorities whilst public or privately owned hotspots are usually set up in a less-controlled environment. These two types of infrastructure access, RSU and HT, also can support different applications types. If neither RSUs nor HT can provide Internet access, OBUs can utilize communication capabilities of cellular radio networks (GSM, GPRS, UMTS, HSDPA, WiMax, 4G) if they are integrated with the OBU particularly for non-safety applications [1, 9, 11, 12].

The individual components of the VANET system architecture (application unit, OBU, roadside unit, sensor and TPM) and their relations to other components are described below.

Application unit (AU): An AU is an in-vehicle entity (embedded or pluggable) that runs applications that could use the OBUs communication capabilities. Examples of AUs are (i) a dedicated device for safety applications, (ii) a navigation system with communication capabilities or (iii) a nomadic device such as a PDA that runs Internet applications. Another type of AUs can dynamically be plugged into the in-vehicle network (e.g., a passenger's PDA). A portable AU should be automatically configured when connected to an OBU. Similarly an AU can dynamically be removed, for example when a passenger leaves a vehicle. Multiple AUs can be plugged in with a single OBU simultaneously and share the OBUs processing and wireless resources [9, 13].

On-board unit (OBU): The OBU is responsible for vehicle-to-vehicle and vehicle-to-infrastructure communications. It also provides communication services to AUs and forwards data on behalf of other OBUs in the ad hoc domain. An OBU is equipped with at least a single network device (that can be used to send, receive and forward safety-related data in the ad hoc domain) for short range wireless communications based on IEEE 802.11p radio technology [14]. An OBU can be equipped with more network devices, e.g. for non-safety communications, based on other radio technologies like IEEE 802.11a/b/g/n. OBU functions and procedures include wireless radio access, geographical ad hoc routing, network congestion control, reliable message transfer, data security, IP mobility support and others. An OBU can be called public safety OBU when it can execute specific applications authorized to send data with the highest priority [9].

Roadside unit (RSU): An RSU is a physical device located at fixed positions along roads and highways, or at dedicated locations such as gas station, parking places, and restaurants. An RSU is equipped with at least a network device for short range wireless communications based on IEEE 802.11p. An RSU can also be equipped with other network devices in order to allow communications with an infrastructure network. An overview of the main functions of an RSU is given below[†] [9, 13].

–   Extending the communication range of an ad hoc network by redistributing information to other OBUs and by cooperating with other RSUs in forwarding or in distributing safety information. This functionality includes the case where an RSU directly forwards data over a multi-hop wireless link to other vehicles (Figure 3.3).
–   Running safety applications, such as for V2I warning (e.g., low bridge warning, work-zone warning), when the RSU can act as an information source or receiver (Figure 3.4).
–   Providing Internet connectivity to OBUs (Figure 3.5).

Sensor: A sensor is a physical device installed on each vehicle that is used to measure its own status (e.g., fuel consumption) and its environment (e.g., slippery road, safety

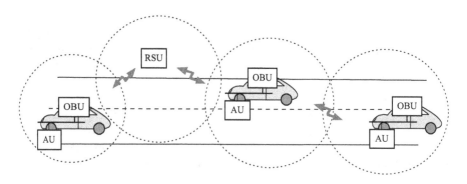

Figure 3.3   An RSU extends the communication range of OBU by forwarding data [9]

[†]The order does not imply priority.

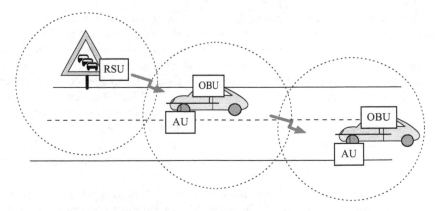

Figure 3.4 RSU acts as an information source [9]

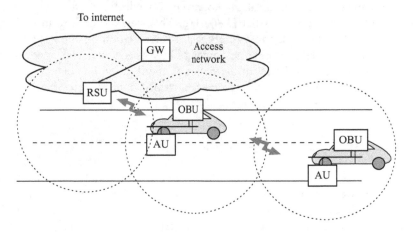

Figure 3.5 An RSU provides Internet access [9]

distance). Such sensori data can be shared with other vehicles to increase their awareness and improve road safety [12].

Trusted Platform Module (TPM): A TPM is a physical device that is often mounted on vehicles and is used for security purposes, and offers reliable storage and computation. It usually has a reliable internal clock and is supposed to be tamper-resistant or at least tamper-evident [12].

3.2.4 Standards for wireless access in VANETs

As mentioned previously, the various characteristics of VANETs impose several unique requirements on VANET applications. The use of communication standards is needed to enable interconnectivity and interoperability and allow compatibility with the emergence of new products and technologies. There are various standards that relate to wireless access in vehicular environments [11, 12, 15].

Dedicated Short Range Communications (DSRC) is a wireless technology that supports vehicle-to-vehicle and vehicle-to-roadside communications. Such communications cover a wide range of applications, including vehicle-to-vehicle safety messages, traffic information, toll collection, drive-through payment, and several others. DSRC is aimed at providing high data transfers and low communication latency in small communication zones. It works in the 5.9 GHz band with bandwidth of 75 MHz with an approximate range of 1000 m. Different DSRC standards have been in use in United States, Europe, Korea and Japan, mainly for applications such as Electronic Toll Collection (ETC) and automatic vehicle identification. These standards were not designed to support V2V or safety communication in VANETs [1, 11].

Wireless Access for Vehicular Environments (WAVE) is a radio communications system intended to provide interoperable wireless networking services for transportation (which includes services recognized for Dedicated Short Range Communications (DSRC)). It is an approved amendment to the IEEE 802.11 standard and is also known as IEEE 802.11p. This standard defines the enhancements made to 802.11 to support Intelligent Transportation Systems (ITS) applications, including data exchange among high-speed vehicles and among those vehicles and the roadside infrastructure in the licensed ITS band of 5.9 GHz (5.85–5.925 GHz). WAVE supplies real-time traffic information, improves road safety and reduces traffic congestion.

3.3   Security issues in VANET

Mobile nodes in VANETs which may form networks in a variety of environments. Subsequently we cannot assume that vehicular nodes will always be under the control of their owners. Hence, nodes could be stolen or tampered with. The possibility of eavesdropping, spoofing and denial-of-service attacks are more prevalent compared to fixed line networks [1]. A successful attack on VANETs can have catastrophic results (such as the loss of lives) or may lead to financial losses (for payment services). Therefore securing VANETs is crucial to their design, implementation and operations [16].

3.3.1   Adversary model

Before describing the attacks in VANET systems, it is necessary to define the adversaries in order to determine the scope of resources needed to secure a vehicular system. The following broad classes of adversaries are identified in a vehicular environment [17–19]:

1.   *Active versus passive:* An active attacker can generate or modify/drop or replay messages in order to give false information to the network vehicles so that the attacker can maximize his/her gain in the network irrespective of the costs, whereas a passive attacker can only eavesdrop on the wireless channel [18, 19].

2.   *Insider versus outsider:* An insider is an authenticated member of the network who can communicate with other members. Being a part of the network, an insider is already in possession of some network credentials such as public keys [1]. The outsider is considered by the network members as an intruder and hence is limited in the diversity of attacks that can be launched (especially by misusing network-specific protocols) [19].

It is worth noting that an insider can cause more damage to the system by tampering with an OBU than an outsider who has limited access to the system because the latter does not normally possess any cryptographic credentials or direct physical access to the system.

3.   *Malicious versus rational:* A malicious attacker seeks no personal benefits from the attacks and aims to harm the members or the functionality of the network. In contrast, a rational attacker seeks personal profit and is more predictable in terms of the attack means and the attack target [1, 19].

4.   *Independent versus colluding:* Attackers can act independently or in collusion, i.e., exchange information and coordinate their actions, in order to mount a more effective attack. For example, colluding vehicle can report an imaginary traffic (e.g., traffic jam or accident) to convince other drivers and clear way for the attackers [17].

5.   *Local versus extended:* An attacker can be limited in scope even if he/she controls several entities (vehicles or RSU), which makes him/her local due to the limited range of OBUs and RSUs that make the attack scope limited. An extended attacker controls several entities that are scattered across the network, thus extending his/her scope. This distinction is especially important in privacy-violating and wormhole attacks which are explained in the next section [1, 19].

3.3.2   Attacks on VANETs

Attackers can launch attacks by manipulating either the vehicular system or the security protocols. Two kinds of attacks can be launched against vehicular systems: attacks against messages and those against vehicles [1, 6, 11, 16, 20–22].

3.3.2.1   Basic attacks against messages

1.   *Bogus information attacks:* In this attack, the attacker can be an outsider/intruder or an insider/legitimate user. The attacker disseminates wrong information in the vehicular network to influence the behaviour of other vehicles by spreading false information in the network [19, 21]. For example, a vehicle can imitate a heavy traffic on one road to prevent the other vehicles to choose that road (see Figure 3.6).

2.   *Cheating with sensor information:* This attack is launched by attackers by altering their perceived position, speed, direction, etc. in order to escape liability, notably in the case of an accident. In the worst case, colluding attackers can clone each other, but this would require retrieving the security material (such as private keys which should be stored in tamper-proof hardware) and having full trust among the attackers [19, 23].

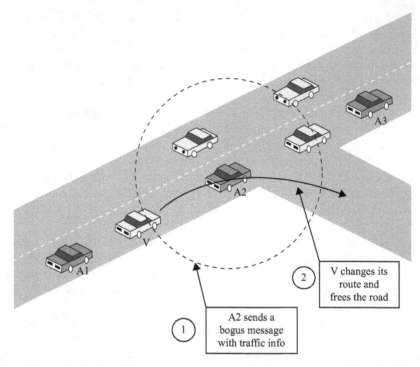

Figure 3.6   Example of Bogus attack where colluding attackers (A2 and A3) disseminate false information to affect the decisions of other vehicles (V) and thus clear the way of attacker A1 [19]

3. *Black hole attack:* A black hole is formed when nodes refuse to participate in the network or when an established node drops out. When the node drops out, all routes it participated in are broken leading to a failure to propagate messages [11, 21].

4. *Masquerading:* The attacker actively pretends or impersonates to be another vehicle by using false identities and can be motivated by malicious or rational objectives. To perform masquerading attacks, all that is required for an attacker to join the network is a functioning OBU. By posing as legitimate vehicles in the network, after some time period, outsiders can conduct a variety of attacks in network such as forming black holes or producing false messages [1, 11, 24].

5. *Privacy violation:* Privacy refers to the ability of the drivers to protect sensitive information about them against unauthorized observers. However, with vehicular networks deployed, the collection of vehicle-specific information overheard from vehicular communications becomes particularly easy. Therefore, inferences on the drivers personal data could be made and consequently, violate her/his privacy. The vulnerability lies in the periodic and frequent transmissions

of vehicular network traffic. On these occasions, messages will include, by default, information (e.g., time, location, vehicle identifier, technical description, trip details) that could precisely identify the originating node (vehicle) as well as the drivers actions and preferences [1, 23].

6. *Replay attack:* Using previously received packets, the attacker re-injects them back into the network, poisoning a nodes location table by replaying beacons. A malicious user can capture a generated packet and use it in other parts of the vehicular network. The main objective of this attack is to confuse the authorities and prevent identification of vehicle in any accident [11, 21, 25].

7. *Denial of Service (DoS):* DoS attack can be carried out by network insiders and outsiders and is one of the key attacks related to availability of the network. The attacker may want to bring down the VANET or even cause an accident. This attack could be performed in many ways, either by sending messages that would lead to improper results or by jamming the wireless channel (through a DoS attack) so that vehicles cannot exchange safety messages [12, 22, 24].

8. *Illusion attacks:* An illusion attack is a security threat on VANET applications, where the adversary creates a specific traffic situation and sends false traffic warning messages to decoy other drivers in believing that a traffic event occurred [23]. Since an attacker must create a virtual event to produce an illusion attack, two prerequisite conditions must be achieved by the attacker to create the virtual traffic event [26]. The first condition is to create the prerequisite traffic situation on the road. Second, the false traffic warning messages should be generated and distributed by the attacker.

9. *Traffic analysis attacks:* Considered as one of the serious threats to privacy in VANETs, traffic analysis is a category of attacks against anonymity of communications between the vehicle to vehicle (V2V) and vehicle to road side unit (V2R). An attacker define some goal and achieve their goal through capturing some different types of traffic information packets (such as location of user, vehicle ID, traveling route of user, etc.) and use it for attacks [16, 24, 27].

10. *In-transit traffic tampering:* As any node acting as a relay can disrupt communications of other nodes, it can drop or corrupt messages, or meaningfully modify messages. Therefore, the reception of valuable or even critical traffic notifications or safety messages can be manipulated. Moreover, attackers can replay messages (e.g., to illegitimately obtain services such as traversing a toll check point). In fact, this attack may be simpler and more powerful than forgery attacks [1, 19].

11. *Timing attack:* This attack can be launched when the attacker manipulates the actual content, add some time slots in the original message to create a delay in the message which leads to the recipients receiving the message after the required time [21, 28].

3.3.2.2   Other attacks

In this section, other sophisticated versions of basic attacks or a combination of basic attacks on messages as well as attacks on vehicles are presented [1, 11, 16, 21, 22, 29].

1. *Hidden vehicle attack:* In this attack, a vehicle broadcasting warnings will listen for feed back from its neighbour and stops its broadcast if it realizes that one of its neighbours is better positioned for warning other vehicles. This reduces congestion on wireless channels. As Figure 3.7 illustrates, the hidden vehicle attack consists in deceiving vehicle **A** into believing that the attacker is better placed for forwarding the warning message, thus leading to silencing **A** and making it hidden, in DSRC terms, to other vehicles. This is equivalent to disabling the system [1, 19, 30].

2. *Spamming:* In this attack, an attacker disseminates spam messages to a group of users in the vehicular network with the aim of increasing the transmission latency and consuming network bandwidth. These spam messages are of no concern to the user just like advertisement messages. Spamming is made more difficult to control because of the absence of a basic infrastructure and centralized administration [24, 31].

3. *Global Positioning System (GPS) spoofing attack:* Since a GPS device maintains a location table with the geographic location and identity of all vehicles on the network, an attacker can fool vehicles into thinking that they are in a different location by producing false readings in the GPS devices. This is possible through the use of a GPS satellite simulator to generate signals that are stronger than those generated by the genuine satellite [11, 31, 32].

4. *Tunneling:* Since GPS signals disappear in tunnels, an attacker may exploit this temporary loss of positioning information to inject false data into the OBU once the vehicle leaves the tunnel and before it receives an authentic position update as is illustrated in Figure 3.8 [19].

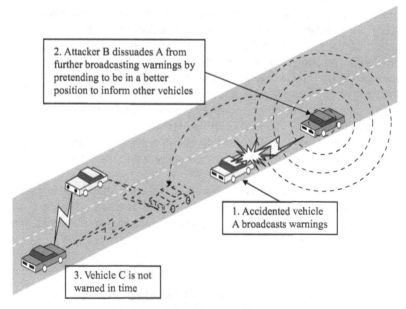

2. Attacker B dissuades A from further broadcasting warnings by pretending to be in a better position to inform other vehicles

1. Accidented vehicle A broadcasts warnings

3. Vehicle C is not warned in time

Figure 3.7   Hidden vehicle attack [19]

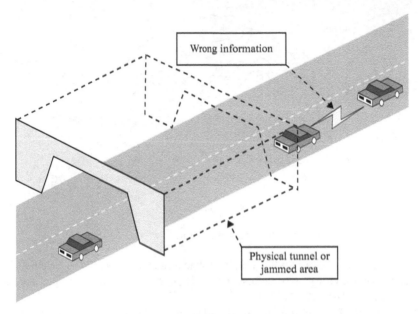

Wrong information

Physical tunnel or
jammed area

Figure 3.8 Tunnel attack [19]

5. *Wormhole attack:* The Wormhole attack is a severe attack in ad hoc networks that is particularly challenging to defend against. It is possible even if the attacker has not compromised any hosts, and even if all communication provides authenticity and confidentiality [33]. In the wormhole attack, an attacker records packets (or bits) at one location in the network, 'tunnels' them to another location in the network, and then retransmits them into the netwok from that location. The tunnel can be established through a single long range wireless link or through a wired link between the two colluding attackers [19, 34, 35].

The wormhole attack can form a serious threat in wireless networks, especially against many ad hoc network routing protocols and location-based wireless security systems. This attack and a possible countermeasure (using the concept of packet leashes) is presented in [33]. A Wormhole attack model is illustrated in Figure 3.9. When node A broadcasts its HELLO message, node X (an attacker) copies this HELLO message and tunnels it to node Y (the colluding attacker) through the constructed wormhole. Y receives A's HELLO message and replays in its area. When node B receives the replayed HELLO message, B deems node A to be its one-hop neighbour [34].

6. *Eavesdropping:* Confidentiality of messages exchanged between the nodes of a vehicular network are particularly vulnerable to techniques such as the illegitimate collection of messages through eavesdropping and the gathering of location information available through the transmission of broadcast messages. Eavesdropping is the most prominent attack in VANETs against confidentiality.

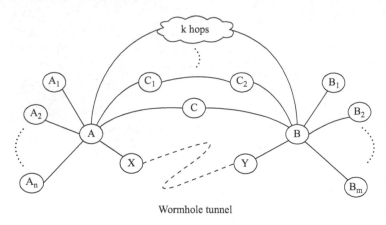

Wormhole tunnel

Figure 3.9   Wormhole attack model [34]

To perform it, insider and/or outsider attackers can be located in a vehicle (stationary or moving) or in a false RSU. Their goal is to illegally get access to confidential data [12, 21, 31].

7. *Sybil attack:* The Sybil attack is aimed at distributed system environments. It is a well-known harmful attack in VANETs, whereby a vehicle claims to be several vehicles either at the same time or in succession. In this way, a single vehicle could report the existence of a false bottleneck. In addition, a Sybil attack refers to an attack where the vehicles identity masquerades as multiple simultaneous identities [1, 11, 12, 16, 21, 36]. Figure 3.10 illustrates the Sybil attack problem in which a node illegitimately claims multiple identities. The attack edge area shows false data and false information between honest and Sybil nodes.

8. *On-board tampering:* The attacker may select to tinker with vehicle/driver-specific data (e.g., velocity, location, status of vehicle parts) and tamper with the on-board sensing devices and other hardware devices. In fact, it may be simpler for the attacker to replace or bypass the real-time clock or the wiring of a sensor in his vehicle rather than modifying the binary code implementation of the data collection and communication protocols [10, 23, 31].

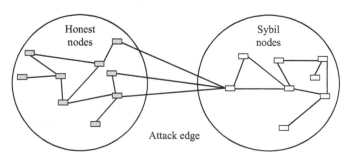

Figure 3.10   Sybil attack [36]

3.4 Security solutions

In order to protect VANETs against the threats mentioned in the previous section and any generic attack, the security mechanisms employed in VANETs should satisfy the following security requirements [1, 19, 25, 31]:

1. *Authentication:* For safety applications, trust is important. Authentication ensures that a message can be trusted by correctly identifying the sender of the message. Network nodes must be authenticated in order to be able to send messages over the network. Before reacting to messages and events a vehicle must verify the legitimacy of the message and its sender which can be achieved with authentication. Without authentication, illegitimate and malicious users can inject false messages into the network and confuse other vehicles by distributing false information. With authentication, vehicles can simply drop messages received from unauthenticated users.

2. *Data consistency:* Data consistency is an important requirement for safety applications to protect users against malicious insider users. In general, the majority of VANET users are honest. However, if one of the vehicle's sensors malfunctions, it will start transmitting messages with wrong information. The same situation applies to legitimate users who have malicious behaviour.

3. *Integrity:* All messages which are sent to and received from the network should be protected against alteration attacks. A secure vehicular network should provide protection against message alteration. A message can be altered in several ways during its transit from source to destinations and all possible attacks must be considered.

4. *Confidentiality:* Confidentiality requires that the information flowing from sender to receiver should not be eavesdropped. Only the sender and the receiver should have access to the contents of the message (e.g., instant messaging between vehicles).

5. *Privacy:* Privacy is a key aspect in VANETs and refers to the ability of the drivers to protect sensitive information about them against unauthorized observers [16]. An in-depth discussion of this requirement is presented later in this chapter.

6. *Availability:* Since vehicular networks require real-time responses, they are vulnerable to DoS attack. Therefore, the communication channel must be available at all times. Availability means that messages not only reach all the targeted recipients but also reach them at the correct time. Therefore, availability should be ensured by all means.

7. *Access control:* Access control is necessary to ensure the reliable and secure operation of a system. Any misbehaving nodes (e.g., by an intrusion detection system using a trust management scheme) should be revoked from the network to protect the safety of other legitimate entities in the network. Moreover, any actions taken by the misbehaving entity should be canceled.

8. *Auditability:* Auditability, the non-repudiation requirement, is the mechanism by which legitimate senders or receivers can prove that messages have been

received or sent, respectively. It may be crucial for an investigation to determine the correct sequence and content of messages exchanged before the
ocurrence of a security incident.

9. *Physical security:* This is essential to prevent unauthorized access of vehicle,
   which could lead to unauthorized use, compromise of radio systems or cryptographic credentials.
10. *Real-time constraints:* At high speeds typical in VANETs, strict time con-
    straints should be met. Out-dated messages carrying information such as traffic
    or road/weather conditions, are of no use in vehicular networks and must be
    eliminated in order to let newly generated messages get to their destinations on
    time.

Based on the above security requirements, Figure 3.11 shows a classification
of attacks on VANETs presented earlier and the major security services that they
can affect. However, some attacks can also have an impact on multiple security
services. A discussion of all possible VANET security solutions proposed in the
literature is beyond the scope of this work. Instead, we focus on security solutions
for VANET attacks that have received the most attention in the literature recently.

In recent years, taking into consideration the security requirements described
above, the research community has proposed different schemes that can be
implemented to thwart VANET attacks.

VANET safety applications require safety messages to be received by all the
targeted vehicles within their lifetime. To deal with *Bogus Information attack*,
Yang *et al.* [37] proposed a piggybacked cooperative repetition approach for reliably broadcasting safety messages in VANETs. This proposal introduces two
policies that help to mitigate the bogus information attack: (a) Full Beacon Piggyback (FBP), where the safety message and the public key cryptography system
(PKCS) data are both piggybacked and (b) Payload Only Piggyback (POP), where
only the safety message is piggybacked.

In general, there are two approaches to prevent *replay attack*. The first
approach is to set up a globally synchronized time for all nodes. Another approach
is to use nonces, which usually refer to a large random number that is used as a
challenge to the communication partner, which must respond with the right
response [38]. Also, Riley [39] proposed an efficient and lightweight symmetric-
key-based authentication scheme for VANETs based on group communication
(called Group-based Lightweight Authentication Protocol (GLAP)) that helps to
prevent replay attacks.

It is important to note that VANETs operating in the WAVE framework are
protected from replay attacks but to continue protection an accurate source of time
must be maintained as this is used to keep a cache of recently received messages,
against which new messages can be compared [11].

Denial of Service (DOS) attack could be prevented using the model proposed
by Hasbullah *et al.* [40] in which the intention is to ensure network availability for
secure communication among the nodes. The model relies on the use of an OBU
that is fitted on each vehicle node, to make decision to deter a DOS attack. A

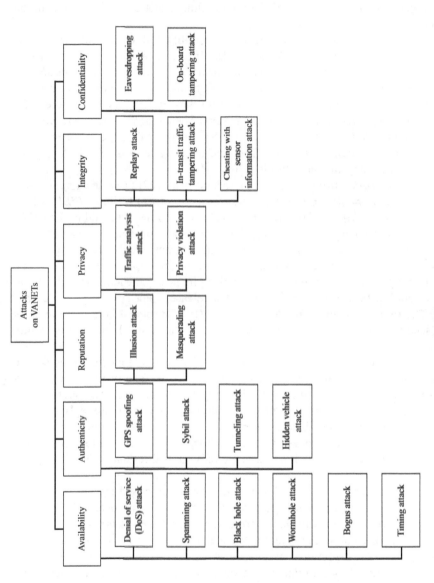

Figure 3.11 Security services impacted by various types of VANET attacks

Processing Unit will suggest to the OBU to switch channel, technology, or to use frequency hoping technique. The OBU can make a decision based on the received attack message using four options: channel switching, technology switching, frequency hopping spread spectrum (FHSS) and multiple radio transceivers. After processing and making a decision, the information is sent to the next OBU in the network.

A new system architecture called the Plausibility Validation Network (PVN) was proposed by Lo *et al.* to check the raw data from sensors and evaluates whether the incoming or generated message is valid or not [26] to protect from an *illusion attack*. The new architecture uses two ways to obtain the application system input. One way is to receive incoming messages from the wireless antenna, whereas the other way is to validate data reported by sensors. Then, when a message is received from the antenna or generated from sensors, depending on the type of message, the system retrieves predefined rule set from rule database to cross-check the plausibility of the incoming message fields [16].

To address *traffic analysis attacks*, Cencioni *et al.* [27] proposed a vehicle-to-infrastructure communication privacy enforcement protocol (called *VIPER*) which is resilient to three kinds of traffic analysis attacks: (a) message coding attack (if messages do not change their coding during transmission they can be linked or traced), (b) message volume attack (the amount of transmitted data, i.e., the message length, can be observed) and (c) timing attack (an opponent can observe the duration of a specific communication by linking its possible endpoints and waiting for a correlation between the creation and/or release event at each possible endpoint). The intuition behind the design of the VIPER protocol is to have vehicles not to send their messages directly to the RSU, but to have vehicles acting as mix nodes [16].

To avoid a *wormhole attack*, Kaur *et al.* [41] proposed a method to detect the wormhole nodes in the network using decision packets. The method computes a value of each packet to maintain the integrity of the packets. The source node broadcasts the decision packet to all nodes after receiving the route reply message from the destination node which contains the list of the route forming nodes. The decision packets from the nodes are then evaluated by the destination node based on the hop count value. If the hop count exceeds some threshold value, it means a wormhole is formed between the nodes.

Sybil attack can be prevented with the solution proposed by Yan *et al.* [42] who argued that if an on-board radar works such that it can detect the physical existence of a vehicle, this physical information can be used to improve the highly abstract information about the vehicle. The authors compute similarity among three kinds of data: radar detections, oncoming traffic reports and reports from neighbours. To average these similarities, each similarity has a weight. When radar works, radar detections are more trustworthy, therefore radar detections have a larger weight. When the radar does not work, reports from neighbours have a larger weight. The average position and velocity will be computed if the similarity is close. A history of the road map is maintained by storing these average positions and velocities over a period of time. When a query (based on the vehicular node's position) needs to be made, vehicles rebuild the target vehicles map history virtually and make their decisions based on this map [16].

Kaur *et al.* [36] discuss various defence mechanisms proposed by different researchers against Sybil attack and then compare these different mechanisms.

3.5 Privacy in VANET

In VANETs it is easy to collect information about the speed, status trajectories and whereabouts of the vehicles. With this information, the traffic administration authorities can optimize the traffic and relieve jams. However, malicious observers could exploit this information to draw inferences about a driver's personality (e.g., someone driving slowly is likely to be a calm person), living habits and social relationships (visited places tell a lot about people's lives). This private information may be traded in underground markets, exposing the observed vehicles and drivers to harassments (e.g., junk advertisements), threats (e.g., blackmail if the driver often visits an embarrassing place such as a red-light district) and dangers (e.g., hijacks) [43]. Therefore, privacy becomes an important factor for the public acceptance and successful deployment of VANETs.

Due to the ad hoc nature of vehicular networks, there will be no centralized infrastructure in order to manage security and privacy issues. Therefore, some IT-based security and privacy countermeasures, such as key management, may not work properly in vehicular networks. New and improved security mechanism are required to prevent unauthorized disclosures of information. Nevertheless, privacy in VANETs should be conditional which means that user-related information such as license plate, current speed, current position, identification number, and the like, should be kept private from other users/vehicles in the system while authorized users (e.g., police others) should have access to it [12, 43].

The trade-off between security and privacy needs remains a challenge. Receivers want to be sure that they can trust the source of information but the availability of such trust might contradict the privacy requirements of a sender.

Privacy, along with security, focuses on private vehicles (e.g., excluding emergency vehicles, buses, etc.) because the operation of all other vehicular nodes, including RSUs, does not raise any privacy concerns, and all the other nodes should be readily identifiable [17]. *Location privacy* is a primary concern for VANET because it aims to prevent others (any *observer*) from learning past or future locations of a vehicular user (vehicle driver or passenger). Anonymity for vehicle message transmissions is a way to protect location privacy.

For any observer, it should be impossible to acquire information about a specific vehicle that transmitted or will transmit a message (more generally, take an action according to a vehicular communication protocol). In addition, it should be impossible for observers to link any two or more messages (in general, actions) of the same vehicle. In the worst case scenario, if an observer attempts to guess, there should be only a low probability of linking a vehicles actions or identifying it among the set of all vehicles, that is, the anonymity set.

Rather than aiming for this strong anonymity, a relatively weaker level of protection should be adequate: messages should not allow for the identification of their sender, and two or more messages generated by the same vehicle should be difficult to link to each other [17].

Since safety messages do not contain any confidential data about their senders, vehicle owners will be only concerned about identity and location privacy. The use of anonymous public keys is the response to these concerns [44–46]. As signed messages can be trivially linked to the certificate of the signing node, it is necessary to remove all information identifying the user/vehicle from node certificates to make communications anonymous.

A set of distinct certified anonymous public keys that do not provide additional identifying information, denoted as *pseudonyms*, can be installed on every private vehicle [45–48]. The private key corresponding to a pseudonym is used by a node to sign outgoing messages, and appends the pseudonym to the messages. Messages signed under the same pseudonym (i.e., using the same corresponding private key) can be trivially linked to each other [1].

As pseudonymous certificates must be issued by a trusted authority, often a *Vehicular Public Key Infrastructure (VPKI)* is assumed for this purpose. VPKI is composed of a set of trusted third parties (TTPs) in charge of managing pseudonymous certificates. It is hierarchically structured. There is a single root Certificate Authority (CA) in each administrative domain (e.g., a country) and a delegated CA in each region within that domain. As vehicles from different regions (or even domains) can meet in a VANET, it is generally assumed that these CAs will be mutually recognized [12]. Figure 3.12 shows the interactions in a vehicular public key infrastructure and the relationships among the various entities that were introduced earlier.

Even if pseudonyms are in use, location information can be employed to trace a vehicle. Therefore, it is necessary to offer the minimum required information to other vehicles, while keeping it useful. To achieve this, *location cloaking techniques* [49, 50] have been proposed recently. With these techniques, location information is only offered when enough protection is achieved, that is, when the attacker is so confused that the probability of tracking is below than a certain threshold. Moreover, *aggregation* is considered for this purpose because it allows sending only aggregated data, thus minimizing the amount of private data sent [12].

Group signatures (GS) is one of the widely acceptable PKI techniques for achieving anonymous authentication in VANETs [31]. In a group signature, there is a group manager (which role can be separated into two parts, namely: the issuer and the opener) and its main function is to maintain the group; members may join or leave the group dynamically. After registering with the group, the member can anonymously sign any message on behalf of the group. A verifier can verify the group signature with only the group public key but cannot know which registered vehicle is the message generator. However, if necessary, the group manager can reveal the originator of any group signature. The main merit of the group signature-based technique over the anonymous certificates approach is that the former overcomes the limitation of pre-storing a large number of anonymous certificates [43].

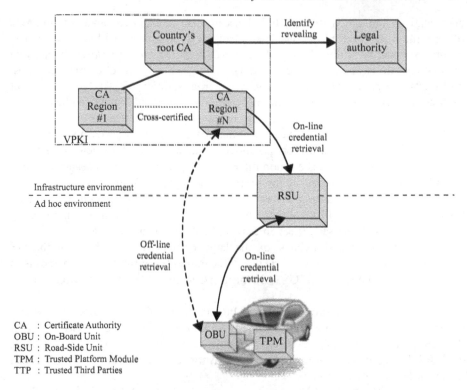

Figure 3.12   Components of a VPKI [12]

Based on the group signature techniques, a novel security framework for vehicular communications was presented by Guo *et al.* [51]. This work is incomplete because the authors do not give details about a concrete instantiation and any experimental analysis. To address these shortcomings Lin *et al.* [52] presented the first concrete instantiation of a group signature-based technique in VANET. The proposal, called Group Signature and Identity-based Signature (GSIS), is a conditional privacy-preserving vehicular communications protocol based on group signatures and ID-based signatures [53]. In the GSIS protocol, a single membership manager who issues secret member keys for vehicles is used. Unfortunately, this approach cannot effectively cope with the exclusion of compromised vehicles from the system. In addition, the solutions proposed by Lin *et al.* [52] to deal with compromised vehicles seem to be insufficient. The first option is to update the group public key pair for all non-revoked vehicles but this option incurs considerable overheads. The other option, called Verifier-Local Revocation (VLR), is similar to the traditional certificate revocation list scheme. Since the signature verification time grows linearly with the number of revoked vehicles, the VLR procedure becomes very time consuming and inefficient when the number of revoked vehicles grows [43].

In Reference 54, Tsang *et al.* proposes the Peer-to-Peer Anonymous Authentication (PPAA) scheme which views a VANET as a form of a P2P system. PPAA is a credential system which attempts to balance user privacy and accountability in terms of both the client and the server. The authors of PPAA identified four key requirements for security within their system as *mis-authentication resistance* (when two peers successfully complete mutual authentication, but only one of them is an honest and registered peer), *peer accountability* (when a coalition of $n \geq 1$ registered but malicious peer(s) attempts to run more than n successful mutual authentication involving the same honest peer A during the same event such that the tags A outputs in those authentications are all pairwise unlinked), *peer privacy* (when an honest peer A involved in an authentication potentially executed with a malicious peer, the adversary, potentially with the group manager's help, attempts to (a) deanonymize A in individual protocol runs, and/or or (b) pseudonymize A in protocol runs with different peers and/or during different events) and *framing resistance* (when an honest peer A is framed by another honest peer B thinking that he/she is mutually authenticating with the same peer in two successful authentication runs) [39].

To overcome the drawback of the large computation overhead of the GS schemes, the *hybrid schemes* can be used. The main idea of the hybrid schemes is to use the private keys of the GS scheme to issue pseudonym certificates for the vehicles [31].

An Efficient Conditional Privacy Preservation (ECPP) protocol for secure vehicular communications was proposed by Lu *et al.* [55]. In ECPP, GS is used at the RSU level, where all the RSUs in the network form the group members (i.e., each RSU has a private group key). The authentication at the vehicle level is based on pseudonym certificates.

Calandriello *et al.* [56] proposed to use GS at the OBU level, where all the OBUs in the network form the group members (i.e., each vehicle has a private group key). The private key of each vehicle is not used for signing outgoing messages as in GSIS, but instead, it is used for signing a short-lifetime pseudonym certificate for itself.

Since the security and privacy is an important issue for safety applications, several studies have been made recently to address these concerns. However, it is also important to study the impact of security and privacy on non-safety applications. A novel Portable Privacy-Preserving Authentication and Access Control Protocol, named PAACP, for non-safety applications in VANETs was proposed by Yeh *et al.* [57]. Besides the essential support of authentication, key establishment and privacy preservation, PAACP was developed to provide a sophisticated differentiated service access control, which will facilitate the deployment of a variety of non-safety applications. Moreover, the portability feature of PAACP can eliminate the backend communications with service providers. Therefore, better performance and scalability can be achieved with PAACP.

3.6   Future security challenges

In traditional networks or other emerging mobile networks, security and privacy failures usually bring only financial losses. However, both security and privacy failures in VANETs could be much more serious. For instance, the failure to detect a tampered vehicular message in time may cause serious traffic accidents, with loss of lives. In case of privacy failures, a driver (e.g., a well-known millionaire or movie star) may become the victim of kidnappers for ransom if organized criminals extract his/her driving routine by collecting and analysing vehicular communications. This implies that every effort must be devoted to security and privacy concerns as a precondition for the wide deployment and adoption of VANETs [43].

Security challenges are mostly concerned with the trade-off between authentication and non-repudiation versus privacy during communication within VANET environments. Another security challenge is delay sensitivity because significant delays prohibit the use of security protocols that have high overheads or rely on multiple stages of full-duplex communication between nodes [16].

Usage of traditional authentication mechanisms to address some security threats (such as illusion attacks) without affecting privacy in VANETs poses a new challenge for those VANET applications that need to authenticate nodes in VANETs. The other challenge is the restriction introduced by the transitory nature of interactions in a vehicular network to use reputation-based schemes [16].

Secure, efficient message exchange and authentication schemes operating for vehicle-to-infrastructure (V2I) and vehicle-to-vehicle (V2V) communications are required. For instance, mechanisms that can perform fast authentications between vehicles and roadside infrastructure units are needed to avoid delays. The use of a central, trusted authority and the use of public/private key-based solutions for vehicle-to-vehicle communication not only suffer high operational costs and response times but are also not scalable. Innovative approaches that can support fast, low-cost message exchanges whose communication overheads remain constant as the number of vehicles in the communication range increases are needed. Novel encryption protocols that can operate at high speeds compared to traditional public key-based solutions, which incur more delays and overheads when encrypting messages from neighbouring vehicles [11] are also required.

The time constraints of the envisioned safety and driver-assistance applications is another important challenge. During emergency braking, milliseconds of delay may cause a serious traffic accident. Hence emergency messages must be generated by the sender and verified by the receiver as soon as possible. For instance, in metropolitan areas with high vehicular density, each node may be flooded by a large number of messages to be verified. Therefore, ideally, the safety-related messages should be generated efficiently and given a high verification priority even if the receiver is overloaded with messages. Unfortunately, very few efforts have been made so far to cater for these compelling concerns in practice [43].

Signatures are usually used in vehicle-generated messages to allow the receiving vehicles to verify that these messages have originated from authentic sources and have not been modified during transmission. However, these signatures do not prevent attackers to identify who generated a vehicular message containing speed, location, direction, time and other driving information. Therefore, security and privacy of V2V communications need to be conciliated with data aggregation/compression [58, 59].

Due to the large number of broadcast messages transmitted in VANETs, broadcasting continues to be a strong research area of focus by VANET researchers. Broadcasting algorithms are required to minimize broadcast storms that arise as a result of packet flooding. More research is required to investigate intelligent flooding schemes, distributed algorithms that can efficiently handle asymmetric communications among vehicles for different transmission ranges. Moreover, to provide reliable broadcast messages with minimal overheads in VANETs, we need to address several other technical challenges including the selection of the next forwarding node, the maintenance of communications among vehicles as they leave and join a group, hidden terminal problems because broadcast messages do not use the typical Request to Sender/Clear to Sender (RTS/CTS) message exchange employed by IEEE 802.11 [11].

Routing schemes such as position-based routing which require vehicles to periodically reveal their locations in order to properly route the messages between the source and the destination, violate the location privacy of the users and it may result in users abstaining from using multi-hop applications in VANETs. Therefore, preserving the location privacy in position-based routing protocols is an open research topic where the main challenge is to investigate how to route the messages between the source and the destination without revealing their exact locations [31].

Electronic health (E-health) is a secure and privacy-aware electronic health system which provides medical service through personal health records. This access is essential to save lives when health records are needed on the spot to provide the necessary medical care. On the other hand, body area network is a set of sensors mounted on the body of the patient to monitor his/her health conditions. E-health and body are network and should be integrated with location-based routing in VANET to enable the aforementioned medical service on the road. Such integration is very important for providing health reports in case of accidents [31, 60]. This is an open research area that should be investigated to create healthcare information infrastructures that could help when accidents occur without disclosing privacy of personal health records.

The modeling of trustworthiness of peers in VANETs introduces several issues some of which include network congestion because vehicles are communicating on a shared channel and information overload – can result from vehicles receiving a lot of data from nearby vehicles in a congested area etc. Therefore, intelligent vehicle communication systems that are scalable and can detect and respond to these potentially hazardous situations by effectively deciding with which peers to communicate are required.

Another key challenge in modeling trust in a VANET environment is that a VANET is a decentralized and an open system (i.e., there is no centralized infrastructure and peers may join and leave the network any time, respectively). If a peer is interacting with a vehicle now, it is not guaranteed to interact with the same vehicle in the future. Therefore, it is not possible to rely on mechanisms that require a centralized system (e.g., the Centralized Certification Authority and the Trusted

Third Party, etc.) or social networks to build long-term relationships. However, in such an environment, there is a lot of uncertainty in deciding whom to trust [61].

Robust trust management is an issue that still needs attention from researchers. Trust models that are robust against various attacks need to be developed.

3.7 Conclusion

Interests in the development and improvement of vehicular networks have increased significantly in recent years. The convergence of computing, tele-communications (fixed and mobile) and various kinds of services are enabling the deployment of different kinds of VANET technologies and applications. However, as those applications and technologies have a direct impact on road traffic safety, it is essential that the communication protocols meet their performance and security requirements. Security mechanisms implemented for the VANET environment must take into consideration the inherent features (such as high node speed, decentralized infrastructure, etc.) of VANETs. In this chapter, we have presented an overview of the current security issues in vehicular ad hoc networks that will enable VANET designers and developers to design more secure and robust VANET archi-tectures, protocols and applications in the future. Furthermore, we have identified several attacks that can be launched on VANETs. Finally, we have described and analysed security solutions that have been proposed in the literature to mitigate the aforementioned attacks on VANETs.

Although several VANET security solutions have been proposed by the research community, we have also identified several security challenges and open research issues that still need to be addressed to support and enable a highly secure VANET infrastructure, secure VANET communications and robust trust models against attacks. Moreover, we argue that it is necessary to investigate mechanisms that can avoid delays during message exchanges and authentications between vehicles and roadside infrastructure units, and to allow the receiver of an emer-gency message to verify it as soon as possible in driver-assistance applications.

Current trust management models for VANET are inadequate because of the lack of support of important characteristics such as decentralized trust establishment, system level security and sensitivity to privacy concerns. We need to design efficient and robust trust management techniques and models that support all the aforemen-tioned characteristics to improve road safety and reduce the number of car accidents.

Acknowledgements

The authors thank the anonymous reviewers for their comments which helped to improve the content and quality of this chapter. We also thank the editors Professor Habib Rashvand and Professor Han-Chieh Chao for their support and encourage-ments throughout the preparation of this chapter. Sherali Zeadally was partly sup-ported by a District of Columbia NASA Space Grant during the course of this work.

References

1. Abdul Kalam Kunnel Aboobaker. 'Performance analysis of authentication protocols in vehicular ad hoc networks (vanet)'. Technical report, Royal Holloway, University of London Egham, Department of Mathematics, 2010

2. Jesús Téllez Isaac, José Sierra Cámara, Antonio Izquierdo Manzanares and Joaquín Torres Márquez. 'Anonymous payment in a kiosk centric model using digital signature scheme with message recovery and low computational power devices'. *Journal of Theoretical and Applied Electronic Commerce Research*, 1(2):1–11, 2006

3. Hannes Hartenstein and Kenneth Laberteaux. *VANET: Vehicular Applications and Inter-Networking Technologies*. Wiley Online Library, 2010

4. Jesús Téllez Isaac, José Sierra Cámara, Sherali Zeadally and Joaquín Torres Márquez. 'A secure vehicle-to-roadside communication payment protocol in vehicular ad hoc networks'. *Computer Communications*, 31(10):2478–2484, 2008

5. Panos Papadimitratos, Antonio Kung, Jean-Pierre Hubaux and Frank Kargl. 'Privacy and identity management for vehicular communication systems: A position paper'. In *Proceedings of the Workshop on Standards for Privacy in User-Centric Identity Management*, PRIME Project, Belgium, 2006

6. Maxim Raya and Jean-Pierre Hubaux. 'The security of vehicular ad hoc networks'. In *Proceedings of the 3rd ACM Workshop on Security of ad hoc and Sensor Networks (SASN 2005)*, New York, NY 10121–0701, USA, pp. 11–21, 2005

7. Saleh Yousefi, Mahmoud Siadat Mousavi and Mahmood Fathy. 'Vehicular ad hoc networks (vanets): Challenges and perspectives'. In *Proceedings of the 6th International Conference on ITS Telecommunications Proceedings IEEE press*, Hoboken, NJ 07030–5774, USA, pp. 761–766, 2006

8. Florian Dötzer. 'Privacy issues in vehicular ad hoc networks'. In *Proceedings of the 5th International Workshop on Privacy Enhancing Technologies (PET 2005)*, pp. 197–209, 2005

9. CAR 2 CAR Communication Consortium. 'Overview of the c2c-cc system (version 1.0)'. Technical report, Car2Car Communication Consortium, http://www.car-to-car.org/, 2007. Last accessed: Aug. 2012

10. Yi Qian and Nader Moayeri. 'Design of secure and application-oriented vanets'. In *Proceedings of the 67th IEEE Vehicular Technology Conference (VTC Spring 2008) IEEE press*, Hoboken, NJ 07030-5774, USA, pp. 2794–2799, 2008

11. Sherali Zeadally, Ray Hunt, Yuh-Shyan Chen, Angela Irwin and Aamir Hassan. 'Vehicular ad hoc networks (vanets): Status, results, and challenges'. *Telecommunication Systems*, pp. 1–25, 2012. 10.1007/s11235-010-9400-5

12. José María de Fuentes, Ana Isabel González-Tablas and Arturo Ribagorda. 'Overview of security issues in vehicular ad-hoc networks'. In *Handbook of Research on Mobility and Computing: Evolving Technologies and Ubiquitous Impacts*, pp. 894–911, 2010

13. Andreas Festag, Gerhard Noecker, Markus Strassberger, Andreas Lübke, Bernd Bochow, Marc Torrent-Moreno, *et al.* 'Now – network on wheels: Project objectives, technology and achievements'. In *Proceedings of the 6th International Workshop on Intelligent Transportation (WIT 2008) IEEE press*, Hoboken, NJ 07030-5774, USA, pp. 211–216, 2008

14. Marco Di Felice, Ali J. Ghandour, Hassan A. Artail and Luciano Bononi. 'Enhancing the performance of safety applications in ieee 802.11p/wave vehicular networks'. In *Proceedings of the IEEE International Symposium on a World of Wireless, Mobile and Multimedia Networks (WoWMoM 2012)*, San Francisco, CA, USA, pp. 1–9, 2012

15. Kathrin Bilstrup. 'A survey regarding wireless communication standards intended for a high-speed vehicle environment'. Technical report, School of Information Science, Computer and Electrical Engineering, Halmstad University, Sweden, 2007

16. Jesús Téllez Isaac, Sherali Zeadally and José Sierra Cámara. 'Security attacks and solutions for vehicular ad hoc networks'. *IET Communications*, 4(7): 894–903, 2010

17. Panagiotis Papadimitratos, Levente Buttyán, Tamás Holczer, Elmar Schoch, Julien Freudiger, Maxim Raya, *et al.* 'Secure vehicular communication systems: Design and architecture'. *IEEE Communications Magazine*, 46(11): 100–109, 2008

18. Bryan Parno and Adrian Perrig. 'Challenges in securing vehicular networks'. In *Proceedings of the Workshop on Hot Topics in Networks (HotNets-IV)*, New York, NY 10121-0701, USA, 2005

19. Maxim Raya and Jean-Pierre Hubaux. 'Securing vehicular ad hoc networks'. *Journal of Computer Security*, 15:39–68, 2007

20. Amer Aijaz, Bernd Bochow, Florian Dötzer, Andreas Festag, Matthias Gerlach, Rainer Kroh, *et al.* 'Attacks on inter vehicle communication systems – an analysis'. In *Proceedings of the International Workshop on Intelligent Transportation (WIT 2006), IEEE press*, Hoboken, NJ 07030-5774, USA, pp. 189–194, 2006

21. Ajay Rawat, Santosh Sharma and Rama Sushil. 'Vanet: Security attacks and its possible solutions'. *Journal of Information and Operations Management*, 3(1):301–304, 2012

22. Ghassan Samara, Wafaa A.H. Al-Salihy and Sureswaran Ramadas. 'Security issues and challenges of vehicular ad hoc networks (vanet)'. In *Proceedings of the 4th International Conference on New Trends in Information Science and Service Science (NISS 2010) IEEE press*, Hoboken, NJ 07030–5774, USA, pp. 393–398, 2010

23. Maxim Raya, Panos Papadimitratos and Jean-Pierre Hubaux. 'Securing vehicular communications'. *IEEE Wireless Communications Magazine, Special Issue on Inter-Vehicular Communications*, 13(5):8–15, 2006

24. Irshad Ahmed Sumra, Iftikhar Ahmad, Halabi Hasbullah and Jamalul lail bin Ab Manan. 'Behavior of attacker and some new possible attacks in

vehicular ad hoc network (vanet)'. In *Proceedings of the 3rd International Congress on Ultra Modern Telecommunications and Control Systems and Workshops (ICUMT 2011) IEEE press*, Hoboken, NJ 07030-5774, USA, pp. 1–8, 2011

25. Kasra Amirtahmasebi and Seyed Reza Jalalinia. 'Vehicular networks security, vulnerabilities and countermeasures'. Master's thesis, Chalmers University of Technology, 2010

26. Nai-Wei Lo and Hsiao-Chien Tsai. 'Illusion attack on vanet applications – a message plausibility problem'. In *Proceedings of the IEEE Globecom Workshops, IEEE press*, Hoboken, NJ 07030-5774, USA, pp. 1–8, 2007

27. Paolo Cencioni and Roberto Di Pietro. 'A mechanism to enforce privacy in vehicle-to-infrastructure communication'. *Computer Communications*, 31(12):2790–2802, 2008

28. Irshad Ahmed Sumra, Jamalul-Lail Ab Manan and Halabi Hasbullah. 'Timing attack in vehicular network'. In *Proceedings of the 15th World Scientific and Engineering Academy and Society (WSEAS) International Conference on Computers*, WSEAS Press, 960-6766, USA, pp. 151–155, 2011

29. Christine Laurendeau and Michel Barbeau. 'Threats to security in dsrc/wave'. In *Proceedings of the 5th International Conference on Ad-Hoc, Mobile, and Wireless Networks, (ADHOC-NOW 2006)*, Springer-Verlag, Berlin-Heidelberg, Germany, pp. 266–279, 2006

30. Sandhya Kohli and Rakesh Dhiman. 'Secure message communication using digital signatures and attribute based cryptographic method in vanet'. *International Journal of Information Technology and Knowledge Management*, 2(2):591–594, 2010

31. Albert Wasef. 'Managing and complementing public key infrastructure for securing vehicular ad hoc networks'. PhD thesis, University of Waterloo, 2011

32. Joo-Han Song, Vincent W.S. Wong and Victor C.M. Leung. 'Secure location verification for vehicular ad-hoc networks'. In *Proceedings of the IEEE Global Telecommunications Conference, (GLOBECOM 2008) IEEE press*, Hoboken, NJ 07030-5774, USA, pp. 1–5, 2008

33. Yih-Chun Hu, Adrian Perrig and David B. Johnson. 'Packet leashes: A defense against wormhole attacks in wireless ad hoc networks'. In *Proceedings of the Twenty-Second Annual Joint Conference of the IEEE Computer and Communications (INFOCOM 200)*, *IEEE press*, Hoboken, NJ 07030-5774, USA, pp. 1976–1986, 2003

34. Farid Nait-Abdesselam, Brahim Bensaou and Tarik Taleb. 'Detecting and avoiding wormhole attacks in wireless ad hoc networks'. *IEEE Communications Magazine*, 46(4):127–133, 2008

35. Nisha S. Raote and Kapil N. Hande. 'Approaches towards mitigating wormhole attack in wireless ad-hoc network'. *International Journal of Advanced Engineering Sciences and Technologies*, 2(2):172–175, 2011

36. Karamjeet Kaur, Sanjay Batish and Arvind Kakaria. 'Survey of various approaches to countermeasure sybil attack'. *International Journal of Computer Science and Informatics*, 1(4):96–100, 2012

37. Lin Yang, Jinhua Guo and Ying Wu. 'Piggyback cooperative repetition for reliable broadcasting of safety messages in vanets'. In *Proceedings of the 6th IEEE Conference on Consumer Communications and Networking Conference*, Las Vegas, Nevada, USA, pp. 1165–1169, 2009

38. Florian Dötzer, Florian Kohlmayer, Timo Kosch and Markus Strassberger. 'Secure communication for intersection assistance'. In *Proceedings of the 2nd International Workshop on Intelligent Transportation (WIT 2005)*, Hamburg, Germany, 2005

39. Marshall K. Riley. 'Group-based authentication mechanisms for vehicular ad-hoc networks'. Master's thesis, Southern Illinois University, 2010

40. Jamalul-lail Ab Manan Halabi Hasbullah, Irshad Ahmed Soomro. 'Denial of service (dos) attack and its possible solutions in vanet'. *World Academy of Science, Engineering and Technology (WASET)*, 65:411–415, 2010

41. Harbir Kaur, Sanjay Batish and Arvind Kakaria. 'An approach to detect the wormhole attack in vehicular adhoc networks'. *International Journal of Smart Sensors and Ad Hoc Networks*, 1(4):86–89, 2012

42. Gongjun Yan, Stephan Olariu and Michele C. Weigle. 'Providing vanet security through active position detection'. *Computer Communications*, 31(12):2883–2897, 2008

43. Lei Zhang. 'Research on security and privacy in vehicular ad hoc networks'. PhD thesis, Universitat Rovira i Virgili, 2010

44. Jean-Pierre Hubaux, Srdjan Capkun and Jun Luo. 'The security and privacy of smart vehicles'. *IEEE Security & Privacy Magazine*, 2(3):49–55, 2004

45. Matthias Gerlach, Andreas Festag, Tim Leinmüller, Gabriele Goldacker and Charles Harsch. 'Security architecture for vehicular communication'. In *Proceedings of the 4th International Workshop on Intelligent Transportation (WIT2007), IEEE press*, Hoboken, NJ 07030-5774, USA, 2007

46. Klaus Plöil and Hannes Federrath. 'A privacy aware and efficient security infrastructure for vehicular ad hoc networks'. *Computer Standards & Interfaces*, 30(6):390–397, 2008

47. David Chaum. 'Security without identification: Transaction systems to make big brother obsolete'. *Communications of the ACM*, 28(10):1030–1044, 1985

48. Panagiotis Papadimitratos, Levente Buttyan, Jean-Pierre Hubaux, Frank Kargl, Antonio Kung and Maxim Raya. 'Architecture for secure and private vehicular communications'. In *Proceedings of the 7th International Conference on ITS Telecommunications (ITST 2007), IEEE press*, Hoboken, NJ 07030-5774, USA, 1–6, 2007

49. Baik Hoh, Marco Gruteser, Hui Xiong and Ansaf Alrabady. 'Preserving privacy in gps traces via uncertainty-aware path cloaking'. In *Proceedings of the 14th ACM Conference on Computer and Communications Security (CCS 2007)*, New York, NY 10121-0701, USA, pp. 161–171, 2007

50. Ge Xu. 'Location cloaking for location privacy protection and location safety protection'. PhD thesis, Iowa State University, 2010

51. Jinhua Guo, John P. Baugh and Shengquan Wang. 'A group signature based secure and privacy-preserving vehicular communication framework'. In

Proceedings of the 2007 Mobile Networking for Vehicular Environments IEEE press, Hoboken, NJ 07030-5774, USA, 2007

52. Xiaodong Lin, Xiaoting Sun, Pin-Han Ho and Xuemin Shen. 'Gsis: A secure and privacy preserving protocol for vehicular communications'. *IEEE Transactions on Vehicular Technology*, 56(6):3442–345, 2007

53. Adi Shamir. 'Identity based cryptosystems and signature schemes'. In *Proceedings of the CRYPTO 84 on Advances in Cryptology*, Springer-Verlag New York, Inc. New York, NY, USA, pp. 47–53, 1984

54. Patrick P. Tsang and Sean W. Smith. 'Ppaa: Peer-to-peer anonymous authentication'. In *Proceedings of the 6th International Conference on Applied Cryptography and Network Security (ACNS 2008)*, Springer-Verlag New York, Inc. New York, NY, USA, pp. 55–74, 2008

55. Rongxing Lu, Xiaodong Lin, Haojin Zhu, Pin-Han Ho and Xuemin Shen. 'Ecpp: Efficient conditional privacy preservation protocol for secure vehicular communications'. In *Proceedings of the 27th IEEE International Conference on Computer Communications, Joint Conference of the IEEE Computer and Communications Societies (INFOCOM 2008))*, Phoenix, Arizona, USA, pp. 1229–1237, 2008

56. Giorgio Calandriello, Papadimitrato, Jean-Pierre Hubaux and Antonio Lioy. 'Efficient and robust pseudonymous authentication in vanet'. In *Proceedings of the Fourth ACM International Workshop on Vehicular Ad Hoc Networks*, New York, NY 10121-0701, USA, pp. 19–28, 2007

57. Lo-Yao Yeh, Yen-Cheng Chen and Jiun-Long Huang. 'Paacp: A portable privacy-preserving authentication and access control protocol in vehicular ad hoc networks'. *Computer Communications*, 34(3):447–456, 2011

58. Alexandre Viejo, Francesc Seb and Josep Domingo-Ferrer. 'Aggregation of trustworthy announcement messages in vehicular ad hoc networks'. In *Proceedings of the IEEE 69th Vehicular Technology Conference (VTC Spring 2009)*, Honolulu, Hawaii, USA, pp. 1–5, 2009

59. Albert Wasef Wasef and Xuemin Shen. 'Asic: Aggregate signatures and certificates verification scheme for vehicular networks'. In *Proceedings of the IEEE Global Telecommunications Conference (GLOBECOM 2009)*, New York, NY 10121-0701, USA, pp. 1–6, 2009

60. Gongjun Yan, Ye Wang, Michele C. Weigle, Stephan Olariu and Khaled Ibrahim. 'Wehealth: A secure and privacy preserving ehealth using notice'. In *Proceedings of the International Conference on Wireless Access in Vehicular Environments (WAVE)*, at the University of Michigan-Dearborn, MI. USA, December 8–9, 2008

61. Jie Zhang. 'A survey on trust management for vanets'. In *Proceedings of the IEEE International Conference on Advanced Information Networking and Applications (AINA 2011)*, Biopolis, Singapore, pp. 105–112, 2011

Chapter 4*

INT Internet-gateway discovery in mobile ad hoc networks

Alicia Triviño[a] and Antonio J. Yuste[b]

Abstract

The applications where mobile ad hoc networks are connected to the Internet are gaining popularity. However, several technologies should be applied in order to guarantee a reliable connectivity. Particular cares should be applied to the gateway discovery process. The enhancements related to the gateway discovery process are mainly achieved by controlling the propagation of the gateway messages in the network. Two specific parameters need to be controlled in this process: the frequency of the messages and the area in which they are propagated. This chapter explains how these two parameters are tuned to adapt to the dynamic characteristics of the network. Although the techniques are proposed for the integration of a MANET into the Internet, its applicability could be extended to any other mechanism where broadcast messages are used in a multihop wireless communication.

4.1   Introduction: MANETs connected to the Internet

The principal objective of the fourth generation or 4G networks is to guarantee a reliable communication among all the users at a reasonable cost independently of the network from where they access [1]. Among the networks included in 4G, we can find the mobile ad hoc networks. A mobile ad hoc networks or MANET is formed by autonomous mobile nodes, which are able to communicate among themselves without any infrastructure (e.g. base stations or access points). The capability of operating without previous planning has made MANETs especially

*H. F. Rashvand and H.-C. Chao (Eds.), *Dynamic Ad Hoc Networks*, The IET Book Publishing Department, 2013, ISBN 978-1-84919-647-5, eISBN 978-1-84919-648-2
[a]Dpto. Ingeniería Eléctrica, Escuela de Ingenierías, Campus de Teatinos, the University of Málaga, Málaga, Spain
[b]Dpto de Ing. Telecomunicación, the University of Jaén, Escuela Politécnica Superior de Linares, C/Alfonso X el Sabio, Linares, Spain

suitable for emergency scenarios. For instance, Figure 4.1 shows a typical situation where a catastrophe has occurred. Under these circumstances, the military, the fireman and the medical services need to work in the area. Although a MANET helps communicate among the colleagues in the zone, this specialized staff may also contact to a hospital, the headquarters or the emergency coordinators. For the communication with these external members, the connection to the Internet or to any IP-based access networks such as the 3G telephony systems should be guaranteed.

Therefore, it is a current requirement that the MANET is integrated into IP-based access networks, such as the Internet. Towards an efficient interconnection of both networks, it is necessary to incorporate new mechanisms in the MANET nodes. Among these mechanisms, the gateway discovery outstands. Essentially, the gateway discovery must provide the MANET nodes with an IP address and with the routing information to access to the Internet. To do so, the gateway is responsible for propagating a specific message with the configuration parameters. This message is generically known as the Modified Router Advertisement (MRA). Although the configuration of the IP address is executed the first time the node attaches to the gateway, the reception of the MRA message is continuously required to update the routing information. Since the routes in the MANET change unpredictably, the successive reception of the MRA messages helps the mobile nodes update their routing entries and, consequently, to efficiently transmit their data to the Internet.

Two important parameters affect the MRA propagation process. These parameters are: (i) the frequency of generation of the messages and (ii) the area in which these messages are propagated in the MANET. The most recent research

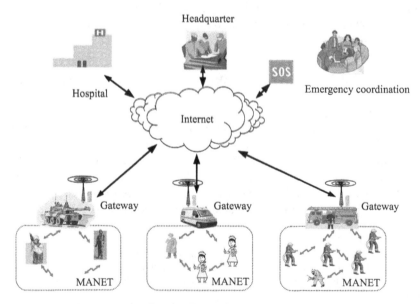

Figure 4.1   Integration of several mobile ad hoc networks into the Internet

works show that the dynamics of the network should be taken into account when configuring these two parameters.

Concerning the element that performs the adjustment, the frequency of the MRA messages is always set by the Gateway. In this sense, the period of transmission could be a multiple of a predetermined configuration parameter or it could be set to any value. On the other hand, the scope of the MRA messages could be determined by the Gateway or by the mobile nodes. In this last case, the mobile nodes decide about the suitability of retransmitting an MRA message upon its reception.

This chapter aims at describing some significant techniques that adjust these two configuration parameters. Although the techniques are proposed for improving the gateway discovery mechanism in mobile ad hoc networks, the mechanisms can be used in any other broadcast communication that implies multihop wireless transmissions.

The rest of the chapter is structured as follows. Section 4.2 reviews the requirements for achieving the integration. Section 4.3 describes the functionalities of the gateway. Sections 4.4 and 4.5 detail the proposals to adapt the frequency and the scope of the MRA messages, respectively. Section 6 explains the techniques that allow the adjustment of both configuration parameters. Section 7 describes some further developments that can be done in this research area. Finally, Section 8 draws the main conclusions of this chapter.

4.2   Requirements for connecting a MANET to the Internet

The protocol in charge of allowing the auto-configuration of the mobile devices is the Neighbour Discovery Protocol [2]. According to this protocol, the Access Router generates a Router Advertisement (RA) message for this purpose. Since the RA messages are generated with link local addresses, they cannot be retransmitted [3]. Consequently, the Neighbour Discovery Protocol as itself does not support the access in a multihop wireless networks such as a MANET. As illustrated in Figure 4.1, the integration of a MANET into an IP-based access networks is supported by the inclusion of a gateway.

The functionalities of the gateway are twofold. First, the gateway generates a specific message, known as Modified Router Advertisement (MRA) message, with the information derived from the RA message. The main difference is that MRA messages can be retransmitted so that all the nodes in the MANET could receive them. Second, the gateway executes the ad hoc routing, which is a functionality that the access router (AR) does not implement. When the AR receives a packet whose destination is a MANET node that is not in its coverage area, it is forced to transmit the packets to the gateway. Then, the gateway will consequently execute the ad hoc routing procedures.

Some additional mechanisms should be also incorporated in the mobile nodes to enable the connection to the Internet. Among these mechanisms, we can outline the selection of the gateway [4, 5], the identification of the network prefix, the construction of the IPv6 address [6, 7], the address resolution or the mobility management [8].

4.3   Internet-gateway discovery in a MANET

As remarked, the gateway is responsible for routing the download traffic and for the propagation of the configuration parameters (network prefix, mechanism to acquire the IP address, etc.). The process by which the route to the gateway and the configuration parameters are learnt is referred to as the gateway discovery.

The gateway discovery is achieved by the reception of the MRA messages in the mobile devices. This reception helps nodes discover, update and optimize the routes to the Internet gateway. Additionally, the MRA messages provide the configuration parameters to access to the Internet.

The different techniques for the Gateway discovery are associated to the methods by which the MRA messages are generated [3, 9, 10]. Specify the features of the gateway and the conditions that trigger the emission of the MRA messages. By far, the Global Connectivity mechanism [11] is the most popular integration approach. The Global Connectivity mechanism differentiates the following three types of gateway discoveries in a MANET:

Reactive: The gateway generates a unicast MRA message only when it receives a request. The request, known as the Modified Router Solicitation (MRS), generated by a node when it does not keep an updated route to the gateway in its routing table. Although the MRS is a multicast message that reaches all the nodes in the MANET, the response generated by the gateway is exclusively transmitted through the path by which the gateway received the MRS.

Proactive: The MRA messages are periodically generated every T seconds. These messages are broadcast and their scope is the complete network. In the interval between two consecutive MRA messages, a route to the gateway learnt from the last MRA may become invalid due to the mobility of the nodes. Under these circumstances, a reactive approach is triggered. Thus, the invalidity of needed routes incurs in an MRS process solved with a unicast MRA message.

Hybrid: This approach combines the previous strategies. First, the gateway periodically generates an MRA message every T seconds. The TTL of the messages, which determines the number of retransmissions that the MRA messages can experiment, is restricted so that not all the nodes receive the MRA messages. The TTL defines a proactive area. Nodes outside this area are forced to proceed in a reactive way every time they need to start a communication to the Internet. Additionally, the nodes in the proactive area that require an updated route to the gateway also activate a reactive process. This approach was not initially included in the specifications but further research work developed this scheme [12].

The most convenient values for the two configuration parameters (T and TTL) depend on the network conditions. For instance, Figure 4.2 shows the overhead (number of MRA, MRS and route error messages) in a typical MANET for different values of T. The mobility conditions leads to different optimal values of the interval of the MRA messages. The optimum T value that minimizes the overhead could

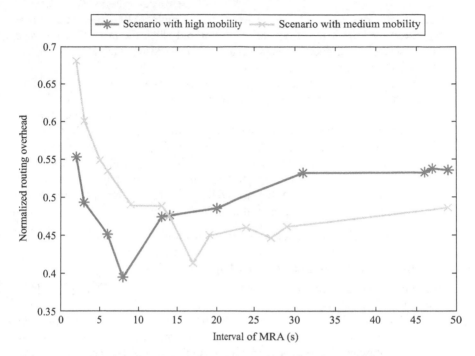

Figure 4.2   Overhead as a function of the T value in a typical MANET scenario

change when the mobility of nodes varies, when the traffic comes from different sources or when the nodes become closer to the gateway. Since these network conditions vary unpredictably in most MANET applications, there is a need for including some algorithms in the gateway or in the MANET nodes that dynamically adjust the gateway discovery process to the instantaneous network variables.

Concerning the elements that are responsible for the adaptive technique, the adjustment of T is exclusively carried out by the gateway. However, the area in which the MRA message is propagated can be determined by the gateway or by the MANET nodes. Transferring the decision to the MANET nodes, the distributed tuning is expected to outperform a centralized approach as more features of the network can be used in the adaptation process.

The next section reviews the techniques proposed to adapt both parameters.

4.4   Techniques to adjust the frequency of the gateway messages

In a proactive and hybrid gateway discovery, the gateway generates a multicast MRA message every T seconds. Two main strategies are followed for the adjustment of T:

- Decide the next instant to generate the following MRA message. In this case, the value of T dynamically changes every time that an MRA is generated. The gateway decides the next instant when the following MRA message will be generated basing on the observed data captured since the last MRA message was broadcast. The decision is taken once that the MRA generation timer (set with the previous value of T) is over.

Figure 4.3 shows a generic scheme where this kind of adaptation takes place. The MRA messages are generated at t_{j-1}, t_j and t_{j+1} instants. At the t_{j-1} instant, the $(j-1)$th MRA is transmitted to the network. At the same time, the new value of T is decided. This new value, which determines when the j-th MRA message will be generated, corresponds to T_{j-1}. The process is repeated at the jth instant. The new value decided for T, that is, T_j could differ from T_{j-1}.

- Decide about the suitability of generating the MRA. The gateway determines every T seconds whether an MRA should be generated or not. In contrast to the previous adaptation process, the value of T is a constant.

Next, the most significant adaptive techniques are summarized.

4.4.1   Adaptive discovery based on quality of service

This technique tries to guarantee the delay requirements for the traffic sources [13]. According to this proposal, the destination of the data traffic generates a specific message called QS_LOST when it detects that the delay requirement is about to be exceeded. The destination, as it is placed in the Internet, transfers the message to the MANET gateway that routes it to the original data source. Thus, the source triggers the procedures to discover alternative routes in the MANET that could satisfy the delay requirements.

The tuning of the periodicity of the MRA messages is performed by the gateway, which analyses the number of QS_LOST messages received along the last interval and the number of traffic sources. When the ratio of these two magnitudes exceeds a threshold, the network is assumed to be congested. Consequently, the generation of a new MRA message would deteriorate the network performance.

4.4.2   Algorithm based on the stability factor

The supporting idea of this algorithm relies on the fact that stable paths require to be updated less frequently [14]. A path is assumed to be stable when the mobility of nodes composing the path is minimal and, in turn, the duration of the path is significantly high. On these conditions, the update of the routes, that is, the generation of an MRA message could be deferred.

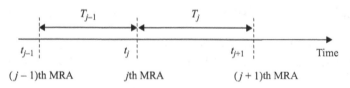

Figure 4.3   *Generic scheme to decide the next instant to generate an MRA message*

An indicator of the network stability is the number of nodes that continue being the gateways neighbours. To know this parameter, the gateway analyses the retransmitted MRA messages and it computes the stability factor (*SF*) at an instant *t* defined as:

$$SF = \frac{2p - d}{NMRA_{j-1} + NMRA_j} \tag{4.1}$$

where, *p* is the number of nodes that were in the gateway's neighbourhood at instants $t - 1$ and *t*. *d* corresponds to the number of mobile nodes that were the gateway's neighbours at the instant $t - 1$ but they have left its coverage area at instant *t*. $NMRA_x$ stands for the number of MRA messages received between the generation of the $(x - 1)$-th MRA and the *x*-th MRA message.

The stability factor determines the value of the next *T* basing on a linear relationship shown in Figure 4.4. The function also defines two limiting values for *T* (T_{min} and T_{max}), which are associated to two values of the stability factor (SF_{min} and SF_{max}).

4.4.3 Fuzzy-logic-based adaptive algorithm

According to this proposal, the gateway executes a fuzzy-logic-based system to determine the following instant when the MRA should be generated [15]. The system employs three variables: the stability factor (defined in the previous proposal), the route request factor and the connectivity factor. The route request factor (RRF) is defined as:

$$RRF = \frac{NMRS_j}{N_s} \tag{4.2}$$

where $NMRS_j$ is the number of MRS messages by the gateway from the $(j - 1)$-th MRA message to the instant *t* according to a scheme as described in Figure 4.3. The N_s parameter corresponds to the number of traffic sources in the MANET.

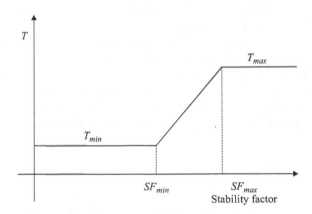

Figure 4.4 Relationship between the stability factor and the T value

The connectivity factor (CF) is computed as:

$$CF = \frac{NMRA_j}{E[NMRA]} \tag{4.3}$$

where the $E[\cdot]$ is the expected value and NMRA is the discrete variable that captures the number of MRA messages retransmitted by the gateway's neighbours once the gateway has generated it.

To compute these three parameters, the gateways need to monitor the MRS received since the last generation of the MRA, the number of MRAs retransmitted by the gateway's neighbour and the precedence of the retransmitted MRA. Therefore, no additional overhead is incurred in the network.

4.5   Techniques to adjust the scope of the gateway messages

The area in which the MRA messages are propagated can be controlled by a centralized or distributed technique. In the centralized schemes, the gateway generates the message accordingly to the area in which the message is desired to be received. Thus, the TTL in the IP header of the MRA is set taking into account the maximum number of retransmissions that the message should experiment. On the other hand, a distributed adjustment transfers the decision about the scope of the MRA messages to the MANET nodes. Specifically, the nodes in the MANET that receive the MRA message decide about the suitability of retransmitting it and they react accordingly.

Next, the most relevant techniques for the adjustment of the TTL parameter are presented.

4.5.1   *Maximal source coverage*

The first adaptive technique is due to Ruiz and Gomez-Skarmeta [12]. In this proposal, known as maximal source coverage, the gateway analyses the distance to the MANET sources. The distance is measured as the number of hops. Then, the TTL of the MRA messages is set to the farthest distance. Figure 4.5 shows a MANET where two gateways provide access to the Internet. In this illustration and according to the maximal source coverage algorithm, the gateway named GW1 sets the TTL to 4, whereas the gateway GW2 fixes this parameter to 2.

Despite its simplicity, the algorithm is able to improve the network performance when there are a significant number of sources in the wireless network. Conversely, a reduced number of traffic generators in the MANET would provoke an increased overhead in the network in comparison to a pure reactive gateway discovery.

4.5.2   *Maximal benefit coverage*

In this algorithm [12], the goal is to avoid the deterioration of the network performance when the maximal source coverage is employed in scenarios with a low number of traffic sources at far distances. For this purpose, the gateway tries to

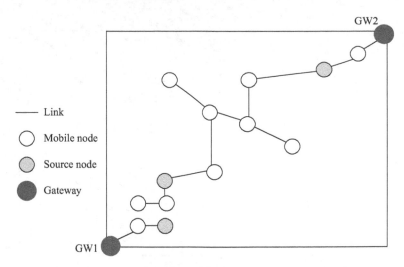

Figure 4.5   Illustration of a MANET connected to the Internet to show how the maximal source coverage works

minimize the overhead incurred because of the propagation of the MRA messages and because of the reactive procedures. The exact computation of this value would demand considerable data that are not always available. For instance, the topology of the MANET would be required for this computation. Therefore, the authors propose a heuristic based on the parameters that the gateway easily computes. This heuristic, $\beta(t)$, is defined as:

$$\beta(t) = \frac{N \cdot S(t)}{t \cdot (t + 3)} \tag{4.4}$$

where N stands for the cost of flooding an MRA message in the network and $S(t)$ is a function that computes the number of sources at a distance (in terms of number of hops) lower or equal to t. To compute the cost of propagating an MRA message in the network, a grid model for the topology of the network is used.

4.5.3   Low overhead and scalable proxied

According to the present proposal [16], the nodes in the boundaries of the proactive zone are enabled to reply to the MRS messages. Figure 4.6 shows how this technique works.

In this figure, the gateway GW1 has set its TTL to 3. Node 1 needs to start a communication with a host in the Internet and it does not possess a routing entry for this destination. Thus, it transmits an MRS message. The message is received by node A. With the conventional global connectivity mechanism, the node A retransmits the MRS until it reaches the gateway, which is the only element that can reply to this request. However, the present proposal allows node A to reply transmitting a unicast MRA to node 1.

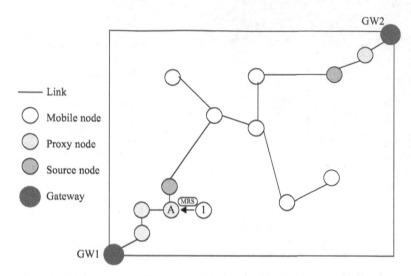

Figure 4.6   Scheme of a MANET connected to the Internet to illustrate the behaviour of the low overhead and scalable proxied technique

4.5.4   Mobile-IP-based adaptive discovery

To improve the network performance when the Mobile IPv6 protocol is executed, the technique in [17] proposes that the gateways providing access to the Internet share the information concerning the distance of the traffic sources. Once this information is exchanged, the gateways are configured to set a value for the TTL parameter equal to the mean distance at which the source nodes are attached to the different gateways.

4.5.5   Centralized TTL adaptation

In this proposal [18], the gateway considers the following measurements to tune the value of the TTL:

- The number of MANET sources communicating with the Internet
- The most frequent distance (in terms of number of hops) from the sources to the gateway
- The average value of the distance from the sources to the gateway
- The maximum distance from the sources to the gateway

Once the gateway has obtained these parameters, an algorithm is executed to know the exact value of the TTL.

4.5.6   Load-based gateway discovery

The proposal in [19] aims at maintaining the network in a low level of congestion. Thus, when the gateway detects that the traffic that it is routing increases, it decreases the value of the TTL. In this way, the scarce wireless resources are left for the data traffic. In contrast, when the gateway identifies that the traffic that it is processing is lower than a predetermined threshold, it opts for generating MRA messages with an increased value of the TTL parameter. In this way, the low congested networks can benefit from low activity cycles to update their routing information upon receiving the MRA messages.

The congested level is also used to tune the value of T in an enhanced version of this algorithm in [20].

4.5.7   Signal-to-noise-based adaptation

In this algorithm [21], the gateway tunes the value of the TTL basing on the distance to the traffic sources. In addition, the gateway also measures the signal-to-noise ratio in its vicinity in order to identify the scenarios where there are unstable links. Unstable links require the frequent update of their routing information.

4.5.8   Adaptive distributed discovery

The main contribution of this technique [22] relies on the fact that it was the first proposal that adjusts the scope of the MRA messages in a distributed way. The adaptive distributed gateway discovery (ADD) is based on exclusively retransmitting the MRA messages through the paths that are currently in use. Figure 4.7 depicts how this procedure works.

In Figure 4.7 we can observe that only four nodes will retransmit the MRA messages. These nodes are marked in the figure as intermediate nodes.

This strategy is not valid for time-varying-traffic sources as it is difficult to determine the future active routes.

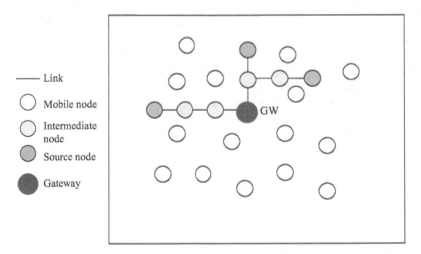

Figure 4.7   Illustration of a MANET connected to the Internet to show the behaviour of the adaptive distributed gateway discovery

4.5.9   *Selective retransmission of the MRA messages*

In this technique [23], the gateway periodically generates an MRA message every T seconds. The mobile nodes decide about the convenience of retransmitting them basing on the remaining lifetime of the route to the gateway. When a mobile node receives an MRA through a route more efficient than the one it knows, it updates the route to the gateway with the routing information derived from this message. Under these circumstances, the conventional gateway discovery forces the retransmission of the MRA. In this proposal, the nodes estimate the remaining lifetime of the route (RRL) that could be learnt from the MRA message. This estimation is computed basing on the Mean Residual Lifetime and the statistical characterization of the perceived link durations. Then, the nodes check if the following expression holds to transmit the MRA message:

$$RRL \leq T.hops \tag{4.5}$$

where the number of hops of the route corresponds to the variable *hops*.

The most important novelty of this proposal is that the mobile nodes are not always enabled to decide about the retransmission. In fact, the gateway includes a new field in the MRA messages to let the nodes know if they are allowed to decide about this forwarding. In addition, the mobile devices that are acting as relaying nodes for a traffic source will always retransmit the MRA message in order to promote the optimization of the ongoing traffic.

4.5.10   *Gateway discovery based on stable links*

Aiming at improving the network performance for the proactive gateway discovery procedures, the paths to the gateway that are expected to endure longer should be preferred to route the packets to the Internet [24]. With this objective, the proposed algorithm obliges the mobile devices to retransmit the multicast MRA messages basing on the remaining lifetime of the path to the gateway. Accordingly, a node is allowed to forward an MRA message only when the link from which the message has been received is estimated to remain active along the next interval T. T is the period of the generation of the MRA messages.

The analysed link would be part of the route to the gateway if the MRA is retransmitted and the link is also used to update the route information in the receiving node. As this decision is successively taken along the paths in which the MRA messages are forwarded, only the routes that are expected to remain stable during the next period (T) are discovered.

To study the remaining duration of the link through which they have received the MRA messages, the nodes compute the Mean Residual Lifetime (MRL) of this link. The computation of this parameter requires the statistical characterization of the duration of the wireless links. The authors demonstrate that it is possible to model the duration of the links without incurring in additional overhead.

4.5.11 Type-2 fuzzy-logic-based adjustment

Several proposals have adjusted the TTL by means of a fuzzy-logic control system. However, this kind of system assumes that the entries correspond to an exact measurement. Since a type-2 fuzzy logic can work with uncertainties in its entries, this type of control outstands as more adequate for a MANET, where the measurements may be partially erroneous. For instance, the exact computation of the duration of the established links requires the inclusion of additional control messages in the MANET. As this additional overhead should be avoided, the gateway estimates this parameter with partial information obtained from the routing protocol. The estimation could be inexact.

Specifically, the work in [25] explains the configuration of a type-2 fuzzy system to implement the decision about retransmitting the periodic MRA messages in the mobile nodes. The system takes the local connectivity to the gateway, the route length and the source spreading as inputs.

The system output corresponds to two values. Depending on the activity of the nodes (if it is transmitting data packets or not), one of the outputs is chosen and compared to a threshold. If the selected output exceeds the threshold, the received MRA is propagated.

4.6 Adjustment in the hybrid gateway discovery

Although three types of gateway discovery could be configured in the global connectivity mechanism, all of them can be always modelled by a hybrid approach. In this sense, a proactive gateway discovery is just a hybrid discovery where the TTL is set to the network diameter. On the other hand, a reactive gateway discovery is equivalent to a hybrid gateway discovery where T is infinite. In an adaptive hybrid gateway discovery, two parameters need to be adjusted: the periodicity of the MRA messages (T) and the scope (controlled by the TTL value).

In the next subsections, we explain how these two parameters are simultaneously adjusted.

4.6.1 Generic algorithm

In Reference [26], Ghassemian *et al.* defend that the optimal selection of the TTL and T can be achieved by a control system. The control system studies the received MRS messages. Specifically, it focuses on how far the sources generating the MRS messages are in comparison with the defined TTL value. Analysing the difference, the TTL should be increased or decremented. Concerning the value of T, the control system should take into account several parameters such as the number of MRS messages received, the distance to the sources generating them or the traffic routed by the gateway.

The most significant drawback of the proposal relies on the fact that the exact procedure by which these parameters should be used by the control system is not specified.

4.6.2   Regulated mobility degree

This proposal [27] defends that the MRA messages should not be generated periodically but only when the routes to the gateway are demanded. The basis is supported by the fact that the network will benefit from an MRA message only when a movement of the nodes has occurred. Under these circumstances, a refreshment of the routes to the gateway may be necessary.

The algorithm is supported by a heuristic that considers how far the traffic sources are and how many traffic sources are active. The heuristic, name regulated mobility degree (RMD), is:

$$RMD = \frac{1}{\sum_{i=1}^{N_f} dist_i - 1} \tag{4.6}$$

where N_f is equal to the number of sources. Every source i is at a distance $dist_i$ (in terms of number of hops), where $1 \leq i \leq N_f$.

When the heuristic exceeds a threshold, the algorithm opts for retransmitting the MRA message. The computation of the heuristic is performed every T seconds.

Figure 4.8 shows a MANET scenario where two gateways are available. For gateway GW1, the RMD corresponds to 1/3, whereas GW2 has an RMD equal to 1.

On the other hand, the TTL is adjusted basing on the maximal benefit coverage algorithm.

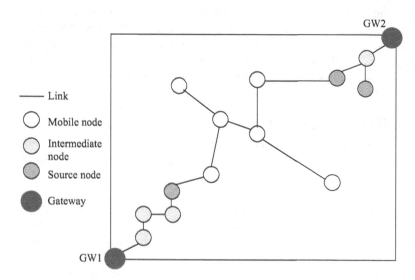

Figure 4.8   *A MANET scenario where the computation of the RMD is illustrated on the other hand, the TTL is adjusted basing on the maximal benefit coverage algorithm*

4.6.3   *Auto-regressive-filter-based algorithm*

By means of an auto-regressive filter [28], the algorithm adjusts the value of *T*. In particular, the system uses the number of MRS as an indicator of the need for updates routes, that is, for the generation of a multicast MRA message. Therefore, the higher the number of MRS messages received in the gateway is, the shorter the periodicity of the MRA generation becomes. The most important drawback of the proposal relies on the difficulty of configuring the auto-regressive filter when the network features vary.

Concerning the TTL, the maximal source coverage is employed.

4.6.4   *Adaptive discovery based on the neighbourhood*

In this proposal, the TTL value is fixed according to the maximal source coverage. Alternatively, the value of *T* is set basing on the percentage of the number of network nodes that are in the gateway neighbourhood. The number of nodes placed in this area can be easily estimated by the gateway. It just has to count the number of MRA retransmissions.

Since the nodes accessing to the Internet transfer the data through the gateway, this element also estimates the members of the network. From these two estimations, the gateway determines if the nodes are keeping short routes to access to the Internet. Under these circumstances, identified because a high percentage of nodes are in the gateway's neighbourhood, the routes are assumed to be more stable. Consequently, these routes do not need to be frequently updated. Accordingly, the gateway increases the interval between consecutive MRA messages, that is, the value of *T*. Alternatively, when the gateway detects that the percentage of nodes in its neighbourhood has decreased, it assumes that the routes to the gateway are composed of more intermediate nodes and it reduces the value of *T*.

In order to specify how the value of *T* is increased or decreased two strategies have been proposed. First, a genetic algorithm was applied in [29]. The work in [30] analytically derives the equation for the increment basing on the study of a mobility model such as the Random Waypoint. The work in [31] extends this last study when other mobility conditions characterize the network.

4.6.5   *GPS-assisted hybrid gateway discovery*

An application of a MANET is a Vehicular ad hoc Network (VANET). The proposal in Reference 32 defends that an improved gateway discovery in a VANET should take into account the positions of the vehicles in the network. Thus, the vehicles are provided with a global positioning system (GPS) to exchange their coordinates. The algorithm is able to tune the value of T and TTL.

4.6.6   *Fuzzy-logic-based hybrid gateway discovery*

This work [33] regulates the value of *T* while the TTL is set according to the maximal source coverage algorithm. Every second, the gateway executes the control system to decide about the suitability of broadcasting an MRA at that instant.

The entries of the fuzzy system are the number of route request, the number of local link changes and the variations of the distance to reach the traffic sources.

Since the gateway is expected to be a fixed element without energy constraints in most of the integration supports, the continuous execution of the algorithm is feasible.

4.7   Further developments

This chapter has reviewed the most significant contributions related to the adaptation of the gateway discovery process to the MANET features. This work could be extended in the following guidelines:

- Inclusion of more parameters to adjust the value of T. In particular, the need for updated routes in the MANET should be supported by the instantaneous data losses, delay communications and overhead. New metrics that take into account these features could improve the gateway discovery process. In addition, when more than one gateway is available in a MANET, the gateways could exchange measurements related to these parameters to adapt to the dynamics of the network.
- Propagation of the MRA messages basing on the QoS requirements of the traffic sources. The most convenient propagation of the MRA messages is related to the need of the traffic sources for updated communication paths. However, the requirements of the sources are dependent on the QoS constrains of their communication. In this sense, the propagation of the MRA should consider the necessity of a source for bounded-delay paths or low-losses routes.
- Simultaneous adjustment of the values of T and TTL in a distributed way. Although there exist several proposals that adjust the values of T and TTL simultaneously, the proposed techniques tune the TTL in a centralized way. A distributed approach for this adaptation is expected to improve the network performance.
- Extending the techniques to other periodic broadcast process in MANETs. The gateway discovery is a process to transmit periodic broadcast messages in a multihop wireless network. The presented techniques could be useful for their application in other periodic broadcasting processes for this kind of network.

4.8   Conclusion

Mobile ad hoc networks are characterized by unpredictable and continuous changes of their link states. These dynamic features recommend the use of adaptive algorithms for the protocols intended for this kind of network. In particular, the interconnection of MANETs to the Internet through a gateway can greatly benefit from adaptive techniques that control the propagation area and the periodicity of the gateway messages. This chapter has reviewed the main techniques proposed for the adjustment of these two parameters relating to the gateway messages. These two configuration parameters can be adapted simultaneously or individually. In addition, we have observed that the periodicity of the MRA messages is always controlled by the gateway. Conversely, the scope of the messages is determined by the gateway or the MANET nodes. The proposed techniques infer the need for the messages from the measurements related to the stability of the communication paths, the traffic status or the network overhead. These measurements give hints about the need for updated routes in the MANET. Although the presented techniques were proposed for mobile ad hoc networks connected to the Internet, they can also be of utility for any periodic broadcasting process in a multihop wireless network.

References

1. Ding, S.: 'A Survey on Integrating MANETs with the Internet: Challenges and Designs'. *Computer Communications*, 2008, 31(14), pp. 3537–3551
2. Narten, T., Nordmark, E. and Simpson, W.: 'Neighbor Discovery for IP Version 6 (IPv6)'. 2007, RFC 4861
3. Wakikawa, R., Malinen, J.T., Perkins, C.E., Nilsson, A. and Tuominen, A.J.: 'Global Connectivity for IPv6 Mobile Ad Hoc Networks'. Internet Engineering Task Force, Internet Draft (work in progress), 2006
4. Bouk, S.H., Sasase, I., Ahmed, S.H. and Javaid, N.: 'Gateway Discovery Algorithm Based on Multiple QoS Path Parameters between Mobile Node and Gateway Node'. *Journal of Communications and Networks*, 2012, 14(4), pp. 434–442
5. Benslimane, A., Taleb, T. and Sivaraj. R.: 'Dynamic Clustering-Based Adaptive Mobile Gateway Management in Integrated VANET – 3G Heterogeneous Wireless Networks'. *IEEE Journal on Selected Areas in Communications*, 2011, 25(3), pp. 559–570
6. Korhonen, J., Soininen, J., Patil, B., Savolainen, T., Bakjo, G. and Iisakkila, K.: 'IPv6 in 3rd Generation Partnership Project (3GPP) Evolved Packet System (EPS)'. IETF RFC 6459, January 2012
7. Baig, Z.A. and Adeniye, S.C.: 'A Trust-based Mechanism for Protecting IPv6 Networks against Stateless Address Auto-Configuration Attacks'. *Proceedings of IEEE Internatioal Conference on Networks (ICON)*, Singapore, Dec. 2011, pp. 171–176
8. Bo, L., Bin, Y. and Bin, S.: 'Adaptive Discovery of Internet Gateways in Mobile Ad Hoc Networks with Mobile IP-based Internet Connectivity'. *Proceedings of International Conference on Wireless Communications, Networking and Mobile Computing*, Beijing, China, Sep. 2009, pp. 1–5
9. Jelger, C., Noel, T. and Frey, A.: 'Gateway and Address Autoconfiguration for IPv6 Ad Hoc Networks' (work in progress). IETF Internet-Draft, April 2004
10. Singh, S., Kim, J.H., Choi, Y.G., Kang, K.L. and Roh, Y.S.: 'Mobile Multi-Gateway Support for IPv6 Mobile Ad Hoc Networks'. IETF Internet Draft, work in progress, June 2004

11. Yuste, A.J.: 'Descubrimiento Adaptativo de pasarelas en redes MANET conectadas a Internet'. PhD thesis, Málaga University, 2012
12. Ruiz, P.M. and Gomez-Skarmeta, A.F.: 'Adaptive Gateway Discovery Mechanisms to Enhance Internet Connectivity for Mobile Ad Hoc Networks'. *Ad Hoc and Sensor Wireless Networks*, 2005, 1(1), pp. 159–177
13. Domingo, M.C. and Prior, R.: 'An Adaptive Gateway Discovery Algorithm to Support QoS When Providing Internet Access to Mobile Ad Hoc Networks'. *Journal of Networks*, 2007, 2(2), pp. 33–44
14. Trujillo, F.D., Triviño, A., Casilari, E., Díaz-Estrella, A. and Yuste, A.J.: 'Interconnecting MANET and the Internet a Mobility Approach'. *Proceedings of IEEE Conference on Local Computer Networks*, Montreal, Canada, Oct. 2008, pp. 581–582
15. Yuste, A.J., Trujillo, F.D., Triviño, A., Casilari, E. and Díaz-Estrella, A.: 'An Adaptive Genetic Fuzzy Control Gateway Discovery to Interconnect Hybrid MANETs'. *Proceedings of IEEE Conference on Wireless Communications & Networking Conference*, Budapest, Hungary, Apr. 2009, pp. 2810–2815
16. Ros, F.J. and Ruiz, P.M.: 'Low Overhead and Scalable Proxied Adaptive Gateway Discovery for Mobile Ad Hoc Networks'. *Proceedings of IEEE International Conference on Mobile Ad-hoc and Sensor Systems*, Vancouver, Canada, Oct. 2006, pp. 226–235
17. Shen, B., Shi, B., Li, B., Hu, Z. and Zou, L.: 'Adaptive Gateway Discovery Scheme for Connecting Mobile Ad Hoc Networks to Internet'. *Proceedings of the Wireless Communications, Networking and Mobile Computing*, Wuhan, China, Sept. 2005. vol. 2, pp. 795–799
18. Bin, S., Haiyan, K. and Zhonggong, H.: 'Adaptive Mechanisms to Enhance Internet Connectivity for Mobile Ad Hoc Networks'. *Proceedings of International Conference on Wireless Communications, Networking and Mobile Computing*, Wuhan, China, Sep. 2006, pp. 1–4
19. Park, B.N., Lee, W., Lee, C., Hong, J. and Kim J.: 'LAID: Load-Adaptive Internet Gateway Discovery for Ubiquitous Wireless Internet Access Networks'. *Proceedings of International Conference on Information Networking (ICOIN 2006)*, Sendai, Japan, Jan. 2006, pp. 684–702
20. Park, B.N., Lee, W. and Lee, C.: 'QoS-aware Internet Access Schemes for Wireless Mobile Ad Hoc Networks'. *Computer Communications*, 2007, 30(2), pp. 369–384
21. Xie, F., Du, L., Bai, Y. and Chen, L.: 'Adaptive Gateway Discovery Scheme for Mobile Ubiquitous Networks'. *Proceedings of the Wireless Communications and Networking Conference*, Las Vegas, USA, Mar. 2008, pp. 2916–2920
22. Javaid, U., Rasheed, F., Meddour, D.-E. and Ahmed, T.: 'Adaptive Distributed Gateway Discovery in Hybrid Wireless Networks'. *Proceedings of IEEE Wireless Communications and Networking Conference*, Las Vegas, USA, Apr. 2008, pp. 2735–2740
23. Yuste, A.J., Triviño, A., Trujillo, F.D., Casilari, E. and Díaz-Estrella, A.: 'Optimized Gateway Discovery in Hybrid MANETS'. *International Journal of Computer Networks & Communications (IJCNC)*, 2009, 1(3), pp. 78–91

24. Yuste, A.J., Triviño, A., Casilari, E. and Trujillo, F.D.: 'Adaptive Gateway Discovery for MANETs Based on the Characterization of the Link Lifetime'. *IET Communications*, 2011, 5(15), pp. 2241–2249

25. Yuste, A.J., Triviño, A. and Casilari, E.: 'Type-2 Fuzzy Logic Control to Optimize Internet-Connected MANETs'. *Electronics Letters*, 2011, 47(12), pp. 727–728

26. Ghassemian, M., Friderikos, V. and Aghvami, A.H.: 'A Generic Algorithm to Improve the Performance of Proactive Ad Hoc Mechanisms'. *Proceedings of IEEE International Symposium on a World of Wireless Mobile and Multimedia Networks*, Taormina, Greece, Jun. 2005, pp. 362–367

27. Rakeshkumar, V. and Misra, M.: 'An Eficient Mechanism for Connecting MANET and Internet through Complete Adaptive Gateway Discovery'. *Proceedings of International Conference on Communication System Software and Middleware*, New Delhi, India, Jun. 2006, pp. 1–5

28. Triviño-Cabrera, A., Ruiz-Villalobos, B. and Casilari, E.: 'Adaptive Gateway Discovery in Hybrid MANETs'. *Proceedings of the Workshop on Applications and Services in Wireless Networks*, Santander, Spain, May 2007, pp. 9–14

29. Yuste, A.J., Trujillo, F.D., Triviño, A. and Casilari, E.: 'An Adaptive Gateway Discovery for Mobile Ad Hoc Networks'. *Proceedings of ACM International Workshop on Mobility Management and Wireless Access*, Chania, Greece, Oct. 2007, pp. 159–162

30. Yuste, A.J., Trivino, A., Trujillo, F.D. and Casilari, E.: 'Improved Scheme for Adaptive Gateway Discovery in Hybrid MANET'. *Proceedings of the IEEE International Conference on Distributed Computing Systems Workshops*, Genoa, Italy, Jun. 2010, pp. 270–275

31. Yuste, A.J., Triviño-Cabrera, A., Trujillo, F.D., Casilari, E. and Estrella, A. D.: 'Connectivity Gateway Discovery in MANETs', in Llorent Cerdá-Alabern (Ed.): 'EuroNGI Workshop' (*Lecture Notes in Computer Science*, Springer, 2008, vol. 5122), pp. 128–141

32. Boukerche, A., Abrougui, K. and Pazzi, R.W.: 'An Efficient Hybrid Adaptive Location-aided Gateway Advertisement and Discovery Protocol for Heterogeneous Wireless and Mobile Networks'. *Proceedings of IEEE Global Telecommunications Conference (GLOBECOM)*, Honolulu, USA, Nov.-Dec. 2009, pp. 1–6

33. Yuste, A.J., Triviño, A., Casilari, E. and Trujillo, F.D.: 'An Optimized MANET Gateway Discovery Based on Fuzzy Logic', in: Abdulkadir Özcan, Nabendu Chaki, and Dhinaharan Nagamalai (Eds.), 'Recent Trends in Wireless and Mobile Networks' (*Communications in Computer and Information Science*, Springer Berlin Heidelberg, vol. 84, 2010), pp. 273–282

Chapter 5*

Capacity of wireless ad hoc networks

Roya E. Rezagah[a] and Abbas Mohammadi[a]

Abstract

The objective of this chapter is to provide a general and flexible analysis method for the capacity of a wireless ad hoc network. First of all, the total capacity of a typical ad hoc network is defined, characterized and formulated as a function of the cumulative distribution function (CDF) of the received SIR. Then, a closed form expression for the CDF of signal to interference power ratio (SIR) is approximated, which directly results in a closed form solution for the total network capacity. Among various capacity metrics, the focus of this chapter is on the total outage capacity as a practical example. The effect of the outage threshold, β, on the total capacity of the network is studied and the optimum β that maximizes the capacity is determined.

5.1 Introduction

The capability of rapid deployment without any infrastructure makes a wireless ad hoc network an attractive choice for many applications, especially where no backhaul is available [1]; but, the lack of any predetermined topology as well as dynamic changes in wireless channel bring about many difficulties in estimating and guaranteeing the performance of such networks [2]. This chapter focuses on the capacity of wireless ad hoc networks as one of the most important performance metrics.

The complete solution for the capacity of an ad hoc network is to find a set of possible rates at which every two nodes in the network can communicate as studied in Reference 3. For a network consisting of N nodes, the rate region is of the dimension of $N(N - 1)$. Even for a small number of nodes this solution is very complicated and for a large network finding the rate region would even be unobtainable [3].

*H. F. Rashvand and H.-C. Chao (Eds.), *Dynamic Ad Hoc Networks*, The IET Book Publishing Department, 2013, ISBN 978-1-84919-647-5, eISBN 978-1-84919-648-2
[a]Microwave and Wireless Communications Research Lab., Electrical Engineering Department, Amirkabir University of Technology (Tehran Polytechnic), Tehran, Iran

As a result, many studies concentrate on the total capacity of the network or the transmission capacity of a typical node instead of the rate region, e.g. References 4–8, 9–11, or more recent studies of References 12–17. Although this approach does not discuss fairness or how the total capacity is divided among the nodes, it gives an insight to the overall performance of the network. In References 4–8, the asymptotic capacity or the *order* of the capacity has been determined. Particularly, Reference 4 is one of the pioneering studies, which model and examine the asymptotic capacity of a static ad hoc network. Authors of Reference 4 show that, the throughput for every node is of the order of $1/\sqrt{N}$, where N is the number of nodes in the network. This result shows that the capacity offered to each node will degrade by increasing number of nodes. However, in Reference 5 mobility of nodes was added to the analysis and it was shown that mobility can improve the capacity and keep it constant irrelevant to the number of nodes in the network. In Reference 16, beside the mobility, some fixed nodes (base stations) are added to the network to further improve the capacity.

References 9–11 follow the same definition for capacity as introduced in Reference 4 and investigate the scaling laws of network and total capacity as a function of number of nodes. There are also studies, e.g. References 18–21, which explore total capacity of the network and a more recent study in Reference 12 extends the asymptotic capacity to the case of multi-hop MIMO ad hoc networks. Beside these studies of the asymptotic capacity, in Reference 22, the total capacity has been examined through Monte Carlo simulation. However, Monte Carlo simulation is based on a number of recurrences and sometimes it takes a long time to give an accurate result.

In References 23 and 24, based on the outage constraint the transmission capacity of the network has been determined. Such studies are interesting in that they establish a clear connection between outage probability and the network capacity. This connection is also emphasized in this chapter by defining and ana- lysing the 'total outage capacity' of the network.

This chapter is organized as follows. First, a model for a typical ad hoc net- work is introduced and the capacity is defined and formulated. Then, the statistics of the received SIR is extracted and the CDF of SIR is analytically derived; and finally, the capacity is studied.

5.2   Fundamental concepts

Before proceeding to analyse the capacity of an ad hoc network, we need to pre- cisely illustrate a suitable model for a general ad hoc network and explain what we mean when we point out the capacity of such networks. In defining a network scenario, the objective is to facilitate the mathematical analysis while maintaining the generality of a typical network.

Obviously, analysing the capacity also requires a precise definition for the capacity of such networks. This issue will be discussed separately in Section 5.2.2, where a general formulation and some practical examples are introduced.

5.2.1   Ad hoc network scenario

In the analyses and evaluations in this chapter, it is assumed that nodes do not move during one transmission/reception. Note that this does not mean that the network is static, i.e., the network is still dynamic since the location of nodes changes from time to time.

Another common assumption is that the nodes are randomly located in the network coverage area with uniform distribution. To make the mathematical analysis more tractable, the network coverage area is considered as a planar circular disk with radius R. This makes it easier to formulate the cumulative distribution function (CDF) of the distance of the location of each node from the centre of the network, r:

$$F_r(x) = Prob.\{r \leq x\} = \begin{cases} 0, & x < 0 \\ \dfrac{\pi x^2}{\pi R^2}, & 0 \leq x \leq R \\ 1, & x > R \end{cases} \tag{5.1}$$

where, $Prob.\{A\}$ is the probability of event A.

Therefore, the polar coordinates of each node, (r, θ), will have the following probability density functions (PDF) [25]:

$$\begin{cases} f_r(r) = \dfrac{dF_r(r)}{dr} = \dfrac{2r}{R^2}, & 0 \leq r \leq R \\ f_\theta(\theta) = \dfrac{1}{2\pi}, & 0 \leq \theta \leq 2\pi \end{cases} \tag{5.2}$$

where, r is the distance from the origin and θ is the angle between the positive x-axis and the ray from the origin to the location.

It is also assumed that every transmitter uses an omnidirectional antenna and randomly chooses its receiver from nodes no closer than ε and no farther than D with equal probability (Figure 5.1).

We assume that $D \ll R$ and thus the effect of nodes in the edge of coverage area is negligible. Therefore the probability that a node W chooses a destination within $\rho \geq \varepsilon$ distance away is proportional to the number of nodes in the disk centred at W with radius from ε to ρ. Since the nodes are uniformly distributed in the coverage area we can write:

$$F_d(\rho) = Prob.\{d \leq \rho\} = \begin{cases} 0, & \rho \leq \varepsilon \\ \dfrac{\pi \rho^2 - \pi \varepsilon^2}{\pi D^2 - \pi \varepsilon^2}, & \varepsilon \leq \rho \leq D \\ 1, & \rho \geq D \end{cases} \tag{5.3}$$

where, $F_d(\rho)$ is the probability distribution function (CDF) of the distance between a transmitter to its intended receiver.

An *interference-limited environment* is assumed where the noise power is negligible compared to the interference and no interference cancellation technique is considered. Therefore, in our scenario we have to deal with signal-to-interference

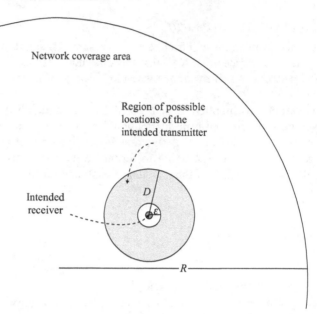

Figure 5.1   A typical scenario for an ad hoc network

power ratio (SIR). Neglecting noise in the presence of interference is a usual assumption in ad hoc networks. In fact every ad hoc network can be interference-limited if all transmission powers are high enough [26].

Other assumptions can be added to the scenario to reflect communication schemes among nodes. For example, each transmitter can be assigned with a unique code and all nodes may use direct sequence code division multiple access (DS-CDMA) with the same finite processing gain of L, in order to reduce the destructive effect of interference. Such a communication scheme reduces the amount of total interference power at each receiver with a factor of L.DS-CDMA also transforms the interfering signals into pseudo-noise signals. In our SIR analysis, we will consider this processing gain of L. One can set L to 1 to remove DS-CDMA from the scenario.

As another example, one can develop the scenario further by adding multi-antenna capability to the transceivers. To show the analysis methodology, we will also investigate two examples of multi-antenna communications in the end of this chapter.

5.2.2   *Capacity definition*

The goal of this chapter is to introduce a simple, yet general analysis method that can be used to approximate the capacity of wireless ad hoc networks. To achieve this, a general and simple formulation of capacity in various conditions is required.

To define the total capacity of the network, we start by characterizing the *rate function*, which is the communication rate of a single wireless link as a function of the signal-to-interference-plus-noise ratio (SINR) at the receiver [3]. The rate function can be defined in various forms according to the capabilities of the transmitters and receivers in the network. This function is upper bounded by the Shannon rate: $\log_2(1+\text{SINR})$ [bps/Hz]. In the best case, the transmitter and the receiver can adapt themselves to communicate with the Shannon rate according to the current SINR of the link and therefore achieve the upper bound.

A more realistic example for the rate function is a step function, in which when the received SINR is higher than a threshold, the rate is equal to a positive constant, and otherwise it is zero. A more complicated, but still practical function is a multi-step or staircase-form function. In this case, the transmitter and the receiver have the capability to adapt their communication rate to the discrete rates according to the SINR or equivalently the link quality. These examples beside the upper bound are shown in Figure 5.2.

Obviously, the step function is a special case of the general staircase-form function. Therefore, it is sufficient to formulate a general rate function with m discrete possible rates, $k_1 > k_2 > \ldots > k_m$, corresponding to m thresholds on the received SINR, $\beta_1 > \beta_2 > \ldots > \beta_m$:

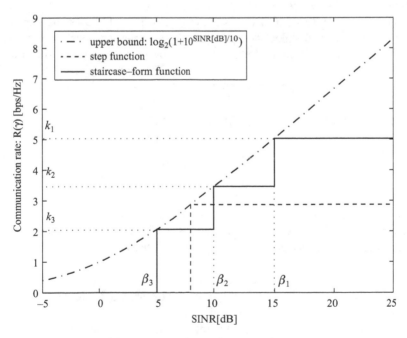

Figure 5.2   Two possible examples of rate function for a wireless communication link are shown beside the upper bound of this function [28]

$$
\begin{aligned}
R(\gamma) = & \; k_1 \times u(\gamma - \beta_1) + \\
& k_2 \times [u(\gamma - \beta_2) - u(\gamma - \beta_1)] + \\
& k_3 \times [u(\gamma - \beta_3) - u(\gamma - \beta_2)] + \ldots + \\
& k_m \times [u(\gamma - \beta_m) - u(\gamma - \beta_{m-1})], \; [bps/Hz]
\end{aligned}
\tag{5.4}
$$

In (5.4), $R(\gamma)$ is the rate function, γ is the received SINR and $u(x)$ is the step function as follows:

$$
u(x) = \begin{cases} 0, & x \le 0 \\ 1, & x > 0 \end{cases}
\tag{5.5}
$$

Since the received SINR is a random variable in an ad hoc network, the communication rate of each link is a function of a random variable. The capacity of each link is defined as the expected value of its communication rate:

$$
C_{link} = \int_0^\infty R(\gamma) f_{SINR}(\gamma) d\gamma, \; [bps/Hz]
\tag{5.6}
$$

where, γ is the value of the received SINR and $f_{SINR}(\gamma)$ is its probability density function (PDF). As before, $R(\gamma)$ is the rate function.

The total capacity of a wireless network can be defined as the sum of the capacities of all active links. According to the symmetry of our wireless ad hoc scenario, the PDF of SINR is the same for all the receivers. As a result, the total capacity of the network with N nodes is $N.C_{link}$. Therefore, replacing (5.4) in (5.6), the total network capacity is obtained as:

$$
\begin{aligned}
\text{Total network capacity} = & \; [1 - F_{SINR}(\beta_1)]Nk_1 \\
& + [F_{SINR}(\beta_1) - F_{SINR}(\beta_2)]Nk_2 \\
& + [F_{SINR}(\beta_2) - F_{SINR}(\beta_3)]Nk_3 \\
& + \cdots + [F_{SINR}(\beta_{m-1}) - F_{SINR}(\beta_m)]Nk_m, \; [bps/Hz]
\end{aligned}
\tag{5.7}
$$

In the above equation, $F_{SINR}(\gamma)$ is the cumulative distribution (CDF) functions of the received SINR, γ, and β is the threshold. The final result of the equation is written using the fact that the CDF is by definition the integral of the PDF, $f_{SINR}(\gamma)$ [10].

It should be noted that the rates associated to various intervals of SINR ($k_1 > k_2 > \ldots > k_m$ in Figure 5.2) are functions of threshold values ($\beta_1 > \beta_2 > \ldots > \beta_m$) and also depend on nodes capabilities.

So far the general concept of rate function has been described. With this tool the capacity can be analysed for a wide family of scenarios, from single step rate function to Shannon rate. In the case of Shannon rate the capacity is called *ergodic capacity*. On the other hand, one may obtain *outage capacity* by considering the rate function as a single-step function. In this case, there is only one threshold, β_1, and only one corresponding communication rate, k_1. In other words, only the first line of (5.7) exists.

Although in the general case, where nodes have the capability of adaptive modulation and adaptive rate may be attractive, in the rest of this chapter we focus on analysis for the special case where the rate function is a single step function. In other words, we limit our analysis to the outage capacity, unless otherwise clearly emphasized. Extension to more complicated rate functions is tedious, yet straightforward.

From a different point of view, the outage capacity can be defined based on the definition of outage event. Nonetheless, both definitions lead to the same concept. In Section 5.2.2.1, we will have a deeper look at the outage capacity. We will also include nodes' practical limitations in calculating the communication rate of each link.

5.2.2.1 Outage capacity

The outage event is defined as the event when the signal-to-interference ratio (SIR) at the receiver's output drops below a threshold [27]. Then, if the network condition is such that at most M simultaneous communications can take place with a predetermined rate of R bits per second, while ensuring that a certain target SIR is maintained at each receiver, the total capacity of the network would be MR bits per second [4, 28, 29].

In general, the predetermined rate of each communication, R, depends on the outage threshold, β. The higher this threshold the better the quality of an active link, and consequently a higher communication rate can be set. Theoretically, the maximum possible value for R can be obtained as a function of β as follows:

$$R(\beta) = \log_2(1 + 10^{\beta/10}) \text{ [bps/Hz]} \tag{5.8}$$

Equation (5.8) represents the Shannon capacity, which is the maximum communication rate when the received signal-to-noise power ratio (SNR) equals to β in dB units.

On the other hand, in practical systems, the modulation scheme affects the communication rate. In fact, (5.8) is an upper bound on the practical rate. The practical rate is determined based on the maximum acceptable bit error rate (BER) and the modulation that meets that BER constraint.

To be more explicit, based on the maximum acceptable BER and for a fixed outage threshold, a modulation scheme is selected among the available schemes so that the communication rate is maximized.

Example: It is assumed that eight modulation including BPSK and M-QAM for $M = 2^2, 2^3, \ldots, 2^8$ are feasible and consequently, the possible communication rates are $R = 1, 2, 3, \ldots, 8$ bits per second per hertz (bps/Hz), respectively. For BPSK, the BER or bit error probability, P_e, is calculated as follows [1]:

$$P_e = Q\left(\sqrt{2\gamma}\right) \tag{5.9}$$

where, γ is the received SNR and $Q(x)$ is the Q-function defined as:

$$Q(x) = \int_{t=x}^{+\infty} \frac{1}{\sqrt{2\pi}} e^{-t^2/2} dt \tag{5.10}$$

For the case of M-QAM, an approximate upper bound for the P_e is used [1]:

$$P_e = 0.2e^{\frac{-1.5\gamma}{M-1}} \tag{5.11}$$

where, γ is the received SNR as before.

Now, for instance, if the BER should be less that 10^{-3} and the outage threshold is 15 dB, according to (5.9) and (5.11) only BPSK and 4QAM among our eight feasible modulations can be used. Therefore the possible communication rates are 1 and 2 bps/Hz and the highest practical rate is 2 bps/Hz. Similarly, by means of (5.9) and (5.11) for the maximum BER of 10^{-3} and a range of outage thresholds, the highest possible communication rate can be obtained. In other words, the practical communication rate of a link is determined as a function of the pre-determined outage threshold. Interested reader is referred to Reference 30 for more detail of such analysis.

To formulate total outage capacity, we also need to express the outage probability:

$$Pr_{outage} = Prob.\{SIR \leq \beta\} = F_\gamma(\beta) \tag{5.12}$$

where, $F_\gamma(\beta)$ is the cumulative distribution function (CDF) of the received SIR and β is the outage threshold.

SIR of each link is a stochastic process and by ignoring the edge effects of the coverage area, we assume that *'probability distribution of SIR'* is the same for all nodes in the network due to the symmetry of the assumed scenario. Although the SIRs of links may be different from each other at every particular moment, the *distribution of the SIR* can be considered to be the same for all links.

According to (5.8), the probability that the communication can take place while the minimum required SIR is met at the receiver equals to $(1 - Pr_{outage})$ or equivalently $(1 - F_\gamma(\beta))$. If there are N *simultaneously active* transmitter–receiver pairs in the network, the number of *successful* communications, n, follows a binomial probability distribution and assuming that each communication occurs at the rate of $R(\beta)$ bits per second, the total outage capacity would be:

$$Total\ outage\ capacity = \sum_{n=0}^{N} \left\{ \binom{N}{n} \left(1 - F_\gamma(\beta)\right)^n \left(F_\gamma(\beta)\right)^{N-n} \right.$$
$$\left. \times n \times R(\beta)\ [bps/Hz] \right\}$$
$$= (1 - F_\gamma(\beta)) \times N \times R(\beta)\ [bps/Hz] \tag{5.13}$$

Inspecting the final result of (5.13) beside the first line of (5.7) shows that both point of views to outage capacity are equivalent.

5.3 Analytical modelling

So far we have introduced a typical scenario of an ad hoc network as well as a mathematical formulation for the total capacity of a wireless network. The objective is to find a general and tractable mathematical tool that connects the capacity to the network parameters such as number of nodes in the networks area and wireless channel parameters. In this section, we concentrate on the analytical modelling to obtain a closed form approximation of the capacity of a typical wireless ad hoc network.

5.3.1 Modelling of the received signals in ad hoc networks

According to the definitions of the network capacity in (5.7) or (5.13), it is apparent that the knowledge of the cumulative distribution function (CDF) of SNR at the receiver location is sufficient to calculate the capacity. Here, an interference-limited environment has been assumed and therefore SNR is replaced by the SIR. Therefore, the first step towards the capacity is to model and analyse the CDF of the received SIR.

We begin with the definition of the SIR. It is assumed that there are N pairs of transmitter–receiver nodes in the network. And, with no loss in generality, the first pair can be taken as the intended pair for which the receiver's SIR after dispreading is written as:

$$\text{SIR} = \frac{P_t/d^\alpha \times L}{\sum_{i=2}^{N} P_t/r_i^\alpha} = \frac{L/d^\alpha}{\sum_{i=2}^{N} 1/r_i^\alpha} \tag{5.14}$$

where, P_t is the power of each transmitter, d is the distance between the intended transmitter (the first transmitter) and the intended receiver and r_i $(2 \leq i \leq N)$ is distance from the ith transmitter to the intended receiver. Also, L is the processing gain or the spreading factor of DS-CDMA. A free space path loss model is considered in all interfering paths as well as the desired link with path loss exponent of α [27].

The interfering power at the receiver, I, is defined as follows:

$$I = \sum_{i=2}^{N} 1/r_i^\alpha \tag{5.15}$$

In References 31 and 32, it has been suggested that using the law of large numbers, I can be replaced by $(N - 1)E\{1/r^\alpha\}$, where $E\{.\}$ stands for the expected value.

A short simulation study shows that for small values of α (around 1 or less), I approaches to $(N-1)E\{1/r^\alpha\}$ as N is increased. However, for most common wireless channels, the path loss exponent, α, is larger than 2 (actually $2 \le \alpha \le 4$) [27]. Monte Carlo simulation shows that for these values of α, the variance of I will tend to infinity and the law of large numbers or even the central limit theorem is inapplicable.

The fact that the variance of I is too large, directs us to use logarithm and study the powers in dBm and SIR in dB units. Therefore, we define I_{dB} as follows:

$$I_{dB} = 10\log_{10}I = 10\log_{10}\left(\sum_{i=2}^{N} 1/r_i^\alpha\right) \tag{5.16}$$

Monte Carlo simulation study shows that I_{dB} tends to follow some sort of *extreme value* distribution. In fact, since $R \gg \varepsilon$ and r_i varies in a wide range from ε to R, in the above equation the smallest r_i or in other words, the nearest interferer has the dominant effect. This motivates us to approximate the summation by this dominant part. It should be noted that the larger the value of α is, the more accurate this approximate is. Later, by comparing the analytic results with the simulation, it will be shown that for $2 \le \alpha \le 4$, this estimate is accurate enough to estimate the capacity. Consequently, we approximate I_{dB} as follows:

$$I_{dB} \cong 10\log_{10}\left(\max_{i(2 \le i \le N)}\{1/r_i^\alpha\}\right)$$

$$= 10\log_{10}\left(\frac{1}{\min_{i(2 \le i \le N)}\{r_i^\alpha\}}\right) = 10\log_{10}\left(\left[\min_{i(2 \le i \le N)}\{r_i\}\right]^{-\alpha}\right) \tag{5.17}$$

where $\max_i\{a_i\}$ and $\min_i\{a_i\}$ are the maximum and minimum of the a_i for $2 \le i \le N$, respectively. Hence, the CDF of I_{dB} can be estimated as:

$$F_{I_{dB}}(x) = Prob.\{I_{dB} \le x\} \cong Prob.\left\{10\log_{10}\left[\left(\min_{i(2 \le i \le N)} r_i\right)^{-\alpha}\right] \le x\right\}$$

$$= Prob.\{r_i \ge 10^{-\frac{x}{10\alpha}}, \quad for\ 2 \le i \le N\}$$

$$= \left[1 - F_r\left(10^{-x/10\alpha}\right)\right]^{(N-1)} \tag{5.18}$$

$F_r(r)$ is the CDF of the distance between each interferer and the intended receiver that depends on the network scenario. Interested reader is referred to Reference 28 for details of extracting the following approximation for $F_{I_{dB}}(x)$ for the network scenario of this chapter:

$$F_{I_{dB}}(x) \cong \left(\frac{R^2 - 10^{-x/5\alpha}}{R^2 - \varepsilon^2}\right)^{(N-1)}, \quad -10\log_{10}R \le x \le -10\log_{10}\varepsilon \tag{5.19}$$

where, ε is the minimum distance between every two nodes in the network and R is the network radius.

In a similar way, SIR is also considered in dB and after following mathematical steps as in Reference 28, $F_\gamma(\gamma)$ is obtained as:

$$
F_\gamma(\gamma) = \begin{cases}
0, \quad \gamma \leq 10\alpha\log_{10}(\varepsilon/D) + 10\log_{10}L \\[2mm]
\left[H\left(D^2 10^{\frac{\gamma - 10\log_{10}L}{5\alpha}}\right) - H(\varepsilon^2) \right] - \dfrac{10^{-\gamma - 10\log_{10}L/5\alpha}}{D^2 - \varepsilon^2} \\[3mm]
\quad \times \left[G\left(D^2 10^{\frac{\gamma - 10\log_{10}L}{5\alpha}}\right) - G(\varepsilon^2) \right], \\[2mm]
\quad 10\alpha\log_{10}(\varepsilon/D) + 10\log_{10}L \leq \gamma \leq 10\log_{10}L \\[3mm]
\left[H\left(\varepsilon^2 10^{\frac{\gamma - 10\log_{10}L}{5\alpha}}\right) - H(\varepsilon^2) \right] + \dfrac{D^2}{D^2 - \varepsilon^2} \\[3mm]
\quad \times \left[H\left(\min\{R^2, D^2 10^{\frac{\gamma - 10\log_{10}L}{5\alpha}}\}\right) - H\left(\varepsilon^2 10^{\frac{\gamma - 10\log_{10}L}{5\alpha}}\right) \right] \\[3mm]
\quad - \dfrac{10^{-\gamma - 10\log_{10}L/5\alpha}}{D^2 - \varepsilon^2} \times \left[G\left(\min\{R^2, D^2 10^{\frac{\gamma - 10\log_{10}L}{5\alpha}}\}\right) - G\left(\varepsilon^2 10^{\frac{\gamma - 10\log_{10}L}{5\alpha}}\right) \right], \\[3mm]
\quad 10\log_{10}L \leq \gamma \leq 10\alpha\log_{10}(R/\varepsilon) + 10\log_{10}L \\[3mm]
0, \quad \gamma \geq 10\alpha\log_{10}(R/\varepsilon) + 10\log_{10}L
\end{cases}
$$

$$(5.20)$$

where, $H(x)$ and $G(x)$ are defined as follows:

$$
\begin{cases}
H(x) = \displaystyle\int (N-1) \frac{(R^2 - x)^{(N-2)}}{(R^2 - \varepsilon^2)^{(N-1)}} dx = -\frac{(R^2 - x)^{(N-1)}}{(R^2 - \varepsilon^2)^{(N-1)}} \\[4mm]
G(x) = \displaystyle\int x(N-1) \frac{(R^2 - x)^{(N-2)}}{(R^2 - \varepsilon^2)^{(N-1)}} dx \\[4mm]
\quad = -\frac{(N-1)}{(\varepsilon^2 - R^2)^{(N-1)}} \left[\frac{(x - R^2)^N}{N} + \frac{R^2(x - R^2)^{(N-1)}}{N-1} \right]
\end{cases}
$$

$$(5.21)$$

Equation (5.20) for $F_\gamma(\gamma)$ is a straight closed form that can be used in (5.7) or (5.13), to calculate total network capacity.

5.3.2   Model verification

A Monte Carlo simulation can be conducted to verify the accuracy of the obtained approximation [22, 28, 29]. In Figure 5.3, the resultant CDF's from both simulation and analysis are shown for various values of the path loss exponent, α, for 20 active transmitter–receiver pairs in the network ($N = 20$). Note that in the analysis only the strongest interfering power is considered as the dominant term while in simulation all interfering powers are taken into account as well as the noise power.

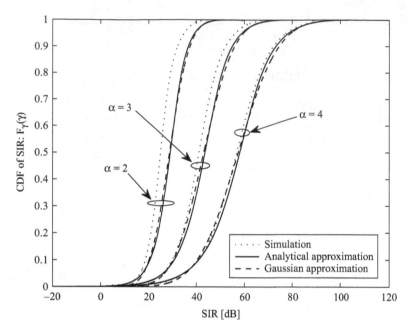

Figure 5.3   *Analytically approximated cumulative distribution of SINR beside the result of the Monte Carlo simulation for various values of path loss exponent, 'α' for 20 active transmitter–receiver pairs in the network [30]*

It can be seen that, increasing α makes the analytical approximate more accurate. Since the interfering power of a transmitter located in the distance of r from the receiver is proportional to $r^{-\alpha}$, it decays faster when α is higher. Therefore, in such a case, neglecting the effects of far interferers has less destructive effect in the accuracy of the analysis.

In addition to (5.20) and simulation results, in Figure 5.3 Gaussian distribution is plotted for each case, as well. The Gaussian distribution is a well-known distribution that is fully characterized by only first and second order moments. The probability density function (PDF) of the Gaussian distribution has the following general format [29]:

$$f_x(x) = \frac{1}{\sqrt{2\pi\sigma^2}} e^{\frac{-(x-m)^2}{2\sigma^2}} \tag{5.22}$$

which is completely characterized by its mean, m, and variance, σ^2.

The mean and variance of the Gaussian distributions in Figure 5.3 are calculated according to network conditions based on the assumptions made in previous section. In other words, in each case, the mean and variance of the Gaussian distribution is selected equal to the mean and variance that are calculated from (5.20). Figure 5.3 shows that the Gaussian approximation is close to the result of (5.20).

5.4 Capacity analysis in ad hoc networks

In previous sections, network scenario and corresponding total capacity have been modelled and then the capacity has been characterized as a function of the CDF of the received SIR ((5.7) and (5.13)). This modelling enables us to evaluate capacity and investigate effects of various parameters on the capacity. Among system and channel parameters, in this section we focus on a system design parameter, the outage threshold, and study the effect of chosen threshold on the total capacity. We start by setting the parameters of the network and evaluating the total capacity. During this evaluation the importance of the outage threshold will be more evident.

5.4.1 Capacity analysis

The CDF of the received SIR ((5.20) and (5.7)) provides sufficient tool to calculate the capacity for various link rate functions of (5.4) or Figure 5.2. One can easily apply this analysis to various scenarios in which nodes are capable of rate adaptation. In the most basic case that the rate function is a single step, the resultant capacity is the outage capacity. The concept of outage capacity has been discussed in Section 5.2.2.1. In the followings, we take the advantage of (5.13) to study the total outage capacity of the network and the effect of the preset outage threshold on this quantity.

In order to examine the capacity, first the parameters are set for the scenario introduced in Section 5.2, and then for several number of transmitter–receiver pairs, N, the capacity is calculated. Here, the path loss exponent, α, is set to 4 and the distances ε, D and R are chosen proportional to 1 : 10:100. Also, in this Section, the processing gain of DS-CDMA, L, is set to 128.

With these assumptions, the total outage capacity of the network versus number of active transmitters, N, is plotted in Figure 5.4 for various outage threshold values, β, of 10, 20 and 30 dB. It should be noted that β is the minimum acceptable SIR at the receiver's location after de-spreading. In Figure 5.4, the constant communication rate in (5.9), $R(\beta)$, is set to its maximum theoretical value which is calculated using (5.8). On the other hand, one could assume that only a limited number of QAM modulations are available to the transmitters and receivers and determine the practical communication rate for each β.

5.4.2 Optimum outage threshold

Inspecting Fig. 5.4 shows that increasing the outage threshold, β, does not necessarily increase the capacity. In this figure, the communication rate, $R(\beta)$, has been set to its maximum theoretical values, the Shannon rate. However, it should be mentioned that in case of practical system, in which the nodes are only capable of implementing some particular modulation schemes, the same trend is detected [28]. In fact, the total capacity in (5.13) consists of two factors, the first factor is $[1 - F_{SINR}(\beta)]$ which is a descending function of β. The second factor is the communication rate, $R(\beta)$, which is an ascending function of β. Hence, there is a trade-off on the value of β.

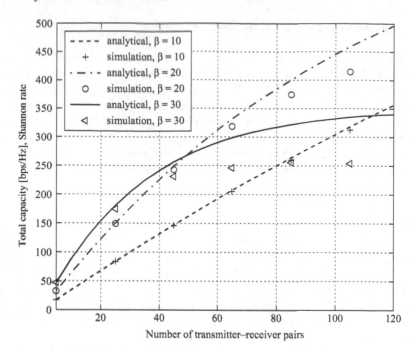

Figure 5.4   Total capacity of the network as a function of number of active transmitters, N, for various values of the outage threshold, β [28]

This observation leads us to the conclusion that for a particular number of active transmitters in the network, there is a particular β that maximizes the capacity. Figure 5.5 illustrates this fact. In this figure, capacity of the network is plotted versus outage threshold, β, for various number of transmitter–receiver pairs. It can be seen that independent of using the Shannon bound or a practical system with limited modulation schemes, an optimum β exists [28].

To conclude this section, in Figure 5.6 the optimum outage threshold is depicted versus number of transmitter–receiver pairs. It can be seen that when there are only a few nodes in the network, β must be set to a higher value to obtain the maximum possible capacity from the network. In this case, less simultaneous communications, each with higher communication rate take place. As the number of nodes increases, the optimum β decreases, which means that in such a case more simultaneous communications, each at a lower rates, maximizes the overall capacity of the network.

5.5   Further developments

In this chapter, we saw that the capacity of a plain ad hoc network is very limited. This result is in agreement with the essential results of Reference 4 on the asymptotic performance of such networks. Capacity enhancement is a matter of

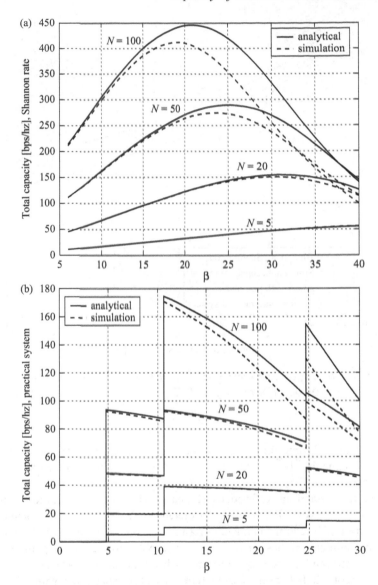

Figure 5.5 *Total capacity of the network as a function of the outage threshold, β, in dB: (a) nodes can communicate with the Shannon rate; (b) nodes are only capable of implementing particular modulation schemes [28]*

concern in many researches in the field of wireless ad hoc networks. To be more explicit, in parallel to studies on the capacity, various methods and schemes are being introduced to improve the capacity, e.g. recent works of References 12, 13 and 16, 17. For example, Reference 13 studies the improvement in outage probability and transmission capacity due to interference management. In Reference 16

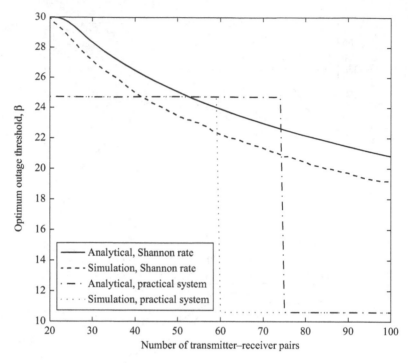

Figure 5.6   Optimum outage threshold, β, in dB versus number of transmitter-receiver pairs in the network [28]

an infrastructure of some fixed base stations has been added to the network which enhances the capacity, but on the other hand destroys the flexible nature of a pure ad hoc network.

On the other hand, in References 12 and 17 MIMO communications has been included in the network. Especially in Reference 17, the receiver uses some of its spatial degrees of freedom to cancel certain interferers, e.g. the nearest interferers. MIMO communication has proven its remarkable efficiency in point to point communications and therefore including MIMO in ad hoc networks seems an attractive option. It has been shown that providing each node with M antenna multiplies the asymptotic capacity by a factor of M [12].

Beside researches on the techniques for improving capacity, there are studies about modelling wireless ad hoc networks. For example, a very common assumption in the theoretical research on the ad hoc networks is to assume a two-dimensional network area. This assumption has been used in this chapter as well. Nonetheless, in Reference 14 the authors extended the capacity analysis of Reference 4 to a network in a three-dimensional space and obtained a higher capacity. It seems that in order to obtain reliable results for a practical implementation, every assumption should be revisited carefully.

5.6   Conclusion

The main goal of this chapter was to introduce a tractable yet general analysis method for the capacity of a wireless ad hoc network. First, the capacity of the ad hoc network was defined and mathematically formulated. Then, a statistical model was described to derive a closed form expression for the cumulative distribution function (CDF) of the received SIR. This closed form directly results in a closed form solution for the total network capacity.

The strength of the analysis lies in the suitable formulation of the capacity as well as network modelling. Particularly, formulating the capacity based on the rate function provides the flexibility to study the capacity in various practical scenarios. Not only rate adaptation but also more advanced communication schemes can be analysed with the same methodology. Modelling rate adaptation is straightforward and only changes the rate function itself, while analysing advanced communication schemes requires that the effect on the CDF of SIR is analysed first.

In this chapter the main focus was on the total outage capacity. Furthermore, as an example of how to utilize such an analysis, the effect of the outage threshold, β, on the total capacity of the network was studied and the optimum β that maximizes the capacity was determined.

References

1. Goldsmith, A. *Wireless Communications* (Cambridge University Press, USA, 2005)
2. Ramanathan, R., Redi, J.: 'A Brief Overview of Ad Hoc Networks: Challenges and Directions', *IEEE Communications Magazine*, 2002, vol. 40, no. 5, pp. 20–22
3. Toumpis, S., Goldsmith, A.: 'Capacity Regions for Wireless Ad Hoc Networks', *IEEE Transactions on Wireless Communications*, 2003, vol. 24, no. 5, pp. 736–748
4. Gupta, P., Kumar, P. R.: 'The Capacity of Wireless Networks', *IEEE Transactions on Information Theory*, 2000, vol. 46, pp. 388–404
5. Grossglauser, M., Tse, D.: 'Mobility Increases the Capacity of Ad-Hoc Wireless Networks', *IEEE/ACM Transactions on Networking*, 2002, vol. 10, no. 4, pp. 477–486
6. Lozano, A. C., Kulkarni, S. R., Viswanath, P.: 'Throughput Scaling in Wireless Networks with Restricted Mobility', *IEEE Transactions on Wireless Communications*, 2007, vol. 6, no. 2, pp. 670–679
7. Liang-Liang Xie, Kumar, P. R.: 'A Network Information Theory for Wireless Communication: Scaling Laws and Optimal Operation', *IEEE Transactions on Information Theory*, 2004, vol. 50, no. 5, pp. 748–767
8. Gupta, P., Kumar, P. R.: 'Towards an Information Theory of Large Networks: An Achievable Rate Region', *IEEE Transactions on Information Theory*, 2003, vol. IT-49, pp. 1877–1894

9. Jovicic, A., Viswanath, P., Kulkarni, S.: 'Upper Bounds to Transport Capacity of Wireless Networks', *IEEE Transactions on Information Theory*, 2004, vol. 50, no. 11, pp. 2555–2565

10. Leveque, O., Teletar, I. E.: 'Information-theoretic Upper Bounds on the Capacity of Large Extended Ad Hoc Wireless Networks', *IEEE Transactions on Information Theory*, 2005, vol. 51, no. 3, pp. 858–865

11. Franceschetti, M., Dousse, O., Tse, D., Thiran, P.: 'Closing the Gap in the Capacity of Wireless Networks via Percolation Theory', *IEEE Transactions on Information Theory*, 2007, vol. 53, no. 3, pp. 1009–1018

12. Jiang, C., Shi, Y., Hou, Y. T., Kompella, S.: 'On the Asymptotic Capacity of Multi-Hop MIMO Ad Hoc Networks', *IEEE Transactions on Wireless Communications*, Apr. 2011, vol. 10, no. 4, pp. 1032–1037

13. Liu, C.-H., Andrews, J. G.: 'Ergodic Transmission Capacity of Wireless Ad Hoc Networks with Interference Management', *IEEE Transactions on Wireless Communications*, Jun. 2012, vol. 11, no. 6, pp. 2136–2147

14. Li, P., Pan, M., Fang, Y.: 'Capacity Bounds of Three-Dimensional Wireless Ad Hoc Networks', *IEEE/ACM Transactions on Networking*, Aug. 2012, vol. 20, no. 4, pp. 1304–1315

15. Nardelli, P. H. J., Kaynia, M., Cardieri, P., Latva-aho, M.: 'Optimal Transmission Capacity of Ad Hoc Networks with Packet Retransmissions', *IEEE Transactions on Wireless Communications*, Aug. 2012, vol. 11, no. 8, pp. 2760–2766

16. Chen, X., Huang, W., Wang, X., Lin, X.: 'Multicast Capacity in Mobile Wireless Ad Hoc Network with Infrastructure Support', *Proceedings of (IEEE INFOCOM 2012)*, Orlando, Florida USA, Mar. 2012, pp. 271–279

17. Vaze, R., Heath, R. W.: 'Transmission Capacity of Ad-hoc Networks with Multiple Antennas Using Transmit Stream Adaptation and Interference Cancellation', *IEEE Transactions on Information Theory*, Feb. 2012, vol. 58, no. 2, pp. 780–792

18. Baccelli, F., Błaszczyszyn, B.: 'Stochastic Geometry and Wireless Networks Volume 1: Theory', *Foundations and Trends® in Networking*: 2009, vol. 3, no 3–4, pp. 249–449

19. Haenggi, M., Andrews, J. G., Baccelli, F., Dousse, O., Franceschetti, M.: 'Stochastic Geometry and Random Graphs for the Analysis and Design of Wireless Networks', *IEEE Journal on Selected Areas in Communications*, 2009, vol. 27, no. 7, pp. 1029–1046

20. Haenggi, M., Ganti, R. K.: 'Interference in Large Wireless Networks', *Foundations and Trends® in Networking*: 2008, vol. 3, no. 2, pp. 127–248

21. Wang, C., Jiang, C., Li, X.-Y., Tang, S., Tang, X.: 'Achievable Multicast Throughput for Homogeneous Wireless Ad Hoc Networks', *Proceedings of IEEE WCNC 2009 – Wireless Communications and Networking Conference*, Budapest, April 2009, pp. 1–6

22. Ebrahimrezagah, R., Mohammadi, A.: 'The Capacity of Wireless Ad Hoc Networks Using Statistical Techniques', *Proceedings of IEEE ICC 2006 – IEEE International Conference on Communications*, vol. 1, Istanbul, Turkey, 2006, pp. 337–342

23. Weber, S., Yang, X., Andrews, J. G., de Veciana, G.: 'Transmission Capacity of Wireless Ad Hoc Networks with Outage Constraints', *IEEE Transactions on Information Theory*, 2005, vol. 51, no. 12, pp. 4091–4102

24. Weber, S., Andrews, J. G.: 'Transmission Capacity of Wireless Networks', *Foundations and Trends® in Networking*, vol. 5, issue 2–3, Now Publishers Inc., 2010, pp. 109–281

25. Tranter, W. H., Shanmugan, K. S., Rappaport, T. S., Kosbar, K. L.: *Principles of Communication System Simulation with Wireless Applications* (Prentice Hall PTR, New Jersey, 2004)

26. Jindal, N., Andrews, J. G., Weber, S.: 'Energy-Limited vs. Interference-Limited Ad Hoc Network Capacity', *Proceedings of ACSSC 2007 – Forty First Asilomar Conference on Signals, Systems and Computers*, Pacific Grove, CA, Nov. 2007, pp. 148–152

27. Rappaport, T. S.: *Wireless Communications, Principles and Practice* (Prentice Hall PTR, New Jersey 2nd edn. 2002)

28. Rezagah, R. E., Mohammadi, A.: 'Outage Threshold Extraction for Maximizing the Capacity of Wireless Ad Hoc Networks', *IET Communications*, 2011, vol. 5, no. 6, pp. 811–818

29. Papoulis, A., Pillai, S. U.: *Probability, Random Variables and Stochastic Processes* (TATA McGraw-Hill, 4th edn., New Delhi, 2002)

30. Rezagah, R. E., Mohammadi, A.: 'Analysing the Capacity of Wireless Ad Hoc Networks', accepted to be published in Springer Telecommunication Systems Journal, vol. 63: 1–2: Sep./Oct. 2016, scheduled for online publication in 2013

31. Comaniciu, C., Poor, H. V.: 'On the Capacity of Mobile Ad Hoc Networks with Delay Constraints', *IEEE Transactions on Wireless Communications*, 2006, vol. 5, no. 8, pp. 2061–2071

32. Rezagah, R. E., Mohammadi, A.: 'The Capacity Estimation of Wireless Ad Hoc Networks in Fading Channels', *IET Communications*, 2009, vol. 3, no. 2, pp. 293–302

Part II

Networking methods and techniques

Chapter 6*

VANET dynamic routing protocols: evaluation, challenges and solutions

Michael Barros[a], Reinaldo Gomes[b] and Anderson Costa[c]

Abstract

Routing plays important roles in dynamic VANET and becomes more critical than conventional mobile dynamic ad hoc networks. Thus, the design of new routing protocols for these networks requires actual research efforts associated within this chapter, since there is no considerable previous evaluation of routing for VANET. This chapter presents the state-of-art of routing for VANET, with a performance evaluation of some of the proposed protocols. It is identified that new research trends and some issues regarding this new technology are highlighted.

6.1 Introduction

Vehicular Dynamic ad hoc Networks (VANET) represents a specialized type of communication systems composed of vehicles. These vehicles possess the ability to interconnect themselves, and to support infrastructure at roadsides and streets corners. The main objective of this new network is to allow vehicles to operate as mobile devices, offering a communication infrastructure to users' applications, e. g., driver assistance, tourist information propagation, location of gas stations and automated toll collection. VANET can also be applied into entertainment technology, most eminently to systems of video sharing among vehicles, and applications for transit security, which would prevent accidents and congestions [1, 2].

Contemplating this communication model, VANET is a practical example of Mobile Dynamic ad hoc Networks (MANET), since they do not require an earlier formed network to allow communication among vehicles. However, VANET differs from other wireless networks due to the fact that the elements themselves are

*H. F. Rashvand and H.-C. Chao (Eds.), *Dynamic Ad Hoc Networks*, The IET Book Publishing Department, 2013, ISBN 978-1-84919-647-5, eISBN 978-1-84919-648-2
[a]*Telecommunications Software and Systems Group, Waterford Institute of Technology, Waterford, Ireland.*
[b]*Systems and Computing Department, Federal University of Campina Grande, Campina Grande, Brazil.*
[c]*Federal Institute Education, Science and Technology of Paraiba, Campina Grande, Brazil*

composed of systems or networks, e.g., automobiles, motorcycles, traffic lights, trucks, etc.

To support these specific communication characteristics and applications, VANET's nodes should have sensor to obtain information about the environment. They should be capable of processing this information to actuate and control their operations. The collected information can also be shared with other vehicles or to a central processor, responsible for inferring traffic conditions and for notifying interested users.

VANET might be compatible with the Dedicated Short Range Communications (DSRC) allowing more accurate communication among vehicles. DSRC enables communication modes like vehicle-to-vehicle (V2V) and vehicles-to-infrastructure (V2I), and the vehicular communication standard. The IEEE 802.11p Wireless Access in the Vehicular Environment (WAVE) architecture also uses the DSRC [3].

Although the standard set in June 2010, there is a challenge to determine routes for packets forwarding due to the high mobility of nodes, instability of wireless links, new applications and mobility patterns. The existing protocols for VANET try to increase the performance of the packets routing by relying on specific characteristics. Some of them include: carrying large scales in the network on situations with high vehicle density to improve the routing performance [4]; support to the intense vehicles mobility, adapts quickly to the new topologies and enables a greater connection minimizing a possible link breakage [5]; adaptation system to the constantly position exchange of nodes in the network [6]; passivity [7] and dynamically [8].

This chapter presents an overview of routing solutions used in VANET, organized in the following way. Initially the requirements necessary by routing protocols in this specific type of network are discussed. Then, a survey of VANET routing protocols is presented. It is noteworthy that, some of the presented protocols are not specific for VANET, but they are worthy of consideration because they are largely used and referenced by many academics. After, information about the performance of some of these protocols is presented and discussed, showing what can be expected from the various methodologies of protocols operating in diverse situations. And finally, research trends and challenges and final conclusions are presented.

6.2   Requirements for a routing protocol for VANET

Routing in VANET presents many specific issues that are not contemplated by conventional MANET routing protocols. Most significant ones include different mobility pattern, diversity of involved elements, device energy restriction and instability of communication links.

The vehicle mobility pattern is expected to be different from conventional MANET since they are applicable to different environments. Individual mobility represents how the node will change its own position within a specified area and group mobility is related with movement of nodes that are involved with each other. These mobility patterns in MANET usually do consider a well-defined set of obstacles to define possible directions that can be chosen by the nodes. However, VANET might use restricted environments, with a rigorous definition of the available paths to represent the streets and roads.

The second aspect is the diversity of the elements. VANET are expected to involve vehicles as much as possible and support elements in a certain area, such as, automobiles, motorcycles, traffic lights, traffic signs, etc. This diversity of devices also brings another feature - energy restriction, which differentiates VANET from conventional MANET.

The last characteristic is the instability of the communication links. In VANET nodes, velocity values change from almost zero up to hundred kilometres per hour in traffic jam situations. This considerable change needs to be considered to control vehicle connectivity and transmissions by the communication technologies. Another issue that is influential to vehicle connection is the presence of the obstacles, which can mitigate link transmission quality or even disallow them to operate.

Routing solutions are important to guarantee accurate communication among vehicles. Because of those specific characteristics and, most important, the specific interaction from all involved elements necessary to obtain and disseminate information of traffic, weather, car crashes, etc. Many works presenting solutions consider diverse techniques to improve communication quality. More details of the protocols are presented in Section 6.3. Based on above points some important requirements for routing solutions in VANET include dynamicity performed in the origin, support of operations for small-scale and large-scale situations, control of link connectivity improving routing performance, incorporation of geographical information in routing decisions and support of heterogeneous communication modes.

Different routing protocols present the aforementioned vehicle partners' characteristics, but none of them integrate all those. Network nodes cannot switch protocols to change their decision process according to certain events. To integrate those characteristics in one routing strategy, a modularized architecture able to have new modules dynamically 'plugged' could adapt to different environments in a very flexible and easy way.

More details of these desired characteristics and the main features of the most important routing protocols in VANET area are discussed later. It is important to note that some of these protocols belong to MANET, but their relevance and frequent utilization in VANET works brought attention to them in the behalf of comparison.

6.3 State-of-art in routing protocols for VANET

Routing in VANET is an object of recent research [1, 9]. There are algorithms developed for large-scale networks, in which high density of vehicles is found. Here, enhancement of routing is to provide greater objectivity [10], supporting the intense mobility of vehicles, adapting quickly to new topologies and allowing a longer connection without a possible drop of the connection [5]. They should be capable of adapting themselves to the constant position switching of network nodes [6], its passivity [7] and dynamics [8, 10]. The routing protocols can be classified into the following categories: topology-based, geographic routing and routing architectures.

6.3.1   Topology-based routing

The topology-based routing protocols use links information that exists in the network to perform packet forwarding; in other words, these protocols determine the route and retain it in a table before the sender starts transmitting data. They are classified into two approaches: proactive and reactive.

6.3.1.1   Proactive approach

Proactive routing protocols, also known as table-driven routing protocols, periodically update the routing table, thus generating sustained routing overhead. The proactive protocols do not have initial route discovery delay but consume lot of bandwidth due to the continual updates of topology.

Optimized link-state routing protocol (OLSR)
OLSR is an optimization of the classical link state algorithm adapted for the use in MANET. Each node in the network chooses a set of neighbour nodes called as multipoint relays (MPR) which retransmits its packets. The neighbour nodes that are not in its MPR set can only read and process packets. This is in contrast to what is in conventional flooding mechanism, where every node broadcasts the messages and generates a lot of overhead traffic. MPR also reduces retransmission in broadcast communication [11].

Topology dissemination based on reverse-path forwarding (TBRPF)
TBRPF is a link-state routing protocol planned for MANET [7]. In this protocol, each node builds a source tree that contains paths to all accessible nodes by using a topology table. Nodes update themselves periodically using HELLO messages. Hence, routing messages are slighter, being frequently sent to neighbouring nodes.

Destination-sequenced distance vector (DSDV)
In DSDV [12], there is a table in each node with all possible destinations as well as the set of hops to every node in the network. Each entry in its table is marked with a sequence number determined by the destination node. This number serves to distinguish old routes from new ones, avoiding the formation of loops. DSDV requires periodic updates in routing tables, which may affect its performance, since there is a large power consumption and a low transmission rate even if the network is idle.

6.3.1.2   Reactive approach

In reactive routing protocols, a route is requested only when it is necessary, also regarded as an on-demand approach. Typically, reactive routings use flooding process for route discovery, where query packets inundate the network in search of an available path. This type of approach causes routing overhead and it is badly influenced by the initial delay from the route discovery step.

Ad hoc On-Demand Distance Vector (AODV)

The AODV [12] is a major routing protocol proposed for MANET. This protocol makes the use of sequence numbers for each destination, checking unavailable routes and preventing loops. Every routing packet has those sequence numbers, ensuring to update specific points of the network. An important feature of AODV is the route states management technique that underlies on the timing of each node usage. Establishing its validity and making a route expire if not used recently. Backup lists of previous nodes are maintained for each entry, showing the set of neighbours who use this entry to forward packets. Every connection detected with a broken link caused by any change in topology will have the source node notified via an error message.

Dynamic MANET on demand (DYMO)

DYMO [10] is another reactive routing protocol that works in MANET. It is considered as a successor to the AODV routing protocols. It has a simple design and is easy to implement. The basic operations of DYMO protocol are the discovery and the maintenance route. DYMO handles diversity of mobility and traffic patterns. It is a reactive protocol in nature; thus, it employs very slight resources, and is ideal for memory-constrained devices.

Dynamic source routing (DSR)

DSR [13] is a routing protocol developed for MANET by the Internet Engineering Task Force (IETF). It is a simple and efficient routing protocol specifically designed for the use in MANET. DSR allows the network to be completely self-organized and self-configured. The node initiates a route discovery by broadcasting a route request that contains the destination's address, the source node's address and a unique identification number. Each node receiving that packet checks whether it knows a route to the destination. If it does not, it adds its own address to the route record and then it retransmits the packet. Generation of route replies occurs when the route request reaches either the destination itself or an intermediate node that contains in its route cache an unexpired route response to the destination.

6.3.2 Geographic routing

Geographic routing uses positioning information to select the next forwarding hops. No global route between the source and the destination needs to be created and maintained. Routes are selected based on the geographic location of neighbouring nodes, before the packet is forwarded. There is no need of link state switch or route setup. This is a typical scenario of VANET, thus most of the routing algorithms follow the geographic approach, since these types of protocols are more robust and promising to the highly dynamic environments like VANET.

Generally, the geographic routing protocols assume that all nodes in the network have a locating system such as GPS [14]. Additionally, some protocols use topology information of traffic routes through digital maps.

6.3.2.1   Greedy perimeter stateless routing (GPSR)

GPSR [15] uses the positions of routers and a packet's destination to make packet-forwarding decisions. In this protocol, a node forwards a packet to an immediate neighbour, which is geographically closer to the destination node. This type of forwarding is the greedy mode. This is caused by the protocol, which makes greedy forwarding decisions using only information about a router's immediate neighbours in the network topology. The position of a packet's destination and positions of the candidate next hops are enough to make correct forwarding decisions, without any other topological information.

6.3.2.2   Geographic source routing (GSR)

GSR [16] was the first protocol to use a digital map of the streets to calculate a route. It is mostly applicable for urban environments, avoiding related issues as those from the GPSR protocol. GSR attempts to overcome the weaknesses of position-based routing approaches designed for MANET when used to VANET in urban scenarios.

The routing starts at the source node. It has the following modes, route in the packet header or hop-by-hop. GSR has the disadvantage that it does not consider vehicles movement to the management of stable connections, and with no guarantee that all vehicles have digital maps for the use in obtaining the route.

6.3.2.3   Anchor-based street and traffic aware routing (A-STAR)

The A-STAR is different from GSR regarding packets that are routed throughout anchor points of the overlay [17]. A-STAR improves the trouble where the perimeter mode of GPSR uses next-neighbour hops along a street as an alternative of choosing the furthest neighbour along a street for the subsequent hop [15].

The protocol A-STAR uses information about the bus routes, prioritizing roads that are part of these routes because these pathways have higher density of vehicles, which in principle provides greater connectivity. The recovery of local maxima is performed by calculating a new way to package anchors. Furthermore, the route in which the local maximum occurs is marked 'out of service' temporarily. This information is added to data packets to inform other nodes. To prevent the movement of data on the network indefinitely, there is a maximum number of allowed recoveries. Besides, using the scheme anchors, the protocol also makes use of digital maps and the Dijkstra algorithm among the anchors. A-STAR uses anchor-based street information to discover the routes in large city locations; consequently, it is not a good option for highway scenarios.

6.3.2.4   Connectivity-aware routing (CAR)

The CAR is an adapted version of Preferred Group Broadcasting (PGB) to minimize broadcast from AODV route discovery and Advanced Greedy Forwarding (AGF) to account for node mobility in VANET scenarios [9]. CAR uses AODV-based path discovery to find routes with limited broadcast from PGB. The CAR does not depend on a service location. An identifier for the request is added to the message to avoid cycles. The CAR uses a geographic marker that is stored and forwarded among vehicles to disseminate information on a node that has changed its position. This marker, called guard, is a temporary message containing an ID, a TTL, a propagation radius and some state information. The static guards are fixed without specific geographic coordinates while the guards have coordinated furniture, vector time and initial speeds.

This algorithm performs better than GPSR in many respects, but there are two points to be improved: First, selecting anchor points might possibly add some unnecessary nodes in the path increasing the number of hops; Second, movements of intermediate nodes can also lead link breakage to destination nodes.

6.3.3   Routing architecture for VANET

Different routing protocols present the aforementioned routing characteristics in Section 6.2. To integrate those characteristics in one routing protocol a routing architecture is proposed in [18], enabling a new trend of routing protocols for VANET. Figure 6.1 shows the architecture.

The routing protocols that rely on the architecture must follow it with the top-down approach. The architecture contains three layers but four components, the components include: dynamic routing, small-large scale, connectivity time and routing strategy. The principal component and the basis of any protocol developed based on the architecture is the dynamic routing component. All packets headers are defined in this component, as well as the routing methodology.

6.3.3.1   Generic vehicular dynamic source routing (GVDSR)

A new protocol proposed in [19] used while the routing architecture is instantiated: the GVDSR. The selected protocols which present the techniques compose the GVDSR

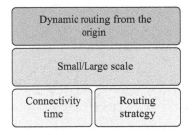

Figure 6.1   Proposed routing architecture

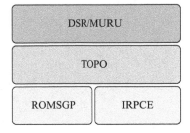

Figure 6.2   Used algorithms in the architecture

are shown in Figure 6.2. These techniques can be replaced in every moment. The GVDSR protocol is an extension of the DSR protocol [13], but specifically designed for VANET. GVDSR also incorporates the features of the other protocols founded in its protocol stack, Figure 6.2. The chosen protocols are based in the specific steps of the routing architecture. Every component presents a specification and the chosen protocol should satisfy it. The used techniques in each component of the GVDSR's stack are explained in the next subsections.

The dynamic routing component

To provide a dynamic routing from the origin the select protocol is DSR with the strength link control technique, found in MURU protocol [20]. The proposed algorithm has the following three phases, which follows the DSR specification: Request, Reply and Packet, as presented in Figure 6.3. Request is the phase when a certain source node wants a new route. Reply is a phase to respond nodes with the destination path before updating the routing table. And routing packets are possible when the next node of the path is available. If the next node is not available, it is necessary to store the packet in a buffer until the node finds another available path.

Similar to DSR, GVDSR starts sending broadcasts requests to find a route to the requested destination. The node that receives the requests does the same process until the destination node or an intermediate node that has a valid route to it responds. Also, when a node receives a request message it verifies if the source node is yet in the broadcast area to route the information. A response message, containing destination's location is then transmitted. When the source node receives the response with the path, it starts to send information to the destination

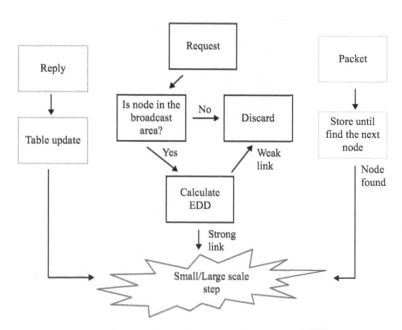

Figure 6.3   The dynamic routing step

through the discovered path. The connection drops if the link breaks and a new path request process is necessary. To solve this problem, the MURU protocol calculates the strength of the link with a metric called Expected Disconnection Degree (EDD). The source can choose the shortest path with more link connection reliability.

The small-large scale component

Possibly the information needs to travel through the whole city to reach the desired destination. Normally, when a node starts the requests to find the destination path, it creates a huge overhead, increasing the path request time. Also, when a path node is not available, the whole process will be started again. To solve these problems the Two-Phase Routing Protocol (TOPO) algorithm, developed by Reference 8, is used.

Figure 6.4 shows the flowchart of the small-large scale component. TOPO verifies if the destination node is in the broadcast area captured by the vehicle's antenna. If it is, the packet is transmitted to it. Otherwise, then if the source node is in an access area the small-scale routing is activated, otherwise, the large-scale routing is chosen.

A neighbour's list is the reference for routing on the access phase. Based on that list and verifying all the nodes that it has, the algorithm searches for the destination. The node should use the overlay routing in the case if the destination is not available. The overlay routing uses the cognitive routing presented by the IRPCE protocol, discussed in Section 6.3.3.1. When a destination node is in another access area, the route should include nodes in some overlay areas are between access areas. The cognitive routing is applied inside the overlay areas.

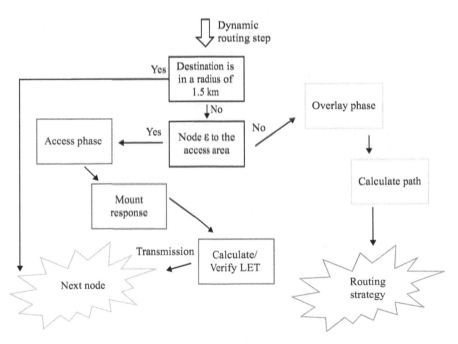

Figure 6.4   The small-large scale situation and the connectivity time steps

The connectivity time component

The Receive on Most Stable Group-Path (ROMSGP) protocol proposed in [21] predicts the link breakage during the transmission by a metric called link expiration time (LET). The LET, with the help of a GPS, calculates the distance between those vehicles and, through the car's direction verifies the link breakage probability. If the connection has a high probability to be dropped the protocol tries an alternative route. This enables the possibility to find another path if the link is not trustful enough to send information. With this mechanism, it is expected an increase on the end-to-end delay but a decrease on the loss probability.

The routing strategy component

The Intelligent Routing Protocol for City Environments (IRPCE) protocol, proposed in [6], is responsible to forward packets in the overlay phase. The greedy method in the TOPO algorithm presents a large overhead in the network to route information among access areas. To provide a lower end-to-end delay and decrease the overhead, IRPCE protocol presents a method to move information in a better way.

Figure 6.5 shows how the IRPCE method route packets in the large-scale situation and how it connects to the proposed architecture. The algorithm finds the junctions to the destination in different paths and route the packet to the node that has the same direction and highest velocity. This information about the nodes is obtained inside the packets. It also provides the best effort routing.

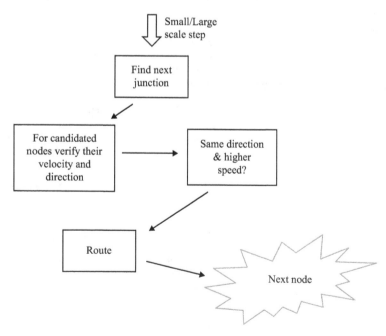

Figure 6.5   The routing strategy step

6.4   Performance evaluation of routing protocols for VANET

The main objective of the simulation is regard to the viability of the routing methodologies in a VANET scenario. Researchers have the common sense that the results for MANET will be the same in VANET. This information is clearly unverified that the presented performance evaluation intends to clarify.

The research questions to be answered include: RQ1 – The routing methodologies have same performance? RQ2 – Which is the best routing methodology for real VANET scenarios? A hypothesis is formulated for every question. The results obtained by the simulation model will show the statistical and importance significance to refute or accept the null hypotheses. The hypotheses for RQ1 are: H1-0 – The methodologies have no statistically significant difference. H1-A – The methodologies have statistically significant difference. The hypotheses for RQ2 are: H2-0 – Based on the results for MANET in [22], the reactive methodology is not the best for real VANET scenarios. H2-A – The reactive methodology is the best for real VANET scenarios.

The metrics for comparison include: Packet Delivery Ratio, Application Throughput, Delay, Percentage of Dropped Packets and Total Packets. The independent variables used in the experiments are: The velocity of the vehicles and the type of traffic. Velocity random values are in the range of five to 30 meters per second. The type of traffic is important to help us to analyse the network. The File Transfer Protocol (FTP) using TCP and the Constant Bit Rate (CBR) using UDP were the types chosen for the experiments.

The routing methodologies are the object of study of this evaluation. The methodologies are represented by routing protocols. Therefore, the experimental unities of this experimental approach are: the Generic Vehicular Dynamic Source Routing (GVDSR), ad hoc On-Demand Distance Vector (AODV) [23] and Destination Sequenced Distance Vector (DSDV) [13].

The population used in this experiment is the data traffic, which is also an independent variable. FTP and CBR connections are used in different scenarios with the rate of 4 packets per second.

In the scenario A, vehicles follow the urban perimeter traffic model of the Malaga City, Andaluzia, Spain. They can vary their velocity between 5 and 30 m/s, appropriate range for the mobility standards in vehicular scenarios. The number of nodes per vehicles in this scenario is 30 since 20 are communicating nodes. The scenario B presents the same basic characteristics of the scenario A. But in the scenario B, the perimeter of the Malaga City is on a highway environment. Table 6.1 presents further information about both scenarios.

The two independent variables are combined with each other, as a full factorial design. In this way, there is randomness and blockage in the experiments, which are enough to avoid some mistakes in the experimentation and hidden variables that cannot be analysed.

Table 6.1 shows the simulation configuration. The number of trials, for all values of speed, on each scenario and each protocol is 50, changing the seed of each execution presenting 90% of reliability.

Table 6.1   Simulation parameters for all scenarios

Metric	Value
Number of nodes	30
Velocity	5–30 m/s
Number of communicating nodes	20
Simulation area	1000 × 1000 m
Transceivers	IEEE 802.11 standard
Propagation model	Two-ray model
Antennas	Omnidiretionals
Routing protocols	AODV/DSDV/GVDSR
Queue	Priority
Traffic protocol	UDP, TCP
Application protocol	CBR, FTP
Packet rate	4 packets/s
Simulation time	900 s

6.4.1   Results

6.4.1.1   Results for TCP traffic

According to the evaluated topologies, it is possible to identify different behaviours of the evaluated algorithms depending on the selected scenario. In scenario A, which represents the scenario of the urban perimeter of Malaga, the results are present in Figure 6.6. On the packet delivery rate, equivalence among the algorithms evaluated is founded, indicating that because of the reduced number of vehicles as well as the low level of mobility found in urban environments, there were no representative differences in the results.

Regarding to delay and the discarded packets, it is observed some differences according to the used routing technique. About the delay, the techniques based on routing tables, instead of creating a list of jumps, obtained better results. On the dropping packets, AODV showed the best results, since node mobility is low, but when they happen, routes updates are more efficiently than both DSDV and GVDSR.

About the throughput, the GVDSR presents the best application throughput for the urban perimeter scenario. The integrated mechanisms of GVDSR's protocols benefit the route discovery mechanism. With an available route in hands, the application packets drive to the destiny more efficiently, since routing errors are harder to happen because of the link control mechanism executed by the connectivity time component. DSDV reached an intermediate result and AODV was the worst of all, what is expected to an on-demand protocol in a constant transmission scenario.

In the scenario B, which considers the topology Malaga in a stretch of highway, Figure 6.7, it is visualized results completely different compared to those observed initially. In this scenario, all evaluated metrics presented better results

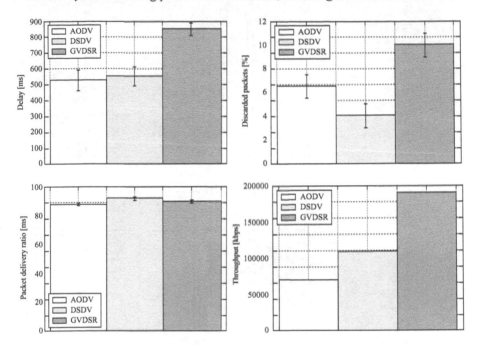

Figure 6.6   Graphs of delay, discarded packets, packet delivery ratio and throughput with TCP traffic connections for the urban perimeter of the Malaga city

than those from scenario A. In all evaluated metrics all protocols lead to more approximate results, since none of the protocols have been overloaded during their operation. However, protocols presented the same general behaviours of the first scenario: DSDV obtained the higher packet delivery and the lower packets discard; AODV had the lower delay; and GVDSR presents the best results for throughput. From the graphical analysis, it is possible to refute the hypothesis H1-0 and H2-0. The reactive methodology is not the best for VANET since exists an assimilation of the AODV and GVDSR protocols.

6.4.1.2   Results for UDP traffic

According to the evaluated topologies, it is possible to identify different behaviours of the evaluated algorithms. For the scenario A, which represents Malaga in an urban perimeter, it is observed equivalence between the algorithms evaluated on throughput and delivery rate. This shows that because of the increased number of vehicles as well as the low level of mobility found in urban environments, there were no differences in the representative results, Figure 6.8. Now regarding the delay and the discarded packets, it is observed that according to the routing tech-nique used representative differences appears. About the delay, the techniques

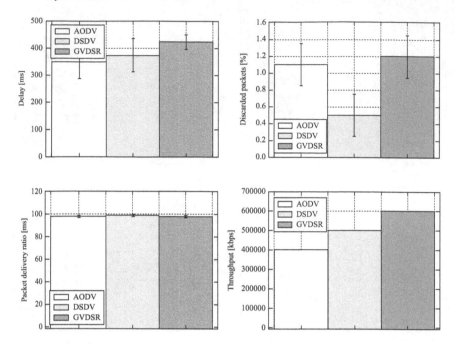

Figure 6.7   Graphs of delay, discarded packets, packet delivery ratio and throughput with TCP traffic connections for the highway perimeter of the Malaga city

based on routing tables instead of creating a list of hops had better results. On dropping packets, AODV showed the best results, since mobility is low. But, when they happen, the AODV route update mechanism was more efficient than DSDV and GVDSR.

In the scenario B, which considers the topology of Malaga in a highway environment, it is observed a completely different behaviour from that observed initially. In the four evaluated metrics, all protocols lead to similar results, as shown in Figure 6.9. It is observed a degradation of the network performance, reducing the throughput and delivery rate. Also, there is a considerable increase on the discarded packets. About the delay, the technique that presents a list of hops performed better, since only a small number of packets delivered generally through direct communication among vehicles. These changes occur because of large differences in the pattern of mobility, speed and dispersion of vehicles. Road environments have a degree of mobility much higher than the urban environment. Also, vehicles with higher speed and more distant from other vehicles are affected too, which undermines the quality of communication.

The hypotheses H1-0 and H2-0 are refuted by the graphical analysis. The reactive methodology is not the best for VANET, since it is an assimilation of the AODV and GVDSR protocols. This fact guides us to more simulation analysis, to guarantee the contribution of the architecture methodology for VANET.

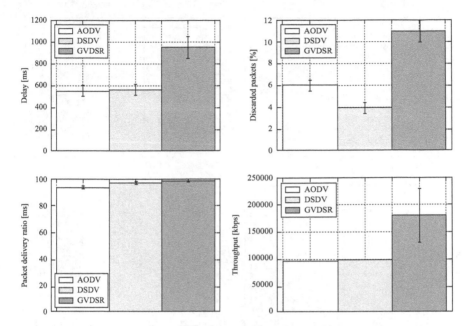

Figure 6.8   Graphs of delay, discarded packets, packet delivery ratio and throughput with UDP traffic connections for the urban perimeter of the Malaga city

6.5   Research trends and challenges

6.5.1   Mobility modelling and predication

As already discussed, VANET presents a high mobility of nodes, what makes many conventional operations more complicated of being executed. Nodes mobility has being studied since MANET, and many models were proposed since then.

However, those mobility models are not applicable to VANET, since the basic characteristics of these networks are different from conventional MANET. Some works were developed trying to improve VANET mobility representation. Most important limitations presented from the simplifications by MANET mobility models are the reduced number of nodes and speed, error-free transmission environment and open communication field, instead of a large number of vehicles which have their mobility restricted by roads and their velocities adjusted speed limits, traffic jams and traffic control mechanisms as traffic lights.

Some works also present new mobility models specifically designed to VANET, such as MOVE [1], Vanetmobisim [24] and STRAW [25].

6.5.2   Applications support

VANET applications are generally classified into two groups, which represent the simplification of the applications defined by [26] intelligent transportation applications and comfort applications.

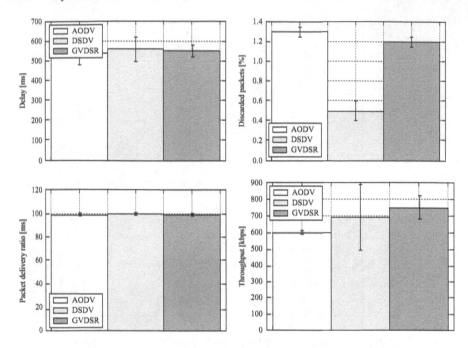

Figure 6.9 *Graphs of delay, discarded packets, packet delivery ratio and throughput with UDP traffic connections for the highway perimeter of the Malaga city*

Intelligent transportation applications are most of the vehicular networks applications. These applications represent many categories defined by DSRC applications, such as on-board navigation, co-operative traffic monitoring, control of traffic flows, driving assistance, etc. These applications have in common its relevance to life-critical situations through services, which help or interfere in driving with the intention of preventing accidents. Consequently, these applications need a more restricted variation of the connectivity quality from network level and the support to a differentiation to privilege these applications.

Comfort applications are applications which offer entertainment to vehicles passengers using communication with other vehicles to obtain information already stored by them, with an infrastructure to access services offered by control agencies or with Internet, which can be done by the two previous connections or by an alternative communication, such as 4G. These applications usually have more flexible communication constraints than the first ones, since they are not critical to vehicles operation and their eventual fail will not bring any major consequences. On the other hand, some of these applications need to have some communication requirements to improve passengers' experience, such as audio and video applications.

6.5.3   Simulation environments

VANET simulation environments still present many restrictions regarding the simulations control. Most of the simulation environments don't support natively the protocols developed to VANET and because of it the interaction among different tools is necessary. VANET simulation environments can be grouped in according to their specific functionalities in simulation process [27]: mobility generators, network simulators and VANET simulators.

Mobility generators [1, 24, 25] are responsible by generating vehicles mobility traces to be used as input for a simulator to represent vehicles movements during the entire simulation time according to the road model and simulation parameters, i.e., maximum/minimum vehicular speed, vehicle arrivals and departures, radio model, etc.

Network simulators are responsible to the 'conventional' simulation of the environment, controlling applications traffic transmission/reception, routing, propagation models, channel allocation, etc. However, these simulators were not designed to support VANET solutions and because of it they require extensions, which do not always represent correctly VANET operation, to simulate this type of networks. Examples are NS-2 [28] and GloMoSim [29].

Last group is of the specific VANET network simulators. These environments provide traffic flow simulation and network simulation. To do so, some of them work with a co-simulation process, where one layer controls each part of the simulation: VANET specific traffic is conducted by VANET simulator and network traffic by the network simulator [26, 30]. Other solutions are implemented to be a complete solution and are responsible for both operations [31].

6.6   Conclusion

Requirements that might be considered by VANET routing protocol were discussed to summarize relevant aspects presented in many relevant papers of the literature. This may facilitate design and implementation of new solutions based on the most important characteristics in performance, scalability and users applications and communication patterns heterogeneity.

An evaluation was also presented regarding most important routing techniques behaviour. Based on the two used scenarios, a match between the routing protocols AODV and GVDSR is observed. We note that the main difference between these two protocols is the delay, but which in fact may be impacting on these networks is the jitter that was not measured in the experiments. In order to a just conclusion of the methodologies and reactive routing by a routing architecture, and as the basis for the protocol is DSR the GVDSR in which all the features of DSR are preserved only by adding new technologies. It is noted in the literature, but particularly [22] a significant difference between protocols DSR and AODV, in which the architecture has raised the performance of DSR in the form of GVDSR to match in some metrics such as AODV.

It is important to highlight that the research activities in VANET are growing but it still lacks further capabilities to encourage products commercialization, being the motivation for more research in this subject. Some aspects still need a more detailed study as security, data dissemination, applications performance evaluation, delay-constrained routing and network fragmentation.

References

1. Lee K., Lee S.-H., Cheung R., Lee U., Gerla M. 'First Experience with CarTorrent in a Real Vehicular Ad Hoc Network Testbed'. Mobile Networking for Vehicular Environments (MOVE), 2007
2. Hertenstein H., Labertaux K. P. 'A Tutorial Survey on Vehicular Ad Hoc Networks'. *IEEE Communications Magazine*, 46(6), 164–171, 2008
3. IEEE Std 1609.3. 'IEEE Trial-Use Standard for Wireless Access in Vehicular Environments (WAVE) – Networking Services'. Intelligent Transportation Systems Committee, 2007
4. Wang W., Xie F., Chatterjee M. 'TOPO: Routing in Large Scale Vehicular Networks'. IEEE 66th Vehicular Technology Conference, pp. 2106–2110, 2007
5. Taleb T., Sakhaee E., Jamalipour A., Hashimoto K., Kato N., Nemoto Y. 'A Stable Routing Protocol to Support ITS Services in VANET Networks'. *IEEE Transactions on Vehicular Technology*, 56(6, pt. 1), 3337–3347, 2007
6. Ali S., Bilal S. M. 'An Intelligent Routing Protocol for VANET in City Environments'. 2nd International Conference Computer, Control and Communication, Karachi, Pakistan. IEEE Computer Society, USA pp. 1–5, 2009
7. Xue G., Feng J., Li M. 'A Passive Geographical Routing Protocol in VANET'. IEEE Asia-Pacific Services Computing Conference, Yilan, Taiwan. IEEE Computer Society, USA, pp. 680–685, 2008
8. Xi S., Li X.-M. 'Study of the Feasibility of VANET and its Routing Protocols'. 4th International Conference on Wireless Communications, Networking and Mobile Computing, Dalian, China. IEEE Computer Society, USA, pp. 1–4, 2008
9. Lee K. C., Lee U., Gerla M. 'Survey of Routing Protocols in Vehicular Ad Hoc Networks', *Advances in Vehicular Ad-Hoc Networks: Developments and Challenges*, IGI Global, Oct. 2009
10. Sommer C., Dressler F. 'The DYMO Routing Protocol in VANET Scenarios'. IEEE 66th Vehicular Technology Conference, pp. 16–20, 2007
11. Clausen T., Jacquet P. 'Optimized Link State Routing Protocol (OLSR)'. RFC 3626, Network Working Group, Oct. 2003
12. Perkins C., Belding-Royer E., Das S. 'Ad Hoc On-Demand Distance Vector (AODV) Routing'. http://tools.ietf.org/html/rfc3561 IETF. RFC 3561. 1999
13. Johnsort D. 'Routing in Ad Hoc Networks of Mobile Hosts'. In First Workshop on Mobile Computing Systems and Applications, 1994. WMCSA 1994, pp. 158–163

14. Hein G. W., Godet J., Issler J. L., Martin J. C., Erhard P., Lucas R., *et al.* 'Status of Galileo Frequency and Signal Design'. In International Technical Meeting of the Satellite Division of the Institute of Navigation ION GPS, pp. 266–277, 2002

15. Bernsen J., Manivannan D. 'Greedy Routing Protocols for Vehicular Ad Hoc Networks'. In *Proceedings of the 7th International Conference on Wireless Communications and Mobile Computing (IWCMC)*, pp. 632–637, Aug. 2008

16. Lochert C., Hartenstein H., Tian J., Füßler H., Hermann D., Mauve M. 'A Routing Strategy for Vehicular Ad Hoc Networks in City Environments'. In *Proceedings of the IEEE Intelligent Vehicles Symposium*, pp. 156–161, Jun. 2003

17. Seet B.-C., Liu G., Lee B.-S., Foh C.-F., Wong K.-J., Lee K.-K, 'A-STAR: A Mobile Ad Hoc Routing Strategy for Metropolis Vehicular Communications'. In *Proceedings of the 3rd International IFIP-TC6 Networking Conference (Networking)*, pp. 989–999, May 9–14, 2004

18. Barros M. T., Gomes R. C. M., Costa A. F. B. F. 'Routing Architecture for Vehicular Ad-Hoc Networks'. *IEEE Latin America Transactions*, 10(1), 1411–1419, Jan. 2012

19. Barros M. T., Costa A. F. B. F., Gomes, R. C. M. 'GVDSR: A Dynamic Routing Strategy for Vehicular Ad-Hoc Networks'. In IADIS International Conference WWW/INTERNET, Timisoara, Romania, 2010

20. Mo Z., Zhu H., Makki K., Pissinou N. 'MURU: A Multi-hop Protoccol for Urban Ad-hoc Networks'. Third International Conference on Mobile and Ubiquitos System: Networking and Services, (MOBIQUITOUS 2006) July 17–21, 2006 - San Jose, California, USA, pp. 169–176, 2006

21. Lebrun J., Chuah C.-N., Ghosal D., Zhang M. 'Knowledge-based Opportunistic Forwarding in Vehicular Wireless Ad Hoc Networks'. IEEE Vehicular Technology Conference (VTC-Spring), vol. 4, Stockholm, Sweden pp. 2289–2293, 2005

22. Mittal S., Kaur P. 'Performance Comparison of AODV, DSR and ZRP Routing Protocols in Manet's'. In *Advances in Computing, Control, International Conference on Telecommunication Technologies, ACT '09.* pp. 165–168, 2009

23. Perkins C., Bhagwat P. 'Highly Dynamic Destination-Sequenced Distance-Vector Routing (DSDV) for Mobile Computers'. http://www.cs.virginia.edu/cl7v/cs851-papers/dsdv-sigcomm94.pdf, 1994

24. Haerri J., Fiore M., Fethi F., Bonnet C. 'VanetMobiSim: Generating Realistic Mobility Patterns for VANET'. Institut Eurécom and Politecnico Di Torino, 2006. Available at: http://vanet.eurecom.fr/

25. Choffnes D. R., Bustamante F. E. 'An Integrated Mobility and Traffic Model for Vehicular Wireless Networks'. In *Proceedings of the 2nd ACM International Workshop on Vehicular Ad Hoc Networks*, pp. 69–78, 2005

26. Piorkowski M., Raya M., Lugo A. L., Papadimitratos P., Grossglauser M., Hubaux J.-P. 'TraNS (Traffic and Network Simulation Environment)'. Ecole Polytechnique Fédérale de Lausanne, EPFL, Switzerland, 2007. Available at: http://trans.epfl.ch/

27.   Martinez F. J., Toh C. K., Cano J.-C., Calafate Ca. T., Manzoni P. 'A Survey and Comparative Study of Simulators for Vehicular Ad Hoc Networks (VANET)'. *Wireless Communications and Mobile Computing*, 11(7), 813–828, Jul. 2011

28.   Fall K., Varadhan K. 'Ns Notes and Documents.' The VINT Project, UC Berkeley, LBL, USC/ISI, and Xerox PARC, February 2000. Available at: http://www.isi.edu/nsnam/ns/nsdocumentation.html

29.   Martin J. 'GloMoSim. Global Mobile Information Systems Simulation Library.' UCLA Parallel Computing Laboratory, 2001. Available at: http://pcl.cs.ucla.edu/projects/glomosim/

30.   Mangharam R., Weller D., Rajkumar R., Mudalige P., Bai F. 'GrooveNet: A Hybrid Simulator for Vehicle-to-Vehicle Networks'. Carnegie Mellon University, 2006. Available at: http://www.seas.upenn.edu/rahulm/Research/GrooveNet/

31.   MobiREAL, 2008. Available at: http://www.mobireal.net/

Chapter 7*

Exploiting cooperative relays in MIMO ad hoc networks

Shan Chu[a], Xin Wang[b] and Yuanyuan Yang[b]

Abstract

With the popularity of wireless devices and the increase of computing and storage resources, there are increasing interests in supporting mobile computing techniques. Particularly, ad hoc networks can potentially connect different wireless devices to enable more powerful wireless applications and mobile computing capabilities. To meet the ever-increasing communication need, it is important to improve the network throughput while guaranteeing transmission reliability. Multiple-input-multiple-output (MIMO) technology can provide significantly higher data rate in ad hoc networks where nodes are equipped with multi-antenna arrays. Although MIMO technique itself can support diversity transmission when channel condition degrades, the use of diversity transmission often compromises the multiplexing gain and is also not enough to deal with extremely weak channel. Instead, in this work, we exploit the use of cooperative relay transmission (which is often used in a single antenna environment to improve reliability) in a MIMO-based ad hoc network to cope with harsh channel condition. We design both centralized and distributed scheduling algorithms to support adaptive use of cooperative relay transmission when the direct transmission cannot be successfully performed. Our algorithm effectively exploits the cooperative multiplexing gain and cooperative diversity gain to achieve higher data rate and higher reliability under various channel conditions. Our scheduling scheme can efficiently invoke relay transmission without introducing significant signalling overhead as conventional relay schemes, and seamlessly integrate relay transmission with multiplexed MIMO transmission. We also design a MAC protocol to implement the distributed algorithm. Our performance results demonstrate that the use of cooperative relay in a MIMO framework could bring in a significant throughput improvement in all the scenarios studied, with the variation of node density, link failure ratio, packet-arrival rate and retransmission threshold.

H. F. Rashvand and H.-C. Chao (Eds.), Dynamic Ad Hoc Networks, The IET Book Publishing Department, 2013, ISBN 978-1-84919-647-5, eISBN 978-1-84919-648-2
[a]Motorola Solutions, One Motorola Plaza, Holtsville, NY, USA
[b]Department of Electrical and Computer Engineering, Stony Brook University, Stony Brook, NY, USA

7.1   Introduction

There are increasing interests and use of mobile ad hoc networks (MANETs) with the proliferation of mobile, network-enabled wireless devices, and the fast progress of computing techniques and wireless networking techniques. In a MANET, wireless devices could self-configure and form a network with an arbitrary topology. The network's topology may change rapidly and unpredictably. Such a network may operate in a stand-alone fashion, or may be connected to the larger Internet. MANETs became a popular subject for research in recent years, and various studies have been made to increase the performance of ad hoc networks and support more advanced mobile computing and applications.

As the number, Central Processing Unit [CPU] power and storage space of wireless devices continue to grow, there is a significant increase in data transmission demand to support data intensive mobile computing and applications, such as multimedia streaming, gaming, transmission of a large amount of event data during environmental monitoring, and distributed and collaborative processing among a set of wireless devices. Wireless communication systems using multiple antennas at the transmitter and/or receiver have recently emerged as one of the most significant advances in wireless communications. Multiple-input multiple-output (MIMO) systems are presently at the leading edge of wireless systems research and are considered as one of the best approaches for increasing the capacity of wireless networks. MIMO technology is also prominently regarded as a technology of choice for next generation commercial wireless networks such as IEEE 802.16 [1], IEEE 802.11 [2] and cellular third generation (3G) systems such as Universal Mobile Telecommunications System (UMTS) or $1 \times$ EV-DO system [3]. Moreover, to fully support cellular environments MIMO research consortia including IST-MASCOT have proposed to develop advanced MIMO techniques, i.e., multi-user MIMO (MU-MIMO).

A MIMO wireless communication system is defined as a transmission link where the transmitter and the receiver are equipped with multiple antenna elements to supplement traditional time processing with spatial signal processing, with the aim of improving transmission reliability and providing higher raw data rates. As a rich scattering environment can provide independent transmission paths (multichannels) between different transmitting and receiving antenna pairs, an intended receiver node can separate and decode its received data streams based on their unique spatial signatures. This allows MIMO systems to efficiently take advantage of random fading and multi-path propagation to improve the performance of wireless transmission links by several orders of magnitude without requiring any additional bandwidth. A transmitter node can divide its data into multiple data streams and transmit them simultaneously over multiple antenna elements, which is known as spatial multiplexing [4, 5] to increase the transmission rate and/or by space-time codes [6–8] to exploit the MIMO channel diversity. In a network with multiple users, the channels between different users and antenna pairs are different and vary over time. In cellular networks, multi-user diversity could be exploited by scheduling the user with the best channel condition to communicate with the base station [9–11].

With the fast progress of MIMO technology, it is now being considered for ad hoc networks, where all nodes are peer-to-peer in nature and connected through a mesh topology. Different from an infrastructure-based single-hop cellular network, it is difficult for nodes to coordinate in channel evaluations and transmissions in a dynamic meshed ad hoc network. Different nodes may have different number of antennas, and the peer relationship changes as network topology changes. The quick variation of channel condition and network topology as well as the inconsistency in node density would lead to more challenges in ad hoc network design. Traditional networking research has modelled the physical layer by constructing simplified and, in many cases, unrealistic abstractions that make it easier to perform both analytical and simulation-oriented studies of the protocols developed. The transmission pattern using a multiplicity of antennas is complex and difficult to model. Furthermore, a multiplicity of communicating pairs that are in close proximity to one another could share the available bandwidth simultaneously. Given this, the design of a MAC protocol is challenging and should have to account for physical-layer dependencies.

Some recent works have endeavoured to apply MIMO techniques in ad hoc networks [12–21]. Although various MAC schemes have been designed to exploit the intrinsic features of MIMO to improve the throughput and reliability, they may not be able to handle consecutive packet loss due to severe path loss, continuous deep fading or temporary topology changes and link breakages. Continuous packet retransmissions would lead to significant throughout reduction. The severe transmission conditions pose a big threat to the growth of wireless applications. Although beamforming can help improve the transmission reliability, it compromises the potential multiplexing gain and hence reduces the transmission rate. In addition, when the channel condition is extremely weak or the distance between the transmitter and receiver is temporarily very long, even beaming-forming may not be able to ensure the transmission reliability for the direct link. Moreover, the design of MAC scheme to coordinate beamforming transmissions in a multi-hop network is very difficult. As an alternative to MIMO technique, recent efforts have been made to enable cooperative relay transmission to cope with channel degradation, with the assumption that network nodes have single antenna [22–24]. One question to raise: is it beneficial to adopt cooperative relay to facilitate transmission in a MIMO-based ad hoc network?

The introduction of cooperative relay transmission into a network where nodes are equipped with multiple antennas could bring in benefits far beyond that of simply combining the two techniques together. It would not only allow joint exploitation of multiplexing gain of MIMO and cooperative diversity gain of relay transmission, but would also help mitigate many issues presenting in conventional relay transmissions. First, with the support of relay nodes, transmissions on MIMO links with harsh conditions or temporary breakages can possibly be bridged through relay links over source-relay-destination paths. Without being impacted by a poor link for a continuous time period, traffic can be scheduled more efficiently to avoid a significant transmission delay and extra consumption of precious network resources. Second, with a careful relay selection, the channel quality of a relay link would be generally better thus allow for a higher rate, which reduces the cost of using relay transmission. Third, taking advantage of multi-packet transmission/reception capability enabled by MIMO technique, a relay node that has multiple antennas can overhear the transmission from a source while receiving its own packets, which avoids the need for the source to forward the packet explicitly to the relay node as in conventional cooperative transmission. Meanwhile, a relay node can simultaneously forward packet for others while transmitting its own packets.

Although the benefits of using relay transmission in a MIMO ad hoc network are significant, there are also big challenges in efficiently selecting and triggering cooperative relay transmissions, especially in concert with multi-user-based MIMO transmissions in an ad hoc network environment. Without a properly designed strategy, the use of relay would cost much more transmission time and bandwidth instead of supplementing the spatial multiplexing transmission. In this chapter, our focus is to design algorithms along with a MAC scheme that *opportunistically* use cooperative relay in MIMO-based ad hoc networks to further improve the transmission reliability and throughput when the transmissions between two nodes encounter difficulty. Our proposed strategy is named as Cooperative Relayed Spatial Multiplexing (CRSM). The main contributions of this paper are as follows:

- We mathematically model the problem and provide a centralized algorithm with proved approximation ratio to serve as the performance reference of the distributed algorithm.
- We practically divide the problem into two phases and provide simple but effective distributed scheduling algorithms that seamlessly incorporate the use of cooperative relay into MIMO transmission, which can guide the practical protocol design.
- We propose a simple relay scheme to formulate relay set and invoke relay transmission without extra signalling overhead.
- We design an efficient MAC protocol to support our distributed algorithm.

The rest of the chapter is organized as follows. We introduce the motivation of our work in Section 7.2. We formulate the problem and propose a centralized algorithm with proved approximation ratio in Section 7.3. We then present our scheduling algorithms to support seamless use of cooperative relay with multi-user-based MIMO transmission in an ad hoc network in Section 7.4, and provide more details about relay operation and MAC protocol design in Section 7.5. The performance of the proposed algorithms is studied through simulations in Section 7.6. Finally, we discuss the related work and further development in Section 7.7 and conclude the paper in Section 7.8.

7.2 Background and motivation

In an ad hoc network where nodes are equipped with multiple antennas, there are generally two types of gain achieved by MIMO transmission. *Multiplexing gain* refers to the increase in raw data rate by concurrent transmission of multiple data streams between a node pair, and *diversity gain* is achieved by space-time coding or antenna selection which may be exploited to improve the transmission reliability. In this work, we make an effort to leverage the multiplexing gain and diversity gain brought by MIMO transmission along with multi-user diversity in a network with mesh topology. Instead of only allowing multiplexed transmission between a pair of nodes as in traditional MIMO scheme, we consider cooperative MIMO multiplexed transmission in which multiple nodes can simultaneously transmit to a receiver that has multiple antennas, i.e. forming a virtual MIMO array [25], and a sender with multiple antennas can also transmit multiple streams to a set of nodes. In this way, many-to-many transmissions are allowed between node pairs to better exploit multiplexing gain. Moreover, among the transmission links between node pairs, those whose channel qualities are higher can be selected for transmission to exploit multi-user diversity gain. When the information of channel coefficients is available for a node pair, a subset of antennas that transmit signals at better quality can be opportunistically selected for transmissions. A framework is proposed in Reference 20 to allow the exploration of multi-user diversity and antenna selection diversity to further improve the capacity and reliability of the network. These diversity techniques, however, are insufficient when the channel condition is extremely weak, the existence of correlated fading between a sender and receiver pair, or the distance between a node pair changes as a result of temporary topology change. If the channel degradation is short term, it would be inefficient to change the transmission path immediately. Although schemes such as beamforming could be used between the transmission pair that has severe channel condition, it may prevent concurrent transmissions from the same or other nodes and compromise the potential throughput gain of the network that could be achieved with multiplexed transmissions. Also, sometimes the beamforming finds it too hard to handle a weak transmission between two nodes when their distance is large enough or the channel is very weak, although the two nodes are within two-hop transmission distance.

In order to alleviate the problem of data rate reduction and excessive queuing delay caused by severe channel condition and/or link breakage as a result of temporary network topology change, in this work, we propose to adaptively invoke *cooperative relay* in conjunction with *cooperative multiplexing MIMO communications* when direct transmission cannot be successfully pursued. There are some unique benefits by taking advantage of both techniques.

Concurrently exploiting cooperative diversity and spatial multiplexing for transmission robustness and higher throughput: Different from the literature work that exploits cooperative diversity in a single antenna case only to improve the transmission quality, in the proposed work, the relay transmissions coordinate with the transmissions in a neighbourhood and take advantage of *cooperative multiplexing* to improve the overall network throughput.

Obtaining relay packets without extra overhead: With multi-packet reception capability brought by multiple antennas, a relay node can obtain the packet to be relayed through overhearing during its own data receiving when the sender attempts for initial direct transmission. As an example, in Figure 7.1(a), *R* receives

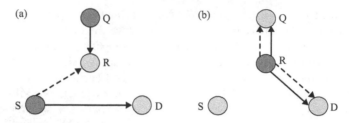

Figure 7.1   An illustration of cooperative relay transmission

the relay packet as an interference stream while it is receiving data stream from Q. Assume R has 2 antennas, it is therefore able to decode the packet from Q as well as the relay packets from S.

Relay packet forwarding in conjunction with normal packet transmissions: Instead of simply postponing the transmissions of packets with relay nodes as the direct sender, which is often the case in the conventional cooperative diversity study, a relay node can transmit a relay packet concurrently with its own packets therefore avoid excessive delay for its own packets. As shown in Figure 7.1(b), node R can simultaneously transmit to Q when it serves as a relay node to transmit the relay packet to D. A relay node can even have a higher transmission probability driven by our priority-based scheduling, as the priority of a relay node increases when its packets experience longer delay due to relay transmissions.

Relaxed synchronization requirements taking advantage of multi-stream reception capability of receivers: The direct transmissions and relayed transmissions are performed independently, and a receiver node takes advantage of multiple antennas to decode transmissions from multiple streams without requiring synchronization at the symbol level between neighbouring nodes as in conventional cooperative diversity schemes.

With use of coded cooperation, the network performance can be further improved. As our focus is to investigate the benefit and strategy of incorporating relay into multiplexed MIMO transmission, we consider decode and forward cooperative strategy here for simplicity.

7.3   Problem formulation and a centralized solution

In this section, we first describe the system model and introduce some notations to use in the paper. We then provide a mathematical formulation of the problem to guide the design of scheduling algorithms. The modelling of transmission opportunities and constraints to enable cooperative MIMO transmissions in multi hop wireless mesh network involves a big challenge, while the need of incorporating relay transmissions makes the problem even harder. Finally, we provide a centralized algorithm with provable approximation ratio to serve as the performance reference of the distributed algorithm to be introduced in the next section.

7.3.1   Problem formulation

To enable concurrent many-to-many stream transmission, our MAC design is TDMA-based, in which the time domain is divided into transmission durations (TD). A TD covers one round of control signal exchange and data frame transmission and consists of a fixed sequence of phases each with a fixed length. Channel conditions are supposed to be quasi-static during a TD. The data transmission rate within a TD can vary for different links based on the their channel conditions, i.e. more efficient coding can be used to encode the symbols at a higher rate for a channel with higher quality. As the total transmit power of each node is generally fixed, the transmit power of each antenna is different when a node uses a different number of antennas for transmission.

As the complete information about future traffic is unavailable, it is a practical option to schedule the transmission of packets in each TD considering the existing traffic and queueing delay, and the scheduling scheme is consecutively executed during the lifetime of the network. In a TD, suppose there is a set of N_n nodes $N = \{1, 2, \ldots, N_n\}$ in the network, and there are N_p packets waiting for transmission which are contained in the set $P_{pkt} = \{1, 2, \ldots, N_p\}$. A node j has an antenna array of size N_j^{ant}. There is a buffer queue at each node where data packets are stored. For a packet i, a parameter called *priority* $\mathcal{P}(i)$ is used to capture both its service type and queuing delay. For the convenience of calculation, $\mathcal{P}(i)$ is measured in the unit of TD. A possible way to integrate both factors into the priority calculation is to equate the service priority of i to an initial value of $\mathcal{P}(i)$ in terms of TD, and $\mathcal{P}(i)$ increases as the queuing time of p_i increases. A higher value of $\mathcal{P}(i)$ indicates that the packet i has a higher priority.

The transmissions of packets are organized as *streams*. For spatial multiplexed transmission, a stream s is defined to be an independent data flow transmitted from an antenna of a transmitter node to a receiver node and identified by a triplet $s = (I_t, I_r, I_{ant})$, where $I_t / I_r / I_{ant}$ is the index of the transmitter/receiver/antenna that involves in the transmission of the stream. Suppose the signal to noise and interference ratio (SINR) at the receiver node is $\rho_{I_r}(s)$ for stream s, the data rate of s can be calculated as $\mathcal{R}(s) = \log(1 + \rho_{I_r}(s))$. In a practical system, a receiver can include its estimated $\rho_{I_r}(s)$ in its feedback message, and a transmitter can then decide the actual data rate based on the SINR information, i.e. by looking up a preset table. The transmissions in the network are half-duplex, so a node cannot be a transmitter and receiver at the same time. In a TD, a subset of nodes, denoted as T, are selected as transmitter nodes.

The notations used in the problem formulation are summarized in Table 7.1. Denote the set of neighbouring nodes of node j as $\mathcal{V}_j$. Suppose the transmission of a packet i is through stream $s(i)$, and the reception is successful when the receiving SINR $\rho_{I_r}(s(i))$ is above a certain threshold Γ. After a direct transmission of a packet i from s_i to d_i, nodes that successfully overhear the packet while are in the transmission range of s_i and the receiving range of d_i, i.e. those in the set $R_i = \{r \mid \forall r \in N \backslash T, s.t. \ s_i \in \mathcal{V}_r, d_i \in \mathcal{V}_r, \rho_{I_r}(s(i)) \geq \Gamma\}$, store the packet in their own buffers. These nodes become candidate relay nodes for packet i. The packet

Table 7.1   List of notations used in problem formulation

Notation	Definition
$i = 1, \ldots, N_p$	Index of packets
$j = 1, \ldots, N_n$	Index of nodes
$h_j \in 0, 1$	$h_j = 1$ if and only if node j is selected as a receiver
$t_j \in 0, 1$	$t_j = 1$ if and only if node j is selected as a transmitter
$y_{ij} \in 0, 1\pi$	$y_{ij} = 1$ if and only if packet i is assigned to be transmitted from node j
$a_{ijk} \in 0, 1$	$a_{ijk} = 1$ if and only if packet i is assigned to be transmitted from the kth antenna of node j
$s = (I_t, I_r, I_{ant})$	Stream from the I_{ant}th antenna of transmitter I_t to receiver I_r
R_i	The set of candidate relay nodes for packet i
$\mathcal{P}(i)$	Priority of packet i
$\mathcal{R}(s)$	Data rate of stream s
$\mathcal{I}(d_i)$	Interference at receiver node d_i when receiving packet i

i becomes available to nodes in $R_i \cup \{s_i\}$, which store the packet with the consistent priority. R_i is updated to include more qualified relay nodes whenever there is any direct transmission of i. When $y_{ij} = 1$, it implicitly indicates that $j \in R_i \cup \{s_i\}$.

Note that if $a_{ijk} = 1$, the transmission rate of packet i depends on the channel condition of the stream $s(i) = (j, d_i, k)$ and the interference at node d_i when receiving the stream, denoted as $\mathcal{I}(d_i)$. Therefore, the rate of stream $s(i)$ is denoted as $\mathcal{R}(s(i), \mathcal{I}(d_i))$.

We now can formulate the constraints for the problem of cooperative relayed spatial multiplexing in a MIMO ad hoc network to capture the features of MIMO transmissions and conditions of relay transmissions. First, it is necessary to ensure that a packet i is assigned to at most one transmitter node among all the candidate ones (including the source node s_i and candidate relay nodes in R_i) to avoid redundant transmission,

$$\sum_{j \in R_i \cup \{s_i\}} y_{ij} \leq 1, i \in P_{pkt} \tag{7.1}$$

As the *transmitting constraint*, an antenna k at a transmitter j can only accommodate the transmission of at most one stream in a TD,

$$\sum_{i \in P_{pkt}} a_{ijk} \leq 1 + (1 - t_j)M, j \in N, k = 1, \ldots, N_j^{ant} \tag{7.2}$$

where M is a sufficiently large number introduced to relax the constraint when node j is not selected as the transmitter, i.e. $t_j = 0$. Similarly, the *receiving constraint* is used to model the impact of interference at the receiver end of a MIMO link, where the total number of receiving streams (data streams plus interference streams) at a receiver node j is restricted to be no more than its number of antennas in order to decode the receiving data packet,

$$\sum_{i \in P_{pkt}} \sum_{m \in V_j} \sum_{k=1}^{N_m^{ant}} a_{imk} \leq N_j^{ant} + (1 - h_j)M, \, j \in N \tag{7.3}$$

To ensure that the transmission is half-duplex, t_j and h_j for each j have to satisfy:

$$t_j + h_j \leq 1, j \in N \tag{7.4}$$

It is also important to constrain the relation between the parameters,

$$\begin{aligned}
&a_{ijk} \leq y_{ij} \leq t_j, a_{ijk} \leq y_{ij} \leq h_{d_i}, \\
&i \in P_{pkt}, j \in N, k = 1, \ldots, N_j^{ant}
\end{aligned} \tag{7.5}$$

Finally, following the scheduling framework in Reference 26, our scheduling aims to maximize the sum of priority-weighted capacity so that both data rate and priority can be jointly optimized. The objective function is:

$$\max \sum_{i \in P_{pkt}} \sum_{j \in R_i \cup \{s_i\}} \sum_{k=1}^{N_j^{ant}} a_{ijk} \mathcal{R}(s(i), \mathcal{I}(d_i)) \mathcal{P}(i) \tag{7.6}$$

With this formulation, the nodes without packets will have the priority set to 0 and not be scheduled to transmit, while the packets associated with worse quality links will still get chance to transmit as their priority increases.

So far, we formulate the problem of cooperative transmission with relays in a MIMO ad hoc network as an integer linear programming (ILP) problem with objective function in (7.6) subject to constraints (7.1), (7.2), (7.3), (7.4) and (7.5). As an ILP problem is NP-hard in general and needs exponential time complexity to find a solution, an efficient heuristic algorithm is required for the practical implementation.

7.3.2 A centralized algorithm

In Algorithm 2, we propose a centralized scheme to schedule packet transmissions in a single TD. As the interference streams which can transmit simultaneously with stream i are unknown before the scheduling is finalized, it makes the accurate determination of $\mathcal{R}(s(i), \mathcal{I}(d_i))$ difficult. On the other hand, as the transmission rate is only used as a guidance to select the streams that potentially support higher throughput for transmissions, it is not necessary to know the accurate transmission rate at scheduling time. Therefore, we consider the maximum possible receiving interference and use it for the conservative estimation of rate for each candidate stream. Specifically, as the number of interference and data stream could not exceed $N_{d_i}^{ant}$ for correct decoding, $N_{d_i}^{ant} - 1$ strongest candidate streams around d_i are considered to calculate the interference strength. The estimated value of $\mathcal{R}(s(i), \mathcal{I}(d_i))$ is then calculated based on the channel condition of the stream and the interference strength, and is then used in the centralized algorithm. Note that our algorithm does not prevent using other model for stream rate determination.

When channel conditions from all the potential transmitters are estimated in advance, more sophisticated techniques could be used to cancel the majority of interference, and thus further improve the transmission rate.

The algorithm is to be executed by a central controller of the network which has the complete information of packets and channels, as shown in Figure 7.2. To facilitate scheduling, a parameter $w(ijk)$ is introduced to represent the priority weighted data rate achieved with the transmission of packet i from transmitter j using antenna k as in (7.6), and the set W consists of the weighted rates of all candidate streams. The algorithm greedily schedules a packet i^* to transmit from antenna k^* of transmitter node j^*, which has the highest weighted rate among all candidate and guarantees the constraints (7.2) and (7.3). P is the set of scheduled packets and T contains all selected transmitters. All the candidate streams that have transmission conflict with the scheduled stream $s = (j^*, d_{i^*}, k^*)$ are then removed from the set W, including the ones that have the node j^* as the receiver, have d_{i^*} as

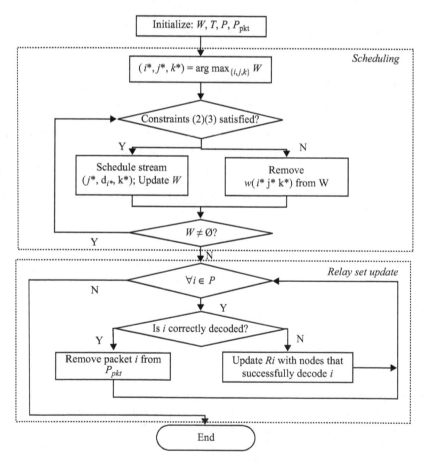

Figure 7.2   Centralized scheduling

the transmitter, or have node j^* as the transmitter but are associated with the antenna k^*. A packet may be queued at multiple candidate transmitting nodes, i.e. source and candidate relay nodes. To avoid repetitive transmission of a packet and satisfy constraint (7.1), all other candidate streams for the selected packet i^* are also removed from W after i^* is successfully scheduled in the current TD. The algorithm then checks if packets are correctly received at destinations, and successfully received packets are removed from the packet set P_{pkt}. For any incorrectly received packet i, its candidate relay list R_i is updated to add in nodes that are within the range of both the source and destination of i and have correctly overheard the direct transmission, so that nodes in R_i would assist in the transmission of i in the following TDs.

Proposition: The centralized scheduling algorithm can achieve an approximation ratio of $1/((2 + \mathcal{D}) \max_i \{N_i^{ant}\} + 2)$, where $\mathcal{D}$ is the maximum node degree in the network.

The proof of the proposition can be found in Reference 27. Note that the approximation ratio represents the worst case that can be achieved for the centralized algorithm and is rather conservative. In general, there are not many idle nodes in the network and nodes are either transmitters or receivers, especially when many-to-many communication is enabled. In that case, it is unnecessary to consider the suppression of a potential idle node when a stream is selected, and the approximation ratio can be improved to $1/(2 \max_i \{N_i^{ant}\} + 2)$ when all the nodes are active transmitter or receivers.

7.4 Packet scheduling with relay transmission

In order to achieve the optimum system performance, it is essential for a scheduling scheme to determine the set of nodes that serve as the transmitters and the packets to be transmitted in a transmission duration, and assign them to the appropriate antennas for transmissions. The coordination among nodes and the selection of antennas to complete these procedures in a distributed manner are highly nontrivial. The need of invoking relay transmissions upon severe channel conditions adds in significantly more challenges. In this section, we design a distributed scheduling algorithm to fully exploit the multiplexing gain enabled by cooperative MIMO transmission and diversity gain enabled by cooperative relay transmission for overall higher system performance. Specifically, our scheduling has the following features for relay handling.

Simple formulation of a candidate relay set for a packet: The nodes in a neighbourhood collaboratively determine if a relay transmission is needed without sophisticated signalling.

Simple priority-based relay selection without extra signalling: A candidate relay node schedules the transmissions of relay packets with its own packets based on their relevant priorities. As the relevant priority of relay packets to existing packets in different candidate relay nodes are different, our scheduling naturally selects the relay transmission among a group of candidate relay nodes.

Support of load balancing and reduction of delay impact on relay nodes: By incorporating delay into priority in our scheduling, a packet that experiences a longer delay as a result of repeated transmission failures of its source node has its priority increased, which may be higher than some packets at a candidate relay node (especially when the relay node has a lower load). It is therefore more likely for a relay node with lower traffic to forward the relay packets, which would balance the load of nodes in a neighbourhood and the relay transmission would not significantly impact the transmission of an overloaded candidate relay node. In addition, with extra packets buffered to forward for other nodes, a candidate relay node could have a higher priority of being scheduled for transmission.

Receiver-facilitated reduction of redundant relay transmission: As a node self-determines if it can be a relay in a time slot based on the priority of the cached packet to avoid signalling overhead, there is a likelihood that multiple nodes may attempt to perform relay transmission. Our MAC scheme let the receiver to select the relay as discussed at the end of Section 7.4.1.2.

From the problem formulation in Section 7.3, it is clear that the scheduling problem has to determine the values of the four parameter set: $\{t_j\}$, $\{h_j\}$, $\{y_{ij}\}$ and $\{a_{ijk}\}$ to assign a packet to an appropriate transmitter antenna in order to maximize the total weighted rate of the network. In a practical half-duplex network, it is reasonable to divide the problem into two parts: transmitter selection and stream allocation. In the first phase, a set of nodes are selected as transmitter nodes, and for each selected node, it needs to determine the number of packets to transmit in the current transmission duration. Thus the values of $\{t_j\}$, $\{h_j\}$ and $\{y_{ij}\}$ are determined. The decision in our scheduling is made based on the transmission priority of the packets in queue, and the antenna constraints of the transmitter nodes and receiver nodes. In the second phase, each selected transmitter node needs to assign its packets to appropriate antennas for transmission based on the number of streams it is allowed to transmit, the priority of the packets, and the channel conditions. Thus, the value of $\{a_{ijk}\}$ is determined. In the next two subsections, we introduce the problem and algorithm for each scheduling phase.

7.4.1 Determination of transmitter nodes and the number of transmission streams

Instead of randomly selecting the transmitter nodes in a TD, in this phase, we propose a *priority-based self-selection* strategy with which an active node self-determines if it can serve as the transmitter and the number of streams to transmit based on the priority of its packets, its transmitter constraint and the decoding constraints of its neighbours. A candidate relay node incorporates the relay packet with its own transmission and participates in the transmitter selection process.

As the selection is performed at the beginning of each TD before any transmissions, the rate information for candidate streams is unavailable. The transmitter node assignment and the number of streams are thus determined with the goal of optimizing the overall priority performance, and the goal of rate optimization is addressed later in the stream allocation phase. The problem in (7.1)–(7.6) is then reduced to the sub-problem formulated as follows:

$$\max \sum_{i \in P_{pkt}} \sum_{j \in R_i \cup \{s_i\}} y_{ij} \mathcal{P}(i) \tag{7.7}$$

$$\sum_{j \in R_i \cup \{s_i\}} y_{ij} \leq 1, i \in P_{pkt} \tag{7.8}$$

$$\sum_{i \in P_{pkt}} y_{ij} \leq N_j^{ant} + (1 - t_j)M, j \in N \tag{7.9}$$

$$\sum_{m \in V_j} \sum_{i \in P_{pkt}} y_{im} \leq N_j^{ant} + (1 - h_j)M, j \in N \tag{7.10}$$

$$t_j + h_j \leq 1, j \in N \tag{7.11}$$

$$y_{ij} \leq t_j, y_{ij} \leq h_{d_i}, t_j, h_j, y_{ij} \in \{0,1\},$$

$$i \in P_{pkt}, j \in N \tag{7.12}$$

where M is a sufficiently large number as defined in Section 7.3. Corresponding to constraints (7.1)–(7.3), (7.8) limits a packet to only one transmitter to avoid simultaneous transmissions of a packet from multiple relay nodes for improved transmission throughput, (7.9) and (7.10) represent degree constraints at a transmitter and a receiver respectively. Note that the set P_{pkt} is updated at the beginning of each TD so that the packets that arrive during the previous TD can be included.

7.4.1.1 Distributed transmitter node selection

A distributed solution for the problem aims at maximizing the objective in (7.7) while probabilistically satisfying constraints (7.8)–(7.12). Let Q_j denote the packet queue at node j, where original packets and relay packets are sorted in a descending order of their priorities. Let N_j^0 be the proposed number of transmission streams, obviously $N_j^0 = \min\{N_j^{ant}, |Q_j|\}$. Denote the l-th packet of node j as $p(j, l)$. Parameter U_j is defined to be the priority of the head-of-the-line packets in node j's queue, i.e. $U_j = \sum_{l=1}^{N_j^0} \mathcal{P}_{p(j,l)}$, which is used as the priority of j for scheduling.

In order to avoid unnecessary channel measurement and message processing at a receiver, our algorithm first selects a candidate set of transmitters. To guide the transmitter selection, we introduce a probability P_j^{TX}, below which an active node j can be selected as a transmitter node. Suppose m, a neighbouring node of j, has N_m^{active} neighbouring nodes and can decode N_m^{dec} concurrent streams, which can be obtained from periodic Hello messages sent in the two-hop neighbourhood of j at the network layer. If the average number of streams from a single transmitter node around a receiver m is known and denoted as $\bar{N}_{V_m}^{allo}$, in order to not exceed its decoding capacity, m generally only allows $\tilde{N}_m = N_m^{dec}/\bar{N}_{V_m}^{allo}$ nodes among its N_m^{active} neighbours to transmit in a TD. That is, each of the nodes around m is allowed to have a probability of $N_m^{dec}/(\bar{N}_{V_m}^{allo} N_m^{active})$ to serve as the transmitter.

As $\bar{N}_{V_m}^{allo}$ is hard to know before scheduling is performed, a node can at most have a probability of N_m^{dec}/N_m^{active} to serve as the transmitter. The parameter P_j^{TX} of j can then be calculated as follows to consider the decoding capability of all its neighbouring receiver nodes:

$$P_j^{TX} = \min_{m \in \mathcal{V}_j}(N_m^{dec}/N_m^{active}) \tag{7.13}$$

Instead of only considering the decoding capability of the selected receiver nodes which is not available at the selection time, our selection considers the decoding capability of all the neighbouring nodes and is more conservative.

With this calculation, when there is only a small number of nodes around each receiver, e.g. P_j^{TX} calculated in (7.13) has a value larger than 1, there is a possibility that all the nodes within a neighbourhood are selected as the transmitters. For example, if the network has only two nodes and each node can decode up to four streams, both nodes may be selected as transmitters and it is not possible to complete the transmission. To avoid this problem, when $P_j^{TX} \geq 1$, the value of P_j^{TX} is replaced with $P_j^{TX} = \max_{m \in \mathcal{V}_j}(N_m^{active}/(N_m^{active} + 1))$, so that at least one node will be kept as the receiver.

The priority of a node can be attached with periodic Hello messages sent at the network layer, and updated with the data packets sent. The priority of the active nodes not having packets sent in a TD can be predicted as the time moves forward. A node j can then record the maximum priority U_j^{max} and the minimum priority U_j^{min} of all the N_j^{active} active nodes in its neighbourhood and itself, and also calculate the average priority $\bar{U}_j$ as $\bar{U}_j = (\sum_{m=1}^{N_j^{active}} U_m + U_j)/(N_j^{active} + 1)$.

To avoid extra signaling and control overhead, an active node j *self-decides* if it should be selected as a transmitter node by calculating an index number r_j^{TX} as follows:

$$r_j^{TX} = \begin{cases} (\bar{U}_j - U_j)/(U_j^{max} - U_j^{min}) + \gamma_j & \text{if } U_j^{max} \neq U_j^{min} \\ \gamma_j & \text{if } U_j^{max} = U_j^{min} \end{cases} \tag{7.14}$$

where the parameter γ_j is uniformly distributed in the range $[0, 1]$ and randomly generated by a node j in each transmission duration (TD) to provide some fairness among nodes. The factor $(\bar{U}_j - U_j)/(U_j^{max} - U_j^{min})$ is used to give the higher priority node a larger probability for transmission. In a TD, if $r_j^{TX} < P_j^{TX}$, node j is selected as a transmitter node; otherwise, it has no right of transmission. Our transmitter selection algorithm gives preference to a node with a higher service priority and/or a larger load and hence longer delay, and thus supports load balancing. Moreover, as the priority parameter dynamically reflects the queuing status of nodes so a node does not always have higher priority than its neighbours, it helps ensure fairness over the network.

Note that in this phase relay packets and original packets are treated equally, and the value of $\{x_j\}$ is determined.

7.4.1.2   Distributed determination of the number of streams

Through the procedure described next in Section 7.5, a receiver node estimates the total number of candidate streams it may receive N_j^{rec} and broadcasts it together with the number of streams it is able to decode N_j^{dec}. These two parameters are used at a transmitter node to determine the actual number of transmission streams it is allowed to transmit.

Denote the set of receiver nodes within the transmission range of a transmitter node j as X_j^{rc}. In order to ensure all the receiver nodes in its neighbourhood to have high probability of meeting their degree constraints, j constrains its number of sending streams to a number N_j^{allo} as follows:

$$N_j^{allo} = N_j^0 \min_{m \in X_j^{rc}} \left(\frac{N_m^{dec}}{N_m^{rec}} \right) \tag{7.15}$$

Note that the value N_j^{allo} may be a fractional number. To achieve a higher accuracy in calculating N_j^{allo} than using simple rounding, let $N_{j,0}^{allo} = N_j^{allo} - \lfloor N_j^{allo} \rfloor$. If $N_{j,0}^{allo} > 0$, generate a random variable β_j uniformly distributed in $[0, 1]$. If $\beta_j \le N_{j,0}^{allo}$, $N_j^{allo} = \lfloor N_j^{allo} \rfloor + 1$; otherwise, $N_j^{allo} = \lfloor N_j^{allo} \rfloor$. So far, the number of streams to be transmitted is determined.

7.4.2   Allocation to antennas

In this phase, N_j^{allo} data packets of node j are allocated to N_j^{allo} out of N_j^{ant} antennas for transmission. For a node that does not serve as a relay, it simply considers the first N_j^{allo} data packets in the queue. For a potential relay node, it would waste network resource if it forwards the same packet concurrently with other relay nodes. Our scheduling scheme naturally selects the forwarding nodes based on the relevant priority of the to-be relayed packet and the priorities of the other packets of a relay node. After this self-selection process, there is still the possibility that some relay nodes choose the same TD to forward i. To further reduce the chance of unnecessary relay forwarding, when the destination receiver receives multiple relay transmission requests, it selects the relay node with the best channel condition to forward the packet. The rest of the requesting relay nodes can use the slot to send other packets. More details of the relay selection operation are presented in Section 7.5.

The packets may have different destination nodes thus varied link loss, and the spatial channels from different elements of the antenna array undergo different fading. As discussed in [20], the data rate can be improved by opportunistically allocating the packets to transmitted antennas. Moreover, with channel information available at transmitters' side, selection diversity is shown to outperform space-time coding in improving the link reliability [28]. With the goal of maximizing transmission rate, the stream allocation problem is essentially a bipartite maximum matching problem.

Construct a graph $G = (V_1 \cup V_2, E)$ for a transmitter node j. V_1 denotes the set of packets to be allocated to antennas and V_2 denotes the set of transmitting antennas of j. Thus $|V_1| = N_j^{allo}$ and $|V_2| = N_j^{ant}$. Form an edge (v, u) between v and u where $v \in V_1$ and $u \in V_2$, and the weight of the edge is $w_{vu} = \mathcal{R}(v, u)$. Here $\mathcal{R}(v, u)$ is the rate of the stream to transmit a packet represented by node v to its destination node through the antenna represented by node u, which is estimated through signal exchange as discussed in Section 7.5. If $|V_1| \neq |V_2|$, add dummy nodes to make $|V_1| = |V_2|$ and the edges connected to a dummy node has weight 0.

By solving the maximum weight-matching problem formulated above (i.e. using successive shortest path algorithm [29]) and then deleting the dummy nodes and edges connected to them, the optimum solution of the allocation is derived. Let $|V| = |V_1| + |V_2|$, the complexity of the algorithm is bounded by $O(|V|\log|V|)$.

7.5 Protocol design

In the previous section, the scheduling is performed in each transmission-duration to determine the transmission schedule of the packets, including original packets and relay packets, in the queue of each node. However, the details about cooperative relay transmission, i.e., how to maintain the queue to store relay packets, how to trigger and enable a relay node to transmit relay packets have not been addressed yet. In this section, we propose the protocol to facilitate cooperative relay transmission in a MIMO-based ad hoc network and implement the distributed scheduling algorithm described in Section 4. We first give an overview of the relay operations in Section 7.5.1, and then describe the details of the protocol in Section 7.5.2. An example is presented in Section 7.5.3.

7.5.1 Relay operations

There are several challenges arising in integrating the cooperative relay transmission with the cooperative MIMO multiplexing transmission scheme. We propose a few strategies to address the issues, some of which are also mentioned in previous sections, and we summarize them here for the protocol design.

7.5.1.1 Finding candidate relay nodes

In a conventional relay strategy, a source often broadcasts a relay request explicitly, and waits for replies from the potential relay nodes. This process not only introduces extra signalling overhead but also adds in delay for relay transmission. Instead, the process of finding candidate relays in our scheme is automatically performed at qualified nodes without involving the source and destination of a packet. Specifically, a node r_l identifies its potential of being a candidate relay node of a packet i which is targeted to d_i when successfully receiving the packet from its sender s_i, either because r_l is idle or because r_l could decode i when receiving its own packet with its multi-packet reception capability. If the destination of the data packet i is also in r_l's neighbour list, r_l temporarily stores i in its buffer with the current priority of i. If i is successfully received by d_i, r_l removes i from its buffer; otherwise, the priority of i is updated as its buffering time in r_l increases. In a dense network where a packet could be overheard and buffered by too many potential relay nodes, to avoid excessive and unnecessary buffering, a node may only buffer a packet with certain probability, or a sender could tag the packets that may need relay.

7.5.1.2 Triggering of relay transmission

Instead of explicitly invoking relay transmission, in our scheme, triggering of relay transmission and selection of relay node is incorporated with normal packet scheduling. If a failed direct transmission is detected, i.e. a candidate relay r_i receives packet i from s_i but does not receive the successful reception acknowledgement for packet i (either through ACK-I or through ACK-II as described in Section 7.5.1.4) in the same TD, r_i immediately moves the relay packet i from the buffer to its MAC queue, and treats it as a normal packet waiting for transmission. The node then serves as a relay node in the following TDs. There may be multiple candidate relay nodes for a packet, and the packet to relay is generally placed in different positions of the packet queues in different candidate relay nodes depending on the relative priority of the packets. In a TD, a candidate relay node that has the relay packet scheduled to transmit is implicitly selected as the relay node of the packet. With multiple candidate relay nodes, as long as a subset of the nodes receives a packet from the source, the packet can be relayed to the receiver. Multiple relay nodes and maybe also the source node of i may intend to transmit it in the same TD, if i happens to be a head-of-the-line packet in all of their queues. In order to reduce the chance of unnecessary concurrent transmission, the targeted receiver node counts the number of successful transmission requests for the same packet. The node with the best channel condition is selected to serve as the packet sender and the selection is broadcasted by the receiver. In summary, our scheduling strategy triggers relay transmission through the implicit self-selection by candidate relay nodes and explicit selection by the destination receiver to reduce the signalling overhead as well as to avoid redundant transmission.

7.5.1.3 Constraining the delay of relay transmission

To avoid excessive traffic increase and occupation of network resource, a retransmission threshold F is introduced that a packet is dropped if its reception fails after F TDs has elapsed since its first direct transmission. To ensure that the source node and all candidate relay nodes have a consensus on the packet transmission status, a packet transmitted from its source node is attached with a time-stamp indicating the current elapsed time since its initial transmission, so that candidate relays can record this stamp and update it as the queuing time increases. If the transmission fails continuously over a period of time, e.g. longer than $3F$ TDs since the first direct transmission, a source node may even give up its transmission towards a particular receiver as the continuous failure indicates a long-term breakage of the link, e.g. topology change due to mobility. It may then look for an alternative path to the destination, e.g. through multi-hop relays.

7.5.1.4 Broadcast of packet reception status

The information about successful or failed reception of a packet is usually broadcast through ACKs. However, as all receivers in a TD send ACK simultaneously as described in Sections 7.5.2, only nodes that are not receivers in the current TD can receive the ACKs. As a candidate relay node may serve as a either transmitter or a receiver in a TD, it is necessary to inform all of them about the updated reception status, so that successfully received packets can be removed while unsuccessfully received packets can have their priority increased. In addition, a source may not be able to get the ACK if the channel condition from the destination to it is very poor, and a potential relay node also needs the reception status to determine whether the packet should be moved from the buffer to the MAC queue. To address those issues, an extra ACK phase is introduced into the protocol, during which the information included in the first ACK is rebroadcast by nodes that receive it in the current TD. Through the two phases of ACK from multiple nodes, extra diversity is provided to guarantee the correct update of the packet reception status for all the nodes in concern. To differentiate between the two ACK messages, they are named ACK-I and ACK-II, respectively. In the proposed MAC scheme, the data transmission can be in burst, so the overhead of ACK signalling is relatively small.

7.5.1.5   Rate determination

As described in the protocol, both transmitter nodes and receiver nodes are able to estimate the full channel condition matrix through training sequences. Also, a receiver node can estimate the interference and noise around it, and announce this information to the corresponding senders. With the channel matrix and the interference and noise at the receiver, a transmitter can determine the rate to use for transmission. If a packet is scheduled for its first direct transmission and the link to its destination is estimated to be severe, the source node uses a default moderate transmission rate for its transmission, so as to increase the chance of having some relay node successfully receive the packet as well as avoid wasting the transmission opportunity in the current TD. Note that the transmission of a specific packet is cancelled for the current TD if a sender node could not receive response, i.e. CTS, from the corresponding receiver after sending an initial handshaking signal, as it can be expected that the requested receiver is currently a transmitter or the link condition is temporarily poor. However, if the response from a receiver is consecutively missing, e.g. for more than F of transmission requests, it is indicated that the link between the source and destination undergoes relatively long term degradation. In such a case, the source node may still initiate transmission in the following $2F$ TDs and send out the packet using the default moderate transmission rate, in the hope that it can be received and forwarded by some relay nodes in the neighbourhood.

7.5.2   Protocol details

Based on the above operations, we propose a TDMA-based MAC protocol to support the cooperative relay transmission in a MIMO-based ad hoc network. A time frame is divided into five phases with different transmission duration, namely RTS, CTS, DATA, ACK-I and ACK-II. Note that slot synchronization is currently achievable in the IEEE 802.11 family of protocols. By taking advantage of various diversity techniques, our scheme effectively increases the SINR of received signals, which helps improve the accuracy of synchronization as well as mitigate the impact of asynchronicity in a distributed scenario. A group of random access codes, called ID code, which are almost orthogonal for different nodes and assigned similarly to that in Reference 30, are used to mask and differentiate simultaneously transmitted control signals from selected nodes, and used for transmission coordination and channel estimation.

RTS: Using algorithm in Section 7.4.1.1, nodes that determine themselves to be transmitter nodes broadcast RTSs in an RTS transmission phase. For a transmitter node j, the RTS message contains the number of streams it plans to transmit N_j^0, its node ID and the IDs of the destination nodes. The preamble of a packet is used as the training sequence (without incurring extra overhead for adding in pilot signal) for channel estimation purpose. The preamble of an RTS message is transmitted rotationally from each antenna so the full channel condition matrix can be estimated at receiver nodes. RTS messages sent from different transmitters are masked by different ID code to allow a receiver to differentiate the messages. As the number of antennas is generally small and only the preamble of the RTS message is transmitted through all antennas, the total transmission delay for channel estimation purpose is small. The full knowledge of the channel as a result of the estimation, however, could enable simultaneous transmission of multiple spatial streams and bring in multi-fold capacity gain [20] and thus delay reduction.

CTS: The RTSs are received at receiver nodes, where channel matrices are estimated by extracting the preambles. A receiver node m also estimates the number of streams it may receive $N_m^{rec} = \sum_{j \in \mathcal{V}_m, x_j = 1} N_j^0$. Constrained by its degree of freedom, m can decode at most N_m^{dec} streams simultaneously. An RTS message can be from the source and/or candidate relay nodes. If m receives multiple RTSs on the transmission of i in current TD and is the target receiver of i, it then selects the node r_i which has the best channel condition between r_i and m to forward the packet. Based on the decoding capability and the signal strength received, m estimates the interference plus noise level (SINR) for candidate transmission nodes. In general, SINR can be quantized into different levels and only the index of level is needed in feedback instead of its absolute value, which can effectively reduce the amount of overhead. Finally, m broadcast a CTS message including SINR, N_m^{rec}, N_m^{dec} and r_i. Note that CTS message is also masked by ID code and the preamble is transmitted rotationally from each antenna of m for transmitter nodes to estimate the full channel condition matrix.

DATA: In the DATA phase, a sender first determines the number of streams it is allowed to transmit using the algorithm in Section 7.4.1.2, based on the information received from CTSs sent by neighbouring receivers. It should also select the packets to be transmitted based on the receivers' confirmation for the initial handshaking messages. Specifically, a node should check if it has been selected as the sole forwarder by the receiver if a request for relay transmission is sent earlier. If a node is the source for a packet and the CTS has been missing for more than F times, it would also send out this packet for relay purpose. The transmitter then estimates the transmission rate from each antenna based on the estimated channel condition and interference at a destined receiver, and transmits the packets from the antennas selected using the maximum weight-matching algorithm in Section 7.4.2. A receiver node then differentiates all streams it receives and extracts the data packets targeted for it. Instead of discarding packets transmitted through interference streams, a receiver buffers an overheard packet if it is within the transmission range of the packet destination for potential relay transmission.

ACK-I: Receiver nodes broadcast ACKs about those successfully received packets, which include the original sources of the packets. These messages are received by nodes that are not receivers of the current TD.

ACK-II: If a relayed packet is received successfully, the source node as well as all the potential relay nodes should remove it from their buffers and queues in order to avoid redundant transmissions. Some of these nodes may not be able to receive the ACKs as they are also in transmitting states during the transmission of ACKs. After the transmission of ACK-I, ACK-II is rebroadcast by non-receiver nodes in the current TD. With the transmission of ACKs in consecutive phases, it not only ensures all candidate relay nodes to learn the packet transmission status but also guarantees that the original packet sender is informed about the successful transmission of the relay packet. In the case that the channel condition between the source and the destination is poor and ACK-I message from the destination cannot be received by the source node, the rebroadcast of ACK-II messages from intermediate nodes plays an important role to avoid the continuous redundant retransmissions and thus more waste of wireless resources. In this way, a potential relay node that successfully overhears a packet but does not have a functional link towards the destination will also be informed by the sender through ACK-II, so that it will not vainly consider relaying the packet.

7.5.3   An example

In this section, we give a brief example to explain the process of cooperative relay transmission. In the simple topology shown in Figure 7.3, node 1 has a packet to transmit to node 4, nodes 2 and 3 are in the neighbourhood of both nodes 1 and 4 but are not in each other's neighbourhood. Assume the channels are with good quality between node 1 and node 2/3 and between node 2/3 and node 4, but the channels between nodes 1 and 4 experiences severe fading. In the transmission duration shown in Figure 7.3(a), node 1 initiates a direct transmission towards node 4. As node 2 and 3 are both in the receiving mode, they overhear the packet, as

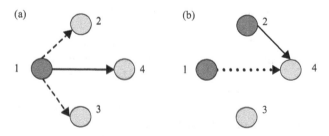

Figure 7.3   An example of cooperative relay transmission

indicated by the dashed edges. Perceiving that there is no ACK for the packet from node 4 due to the link failure, nodes 2 and 3 both store the packet into their own MAC queue and treat it equally with their own direct packet so that they are potential relays for the packet. In a following transmission duration shown in Figure 7.3(b), according to the transmitter selection criterion, nodes 1 and 2 could both be selected as transmitters and nodes 3 and 4 are still in the receiving mode. Suppose that the priority of the packet from node 1 to node 4 is relatively high, and both nodes 1 and 2 indicate their preference to send it to node 4 in the RTSs. By receiving the RTSs and completing channel estimation, node 4 selects node 2 as the transmitter for the packet as the channel condition from node 2 to node 4 is better than that from node 1 to node 4, in order to avoid redundant transmission. Therefore, node 1 withholds the transmission, as indicated by the dotted edge, and node 2 successfully relays the packet to node 4. In the ACK-I phase, node 4 feeds back the information about the successful reception. After receiving the ACK, potential nodes (original source or relays) that are currently transmitters, i.e. nodes 1 and 2, remove the packet from their queues. In order to make sure the packet is also removed from the queues of candidate relay nodes that currently serve as receivers (which are also in the process of sending out ACK to their corresponding transmitters) and are not able to receive ACK-I, e.g. node 3, transmitter nodes that have received the ACK-I, i.e. nodes 1 and 2, send out ACK-II to further rebroadcast the successful reception information. To this end, the packet is successfully transmitted through the cooperative relay transmission and removed from all queues.

7.6 Performance evaluation

In this section, we evaluate the performance of our proposed algorithms through simulations based on a detailed MATLAB simulator we have built. We consider an ad hoc network with random topology where nodes are distributed uniformly over a 1250 m × 1250 m area. Each node is equipped with an array of 4 antennas and has a reference transmission range of 250 m as in a standard IEEE 802.11 wireless network. Both path loss and independent Rayleigh fading are incorporated for each wireless link between an antenna pair. For each node, the number of incoming data packets is Poisson distributed with a given mean value λ and the destination of each packet is chosen at random. The size of a packet is 200 bytes. A simulation result is obtained by averaging over ten runs of simulations with different seeds.

The two-phase scheduling algorithm proposed in Section 7.4 is implemented based on the MAC protocol described in Section 7.5. The Cooperative Relayed Spatial Multiplexing schemes proposed in this paper are named as CRSM-C or CRSM-D, respectively, depending on whether a centralized scheme or a distributed scheme is used for the determination of transmitter nodes and the number of transmission streams. Correspondingly, we implemented two reference TDMA-based schemes in the distributed manner for performance comparison. One scheme is the Distributed Opportunistic and Cooperative Spatial Multiplexing (OCSM-D) scheme proposed in Reference 20, which does not involve a relay transmission, the other scheme is also based on OCSM-D but have random relay selection enabled for performance enhancement, which is denoted as Distributed Random Relayed Spatial Multiplexing (RRSM-D). The metrics we use are throughput and normalized delay. Throughput is the total effective data rate of the network averaged over the number of transmission durations. Delay time is defined as the number of transmission durations a packet waits in the queue before it is removed from the MAC queue. The transmission delay includes the time for transmission of control packets. For the convenience of comparison, the results of delay are normalized to the maximum value in each figure. We investigate the impact on network performance due to four factors, namely node density, link failure ratio, packet arrival rate and retransmission threshold. The retransmission threshold defined in Section 7.5.1 is in the unit of TD, and a packet is dropped from both the source queue and queues of candidate relay nodes when the time lasted from the initial packet transmission exceeds the threshold. If not otherwise specified, the number of nodes in the network is 100, the link failure ratio is 0.3, the average packet arrival rate λ is 0.5 and the retransmission threshold is 8.

The impact of node density is shown in Figure 7.4. Increased node density leads to heavier traffic and also provides more links among nodes in a network. In case of severe links, the two CRSM schemes have a higher possibility of finding candidate relay nodes to assist in transmission by taking advantage of the improved connectivity. In Figure 7.4(a), CRSM-D is observed to improve the throughput up to 53% compared to OCSM-D. Effective scheduling of packets with relay also reduces the queuing delay as seen in Figure 7.4(b). Compared with RRSM-D that uses a preselected relay, CRSM-D implicitly and adaptively selects the node scheduled to transmit the first as the relay, which not only helps to speed up relay forwarding but also helps to balance load among nodes. These benefits are reflected in the up to 14% improvement in throughput and 13% reduction in delay.

A link is considered to be failed if a packet transmitted through it cannot be received successfully by its receiver. Link failure can be a result of path loss, deep

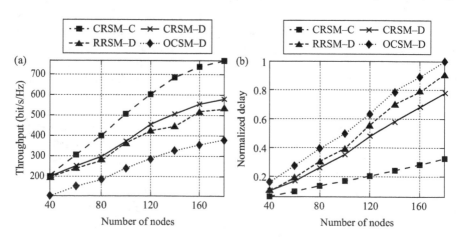

Figure 7.4   Impact of node density: (a) throughput, (b) normalized delay

fading of channels, mobility of nodes, etc. We use link failure ratio (LFR) to model the percentage of failed links over all direct data transmission links between each pair of source and destination in the network. The failed links are randomly selected based on the link failure ratio and they are disconnected throughout the current run of simulation. The two CRSM schemes are shown to have a robust performance under different link failure ratios, as in Figure 7.5. In Figure 7.5(a), while the throughput of OCSM-D degrades tremendously with increasing LFR, only a slight degradation in throughput is observed with both CRSM schemes. As the CRSM schemes can smartly leverage the functional relay links to send packets out, it helps maintain the throughput performance. The throughput of CRSM-D is three times that of OCSM-D when a frequent link breakage occurs at $LPF= 0.6$, and the delay reduction is up to 50%. A higher link breakage ratio would lead to increased delay. The significant performance improvement demonstrates the effectiveness of adaptively using relay in MIMO transmissions to improve reliability in a harsh transmission environment. Although RRSM-D also supports the use of relay, the random relay selection which does not take advantage of the channel conditions to select node for more reliable relay transmission is observed to be less effective than the adaptive scheme of cooperative relay proposed in this paper, as the throughput drops faster with increasing LFR compared with CRSM-D. RRSM-D has up to 26% lower throughput and 25% higher delay compared with CRSM-D.

The mean packet arrival rate λ captures the traffic load in a network. By adaptively using cooperative relay transmissions, high rate links are more efficiently utilized to schedule heavier traffic load. In Figure 7.6(a), even with the heaviest traffic load, CRSM-D still achieves 35.7% higher throughput than OCSM-D. Although higher traffic increases queuing delay of packets due to limited network capacity, the delay of CRSM-D scheme is about 30% lower than that of OCSM-D. This demonstrates that even in the heavy traffic load condition, the relay can effectively improve performance. The node with the lowest load will be

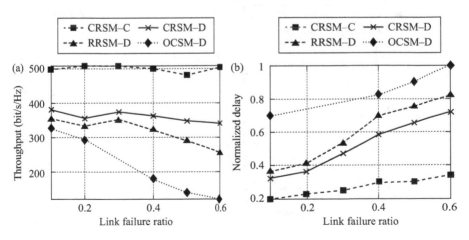

Figure 7.5   Impact of link failure ratio: (a) throughput, (b) normalized delay

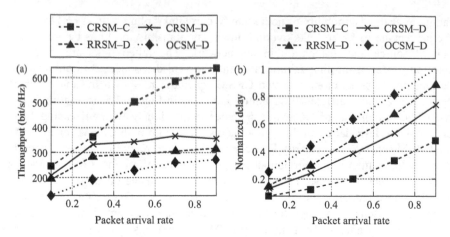

Figure 7.6   Impact of packet arrival rate: (a) throughput, (b) normalized delay

naturally selected as the relay. Meanwhile, CRSM-D consistently outperforms RRSM-D by up to 20% higher throughput and 19% lower delay, which further demonstrates the advantages of using adaptive cooperative relay instead of conventional relay schemes. In the case of heavy load, the packets are backlogged in the queue of nodes, and the delay increases significantly.

Retransmission is a common strategy used to deal with temporary transmission failure. The performances of CRSM and OCSM are compared in Figure 7.7 under different values of the retransmission threshold F, as introduced in Section 7.5. In CRSM schemes, packets experienced direct transmission failure can be forwarded through relay links, which may have better link conditions than the direct link. With increased value of F, both CRSM schemes keep a nearly constant throughput values, while OCSM-D undergoes 33.5% throughput reduction from $F= 2$ to

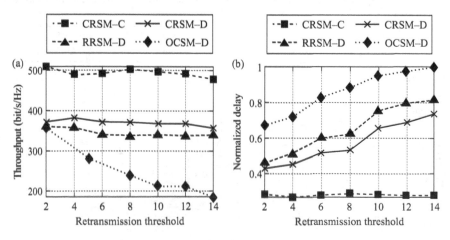

Figure 7.7   Impact of retransmission threshold: (a) throughput, (b) normalized delay

$F = 14$. Even though more retransmissions help to increase the probability of successful packet reception, transmissions over poor links for a longer period of time would consume more network resources. On the contrary, both CRSM schemes actually take advantage of a larger F to conduct relay transmissions through adaptive scheduling. The delays of two OCSM schemes and CRSM-D scheme all increase with F with the increase of time to keep the packets in buffers, while CRSM-D remains to have much lower delay (up to 40%) than OCSM-D under all values of F. With varied values of F, CRSM-D still takes advantage of the adaptive relay selection to achieve both higher throughput and lower delay than RRSM-D.

7.7   Further development

In recent years, many efforts have been made in developing MAC schemes to support MIMO transmission and cooperative diversity in ad hoc networks.

In Reference 12, spatial diversity is explored to combat fading and achieve robustness. Layered space-time multi-user detection and its role in PHY-MAC cross-layer design are analysed in Reference 14. In Reference 15, spatial multiplexing with antenna subset selection for data packet transmission is proposed. The optimization considerations for MAC layer design in ad hoc networks with MIMO links is discussed in Reference 16, and unified representation of the physical layer capabilities of different types of smart antennas, and unified medium access algorithms are presented in Reference 31. The authors of Reference 18 exploits the benefits of using multiple antennas to achieve flow-level QoS in multi-hop wireless networks. In Reference 20, an opportunistic and cooperative multiplexing scheme is proposed to better exploit spatial/multi-user diversity to improve transmission capacity and support different traffic demands in the network. An adaptive and distributed solution considering the heterogeneity of antenna array sizes of network nodes is presented in Reference 32. However, none of these solutions considers the potential benefits of using cooperative relay in MIMO-based ad hoc networks.

Though cooperative diversity has been extensively studied theoretically [22], there are limited work that investigate the solution of scheduling in practical network implementations. In Reference 23, the authors proposed relaying strategies to increase the system reliability and the work in Reference 33 tries to emulate the function and achieve the transmit diversity gain of using space-time codes in a distributed manner through node cooperation without the use of multi-antenna arrays. A multi-layer approach for exploiting virtual MISO links in ad hoc networks is presented in Reference 17 and an optimal relay assignment is discussed in Reference 34. A relay selection scheme is proposed in Reference 35 for multi-node decode-and-forward cooperative scenarios via the available partial channel state information (CSI) at the source and the relays, and a distributed relay selection scheme is proposed in Reference 36 using finite-state Markov channels. However, the scale of network considered in these studies is relatively small, and they do not provide MAC protocols to implement in a wireless multi hop wireless mesh network. The utilization of cooperative relay in wireless cognitive radio networks is investigated in Reference 24 and a new MAC protocol is proposed. In this work, cooperative relay is only considered for networks with single antenna nodes, while it requires specific strategies to leverage the benefits of cooperative relay in a MIMO-based network. In Reference 37, the authors analytically considers a general multiple-antenna network with multiple relays in terms of the diversity-multiplexing trade-off. In Reference 19, retransmission diversity through node cooperation is investigated in specific homogeneous omni-directional and smart antenna networks. Cooperative spatial multiplexing is systematically implemented with hybrid ARQ in Reference 38, however, it lacks a detailed algorithm and protocol to specifically enable cooperative transmission which is generally very challenging to achieve in a dynamic network.

Our work distinguishes itself from the aforementioned work in that it adaptively adopts relay forwarding with cooperative MIMO multiplexing to significantly improve the throughput while supporting transmission reliability. Based on the framework proposed in this chapter, more aspects can be taken into consideration when designing a cooperative relay enabled MAC protocol. For example, power consumption may be considered when selecting the relay nodes to favour nodes with higher remaining power. The mechanism of integrating adaptive relay and cooperative MIMO multiplexing may also be extended to other types of networks, such as wireless sensor networks, wireless mesh network and Femtocell networks, with the benefits of significantly improved reliability. These could all be the directions for further development of the proposed mechanism.

7.8 Conclusion

Ad hoc networks are popularly used in military and emergency rescue environments. In addition, there are increasing interests in applying ad hoc networks to connect various wireless devices to enable more effective wireless applications and mobile computing capabilities. All these applications require higher network throughput and reliability. In this work, we design scheduling algorithms and MAC protocol to enable cooperative relay transmission in MIMO-based ad hoc networks, in order to jointly exploit the cooperative multiplexing gain and cooperative diversity gain to achieve overall higher data rate and lower delay under harsh channel conditions. We formulate the problem of packet scheduling with cooperative relay in MIMO ad hoc networks as an integer-programming problem, and propose both centralized and distributed solutions to support relay transmissions. We also design an effective MAC protocol to facilitate the implementation of the distributed scheduling algorithm. Through extensive simulations, our scheme is shown to outperform the reference MIMO scheme that does not use relay or employs random relay selection, with significantly higher throughput and reduced average delay. This demonstrates the importance of incorporating relay transmissions in MIMO-based ad hoc networks and the effectiveness of the proposed algorithm in enabling concurrent MIMO and relay transmissions.

References

1. IEEE Strandards. *IEEE Standard 802.16e*
2. IEEE Strandards. *IEEE Standard 802.11n*
3. Gesbert D., Shafi M., Shiu D., Smith P. J., and Naguib A. 'From theory to practice: an overview of MIMO space-time coded wireless systems'. *IEEE J. Select. Areas Commun.*, 21(3):281–302, Apr. 2003
4. Foschini G. J. 'Layered space-time architecture for wireless communication in fading environments when using multi-element antennas'. *Bell Labs Tech. J.*, 1(2):41–59, 1996
5. Wolniansky P. W., Foschini G. J., Golden G. D. and Valenzuela R. A. 'V-BLAST: An architecture for realizing very high data rates over the rich-scattering wireless channel'. In *Proc. of ISSSE-98*:295–300, Sep. 1998
6. Alamouti S. M. 'A simple transmit diversity technique for wireless communications'. *IEEE J. Select. Areas Commun.*, pp. 1451–1458, Oct. 1998
7. Tarokh V., Seshardi N. and Calderbank A. 'Space-time codes for high data rate wireless communication: Performance criteria and code construction'. *IEEE Trans. Inform. Theory*, 44(2):744–765, Mar. 1998
8. Tarokh V., Seshardi N. and Calderbank A. 'Space-time block codes from orthogonal designs'. *IEEE Trans. Inform. Theory*, (5):1456–1467, Jul. 1999
9. Ajib W. and Haccoun D. 'An overview of scheduling algorithms in MIMO-based fourth-generation wireless systems'. *IEEE Network*, (5):43–48, Sept.–Oct. 2005
10. Lau V. K. N., Liu Y. and Chen T. A. 'Optimal multi-user space time scheduling for wireless communications'. In *Proc. IEEE VTC 2002-Fall*, pp. 1939–1942, 2002
11. Aktas D. and El Gamal H. 'Multiuser scheduling for MIMO wireless systems'. In *Proc. IEEE VTC 2003-Fall*, pp. 1743–1747, 2003
12. Hu M. and Zhang J. 'MIMO ad hoc networks: Medium access control, saturation throughput, and optimal hop distance'. *Journal of Communications and Networks, Special Issue on Mobile Ad Hoc Networks*, pp. 317–330, 2004
13. Bhatia R. and Li L. 'Throughput optimization of wireless mesh networks with MIMO links'. In *Proc. IEEE INFOCOM 2007*, May 2007
14. Levorato M., Tomasin S., Casari P. and Zorzi M. 'Analysis of spatial multiplexing for cross-layer design of MIMO ad hoc networks'. In *Proc. IEEE VTC-2006* Spring, pp. 1146–1150, May 2006
15. Park M., Heath R. and Nettles S. 'Improving throughput and fairness of MIMO ad hoc networks using antenna selection diversity'. In *Proc. IEEE Globecom 2004*, Nov. 2004
16. Sundaresan K., Sivakumar R., Ingram M. and Chang T.-Y. 'A fair medium access control protocol for ad-hoc networks with MIMO links'. In *Proc. IEEE INFOCOM 2004*, Jun. 2004

17. Jakllari G., Krishnamurthy S. V., Faloutsos M., Krishnamurthy P. V. and Ercetin O. A. 'Framework for distributed spatio-temporal communications in mobile ad hoc networks'. In *Proc. IEEE INFOCOM 2006*, pp. 1–13, Apr. 2006

18. Hamdaoui B. and Ramanathan P. 'A cross-layer admission control framework for wireless ad-hoc networks using multiple antennas'. *IEEE Trans. on Wireless Communications*, Nov. 2007

19. Sundaresan K. and Sivakumar R. 'Cooperating with smartness: Using heterogeneous smart antennas in ad-hoc networks'. In *Proc. INFOCOM 2007*, pp. 303–311, May 2007

20. Chu S. and Wang X. 'Opportunistic and cooperative spatial multiplexing in MIMO ad hoc networks'. *IEEE Trans. on Networking*, 18(5):1610–1623, Oct. 2010

21. Chu S., Wang X. and Li M. 'Enforcing high-performance operation of multihop wireless networks with MIMO relays'. In *Proc. ICDCS 2012*: 376–385, Jun. 2012

22. Sendonaris A., Erkip E. and Aazhang B. 'User cooperation diversity' part I and part II. *IEEE Trans. Commun.*, 51(11):1927–1948, Nov. 2003

23. Laneman J. N., Tse D. N. C. and Wornell G. W. 'Cooperative diversity in wireless networks: Efficient protocols and outage behavior'. *IEEE Trans. Inform. Theory*, (12):3062–3080, Dec. 2004

24. Zhang Q., Jia J. and Zhang J. 'Cooperative relay to improve diversity in cognitive radio networks'. *IEEE Communications Magazine*, (2):111–117, Feb. 2009

25. Tse D. and Viswanath P. *'Fundamentals of Wireless Communication'*. Cambridge University Press, May 2005

26. Schwartz M. *'Mobile Wireless Communications'*. Cambridge University Press, 2005

27. Chu S., Wang X. and Yang Y. 'Exploiting cooperative relay for high performance communications in MIMO ad hoc networks'. *IEEE Trans. on Computers*, 62(4):716–729, Apr. 2012

28. Pan Y. and Aissa S. 'Performance analysis of selective space-time coding and selection diversity under perfect and imperfect CSI'. In *Proc. PIMRC 2005*, pp. 2371–2375, Sep. 2005

29. Ahuja R. K., Magnanti T. L. and Orlin J. B. *Network Flows: Theory, Algorithms and Applicationss*. Prentice Hall, 1993

30. de Moraes R. M., Sadjadpour H. R. and Garcia-Luna-Aceves J. J. 'Many-to-many communication: A new approach for collaboration in MANETs'. In *Proc. IEEE INFOCOM 2007*, pp. 1829–1837, May 2007

31. Sundaresan K. and Sivakumar R. 'A unified MAC layer framework for Ad-Hoc networks with smart antennas'. In *Proc. ACM MobiHoc 2004*, pp. 244–255, May 2004

32. Chu S. and Wang X. 'Adaptive and distributed scheduling in heterogeneous MIMO-based ad hoc networks'. In *Proc. IEEE MASS 2009*, pp. 217–226, Oct. 2009

33. Cui S., Goldsmith A. J. and Bahai A. 'Energy-efficiency of MIMO and cooperative MIMO in sensor networks'. *IEEE J. Select. Areas of Commun.*, 22(6):1089–1098, August 2004

34. Shi Y., Sharma S., Hou Y. T. and Kompella S. 'Optimal relay assignment for cooperative communications'. In *Proc. ACM Mobihoc 2008*, May 2008

35. Ibrahim A. S., Sadek A. K., Su W., and Liu K. J. R. 'Cooperative communications with relay-selection: When to cooperate and whom to cooperate with?'. *IEEE Trans. on Wireless Commun.*, 7(7):2814–2827, July 2008

36. Wei Y., Yu F. R. and Song M. 'Distributed optimal relay selection in wireless cooperative networks with finite-state markov channels'. *IEEE Trans. on Vehicular Technol.*, 59(5):2149–2158, Jun. 2010

37. Yuksel M. and Erkip E. 'Multiple-antenna cooperative wireless systems: A diversity mmultiplexing tradeoff perspective'. *IEEE Trans. Inform Theory*, Octorber 2007

38. Levorato M., Tomasin S. and Zorzi M. 'Cooperative spatial multiplexing for ad hoc networks with hybrid ARQ: System design and performance analysis'. *IEEE Trans. Commun.*, (9):1545–1555, Sep. 2008

Chapter 8*

Single-path and multipath routings in mobile ad hoc networks

Haseeb Zafar[a], Ivan Andonovic[b], Inayatullah Babar[c] and Sahibzada Mahmud[c]

Abstract

The provisioning of real-time applications such as voice and video over ad hoc networks have received a lot of attention among researchers mainly due to the increasing demand of this service among users. This is particularly challenging due to capacity requirements and stringent delay constraints. In general, wireless nodes have limited resources like capacity and battery power. In multi-hop wireless mobile networks, one of the key issues is how to route packets efficiently. Some of the important factors that need to be considered in designing a routing scheme for ad hoc networks are: minimum delivery latency, higher probability of packet delivery, energy efficiency and adaptability. Therefore, the design of an efficient and reliable routing scheme for such applications is a major challenge. This chapter provides background and describes related research efforts in single path and multipath routing in Mobile ad hoc Networks (MANETs). A brief outline of the operation as well as strengths and limitations of each scheme is presented. In addition, the open issues that must be addressed in the design of efficient routing algorithms are discussed.

8.1 Introduction

MANETs [1] are a key part of the ongoing evolution of wireless communications. In contrast to the traditional infrastructure-based cellular systems, ad hoc networks

*H. F. Rashvand and H.-C. Chao (Eds.), *Dynamic Ad Hoc Networks*, The IET Book Publishing Department, 2013, ISBN 978-1-84919-647-5, eISBN 978-1-84919-648-2
[a]Department of Computer Systems Engineering, University of Engineering and Technology, Peshawar, Pakistan
[b]Department of Electronic & Electrical Engineering, University of Strathclyde, Glasgow, United Kingdom
[c]Department of Electrical Engineering, University of Engineering and Technology, Peshawar, Pakistan

comprise mobile/semi-mobile nodes that do not rely on infrastructure and are free to move, appear and disappear randomly. Each node has the capability to communicate directly with other nodes, acting not only as a mobile wireless host but also as router, forwarding data packets for other nodes. In other words, ad hoc networks are self-creating, self-organizing and self-administrating multi-hop wireless networks, with a dynamically changing topology.

Routing is one of the most fundamental aspects of any network. Routing in ad hoc wireless networks plays an important role for data forwarding, where each mobile node can act as a relay in addition to being a source or destination node. Because nodes are usually multiple hops away from each other, routing schemes are usually needed for a source to find a route to the destination before it can send any data to the destination.

Reactive or on-demand routing protocols have been widely studied because they consume less capacity than their pro-active or table-driven counterparts [2, 3]. The reason is that table-driven protocols waste the limited system resources to discover routes that are not needed. On the other hand, on-demand routing protocols have been proposed as an effective solution to this problem. Their main advantage is that a route discovery is performed only when there is a request for communication between two network nodes. However, on-demand routing protocols do not exploit the fact that the route discovery has already been performed and does not discover multiple paths. This results in a higher frequency of route discoveries, which in turn, increases delay and overheads.

Multipath routing has the potential to alleviate these problems by establishing multiple paths between source and destination within a single route discovery process. Such schemes are typically proposed in order to increase the reliability of data transmission or to provide load balancing.

The rest of the chapter is organized as follows: Section 8.2 gives basic definitions used in ad hoc networks. Section 8.3 highlights common routing protocols used in fixed networks and explains why such protocols cannot be used in ad hoc networks. Section 8.4 presents taxonomy of ad hoc routing protocols and provides a review of commonly used routing protocols that has the status of Internet Engineering Task Force (IETF) experimental Request for Comments (RFCs). Section 8.5 of this chapter gives a full description of the implementation issues associated with the development and design of a multipath routing and discusses related published work. Section 8.6 presents further developments in MANETs. Finally, Section 8.7 concludes the chapter.

8.2   Mobile ad hoc networks

MANET is typically represented as a dynamic graph $G = \{V, E(t)\}$, where V is the set of vertices or nodes and $E(t)$ is the set of edges at time t. Let $n = |V|$ be the number of mobile nodes participating in wireless communication. Node $i \in V$ can hear node $j \in V$ if node i is within radio range of j. Let $H(i)$ to be a set of nodes in which node i can hear and $H(j)$ to be a set of nodes in which node j can hear. It is obvious that nodes i and j can hear each other if and only if $i \in H(j)$ and $j \in H(i)$.

The radio range of a node is the geographic distance over which packets sent by the node can be received. The distance used is the Euclidean distance or Euclidean metric. Thus, if the range of a node A is r, then a packet sent by A can be received only by the nodes that are within or on the circle of radius r cantered at the point occupied by A. Different nodes may have different ranges. Therefore, in the light of the above definition, it is not true that if $i \in H(j)$ then $j \in H(i)$ or vice versa, though it is a frequent assumption for many routing and Medium Access Control (MAC) protocols.

8.2.1 Applications

Originally MANETs were studied in relation to military and defence research, often under the name of Packet Radio Networks (PRNet) which evolved into the Survivable Adaptive Radio Networks (SURAN) [4]. In this context, MANETs have played an important role in military applications and related research efforts, for example, the Global Mobile Information Systems (GloMo) programme [5] and the Near-term Digital Radio (NTDR) [6] programme. However, the widespread success of IEEE 802.11 Wireless Local Area Network (WLAN) technology [7] in the consumer, enterprise and service provider markets, as well as the common availability of low cost Personal Digital Assistance (PDAs), laptops and palmtops with radio interfaces, have sparked renewed interest in the field. Internet or intranet connectivity, therefore, are significant factors to be taken into account in the utilization of ad hoc network technology. Therefore, the IETF MANET working group's main task is to develop a framework of IP-based routing protocols for ad hoc networks.

There are a growing number of real time applications using wireless ad hoc and sensor networks, and they are being taken seriously by the industries. Some of the potential applications of ad hoc networks that might provide the basis for commercially successful products are:

Conferencing: Perhaps the prototypical application requiring the establishment of an ad hoc network is mobile conferencing enabling notebook or palmtop for spreading or sharing information among participants in a conference.

Home networking: It might be possible to deploy ad hoc technology to enable direct communication between devices at home. This would make possible the exchange of information such as voice, video-alarms and configuration updates.

Internet hot spots: Ad hoc networks can be linked to a fixed infrastructure via access points to provide extended wireless Internet access.

Personal area networks: Short-range ad hoc networks can be formed to simplify intercommunication between various mobile devices by forming a personal area network (PAN).

Emergency services: Ad hoc networks can help to overcome network impairment during disaster emergencies. Mobile units will probably carry networking equipment in support of routine operations for the times when the Internet is available and the infrastructure has not been impaired.

Vehicular networks: Vehicles on a highway can form an ad hoc network in order to propagate information such as traffic and road conditions. This information can be generated by an individual vehicle and subsequently broadcast to other vehicles. Alternatively, the information can be transmitted to and received from fixed network access points placed near the road.

Sensor dust: Recent advances in sensor, computing and networking technology have enabled the mass production of intelligent, wireless communicating sensors. Networks of these sensors can be used in many different ways:

- *Monitoring space:* Environmental and habitat monitoring, precision agriculture, indoor climate control, surveillance and intelligent alarms.
- *Monitoring objects:* Structural monitoring, condition-based equipment maintenance, medical diagnostics, etc.
- *Monitoring interactions:* Between objects and between objects and their environment, e.g. wildlife habitats, disaster management, emergency response, healthcare and manufacturing process flow.

8.2.2   Open challenges

MANETs pose numerous challenges and generate new research problems compared with the fixed wireless networks. These are due to the following reasons:

Mobility: Each node in MANETs tends to have a mobility pattern with changeable speeds. This phenomenon adds another aspect to the problems that is of routing and supporting Quality of Service (QoS) [8].

Variable topology: The network topology can change rapidly and unpredictably. This is because, as previously stated, nodes are free to move arbitrarily. Moreover, radio propagation conditions can change rapidly.

Inexact state information: The link state information required for effective (QoS) routing is subject to change mainly due to user mobility and changeable channel conditions.

Capacity constraints: Wireless links have significantly lower capacity than wired links and hence congestion is more problematic.

Variable link capacity: The capacity of wireless links can vary over time due to effects such as multiple access, multipath fading, noise, and signal interference.

Energy constrained nodes: Nodes participating in the network rely on batteries for power. If the energy in the batteries is depleted, there is an adverse effect on the network's performance.

Limited security: Mobile wireless networks are generally more vulnerable than wired networks to security threats, such as eavesdropping, spoofing and denial-of-service (DoS) attacks.

Scalability: Because MANETs do not typically allow the same kind of aggregation techniques that are available to standard Internet routing protocols, they are vulnerable to scalability problems. This issue in MANETs can be generally defined as whether the network is able to provide an adequate level of service to packets even in the presence of a larger number of mobile nodes in the network.

Keeping in view the aforementioned challenges, there are still quite a number of open issues. These include medium access scheme, transport layer protocol, energy management, mobility management, security, QoS issues and, of principal interest here, efficient routing.

8.3   Routing in fixed networks

Many ad hoc routing protocols use the same concepts and underlying algorithms as traditional routing protocols for fixed networks. Therefore, it is appropriate to present an overview of the traditional routing protocols and their basic operation. Traditional protocols can be categorized by several criteria:

Static vs. dynamic: In static protocols, the routing tables construct a priori possibly enabled by a network administrator. In contrast to dynamic protocols, these tables do not change in response to small topological changes, which can be caused by broken links and node failures, or changes in traffic patterns.

Centralized vs. distributed: In centralized routing a single node collates all the information about the network topology, computes the relevant routes and then passes them to the other nodes of the network. In distributed routing, adjacent nodes exchange information to update routing tables.

Single-path vs. multipath: Single-path routing is performed via obtaining the one best possible path for a packet to travel from source to destination. Multipath routing, on the other hand, acknowledges that there is more than one possible route between source and destination. It is therefore more reliable than single-path routing but may not always use the best possible route.

From the above, it is clear that, with respect to the characteristics of ad hoc networks, the most suitable protocols are dynamic and distributed. The two most prevalent examples of dynamic, distributed routing are distance vector and link state routing.

8.3.1   Distance vector

In distance vector routing each node maintains a routing table containing the next hop and length of the shortest path to every other node in the network. Nodes determine the 'distance' between themselves and adjacent nodes using periodic message exchanges. Furthermore, each node's routing table is periodically broadcast to all adjacent nodes. Upon receiving a neighbouring node's routing table, a node can use this information to update the shortest path in its routing table.

Compared to link state, distance vector is more computation efficient, easier to implement and requires much less storage space. However, it can create long-lived routing loops, due to the fact that nodes choose their next hops to a completely distributed manner, based on information that can be out of date. Distance vector is used in the Routing Information Protocol (RIP) [9] that is used for Internet routing.

8.3.2   Link state

In link state routing, each node maintains a table of links to adjacent nodes, with some measure of the state, or cost, of each link. This table is periodically flooded throughout the network, such that each node in the network has full knowledge of the network topology. With this knowledge, the nodes are able to construct and update routing tables containing the next hops of the best paths to all other nodes in the network using an appropriate shortest path algorithm. Typically the shortest path algorithm is that developed by Dijkstra [10].

Link state routing overcomes some of the shortcomings of distance vector, such as long-lived routing loops that can cause packets to circulate in the network indefinitely. It forms the basis of the Open Shortest Path First (OSPF) protocol [11], which is used for Internet routing.

8.4   Routing in ad hoc networks

Design of appropriate routing protocols for ad hoc networks is one of the major challenges. To support ad hoc mobile communications, an ad hoc routing protocol will need to perform the following functions:

- Determine and detect changes in network topology.
- Maintain network topology and connectivity.
- Schedule packet transmissions and channel assignment.
- Compute updated routes to the destination

8.4.1   Characteristics of an ideal ad hoc routing protocol

The existing routing protocols, designed for conventional wired packet switched networks, are very mature, having been in use for a considerable amount of time. These protocols, which make use of distance vector or link state algorithms, could be used in ad hoc networks. Nevertheless, the particular characteristics of the wireless medium make the following properties desirable for ad hoc routing protocols:

Distributed implementation: MANETs are autonomous and self-organizing systems, which do not rely on centralized authorities. Therefore, routing protocols must be based on distributed routing techniques.

Adaptability to changing topology: Routing protocols should be able to react to changes in topology and provide new and stable routes promptly. For example, in distance vector routing, the speed of convergence to a new route is slow, leading to inaccurate route information due to the presence of out of date routes.

Efficient capacity utilization: Since the capacity of wireless networks is limited, reduction of control overhead is an important factor. That is, if a routing protocol generates excessive control traffic, the capacity available for data traffic will be greatly reduced. Moreover, the larger the network, the more capacity is consumed during the propagation of routing information. The above can have a serious impact on communication performance. For example, table driven ad hoc routing protocols transmit routing information periodically, generating significant control overhead.

Energy conservation: The lifetime of mobile nodes has a strong impact on the performance of MANETs, since nodes need to relay their messages towards their destinations through other nodes. Therefore, a decrease in the number of available nodes could lead to a degradation of network performance or even partitioning of the original network into smaller networks. Consequently, one of the most important considerations of ad hoc routing protocols should be power consumption. For example, routing protocols should be able to accommodate sleep periods without causing any adverse consequences.

Freedom from loops: Routing algorithms can cause a small fraction of packets circulating around the network for an arbitrary period of time. Looping of such packets can result in considerable capacity and power consumption. These cause many problems and are highly undesirable.

Unidirectional link support: A number of factors, such as the presence of different radio capabilities and signal interference, can cause wireless links to be unidirectional. Hence, the ability to utilize unidirectional links is important [12].

8.4.2   Taxonomy of ad hoc routing protocols

The recognition of the requirements mentioned in the previous section has led to a large body of work on the subject of ad hoc routing. A large number of competing protocols have emerged. Some of them have become Internet Engineering Task Force (IETF) Request for Comments (RFCs); others have draft status in the IETF but many dropped by the research community.

Consequently there are many ways in which the protocols can be categorized according to various characteristics they have. The most prevalent taxonomies found in literature [2, 3, 13, 14] are depicted in Figure 8.1. This taxonomy is based on to divide protocols according to following criteria, reflecting fundamental design and implementation choices:

Communication model: Protocols can be divided according to communications model to protocols that are designed for *single-channel* or *multi-channel* communications. A large class of protocols assumes that nodes communicate over a single logical wireless channel. The IEEE 802.11 MAC method is the most widely used example for such a shared channel link layer. *Multi-channel* protocols are low-level routing protocols that combine channel assignment and routing functionality.

Multi-channel protocols utilize CDMA, FDMA or TDMA to form specific channels. Although communication can be much more efficient using such a method, it is difficult to be used in an ad hoc network since, usually, a distinguished controlling station is required to assign the channels.

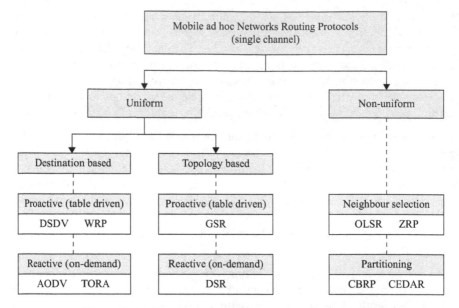

Figure 8.1   Taxonomy of ad hoc routing protocols [3]

Structure: Routing protocols can be categorized according to node uniformity. Some protocols treat all the nodes uniformly, other make distinctions between different nodes. In *uniform* protocols, there is no hierarchy in network; all nodes send and respond to routing control messages at the same manner. *Non-uniform* protocols attempt to limit routing complexity by reducing the number of nodes participating in the route computation. *Non-uniform* protocols fall into two categories: *neighbour selection* – protocols in which each node focuses routing activity on a subset of its neighbours and *partitioning* – protocols in which the network is topologically partitioned.

State information: Protocols may be described in terms of the state information obtained at each node and/or exchanged among nodes. Nodes participating in *topology-based* protocols maintain large-scale topology information. This principle is the same as applied in link state protocols. *Destination-based* protocols do not maintain large-scale topology information. They only maintain topology information that is needed to know the nearest neighbours. The best known of such protocols are distance vector protocols, which maintain a distance and a vector to a destination.

Scheduling: Obtaining route information can be continuous or regular or it can be triggered on-demand. Thus, protocols can be classified to proactive and on-demand protocols. *Proactive* or *table-driven* protocols constantly maintain knowledge of the status of the whole network, regardless of communication requests. In *on-demand* or *reactive* protocols, the routes are only calculated on an on-demand basis that means no unnecessary routing information is maintained. The route calculation process is divided into route discovery and route maintenance phases. The route discovery process is initiated when a source needs a route to a destination.

Table 8.1 Proactive and reactive comparison

Parameters	Proactive (table-driven)	Reactive (on-demand)
Route availability	Always available irrespective of need	Computed when needed
Routing philosophy	Flat	Flat, except for CBRP
Periodic updates	Always required	Not required
Handling mobility	Updates occur at regular intervals	Uses localized route discovery
Control traffic generated	Usually higher than on-demand	Increases with mobility of active routes
Storage requirements	Higher than on-demand	Depends on the number of routes maintained or needed
Delay	Small as routes are predetermined	High as routes are computed when needed
Scalability	Usually up to 100 nodes	Usually higher than table-driven

The route maintenance process deletes failed routes and re-initiates route discovery. Table 8.1 summarizes and compares the proactive and reactive characteristics.

Table 8.2 summarizes the salient feature of ad hoc routing protocols mentioned in Figure 8.1 that cover a range of design choices. Discussing in detail all of the above is not appropriate for the chapter and thus only a selection will be considered. The prerequisites used for selection are:

- The protocols must be mature, with valid and well-documented performance evaluation.
- They must be under active development.
- For obvious reasons, it is preferable to have protocols adopted by the IETF MANET working group.
- The protocols must be as representative of different categories as possible.
- Protocols too similar to each other or which have been shown to perform poorly with respect to the others are excluded; their inclusion would not add to existing knowledge.

Section 8.4.3 introduces two commonly used routing protocols: Dynamic Source Routing (DSR) and ad hoc On-demand Distance Vector (AODV), which has the status of IETF Experimental RFCs. Finally, IETF is developing Dynamic MANET On-demand (DYMO) [29] routing protocol, which is successor to the popular AODV and DSR protocols and shares many of its benefits.

8.4.3 On-demand single-path routing schemes

8.4.3.1 Dynamic source routing

Dynamic Source Routing (DSR) [17, 21–23] is a reactive protocol. It has a flat structure, with all nodes treated equally by the routing algorithm. In DSR routing, the source node appends the complete routing path to each data packet before transmitting. Additionally, each node uses a caching technique to maintain the

Another important feature for AODV is the route management through caching scheme. A node maintains cache information in order to keep track of the RREQ packets it has received and as well as to store the paths pointing back to the originator of RREQ packet. A RREQ packet is deemed fresh if the new destination sequence number is at least equal or greater than the value indicated in previous RREQ packet. A node, either the destination or the intermediate node, which receives a fresh RREQ packet, replies with a RREP packet. The RREP packet is propagated in reverse, along the forward path created by the RREQ packet, resulting in a symmetrical routing path between the source and destination. Along the reverse path, each intermediate node updates its routing table entry, adding information such as next-hop node and hop count with respect to the destination node.

The neighbour status update in AODV is either periodically sent or on demand. As for periodic update, a HELLO message is sent from a node to its neighbours to notify its existence. This way, the status of link to the next hop is actively monitored although it generates more traffic packet. On the other hand, the AODV also allows a node to passively monitor the link using the data link layer message feedback. When a particular node discovers that an active link along the route has been disconnected or is unavailable for communication, it either repairs the route locally or broadcasts a route error (RERR) packet. The local repair is invoked if it is deemed that the point of failure along the route is closer to the destination than to the source. Otherwise, the node releases a broadcast RERR packet to its neighbours. As a result, every node that receives the RERR propagates the packet to all intermediate nodes whose routes may be affected by the disconnected link. Upon reception of RERR, the source node will then reinitiate another route discovery operation if it still has data to be transmitted.

A large number of ad hoc related papers cite AODV as a reference. However, some papers did an independent comparison between some ad hoc routing protocols including AODV [32–34]. The main advantage of this protocol is that routes are established on demand and sequence numbers are used to find the latest route to the destination. The connection setup delay is less. One of the disadvantages of this protocol is that intermediate nodes can lead to inconsistent routes if the source sequence number is very old and the intermediate routes have a higher but not the latest destination sequence number, thereby indicating stale entries. Additionally, multiple RREP packets in response to single RREQ packet can lead to a heavy control overhead. Another disadvantage of AODV is that the periodic beaconing leads to unnecessary capacity consumption.

8.5   Multipath routing

Multipath routing is a concept that has been applied to several applications. However, the fundamental difficulties presented in MANETs caused by node mobility and communication over a wireless medium make new study of multipath routing schemes within this context interesting. This section briefly describes benefits and components of multipath routing, related published work and open issues.

8.5.1   Benefits of multipath routing

Fault tolerance: Multipath routing schemes can provide fault tolerance in the presence of route failures by routing redundant information to the destination through alternative paths. This increase in route resiliency is largely dependent on factors such as the degree of the network and disjointness of the available paths.

Load balancing: Load balancing is of special importance in MANETs because of the limited bandwidth between the nodes. Load balancing can be achieved by distributing the traffic along multiple routes [38]. This can alleviate congestion and bottlenecks and improve the overall QoS.

Bandwidth aggregation: The effective bandwidth can be aggregated by the distributing traffic to the same destination into multiple paths. This approach is particularly useful when a node has multiple low bandwidth links but requires a bandwidth greater than an individual link can provide. End-to-end delay may also be reduced directly as a result of the availability of increased aggregate bandwidth.

Reduced delay: Single-path on-demand routing protocols use a single route for each session. However, in case of a failure of an active link between source and destination, the routing protocol must invoke a route maintenance process followed by route discovery process and, in so doing, additional delay is incurred. Multipath routing schemes alleviate this problem by establishing multiple paths between a source and a destination within a single route discovery process.

8.5.2   Components of multipath routing

The following components are identified as fundamental to multipath routing algorithms [39–42]. Although all of them need not be present in a routing scheme, they all ought to be considered in any multipath design. These concepts can be used as building blocks for designing a new multipath scheme or as features for comparison among existing multipath routing schemes.

Route discovery: Route discovery is the process of determining the available routes between a source and destination node. This procedure generally includes provisions to avoid route looping and heuristics to generate disjoint multipath sets. There are three main types of path disjointness, namely link-disjoint, node-disjoint and partially disjoint. A set of link-disjoint routes have no common links and may share some common intermediate nodes as shown in Figure 8.2. Link-disjoint routes are not as resilient to geographically localized and correlated failures. Node-disjoint routes, as shown in Figure 8.3, have no common nodes except the source and the destination. Node-disjoint routes are least abundant and are hardest to find. It has been shown that in moderately dense networks, only a small number of node-disjoint routes may exist between any two arbitrary nodes, especially as the distance between the nodes increases [50]. A more relaxed form of the multipath routing scheme is to construct partially disjoint or non-disjoint routes as shown in Figure 8.4. The formation of partially disjoint routes is mostly for reliability purposes. The primary route is used for data transmission, while other partially disjoint routes are backup routes for failure recovery. Because there are no

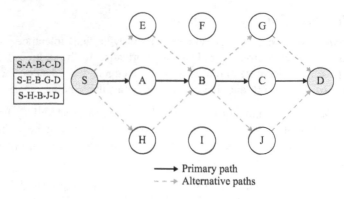

Figure 8.2   Link-disjoint multiple paths

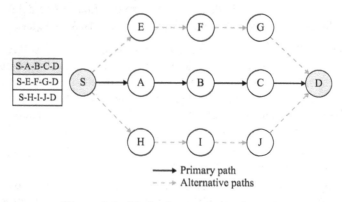

Figure 8.3   Node-disjoint multiple paths

restrictions that require the routes to be node-disjoint or link-disjoint, a greater number of partially disjoint routes exist in a given network than node-disjoint or link-disjoint routes.

Filtering provision: Filtering provision is the option of choosing a subset of alternative paths according to certain quality of the paths. Some filtering provisions are path length or hop-count, shortest multipath, disjointness, available capacity or a combination of metrics. In QoS routing, a subset of paths is selected only if the combined metric satisfies the QoS requirement.

Route usage policy for traffic distribution: There are various policies of distributing traffic over available routes. Examples of such a policy are path redundancy and allocation granularity. In the case of redundant path usage, the source node can choose to use a single path and keep the rest as backups, or it can utilize multiple paths in a round-robin fashion, with only one path sending at a time. If multiple paths are used simultaneously to carry traffic, the protocol needs to decide how traffic is split over the paths and how to handle out-of-order packets at the destination. Some possible choices of traffic granularity include, in order of increased control overhead, per source-destination pair, per flow, per packet, per segment. With a fine granularity, load balancing can be more efficient, since traffic fluctuation can be adapted to

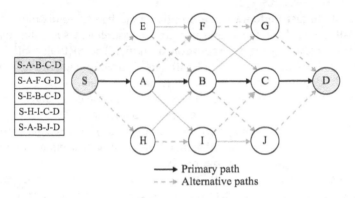

| S-A-B-C-D |
| S-A-F-G-D |
| S-E-B-C-D |
| S-H-I-C-D |
| S-A-B-J-D |

⟶ Primary path
- - -▶ Alternative paths

Figure 8.4   Partial-disjoint multiple paths

quickly [43]. However, per packet or finer granularity requires reordering at the destination, which may not suit some applications.

Route maintenance: Routes may fail due to link/node failures or, in ad hoc networks, node mobility. Route maintenance is the process of re-establishing routes after the initial route discovery. It can be initiated after each route failure or when all the routes have failed to enable efficient use of multipath. Some multipath schemes use dynamic maintenance algorithms to constantly monitor and maintain the quality or combined QoS metric of available paths.

8.5.3   On-demand multipath routing schemes

Numerous multipath routing schemes have been proposed for ad hoc networks [38–41, 44–50]. Most of these schemes compute link-disjoint and node-disjoint paths. This section presents a selection based on DSR and AODV.

Schemes based on DSR: *Multipath-DSR (M-DSR)* [44] presents two slightly varied versions of multipath extensions of the popular DSR. Instead of replying when the first RREQ is received as with DSR, the destination node sends an additional RREP for a RREQ that carries a link-disjoint route compared with the primary path. In the first of the proposed extensions, only the source node has the responsibility to switch to an alternative route in response to intermediate link failures. Such a situation will cause a temporary loss of route until the source receives a RERR message and switches to a new route. The second proposed extension alleviates this problem by allowing intermediate nodes to have one alternative route and to switch route as soon as the primary path fails. Upon link failure, intermediate nodes do not send a RERR message to the source node but adjust the packet's header with the alternative route. In such a way, traffic currently in transit is not lost. It was shown analytically that multipath outperforms single-path routing in terms of route re-discovery and longer alternative routes are less beneficial. However, in many cases, M-DSR cannot compute link-disjoint paths because intermediate nodes drop every duplicate RREQ that may invoke another link-disjoint path.

Multipath Source Routing (MSR) [45] extends DSR's route discovery and route maintenance phases to compute multiple node-disjoint paths, which are used simultaneously to distribute traffic. It proposes a mechanism to distribute load over multiple paths, based on the round-trip time measurement such that paths with lower delays receive a greater proportion of traffic. The SRPing tool[1] is used to estimate the end-to-end delay. A multipath table is used to maintain information of routes to a destination. This table contains for each route to the destination: the index of the path in the route cache, the destination ID, the delay and the calculated cost weight based on the delay of all paths to the same destination. Such an approach has the disadvantage, pertinent to real-time services, that traffic flows over the different paths may be unbalanced and require re-sequencing and subsequently incur additional delay at the receiver.

Split Multipath Routing (SMR) [46] scheme is an on-demand multipath source routing that provides a way of determining maximally disjoint paths. Unlike DSR intermediate nodes are not allowed to respond to RREQs from their cache. In order to maximize the number of RREQs reaching the destination, it uses a modified RREQ packet-flooding scheme in the route query process. Intermediate nodes do not necessarily discard any duplicate RREQ packets received. The destination node, upon reception of first RREQ, responds immediately to the source node and then waits for a pre-allocated time to receive additional RREQs to determine a second maximally disjoint route. Once the source node receives the first RREP, it starts sending traffic to the destination to avoid additional delay to the currently buffered packets. When the second RREP is received, the source node splits traffic using per-packet allocation scheme [43] in a round-robin fashion. This approach has the disadvantage of transmitting a large number of RREQ packets.

Shortest Multipath Source (SMS) routing scheme [47] is a reactive source routing scheme that is designed to build on the strengths of DSR and SMR, while reducing the restrictions on the route selection scheme used in SMR to increase the number of multipath possible. Rather than selecting routes that are node disjoint throughout as in SMR, SMS increases the number of routes possible between a source and destination by requiring that the alternative routes be partially disjoint only, i.e. that they bypass at least one intermediate node on the primary path [47]. The primary path here is simply the first path to be established, i.e. the path for which the source receives the first route reply message. Increasing the number of paths possible between a source and a destination makes the scheme more resistant to faults, and helps speed up recovery when a link along the path breaks. In Reference 47, a mathematical analysis is used to prove that using a larger number of partially disjoint paths increases the network's tolerance to faults, compared to link or node disjoint multiple paths. Details of the simulation scenarios and set up and the results of the three sets of simulations namely mobility, offered load and network size in terms of goodput or packet delivery ratio, average end-to-end delay, normalized routing load and packet loss are described in References 3, 47.

Schemes based on AODV: Ad hoc On-demand Multipath Distance Vector *(AOMDV)* [48] routing is an extension to AODV. It computes multiple loop-free, link-disjoint or node-disjoint paths during route discovery. AOMDV uses the

---

[1]SRPing is a measurement tool to get the round trip time between two arbitrary nodes.

notion of advertised hop-count and last hop that ensures loop freedom and path disjointness respectively. Unlike AODV, in AOMDV the intermediate node does not simply drop the duplicate RREQ packet but examines it to see if it contains a node-disjoint path to the destination. If so, then the node checks to see if the reverse path to the source is available. If this is also true, then the path is added in the table. In the case of a link-disjoint path, the node applies a slightly lenient policy and replies to a certain number of RREQs, which come from disjoint neighbours. AOMDV can only discover equal length multiple paths, which may not be possible when the network is moderately-to-sparsely connected.

Node-Disjoint Multipath Routing (NDMR) [49] modifies and extends AODV to enable the path accumulation feature of DSR to build multiple node-disjoint paths. It exhibits a low routing overhead during the route discovery process by recording the shortest routing hops of loop free paths. The source node selects one of the alternative paths in case of a link-failure. This approach, however, has similar disadvantages as schemes based on AODV and DSR and suffers from scalability issues.

Scalable Multipath On-demand Routing (SMORT) [50] scheme reduces the routing overhead incurred in recovering from route breaks through the use of secondary paths. SMORT computes fail-safe multiple paths, providing all intermediate nodes on the primary path with multiple routes to the destination. A path between source and destination is said to be fail-safe with respect to the primary path, if it bypasses at least one intermediate node on the primary path. The number of RERR packets transmitted during route break recovery is reduced which, in turn, reduces end-to-end delay and overheads whilst providing improved scalability. This approach has the disadvantage of generating/recording multiple copies of RREQ packets at each node, thus increasing memory overheads.

8.5.4 Comparison and open issues

Table 8.3 summarizes and compares the main characteristics of multipath routing schemes presented.

Although on-demand multipath routing schemes can build multiple routing paths between source and destination, most of them will encounter a broadcast storm of routing packets in the process of discovering multiple disjoint routing paths. This increases considerably routing overhead in the network [45, 46, 48–50]. Also, disjoint multipath routing schemes discussed previously compute maximally disjoint multiple paths, whose availability is lower due to the disjointness restriction imposed in the path selection. Hence, disjoint multiple paths cannot provide efficient fault-tolerance towards route breaks. Also, these schemes involve significant delay and overhead in selecting disjoint multiple paths. On the other hand, SMS routing scheme can build multiple partial-disjoint paths from source to destination in order to reduce delays, overhead of additional route discoveries and recover quickly in case of route breaks. This scheme addresses the problem of wireless broadcast storm by simple hop count mechanism.

Further work on MANETs is likely to uncover techniques that would be appropriate for stabilizing routing schemes, leading to faster route convergence and reduced route flaps. Creating ad hoc routing schemes which experience minimal performance degradation when used for real-time services is a challenge, and there

Table 8.3 Summary of multipath routing schemes [47]

	M-DSR [44]	MSR [45]	SMR [46]	SMS [47]	AOMDV [48]	NDMR [49]	SMORT [50]
Base protocol	DSR	DSR	DSR	DSR	AODV	AODV	AODV
Alternative / backup paths	Link-disjoint	Node-disjoint	Maximally link- or node-disjoint	Partially disjoint	Link- or node-disjoint	Node-disjoint	Fail-safe
Routing choice made at	Source and intermediate nodes	Source	Source	Source	Intermediate nodes	Source	Intermediate nodes
Complete routes known at source	Yes	Yes	Yes	Yes	No	Yes	No
Delay known	No	Yes	No	No	No	No	No
Paths used simultaneously	Possibly (not specified)	Yes	Yes	No	Possibly (not specified)	Possibly (not specified)	No
TTL limitation	Yes	Yes	Yes	Yes	Yes	Yes	Yes
QoS support	No	Possibly	No	No	No	No	No
Multicast support	No	No	No	No	No	No	No
Power management	No	No	No	No	No	No	No
Security support	No	No	No	No	No	No	No
Motivation / application	Reduce frequency of route discovery floods	QoS applications with soft end-to-end reliability	Splitting traffic provides better load distribution	Fault-tolerant routes	Discovers disjoint paths without using source routing	Reduce routing overheads using path accumulation feature of DSR	Discovering fail-safe paths provides better scalability

remains a significant amount of work to reach this goal. Capacity estimation, route discovery, route maintenance and feasible path selection are some of the issues that require further exploration. An effective QoS provisioning mechanism is highly desirable to further improve the performance of routing schemes and to support real-time services under the dynamically changing environment of MANETs.

8.6   Further trends

Due to the explosive growth in the market for handheld devices, i.e. smart phones, tablets, phablets, etc. the challenges put forth towards the existing single and multi-path routing protocols as well as designing new ones have increased. Due to the competitive trends being observed between various handheld vendors, the race for bigger market shares have led to an unprecedented pace in surfacing of new operating systems and applications. A higher number of mobile and multi-interface devices also mean more congestion in the allocated radio frequency spectrum for the existing wireless communication technologies, e.g. Zigbee, WLANs, etc. The evolution in hardware of handheld devices has led to higher processing ability that is good enough to manage high definition (HD) multimedia content. The popularity and use of social media and content sharing especially multimedia content, as well as the increased access to online multimedia streaming means the corresponding increase in the throughput requirements. Interactive gaming is also becoming prevalent with demands coming from the wireless network. Here, with the multipath routing protocols not only we get higher throughput but also better group mobility management.

Recent statistics have shown that the carbon footprint of the ICT industry is estimated to contribute towards >3% of the world's total [51]. To address these concerns focus has shifted towards inducing energy efficiency in the communication protocols and the ICT infrastructure. For similar reasons, the routing protocols are also envisaged to consider energy efficiency as one of the key metrics. For congested networks, not only does the interference among nodes increase along with higher demand for throughput, but also fair allocation of channel time to nodes that require access to the network. Therefore, the use of game theoretic approaches, and multi-radio/multi-channel techniques in routing protocols to determine fair access to the network and reduce interference respectively, have become popular in the research community. Some of the key envisaged future research trends for single path and multipath routing protocols are summarized as:

- Application centric routing protocols
- Routing in heterogeneous networks
- Ability of a routing protocol to adapt in presence of multiple wireless interfaces
- Ensuring seamless multi-hop communication across various software platforms
- Spectrum efficient routing protocols
- Game theoretic approaches to handle fair access
- Cooperative routing protocols
- Energy efficient routing protocols for Green ICT
- Routing in dense machine-to-machine (M2M) communication networks

- Routing in cloud-based networks
- Routing in cognitive networks
- Effectively managing group-based mobility in multicast routing protocols
- Multi-channel/Multi-radio-based single and multipath routing protocols for Wireless Mesh Networks
- Hybrid disjoint multipath routing protocols, i.e. a combination of all/some
- Intelligent selection of multiple routing algorithms in the same networks

8.7   Conclusion

In this chapter, the basic concepts of ad hoc networks were discussed. Further, the major issues involved in the design of a routing protocol and the different classifications of routing protocols for MANETs were described. The major challenges that an ad hoc routing protocol must address are the mobility of nodes, rapid changes in topology, limited capacity, hidden and exposed terminal problems, limited battery power and time-varying channel properties. The different approaches upon which the protocols can be classified include classification based on the type of communication model, the structure used, the use of state information and the scheduling mechanism that include proactive and reactive approaches. The protocols belonging to each of these categories were highlighted and key protocols were discussed.

The next part of the chapter presented the concept of multipath routing with emphasis on its applications on MANETs. The benefits of employing multipath algorithms in routing, and its four components, namely route discovery, filtering provision, route usage policy and route maintenance are described. A number of multipath routing schemes proposed for MANETs are discussed, aiming at showing various strategies of utilizing multiple routings in wireless networks. A summary of these schemes is given, highlighting their features and characteristics. Several areas in multipath routing have been identified to improve the performance in terms of delay bounds or guarantees and lower routing overheads.

References

1. IETF Mobile Ad-Hoc Networks (MANET) Working Group. Available from http://www.ietf.org/html.charters/manet-charter.html [Accessed 1 Sep. 2012]
2. Murthy C.S., Manoj B.S. *Ad-Hoc Wireless Networks Architectures and Protocols*, Prentice Hall, NJ, USA, 2004
3. Zafar H., Alhamahmy N., Harle D., Andonovic I. 'Survey of Reactive and Hybrid Routing Protocols for Mobile Ad-Hoc Networks', *Int. J. Commun. Netw. Info. Security*, Dec. 2011, vol. 3(3), pp. 193–216
4. Kahn R.E., Gronemeyer S.A., Burchfiel J., Kunzelman R.C. 'Advances in Packet Ratio Technology', *Proc. IEEE*, Nov. 1978, vol. 66(11), pp. 1468–96
5. Leiner B., Ruth R., Sastry A.R. 'Goals and Challenges of the DARPA GloMo Program', *IEEE Personal Commun.*, Dec. 1996, vol. 3(6), pp. 34–43

6. Ruppe R., Griswald S., Walsh P., Martin R. 'Near Term Digital Radio (NTDR) System', *Proc. IEEE Military Commun. Conf. (MILCOM)*, Nov. 1997, vol. 3, pp. 1282–87

7. 'IEEE Standard for Information Technology-Telecommunications and Information Exchange between Systems-Local and Metropolitan Area Networks-Specific Requirements – Part 11: Wireless LAN Medium Access Control (MAC) and Physical Layer (PHY) Specifications', *IEEE 802.11*, Jun. 2007

8. Zafar H., Zuhairi M., Harle D., Andonovic I. 'A Survey of Quality of Service-aware Routing Approaches for Mobile Ad-Hoc Networks', *IETE Tech. Rev.*, May-Jun. 2012, vol. 29(3), pp. 188–95

9. Malkin G. 'RIP Version 2', *RFC 2453*, Nov. 1998

10. Leon-Garcia A., Widjaja I. *Communication Networks*, 2nd edn., McGraw-Hill Science Engineering, New York, NY, USA, Jul. 2003

11. Moy J. 'OSPF Version 2', *RFC 2328*, Apr. 1998

12. Zuhairi M., Zafar H., Harle D. 'Wireless Machine-to-Machine Routing Protocol with Unidirectional Links', *Smart Comput. Rev.*, Oct. 2011, vol. 1(1), pp. 58–68

13. Feeney L.M. 'A Taxonomy for Routing Protocols in Mobile Ad-Hoc Networks', *SICS Technical Report T99/07*, Oct. 1999

14. Zuhairi M. 'On-demand Routing with Unidirectional Link Support for Mobile Ad-Hoc Networks', *Ph.D. Thesis*, Department of Electronic and Electrical Engineering, University of Strathclyde, Glasgow UK, Aug. 2012

15. Perkins C.E., Bhagwat P. 'Highly Dynamic Destination-Sequenced Distance Vector (DSDV) for Mobile Computers', *ACM SIGCOMM Computer Commun. Rev.*, Oct. 1994, vol. 24(4), pp. 234–44

16. Murthy S., Garcia-Luna-Aveces J.J. 'An Efficient Routing Protocol for Wireless Networks', *AACM/Baltzer J. on Mobile Netw. and Applications*, Oct. 1996, vol. 1(2), pp. 183–97

17. Perkins C.E. *Ad-Hoc Networking*, Addison-Wesley, Upper Saddle River, NJ, USA, 2001

18. Perkins C.E., Royer E.M., Das S. 'Ad-Hoc On-demand Distance Vector (AODV) Routing', *RFC 3561*, Jul. 2003

19. Park V., Corson S. 'Temporally-Ordered Routing Algorithm (TORA) Version 1', *Internet Draft* <draft-ietf-manet-tora-spec-04.txt>, Jun. 2001

20. Gerla M., Chen T. 'Global State Routing: A New Routing Scheme for Ad-Hoc Wireless Networks', *Technical Report*, Computer Science Department, University of California, Los Angeles, 1998

21. Johnson D.B., Maltz D.A. 'Dynamic Source Routing in Ad-Hoc Wireless Networks', *Technical Report*, Computer Science Department Carnegie Mellon University, 5000 Forbes Avenue Pittsburgh, PA, 1996

22. Maltz D.A., Broch J., Johnson D.B. 'Experiences Designing and Building a Multi-hop Wireless Ad-Hoc Network Testbed' *Technical Report*, The CMU Monarch Project, Computer Science Department, Carnegie Mellon University, Pittsburgh, PA, 1999

23. Johnson D.B., Hu Y., Maltz D.A. 'Dynamic Source Routing in Ad-Hoc Wireless Networks', *RFC 4728*, Feb. 2007

24. Jacquet P., Muhlethaler P., Qayyum A., Laouiti A., Viennot L., Clausen T. 'Optimized Link State Routing Protocol', *Internet Draft* <draft-ietf-manet-olsr-04.txt>, Mar. 2001

25. Clausen T., Dearlove C., Jacquet P. 'The Optimized Link State Routing Protocol version 2', *Internet Draft* <draft-ietf-manet-olsrv2-07>, Jul. 2008

26. Haas Z.J., Pearlman M.R., Samar P. 'The Zone Routing Protocol (ZRP) for Ad-Hoc Networks', *Internet Draft* <draft-ietf-manet-zone-zrp-04.txt>, Jul. 2002

27. Jiang M., Li J., Tay Y.C. 'Cluster Based Routing Protocol (CBRP)', *Internet Draft* <draft-ietf-manet-cbrp.txt>, Jun. 1999

28. Sivakumar R., Sinha P., Bharghavan V. 'CEDAR: A Core-Extraction Distributed Ad-Hoc Routing Algorithm', *IEEE J. on Selected Areas in Commun.*, Aug. 1999, vol. 17(8), pp. 1454–65

29. Perkins C., Chakeres I. 'Dynamic MANET On-demand (AODVv2) Routing', Internet Draft <draft-ietf-manet-dymo-23>, Oct. 2012

30. Boukerche A. *Algorithms and Protocols for Wireless and Mobile Ad-Hoc Networks*. John Wiley & Sons, Inc., Hoboken, New Jersey, 2009

31. Dyer T.D., Boppana R.V. 'A Comparison of TCP Performance over Three Routing Protocols for Mobile Ad-Hoc Networks', *Proc. ACM Symposium on Mobile Ad-Hoc Netw. & Comput. (MOBIHOC)*, Long Beach, CA, Oct. 2001

32. Broch J., Maltz D.A., Johnson D.B., Hu Y., Jetcheva J. 'A Performance Comparison of Multi-hop Wireless Ad-Hoc Network Routing Protocols', *Proc. Fourth Annual ACM/IEEE Int. Conf. on Mobile Comput. and Netw.*, Dallas, TX, Oct. 1998, pp. 85–97

33. Johansson P., Larsson T., Hedman N., Mielczarek B., Degermark M. 'Scenario-based Performance Analysis of Routing Protocols for Mobile Ad-Hoc Networks', *Proc. Fifth Annual ACM Int. Conf. on Mobile Comput. and Netw. (MOBICOM)*. Seattle, Washington, Aug. 1999, pp. 195–206

34. Perkins C., Royer M., Das S., Marina M. 'Performance Comparison of Two On-demand Routing Protocols for Ad-Hoc Networks', *IEEE Personal Commun.*, Feb. 2001, vol. 8(1), pp. 16–28

35. Adibi S., Agnew G.B. 'Multilayer Flavoured Dynamic Source Routing in Mobile Ad-Hoc Networks', *IET Commun.*, May 2008, vol. 2(5), pp. 690–707

36. Bouhorma M., Bentaouit H., Boudhir A. 'Performance Comparison of Ad-Hoc Routing Protocols AODV and DSR', *Proc. Int. Conf. on Multimedia Comput. and Systems*, Tanger, Morocco, Apr. 2009, pp. 511–14

37. Taksande V.K., Kulat K.D. 'A Simulation Comparison among AODV, DSDV, DSR Protocol with IEEE 802.11 MAC for Grid Topology in MANET', *Proc. Int. Conf. on Computational Intelligence and Commun. Netw.*, Nagpur, India, Oct. 2011, pp. 63–7

38. Tachtatzis C., Harle D. 'Performance Evaluation of Multi-path and Single-path Routing Protocols for Mobile Ad-Hoc Networks', *Proc. 2008 Int. Symp. on Performance Evaluation of Computer and Telecommun. Systems*, Edinburgh, Jun. 2008

39. Tsai J., Moors T. 'A Review of Multipath Routing Protocols: From Wireless Ad-Hoc to Mesh Networks', *Proc. ACoRN Early Career Researcher Workshop on Wireless Multihop Netw.*, Jul. 2006

40. Zafar H., Harle D., Andonovic I., Ashraf M. 'Performance Evaluation of On-demand Multipath Routing Protocols for Mobile Ad-Hoc Networks', *Proc. Seventh IASTED Int. Conf. of Wireless & Optical Commun. (WOC)*, Montreal, Canada, May 2007, pp. 325–29

41. Tarique M., Tepe K.E., Adibi S., Erfani S. 'Survey of Multipath Routing Protocols for Mobile Ad-Hoc Networks', *J. of Netw. and Computer Applications*, Nov. 2009, vol. 32(6), pp. 1125–43

42. Zahary A., Ayesh A. 'An Analytical Review for Multipath Routing in Mobile Ad-Hoc Networks', *Int. J. of Ad-Hoc and Ubiquit. Comput.*, Jan. 2010, vol. 5(2), pp. 69–85

43. Krishnan R., Silvester J.A. 'Choice of Allocation Granularity in Multipath Source Routing Schemes', *Proc. 12th Annual Joint Conf. of the IEEE Computer and Commun. Societies (INFOCOM)*, San Francisco, CA, Mar. 1993, pp. 322–29

44. Nasipuri A., Castaneda R., Das S. 'Performance of Multipath Routing for On-demand Protocols in Mobile Ad-Hoc Networks', *ACM/Kluwer Mobile Netw. and Applications J.*, 2001, vol. 6(4), pp. 339–49

45. Wang L., Zhang L., Shu Y., Dong M. 'Multipath Source Routing in Wireless Ad-Hoc Networks', *Proc. Canadian Conf. on Electrical and Computer Engineering*, 2000, pp. 479–83

46. Lee S., Gerla M. 'Split Multipath Routing with Maximally Disjoint Paths in Ad-Hoc Networks', *Proc. IEEE Int. Conf. on Commun., Helsinki, Jun. 2001*, pp. 3201–05

47. Zafar H., Harle D., Andonovic I., Khawaja Y. 'Performance Evaluation of Shortest Multipath Source Routing Scheme', *IET Commun. in Special Issue on Wireless Ad-Hoc Networks*, May 2009, vol. 3(5), pp. 700–13

48. Marina M., Das S. 'On-demand Multipath Distance Vector Routing in Ad-Hoc Networks', *Proc. 9th IEEE Int. Conf. on Netw. Protocols*, California, 2001, pp. 14–23

49. Li X., Cuthbert L. 'A Reliable Node-Disjoint Multipath Routing with Low Overhead in Wireless Ad-Hoc Networks', *Proc. 7th ACM/IEEE Int. Symp. on Modelling, Analysis and Simulation of Wireless and Mobile Systems*, Venezia, 2004, pp. 230–33

50. Reddy L.R., Raghavan S.V. 'SMORT: Scalable Multipath On-demand Routing for Mobile Ad-Hoc Networks', *Elsevier Ad-Hoc Netw.*, 2007, vol. 5(2), pp. 162–88

51. C02 footprint of the ICT Industry (report). Available from http://www.parliament.uk/documents/post/postpn319.pdf [Accessed 1 Sep. 2012]

Chapter 9*

Ant colony inspired routing for mobile ad hoc networks

P. Venkata Krishna[a] and V. Saritha[a]

Abstract

Although ant-based routing protocols for MANETs have been widely explored but most of them are essentially single-path routing methods that have heavy burden on the hosts along the shortest path from source to destination. The robustness of these protocols is comparatively not good which is further weakened by the positive feedback mechanism of ant. Link-disjoint multipath routing is more robust and can support QoS better than single-path routing in MANETs. In this chapter, we present swarm intelligence and link disjoint multipath routing to solve the problem of dynamic routing issues of MANET. A novel approach named Ant Colony Inspired Routing for Mobile ad hoc Networks (QAMR) is discussed. In this approach, forward ants and backward ants are used to determine the paths with QoS properties satisfied. QAMR establishes and utilizes multiple routes of link-disjoint paths to send data packets concurrently and adopts pheromone to disperse communication traffic, thus it can adapt to the dynamic changes of the network and better support for QoS.

9.1   Introduction

MANETs are being widely used for military applications, wearable devices, and rescue operations and in places where there is no pre-installed infrastructure, it is dynamic in nature and self-configuring networks. In a dynamic network, it is difficult to use multimedia and other advanced applications without QoS constraint. QoS can be defined as a set of service requirement that a given network should satisfy while transmitting packets from source to destination [1]. It is difficult to design a path with multiple QoS constraints as there can be conflicting parameters

*H. F. Rashvand and H.-C. Chao (Eds.), *Dynamic Ad Hoc Networks*, The IET Book Publishing Department, 2013, ISBN 978-1-84919-647-5, eISBN 978-1-84919-648-2
[a]School of Computing Science and Engineering, VIT University, Vellore, India.

and race conditions among various parameters [2]. Many of the popular protocols like AODV, DSR and TORA are designed without considering QoS constraints for the path they generate.

Any given QoS metric can be classified as additive, concave or multiplicative. Bandwidth and energy are concave metric, while cost, delay and jitter are additive metrics. Bandwidth and energy are concave as end-to-end bandwidth and energy of the path is the minimum of all the links along the path. The end-to-end delay is an additive constraint because it is the accumulation of delays caused at all intermediate nodes and the links along a path [3]. The reliability or availability of a link is a multiplicative metric, which is based on some criteria such as link break probability.

9.1.1   Routing issues in mobile ad hoc networks

In MANETs, designing a routing algorithm with given QoS constraint is NP-hard because of the unavailability of accurate path information and it is difficult to keep up-to-date information about the link due to its dynamic nature and depletion of energy at node that causes link breakage. There are many challenges in the design of routing protocol in MANET. Some of them are the dynamic topology of the network, the asymmetric property of the links among nodes in MANET, the routing overhead in maintaining musty routes in the routing tables because of the mobility of the nodes in the network, due to the infrastructure less property of MANET interference problem need to be handled, guaranteeing delivery because of the mobility and infrastructure less property of the network and battery-powered nodes of the network etc.

9.1.2   Need for multipath routing in mobile ad hoc networks

The provision for selecting a path from all the possible paths is given by multipath routing technique. This yields in advantages like managing fault tolerance, bandwidth effective usage, load balancing and security improvement. By spreading the traffic among the different multiple routes using the multipath routing technique, load balancing can be achieved. When multiple paths are determined from a particular source to a particular destination, these paths might be node disjoint, edge disjoint or part of a path overlapped [4].

On an average the bandwidth required by unipath routing technique is more when compared to the multipath routing techniques. So, multipath routing will be more effective for limited bandwidth availability. In high-density networks, multipath routing performs better in terms of throughput when compared to unipath routing [5].

Multipath routing is useful in many applications like traditional circuit switched telephone networks. Multipath routing is useful in reducing the call blocking probability and improves the utilization factor of the network.

9.1.3   Ant colony optimization for multipath routing

Swarm intelligence algorithms are used to optimize different algorithms. One of the most popular and swarm intelligence algorithms used is ant colony optimization algorithm. Ants don't communicate directly to indicate the path they choose to search for food but they do with the help of pheromone. This pheromone is also used to identify the chosen path, shortest path and to choose another path in case of hurdles in the initially chosen path. In this way, the ant colony algorithm supports multipath routing also. Technically speaking, a node maintains pheromone concentration also along with the general routing table information to support and optimize multipath routing algorithms. The pheromone concentration in the routing table is used to decide the node to which the packets need to be forwarded next [6].

9.1.4 Performance issues of multipath routing

Due to the dynamic nature of the network topology and the resource constraints, routing in MANETs is a challenging task. Also for the application such as multimedia finding the best path with multiple QoS constraints is an N-complete problem. The use of Ant colony Optimization in the system, which was inspired by the behaviour of the real ant colony making the probabilistic movement of ants in the system to explore all the paths from source to destination. As the size of the network increases on-demand routing protocols provide low performance due to large routing overhead generated while repairing route breaks. Maintaining routes in large networks becomes unmanageable due to longer path lengths between node pairs, possibility of route breaks as there are more number of nodes along the path, limited energy level problem as nodes in MANETs are battery driven, link breakages which occur due to node dying of energy depletion and node moving out of its neighbouring node and presence of malicious node in the network degrading the performance of MANETs.

9.2 Background

9.2.1 On-demand multipath routing protocols

The recent studies extensively focused on the multipath discovering and QoS extension of the on-demand routing protocols in order to address problems related with single path routing protocols like AODV and DSR [1]. Many On-demand multipath routing protocols have been proposed for MANETS including Split Multipath Routing (SMR) [7], Ad hoc On-demand Multipath Distance Vector (AOMDV) [8], Cross-Layered Multipath AODV (CM-AODV) [9] and cooperative packet caching and shortest multipath (CHAMP) [10]. SMR and MDSR are based on Dynamic Source Routing (DSR) while TORA, ROAM, AODV-BR and AOMDV routing protocols are based on AODV. Node-Disjoint Multipath Routing (NDMR) [11] provides with node-disjoint multiple paths. Other energy aware multipath protocols that give disjoint-paths are Grid-based Energy Aware Node-Disjoint Multipath Routing Algorithm (GEANDMRA) [12], Energy Aware Source Routing (EASR) [13] and Energy Aware Node Disjoint Multipath Routing (ENDMR) [14]. The Lifetime-Aware Multipath Optimized Routing (LAMOR) [15] is based on the lifetime of the node that is related to its residual energy and current traffic conditions.

In Reference 16, Shunli *et al.* proposed an algorithm for multipath routing based on the standard on-demand routing protocol AODV. The authors tried to reduce the routing overhead during the re-route discovery process by identifying the multiple node-disjoint paths while conserving the energy levels of the nodes.

9.2.2   Ant colony–based multipath routing protocols

Ant colony optimization has also been used for fault tolerance routing in MANETs. FTAR [17] proposed by Misra *et al.* discusses about fault tolerance routing in MANET using ant like agent. LAFTRA [18] proposed by Misra *et al.* looks at fault tolerance routing in MANET from a learning automata perspective.

FACO introduced by Goswami *et al.* uses a fuzzy logic and ACO for optimizing various parameters used for selecting optimal path between source and destination [19].

Luis *et al.* proposed an algorithm for wireless sensor networks that is based on QoS routing model in Reference 20. The author used ant colony optimization process for presenting the new metric referred as AntSensNet. This algorithm utilizes hierarchical structure in order to have maximum network utilization and the distortion in transmission of video is reduced using the multipath video packet scheduling.

In Reference 21, Na Lin *et al.* proposed an algorithm based on ant colony optimization for determining multiple routes. In this chapter, the ant colony optimization is improved in three different aspects. The next hop selected by the forward ant based on the utilization of router's buffer queue during transfer of data. The metric on which the proposed algorithm in Reference 21 is tested are the load balance, congestion, and network resource utilization.

9.2.3   QoS enabled multipath routing protocols

ARMAN [2] is an on-demand QoS aware routing protocol, the path is selected based on the path preference probability metric calculated at each node using multiple QoS parameters. In NDMLNR [22], Node Disjoint Multipath Routing considering link and node stability had taken link and node stability in to account for multipath routing. Here bandwidth is taken as QoS parameter for path selection. In QOLSR [23], QoS routing over OLSR protocol, delay and bandwidth metrics are considered for QoS routing. AMQR by Liu *et al.* combines link-disjoint multipath routing and swarm intelligence to select multiple paths for providing QoS services [24].

In Reference 25, Jie Wu proposed a multipath routing for delay tolerant networks. This algorithm is based on social features. The author describes how people having common social features contact each other frequently; similarly the nodes with common social features help in improving the performance of the system. The two steps in this algorithm are the extraction of social features from the nodes and multipath routing based on these features. The routing process in this algorithm is a feature difference resolving process gradually. The author discusses two different multipath routing schemes such as node-disjoint-based routing and delegation-based routing.

Challal *et al.* proposed a multipath routing for wireless sensor networks, which is also fault tolerant as in Reference 26. The scheme presented in this paper is based on distributed nature and the verification is in-network that requires no base station to be involved. The author showed that the proposed scheme is good in tolerance and it also conserves energy, both being important factors in sensor nodes.

In Reference 27, the authors Stefan *et al.* proposed an algorithm that focuses on multipath slot allocation static resource reservations. The authors used various routing strategies to improve the efficiency. The network-on chip is used to test the proposed scheme that makes the implementation simpler and cost effective. This TDM slot allocation flow overall performance is better but it does not give guarantee in all instants.

9.3   System model

9.3.1   *Notations*

Various notations used in this chapter are given in Table 9.1:

Table 9.1   Notation table

Notation	Meaning
B_r	Remaining battery lifetime of node N_i
B_m	Lifetime of a fully charged battery
D_T, D_C, d_g	Threshold, calculated and goodness value for delay
B_T, B_C, b_g	Threshold, calculated and goodness value for bandwidth
H_T, H_C, h_g	Threshold, calculated and goodness value for hop count
$P(i)$	Path preference probability
FANT, BANT	Forward ants, backward ants
T_w	Time delay between arrival of first and last FANT

9.3.2   *QoS model*

We are representing MANET as a connected undirected graph $G = (V, E)$ as shown in Figure 9.1, where V denotes the set of nodes in the network and E denotes the set of bi-directional links.

For each link $e \in E$ the QoS metrics associated with it are *bandwidth (e)* and *delay (e)* and *hop count metric* for the whole path. Similarly *bandwidth (e)* represents the available bandwidth of the link *e* and *bandwidth (path (i, j))* represents the bandwidth available for the entire path from *i* to *j* [2]. The metrics delay and bandwidth from a node *i* to an arbitrary node *j* are calculated as

$$Delay(path(i,j)) = \sum_{e \in p(i,j)} delay(e) + \sum_{n \in p(i,j)} delay(n) \qquad (9.1)$$

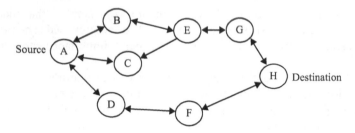

Figure 9.1   Mobile ad hoc network

For example, let us assume that the delay at

> node A = 2 ms; node B = 3 ms; node C = 1 ms; node D = 2 ms;
> node E = 2 ms; node F = 3 ms; node G = 4 ms; node H = 1 ms

Let us assume that the delay at edge

> A→B = 2 ms; B→A = 1 ms; A→C = 3 ms; C→A = 4 ms; B→E = 2 ms;
> E→B = 2 ms; E→G = 1 ms; G→E = 2 ms; G→H = 2 ms; H→G = 1 ms;
> A→D = 4 ms; D→A = 2 ms; D→F = 3 ms; F→D = 3 ms; F→H = 2 ms;
> H→F = 2 ms; E→C = 3 ms

Let us calculate the delay of path (A, H)
There are two possible paths

Path 1 (A, H) = A → B → E → G → H.

According to (9.1),

Delay (path 1 (A, H)) = delay (A → B) + delay (B → E) + delay (E → G)+
delay (G → H) + delay (A) + delay (B) + delay (E) + delay (G) + delay (H)
= 2 + 2 + 1 + 2 + 2 + 3 + 2 + 4 + 1 = 19 ms

Path 2 = A → D → F → H
The delay along this path is calculated using (9.1) as

Delay (path 2 (A, H)) = delay (A → D) + delay (D → F) + delay (F → H)+
delay (A) + delay (D) + delay (F) + delay (H)
= 4 + 3 + 2 + 2 + 2 + 3 + 1 = 17 ms

Here delay is an additive metric, and bandwidth is a concave metric.

$$bandwidth(path(i,j)) = \min_{e \in p(i,j)} \{bandwidth(e)\} \tag{9.2}$$

Let us assume that the bandwidth along the edges as

> A → B = 6 Mb/s; B → A = 7 Mb/s; A → C = 8 Mb/s; C → A = 6 Mb/s; B →
> E = 7 Mb/s; E → B = 6 Mb/s; E → G = 8 Mb/s; G → E = 6 Mb/s; G → H =
> 9 Mb/s; H → G = 8 Mb/s; A → D = 7 Mb/s; D → A = 9 Mb/s; D → F = 7 Mb/s;
> F → D = 8 Mb/s; F → H = 6 Mb/s; H → F = 6 Mb/s; E → C = 8 Mb/s

Let us calculate the bandwidth of path 1 (A, H) using (9.2) as

Bandwidth (path 1 (A, H) = min{(bandwidth (A → B)), (bandwidth (B → E)), (bandwidth (E → G)), (bandwidth (G → H))} = min(6, 7, 8, 9) = 6

Let us calculate the bandwidth of path 2 (A, H) using (9.2) as

Bandwidth (path 2 (A, H) = min{(bandwidth (A → D)), (bandwidth (D → F)), (bandwidth (F → H))} = min(7, 7, 6) = 6.

Here bandwidth is a concave metric and end-end delay, hop count are additive metric. To specify the amount of bandwidth that is available along the path from the source to the destination, bandwidth metric is used.

As multiple hops are involved to transmit data from source to destination in MANET's hop count is considered as an important metric [2].

If the user had specified threshold for QoS parameters then it is desired to find the goodness of the path by using the QoS metrics. Let D_T, B_T and H_T be the threshold values for delay, bandwidth and hop count values, respectively, and D_C, B_C, H_C be the calculated delay, bandwidth and hop count QoS metrics, respectively, along the path from source to destination. Then for each FANT received the paths should ensure that $D_C < D_T$, $B_C > B_T$, $H_C < H_T$. At this point it is essential to find the best path by finding the path preference probability for the paths that satisfy the QoS constraints. This probability can be calculated by estimating the goodness values of QoS parameters along the path. The goodness of the QoS metrics is estimated by finding the percentage of their deviations from the threshold values. Let d_g, b_g and h_g be the delay, bandwidth and hop count goodness values and are calculated as follows:

$$d_g = \frac{D_T - D_C}{D_T} * 100 \tag{9.3}$$

$$b_g = \frac{B_C - B_T}{B_C} * 100 \tag{9.4}$$

$$h_g = \frac{H_T - H_C}{H_T} * 100 \tag{9.5}$$

The path preference probability $P(i)$ for the path i can be calculated by using the above parameters as below

$$P(i) = \frac{(d_g * b_g * h_g)_i}{\sum_{j \in p_i} (d_g * b_g * h_g)_j} \tag{9.6}$$

where, p_i is set of paths that are explored during the route discovery phase from source to the destination.

Let us consider that the threshold values of delay D_T as 30 ms, bandwidth B_T as 4 Mb/s and hop count H_T as 6. Now let us calculate the path preference probability $P(i)$ for the path 1 (A, H) using (9.3)–(9.6)

Path1 (A, H)
$D_C = 19$ ms; $B_C = 6$ Mb/s; $H_C = 5$

Therefore goodness values of delay, bandwidth and hop count are:

$$d_g = \frac{D_T - D_C}{D_T} * 100 = \frac{30 - 19}{30} * 100 = 36.67 \text{ ms}$$

$$b_g = \frac{B_C - B_T}{B_C} * 100 = \frac{6 - 4}{6} * 100 = 33.333 \text{ Mb/s}$$

$$h_g = \frac{H_T - H_C}{H_T} * 100 = \frac{6 - 5}{5} * 100 = 20$$

$$d_g * b_g * h_g = 36.67 * 33.33 * 20 = 24446.42$$

Now let us calculate the path preference probability $P(i)$ for the path 2 (A, H) using (9.3)–(9.6)

Path 1 (A, H)

$$D_C = 17 \text{ ms}; B_C = 6 \text{ Mb/s}; H_C = 4$$

Therefore goodness values of delay, bandwidth and hop count are:

$$d_g = \frac{D_T - D_C}{D_T} * 100 = \frac{30 - 17}{30} * 100 = 43.33 \text{ ms}$$

$$b_g = \frac{B_C - B_T}{B_C} * 100 = \frac{6 - 4}{6} * 100 = 33.333 \text{ Mb/s}$$

$$h_g = \frac{H_T - H_C}{H_T} * 100 = \frac{6 - 4}{4} * 100 = 50$$

$$d_g * b_g * h_g = 43.33 * 33.33 * 50 = 72209.445$$

Path preference probability $P(i)$ for the path 1(A, H)

$$P(i) = \frac{(d_g * b_g * h_g)_i}{\sum_{j \in p_i} (d_g * b_g * h_g)_j} = \frac{24446.42}{24446.42 + 72209.445} = 0.253$$

Path preference probability $P(i)$ for the path 2(A, H)

$$P(i) = \frac{(d_g * b_g * h_g)_i}{\sum_{j \in p_i} (d_g * b_g * h_g)_j} = \frac{72209.445}{24446.42 + 72209.445} = 0.746$$

As the path preference probability of path 2 (A, H) is better than the path preference probability of path 1(A, H), path 2 is chosen for further communications.

9.3.3 QoS metrics

9.3.3.1 Next hop availability

Next hop availability is defined as the probability to find next hops [28], i.e., the availability of node and link for routing on a path.

Here node probability is expressed in terms of remaining battery time. If B_r represents the remaining battery lifetime of node N_i and B_m represents the lifetime of a fully charged battery, then node probability can be calculated using the following formula:

$$Node \quad probability = \begin{cases} 1 & \text{if remaining battery} \geq 30\% \\ \dfrac{B_r - 10}{90} & \text{if } 30\% > \text{remaining battery} \geq 30\% \\ \dfrac{B_r}{100} & \text{if } 10\% > \text{remaining battery} \geq 30\% \end{cases} \quad (9.7)$$

Link probability is a mobility factor and node's battery remaining time is an energy factor.

If large volumes of data are passed through the same nodes then the energy of the nodes get depleted resulting in dead nodes and link failures/breakages. Here our intension is to select the route that can live for a longer time so that it is available for the network. So we have to select the greater frequency nodes that have the longest remaining battery life.

9.4 Quality of service enabled ant colony–based multipath routing for mobile ad hoc networks

9.4.1 Packet structures of ants

QAMR is a multipath QoS enabled routing protocol. It is based on the foraging behaviour of ant colony. The ant agents (called reactive forward ants) are generated by the source for finding multiple paths to the destination, and backward ants return to set up the paths. The paths are represented in pheromone tables indicating their respective quality. During the route discovery phase Next Hop Availability (NHA) is taken as metric to consider the goodness of the links and nodes that have high availability.

In route discovery phase, when a source node wants to send information to a destination node it first checks for the trusted neighbours. Next the nodes whose next hop availability is greater than threshold are selected. Then the source node broadcasts Forward Ant (FANT) to all its trusted neighbouring nodes those having $NHA > NHA_{thr}$ so that routing overhead is controlled.

The packet structure of FANT consists of source address, destination address, the sequence-number, hop count, bandwidth, start-time and path fields. Path field will contain the address of all the nodes traversed along the path from source to destination and so it is a dynamically growing list.

When the intermediate node receives the FANT it first checks whether its own address is already present in the path field. If present it will discard the FANT to avoid loops. If not then it appends its address to FANT and broadcasts to all its trusted and stable neighbours by its NHA values. While searching for the destination the FANT will collect transmission delay of each link, processing delay at each node, the available capacity of each link, and the number of hops visited.

When the FANT reaches the destination node d the destination node will first calculate path preference value by using QoS parameters only for the paths that meets the QoS threshold values specified by the user and generates Backward Ant (BANT). The packet structure of BANT consists of destination address, original source address, start time, received path field and path preference probability. The FANT contains a stack of visiting nodes in path field. Here the destination node will wait for time T_w to receive all the FANTs. T_w is an integer factor of total end-to-end delay D_C. The BANT is unicasted to the source node by popping up the nodes present in the stack.

When the BANT reaches the intermediate node i from node n the pheromone value gets updated in the routing pheromone table of node i as $T_{i,n}$ and it is updated as

$$T_{i,n} = (1 + T_{i,n})P(k)_d \tag{9.8}$$

where $P(k)_d$ is the path preference value of the kth path that satisfied the QoS requirements for the destination d.

For each BANT that reaches the intermediate node or source node, the node will see path preference probability calculated by using the delay, bandwidth and hop count values from the destination. These were the values received from the FANT. When the source node receives the multiple BANTs then there exist multiple paths to the destination. So during the data session the node with higher pheromone value is selected for data transmission. The routing table update is done as follows, when there is no neighbourhood relationship between nodes the pheromone substance on that link is zero. So the hello messages are periodically broadcasted between the nodes so that each node knows about its neighbours. When the relationship is established between the nodes, the initial pheromone value of 0.1 is deposited on that link of nodes i and j.

The pheromone value on that link is positively reinforced for each intermediate node received FANT. This is given as

$$T_{ij} = T_{ij} + \Delta T_{ij} \quad \text{where } \Delta T_{ij} = 0.05 \tag{9.9}$$

When the data is not transferred for a finite time interval T_{decay} the pheromone value on that link gets decayed by a factor ρ

$$T_{ij} = \begin{cases} (1 - \rho) & if\ 1 \ge (1 - \rho)T_{ij} > 0.1 \\ 1 & if\ (1 - \rho)T_{ij} \ge 1 \\ 0.1 & otherwise \end{cases} \tag{9.10}$$

When a link between two nodes is lost then the pheromone value on that link becomes zero. When the BANT reaches the intermediate node and does not find the node in the path due to mobility of node then the BANT is discarded there itself.

Path Maintenance Phase: Route discovery phase chooses the best and feasible path for data transmission. After some time the load on the nodes of that path may increase and cause more delay, less available bandwidth, depletion of node's energy. For this the $P(i)$ of paths are checked periodically. Then automatically the path preference probability and NHA values are decreased. If the NHA of a node falls below threshold value then the node informs its precursor node by sending a message that the node is off. Then the alternate routes are chosen for data transmission. These alternate Routes are also periodically checked for their validity even though they are not currently used.

9.4.2 QAMR – the algorithm

The routing table that contains the next hop to transfer data and contains the pheromone values, trust pheromone table that contains the trust values of neighbouring nodes and neighbour information table that contains the information of all neighbouring nodes using FANT are maintained in the network.

When the path is to be selected, the source node broadcasts FANT to the neighbouring nodes whose trust pheromone value > threshold *and* NHA > NHA_{thr}. This process is shown in Figure 9.2. Then at the intermediate node FANT

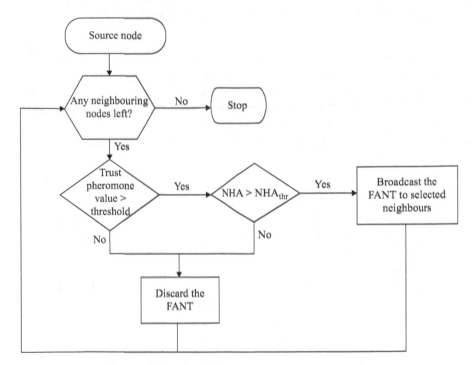

Figure 9.2   The QAMR process at source node

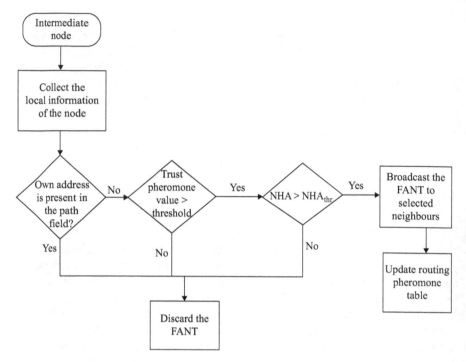

Figure 9.3   The QAMR process at intermediate node

collects the local information of the node. If address of this node is present in the path field, then the FANT is discarded to eliminate loops, repeated forwarding and reduce the traffic. Otherwise check the condition trust pheromone value > threshold and NHA > NHA_{thr} is true or false. If the condition is true then broadcast the FANT to its neighbouring nodes and update the routing pheromone table. If the condition is failed, discard the FANT without forwarding or broadcasting to its neighbours as shown in Figure 9.3.

At last the destination node waits for a certain amount of time in order to receive all the FANTs. For all the generated FANTs, select the path that satisfies the conditions $D_C < D_T$, $B_C > B_T$, $H_C < H_T$. The path preference probability is calculated for all the possible paths and selects the path with minimum path preference probability. Pop the nodes from the path field of this selected FANT. Generate BANT of this selected path and unicast the BANT to the source node as shown in Figure 9.4.

During the travel of BANT from destination to the source node, if the intermediate node is available and is trusted then update the routing pheromone table otherwise discard BANT. During reverse path, the source node selects the path with highest pheromone concentration when multiple BANTs are received.

Finally, start the data transmission by using the updated pheromone values and path preference probability. During each transmission, the pheromone is reinforced

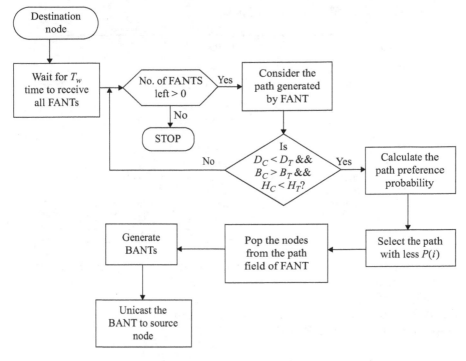

Figure 9.4 The QAMR process at destination node

on the traversed path and gets evaporated on the non-used path using (9.9). On link failure, alternate path is chosen that has next highest path preference probability.

9.4.3 Performance analysis

The following protocols were used for comparing the performance of our proposed protocol, QAMR: AODV [29], ARMAN [2]. AODV is one of the most popular proactive routing protocols for routing in ad hoc networks. ARMAN is an on-demand QoS routing algorithm. The simulations were carried out using NS2 with parameters as shown in Table 9.2.

The following performance metrics were used for the comparisons of the proposed protocol, QAMR with the existing protocols.

(a) QoS path success ratio for different QoS set
(b) Packet delivery ratio with mobility
(c) Packet delivery ratio for varying no of nodes

Figure 9.5 shows the relative performance of three different algorithms, AODV, ARMAN and QAMR in terms of Quality success ratio for different sets of QoS threshold values. In the present routing algorithm the destination node waits for time of $T_w = C * T_d$ for receiving the forward ants, where T_d is end to end delay of the first forward ant received and C is an integer constant. The QoS success ratio

Table 9.2   Simulation parameters

Parameter	Values
Radio range of single node	250 m
Mac layer protocol	IEEE 802.11
Traffic pattern	CBR
Data packet size	512 bytes
Simulation area	500 M * 1000 M
Number of nodes	50
Node mobility speed	0–50 m/s
Simulation time	300 s
Mobility model	Random waypoint mobility model
QoS threshold set	Bandwidth, delay, hop count
Threshold limits	Bandwidth threshold (min 5 Mbps)
	Delay threshold (max. 100 ms)
	Hop count threshold (max. 15)

for wait time of $2T_d$ is more when compared to wait time of $3T_d$ with the increase in wait time, the obtained paths will have more end-to-end delay. Here the QoS success ratio is defined as number of paths that satisfied the user requirements with the total paths explored. The QoS success ratio of QAMR is relatively higher when compared to AODV and ARMAN.

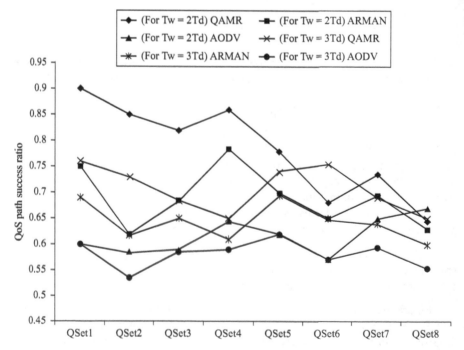

Figure 9.5   Comparison of QoS success ratio for different QoS threshold sets and the waiting time of $2T_d$ and $3T_d$

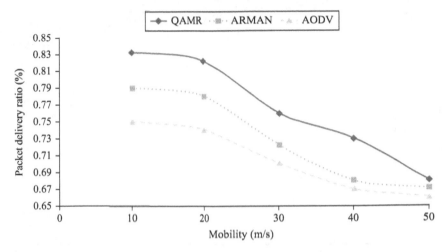

Figure 9.6   Effect of mobility on packet delivery ratio

When there is high mobility there are more chances for link breakages. So frequent routing is required that leads to large routing overhead. Because of the periodic updates of the paths explored, QAMR requires certain amount of routing overhead constantly. The routing overhead is slightly higher than that of AODV due to the use of FANTs and BANTs as control packets.

Packet delivery ratio is a very important metric since it shows the loss rate, which in turn affects the maximum throughput of the network. The packet delivery ratio of the three protocols is shown in Figure 9.6. It shows the effect of mobility on packet delivery ratio. As the node speed increases the packet delivery ratio decreases. In QAMR as link and node stability is considered, the packet delivery ratio is greater than the AODV protocol. As the mobility of the nodes increases, the probability of link failure increases and hence the number of packet drops also increases. QAMR has much higher packet delivery ratio than both AODV and ARMAN. The reason is that QAMR has multiple paths to the destination and the routes are selected based on path preference probability, when an active routing path is broken due to mobility of nodes, the source node of the data flow will receive a notification of link break. The source node at once invalidates the broken routing path in its route table and selects another valid best QoS routing path from its route table to continue to keep communication between source and destination without pause or interrupt.

Figure 9.7 shows the increase in packet delivery ratio with the increase in number of nodes. This is due to more number of intermediate nodes and more stable links available in the networks. The present algorithm shows an increase in packet delivery ratio when compared to AODV and ARMAN.

From the above performance analysis, being an ant-based multipath scheme, the throughput, packet delivery ratio, the QoS success rate of QAMR is higher when compared to AODV and ARMAN.

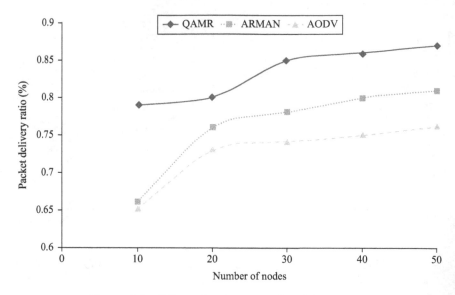

Figure 9.7   Effect of nodes on packet delivery ratio

9.5   Further developments

The QAMR algorithm is tested for mobile ad hoc networks. It can be further refined such that it supports high mobility of nodes and can be validated for the networks like VANET. Similarly it can be refined for the delay sensitive networks, and to be improved as energy efficient process to be supported by sensor nodes in wireless sensor networks.

9.6   Conclusion

In this chapter, the algorithm, QAMR utilizes the concept of forward ant and backward ants to determine the forward paths and reverse paths. Bandwidth, hop count and delay are used to calculate multiple disjoint paths between source and destination to satisfy given QoS constraints. Path preference probability is calculated for all the multiple paths to satisfy the QoS constraints. The path with the highest path preference probability is selected. The next hop availability metric considers both mobility and energy factor to check for the availability of the next hop. The network lifetime is increased as the battery of node is also considered for path computation. ACO used during route discovery phase optimizes the path selection. The best path is strengthened by deposition of pheromone substances on that link. Thus as the routes are selected completely satisfying stability and QoS constraints, it fully complies with quality of service objectives. The performance of the algorithm QAMR is discussed in comparison with the legacy systems like AODV and ARMAN.

References

1. Abolhasan M., Wysocki T. A., Dutkiewicz E. 'A Review of Routing Protocols for Mobile Ad hoc Networks'. *Elsevier Journal of Ad hoc Networks*, 2004, vol. 2, pp. 1–22
2. Deepalakshmi P., Radhakrishnan S. 'Ant Colony Based QoS Routing Algorithm for Mobile Ad Hoc Networks'. *International Journal of Recent Trends in Engineering*, 2009, 1(1), pp. 459–462
3. Asokan R., Natarajan A. M., Nivetha A. 'A Swarm-based Distance Vector Routing to Support Multiple Quality of Service (QoS) Metrics in Mobile Adhoc Networks'. *Journal of Computing Science*, 2007, vol. 3, pp. 700–707, doi: 10.3844/jcssp.2007.700.707
4. Mueller S., Tsang R., Ghosal D. 'Multipath Routing in Mobile Adhoc Networks: Issues and Challenges'. In *Proceedings of Performance Tools and Applications to Networked Systems*, 2004, vol. 2965, pp. 209–234
5. Pham P. P., Perreau S. 'Performance Analysis of Reactive Shortest Path and Multipath Routing Mechanism with Load Balance'. INFOCOM 2003. Twenty-Second Annual Joint Conference of the IEEE Computer and Communications, IEEE Societies, 30 March–April 2003 vol. 1, pp. 251–259, doi: 10.1109/INFCOM.2003.1208677
6. Gunes M., Sorges U., Bouazizi I. 'ARA – The Ant-Colony based Routing Algorithm for MANETs'. In *Proceedings of the 2002 International Conference on Parallel Processing Workshops*, IEEE Computer Society Washington, DC, USA, 2002, pp. 79–85 ISBN: 0-7695-1680-7 Doi: 10.1109/ICPPW.2002.1039715
7. Lee S.-J., Gerla M. 'Split Multipath Routing with Maximally Disjoint Paths in Ad Hoc Networks'. In *Proceedings of IEEE International Conference on Communications*, 2001, vol. 10, pp. 3201–3205 doi: 10.1109/ICC.2001.937262
8. Marina M. K., Das S. R. 'On-demand Multipath Distance Vector Routing in Ad Hoc Networks'. 9th International Conference on Network Protocols, 11–14 Nov. 2001, pp. 14–23 doi: 10.1109/ICNP.2001.992756
9. Jiwon Park., Moh S., Ilyong Chung. 'A Multipath AODV Routing Protocol in Mobile Ad Hoc Networks with SINR-based Route Selection'. ISWCS '08. IEEE International Symposium on Wireless Communication Systems. 21–24 Oct. 2008, pp. 682–686, doi: 10.1109/ISWCS.2008.4726143
10. Valera A., Seah W. K. G., Rao S. V. 'Cooperative Packet Caching and Shortest Multipath Routing in Mobile Ad Hoc Networks'. INFOCOM 2003. 22nd Annual Joint Conference of the IEEE Computer and Communications. IEEE Societies, 30 Mar.–Apr. 2003, vol. 1, pp. 260–269, doi: 10.1109/INFCOM.2003.1208678
11. Li X. 'Multipath Routing and QoS Provisioning in Mobile Ad hoc Networks', Ph.D thesis, Queen Mary University of London, 2006
12. Zhengyu W., Xiangjun D., Lin C. 'A Grid-Based Energy Aware Node-Disjoint Multipath Routing Algorithm for MANETs'. In *Proceedings of International Conference on Natural Computation*, 2007, vol. 5, pp. 244–248

13. Do-Youn Hwang, Eui-Hyeok Kwon, Jae-Sung Lim. 'An Energy Aware Source Routing with Disjoint Multipath Selection for Energy-Efficient Multi-hop Wireless Ad Hoc Networks'. *Lecture Notes in Computer Science*, 2006, vol. 3976/2006, pp. 41–50, doi: 10.1007/11753810_4

14. Lingaiah M. B., Naidu M. M., Sreenivasa Rao D., Varaprasad G. 'Energy Aware Node-Disjoint Routing in Mobile Ad Hoc Networks'. *Journal of Theoretical and Applied Information Technology*, 2009, vol. 5(4), pp. 416–431

15. Tan L., Xie L., Ko K.-T., Lei M., Moshe Z. 'LAMOR: Lifetime-Aware Multipath Optimized Routing Algorithm for Video Transmission over Ad Hoc Networks'. VTC 2006, 63rd IEEE conference on Vehicular Technology, 7–10 May 2006, vol. 2, pp. 623–627, doi: 10.1109/VETECS.2006.1682899

16. Ding S., Liu L. 'A Node-disjoint Multipath Routing Protocol Based on AODV'. (DCABES), 9th International Symposium on Distributed Computing and Applications to Business Engineering and Science, 10–12 Aug. 2010, pp. 312–316, doi: 10.1109/DCABES.2010.70

17. Misra S., Dhurandher S. K., Obaidat M. S., Verma K., Gupta P. 'Using Ant-Like Agents for Fault-Tolerant Routing in Mobile Ad-Hoc Networks'. ICC '09. IEEE International Conference on Communications, 14–18 Jun. 2009, pp. 1–5, doi: 10.1109/ICC.2009.5199555

18. Misra S., Krishna P. V., Bhiwal A., Chawla A. S., Wolfinger B. E., Lee C. 'A Learning Automata-based Fault-Tolerant Routing Algorithm for Mobile Ad-Hoc Networks'. *The Journal of Supercomputing*, Springer, October 2012, vol. 62(1), pp. 4–23, doi: 10.1007/s11227-011-0639-8

19. Goswami M. M., Dharaskar R. V., Thakare V. M. 'Fuzzy Ant Colony Based Routing Protocol for Mobile Ad Hoc Network'. ICCET'09, International Conference on Computer Engineering and Technology, 2009, vol. 2, pp. 438–444, doi: 10.1109/ICCET.2009.168

20. Luis Cobo L., Quintero A., Pierre S. 'Ant-based Routing for Wireless Multimedia Sensor Networks Using Multiple QoS Metrics'. *Computer Networks*, Dec. 2010, vol. 54(17), pp. 2991–3010, ISSN 1389-1286, 10.1016/j.comnet.2010.05.014

21. Lin N., Shao Z. 'Improved Ant Colony Algorithm for Multipath Routing Algorithm Research'. (IPTC), 2010 International Symposium on Intelligence Information Processing and Trusted Computing, 28–29 Oct. 2010, pp. 651–655, doi: 10.1109/IPTC.2010.162

22. Upadhayaya S., Gandhi C. 'Quality of Service Routing in Mobile Ad Hoc Networks Using Location and Energy Parameters'. International Journal of Wireless & Mobile Networks (IJWMN), Nov. 2009, vol. 1(2), pp. 138–147

23. Badis H., Agha K. A. 'Quality of Service for Ad Hoc Optimized Link State Routing Protocol (QOLSR)'. http://www.ietf.org/rfc/rfc3561.txt, IETF, RFC draft 01, Apr. 2005

24. Liu L., Feng G. 'A Novel Ant Colony Based QoS-Aware Routing Algorithm for MANETs'. *Lecture Notes in Computer Science*, 2005, vol. 3612/2005, pp. 457–466, doi: 10.1007/11539902_56

25. Wu J., Wang Y. 'Social Feature-based Multi-path Routing in Delay Tolerant Networks'. In *Proceedings of IEEE INFOCOM*, 2012, 25–30 Mar. 2012, pp. 1368–1376, doi: 10.1109/INFCOM.2012.6195500

26. Challal Y., Ouadjaout A., Lasla N., Bagaa M., Hadjidj A. 'Secure and Efficient Disjoint Multipath Construction for Fault Tolerant Routing in Wireless Sensor Networks'. *Journal of Network and Computer Applications*, Jul. 2011, vol. 34(4), pp. 1380–1397, ISSN 1084-8045, 10.1016/j.jnca.2011.03.022

27. Stefan R., Goossens K. 'A TDM Slot Allocation Flow Based on Multipath Routing in NoCs'. *Journal of Microprocessors and Microsystems*, Mar. 2011, vol. 35(2), pp. 130–138, ISSN 0141-9331, 10.1016/j.micpro.2010.09.007

28. Mehfuz S., Doja M. N. 'Swarm Intelligent Power-Aware Detection of Unauthorized and Compromised Nodes in MANETs'. *Journal of Artificial Evolution and Applications*, January 2008, Article ID 236803, pp. 1–16, doi: 10.1155/2008/236803

29. Chakeres I. D., Belding-Royer E. M. 'AODV Routing Protocol Implementation Design'. In *Proceedings of 24th International Conference on Distributed Computing Systems Workshops*, 23–24 Mar. 2004, pp. 698–703, doi: 10.1109/ICDCSW.2004.1284108

Chapter 10*

Reliable multipath routing in mobile ad hoc networks using hybrid computational intelligence algorithms

Mansour Sheikhan[a] and Ehsan Hemmati[a]

Abstract

Due to mobility and frequent node failure, the topology of a mobile ad hoc network (MANET) is highly dynamic. Routing protocols should adapt to such dynamism, and continue to maintain connection between the source and the destination. A hybrid computational intelligence-based multipath routing algorithm is presented in this chapter. The proposed method employs Hopfield neural network (HNN) as a disjoint path set selection tool for choosing disjoint paths that maximise the network reliability. The parameters of Hopfield model are also optimised by particle swarm optimisation (PSO) algorithm. This method selects disjoint paths in such a way that the network reliability is maximised. For this purpose, each node in the network is equipped with an HNN. Simulation results show that the proposed PSO-optimised HNN-based routing algorithm has better performance as the reliability of multiple paths is increased while the number of algorithm iterations is reduced as compared with the non-optimised HNN multipath routing. In addition, the PSO-optimised HNN-based routing algorithm shows better performance in terms of reliability and number of paths when compared with the backup path set selection (BPS) algorithm.

10.1 Introduction

In structured wireless networks, such as cellular networks, the wireless connection goes only one-hop and the remainder of routing happens in the wired domain. However, mobile ad hoc network (MANET) is a set of wireless mobile nodes forming a temporary network without the use of any fixed infrastructure. Nodes typically communicate with each other in multi-hopping fashion. In a MANET,

*H. F. Rashvand and H.-C. Chao (Eds.), *Dynamic Ad Hoc Networks*, The IET Book Publishing Department, 2013, ISBN 978-1-84919-647-5, eISBN 978-1-84919-648-2
[a]Department of Electrical Engineering, Islamic Azad University, South Tehran Branch, Tehran, Iran.

mobile nodes that have limited resources of computing, storage and power perform the network tasks such as relaying packets, discovering routes, network monitoring and securing communication. There are several applications for a MANET such as mobile conferencing, emergency services, home networking, embedded computing, personal area networking and Bluetooth [1].

In recent two decades, several routing protocols have been proposed for MANET [2]. A promising approach is to use a set of redundant paths, instead of using a single path, to alleviate the effects of failures in the network. Common links and nodes between paths are common failure points in the set; therefore, multiple paths should be considered as link-disjoint or node-disjoint to decrease the possibility of concurrent failures in different paths.

On the other hand, adaptation, fault tolerance, error resilience and high computational speed are the important characteristics of computational intelligence (CI) methods. Neural computing, fuzzy logic, evolutionary computing and swarm intelligence (SI) are the core methods of CI. In this chapter, Hopfield neural network (HNN) [3] that its parameters optimised by particle swarm optimisation (PSO) algorithm is used for disjoint path selection in MANET.

An artificial neural network (ANN) consists of a collection of processing units called neurons that are highly interconnected in a given topology. Neural networks have been successfully used in function approximation, classification and optimisation problems. On the other hand, SI refers to artificial intelligence techniques involving the study of collective behaviour in decentralised systems.

The possibility of using HNN and its modified variants as a disjoint path set selection algorithm for choosing disjoint paths that maximise the network reliability is investigated in this chapter. Each node in the network can be equipped with an HNN. One of the most important features of the proposed model is that HNN can be easily implemented in hardware; therefore, neural computations are done in parallel and the solution is found more quickly.

In Section 10.2, the classification of routing protocols in MANET including multipath protocols and related work are presented. Section 10.3 provides an overview of HNN and PSO as the CI algorithms used in this chapter. Section 10.4 describes the proposed path set selection algorithm. The implementation details and parameters tuning of HNN are described in Section 10.5. Section 10.6 reports the simulation results and comparisons with similar works. Finally, Section 10.7 concludes the work.

10.2 Multipath routing protocols in MANETs

Several routing protocols have been proposed for MANET emphasising different implementation scenarios. The general categories of these protocols are as follows:

(a) source-initiated (reactive or on-demand) such as ad hoc on-demand distance vector (AODV) [4],
(b) table-driven (proactive) such as destination-sequenced distance-vector (DSDV) [5],
(c) location-aware (geographical) such as location-aided routing (LAR) [6],
(d) multipath such as quality of service (QoS)-enabled ant colony-based multipath routing (QAMR) [7],

(e) hierarchical such as hierarchical state routing (HSR) [8],
(f) multicast such as probabilistic predictive multicast algorithm (PPMA) [9],
(g) geographical multicast (geocast) such as direction guided routing (DGR) [10],
(h) power-aware such as device and energy-aware routing (DEAR) [11],
(i) hybrid such as multipath multicast using reliable neighbour selection (MMRNS) [12].

The main objectives of multipath routing protocols are to provide reliable communication and to ensure load balancing as well as to improve QoS. These protocols are classified into delay-aware, reliable, minimum overhead, energy efficient and hybrid multipath routing protocols [13]. The proposed method in this chapter is reliable with hybrid structure (by combining two CI-based methods, not combining two protocols), so the description of some reliable and hybrid protocols is given in Tables 10.1 and 10.2, respectively.

Table 10.1   Description of some reliable multipath routing protocols

Protocol	Description
Game theoretic-multipath multimedia dynamic source routing (G-MMDSR) [14]	Using a game theoretic approach to achieve a dynamic selection of the forwarding paths
Greedy-based backup routing (GBR) [15]	Constructing the primary path based on a greedy forwarding mechanism
Shortest multipath source (SMS) routing based on dynamic source routing (DSR) [16]	Achieving shorter multiple partial-disjoint paths
Proposed protocol in this study	Combining ANN and SI techniques for choosing disjoint paths that maximise the network reliability

Table 10.2   Description of some hybrid multipath routing protocols

Protocol	Description
QAMR [7]	Path selection based on the stability of nodes and the path preference probability similar to the foraging behaviour of ant colony for selecting path
MMRNS [12]	Establishment of a mesh of multipath routes from source to multicast destinations using neighbours that have high reliability pair factor
Multipath optimised link state routing (MP-OLSR) [17]	Implementing route recovery and loop detection in order to improve QoS regarding OLSR
Spatially disjoint multipath routing (SDMR) [18]	Finding spatially disjoint paths without the need of location information
Ad hoc on-demand trusted-path distance vector (AOTDV) [19]	Discovering multiple loop-free paths as candidates in one route discovery
Proposed protocol in this study	Combining HNN model and PSO algorithm as two CI-based algorithms for disjoint path set selection

As a related CI-based work, Wang *et al.* [20] used a hybrid routing algorithm based on ant colony optimisation and zone routing framework of broadcasting called HOPNET. On the other hand, many SI and evolutionary algorithms have been proposed for optimisation of structure and parameters of neural networks. As sample researches in this field, Lee and Ko [21] developed a nonlinear time-varying evolution PSO (NTVE-PSO) algorithm to determine the optimal structure of radial basis function neural network (RBFNN). Leung *et al.* [22] used PSO to optimise the structure of RBFNN including the weights and controlling parameters. It is noted that the PSO algorithm is used in this chapter to determine the optimum value of HNN parameters.

10.3   Investigated computational intelligence algorithms

10.3.1   Hopfield neural network

HNN is a neural model in which a sigmoid monotonic increasing function relates the output V_i of ith neuron to its input U_i as (10.1) [3]

$$V_i = g(U_i) = \frac{1}{1 + e^{-\lambda U_i}} \tag{10.1}$$

where λ is a constant called gain factor. The connection matrix that describes the weighted connections of the network is shown by T. For a symmetric connection matrix and for a sufficiently high gain of transfer function, the dynamics of neurons follow gradient descent of the quadratic energy function as (10.2) [3]

$$E = -\frac{1}{2}\sum_{i=1}^{n}\sum_{j=1}^{n} T_{ij}V_iV_j - \sum_{i=1}^{n} I_iV_i \tag{10.2}$$

where I_i is the bias of ith neuron. Hopfield has shown that as long as the state of neural network evolves inside the N-dimensional hypercube, defined by $V_i \in \{0, 1\}$, if $\lambda_i \to \infty$, then the minimum of energy function (10.2) will attain one of the 2^N vertices of this hypercube [3].

10.3.2   Particle swarm optimisation algorithm

PSO is a population-based stochastic optimisation technique in which each particle moves through the D-dimensional problem space by updating its velocities with the best solution found by itself (cognitive behaviour) and the best solution found by any particle in its neighbourhood (social behaviour). Each particle has a velocity and a position update formula as (10.3) and (10.4), respectively [23]

$$v_i(k + 1) = v_i(k) + \gamma_{1i}(P_i - x_i(k)) + \gamma_{2i}(G - x_i(k)) \tag{10.3}$$

$$x_i(k + 1) = x_i(k) + v_i(k + 1) \tag{10.4}$$

where i is the particle index, k is the discrete time index, v_i is the velocity of ith particle, x_i is the position of ith particle, P_i is the best position found by ith particle (personal best), G is the best position found by swarm (global best) and $\gamma_{1,2}$ are random numbers in the interval $[0,1]$ applied to ith particle. In the simulations of this chapter, (10.5) is used for velocity update [24]

$$v_i(k+1) = \varphi(k)v_i(k) + \alpha_1[\gamma_{1i}(P_i - x_i(k))] + \alpha_2[\gamma_{2i}(G - x_i(k))] \qquad (10.5)$$

in which $\varphi(k)$ is the inertia function and $\alpha_{1,2}$ are the acceleration constants. In this chapter, linear decreasing strategy is used in which an initially large inertia weight (i.e., 0.9) is linearly decreased to a small value (i.e., 0.2) as (10.6) [25]

$$\varphi(k) = [\varphi(0) - \varphi(N_T)]\frac{(N_T - k)}{N_T} + \varphi(N_T) \qquad (10.6)$$

where N_T is the maximum number of iterations, $\varphi(0)$ is the initial inertia weight and $\varphi(N_T)$ is the final inertia weight. The steps of PSO algorithm are as follows:

Step 1 (Initialisation): Initialise swarm and randomise the position and velocity of each particle $(x_i, v_i; i = 1, \ldots, M)$.

Step 2 (Fitness function evaluation): Compute the fitness function of each particle $(y(i) = fitness(x_i))$.

Step 3 (Initialisation of the personal best and global best positions): Initialise each P_i and G as $P_{i0} = y_i$ and $G = \min(P_{i0}); i = 1, \ldots, M$.

Step 4 (Velocity and position update): Update the velocity of particle using dynamic inertia weight ((10.5) and (10.6)) and control it by velocity clamping as (10.7)

$$v_i(k+1) = \begin{cases} v_i(k+1) & if\ v_i(k+1) < V_{\max} \\ V_{\max} & if\ v_i(k+1) \geq V_{\max} \end{cases} \qquad (10.7)$$

and update the position of particle using (10.4).

Step 5 (Update of the personal best and global best positions): Update P_i and G based on the new value of fitness function as: $y_{i,new} = fitness(x_{i,new})$, $P_i = y_{i,new}$ and $G = \min(P_i)$.

Step 6 (Test): If the stop conditions are not satisfied, go to Step 4. Otherwise, stop and return G as the best solution.

10.4   Proposed approach

10.4.1   Model and assumptions

A MANET can be modelled as a graph $G = (V, L)$, where V is a set of nodes in the network, L is a set of links connecting nodes and the probability of proper operation is also assigned to the links. The reliability of a network path between a source and a destination is defined as the probability of that path being operational. The probability of proper operation of a link, proper operation of a path and proper operation of a path set is denoted by p^{link}, p^{path} and p^{pset}, respectively. In this protocol, each node continuously monitors the reliability of its incident links.

In order to acquire link reliability estimates, considering a free space propagation model [26], the link expiration time (LET) between two nodes is used. In this model, the wireless signal strength depends only on the distance to the transmitter. Hence, the link duration can be predicted from the motion information of the two nodes.

Assume node i and node j are within the same transmission range, r. The probability of proper operation of a link between node i and node j, p_{ij}^{link}, is defined as the ratio of $LET_{i,j}$ to LET_{max}, where the LET_{max} is the maximum of time duration that two nodes stay connected in the network.

10.4.2 Path set reliability computation method

To compute the path set reliability, the reliability of each path in the path set should be obtained in the first step. The path reliability is obtained by multiplying the reliability of its constituent links as (10.8) [27]

$$p_i^{path} = \prod_{h=1}^{m} p_h^{link} \tag{10.8}$$

where m is the number of links that form this path. The improper operating probability of the path, q^{path}, is obtained by $q^{path} = 1 - p^{path}$.

For the next step, the objective is to compute the path set reliability using each of the path reliabilities obtained in (10.8). Assume that $P = \{Path_1, Path_2, \dots, Path_n\}$ denotes a disjoint path set that consists of n paths. The reliability of the path set is calculated as (10.9) [27]

$$
\begin{aligned}
p^{pset} &= 1 - \prod_{i=1}^{n} q_i^{path} \\
&\simeq \sum_{i=1}^{n} p_i^{path}
\end{aligned}
\tag{10.9}
$$

This equation will be used later to define energy function in the HNN model.

10.4.3 Disjoint path set types

There are two types of disjoint multiple paths between a source and a destination: node-disjoint and link-disjoint. Node-disjoint paths do not have any common node, except the source and destination. Link-disjoint paths do not have any link in common, but may have shared nodes. A set of link-disjoint paths is formed by a series of node-disjoint segments.

In this section, an algorithm is proposed which can compute both node-disjoint and link-disjoint paths. In this way, the HNN can find the maximum number of disjoint paths in order to maximise the path set reliability. For this purpose, the path set reliability is maximised when compared to other possible disjoint paths in the network.

10.4.4   HNN-based multipath routing

The proposed solution is based on two simple steps:

1. *Route discovery*: Finding all paths between source and destination.
2. *Path set selection*: Finding the most reliable disjoint path set by the HNN model.

10.4.4.1   Route discovery algorithm

In this algorithm, a route cache is considered for each node. At the destination node, this cache preserves the order of nodes and probabilities of all paths, p^{path}, from each source. To find the possible routes between a source and a destination, the following steps are followed:

1. The source node broadcasts the route request (RREQ) packet to the nodes that are in its transmission range. This RREQ packet contains the following fields:
   Record: An accumulated record of the sequence of hops taken by this packet.
   Prob: The reliability of the followed path.
   Max_hop: The maximum number of hops that a packet can traverse along the network before it is discarded.
2. When a node receives an RREQ packet, it decrements *Max_hop* by one and performs the following operations:
   2.1 If node is the destination it updates the *Prob* ($Prob\_new = p^{path}_{incoming} \times Prob\_old$) and adds the *Record* and updates *Prob* to its route cash.
   2.2 If *Max_hop* $= 0$, the RREQ packet is discarded. Thus, *Max_hop* limits the number of intermediate nodes in a path.
   2.3 If ID of this node is already listed in the *Record* of route request, the RREQ packet is discarded to avoid looping.
   2.4 Otherwise, the node appends its own node ID to the *Record* in the RREQ packet, updates the *Prob* field and re-broadcasts the request to its neighbours.
3. When the destination node receives the first RREQ packet from a specific source node, it waits for a while to receive other RREQ packets from longer paths.

Now all the needed information to calculate link-disjoint or node-disjoint path set is obtained by a single route discovery. Therefore, there is no need to send extra messages as overhead in the MANET when both link-disjoint and node-disjoint path sets are needed.

For all the paths in destination route cache, we assume a matrix, ρ, with the size of $(n \times n)$ in which n is the total number of RREQ packets received from a specific source. Depending on whether we want to find node-disjoint or link-disjoint path set, the matrix definition will be different. For finding node-disjoint path set, ρ_{ij} is defined as NDp_{ij} in (10.10)

$$NDp_{ij}_{i \neq j} = \begin{cases} 0 \ \textit{if } i^{th} \textit{ path and } j^{th} \textit{ path in} \\ \quad \textit{route cache are node} - \textit{disjointed} \\ 1 \ \textit{otherwise} \end{cases} \qquad (10.10)$$

Similarly, to find link-disjoint path set, ρ_{ij} is defined as $LD\rho_{ij}$ in (10.11)

$$LD\rho_{ij}_{i \neq j} = \begin{cases} 0 \text{ if } i^{th} \text{ path and } j^{th} \text{ path in} \\ \quad \text{route cache are link} - \text{disjointed} \\ 1 \text{ otherwise} \end{cases} \tag{10.11}$$

All the diagonal elements in ρ are set to zero ($\rho_{ij} = 0$; $i = j$).

10.4.4.2 Path set selection by neural network model

In this approach, the most reliable disjoint path set can be decoded from the final stable state of HNN model. The proposed neural network consists of n neurons; each neuron in this model represents a path of discovered paths in the route discovery phase, listed in the destination route cache. Thus, the total number of neurons, n, required in HNN is equal to the total number of paths found in the route discovery phase from a specific source. The output of a neuron at location i is defined in (10.12)

$$V_i = \begin{cases} 1 \text{ if } i^{th} \text{ path in route cache is in the path set} \\ 0 \text{ otherwise} \end{cases} \tag{10.12}$$

The normalised reliability of ith path is defined as (10.13)

$$C_i = \frac{p_i^{path}}{p_{max}^{path}} \tag{10.13}$$

where p_{max}^{path} is the maximum value of path reliability.

In order to solve this problem using the HNN model, an energy function is defined whose minimisation process drives the neural network into its lowest energy state. The energy function includes the states that correspond to disjoint path sets. Among these disjoint path sets, one path set has the highest reliability.

The proposed energy function consists of the following parts:

Part A: This part guarantees that all the selected paths are disjointed which is defined in (10.14)

$$E_A = \frac{\mu_1}{2} \sum_{i=1}^{n} \sum_{j=1}^{n} \rho_{ij} V_i V_j \tag{10.14}$$

where μ_1 is a positive constant. If the elements of each pair of the paths in the solution are disjointed, then all of them will be disjointed with each other. If the paths are disjointed, then this concept minimises E_A which is equal to zero. But if the solution contains k pairs of non-disjoint paths, then $E_A = k\mu_1$; $k = 1, 2, \ldots$.

Part B: The second part maximises the total reliability of a path set by taking into account the reliability of its constitute paths that is defined in (10.15)

$$E_B = -\mu_2 \sum_{i=1}^{n} C_i V_i \tag{10.15}$$

where μ_2 is a positive constant. By selecting each path, this term is reduced by $\mu_2 C_i$. Thus, the total energy function is calculated as (10.16)

$$E = E_A + E_B$$
$$= \frac{\mu_1}{2} \sum_{i=1}^{n} \sum_{j=1}^{n} \rho_{ij} V_i V_j - \mu_2 \sum_{i=1}^{n} C_i V_i \qquad (10.16)$$

By comparing the corresponding coefficients in (10.16) and (10.2), the connection strengths and the biases are derived as (10.17)

$$T_{ij} = -\mu_1 \rho_{ij}$$
$$I_i = \mu_2 C_i \qquad (10.17)$$

As can be seen in (10.17), this model maps the reliability information into the biases and path disjointedness information into the neural interconnections. In node-disjoint path set selection, ρ_{ij} in (10.16) and (10.17) is set to $ND\rho_{ij}$ and in link-disjoint path set selection, ρ_{ij} in (10.16) and (10.17) is set to $LD\rho_{ij}$. The destination node can set the neural interconnections as it received each RREQ packet and then set the biases after all of the RREQ packets have been received. The destination node uses HNN model to find the most reliable path set and returns a copy of path set, found by neural network, in a route reply packet to the source node.

It is noted that other neural structures such as transient chaotic neural network (TCNN) and noisy HNN can also be used for this purpose [28, 29].

10.4.5 Path set selection by PSO-optimised HNN

There are parameters in the proposed algorithm such as μ_1, μ_2, V_{th} and λ. PSO algorithm is employed in this chapter in order to find optimal values for these parameters. The conceptual scheme of this approach in a MANET node is depicted in Figure 10.1 [30].

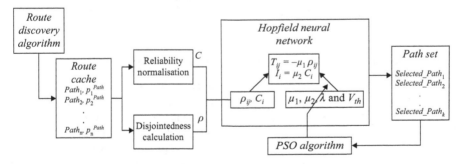

Figure 10.1   Conceptual scheme of path set selection by PSO-optimised HNN model

10.5 Implementation details and parameters tuning

For evaluating the efficiency of proposed routing method, it has been applied to the networks with various transmission ranges, number of nodes and moving characteristics. The simulation consists of three steps: (a) developing the network structure and its mobility model that dictates how the nodes move, (b) finding paths between the source and the destination using the proposed algorithm and (c) finding the best disjoint path set using HNN model.

10.5.1 Ad hoc network model

The MANET is modelled as a set of nodes move as defined by the random way-point model [31]. For this purpose, each node selects a random destination within the working area and moves linearly to that location at a predefined speed. After reaching its destination, the node pauses for a specified time and then selects a new random location and continues the process again.

In the simulations of this work, each node pauses at the current position for 5 s and the speed of individual nodes ranges from 0 to 20 m/s. Simulations for networks have been run with 30 mobile hosts, operating at transmission ranges varying from 150 m to 300 m. The behaviour of the simulated network is studied for 1000 s. The proposed model consists of n neurons, where n is the total number of paths in the destination route cache found in the route discovery phase.

10.5.2 Initialisation of HNN model

The evolution of neural network state is simulated by the solution of a system of n differential equations, where the variables are the neuron outputs V_i. The solution consists of observing the outputs of neurons, V_i, for a specific duration δt. To avoid any bias in favour of a particular path set, it is assumed that all the inputs, U_i, are equal to zero. However, to help the network in rapid convergence, small perturbations should be applied to the initial inputs of neural network. U_i is chosen such that $-0.0005 < U_i < 0.0005$. The calculations are ceased when the neural network reaches a stable state, defined as when the difference between the outputs in two consecutive steps is less than 10^{-6} or after 10^5 epochs. When the neural network is in a stable state, the final value of V_i is rounded off, i.e. it is set to zero if $V_i < V_{th}$; otherwise, it is set to one.

10.5.3 Selecting network parameters by PSO algorithm

As mentioned before, the PSO algorithm is used in this work to find the optimum parameter values of HNN model such as μ_1, μ_2, λ, δt and V_{th}. Each dimension of the PSO particle is used to present a different HNN parameter, thus each particle has five dimensions. To evaluate the fitness of each particle, we compute the percentage error obtained by 500 HNN simulations. The parameters setting of PSO is given in Table 10.3. The result of applying PSO algorithm to obtain the optimum values for HNN parameters is given in Table 10.4 [30].

Table 10.3   Parameters setting of PSO algorithm

Parameter	Maximum number of iterations	Population size	Maximum particle velocity	Initial inertia weight	Final inertia weight	Minimum global error gradient
Value	300	20	4	0.9	0.2	10^{-5}

Table 10.4   Optimum parameter values obtained by PSO algorithm

Parameter	μ_1	μ_2	λ	δt	V_{th}
Value	32	27	0.45	10^{-3}	0.23

10.6   Simulation results

To evaluate the proposed algorithm, the following steps are considered:

1. At the beginning, the nodes are located randomly within a rectangular working area of 1000 m × 500 m.
2. The source and destination nodes are chosen randomly.
3. The random waypoint mobility model is applied for node movements.
4. The number of routes, reliability and lifetime of the path set are computed for various networks with different number of nodes, transmission ranges and node speeds by using the proposed method.

The average number of control messages transmitted in the route discovery phase with *Max_hop* = 3 for different transmission ranges and number of nodes is shown in Figure 10.2.

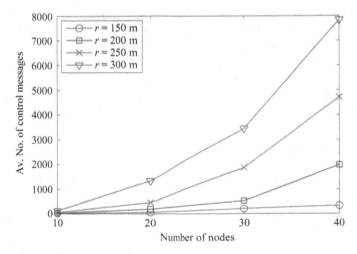

Figure 10.2   Average number of control messages in HNN-based model

Based on the network parameters, two different scenarios are considered. In each scenario, one aspect of MANET characteristics is considered. In the first scenario, the connectivity is considered and the network density is considered in the second scenario. Then, the simulation results for these scenarios, using the PSO-optimised HNN-based routing algorithm are compared with previous works (non-optimised HNN and noisy HNN path set selection algorithms reported in [29, 32]).

In the first scenario, the number and speed of nodes are considered fixed and the transmission range is variable and the effect of this parameter on reliability and number of paths is investigated. As reported in Table 10.5, the reliability of link-disjoint path set is higher than node-disjoint path set with the same range. It should be noted that the reliability of disjoint paths selected by PSO-optimised HNN is higher than two other algorithms. In addition, if the transmission range is increased, then the number of paths in path set is also increased for both link-disjoint and node-disjoint path sets (Table 10.5).

The reliability of node-disjoint and link-disjoint path sets against time is shown in Figure 10.3. As the time passes, some of the paths in the set fail which causes a decrease in the path set reliability.

The average number of iterations for both PSO-optimised and non-optimised settings are reported in Table 10.6 [30]. The PSO-optimised HNN that is reported in this chapter takes less iterations and thus less time to reach the steady state. The reliability of path sets found by PSO-optimised is also higher than those found by non-optimised HNN.

The second scenario considers a fixed transmission range while the number of nodes is variable. In this scenario, the transmission range of all nodes is set to 250 m. The reliability of the set for both the node-disjoint and the link-disjoint paths is shown in Table 10.7.

Although the PSO-optimised HNN has similar or only slightly better results with those of a noisy HNN, but it is noticeable that the implementation of the HNN is simpler than a noisy HNN. It can be found from the simulation results that by fine-tuning of the HNN, better results can be achieved with a simpler implementation and there is no need of an additional hardware.

In this way, Dana *et al.* [27] proposed an algorithm for backup path set selection (BPS) in ad hoc wireless networks. This algorithm only finds the link-disjoint path set. Table 10.8 shows the performance comparison of the proposed PSO-optimised HNN method with the results reported in Reference 27.

10.7   Conclusion

Multipath routing can provide reliable communication in a MANET. The intention of this chapter has been also to find as many disjoint paths as possible that are most reliable. Finding an optimum path set in the network among all the possible path sets is a nondeterministic polynomial time-complete (NP-C) optimisation problem. In the proposed algorithm, HNN has been used to find the most reliable path set. A small-size analogue circuit can implement HNN, so it could be applicable to MANET where time and space are critical and near optimal solution is acceptable.

Table 10.5 *Reliability and number of paths in different HNN-based path selection algorithms*

Transmission range, m	Reliability						Number of paths					
	Link-disjoint			Node-disjoint			Link-disjoint			Node-disjoint		
	HNN	Noisy-HNN	PSO-optimised HNN	HNN	Noisy-HNN	PSO-optimised HNN	HNN	Noisy-HNN	PSO-optimised HNN	HNN	Noisy-HNN	PSO-optimised HNN
150	0.42	0.47	0.48	0.41	0.46	0.47	4.1	4.8	4.9	3.4	4.3	4.3
200	0.73	0.73	0.76	0.72	0.71	0.75	6.1	6.3	6.2	5.6	5.7	5.6
250	0.82	0.83	0.87	0.79	0.81	0.84	6.9	8.4	8.6	6.2	7.4	7.8
300	0.86	0.92	0.95	0.85	0.90	0.95	10.9	12.3	13.1	11.5	11.7	12.6

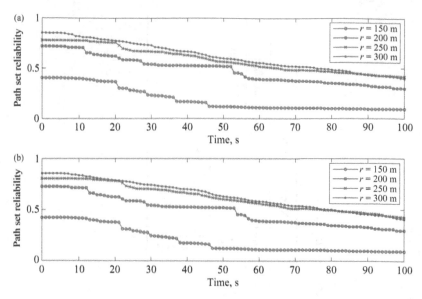

Figure 10.3   *Path set reliability in HNN-based model: (a) node-disjoint,*
(b) link-disjoint

Table 10.6   *Performance comparison between PSO-optimised HNN and*
non-optimised HNN algorithms

Transmission range, m	Number of iterations in HNN-based algorithm			Reliability in HNN-based algorithm		
	Non-optimised	PSO-optimised	Per cent of iterations in optimised to non-optimised model	Non-optimised	PSO-optimised	Per cent of increment in optimised as compared to non-optimised model
150	70,476	8,587	12.2	0.415	0.470	13.3
200	87,944	7,896	9.0	0.723	0.758	4.8
250	83,969	9,601	11.4	0.806	0.837	3.8
300	95,040	11,312	11.9	0.855	0.951	11.1

The proposed algorithm can find both link-disjoint and node-disjoint path sets. This algorithm improves the reliability, when averaged over different transmission ranges, in comparison to BPS algorithm [27], while the computational complexity of the proposed algorithm is less than the BPS algorithm [32].

In addition, to improve the network performance, PSO algorithm has been used to optimise the HNN parameters. The simulation results have shown that PSO is a suitable approach to optimise the HNN for multipath routing, since this method

Table 10.7   Reliability for different number of nodes in investigated HNN-based algorithms

Number of nodes	Reliability					
	Link-disjoint			Node-disjoint		
	HNN	Noisy-HNN	PSO-optimised HNN	HNN	Noisy-HNN	PSO-optimised HNN
10	0.46	0.52	0.57	0.43	0.50	0.52
20	0.66	0.62	0.67	0.62	0.59	0.63
30	0.82	0.83	0.84	0.79	0.81	0.83
40	0.88	0.92	0.94	0.83	0.89	0.94

Table 10.8   Performance comparison between PSO-optimised HNN and BPS algorithms

Transmission range, m	Reliability		Number of paths	
	PSO-optimised HNN	BPS algorithm	PSO-optimised HNN	BPS algorithm
150	0.47	0.38	4.9	4.8
200	0.76	0.48	6.2	6.1
250	0.84	0.67	8.6	7.4
300	0.95	0.71	13.1	10.7

results in fast convergence and produces more accurate results as compared to non-optimised HNN and noisy HNN. The simulation results of PSO-optimised HNN have shown that for different network conditions, the proposed model is efficient in selecting multiple disjoint paths. The PSO-optimised HNN-based routing algorithm has better performance, when averaged over different transmission ranges, as the reliability of multiple paths is increased by 8.3%, while the number of algorithm iterations is reduced to 11.1% as compared to the non-optimised HNN multipath routing. In addition, the PSO-optimised HNN-based routing algorithm has better performance in terms of reliability and number of paths when compared with the BPS algorithm. In this way, it shows up to 58% improvement in the path set reliability and up to 22% improvement in the number of paths in the set.

References

1. Boukerche A., Turgut B., Aydin N., Ahmad M.Z., Bölöni L., Turgut D. 'Routing protocols in ad hoc networks: A survey'. *Comput. Netw.* 2011, vol. 55(13), pp. 3032–80

2. Alotaibi E., Mukherjee B. 'A survey on routing algorithms for wireless ad-hoc and mesh networks'. *Comput. Netw.* 2012, vol. 56(2), pp. 940–65

3. Hopfield J. 'Neurons with graded response have collective computational properties like those of two-state neurons'. *Proc. Natl. Acad. Sci. USA* 1984, vol. 81(10), pp. 3088–92

4. Perkins C.E., Royer E.M. 'Ad-hoc on-demand distance vector routing'. *Proceedings of the 2nd IEEE Workshop on Mobile Computing Systems and Applications*; New Orleans, USA, Feb. 1999 (Los Alamitos, IEEE Computer Society, 1999), pp. 90–100

5. Perkins C.E., Bhagwat P. 'Highly dynamic destination-sequenced distance-vector routing (DSDV) for mobile computers'. *ACM SIGCOMM Comput. Commun. Review* 1994, vol. 24(4), pp. 234–44

6. Ko Y., Vaidya N. 'Location-aided routing (LAR) in mobile ad hoc networks'. *Wirel. Netw.* 2000, vol. 6(4), pp. 307–21

7. Krishna P.V., Saritha V., Vedha G., Bhiwal A., Chawla A.S. 'Quality-of-service-enabled ant colony-based multipath routing for mobile ad hoc networks'. *IET Commun.* 2012, vol. 6(1), pp. 76–83

8. Iwata A., Chiang C., Pei G., Gerla M., Chen T. 'Scalable routing strategies for ad hoc wireless networks'. *IEEE J. Selected Areas Commun.* 1999, vol. 17 (8), pp. 1369–79

9. Pompili D., Vittucci M. 'PPMA: A probabilistic predictive multicast algorithm for ad hoc networks'. *Ad Hoc Netw.* 2006, vol. 4(6), pp. 724–48

10. An B., Papavassiliou S. 'Geomulticast: Architectures and protocols for mobile ad hoc wireless networks'. *J. Parall. Distrib. Comput.* 2003, vol. 63 (2), pp. 182–95

11. Avudainayagam A., Lou W., Fang Y. 'DEAR: A device and energy aware routing protocol for heterogeneous ad hoc networks'. *J. Parall. Distrib. Comput.* 2003, vol. 63(2), pp. 228–36

12. Biradar R.C., Manvi S.S. 'Neighbor supported reliable multipath multicast routing in MANETs'. *J. Netw. Comput. Appl.* 2012, vol. 35(3), pp. 1074–85

13. Tarique M., Tepe K.E., Adibi S., Erfani S. 'Survey of multipath routing protocols for mobile ad-hoc networks'. *J. Netw. Comput. Appl.* 2009, vol. 32(6), pp. 1125–43

14. Igartua M.A., de la Cruz Llopis L.J., Frías V.C., Gargallo E.S. 'A game-theoretic multipath routing for video-streaming services over mobile ad hoc networks'. *Comput. Netw.* 2011, vol. 55(13), pp. 2985–3000

15. Yang W., Yang X., Yang S., Yang D. 'A greedy-based stable multi-path routing protocol in mobile ad hoc networks'. *Ad Hoc Netw.* 2011, vol. 9(4), pp. 662–74

16. Zafar H., Harle D., Andonovic I., Khawaja Y. 'Performance evaluation of shortest multipath source routing scheme'. *IET Commun.* 2009, vol. 3(5), pp. 700–13

17. Yi J., Adnane A., David S., Parrein B. 'Multipath optimized link state routing for mobile ad hoc networks'. *Ad Hoc Netw.* 2011, vol. 9(1), pp. 28–47

18. Gálvez J.J., Ruiz P.M., Skarmeta A.F.G. 'Multipath routing with spatial separation in wireless multi-hop networks without location information'. *Comput. Netw.* 2011, vol. 55(3), pp. 583–99

19. Li X., Jia Z., Zhang P., Zhang R., Wang H. 'Trust-based on-demand multipath routing in mobile ad hoc networks'. *IET Inf. Secur.* 2010, vol. 4(4), pp. 212–32

20. Wang J., Osagie E., Thulasiraman P., Thulasiram R.K. 'HOPNET: A hybrid ant colony optimisation routing algorithm for mobile ad hoc network'. *Ad Hoc Netw.* 2009, vol. 7(4), pp. 690–705

21. Lee C.M., Ko C.N. 'Time series prediction using RBF neural networks with a nonlinear time-varying evolution PSO algorithm'. *Neurocomputing* 2009, vol. 73(1–3), pp. 449–60

22. Leung S.Y.S., Tang Y., Wong W.K. 'A hybrid particle swarm optimization and its application in neural networks'. *Experts Syst. Appl.* 2012, vol. 39(1), pp. 395–405

23. Kennedy J., Eberhart R. 'Particle swarm optimization'. *Proceedings of the 6th IEEE International Conference on Neural Networks*; Perth, Australia, Nov. 1995 (Los Alamitos, Institute of Electrical & Electronics Engineers, 1995), vol. 4, pp. 1942–8

24. Shi Y., Eberhart R. 'Parameter selection in particle swarm optimization'. *Proceedings of the 7th International Conference on Evolutionary Programming*; San Diego, USA, Mar. 1998 (New York, Springer, 1998), pp. 591–601

25. Ratnaweera A., Halgamuge S.K., Watson H.C. 'Self-organizing hierarchical particle swarm optimizer with time-varying acceleration coefficients'. *IEEE Trans. Evolut. Comput.* 2004, vol. 8(3), pp. 240–55

26. Rappaport T.S. *Wireless Communications: Principles and Practice* (New Jersey, Prentice Hall, 2002, 2nd edn.)

27. Dana A., Khadem Zadeh A., Sadat A.A. 'Backup path set selection in ad hoc wireless network using link expiration time'. *Comput. Electr. Eng.* 2008, vol. 34(6), pp. 503–19

28. Sheikhan M., Hemmati E. 'Transient chaotic neural network-based disjoint multipath routing for mobile ad-hoc networks'. *Neural Comput. Appl.* 2012, vol. 21(6), pp. 1403–12

29. Hemmati E., Sheikhan M. 'Reliable disjoint path set selection in mobile ad-hoc networks using noisy Hopfield neural network'. *Proceedings of the 5th International Symposium on Telecommunications*; Tehran, Iran, Dec. 2010 (Los Alamitos, Institute of Electrical & Electronics Engineers, 2010), pp. 496–501

30. Sheikhan M., Hemmati E. 'PSO-optimized Hopfield neural network-based multipath routing for mobile ad-hoc networks'. *Int. J. Comput. Intell. Syst.* 2012, vol. 5(3), pp. 568–81

31. Camp T., Boleng J., Davies V. 'A survey of mobility models for ad-hoc network research'. *Wirel. Commun. Mobile Comput.* 2002, vol. 2(5), pp. 483–502

32. Sheikhan M., Hemmati E. 'High reliable disjoint path set selection in mobile ad-hoc network using Hopfield neural network'. *IET Commun.* 2011, vol. 5(11), pp. 1566–76

Chapter 11*

Dominating set clustering protocols for mobile ad hoc networks

V. S. Anitha[a] and M. P. Sebastian[b]

Abstract

A Mobile ad hoc Network (MANET) is a self-configuring, dynamic, multi-hop network composed of mobile nodes that operate without the need of any established infrastructure. The creation of stable, scalable and adaptive clusters with good performance, faster convergence rate and minimal overhead is a challenging task in MANET. This chapter proposes two clustering techniques for MANET, which are (k, r)-Dominating Set-based, weighted and adaptive to changes in the network topology. The set of dominating nodes functions as the clusterhead (CH) to relay the data and control packets. The proposed scenario-based clustering algorithm for MANETs (SCAMs) is a greedy approximation algorithm, whereas the Distributed SCAM (DSCAM) selects the (k, r)-dominating set through a distributed election mechanism. These algorithms achieve variable degree of CH redundancy through the parameter k, which contributes to reliability. Similarly, flexibility in creating variable diameter clusters is achieved with the parameter r. The performance of these algorithms are evaluated through simulation and the results show that these algorithms create stable, scalable and load-balanced clusters with relatively less control overhead in comparison with the existing popular algorithms.

11.1 Introduction

11.1.1 Mobile ad hoc networks

A Mobile ad hoc Network (MANET) consists of a number of mobile nodes, which communicate with each other through a multi-hop shared radio channel. Each node

*H. F. Rashvand and H.-C. Chao (Eds.), *Dynamic Ad Hoc Networks*, The IET Book Publishing Department, 2013, ISBN 978-1-84919-647-5, eISBN 978-1-84919-648-2
[a]Department of Computer Science and Engineering, Government Engineering College, Wayanad, Kerala, India
[b]Information Technology and Systems, Indian Institute of Management, Kozhikode, Kerala, India

in the network will be able to communicate directly with any other node that resides within its transmission range, whereas intermediate nodes are required for communicating with the nodes that reside beyond the transmission range [1]. All nodes in the ad hoc network take part in the communication process. They are free to move randomly, and arbitrarily organize themselves to create unpredictable network topologies.

The MANET paradigm gains momentum even outside the military field due to the handy size of mobile devices, its low cost, convenience, capacity to run more applications and more network services. This type of network provides effective solutions to home and office automation by dynamically configuring the devices in a short range [2]. A MANET can operate in a stand-alone fashion or can be connected to a fixed infrastructure with the help of gateway devices to facilitate Internet connectivity even in remote places. The MANET is useful in situations where the development of infrastructure is expensive or inconvenient to use or set up, or if absent.

Nodes in MANET are generally battery operated with limited processing power and memory capacity. Wireless networks generally have limited bandwidth and the nodes bear high mobility. The network often experiences high partitioning rate due to the increase in link breakage rate. Instead of using specialized routers for path discovery and traffic routing, each node in the ad hoc network acts as a router and takes part in the communication process.

The routing of messages poses different types of challenges in MANET. Minimizing the routing overhead increases the efficiency of ad hoc networks. Clustering is one of the primary methods for reducing the routing overhead by partitioning the nodes of the MANET into similar size clusters. Clustering can also contribute to energy conservation, load balancing, scalability and low maintenance. Many protocols have been proposed in the literature. Some protocols are application oriented, and some are designed to meet the various objectives like energy conservation, load balancing, mobility awareness, scalability and low maintenance.

In dominating set-based clustering, a set of dominating nodes is selected and they function as clusterhead (CH) to relay data packets and routing information. A dominating set (DS) can create virtual backbone for packet routing and control. Several approximation algorithms were proposed for the selection of minimum DS. All these algorithms are designed to compute a dominating set with minimum number of elements. But none of these algorithms consider the capability of a node to act as CH.

The major objective of this chapter is to introduce efficient and scenario-based clustering algorithms for MANET to support stability and load balancing, with less control overheads.

11.1.2 *Dominating set (DS) graph*

The undirected graph $G = (V, E)$ consists of a set of vertices $V = v_1, \ldots, v_k$, and a set of edges E. An edge is a set (v_i, v_j), where $v_i, v_j \in V$ and $v_i \neq v_j$. A set D, subset of

V of vertices in a graph G, is called a dominating set if every vertex $v_i \in V$ is either an element of D or is adjacent to an element of D [3]. The problem of computing the minimum cardinality DS of any arbitrary graph is known to be NP-complete [4]. A variety of conditions may be imposed on the dominating set D in a graph $G = (V, E)$. Among them, there are multiple domination, and distance domination [3]. Multiple-domination requires that each vertex in V-D be dominated by at least k vertices in D for a fixed positive integer k. Distance domination requires that each vertex in V-D be within distance r of at least one vertex in D for a fixed positive integer r.

The (k, r)-DS problem is defined [5] as the problem of selecting a minimum cardinality vertex set D of a graph $G = (V, E)$, such that every vertex u not in D is at a distance smaller than or equal to r from at least k vertices in D. The problem of computing a (k, r)-DS of minimum cardinality for arbitrary graphs is also NP-complete [5]. Figure 11.1 shows some (k, r)-DS examples. In $(1, 2)$-DS every node in the network other than nodes in DS are at most two hops from at least one node in DS whereas in $(2, 2)$-DS all nodes other than nodes in DS are at most two hops from at least two nodes in DS.

The DS have been proposed as backbones for routing in MANET. A backbone plays an important role in routing where the number of nodes responsible for the routing is reduced to the number of nodes in the DS. To simplify the connectivity management, to reduce the communication overhead and to increase the speed of convergence, it is desirable to find a minimum connected set of a given set of nodes.

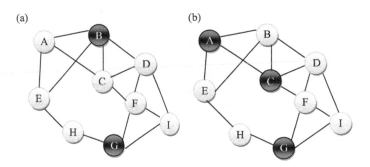

Figure 11.1   DS examples: (a) (1, 2)-DS; (b) (2, 2)-DS

11.1.3   Routing in wireless ad hoc networks

Broadcasting is a fundamental operation in MANET, whereby a source node transmits a message that is to be disseminated to all nodes in the network [6]. William and Camp [7] categorized the broadcasting protocols into blind flooding [8], probability-based methods [9], area-based methods and neighbour-knowledge methods.

Conventional routing protocols can be broadly classified into distance vector [10] and link state protocols. Distance vector routing uses the classical distributed Bellman–Ford algorithm. Link state routing generally requires each host to have the knowledge of the entire network topology. The defining characteristics of ad hoc networks include limited resources, dynamic topology, limited bandwidth and high error rates. Battery power is typically the most constraining among all the resources. Hence, the design goals for ad hoc network routing protocols include dynamic topology maintenance, less control overhead, multi-hop routing capability, less processing overhead and loop prevention.

MANET protocols can be classified as proactive, reactive and hybrid. The proactive routing protocols for ad hoc networks are derived from the traditional distance vector and link state protocols. The main characteristic of the proactive approach is that each node in the network maintains a route to every other node in the network at all times. Proactive routing protocols periodically distribute the routing information throughout the network in order to pre-compute the paths to all possible destinations [11]. Although this approach can ensure higher quality routes in a static topology, it does not scale well to large and highly dynamic networks. The Destination-Sequenced Distance-Vector (DSDV) [12], Source-Tree Adaptive Routing (STAR) [13] and Optimized Link State Routing (OLSR) [14] are examples of proactive routing protocols.

The reactive (on-demand) routing protocols represent the true nature of ad hoc networks, which is much more dynamic than the infrastructure-based networks. Instead of periodically updating the routing information, the reactive routing protocols update the routing information when a routing request is presented, thus reducing the control overhead, especially in high-mobility networks where the periodic update leads to significant overhead. The ad hoc On-Demand Distance Vector (AODV) [15] and Dynamic Source Routing (DSR) [16] protocol are examples of this category.

Hybrid routing protocols try to maximize the benefits of proactive routing and reactive routing by utilizing the proactive routing in small networks, to reduce the delay and the reactive routing in large-scale networks, in order to reduce the control overhead. Hybrid approaches include the Zone Routing Protocol (ZRP) [17] and Core Extraction Distributed ad hoc Routing Protocol (CEDAR) [18]. As the size of the network grows, flat routing schemes do not scale well in terms of performance and result in low-bandwidth utilization in large networks. Hence, hierarchical routing is beneficial in large ad hoc networks.

11.1.4   Clustering and topology control in MANETs

With clustering, the mobile nodes are divided into a number of virtual groups called clusters. Nodes in a cluster can be of type CH, gateway or ordinary node. The CH is the coordinator for the operations within a cluster. Cluster-based virtual network architecture requires many information exchanges to perform routing as well as to create and maintain clusters. A stable clustering algorithm should not change the cluster configuration frequently. Maintaining the cluster structure in a dynamically changing scenario often requires explicit message exchange between the mobile node pairs. Frequent information exchange may consume considerable bandwidth and drain energy of the mobile nodes quickly. Some clustering schemes may cause the cluster structure to be completely re-built over the whole network when some local events take place, such as the movement or death of mobile nodes, which result in some CH re-election. This is called ripple effect of re-clustering. The ripple effect of re-clustering may greatly affect the performance of upper layer protocols. The cost of clustering includes explicit control messages required for cluster creation and maintenance, ripple effect of re-clustering and communication, and computational complexities.

11.2   Scenario-based clustering for MANET

In hierarchical clustering, the nodes are partitioned into several groups called clusters. Each cluster has a CH and is vested with the responsibility of routing data and control messages for all nodes within the cluster. The preferred characteristics of CHs are (i) great reserve of energy in order to avoid that the node becomes dysfunctional after a short duration of election, (ii) low mobility to avoid frequent CH re-election and re-affiliations and (iii) higher connectivity in order to assure CH responsibility. The above-mentioned characteristics of CHs and the cluster formation techniques with load balancing are vital to increase the stability of the created clusters. This section presents scenario-based, adaptive and weighted clustering algorithm for MANETs. The proposed algorithm is named as Scenario-based Clustering Algorithm for MANETs (SCAMs) [17].

Centralized algorithm based on the (k, r)-*dominating set* allows the selection of CHs and gateway nodes in such a way that each node in the network has k CHs within r-*hop* distance. From among the k dominating nodes, the non-CH nodes select the most qualified dominating node as their CH. The quality computation is done using the metrics such as connectivity, residual battery power, stability and transmission range.

11.2.1   Design objectives

Development of a centralized, multi-hop, and adaptive (multi-purpose) clustering algorithm for MANETs, which creates stable clusters and provides good performance and faster convergence rate with minimal overhead, is the main objective of this section. The CH election technique ensures that all other nodes in the network have at least k CHs in the r-*hop* distance. Each non-CH node selects the most suitable CHs among the k CHs as its current CH, based on the quality. Long-term service as a CH depletes its energy, causing it to drop out of the network. Similarly, a CH with relatively high mobility than its neighbours can lead to frequent CH election process. This perturbs the stability of the network and may adversely affect the performance of the network. Load balancing among the CHs and the correct positioning of the CH in a cluster are also vital for increased lifespan of the network.

The main design considerations of SCAM clustering algorithm include selection of an optimal number of CHs, scalability, stability, mechanism to prevent the clusters from growing too large, maintenance mechanism for the existing clusters and quick adaptation with the change of topology. The proposed algorithm must create the clusters in such a way that they are stable for a reasonable amount of time. A stable cluster creation avoids the frequent CH election process. For creating stable clusters, the CH election scheme must be designed in such a way that the elected CH can do its job for a longer period. To select the most powerful node as CH, suitable values are to be set for the various parameters.

The degree of a node is high if it has more number of nodes within its transmission range. The position of a node is also relevant in the CH election process. A large cluster puts too much load on the CH and reduces the system throughput. However, small clusters may increase the size of the backbone structure. Hence, setting upper and lower limits on the number of nodes connected to a CH is important for load balancing.

Since the CHs play a leading role in the communication process, their energy consumption is more compared to the ordinary nodes. Therefore, a node with sufficient battery power is to be selected as CH to minimize the CH re-election and also to avoid node dropping out of the network prematurely. Stability of the CH is another important parameter in selecting the CH. Selection of a less mobile node as CH considerably reduces the number of re-elections. Thus, weighted sum of the above metrics is a better measure of the quality of a dominating node.

11.2.2   Design parameters

The first step in this algorithm is the computation of (k, r)-DS. There are many approximation algorithms for finding the dominating set [19] and connected dominating set [20, 21] of nodes in a MANET. A centralized solution can be found for the (k, r)-DS if the network topology is known. Otherwise distributed solutions are the possibility. Nodes in the (k, r)-DS are the potential candidates to become a CH.

The second step affiliates the ordinary nodes with the CH. This is based on the quality of the CHs and the maximum number of ordinary nodes that a CH can handle. The quality of a dominating node is computed using the metrics such as node degree, residual battery power mobility with respect to the neighbouring nodes and transmission range. It is assumed that the nodes are connected bi-directionally and are capable of measuring its own signal strength.

The following are the parameters used for the computation of quality:

1. *Degree*: The degree of a node v is the total number of nodes within the transmission range of v. The degree of node v in DG_v is computed as

$$DG_v = \sum_{u \in v,\, u \neq v} \{D^{u,v} < T_x\} \tag{11.1}$$

    where $D^{u,v}$ is the distance between node u and v, and T_x is the transmission range.

2. *Residual battery power*: A dominating node with high residual battery power, B_v, can perform well as CH for a longer duration. Hence, residual battery power is a better measure than the consumed battery power [22] or time during which the node acts as CH [23]. But long-term service as CH can deteriorate the battery power and hence B_v of the current CH is to be calculated periodically. If the residual battery power goes below a certain threshold level, all the member nodes need to select the next best qualified dominating node as the new CH, if possible, otherwise a new dominating set finding step is to be initiated. This avoids the total collapse of the current network topology and reduces the number of CH elections and associated overheads.

3. *Mobility*: To compute mobility, each node in the dominating set needs to find out the distance from its neighbouring nodes. For distance computation, Friis [24] free space propagation model is used.

    The received power, P_r, is computed as

$$P_r = P_t G_t G_r \frac{\lambda^2}{(4\pi D)^2} \tag{11.2}$$

where P_r is the power received by the receiving antenna, P_t is the power input to the transmitting antenna, G_t and G_r are the gain of transmitting and receiving antennas, respectively, λ is the wavelength, and D is the distance. P_r is inversely proportional to the square of the distance. Instead of finding the exact physical location, an approximate distance at time t between nodes v and u is calculated using (3.2) as

$$D_t^{v,u} = \frac{K_{\text{const}}}{\sqrt{P_r}} \tag{11.3}$$

where $v \in$ is the dominating set DS, u is an element of the set of neighbouring nodes of v and K_{const} is a constant. $D_t^{v,u}$ is the distance between v and u at time t. The node mobility significantly influences the network performance. The relative mobility between v and u indicates whether they are coming closer to or moving away from each other. The relative mobility of node u with respect to v at time t is given as

$$RM_t^{v,u} = D_t^{v,u} - D_{t-1}^{v,u} \tag{11.4}$$

$RM_t^{v,u}$ is positive if node u is moving away from v and negative if u is coming near to v. Distance from v to u is measured at certain time interval for T times and $RM_1^{v,u}$, $RM_2^{v,u}$, ...,$RM_T^{v,u}$ are calculated. The standard deviation of relative mobility gives the variation of the distances over a time period T as

$$SDRM = \sqrt{\frac{1}{T} \sum_{i=1}^{T} (RM_i - \overline{RM})^2} \tag{11.5}$$

where

$$\overline{RM} = \frac{1}{T}(RM_1^{v,u} + RM_2^{v,u} + \cdots + RM_T^{v,u}) \tag{11.6}$$

The local stability of a node v in *dominating set* DS, LSTAB, with respect to all its neighbours is the mean of standard deviation of relative mobility of all its neighbouring nodes. A low value of this is an indication that the node is stable. This stability is either due to less mobility or due to group mobility (node v and all its neighbouring nodes move in the same direction with more or less same speed). If the CH and the cluster members move with the same speed in the same direction, they remain in the same cluster throughout the communication session. The topology within a cluster used to be less dynamic. This helps in minimizing link breakages and packet losses.

4. *Transmission range*: In a heterogeneous network, the mobile nodes may have differed computational and communication capabilities. The transmission range, T_x, of a node is a factor that affects the quality of a node.

Thus, the quality of a node in the dominating set to work as a CH is computed as

$$Q_v = W_1 * DG_v + W_2 * B_v + W_3 * \text{LSTAB} + W_4 * T_x \tag{11.7}$$

where W_1, W_2, W_3 and W_4 are the weights associated with the various factors affecting the quality. Suitable values are assigned to W_1, W_2, W_3 and W_4 based on the required application such that $W_1 + W_2 + W_3 + W_4 = 1$. If more number of parameters are found to be appropriate, p such parameters can be assigned with weights in such a way that $W_1 + W_2 + \cdots + W_p = 1$. The normalized values of DG_v, B_v, LSTAB and T_x are taken into consideration. To compute the ratio normalized to 1, for each parameter three defined constants DG_{max}, B_{max} and T_{max} are used. The inverse of LSTAB is taken to get a normalized value.

11.2.3   SCAM algorithm

The SCAM works in three phases, the *Clustering Setup* phase, *Cluster Formation* phase and *Cluster Maintenance* phase. The first phase is accomplished by a centralized (k, r)-*dominating set* computation algorithm for choosing the nodes that act as coordinators of the clustering and routing process. While selecting the dominating nodes, redundancy is achieved by choosing the value of parameter k greater than 1 [25]. The parameter r allows increased local availability. These two parameters can be conveniently set depending upon the requirement. The dominating nodes are potential nodes to become CHs and during the *Cluster Formation* phase nodes, which are not in the dominating set, select the best node in the dominating set within the r-*hop* distance as its CH. The selection is based on quality, which is a function of parameters such as stability of the dominating node with respect to its neighbours, remaining energy with the node, connectivity, and transmission range. The selection of the CH based on these parameters helps in maintaining the structure of the created cluster as stable as possible, thus minimizing the topology changes and associated overheads during CH changes. The third phase is *Cluster*

Maintenance that maintains the cluster structure as stable as possible with minimum control overhead.

11.2.3.1 Clustering Setup phase

The first step in the design of SCAM is the selection of some resourceful nodes that can cover the entire network as CHs. This computation is done during the *Clustering Setup* phase. This is accomplished by using a centralized (k, r)-*dominating set computation* algorithm for choosing the dominating nodes. Dominating nodes are potential nodes to become CHs. The centralized algorithm for the (k, r)-DS problem is a greedy approximation algorithm that repeatedly selects the most weighted node in the priority heap as the dominating node. Any node u is said to be (k, r)-*dominated* if node u has at least k neighbours within the *r-hop* distance from the elements in the DS. It is assumed that the nodes have unique identifiers and that they are capable of knowing their neighbours. To learn about the neighbours, they exchange periodic *HELLO* messages as part of the SCAM protocol itself.

To compute a dominating set with parameters k and r, *Required_Ch* value of each node u in the network is calculated. Initially, the *Required_Ch* value for each node is assigned a value k. A node is said to be covered or dominated if it has k nodes in the dominating set within its *r-hop* distance. If node u is not covered, the value of $u.Required\_Ch$ is k minus the number of nodes in the DS within the distance r from u. Once node u is covered, its $u.Required\_Ch$ is set to zero. The *Suitability_Value* of node u depends on the residual battery power, transmission power and the *Required_Ch* value of the *r-hop* neighbourhood. The *Required_Ch* value of the *r-hop* neighbourhood is calculated as $\sum_{v \in Vu} v.required\_Ch$, where V_u is the set of *r-hop* neighbourhood of node u. The computation of the *Suitability_Value* helps in selecting an efficient node with most number of uncovered nodes as the CH. The selection of node u as CH affects the *Suitability_Value* of any node within the *2r-hop* distance from u. This is because the selection of node u reduces the *Required_Ch* value of any node v in node u's *r-hop* distance by 1, if v is not covered.

A priority heap is used as the data structure and all the nodes are inserted in the heap such that the node with the highest *Suitability_Value* is at the root. The root node is selected as the dominating node and is removed from the heap and inserted in the dominating set, DS. After selecting the root node as a member of the dominating set, the *Required_Ch* value of all nodes within the *r-hop* distance from the root node is reduced by 1. When it becomes zero, the node is covered and is removed from the heap. These nodes are the dominated nodes. After this update, the heap is sorted so that the node with the highest *Suitability_Value* is at the root. Ties are broken using the highest residual battery power as the criterion. This process repeats until the heap is empty.

11.2.3.2 Cluster formation phase

The major functions of this phase are quality computation of the dominating nodes and association of the ordinary nodes with the CHs. The *Clustering Setup* phase selects a subset of nodes in the network as dominating nodes. For computing the quality, the dominating nodes send the *FIND_NEIGHBOUR* (*FN*) messages to all neighbouring nodes within the *r-hop* distance. On receiving the *FN* message from a dominating node, each node within the *r-hop* distance sends *T FN_ACK* (*FNA*) messages one after the other in fixed intervals. The details of these messages are used for the calculation of *stability*, which is the relative mobility of the dominating node with respect to its neighbours. The dominating node waits for $2r + (T - 1)$ rounds after sending the *FN* message and then computes its quality. A dominating node uses a list to store the details of all neighbouring nodes within the *r-hop* distance and creates the *Neighbour_List* data structure. After computing the quality, the dominating node advertises its quality through *CLUSTER_HEAD_ ADVERTISEMENT* (*CHA*) message.

The dominating nodes periodically send *CHA* messages to prove its presence. On receiving the *CHA* messages, the *Ordinary* nodes create/modify its CH List, which is a list of CHs within *r-hop* distance. The nodes, which hear the *CHA* message, select the CH with the highest quality and send the *NODE_JOIN* (*NJ*) message to the selected CH. If the total number of nodes attached with that CH is below the maximum allowable number, then the CH accepts this request and sends the *NJ_ACK* (*NJA*) message. The *NJ_ACK* message with *ACCEPT* status *TRUE* indicates a successful CH association. Otherwise, the node should send the *NJ* message to the next qualified node.

11.2.3.3   Cluster maintenance phase

Whenever a new node is switched on, it waits for the *CHA* messages. There are two possible cases depending upon the number of *CHA* messages received. If the number of *CHA* messages received from the different Node ID is greater than or equal to *k*, then the new node selects the most qualified CH node as its CH and sends the *NJ* packet to the selected CH. If the new node receives at least one pair of such *CHA* messages with different Cluster ID then the new node acts as gateway node. If the number of *CHA* messages received is less than *k* then the new node acts as a CH and enters into the quality finding state.

11.2.4   *Performance evaluation*

The performance of SCAM is evaluated through simulation. The parameters used for the simulation are listed in Table 11.1. The nodes under simulation move according to the Random Waypoint Model. The maximum number of nodes that a CH can handle can be suitably adjusted depending upon the processing capability and data rate of the CH and the system requirement. The values assumed for *k* and *r* are 1 or 2 and 1, 2, 3 or 4, respectively. The weights considered for W_1, W_2, W_3 and W_4 are as shown in Table 11.1 [26]. These values are chosen randomly and can be adjusted depending upon the scenario.

Nodes are randomly placed over a terrain. To ensure that the network is connected, a connectivity test is performed. Experiments are repeated for 30 trials with different network topologies and varying number of nodes. The results represent the average of more than 30 trials. The performance metrics evaluated for analysing

Table 11.1   SCAM parameters

Parameter	Value in SCAM
Simulator	Matlab 7.1
Simulation tool	Prowler
Number of nodes	10–500
Network size	1000×1000 m^2, 500×500 m^2
Transmission range	10–150 m
Maximum speed of node movement	20 m/s
W_1, W_2, W_3 and W_4	0.5, 0.3, 0.1 and 0.1
Mobility model	Random way point
Traffic model	128 Bytes packets, 4 packets/s
Simulation time	600 s

SCAM algorithm are cardinality of the dominating, Load Balancing Factor (LBF), number of re-affiliations per unit time and the number of dominating set updates per unit time.

The first experiment provides a report on the average number of CHs or clusters created for different values of the number of nodes in the network. The number of dominating nodes strongly influences the latency, communication overhead and inter- and intra-communication strategies. The number of CHs defines the dominating set. It is observed that the number of dominating nodes increases with the increase in the total number of nodes, as shown in Figure 11.2.

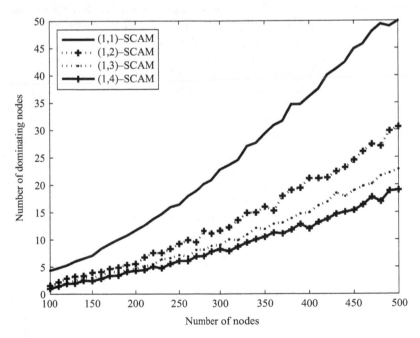

Figure 11.2   Number of dominating nodes for $k = 1$ and $r = 1, 2, 3$ and 4

The number of dominating nodes decreases with the increase in the cluster diameter. This is because with larger values of r, more number of nodes are covered. When the value of r is increased from 1 to 2, the number of dominating nodes is reduced by 51 per cent, which results in lower number of clusters created. The rate of reduction decreases with increase in diameter.

The number of clusters created the number of re-affiliations per unit time and the number of dominant set updates in SCAM is compared with the three popular algorithms: (i) H-degree, (ii) Ruan, and (iii) weighted clustering algorithm WCA. In H-degree, the CH election is based on single criteria. That is, a node with the highest degree than its neighbours is elected as the CH. This In link cluster algorithm (LCA), the clusterhead is selected based on the highest identity number among a group of nodes. H-degree is a modified version of LCA that is designed with an aim to reduce the number of clusters in the network. A higher value of connectivity ensures efficient service to the member nodes by minimizing the number of CHs.

The H-degree algorithm suffers from dynamic network topology, which triggers frequent changes of CHs. Frequent cluster re-configuration and CH re-election incur more number of re-affiliations. The poor cluster stability of the algorithm decreases its application in real-world situations in spite of its reduced delay in data communications. H-degree approach does not have any restriction on the upper bound on node degree in a cluster and does not consider capability as a qualification to become the CH. Hence, heavily loaded CHs with many links easily get deteriorated their power, resulting in CH changes and re-elections.

SCAM is a centralized algorithm and hence for the performance comparison another centralized algorithm, Ruan's algorithm, is considered. Ruan's algorithm is a one step greedy approximation algorithm and is a modified version of the popular algorithm (second algorithm) of Guha and Khuller. The WCA algorithm is a combined weight-metric algorithm. Since SCAM uses a combined weight metric for CH association, WCA is also considered for the performance comparison.

Figure 11.3 shows that the average number of clusters formed in SCAM is relatively high when the transmission range is small. When the transmission range increases, more number of nodes is connected to the same CH and thereby reducing the number of clusters created. A smaller backbone is desirable for minimizing the routing overhead. Hence, transmission power of a node is also to be considered to find the quality of the dominating nodes.

The results of simulation experiments show that the average number of CHs using SCAM (with $k=2$ and $r=2$) is less compared with WCA, Ruan and H-degree. This is because they create less number of clusters when the cluster radius increases and make use of the cluster merging process. But the increase in the value of r leads to increased cluster size, which adversely affects the performance. So the selection of the value of r is critical.

The algorithm achieves load balancing by assigning various time slots for the different CHs based on its quality and by specifying an agreeable threshold on the number of nodes that a CH can handle. The LBF is the inverse of the variance of the cardinality of the clusters [23]. A higher value of LBF signifies a better load distribution. From the simulation result we found that there is a reduction in LBF with increase in the value of r. This is because as the value of r increases, more

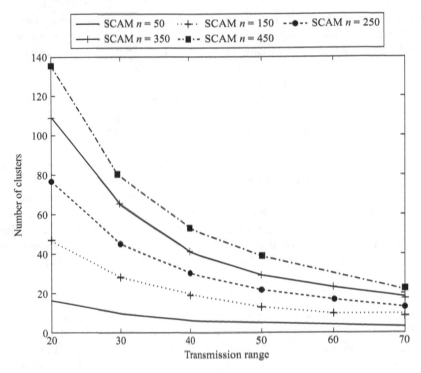

Figure 11.3   Transmission range vs. number of clusters

and more nodes are getting added to the same CH, thus increasing its load. This can be solved putting a limit on the maximum number of nodes that a CH can handle. The threshold value is selected as suggested in Reference 27. This mechanism is used to prevent the clusters from growing too large and the CH can manage its own cluster members without much degradation in performance.

In WCA, a CH election procedure is invoked at the time of system activation, when the current dominating set is unable to cover all nodes and when a node goes into a region not covered by any CH. As a result, the re-affiliation induced by WCA is generally very high. In SCAM, the created clusters preserve their structure for a longer period than in H-degree and WCA. It is observed that the number of re-affiliations increases with the increase in the number of nodes and higher values of displacement in all algorithms. But the number of CH election initiations is less in SCAM compared with Ruan, WCA and H-degree. The dominating node updates are minimal in SCAM compared to the other algorithms.

11.3   Distributed scenario-based clustering for MANET

Unlike cellular networks, no physical backbone infrastructure is needed in MANET. But it is natural to construct a virtual backbone through dominating set formation [28]. The virtual backbone plays a very important role in routing, broadcasting, and cluster formation and management [29]. It has been pointed out that 'The most basic clustering that has been studied in the context of ad hoc networks is based on dominating sets' [30]. The construction of hierarchical topology is an effective solution in topology control [31].

The clustering algorithm provides a logical topology for the routing algorithm. The routing algorithm accepts information from the clustering algorithm to adjust the logical topology and to make clustering decisions. Longer lifetime and network stability are very important performance factors for any MANET. A good clustering scheme should preserve its structure as much as possible when the nodes are moving and the topology is slowly changing. This section proposes a distributed (k, r)-DS based, weighted and adaptive clustering algorithm for MANETs. The proposed algorithm is called Distributed Scenario-based Clustering Algorithm for MANETs (DSCAM). The goals of this algorithm include maintenance of a stable clustering structure, to minimize the overhead for the *Clustering Setup* phase, to maximize the lifetime of the nodes in the system, and thereby achieve good performance. This algorithm resolves some of the limitations of SCAM.

11.3.1   Need for distributed algorithm

Centralized clustering algorithms are suitable for networks with less number of nodes. If the number of nodes in the network is high or if the nodes are highly dynamic then the centralized algorithm incurs more control overhead to learn the topology as well as to cope up with the dynamic topology. In such situations distributed algorithms are needed to reduce the associated overheads. In the distributed approach, the clusters are created with the knowledge of local neighbours. For many MANET applications, distributed dominating set computation is effective due to the lack of centralized administration. Similarly, scalability concern prohibits the centralized DS computation.

It is observed that mobile users in MANETs move in groups, which is known as group mobility. Mobile hosts may get in team collaborations or group activities. All cluster members that move in a similar pattern remain in the same cluster throughout the entire communication session. Thus, highly mobile nodes may appear less mobile. The group mobility consideration can reduce frequent and unnecessary re-affiliations.

However, most of the mobility aware clustering algorithms [32–36] do not consider this group mobility. Topology change occurs when a node is added to the existing network or deleted from the network. A change in the cluster structure affects the performance of the system. Therefore, it is highly essential to develop an effective cluster maintenance scheme. A good cluster maintenance scheme is needed to keep the cluster structure as stable as possible.

11.3.2   Design principles

The proposed algorithm is dominating set-based, distributed and scenario-based. A stable cluster creation avoids frequent CH election process and thereby reduces the overhead associated with this process. For creating stable clusters, the CH election

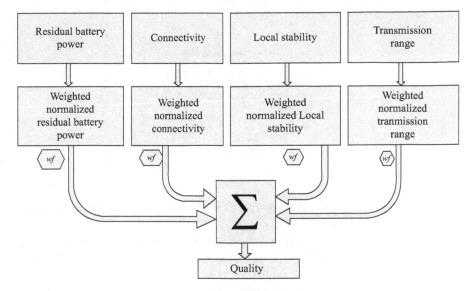

Figure 11.4   The combined weight metrics used in DSCAM

scheme must be designed in such a way that the elected CH can do its job for a longer period. The block diagram for the computation of quality of a node is shown in Figure 11.4.

The proposed DSCAM assumes that the nodes are homogeneous and initially they have the same residual battery power and other resources. Among the k dominating nodes, each *Ordinary* node selects the most qualified dominating node as its CH at any time. DSCAM computes the quality of a dominating node as a function of the above four parameters. Normally, the clustering algorithm based on weight computation [23] computes weights of all nodes participating in the CH election process. This increases the control overhead. In DSCAM, the quality computation is limited to dominating nodes alone to reduce the control overhead.

Many control messages are required for the computation of quality, especially for considering the group mobility. Each member node re-affiliates to the next powerful dominating node on account of the failure of current CH due to its mobility, low battery power or link failure. This local re-affiliation increases the lifespan of the network before requiring a backbone re-computation. DSCAM elects a subset of nodes from the network based on (k, r)-DS to act as CHs. Each ordinary node uses the combined weight metric to select the best CH node from its k choices.

11.3.2.1   Phases of DSCAM

It is assumed that each node in the network has a unique identifier, *NodeID*. The diagrammatic representation of DSCAM methodology is as shown in Figure 11.5. Any node, i in the network is associated with a process, which consists of a *set of states*, a *message generating function*, an *event scheduler* and a *state transition function*.

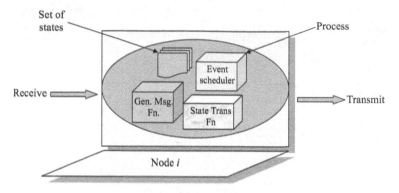

Figure 11.5   Block diagram of DSCAM design methodology

Set of states: A set of states used for describing the current status of node *i*. There are six possible statuses, which are *Unknown, ElectedCh, NominatedCh, Ordinary, CH,* and *Gateway*. Initially, all nodes in the network are assigned with the status *Unknown*. The elected dominating nodes have the status *ElectedCh*. *NominatedCh* status is assigned to nodes where the election into the dominating set is not confirmed. An *Ordinary* node has at least *k* dominating nodes within the *r-hop* distance. *Gateway* nodes have *k* dominating nodes within the *r-hop* distance and can communicate with members of another cluster.

Message generating function: Generates a set of messages that a node should send depending on the current status of the node *i* and specifies to which node it should send.

Event scheduler: Schedules and describes a set of events to be performed at a particular time.

State transition function: Specifies the new state to which node *i* should transit from the current state on receipt of a particular message from the neighbouring node.

The algorithm works in three phases such as *Nomination* phase, *DS-Computation* phase, and *Cluster Formation and Management* phase. During phase I, each node elects a maximum of *k* nodes with the highest residual battery power (smaller *NodeID* is considered in the case of a tie) within the *r-hop* distance. These nodes are nominated to be a member of the DS. Phase II of this algorithm is for finding the minimum number of dominating or CH nodes and gateway nodes. Algorithm proceeds in rounds. A round of message is the successful transmission of a message by any node in the network to all its neighbours within a single hop. DSCAM is suited for both synchronous and asynchronous networks. It is possible to simulate rounds in asynchronous models also, as explained in Reference 37.

During phase III, the CHs compute their quality and send it to all nodes within the *r-hop* distance. From among the *k* CHs, each non-CH node selects the best qualified node as its CH.

Phase I: *Nomination*

The *Nomination* phase takes r rounds to complete. In this phase, each node elects k close nodes with higher weight values within the r-*hop* distance. Initially the *Neighbour_List* of each node contains a structure with single element, which gives the details of itself. In round 1, each node sends its *Neighbour_List* to its *one-hop* neighbourhood. On receiving this list, each node appends its *Neighbour_List* by adding the details of all nodes in its *one-hop* neighbourhood. The process repeats for r rounds and at the end of r rounds all nodes in the network learn about its r-*hop* neighbourhood. The most qualified k elements in the *Neighbour_List* of each node represent its k nominations. In the *Clustering Setup* phase, the *NominationList* elements are selected based on the node weight, which is a function of the residual battery power and the transmission range. In order to reduce the control overhead, mobility is not considered in this phase but in the *cluster formation* phase. If any node has *Neighbour_List* with less than k number of elements in its *Neighbour_List*, then that node changes its status to *ElectedCH*. If node i is in the best k elements of Ni (*Neighbour_List* of node i), then node i changes its status to *NominatedCh*. This node is nominated to be a member of the DS, but the membership is confirmed only during the next phase. If node i is with $|Ni|$ greater than or equal to k and node i is not in the best k elements of Ni then node i gets the *Ordinary* status.

Phase II: *DS-Computation*

The second phase computes the dominating set. Different messages used in this phase are CH Advertisement, CH Advertise Memo and *NominationList*. *CLUSTER_HEAD ADVERTISEMENT* (*CHA*) is the message sent by the CH to its r-*hop* neighbours to show its presence. The *CH Advertise Memo* (*CAM*) is the message sent to inform a node that it should become an *ElectedCh*. The *NominationList* (*NL*) is the message containing the first k *NodeID* of *Neighbour_List*.

   In the $(r + 1)$th round, each node sends to their immediate neighbours a list called *NominationList*, which contains its list of nominated members.

   The transition of an *Ordinary* node i upon receiving a *NominationList* comes as follows:

1. If $(i \in NL_u)$ and $(u \in NH_{1,i})$ and $(i_{status} = Ordinary)$ then $i_{status} = ElectedCh$.

    If node i is in the *NominationList* of any neighbour nodes of i, then node i changes its status to *ElectedCh*. A *CHA* message is advertised to its r-*hop* neighbours to notify its presence.

2. If $(i \notin NL_u)$ and $(u \in NH_{1,i})$ and $(nl \in NL_u)$ and $(u_{nexthop,nl} = i)$ then $i_{status} = Gateway$.

    If node i is not in the *NominationList* of the neighbour nodes of i and i is the next hop to its neighbour's *NominationList* (any node in the *Neighbour_List* of neighbour node of i can be reached only through i) then node i changes its status to *Gateway*.

3. If $(nl \in NL_u)$ and $(u \in NH_{1,i})$ and $(nl \notin NLi)$ then i sends CAM to n_1.

The purpose of *CAM* is to notify the node n_1 about the nomination of n_1 by its *r-hop* neighbour. A node i with *NominatedCh* status can change to *ElectedCh*, *Gateway* or *Ordinary*. *NominatedCh* node changes its status to *ElectedCh* if the cardinality of the confirmed dominating nodes within the *r-hop* distance of i is less than the required minimum number k. A node i with status *NominatedCh* changes its status to *Gateway* if it participates in relaying a *CAM*. If there are enough number of confirmed dominating nodes and if node i does not relay any *CAM* then node i changes its status to *Ordinary*. These transitions are as shown in Figure 11.6.

Phase III: *Cluster Formation and Management*

Phase III activities include quality computation of the CHs and advertisement, CH association, and cluster maintenance. The quality computation starts immediately after completing the dominating set computation. The weighted algorithms proposed so far in the literature compute weights of all nodes participating in the election process and this leads to increase in the control overhead. In DSCAM, only the dominating nodes compute its weight. The dominating nodes send *FIND_NEIGHBOUR* message to all neighbouring nodes within the *r-hop* distance. Whenever an *Ordinary* or *Gateway* node within the *r-hop* distance receives this message from a node with status *ElectedCh*, it sends T consecutive *FN_ACK* messages, piggy-backed with the periodic *HELLO* messages. The details of these messages are used for the computation of the quality of the dominating nodes. The dominating node waits for ($2r + (T + 1) + additional\ wait\ time$) rounds after sending the *FIND_NEIGHBOUR* message. Here T is the number of time slots, which is used for calculating the local stability of dominating nodes.

Each dominating node, v, computes the normalized weighted sum for computing its quality as

$$Q_v = W_1 \times DG_{diffv} + W_2 \times B_v + W_3 \times ILSTAB + W_4 \times T_x \qquad (11.8)$$

The degree difference is defined as

$$DG_{diffv} = |DG_v - Dg_{optv}| \qquad (11.9)$$

Dg_{optv} is a pre-defined threshold for the number of cluster members that a CH can handle. The rate at which the data is transmitted by a node is called the transmission rate or data rate of the node and T_x is the transmission range. All other parameters are the same as in SCAM. A dominating node uses a list to store the details of all neighbouring nodes within the *r-hop* distance and creates a *NeighbourList* data structure. After computing the quality, a dominating node advertises its quality by sending the *CHA* message.

The CHs periodically send *CHA* messages to prove its presence. On receiving the *CHA* message, the *Ordinary* nodes create/modify its *CHList*. An *Ordinary* node gets at least k such *CHA* messages with different *Ch_ID* and selects the CH with the highest quality, and then sends the *NODE_JOIN* (*NJ*) request to the selected CH. If the total number of nodes attached with that CH is below the maximum allowable

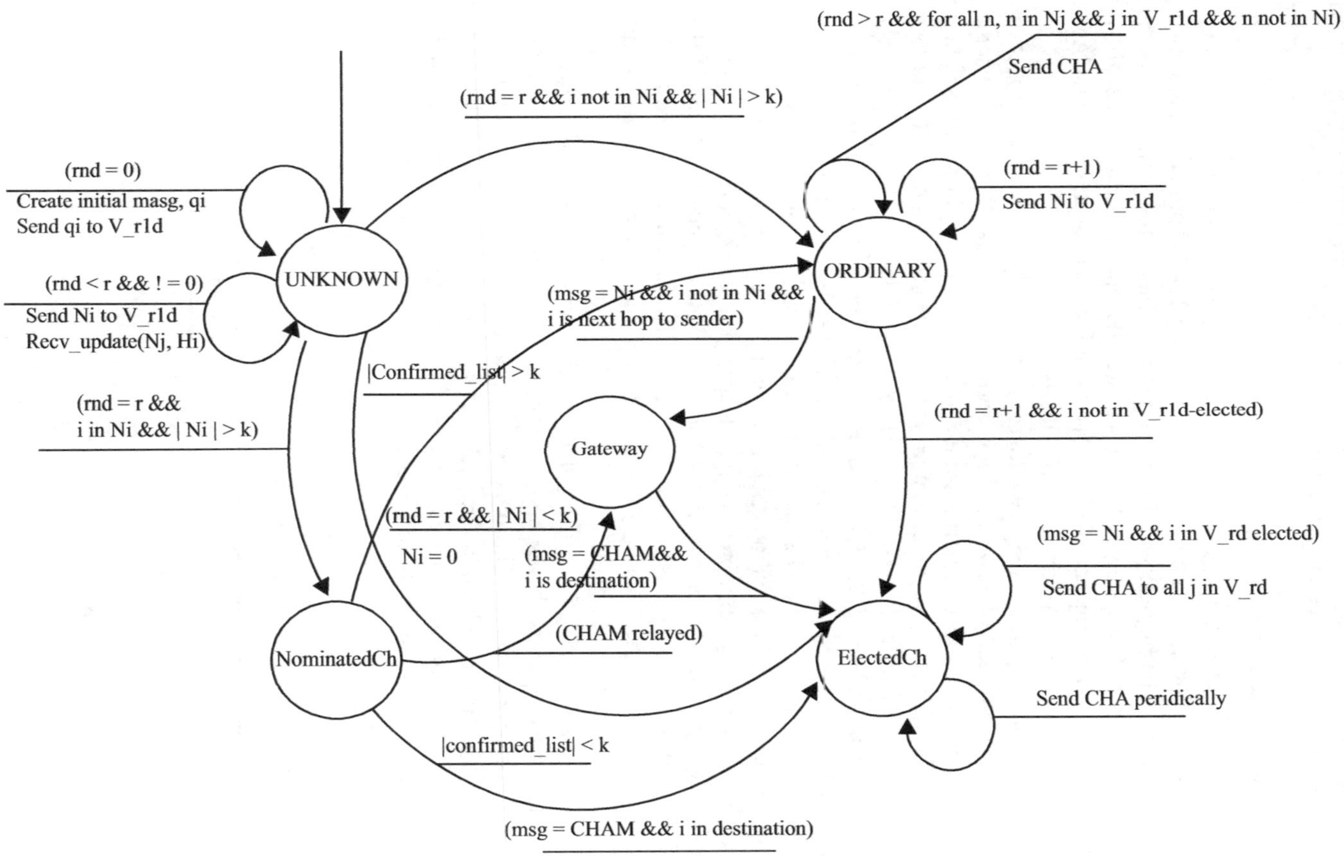

Figure 11.6 DSCAM transition diagram

number then the CH accepts this request and sends the *NJ_ACK* message. The *NJ* message with accept *TRUE* indicates a successful CH assignment, otherwise the node should send the *NJ* message to the next qualified node.

11.3.3   Performance evaluation

The performance of DSCAM is evaluated through simulations. The parameters used for the simulation are listed in Table 11.2. An ideal MAC protocol is assumed with no collisions. The highest weight is assigned for the mobility and the lowest weight for the degree. These values can be adjusted depending upon the scenarios. The flexibility of changing the weight factors allows application of DSCAM algorithm for different networks and applications.

The performance of DSCAM is evaluated using the metrics (i) the number of clusters, (ii) the number of re-affiliations, and (iii) the Load Balancing Factor (LBF). The number of clusters defines the number of elements in the dominating set. The re-affiliation count is incremented when a node selects a new CH and gets dissociated from its current CH. The parameter LBF is used to quantitatively measure how well balanced the CHs are. H-degree, Wu and Li, and WCA algorithms are selected for the performance comparison of DSCAM. DSCAM is a DS-based distributed algorithm. The (k, r)-DS computation algorithm is used for selecting the subset of nodes, which covers the entire network and these nodes form a virtual backbone. The combined weight metric is used for the association of ordinary nodes with the virtual backbone elements. This association results in the formation of disjoint stable clusters with radius r. The algorithm proposed by Wu and Li [38] is one of the popular DS-based algorithms in the literature for the construction of virtual backbones.

WCA [23] is a distributed and combined weight metric clustering algorithm. Here, clusters are created with *one-hop* radius and the most suitable node (based on quality) is elected as the CH. The clusters created using WCA are stable but the number of re-affiliations is high in dynamic networks. H-degree is the earliest well-known distributed algorithm. In this algorithm, a CH may not be able to handle a large number of nodes due to resource limitation even if these nodes lie

Table 11.2   DSCAM parameters

Parameter	Value in DSCAM
Number of nodes	10–500
Network size	1000×1000 m^2, 500×500 m^2
Transmission range	10–150 m
Max speed of node movement	20 m/s
W_1, W_2, W_3 and W_4	0.5, 0.3, 0.1 and 0.1
Mobility model	Random way point
Traffic model	128 Bytes packets, 4 packets/s
Simulation time	600 s

within the transmission range. Here, since the CH is the most heavily loaded node, its battery power deteriorates and results in number of CH changes.

The first experiment provides a report on the average number of elements in the dominating set or clusters created for different values of the number of nodes in the network. The number of dominating nodes strongly influences the latency, communication overhead, and inter- and intra-communication strategies. It is observed that the number of dominating nodes increases with the increase in the total number of nodes in DSCAM, as shown in Figure 11.7. This is because with larger values of *r*, more number of nodes is covered. When the value of *r* is increased from 1 to 2, the number of dominating nodes is reduced by 45 per cent, which results in lower number of clusters created.

DSCAM creates less number of clusters compared with Wu and Li, H-degree and WCA. This is because DSCAM forms less number of clusters with larger values of *r* and uses pruning techniques to reduce the number of CHs. But a larger value of *r* leads to increase in the cluster size, which adversely affects the performance. So the selection of *r* is critical.

To achieve load balancing, DSCAM assigns various time slots for the different CHs based on its quality and an agreeable threshold on the number of nodes that a CH can handle. It is observed that there is a reduction in LBF with increase in the value of *r*. Figure 11.8 compares the LBF for the four algorithms. It is observed that DSCAM with $k=2$ and $r=2$ outperforms the others because of its multi-CH and bounded distance properties.

The average number of clusters remains almost constant for a long duration. The number of dominant set updates is less in DSCAM with $k=2$ and $r=2$

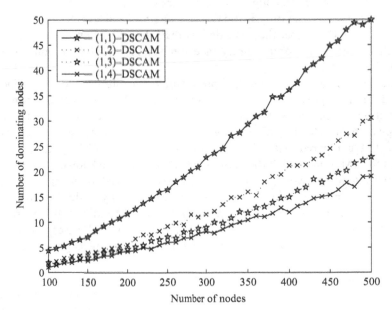

Figure 11.7   Number of dominating nodes for $k=1$ and $r=1, 2, 3$ and 4

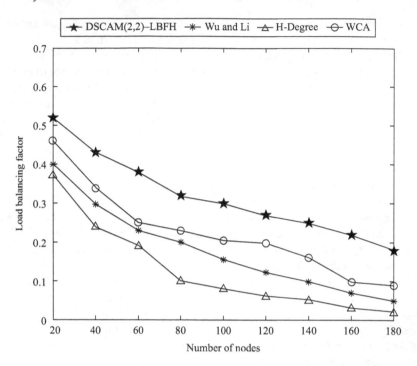

Figure 11.8   Load balancing factor in DSCAM

compared to the other three algorithms. The above results show the stability of the created clusters. This stability in DSCAM is due to the selection of the most capable nodes as CHs so that they can deliver their duty for a longer duration. Similarly, cluster formation and maintenance mechanisms reduce the number of CH election initiations.

The created clusters in DSCAM preserve its structure for a longer period than Wu and Li, H-degree and WCA algorithms. It is observed that the number of re-affiliations increases with increase in the number of nodes and higher values of displacement. Hence, the number of CH election process invoked is less in DSCAM compared with Wu and Li, H-degree and WCA. The centralized solution SCAM requires that the entire network topology be known. In this method, the network topology would have to be broadcast, and the dominating set computed by each node in the network would be the same for any node. But in DSCAM clusters are formed with the knowledge of *r-hop* neighbourhood. It is worth comparing the total number of dominating nodes created in both cases, which would show whether there is any benefit of having the global knowledge of the network topology.

The signalling overhead, which consists of the total number of control packets exchanged for gathering topology information in a centralized algorithm, or for the execution of the two phases in the distributed algorithm, is also considered for performance comparison. The control overheads in SCAM increase rapidly with

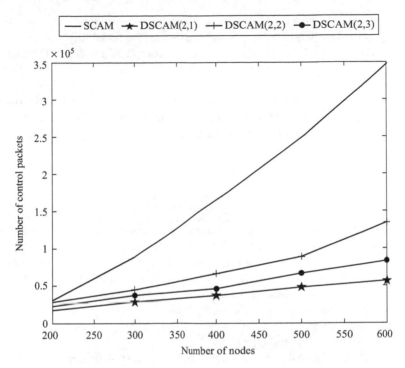

Figure 11.9   Signalling overheads in SCAM and DSCAM

the increase in the number of nodes, whereas the increase is linear in DSCAM as shown in Figure 11.9. The SCAM parameters are $r = 2$ and $k = 2$. The number of control overheads increase with the parameter r.

11.4   Conclusion

SCAM is a multi-hop, (k, r)-DS based and centralized clustering algorithm developed for MANETs. The (k, r)-DS-based algorithm is observed to have improved reliability, variable degree of CH redundancy and less frequent CH re-elections. The SCAM creates stable clusters with minimum control overhead and has improved stability, scalability and load balancing. Various parameters are used in the algorithm to adapt to different network scenarios. The CHs are selected based on the bounded distance parameter and the multi-CH parameter, which improves the scalability. The non-CH nodes select the most suitable CH based on combined-weight metric that improves stability. Load balancing techniques are used to improve the load balancing among the created clusters.

   The availability of a centralized node with sufficient resources is not assured in many MANETs. Similarly, MANETs with static known topology have limited applications. If the topology is not known, the control overhead is high for learning the topology of the entire network. In such situations distributed algorithms are preferred because distributed clustering algorithms can create clusters with the knowledge of *r-hop* neighbours. DSCAM improves the scalability and reduces the control overhead for learning the topology. It computes the (k, r)-DS in a distributed manner where the DS elements are selected based on the quality that is a function of the parameters.

More research is needed to compute and analyse the degree distribution and clustering coefficient of MANETs [39]. Enhancing the algorithms to incorporate security and providing guaranteed QoS are topics suggested for further research.

References

1. Conti M., Giordano S., 'Multi-hop ad hoc networking: The theory'. *IEEE Communications Magazine*. 2007; vol. 45, no. 4: pp. 78–86
2. Imrich Chlamtac, Marco Conti, Jennifer J.-N. Liu, 'Mobile ad hoc networking imperatives and challenges'. *Adhoc Networks*. 2003; 1: 13–64
3. Haynes T. W., Hedetniemi S. T., Slater P. J. *Fundamentals of Domination in Graphs*. Marcel Dekker, New York, 1998
4. Garey M., Johnson D., *Computers and Intractability: A Guide to NP- Completeness*. Freeman and Company, New York, 1979
5. Joshi D., Radhakrishnan S., Narayanan C., 'A fast algorithm for generalized network location problems'. *Proceedings of the ACM/SIGAPP Symposium on Applied Computing*, 1993. ACM, New York, pp. 701–708
6. Basagni S., Conti M., Giordano S., Stojmenvic I., *Mobile Ad hoc networking*, IEEE Press and John Wiley and Sons, Inc., New York, 2004. ISBN 0-471-373133
7. Williams B., Camp T., 'Comparison o broadcasting techniques for mobile ad hoc networks'. *Proceedings of the 3rd ACM International Symposium on Mobile Ad hoc Networking and Computing*. MobiHoc '02: ACM Press, New York, NY, 2002. pp. 194–205
8. Obraczka K., Viswanath K., Tsudik, G., 'Flooding for reliable multicast in multi-hop ad hoc networks'. *Wireless Networks*. 2001; vol. 7, no. 6: pp. 627–634
9. Tseng Y.-C., Ni S.-Y., Chen Y.-S., Sheu, J.-P., 'The broadcast storm problem in a mobile ad hoc network'. *Wireless Networks*. 2002; vol. 8, pp. 151–162
10. Hedrick C., 'Rfc1058-routing information protocol', Internet Request for Comments, 1998. Available online: http://www.faqs.org/rfcs/rfc1058.html
11. Xu H., Wu X., Sadjadpour H. R., Garcia-Luna-Aceves J. J., 'A Unified Analysis of Routing Protocols in MANETs'. *Transactions On Communications*. 2010; vol. 58, no. 3: pp. 911–921
12. Perkins C., Bhagwat P., 'Highly dynamic destination-sequenced distance vector routing (DSDV) for mobile computers'. *Computer Communications Review*. 1994; vol. 1, no. 1: pp. 234–244

13. Garcia-Luna-Aceves J. J., Spohn M., 'Source-tree routing in wireless networks'. *Proceedings of the IEEE International Conference on Network Protocols* IEEE Computer Society Toronto, Canada, 1999. pp. 273–282

14. Clausen T., Jacquet P., Laouiti A., Muhlethaler P., Qayyum A., Viennot L., 'Optimized link state routing protocol for ad hoc networks'. *Proceedings of the IEEE International Multi Topic Conference*, December 2001. Pakistan, pp. 6268–6279

15. Perkins C., Royer E. M., 'Ad hoc on demand distance vector routing'. *Proceedings of 2nd IEEE Workshop on Mobile Computing Systems and Applications*, February 1999. pp. 90–100

16. Johnson D., Maltz D., 'Dynamic source routing ad hoc wireless networks'. *Mobile Computing*. 1996; vol. 1, no. 1: Kluwer Academic Publishers, Dordrecht, The Netherlands, pp. 153–181

17. Anitha V. S., Sebastian M. P., 'SCAM: Scenario-based clustering algorithm for mobile ad hoc networks'. *Proceedings of the First International Conference on Communication Systems and Networks (COMSNET 2009)*, Bangalore, IEEE explore. 2009. pp. 1–8

18. Sinha P., Sivakumar R., Bharghavan V., 'Cedar: A core extraction distributed ad hoc routing algorithm'. *IEEE Journal on Selected Areas In Communications*. 1999; vol. 1, no. 8: pp. 1415–1425

19. Manousakis K. S., Baras J. S., 'Clustering for transmission range control and connectivity assurance for self-configured ad hoc networks'. *Proceedings of IEEE MILCOM*, 2003. pp. 1042–1047

20. Dai F., Wu J., 'On constructing k-connected k-dominating set in wireless networks'. *Journal of Parallel and Distributed Computing*. 2005; vol. 66: pp. 947–958

21. Bandyopadhyay S., Coyle, E. J., 'An energy efficient hierarchical clustering algorithm for wireless sensor networks'. *IEEE INFOCOM, San Francisco*. April 2003; pp. 1713–1723

22. Choi W., Woo M., 'A distributed weighted clustering algorithm for mobile ad hoc networks'. *Proceedings of IEEE ICIW*, 2006; Francis, S.J., Rajsingh, pp. 197–211

23. Chatterjee M., Das S. K., Turgut D., 'WCA: A weighted clustering algorithm for mobile ad hoc networks'. *Cluster Computing*. 2002; vol. 5, no. 1: pp. 193–204

24. Friss H. T., 'A note on simple transmission formula', *Proceedings of IRE*, 1946. pp. 254–256

25. Garey M., Johnson D., *Computers and Intractability: A guide to NP-Completeness*, 1978

26. Watteyne T., Molinaro A., Richichi M. G., Dohler M., 'From MANET to IETF ROLL standardization: A paradigm shift in WSN routing protocols'. *IEEE Communications Surveys & Tutorials*, vol. 13, no. 4: pp. 688–707

27. Gupta P., Kumar P. R., 'The capacity of wireless networks'. *IEEE Transactions on Information Theory*. 2000; vol. 46, no. 2: pp. 388–404

28. Anitha V. S., Sebastian M. P., 'Dominating set based, distributed and adaptive clustering algorithm for mobile ad hoc networks', *IET Communications Journal*, Fourth Quarter 2011; vol. 5: pp. 1836–1853

29. Bhargavan V., Das B., 'Routing in ad hoc networks using minimum connected dominating sets'. *Proceedings of International Conference on Communications*, June 1997; Montreal, Canada

30. Basgni S., Mastrogrovanni M., Petriolic C., 'A performance comparison of protocols for clustering and backbone formation in large scale ad hoc networks'. *Proceedings of MASS' 2004*, October 2004. pp. 70–79

31. Hun P., Jia W., 'Design and analysis of connected dominating set formation for topology control in wireless ad hoc networks'. Proceedings of 14th International Conference on Computer Communications and Networks, 2005. ICCCN 2005, Hong Kong, China, pp. 7–12

32. Choi W., Woo M., 'A distributed weighted clustering algorithm for mobile ad hoc networks'. *Proceedings of IEEE ICIW, IEEEexplore*, Los Alamitos 2006

33. Donald A. A. M., Znati T., 'Mobility based framework for adaptive clustering in wireless ad hoc networks'. *IEEE Journal on Selected Areas in Communications*. 1999, vol. 17, no. 8: pp. 1466–1486

34. Mahasukhon P., Sharif H., Hempel M., Zhou T., Wang W., Chen H. H., 'IEEE 802.11b based ad hoc networking and its performance in mobile channels'. *IET Communications*. 2009; vol. 5, no. 1: pp. 689–699

35. Er I. I., Seah W. K. G., 'Performance analysis of mobility-based d-hop (mobdhop) clustering algorithm for mobile ad hoc networks'. *Computer Networks*. 2006; vol. 50, no. 17, pp. 3375–3399

36. Basu P., Khan N., Little T. D. C., 'A mobility based metric for clustering in mobile ad hoc networks'. *Proceedings of IEEE ICDCW 01*, April 2001. pp. 413–418

37. Gafni E., 'Round-by-round fault detectors unifying synchrony and asynchrony (extended abstract)'. *Proceedings of the Seventh Annual ACM Symposium on Principles of Distributed Computing*. 1998; ACM Press, New York, NY, pp. 143–150

38. Wu J., Li H., 'On calculating connected dominating set for efficient routing in ad hoc wireless networks'. *Proceedings of the 3rd ACM International Workshop on Discrete Algorithms and Methods for Mobile Computing and Communications*; ACM Press, New York, NY, USA, pp. 7–14

39. Tong C., Niu J. W., Niu G. Z., Qu G. Z., Long X., Gao P., 'Complex networks properties analysis for mobile *ad hoc* networks'. *IET Communications*. March 2012; vol. 6, no. 4: pp. 370–380

Part III

Ad hoc network management

Chapter 12*

Reliable approach to prevent Blackhole and Grayhole attacks in mobile ad hoc networks

Rutvij H. Jhaveri[a]

Abstract

Due to user's requirement of wireless connectivity irrespective of his geographical position the dynamic ad hoc networking (DANET) is gaining popularity to its peak today. In mobile ad hoc networks (MANETs), autonomous mobile devices connect with each other forming a temporary network without any centralized administration. The widely accepted ad hoc routing protocols do not address possible security threats at the network layer of MANETs. In this chapter, we investigate Blackhole and Grayhole attacks that cause denial-of-service and badly disrupt normal network functionalities. We present an algorithm that introduces security aspect in the route discovery process of ad hoc On-Demand Distance Vector (AODV) protocol to protect MANETs against these two attacks; a node identifies malicious node by detecting unusual routing information and alerts other nodes about the adversary using default routing packets. The proposed approach detects and isolates multiple malicious nodes during route discovery process to assure safe and secure communication among mobile nodes. We analyse our approach theoretically and evaluate its performance using Network Simulator-2 (NS-2).

12.1 Introduction

Structured wireless networks may break down in critical scenarios such as disaster, flood, cyclone, earthquake, military attacks and other emergency situations [1]. Ad hoc networks open a new dimension and overcome the limitations of structured wireless networks. A MANET is a temporary network formed by collection of mobile nodes connecting anytime and anywhere without any centralized access point [2]. A mobile node such as laptop or mobile phone has limited resources such

*H. F. Rashvand and H.-C. Chao (Eds.), *Dynamic Ad Hoc Networks*, The IET Book Publishing Department, 2013, ISBN 978-1-84919-647-5, eISBN 978-1-84919-648-2
[a]Computer Engineering Department, Shri S'ad Vidya Mandal Institute of Technology, Bharuch, Gujarat, India

as battery power, CPU capacity, storage capacity or bandwidth [3]. The nodes in a MANET have self-configuration ability and therefore they can be deployed on demand [3]; they connect via wireless shared medium and as a consequence of node mobility they form dynamic topologies [1]. Multi-hop links are used for communication between two mobile nodes due to their limited communication range [4]. To stay connected in the network, each node acts both as a host as well as a router, and therefore it must be willing to relay packets for neighbour nodes [1]. The duty of establishing and maintaining routes between the nodes is performed by special routing protocols [5]. Due to link instability, frequently changing topology and node mobility, MANET routing protocols face several challenges [3]. A suitable and effective routing protocol would be helpful to overcome these challenges.

Lots of research work has been carried out to prevent Denial-of-Service (DoS) attacks such as Blackhole and Grayhole attacks against routing protocol at the network layer that seriously disrupt fundamental functionalities of an ad hoc network [6]. After critically analysing the present approaches proposed for handling Blackhole and Grayhole attacks, we find that very little attention has been given to detect and isolate multiple malicious nodes during route discovery process without introducing extra control packets. The limitations of present approaches motivated us to present an algorithm that thwarts Blackhole and Gryahole attacks against MANETs.

The chapter is organized as follows. Section 12.2 describes the scope and objective of our research work. Section 12.3 describes the theoretical background along with related work. Design and analysis of our solution, R-AODV, for improving the route discovery process of AODV to prevent Blackhole and Grayhole attacks, are presented in Section 12.4. Implementation methodology and experimental setup are described in Section 12.5. Section 12.6 presents performance comparison of standard AODV with R-AODV under Blackhole and Grayhole attacks along with simulation results. Further developments and conclusions based on observations are presented in Sections 12.7 and 12.8, respectively.

12.2   Scope and objective

Default routing protocols are prone to various security threats at the network layer. AODV and DSR protocols stand prominent in the category of reactive routing protocols [7], though AODV outperforms DSR in situations with more load and high mobility [7] and provides relative ease of implementation of enhancements compared to DSR [8]. Sequence number and hop count in AODV control packets are the key parameters that affect the route discovery process in a MANET. Many attacks can be carried out just by not following the AODV protocol's rules or lack of modifying the routing information during route discovery process.

Blackhole and Grayhole attacks are widespread DoS attacks against AODV in MANETs [9]; the malicious node accesses the destination sequence number from the received request packet and inserts a fabricated destination sequence number in the corresponding reply packet which causes creation of a bogus route.

Thus, Blackhole and Grayhole attacks can be detected during route discovery process by monitoring the destination sequence number of reply packet sent by malicious node on the reverse path to the source.

The objective of this chapter is to theoretically evaluate the previous research work to thwart Blackhole and Grayhole attacks and present a mechanism to overcome their limitations. In this chapter, we focus on 'introducing reliability into route discovery process of AODV to thwart Blackhole and Grayhole attacks in MANETs'. Efficacy of the mechanism is presented by theoretical as well as experimental analysis as is discussed and peer-reviewed in our publications viz. References 1, 3, 6 and 10.

12.3 Theoretical background and related work

In this section, we introduce MANETs, routing protocols and security threats at the network layer.

12.3.1 Introduction to MANET

In a dynamic ad hoc network (DANET), nodes are connected dynamically in arbitrary manner without a base station [3]. A MANET is a self-organizing dynamic ad hoc network of mobile nodes that communicate with each other via wireless links; it doesn't have predefined boundary or centralized administration [11]. The network topology is unpredictable as it changes frequently due to randomly moving nodes.

Due to self-configurable and rapidly deployable nature, MANETs have become vital in pervasive computing [10]. MANETs can have different forms as following scenarios depict [12]: In first scenario, a MANET is formed by soldiers in battlefield working in a hostile environment where they confidentially operate to track the activities of enemy, impersonate themselves as hostile parties or divert the traffic arbitrarily. In another scenario a MANET is formed between laptop of institute's head and Personal Digital Assistants (PDAs) of professors to show the performance of students over the academic year. Both the scenarios are completely different in terms of security requirements. In the first scenario strong security is required to protect communication in a hostile and demanding setting with unpredictable network conditions, while in the second scenario no special security requirements are there due to safe and friendly setting with predictable network conditions.

12.3.1.1 Challenges
MANETs suffer from several challenges [11, 13] due to their unique characteristics:

- Adapting to traffic conditions and scalability of the mobile nodes due to frequent topology changes
- Providing Quality-of-Service (QoS) levels in a constantly changing environment
- Designing power efficient systems that balance traffic load among nodes to save unnecessary power consumption for light-weight mobile terminals
- Identifying and controlling selfish and malicious nodes that exploit resources

- Designing an effective routing mechanism to establish a smooth transmission in a constantly changing topology
- Developing a standard security mechanism as wireless channel is available to both legitimate users and attackers

These challenges represent the need to develop security solutions that accomplish wider protection and desirable performance of MANET.

12.3.2   Routing protocols

A routing protocol is a standard which specifies how nodes exchange and distribute information that enables them to choose paths between a pair of nodes in a network [14]. Due to completely different characteristics of MANETs from wired networks, protocols of wired network cannot be used. Nodes must rely on ad hoc routing to facilitate communication in the network.

MANET routing protocols are classified into three categories [15]: reactive, proactive and hybrid protocols. Reactive protocols are on-demand protocols that construct route when required. The route remains in the routing table of a node via shortest path until it is no longer needed. They are energy efficient and route maintenance is effective, but need high latency time in route finding [16]. Proactive protocols are table-driven protocols that construct routes in advance; therefore, a route can be selected immediately. However, they periodically update topology which increases bandwidth overhead and exhausts battery power of nodes; moreover, routing tables may needlessly contain multiple entries for a destination; they react slowly during reconstruction or failure of network [16]. Hybrid protocols combine selective features of reactive and proactive protocols [15].

MANETs desire the following properties in ad hoc routing protocols [17]:

- Due to the constraints of limited battery power, it is vital that the routing protocol has support for sleep mode.
- Support for unidirectional links, and not only the bi-directional links, improves performance of the routing protocol.
- Support for multiple routes can reduce the number of reactions to topological changes.
- The mobile nodes enter or leave the network unpredictably and therefore the protocol should not depend on a centralized controlling node; it ought to be distributed.
- It is desirable that the protocol assures loop-free routes to consume lesser bandwidth and power resources.
- It is essential that the protocol brings trust among the nodes and securely transmits data.

12.3.2.1   Ad hoc on-demand distance vector

Ad hoc On-demand Distance Vector (AODV) is a reactive protocol that is capable of both unicast and multicast routing [18]. It is loop-free, self-starting and scales to large numbers of mobile nodes [18]. Sequence numbers are used to ensure the freshness of routes. It establishes route with small delay and link breakages in active routes are efficiently repaired. It only keeps track of next hop using periodic HELLO messages [15]. AODV uses three types of control messages [1]: Route Request (RREQ), Route Reply (RREP) and Route Error (RERR).

Whenever a node wants to discover a route to another node, it broadcasts an RREQ packet to all its neighbours [15]; the packet propagates through the network until it reaches the destination or a node with a fresh enough route to the destination [3]. The distance in hops from the source to the destination is represented as hop count [19]. The node sending RREP increments its own sequence number and updates the sequence number of the source node in its routing table to the maximum of the one in its routing table and the one in the RREQ. The corresponding RREP is unicasted to the source node on the reverse path [3]. When a link breakage is detected in an active route, a peer node notifies other nodes about loss of the link using an RERR message; the message will eventually be received by the affected sources that can choose either to stop sending data or to request for a fresh route by sending out a new RREQ [17].

When a node sends a routing control message, it increases its own sequence number; whichever node sends message with highest sequence number, its information is considered fresher and route is established over that node [19]. AODV doesn't need periodic broadcasts of routes and therefore adds lesser overhead. It is the best-known sequenced distance vector protocol [20].

12.3.3   Security issues in MANET

The basic aspects of security like confidentiality, authentication, integrity, availability and non-repudiation are vital in routing. *Confidentiality* is violated by leakage of sensitive information to adversaries [11]. Impersonation breaches security and affects *Authentication* aspect [21]. Adversaries can intentionally alter information to affect *Integrity* [11]. *Availability* of a network can be violated by dropping off packets and by resource depletion attacks [11]. *Non-repudiation* can be affected when compromised nodes are not detected and isolated [21].

12.3.3.1   Types of security attacks

We can separate the types of attacks by attackers' behaviour viz. passive and active attacks, source of attacks viz. external and internal attacks, as well as number of attackers viz. single and multiple attackers [22].

A passive attack does not disturb the normal network operation while an active attack does that. It is relatively easy to detect active attacks by observing occurrence of unusual network functionalities. External attacks are launched by unauthorized nodes taking part in the network operations with the aim to cause network congestion, to deny access to specific network function or to disrupt network operations [15]; more severe attacks might come from internal attacks which are initiated by authorized nodes [22]. Attackers may launch attacks against ad hoc networks independently or by cooperation of other attackers [22]; single attackers typically produce moderate traffic load and limited resources while colluding attackers make it much harder to protect ad hoc networks against them and they could be residing near the area where they presume high communication rate [23].

12.3.3.2   Attacks on different layers

Several active and passive attacks are possible on different layers of protocol stack as described in References 15 and 24. Application layer is prone to Repudiation, Data corruption, Viruses, Worms and Malicious codes; threats such as Session hijacking and SYN flooding at transport layer breach network security; due to security ignorance in default routing protocols, network layer is prone to attacks such as Sybil, Blackhole, Grayhole, Wormhole, Spoofing, Flooding, Location disclosure, Route table overflow, Route table poisoning and Route cache poisoning; Traffic monitoring and analysis, Disruption MAC (802.11) and WEP weakness may breach the security at data-link layer; while the physical layer may suffer from attacks such as Jamming, Interception and Eavesdropping.

12.3.3.3   Blackhole and Grayhole attacks

In our work, we focus on two well-known DoS attacks on MANETs viz. Blackhole and Grayhole attacks [3]. In Blackhole attack, malicious node sends false routing information to attract source node to establish route through itself; once route is established, malicious node drops all packets [6]. Figure 12.1 [3] shows the behaviour of Blackhole attacker against AODV protocol. Source S wants to communicate with destination D; therefore, S initiates route discovery process by broadcasting an RREQ to its neighbours; intermediate nodes rebroadcast the RREQ until a node having valid fresher route to D or D itself receives it; this node then generates an RREP. As X is a malicious node, it doesn't forward the RREQ ahead; instead, it sends an RREP with abnormally higher destination sequence number, indicating that it has a fresher route to D. Thus, S considers RREP received from X ahead of RREPs received from other genuine nodes. Thus, S considers sending packets to D through X as it believes that X has the shortest valid route to D. X now

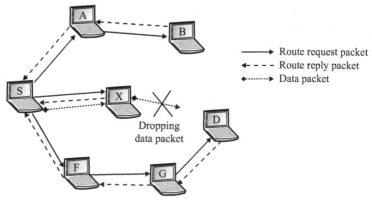

Figure 12.1   Blackhole attack [3][1]

---

[1] Work first published in Infocomp Journal of Computer Science, article *Improving Route Discovery for AODV to Prevent Blackhole and Grayhole Attacks in MANETs. INFOCOMP Journal of Computer Science. March 2012; 11(1): 1–12.*

performs packet-forwarding misbehaviour by dropping all received packets and performance of network is compromised [3].

Grayhole attack is an extension of Blackhole attack in which a malicious node's behaviour is exceptionally unpredictable. A node behaves maliciously and drops packets for a certain time, but later on it behaves just like a genuine node [6]. Due to this unpredictable characteristic, detection of Grayhole node is not an easy task. Grayhole attack can disturb route discovery process and degrade network's performance [25]. As AODV doesn't have any security mechanism, malicious nodes can perform many attacks just by not following the protocol rules [10].

12.3.4 Related work

In our study, we focus on preventing Blackhole and Grayhole attacks as discussed previously. We investigate present mechanisms to prevent these attacks in this section as discussed in References 1, 3 and 10.

Anti-Blackhole Mechanism discussed by Su *et al.* [26] estimates the difference between number of RREQs and RREPs transmitted from a node; the node forwarding RREP, but not re-broadcasting RREQ for a definite route, will have its suspicious value increased in the nearby node's suspicious node table. The node broadcasts a BLOCK message when the suspicious value of a node crosses threshold value, and the suspicious node is isolated cooperatively. However, introduction of BLOCK packet rises normalized routing overhead; furthermore, it also assumes prior existence of authentication mechanism. DPRAODV protocol suggested by Raj *et al.* [5] periodically calculates the difference of destination sequence number of RREP and that of routing table entry and compares it with threshold value; for greater difference than threshold, the node sending RREP is marked as a malicious node. Node detecting the malicious node broadcasts an ALARM packet to inform neighbour nodes about existence of a malicious node. The protocol, though, adds overhead in generating the ALARM packet and broadcasting it leads to higher normalized routing overhead. Mistry *et al.* [8] provided a modification in AODV called MOSAODV that uses heuristic approach to calculate MOS_WAIT_TIME which is the amount of time source node waits for other RREPs after the first RREP is received; a table Cmg_RREP_Tab is used to store all RREPs. Out of all RREPs source node discards RREPs with relatively higher sequence number considering those from malicious nodes. Limitation of this solution is that selecting the key value of sequence number to detect malicious reply is presumed. Vishnu and Paul [27] discussed a solution that establishes a backbone network containing trusted nodes; source node requests an unused IP address from a trusted node; route discovery process includes the unused IP for search of the destination node; detection process is initiated by the source node if an RREP is sent by a malicious node for the unused IP. However, the mechanism assumes high battery power and high communication range of backbone nodes; also, assumption is made that number of adversaries as neighbours must be less than genuine nodes at any time which may not be likely in many scenarios. A one-way hash code is embedded with data packets in the scheme proposed by Mamatha and Sharma [28] that uses simple acknowledgement and principle of flow conservation. For every correctly received packet verified by the hash code, ACK message is sent and for the incorrect one CONFIDENTIALITY LOST is sent. If total transmission time is more than predefined time, a miss counter is incremented and the ratio of the total missed packets to the total sent packets is calculated. If it is out of tolerable range, misbehaviour is detected and replacement node is chosen for future sessions. However, introduction of ACK/CONFIDENTIALITY LOST control packets leads to increase in routing overhead. Agrawal *et al.* [29] discussed a solution that creates a backbone network of strong nodes for monitoring overall traffic using promiscuous mode and carrying out end-to-end checking with destination for every sent data block using Prelude and Postlude messages. In the case of failure in receiving a data block, the backbone network initiates detection process to remove a chain of malicious nodes. However, the mechanism increases routing overhead as it uses additional control packets; also, assumption about strong nodes having powerful battery and high radio range is made; furthermore, requirement that a node has more strong nodes as neighbours than malicious nodes may not be always satisfied when nodes frequently change positions.

From above discussion we find following limitations in the existing approaches:

1. Mechanisms discussed in References 5, 26, 28 and 29 introduce one or more additional routing control packets which lead to increase in normalized routing overhead.
2. Solutions proposed in References 27 and 29 assume high battery power and high communication range of mobile nodes and may not perform well when an intermediate node has more number of adversaries as neighbours than genuine nodes.
3. Algorithm discussed in Reference 26 assumes prior existence of authentication mechanism in the network.
4. Solution discussed in Reference 8 uses heuristic approach and presumes the value of destination sequence number that is a key parameter to detect malicious nodes.

Hence, it is imperative to design a protocol that removes these limitations and finds a secured route to the destination during route discovery phase.

12.4   Reliable-AODV: mechanism to thwart Blackhole and Grayhole attacks

To protect MANETs against Blackhole and Grayhole attacks, we propose modification of AODV protocol, Reliable-AODV (R-AODV), as described in References 1, 3 and 10; R-AODV introduces security and reliability into route discovery process to detect and isolate malicious nodes. We theoretically analyse the algorithm and evaluate its performance under both attacks using Network Simulator-2 (NS-2) and compare it to standard AODV. The objective of R-AODV is to set up a secured route to deliver data packets with higher rate with minimal normalized routing overhead and acceptable average end-to-end delay.

12.4.1 The proposed approach

In order to protect network-layer reactive protocols from Blackhole and Grayhole attacks, it is necessary to discover malicious nodes during route discovery phase as they pass fabricated routing information before data transmission phase to attract source node to send data through itself. Our mechanism does exactly the same.

Traffic conditions in a MANET determine the value of a node's sequence number [30]. Destination sequence number is a key parameter in deciding the fresher valid path to the destination out of the multiple optional paths [5]; this parameter is easily accessible to adversary taking part in the route discovery process. In standard AODV, when a node receives RREP, it checks the sequence number in its routing table; if it is less than the one in the RREP, the routing table is updated [18].

Figure 12.2(a) [10] shows the route discovery process in AODV in the presence of malicious nodes MNs, where source node S broadcasts RREQ; nodes within its communication range receive the RREQ and re-broadcast RREQ to their neighbours until a node having a valid route to the destination or destination D itself receives RREQ which sends RREP to the source node on the reverse path [15]. MNs access the destination sequence number from RREQ, discard RREQ and send RREPs with higher, but fabricated, sequence number to S. Another RREP sent by a node IN when having genuinely higher sequence number. As MNs send RREP with higher sequence number than IN, S unknowingly chooses path through one of the MNs to transfer data packets and therefore the MN can drop some or all received packets which causes disruption in network operations.

Our solution, R-AODV, detects and isolates multiple Blackhole/Grayhole nodes prior to data transfer. We modify the structures of RREQ and RREP, and add a field in the routing table as follows:

- A MALICIOUS_NODE_LIST is appended to RREQ packet to notify other nodes about malicious nodes in the MANET.
- We add a flag called DO_NOT_CONSIDER to RREP to mark/identify reply from a malicious node.
- We add another field to routing table called MALICIOUS_NODE for marking a node as malicious node.

We calculate a PEAK value by adding number of sent out RREQs, number of received RREPs and routing table sequence number to the previous PEAK value. To detect existence of a malicious node, destination sequence number of the received RREP is compared with this PEAK value. We modify functionalities of nodes sending RREQ, nodes receiving RREQ and nodes receiving RREP and put in more responsibilities; functionality for nodes sending RREP remains as it is. R-AODV doesn't add extra control packets; rather, RREQ and RREP routing packets are used to propagate information about malicious nodes to other nodes.

Figure 12.2(b) [10] shows the working of R-AODV in the presence of attackers; intermediate nodes INs receiving RREP from malicious node MNs with sequence number higher than the calculated PEAK value mark that RREP as

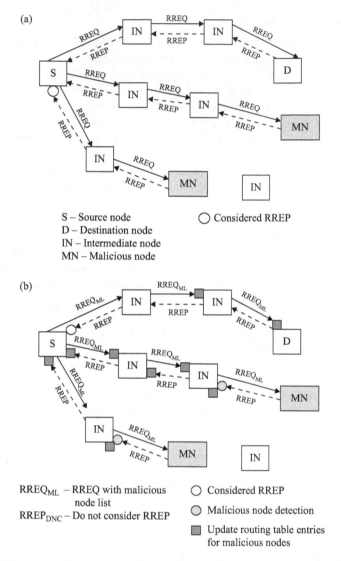

Figure 12.2   Route discovery in (a) AODV and (b) R-AODV in presence of malicious node [3, 10]

DO_NOT_CONSIDER and the node sending RREP is marked as MAL-ICIOUS_NODE in the route table; RREP updates routing tables of INs and S with MALICIOUS_NODE entries on the reverse path to S. When S wants to communicate in future with any other node, it appends a MALICIOUS_NODE_LIST to RREQ during route discovery phase to inform other nodes about the existence of malicious nodes MNs. As a result, replies from those blacklisted nodes remain unconsidered and they remain isolated from genuine nodes unlike standard AODV.

```
                    Mobile Node Receiving RREP
If(Node sending RREP is marked as MALICIOUS_NODE in the ROUTING_TABLE){
Mark RREP as DO_NOT_CONSIDER;

}
Else if(RREP is marked aDO_NOT_CONSIDER){
Mark the node sending RREP as MALICIOUS_NODE in the ROUTING_TABLE;

}
Else if {
    Calculate PEAK value;
    If (RREP_SEQUENCE_NO > PEAK) {
      Mark the node sending RREP as MALICIOUS_NODE in the ROUTING_TABLE;
      Mark RREP as DO_NOT_CONSIDER;
      Append MALICIOUS_NODE information in RREP;

      }
  }
                    Mobile Node Sending RREQ
If (MALICIOUS_NODE entry exists in the ROUTING_TABLE) {
Make MALICIOUS_NODE_LIST and append it to RREQ;

}
                    Mobile Node Receiving RREQ
If (Received RREQ contains MALICIOUS_NODE_LIST) {
Make the blacklisted nodes as MALICIOUS_NODEs in the ROUTING_TABLE;

}
```

Figure 12.3   Design of R-AODV [3, 10] (with kind permission of Springer Science and Business Media)

A mechanism is called *reliable* when it has good resistance to failure of the network while an attack is launched; exhaustive performance evaluation of R-AODV under Blackhole and Grayhole attacks in practical scenarios by varying different network parameters proves the reliability of R-AODV as presented in Reference 3. Figure 12.3 shows design of R-AODV as presented in Reference 10.

12.4.2   Algorithm analysis

The algorithm adds computing overhead in the form of calculation of PEAK value. PEAK value allocates 4 bytes of memory while its calculation uses NO_OF_SENT_RREQ and NO_OF_RECEIVED_RREP and both allocate 2 bytes each. Adding new field MALICIOUS_NODE in the routing table requires 2 bytes for each node entry; an integer flag called DO_NOT_CONSIDER allocates 2 bytes in RREP packet. MALICIOUS_NODE_LIST to be appended to RREQ contains 2 bytes for each entry. The overhead in time is in terms of generation of MALICIOUS_NODE_LIST.

However, under Blackhole and Grayhole attacks, the overhead is worthy for the rise in PDR for MANETs using R-AODV protocol. In addition, R-AODV doesn't generate additional control packets to notify other nodes about malicious nodes, which brings down normalized routing overhead remarkably.

12.5   Implementation methodology

This section describes the implementation methodology of our research work. We discuss simulator choice, implementation of Blackhole and Grayhole behaviour, implementation of R-AODV as well as the simulation parameters and performance metrics used.

12.5.1   Simulator choice

The simulation phase requires meaningful simulation results so that it represents results as close as possible to reality. There may be significant divergence between results of different simulators [31]. There is a range of simulators available to perform simulations of ad hoc network such as GloMoSim, OPNET and NS-2. We chose NS-2 as it provides ease of extensions to default routing protocols and it is the most widely used simulator for MANET simulations [32].

NS-2 includes many network objects such as protocols, applications and traffic source behaviour. At the simulation layer NS uses Object-oriented Tool Command Language (OTCL) to interpret user simulation scripts. In fact, OTCL language is an object-oriented extension of the TCL language, which is fully compatible with C++. At the top layer, NS is an interpreter of TCL scripts of the users that work together with C++ codes [33]. The implementation of the Blackhole behaviour [11] and Grayhole behaviour of the AODV protocol is written in C++.

12.5.2   Experimental setup

We follow steps described in Reference 34 to implement routing protocols *BlackholeAODV*, *GrayholeAODV* and *R-AODV*. To add Blackhole and Grayhole behaviour into the new AODV protocol, we copy and rename respective files and make suitable changes. The nodes should use a new routing protocol that can take part in AODV messaging.

Blackhole and Grayhole behaviour is carried out after the malicious node receives RREQ broadcasted by the source node; when malicious node receives the RREQ packet, it immediately sends RREP packet with bogus routing information on the reverse path as if it has fresh enough path to the destination; it tries to deceive other nodes sending RREPs with a higher destination sequence number. When RREP packet is received by an intermediate node, standard AODV forwards it to the source address, while in R-AODV the routing table is verified, DO_NOT_CONSIDER flag of RREP is checked or destination sequence number of RREP is compared with the calculated PEAK value to confirm that the reply is sent by a genuine node.

12.5.2.1 Simulation parameters

We perform our simulations using NS-2 (Ver.-2.34) [33] that provides implementations of various routing protocols. We use random waypoint model for generating various network scenarios in which each node chooses a random destination and moves towards it with random velocity; *cbrgen* and *setdest* utilities are used to generate traffic and mobility models respectively. Two new routing agents are included in NS-2 containing Blackhole and Grayhole attacks as discussed. We randomly move nodes in the area of 800 m × 800 m for the simulation time of 50 s. Transmission range of each node is 250 m. We use UDP at the transport layer. We vary following network parameters in our simulations:

- Network size: Number of mobile nodes
- Traffic load: Number of sources
- Number of adversaries: Number of Blackhole/Grayhole nodes

Table 12.1 shows simulation parameters and their values.

Table 12.1 Simulation parameters

Parameter	Value
Simulator	NS-2 (ver.-2.34)
Terrain area	800 m × 800 m
Simulation time	50 s
MAC	802.11
Traffic type	CBR (UDP)
Maximum bandwidth	2 Mbps
Routing protocols	AODV and R-AODV
Transmission range	250 m
Data payload	512 Bytes/packet
Pause time	2.0 s
Maximum speed	50 m/s
Number of nodes	20–80
Number of sources	1–9

12.5.2.2 Performance metrics

To evaluate the performance of our solution, we use the following metrics:

Packet Delivery Ratio (PDR): The ratio of number of data packets received by the application layer of destination nodes to the number of packets transmitted by the application layer of source nodes

Average End-to-End Delay: Average time taken by transmitted data packets to reach to corresponding destinations

Normalized Routing Overhead: The ratio of number of routing control packets to the number of data packets

12.6   Simulation results and analysis

We evaluate the performance of our protocol R-AODV under Blackhole and Grayhole attacks and compare it with standard AODV by varying different network parameters. As R-AODV isolates both Blackhole and Grayhole nodes, packet delivery ratio (PDR), average end-to-end delay and normalized routing overhead of R-AODV under both attacks remain same. As our previous results presented in Reference 3, we compare standard AODV in normal condition and R-AODV under attack for average end-to-end delay and normalized routing overhead as AODV under attack gives less end-to-end delay and very high routing overhead.

12.6.1   Effect of network size

Figure 12.4 shows the performance comparison of AODV and R-AODV under attack by varying network size from 20 to 80 with pause time as 2.0 s and maximum speed as 50 m/s.

It can be concluded from the graphs in Figure 12.4(a) and (b) that under Blackhole and Grayhole attacks PDR of standard AODV drops significantly; under both attacks, R-AODV isolates misbehaving nodes and gains back the PDR that is nearly 94 per cent to 99 per cent.

For AODV, as the number of mobile nodes increases average end-to-end delay increases due to increase in the number of hops. The graph in Figure 12.4(c) depicts that compared to AODV the average end-to-end delay for R-AODV under attacks starts increasing when network size exceeds 40.

Normalized routing overhead increases with an increase in the number of nodes due to requirement of relatively more number of routing control packets to establish path. R-AODV doesn't use additional routing control packets and therefore normalized routing overhead of R-AODV almost replicates the behaviour of standard AODV as shown in Figure 12.4(d).

12.6.2   Effect of traffic load

It is imperative that a routing protocol doesn't break out and performs equally well when traffic load increases. Figure 12.5 depicts the effect of traffic load on AODV and R-AODV under attack with network size of 20, maximum speed of 50 m/s and pause time of 2.0 s by varying number of sources from 1 to 9.

From the graphs in Figure 12.5(a) and (b), we can conclude that as the number of sources increases, PDR of AODV decreases due to increase in packet loss because of congestion. Even when traffic load increases, R-AODV proves its reliability by giving noticeably high PDR under attacks that is between 62 and 99 per cent.

Increase in traffic load causes increase in average end-to-end delay as network becomes more and more congested; the graph in Figure 12.5(c) depicts that R-AODV under attack gives higher but acceptable average end-to-end delay compared to standard AODV.

With the increase in number of sources, normalized routing overhead increases as number of control packets are relatively more than number of data packets; the

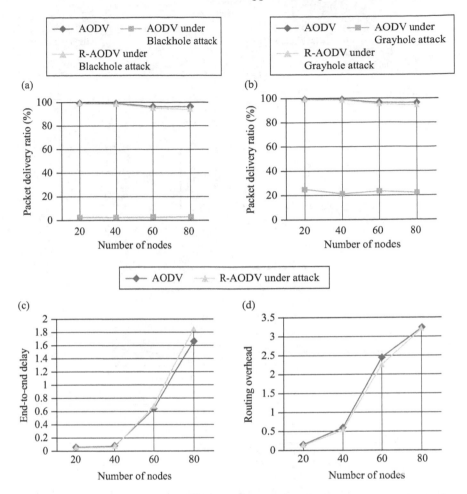

Figure 12.4   Effect of network size: (a) PDR under Blackhole attack; (b) PDR under Grayhole attack; (c) average end-to-end delay and (d) normalized routing overhead

graph shown in Figure 12.5(d) depicts that normalized routing overhead for R-AODV stays within noticeable range even though number of sources increases.

Moreover, simulations carried out by varying other parameters such as mobility, pause time and number of adversaries as presented in Reference 3 emphasize the fact that R-AODV is a reliable protocol and can isolate multiple attackers.

12.7   Further developments

In this section we review updates to thwart Blackhole and Grayhole attacks in MANETs. Jhansi *et al.* [35] presented a scheme to identify cooperative Blackhole attack by modifying AODV protocol; the protocol introduces Data Routing

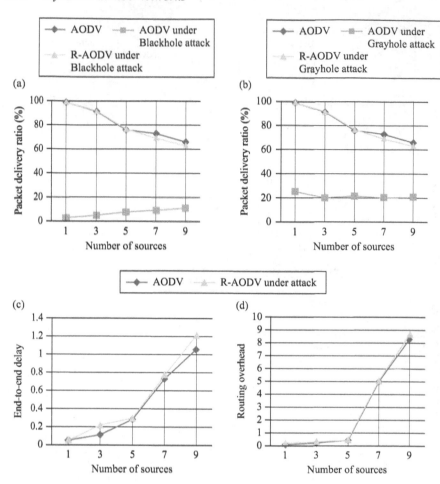

Figure 12.5   Effect of traffic load: (a) PDR under Blackhole attack; (b) PDR under Grayhole attack; (c) average end-to-end delay and (d) normalized routing overhead

Information (DRI) table and cross-checking using Further Request and Further Reply packets to check reliability of an intermediate node. The scheme has the limitation of increasing normalized routing overhead due to additional control packets; moreover, it adds overhead in terms of maintaining DRI table. Uma-parvathi *et al.* [36] proposed a two tier secure AODV protocol; in tier 1, when RREP is received by the intermediate node, the preceding node sends a verification packet to the next hop of the intermediate node and the next hop of the intermediate node sends the verification result to the preceding node. When collaborative attack is not detected in tier 1, tier 2 is used where source node sends control message at a random rate to identify the Blackhole node; the size of the control packet is kept equal to that of the original message; the control message asks the destination to send the acknowledgement; route is replaced if acknowledgement is not received within threshold time. However, the protocol has drawback of increase in routing overhead, delay and cost. A destination-based scheme suggested by Kumar *et al.* [37] uses common neighbour of preceding node and suspicious node along with fresh route request and fresh route reply packets; the scheme verifies the two hop distance node to reach capability to the destination; when reply packet is received by previous node, it attaches the one hop distance node of replying node, otherwise previous node will reject the reply message. The scheme though increases routing overhead due to fresh control packets.

Our work opens new avenues for further research. The research can be extended in several directions that are summarized below:

1. R-AODV is an enhancement of AODV protocol; the concepts of this algorithm can be implemented with little change to other reactive protocols such as DSR; the algorithm can be further extended to the category of hybrid protocols.
2. We used two-ray ground propagation model to obtain simulation results; it would be interesting to note the behaviour of R-AODV with different propagation models such as shadowing model or free space model.
3. In our simulations we measure performance of R-AODV in relatively lesser dense network; simulation results in highly dense network may show interesting outcomes.

12.8   Conclusions

AODV protocol is susceptible to Blackhole and Grayhole attacks. In this Chapter, we discussed an algorithm viz. R-AODV which provides improvement in route discovery process of AODV to isolate Blackhole and Grayhole nodes in MANETs; this has been achieved by adding responsibilities to the nodes taking part in the route discovery process of AODV and by modifying the structures of routing table, RREQ and RREP packets of AODV. AODV fails to remove malicious nodes during route discovery process and therefore doesn't succeed to transfer all data packets to the destination under attack; on the other hand, R-AODV provides an efficient way to detect and isolate multiple malicious nodes without introduction of any new control packet. Simulation results show that AODV performs poorly under both attacks and degrades performance of MANET; on the other hand, R-AODV gives significantly high PDR with noticeable normalized routing overhead and acceptable average end-to-end delay under both the attacks with various network parameters. Moreover, performance of R-AODV under multiple adversaries is remarkable. We conclude that R-AODV would greatly improve overall network performance in real-world and open new avenues for further research in MANET security.

Acknowledgements

We gratefully acknowledge Prof. (Dr.) D. C. Jinwala and Mrs. S. J. Patel of SVNIT, Surat for their constant motivation. Moreover, we would like to thank everyone, including the Institution of Engineering and Technology and the anonymous reviewers.

References

1. Jhaveri R.H., Patel S.J., Jinwala D.C. 'A Novel Approach for Blackhole and Grayhole Attacks in Mobile Ad-hoc Networks'. *Proceedings of International Conference on Advanced Computing & Communication Technologies*; January 2012. Conference Publishing Services; 2012. pp. 556–560
2. Qasim N., Said F., Aghvami H. *Performance Evaluation of Mobile Ad Hoc Networking Protocols*. Lecture Notes in Electrical Engineering, vol. 39. Springer; 2009
3. Jhaveri R.H., Patel S.J., Jinwala D.C. 'Improving Route Discovery for AODV to Prevent Blackhole and Grayhole Attacks in MANETs'. *INFOCOMP Journal of Computer Science*. March 2012; 11(1):1–12
4. Bala A., Bansal M., Singh J. 'Performance Analysis of MANET under Blackhole Attack'. *Proceedings of First International Conference on Networks & Communications*; December 2009. pp. 141–145
5. Raj P.N., Swadas P.B. 'DPRAODV: A Dynamic Learning System against Blackhole Attack in AODV Based MANET'. *International Journal of Computer Science Issues*. 2010; 2(3):54–59
6. Jhaveri R.H., Patel S.J., Jinwala D.C. 'DoS Attacks in Mobile Ad-hoc Networks: A Survey'. *Proceedings of International Conference on Advanced Computing & Communication Technologies*; January 2012. Conference Publishing Services; 2012. pp. 535–541
7. Das S.R., Perkins C.E., Royer E.M. *Performance Comparison of Two On-demand Routing Protocols for Ad Hoc Networks*. IEEE INFOCOM; 2000. pp. 3–12
8. Mistry N.H., Jinwala D.C., Zaveri M.A. 'Improving AODV Protocol againstBlackhole Attacks'. *Proceedings of International Multiconference of Engineers and Computer Scientists*; March 2010. pp. 1034–1039
9. Sophie S., Vincent M., Meshach W.T. 'Preventing Black Hole Attack in MANETs Using Randomized Multipath Routing Algorithm'. *International Journal of Soft Computing and Engineering*. January 2012; 1:30–33
10. Jhaveri R.H., Patel S.J., Jinwala D.C. 'A Novel Solution for Grayhole Attack in AODV Based MANETs'. *Proceedings of Third International Conference on Advances in Communication, Network and Computing*; February 2012. Springer; January 2013. pp. 60–67
11. Shanthi N., Ganesan L., Ramar K. 'Study of Different Attacks on Multicast Mobile Ad hoc Network'. *Journal of Theoretical and Applied Information Technology*. December 2009; 9(2):45–51
12. Revankar M. *Attacks in Ad-Hoc Networks and Modelling in NS-2*. Term Project for ECE 746 Cryptography and Network Security, George Mason University, Department of Electrical and computer Engineering, 2005

13. Goyal P., Parmar V., Rishi R. 'MANET: Vulnerabilities, Challenges, Attacks, Application'. *International Journal of Computational Engineering & Management.* January 2011; 11:32–37

14. Gani A., Hassan M.K., Zaidan A.A., Zaidan B.B. 'Intelligent Routing Information Protocol using Full Triggered Update Mechanism'. *International Journal of the Physical Sciences Vol.* June 2011; 6(11):2750–2761

15. Jhaveri R.H., Patel A.D., Parmar J.D., Shah B.I. 'MANET Routing Protocols and Wormhole Attack against AODV'. *International Journal of Computer Science and Network Security.* April 2010; 10(4):12–18

16. Patil V.P. 'Reactive and Proactive Routing Protocol Energy Efficiency Performance Analysis in Wireless Ad-Hoc Network'. *International Journal of Electronics and Computer Science Engineering.* 2012; 1(4): 2333–2343

17. Kumar V. *Simulation and Comparison of AODV and DSR Routing Protocols in MANETs* [online]. July 2009. http://dspace.thapar.edu:8080/dspace/bit stream/10266/845/1/Final+article.pdf [Accessed February 2011]

18. Patil V.P., Patil K.T., Kharade A.R., Gote D.D. 'Performance Enhancement of Reactive on Demand Routing Protocol in Wireless Ad Hoc Network'. *International Journal of Smart Sensors and Ad Hoc Networks.* 2012; 1(4): 69–74

19. Porwal A., Pal B.L., Maheshwari R., Kakhani G. 'Study and Design of New Reactive Routing Protocol Advance AODV for Mobile Ad hoc Networks'. *International Journal of Engineering Research and Applications.* 2012; 2(3):3195–3204

20. Jamali S., Safarzadeh B., Alimohammadi H. 'SQR-AODV: A Stable QOS-Aware Reliable On-Demand Distance Vector Routing Protocol for Mobile Ad-hoc Networks'. *Scientific Research and Essays.* 2011; 6: 3015–3026

21. Rai A.K., Tewari R.R., Upadhyay S.K. 'Different Types of Attacks on Integrated MANET-Internet Communication'. *International Journal of Computer Science and Security.* July 2010; 4(3):265–274

22. Bhuyan M.H., Bhattacharyya D., Kalita J.K. 'AOCD: An Adaptive Outlier Based Coordinated Scan Detection Approach'. *International Journal of Network Security.* February 2012; 14(6):339–351

23. Gandhewar N., Patel R. 'Review on Sinkhole Detection Techniques in Mobile Adhoc Network'. *Proceedings of International Conference on Soft Computing for Problem Solving*; December 2011. pp. 535–548

24. Madhavi S., Duraiswamy K., Kalaavathi B., Vijayaragavan S. 'Survey of Attacks on AODV and MAODV'. *Proceedings of International Conference and Workshop on Emerging Trends in Technology*; 2010. pp. 320–324

25. Gao X., Chen W. 'A Novel Gray Hole Attack Detection Scheme for Mobile Ad-Hoc Networks'. *Proceedings of IFIP International Conference on Network and Parallel Computing Workshops*; 2007. pp. 209–214

26. Su M.Y. 'Prevention of Selective Black Hole Attacks on Mobile Ad Hoc Networks through Intrusion Detection Systems'. *Computer Communications.* January 2011; 34:107

27.   Vishnu K., Paul A.J. 'Detection and Removal of Cooperative Black/Gray Hole Attack in Mobile Adhoc Networks'. *International Journal of Computer Applications.* 2010; 1(22):38–42

28.   Mamatha G., Sharma S. 'A Robust Approach to Detect and Prevent Network Layer Attacks in MANETs'. *International Journal of Computer Science and Security.* August 2010; 4(3):275–284

29.   Agrawal P., Ghosh R.K., Das S.K. 'Cooperative Black and Gray Hole Attacks in Mobile Ad Hoc Networks'. *Proceedings of Second International Conference on Ubiquitous Information Management and Communication;* 2008. pp. 310–314

30.   Kurosawa S., Nakayama H., Kat N., Jamalipour A., Nemoto Y. 'Detecting Blackhole Attack on AODV-Based Mobile Ad Hoc Networks by Dynamic Learning Method'. *International Journal of Network Security.* November 2007; 5(3):338–346

31.   Weingartner E., Lehn H., Wehrle K. 'A Performance Comparison of Recent Network Simulators'. *Proceedings of IEEE International Conference on Communications;* 2009. pp. 1–5

32.   Abu-Mahfouz A.M., Hancke G.P., Isaac S.J. 'Positioning System in Wireless Sensor Networks Using NS-2'. *Software Engineering.* 2012; 2(4):91–100

33.   *The NS Manual* [online]. http://www.isi.edu/nsnam/ns/doc/ [Accessed August 2011]

34.   Ros F.J., Ruiz P.M. *Implementing a New MANET Unicast Routing Protocol in NS2* [online]. December 2004. http://masimum.dif.um.es/nsrt-howto/pdf/nsrt-howto.pdf. [Accessed January 2012]

35.   Jhansi M., Roopa Devi K., Chandra B.M. 'Effective Measure to Prevent Cooperative Black Hole Attack in Mobile Ad-hoc Wireless Networks'. *International Journal of Engineering Research and Applications.* 2012; 2(4): 204–209

36.   Umaparvathi M., Varughese D.K. 'Two Tier Secure AODV against Black Hole Attack in MANETs'. *European Journal of Scientific Research.* 2012; 72(3):369–382

37.   Kumar A., Chawla M. 'Destination Based Group Gray Hole Attack Detection in MANET through AODV'. *International Journal of Computer Science Issues.* July 2012; 9(4):292–295

Chapter 13*

Distributed channel reservation MAC: A QoS improvement technique for dynamic ad hoc networks

Ali Mahani[a]

Abstract

This chapter covers the problem of negotiation mechanism in IEEE 802.11-based ad hoc networking whose functioning components, being user devices or relay nodes over the wireless or Internet, interchange data using the classic MAC-DCF. In order to overcome the existing bottleneck of negotiation procedure in wireless ad hoc networks, we propose a new channel reservation scheme which basically helps to reduce the negotiation overheads and reduce the transmission delays without any extra bandwidth consumption. Then, the extended multi-channel CRF scheme for new multi-channel applications are discussed for shared controllability and increased multi-channel applications, each on separate frequencies. In order to solve the problem of access identification, a recent distributed channel reservation scheme is explained and reviewed where critical persistent problems such as hidden terminals and coexistence of control and data traffic on different frequency channels have been discussed in detail.

13.1   Introduction

Since MANETs can support a wide range of applications, they appear to have an enormous potential to transform our daily life. Examples of scenarios where such systems can provide a more versatile, affordable solution than the existing technologies are [1, 2] as follows:

• Areas that are unwired, under-wired or hard-to-wire, such as highways, conduits, golf courses or farmlands

*H. F. Rashvand and H.-C. Chao (Eds.), *Dynamic Ad Hoc Networks*, The IET Book Publishing Department, 2013, ISBN 978-1-84919-647-5, eISBN 978-1-84919-648-2
[a]Electrical Engineering Department, Shahid Bahonar University, Kerman, Iran

- Emergency situations such as firefighting, disaster recovery and military operations
- Extensive coverage areas, for example, offices, campuses, stadiums, sprawling facilities

When the size of a MANET increases the average distance between the source and destination nodes increases and so leads to large delay and low capacity. This is due to the large volume of forwarding load through the intermediate nodes. Random access-based MAC protocols, as used in IEEE 802.11 standard, also reduce the network capacity by increasing the amount of competition a node faces for transmissions as discussed in References 3–5.

One suggestion to improve the MANET scalability is using the static relay nodes or Internet gateway. Such relay nodes were originally introduced to provide Internet access to MANETs as proposed in References 6–12, but can be used to facilitate communication between MANET nodes. A large scale MANET is divided into equal sized cells and each cell includes an access point as seen in Figure 13.1. A dynamic ad hoc network resides on subnet 1 and the MANET nodes communicate with one another via their wireless interface. On subnet 2 the relay nodes form a wireless network thus forming a backbone network, as indicated by the solid lines in Figure 13.1. The communication between the MANET nodes can take place via relay nodes through single-hop or multi-hop links.

In Reference 13 the authors have analytically shown that the capacity of a MANET with relay nodes can be improved significantly. In addition to network topology, MAC protocol characteristics affect directly interference levels as well as capacity in ad hoc networks.

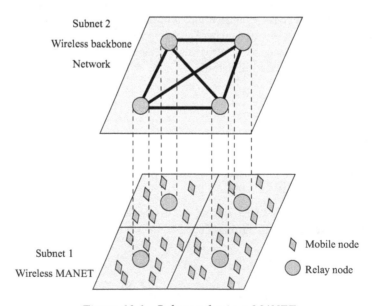

Figure 13.1   Relay nodes in a MANET

13.1.1   Medium access protocol

Medium access (MAC) protocols are needed to regulate communication between nodes through a shared medium. In wireless ad hoc networks, MAC protocols are needed as well to ensure successful operation of the network. With the increased international attention to ad hoc and sensor networks many channel access method have been suggested for these networks in the past few years. Each of these methods may have different priorities for problems to solve, depending on the applications to be supported on higher layers. For example, in sensor networks MAC protocols may primarily attempt to minimize energy consumption [14], whereas in ad hoc networks intended for mobile multimedia, the emphasis is put on packet delay minimization and throughput maximization. One of the key challenge for the success of ad hoc networks is a more suitable design of MAC mechanism for more effective delivery of the upcoming traffic consisting data services and traditional services upon the data networks while satisfying the required quality-of-service (QoS) guarantees by means of assured throughput and mean delay for real-time applications [15].

In this chapter, two different distributed channel reservation-based MAC protocols are proposed in which we focus on the problem of efficient channel access. Our solutions are tailored for IEEE 802.11-based ad hoc networks in which static relay nodes (RNs) are used as infrastructure. Relay nodes can be individual user devices communicating through multi-hop paths, or they can be wireless routers providing access to the rest of the network or acting as gateways towards one or more wired networks.

13.2   Channel reservation: Advantages and drawbacks

One critical factor of economically important challenge is to make more effective use of the bandwidth – provision of user application bandwidth over significantly large coverage areas while making an *efficient use of limited resources* [1, 16–18].

As shown in Figure 13.1, most of the nodes in a dynamic ad hoc network are mobile node and several static nodes serve as relays forwarding traffic from other nodes and maintain network-wide connectivity. Essentially each relay node is equipped with one or more radio systems that can switch among multiple channels, for example IEEE 802.11b has 11 channels of 22 MHz, three of which are non-overlapping channels [19]. The number of concurrent connections can be increased by enabling relay nodes transmitting at the same time to use different channels subject to the constraint that each sender–receiver pairs must be able to tune to the same channel at the time of communications. In order to respond to a highly variable demand, as a critical important function for ad hoc networks, this necessitates to device a new MAC protocol by which coordination between two neighbours allows them to communicate with each other and avoid interfering which could be resolved by, for example, use of different channels or time schedules to avoid interference between communicating relay node pairs [19–21].

In Reference 17, it has been shown that standard IEEE 802.11 MAC functionalities are unable to meet the requirements of the ad hoc network, when multiple channels are available. Thus, several novel access solutions have been proposed, with the aim to provide efficient medium access in multi-channel wireless networks [17–19, 22, 23].

In this chapter, we propose a recently emerged networking mechanism, channel reservation, and advice a new *channel reservation function* (*CRF*) that extends the overall capacity of the network. In order to adapt IEEE 802.11 to the network structure, one has to consider, in addition to arbitrating medium access within the coverage area of one relay node, the challenges of how to increase the network capacity based on channel diversity while a novel reservation scheme used in the IEEE 802.11-based MAC protocol reduces the total average transmission delay in either single or multi-channel application scenarios. Then we assume that RNs are equipped with a single radio interface and study how they can efficiently contend on the common channel and then switch to data channel for data transmission or reception [24].

Afterwards, we present an innovative MAC solution that addresses the two issues:

- First, in the presence of hidden terminals, the negotiation procedure in Reference 23 does not ensure that all neighbours of the candidate transmitter and receiver are correctly informed about the reserved transmission.
- Second, nodes that are communicating on the data channel are unaware of successful reservations taking place on the control channel, thus leading to a mismatch among the information on data channel occupation stored at different network nodes.

We point out that seminal ideas that led to this work were put forward in our previous work [25].

The M-DQDC is used as our scheme [26] which it derives some principles from the well-known DQDB protocol, standardized for wired MAN as IEEE 802.6. Simulation result shows that M-DQDC shows very good performance, and when compared with the standard IEEE 802.11 scheme achieves higher throughput both in the case where all RNs are in each other's radio proximity and in the case where hidden terminals exist.

13.3   Distributed channel reservation without separate control and data channels

In this section we will present new channel reservation function regarding two important scenarios of single channel CRF; for simplicity we use CRF representing this scenario, and multi-channel CRF [27].

13.3.1   Single channel CRF

Basically, in order to reduce the transmission delay, a ready to transmit station waits until a channel is sensed as idle for a DIFS where DIFS in the IEEE 802.11

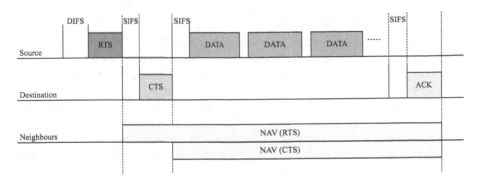

*Figure 13.2   An illustration of negotiation and data transmission according to
the CRF*

wireless LAN is 'DCF Inter-Frame Space' which is a period of time for which a
station waits after it has found the channel idle. DCF is the protocol's distributed
coordination function. Following the backoff rules it preliminarily transmits an
enhanced RTS frame, this RTS frame is like a standard DCF but contains an
additional field, LP,[1] indicating the number of packets present at the time of arrival
at a node. When the destination node receives an RTS frame it replies the CTS
frame after an SIFS period, where SIFS is 'Short Inter-Frame Space', a small gap
between the data frame and its acknowledgment. If the source station receives the
CTS, then it transmits its data packets immediately. The RTS frame is retransmitted
accordingly to binary exponential backoff procedure in the case that the CTS frame
is not received within a predetermined timeout period. All the other neighbours
receiving either the RTS or the CTS frames set their NAV to the duration of LP
transmission time, given in the RTS and/or CTS. Even if a hidden station cannot
hear the RTS from the source station, it will be able to receive the CTS response
from the destination and update its NAV, where NAV here stands for 'Network
Allocation Vector' which is a virtual carrier sensing mechanism used in wireless
network protocols. Figure 13.2 shows an example of negotiation and data transmission according to the CRF.

In DCF, RTS is used by the sender to request a transmission opportunity and
confirmed by the CTS but in proposed method we separate the arrived packets
based on their MAC destination address so that the node has the opportunity to send
all packets in the selected queue. Therefore, to implement the CRF negotiation
method we need to separate the arrival packets based on destination address. Let
the tagged node be denoted by S and its generic neighbour by D. Node S will queue
the packets it receives and destined to D in the queue corresponding to its neighbour D. Besides, the scheduler is needed to make selection among the non-empty
queues which follows Round Robin. We then number those packets that would be
transmitted after a successful negotiation established upon a gated polling strategy.

---

[1] Locked-up packets.

13.3.2   *Multi-channel CRF*

Considering that inclusion of an efficient multi-channel MAC protocol is essential to the success of wireless ad hoc networks so in this section, we can extend our single channel reservation algorithm is extended to supporting multi-channel application scenarios.

In the proposed algorithm we first build a pipeline channel reservation inspired by pipeline parallel processing systems. Pipelining is a category of techniques that provide simultaneous, or parallel, processing within the computer. It refers to overlapping operations by moving data or instructions into a conceptual pipe with all stages of the pipe processing simultaneously. For example, while one instruction is being executed, the computer is decoding the next instruction. Multi-channel CRF protocol takes the key idea of pipeline parallel processing technique.

In multi-channel CRF it is assumed that there are some non-overlapping channels, for example IEEE 802.11b supports three non-overlapping channels. Then source and destination start to negotiate like CRF. When the destination node receives an RTS frame it replies the CTS after SIFS period. If the source station receives the CTS frame subsequently, it then transmits only one data packet and after transmission completion the source and destination nodes switch to the next channel and the source node transmits the second packet after SIFS period and so on. The details of frame exchange and packet transmission algorithm are shown in Figure 13.3.

The theoretical restriction on the maximum number of transmitted packets after a successful negotiation is the number of non-overlapping channels in multi-channel CRF.

13.4   Performance evaluation

We derived some performance results through a simulation process by using the OMNet++ simulator. We considered a WLAN ad hoc network whose nodes are uniformly distributed on a rectangular area. Three scenarios are studied: 4, 8 and 12 neighbours for each node, and each scenario uses two different packet size, 512 bytes and 1024 bytes. Each node is associated with an exponential traffic source whose average generation rate is a varying parameter of the system, but common to all nodes. A node may be either a transmitter or a receiver; when it is a transmitter, the intended destination is randomly chosen among its neighbours. Note that this is reasonable, since we focus on the MAC layer performance.

The Negotiation messages as well as physical headers are transmitted at 1 Mbits per second, while data and acknowledgements on the data channel are sent at 11 Mbits per second. Default values are assumed for all other MAC parameters, for example SIFS $= 10$ µs, physical header size $= 192$ bits and minimum contention window equals 31.

Figure 13.4 shows the delay of the whole network in which the effects of packet size and neighbourhood size are investigated. The results are shown for

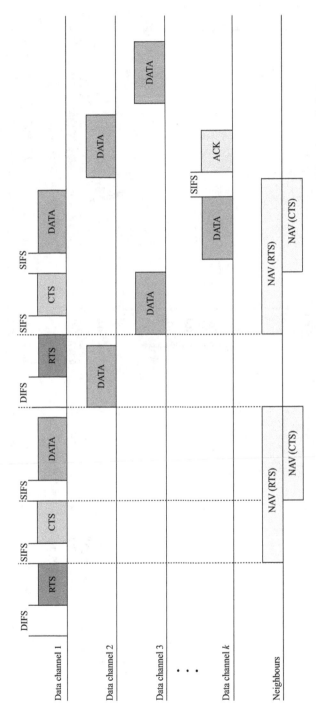

Figure 13.3 An example of negotiation and data transmission according to the multi-channel CRF

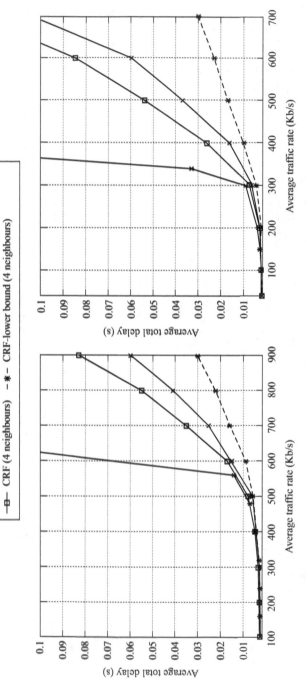

Figure 13.4 The average total delay versus traffic load per node. Results are shown for standard IEEE 802.11, CRF and multi-channel CRF under gated service strategy. In the case of four neighbours in the network

different values of the average node's neighbourhood size, that is average number of nodes in radio proximity of each other and also different packet sizes.

The results have been obtained as the average offered traffic load per node varies, and for different values of the number of nodes in the network, that is under different traffic load conditions. Looking at the plot, we note that the multi-channel CRF total transmission delay is lower than CRF and standard DCF under medium to high traffic load.

The average packet delay versus the offered traffic per node is shown in Figure 13.4. The packet delay is computed as the period between the packet generation and its successful delivery to the destination. Also, the results for different values of the number of nodes show that multi-channel CRF provides lower delay than DCF at high loads, although, when a large number of nodes are present, the benefits of CRF in terms of packet delay become less remarkable due to collisions. At high loads the number of LP is increased and also the transmitted packets per negotiation are increased. So the CRF and multi-channel CRF reduce the average delay at high load effectively.

We also observe that the gap between saturation points of DCF and proposed schemes is approximately robust against doubling packet size. Either simulation result also suggests that increasing the number of nodes in close proximity to each other determines a small gap between saturation point of DCF and CRF.

Indeed, when multi-channel CRF is used, the system saturates at a traffic load that is around *100 per cent higher* than for the standard DCF. Also, we expect that by implementing the low-traffic data channel contention multi-channel CRF can achieve the same performance as the standard DCF at low traffic load.

Using the same channel for negotiation and also packet transmission is the main drawback of the CRF and multi-channel CRF. So in the next section a distributed channel reservation-based MAC protocol with separate control and data channel is presented.

13.5 Distributed channel reservation with separate control and data channels

Since proposed solutions in this chapter are tailored for IEEE 802.11-based ad hoc networks, in which static relay nodes are used as infrastructure, so the relay nodes duty are same as mesh points in the mesh network. Hence, the M-DQDC and its negotiation signalling are completely compatible with the under study ad hoc network.

13.5.1 M-DQDC overview

M-DQDC uses one control channel and one or more data channels on separate frequencies. The control channel accommodates reservations for the data channels, and the data channels carry data packets and acknowledgements. For ease of description, in this section we will refer to one data channel only. The principles of our scheme are as follows:

- On the control channel, RNs contend for future access to the data channel, using a negotiation message exchange.
- Through negotiation, candidate transmitter and receiver (i) agree on a starting time and data transfer duration and (ii) inform neighbouring nodes about such a transmission, thus reserving some radio resources on the data channel.
- All nodes overhearing a successful negotiation store the reservation information such as transmission starting time and duration in a list, so as to maintain a reservation distributed queue (DQ) and avoid collisions on the data channel.
- At the scheduled starting time, the entitled RNs access the data channel without contention, while the rest of the RNs remain on the control channel.

We highlight that in spite of the presence of hidden terminals, the negotiation phase that we envision allows synchronization of the distributed queues among all RNs, which are one-hop away from either the candidate transmitter or the candidate receiver, thus avoiding collisions on the data channel. Furthermore, with regard to the DQ de-synchronization problem caused by the intermittent presence of RNs on the control channel, our scheme operates as follows. Consider the case of two RNs that have just finished communicating on the data channel and wish to exchange additional data. Clearly, the RN pair will be unaware of the reservations that have been placed on the control channel in the meanwhile. To overcome this problem, the M-DQDC negotiation messages include the end time of the furthest reservation, as recorded by the queue of the message sender. By doing so, RNs with outdated queue information that hear a new reservation exchange get updated on the reservation status of the data channel before attempting to access it. In addition, the RN pair that was engaged in data channel transmission performs a post-backoff procedure, as it switches back to the control channel, thus increasing the chance that a reservation exchange is overheard, that is queue information is synchronized. In the following, further details on the M-DQDC protocol are provided. The reader may follow the description alongside Figure 13.5, where the main operations on the control channel are outlined.

13.5.2   *Distributed queue*

In M-DQDC, every relay node maintains a time-ordered reservation list, which is responsible for holding the state of the distributed queue. For each reservation entry, start time, duration, sender and receiver are recorded. The time at which the last reserved transmission is scheduled to end is referred to as DQ threshold and is advertised in reservation messages to maximize the chances that all nodes remain synchronized with the distributed queue. This solution helps system synchronization by feeding up-to-date information to nodes that could not attend recent control channel exchanges and also RNs that have just joined the network. We will refer to the DQ state as the DQ pattern, as shown in Figure 13.6. In the figure, queue pattern sections 1, 2 and 4 correspond to time periods for which the data channel has been already reserved; section 3 represents a time period between two scheduled transmissions during which the data channel is expected to be idle; section 5 is free and available for future reservations. When an RN detects its own reservation at the top

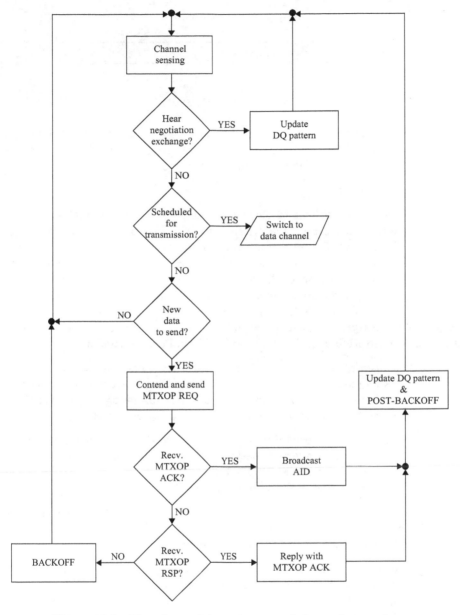

Figure 13.5   Flowchart of the main control channel operations

of the queue, it means that the RN is up next for transmission, and it transmits on the data channel. The transmission occurs after a period of SIFS seconds following the acknowledgement of the previous packet. Note that each reservation is associated with a transmission opportunity that is called mesh transmission opportunity, MTXOP, that is a time interval that can accommodate one or more data packets waiting to be transmitted. To maximize the throughput on the data channel, RNs with several packets to be sent are allowed to have more than one pending

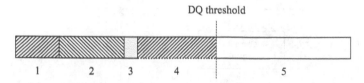

Figure 13.6   A snapshot of a distributed queue pattern

reservation. In other words, they are allowed to occupy several places at once in the distributed queue. After the transmission of a data packet, the DQ is correspondingly updated by popping the reservation at the top of the queue.

13.5.3   Negotiation

Like the RTS/CTS handshake mechanism of IEEE 802.11, the negotiation phase in M-DQDC allows to reserve the wireless medium for pending data exchange. However, the M-DQDC reservation procedure (i) is performed regardless of the size of the data to send and (ii) does not necessarily provide immediate access to the data channel, rather it schedules a future transmission on it. A candidate sender wishing to start a negotiation procedure tries to seize the channel following the standard IEEE 802.11 IFS temporization and backoff procedure; all M-DQDC negotiation messages are then spaced in time by an SIFS time interval. Based on drawing work in Reference 23, we introduce the following notation:

Mesh transmission opportunity request (MTXOP REQ): Similar to the IEEE 802.11 RTS message, it is used by a candidate sender, negotiation initiator, to require a transmission opportunity. Besides the transmitter and receiver ID, it contains the start time and time duration of the requested transmission.

Mesh transmission opportunity response (MTXOP RSP): Like the IEEE 802.11 CTS message, it is a reply message to the negotiation initiator from the intended receiver of the MTXOP REQ. It rejects the original proposal and contains a new proposal for starting time and transmission duration.

Mesh transmission opportunity acknowledgment (MTXOP ACK): An acknowledgment accepting or rejecting the transmission proposal. It can be sent as a reply to either a TXOP REQ or a TXOP RSP.

Agreement indicator (AID): A broadcast message advertising details of the latest transmission agreement reached two RNs. This was sent by the RN receiving the TXOP ACK. A TXOPREQ-negotiation process started by the RN intends to transmit data to one or more destinations. The intended receiving RN may confirm the transmission duration and start time proposed in the MTXOP REQ by sending a TXOP ACK. If, instead, the destination RN rejects the transmission proposal, it sends a TXOP RSP as a reply, including either different values for the transmission parameters or a data exchange refusal [23]. When different values are proposed, the negotiation initiator, in its turn, sends a TXOP ACK message accepting or rejecting the proposal. The RN receiving a positive MTXOP ACK sends out an AID message.

Note that, the negotiation messages being of broadcast nature, all neighbours of the negotiation initiator and receiver will be informed and collision-free access to the data channel will be provided. In particular, neighbouring RNs update their DQ pattern on receiving either a positive MTXOP ACK or an AID message.

To summarize, the MTXOP negotiation can be done either through a three-way or a four-way handshake:

First case, three-way handshake

- The source RN initiates the negotiation by sending a MTXOP REQ.
- The destination RN accepts and replies with a MTXOPACK message.
- The source RN broadcasts the AID to all neighbours, thus informing them about the new agreement.

Second case, four-way handshake

- The source RN initiates the negotiation by sending a MTXOP REQ.
- The destination RN does not accept, so it replies by sending a MTXOP RSP with different values of MTXOP start time and duration.
- The source RN ends the negotiation by sending a MTXOP ACK, accepting or rejecting the new proposal.
- If the new proposal is accepted, the destination RN informs its neighbours by broadcasting the AID.

Figure 13.3 illustrates the three-way and the four-way handshake negotiation. Nodes that receive either MTXOP ACK or AID have to change their DQ pattern according to the new successful negotiation. Figure 13.7 shows an example of successful reservations on the control channel and the associated data transmission on the data channel. As a final remark, we point out that negotiation is started only if the next scheduled transmission or reception of the candidate transmitter does not occur at least for the time that is needed to complete a four-way handshake.

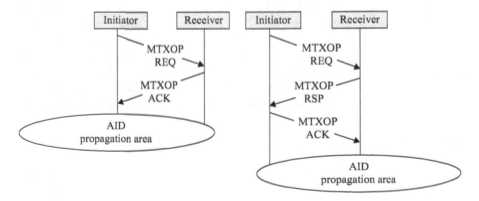

Figure 13.7   Three-way and four-way handshake negotiations

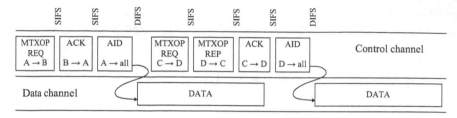

Figure 13.8   Example of negotiation and data transmission according to the protocol M-DQDC

Likewise, an intended receiver only replies either through TXOP ACK or through TXOP RSP if it estimates that negotiation ends before its own upcoming transmission or reception on the data channel.

13.5.4   Post-backoff

According to the M-DQDC protocol, an RN always operates on the control channel unless it has to transmit or receive traffic on the data channel. Collisions on the data channel are avoided, thanks to the negotiation procedure defined above, which enables all RNs, which are neighbours of either the candidate transmitter or the receiver, to store the reservation record in their DQs. However, while two RNs communicate on the data channel, they cannot overhear negotiations on the control channel. It follows that when the RN pair switches back to the control channel, they may be unaware of successful reservations that took place in the meanwhile. To solve this issue, M-DQDC exploits the post-backoff procedure to enhance the RN pair's chances of being exposed to DQ pattern updates through other RN negotiation messages. First, all MTXOP REQ and MTXOP RSP messages used for negotiation carry the value of DQ threshold of the sender's distributed queue.

Second, RNs that have just returned to the control channel must perform a post-backoff procedure. The post-backoff time is extracted according to a uniform distribution, from an interval of values ranging between 0 and the initial value of contention window. During the post-backoff time, if the RNs overhear or receive a negotiation message, they update their DQ pattern accordingly and exit the post-backoff procedure. From then on, the RNs will consider the data channel as busy till the value of DQ threshold is reported in the negotiation message (see Figure 13.8).

If, instead, the RNs do not overhear or receive any negotiation message, they can start contending on the control channel at the end of their post-backoff. Finally, the post-backoff is aborted and reset if the RN has a scheduled transmission or reception and it has to switch to the data channel before the end of the post-backoff.

13.6   Evaluation results

We derived some performance results of MDQDC using the OMNet++ simulator, also more information about mathematical modeling of the proposed protocols could be fined in [24-27]. The packet size is set to 1024 bytes, unless otherwise specified. We assume that each reservation corresponds to the transmission of only one packet on the data channel. MTXOP REQ and MTXOP REP are 23 and 16 bytes long, respectively, while the MTXOP ACK and AID size is equal to 14 bytes. Negotiation messages as well as physical headers are transmitted at rates ranging from 1 Mbits per second up to 11 Mbits per second depending on the control channel capacity, while data and acknowledgements on the data channel are sent at 11 Mbits per second. Default values are assumed for all other MAC parameters, for example SIFS = 10 ms, slot time = 20 ms, physical header size = 192 bits, minimum contention window equals 31.

Results are shown for different values of RNs in each other's radio proximity.

Figure 13.9 shows the normalized throughput of the whole network, as well as the packet delay, in the presence of hidden terminals. To make a fair comparison between M-DQDC and the standard IEEE 802.11 MAC, the throughput is normalized to the aggregate transmission rate required by the access scheme. The results were obtained as the average offered traffic load per RN varies, and for different values of the number of RNs in the network, that is, under different traffic load conditions. Looking at the plots, we note that despite the extra bandwidth required by M-DQDC for the control channel, our solution significantly outperforms the standard DCF under medium/high traffic load. Indeed, thanks to the negotiation phase, the performance loss due to hidden terminals is curbed by M-DQDC: the system throughput under M-DQDC saturates at a traffic load that is 33 per cent higher than that for the standard DCF, when a three-node neighbourhood is considered, that is the case of two neighbours.

When the neighbourhood is composed of 15 nodes, the M-DQDC saturation point corresponds to a traffic load that is 70 per cent higher than that for the standard IEEE 802.11 MAC.

13.7 Further development

According to the new emerging applications of wireless ad hoc networks there are many researches about multi-channel ad hoc networks with QoS provision mechanism. IEEE 802.11p standard draft supports different data rates in each channel [28]. Also, the US FCC divide the overall bandwidth into seven frequency channels: the public Control Channel for delivering the safety information and exchanging control packets and the other six channels are Service Channels which support the transmission of non-safety applications [29].

In Reference 30, authors proposed a Variable CCH Interval MAC scheme to help the IEEE 1609.4 MAC deliver real-time safety packets and accommodate throughput-sensitive services in VANETs by using a multi-channel coordination mechanism and dynamically tuning the duration ratio between CCH and SCHs.

About multi-channel coordination mechanism we have also two sub-channel allocation methods [31]:

1. The fixed allocation method of OFDM-FDMA for multiuser communications was proposed. In such method, different users will be fixedly assigned to

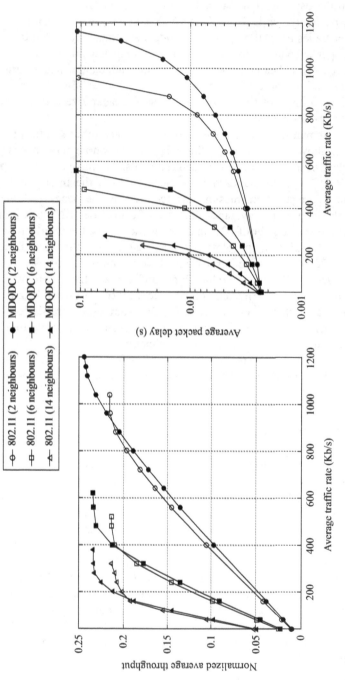

Figure 13.9 Average normalized throughput (left) and packet delay (right) against offered traffic load per node in the presence of hidden terminal comparison of M-DQDC and 802.11 DCF with RTS/CTS

different sub-channels. Therefore, this method has not any anti-interference mechanism.

2. The OFDM-FDMA random allocation method is based on the idle and busy sub-channels allowing users to account different sub-channels. However, it does not have any attention to the network interference. Once a sub-channel is selected, a user starts transmitting using the selected sub-channel. During a transmission process, if a sub-channel does not meet the required QoS, it will be released and assigned to new user. Although the method is simple and it offers an adaptive mechanism, it does not provide co-channel interference (CCI) avoidance, where.

Co-channel interference is crosstalk from more than one different radio transmitters using the same frequency in wireless networks. To avoid CCI and collisions [31], a novel channel allocation algorithm called DSA supports simultaneous transmissions in dynamic ad hoc network among nodes.

In addition to the above channel reservation mechanisms, there are some research works based on topology and channel usage aware. In Reference 32, the authors assume that a prior knowledge of the topology and the channel usages of nodes to be monitored is given to, or can be inferred by, sniffers. On the other hand, Arora *et al.* [33] have studied a trade-off between assigning the radios of sniffers to channels known to be busiest based on the current knowledge versus exploring channels that are under observed. In addition, Shin *et al.* [34] have studied distributed and online solutions to OSCA for large-scale and dynamic networks.

Finally, further research works are proposed about EDCA, which provides a new feature called Transmit Opportunity used to give the nodes opportunity to send more packet for a specific category. TXOP of zero value means that the node can send only one packet after each successful contention [35].

Also some additional research works focus on hybrid MAC RR schemes for EDCA. In general, hybrid MAC RR schemes introduce contention-free channel access for RTSNs with strict QoS requirements while maintaining certain duration of contention-based channel access for other types of traffic sessions in order to ensure their sustainable services. Airtime is split into consecutive service intervals, each of which contains both contention-free period and contention access period. The scheduler of the distributed RR scheme can be part of the MAC layer, with the support of explicit signalling messages that propagate among the nodes in order to determine and configure the reservation parameters [36].

13.8 Conclusion

In order to overcome deficiencies of the DCF as used in the standard IEEE 802.11 WLAN for dynamic ad hoc network technologies, we have devised a new channel reservation mechanism, CRF, that removes the time and bandwidth losses due to the long delays in using the DCF method. To this effect our proposed scheme, aimed at minimizing the negotiation overhead, reduces the overall transmission delay.

The results show that the proposed scheme, the reduction in negotiation overhead, reduces the overall transmission delay. The improvement is considerable especially for the mid-range traffic volume that can be increased for higher average traffic volumes and higher fluctuating mixed services.

Afterwards, a novel MAC scheme, M-DQDC, whose nodes are equipped with a single radio interface is considered. The nodes can use multiple data channels and one control channel. The M-DQDC aims at maximizing the utilization of the data channel by reducing the collision probability on it. In particular, M-DQDC effectively addresses the problem of hidden terminals and of coexisting control and data traffic on different channels. The simulation results show that the protocol scheme offers very good performance and significantly outperforms the standard IEEE 802.11 DCF with handshaking, especially under medium to high traffic load conditions.

References

1. LEE M.J., Zheng J., Co Y.B., Shrestha D.M., 'Emerging Standards for Wireless Mesh Technology'. *Journal of IEEE Wirelreless Communication.* 2006; 13(2): 56–63
2. Camp J., Knightly E., 'The IEEE 802.11s Extended Service Set Mesh Networking Standard'. *IEEE Communication Magazine.* 2008; 46(8): 120–126
3. Li J., Blake C., De Couto D.S.J., Lee H.I., Morris R., 'Capacity of Ad Hoc Wireless Networks'. *Proceeding of International Conference on Mobile Computing and Networking*; Rome, Italy, 2001. pp. 61–69
4. Gupta P., Kumar P.R., 'The Capacity of Wireless Networks'. *IEEE Transactions on Information Theory.* 2000; 46(2): 388–404
5. Mehra S. 'Enhancing the Performance of Mobile Ad Hoc Network with Internet Gateway'. M.Sc. thesis; University of Bombay, India, 2000
6. Xu K., Gerla M., 'A Heterogeneous Routing Protocol based on a New Stable Clustering Scheme'. *Proceedings of IEEE Military Communication (MILCOM)*; Los Angeles, CA, USA, 2002. pp. 838–843
7. Broch J., Maltz D., Johnson D., 'Supporting Hierarchy and Heterogeneous Interfaces in Multi-Hop Wireless Ad Hoc Networks'. *Proceedings of International Symposium on Parallel Architectures, Algorithms and Networks*; Fremantle, Australia, 1999. pp. 370–375
8. Garcia-Luna-Aceves J.J., Fullmer C.L., Madruga E., Beyer D., Frivold T., 'Wireless Internet Gateways (WINGS)', *Proceedings of IEEE Military Communication (MILCOM)*; Monterey, CA, USA, 1997, 3: 1271–1276
9. Jonsson U., Alriksson F., Larsson T., Johansson P., Maguire G., 'MIPMANET – Mobile IP for Mobile Ad-Hoc Networks'. *Proceedings of Workshop on Mobile Ad Hoc Networking (MobiHOC)*; Boston, USA, 2000. pp. 75–85
10. Lei H., Perkins C.E., 'Ad Hoc Networking with Mobile IP'. *Proceedings of European Personal Mobile Communication Conference*; Bonn, Germany, 1997. pp. 197–202
11. Sun Y., Belding-Royer E., Perkins C.E., 'Internet Connectivity for Ad Hoc Mobile Networks'. *International Journal of Wireless Information Networks* (special issues on Mobile Ad hoc Networks). 2002; 9(2): 465–482

12. Liu B., Liu Z., Towsley D., 'On the Capacity of Hybrid Wireless Networks'. *Proceedings of IEEE INFOCOM*. San Francisco, USA, 2003. pp. 1543–1552

13. Belding-Royer E., Sun Y., Perkins C.E., 'Global Connectivity for IPv4 Mobile Ad Hoc Networks'. IETF Internet Draft, draft-royer-MANET-globalv4-00.txt. 2001

14. Ye W., Heidemann J., Estrin D., 'Medium Access Control with Coordinated Adaptive Sleeping for Wireless Sensor Networks'. *IEEE/ACM Transactions on Networking*. 2004; 12: 493–506

15. Perkins C. E., *Ad Hoc Networking*. Addison Wesley Professional; Boston, MA, USA, 2000

16. So J., Vaydia N.H., 'Multi-channel MAC for Ad Hoc Networks: Handling Multi-channel Hidden Terminals Using a Single Transceiver'. *Proceeding of International Conference on Mobile Ad Hoc Networking and Computing*; New York, USA, 2004. pp. 222–233

17. Lee S.W., Lee J., Zhu C., Taori R., '802.11 TGs MAC Enhancement Proposal'. IEEE 802 11-05/0589r0. 2005

18. Conner W.S., Agre J., Audeh M., Chari N., Hasty V., Hiertz G.R., Joshi A., Ozer S.Z., Rayment S., Sakoda K., Sastry A., So T., Yang L., Zuniga J.C., 'EEE 802.11 TGs Functional Requirements and Scope'. IEEE 802 11-04/1174r13. 2005

19. Kim H., Hou J.C., Hu C., Ge Y., 'QoS Provisioning in IEEE 802.11-Compliant Networks: Past, Present, and Future Computer Networks'. *The International Journal of Computer and Telecommunications Networking*. 2007; 51(8): 1922–1941

20. Zeng G., Wang B., Ding Y., Xiao L., Mutka M., 'Multicast Algorithms for Multi-Channel Wireless Mesh Networks'. IEEE International Conference on Network Protocols (ICNP); 2007. pp. 1–10

21. Shi J., Salonidis T., Knightly E.W., 'Starvation Mitigation through Multi-channel Coordination in CSMA Multi-hop Wireless Networks'. *Proceedings of the 7th ACM International Symposium on Mobile Ad Hoc Networking and Computing*; Florence, Italy, 2006. pp. 214–225

22. Abraham S., Agre J., Aoki H., Bahr M., Chari N., Cheng R.G., Chu L., Conner W.S., Faccin S.M., '802.11 TGs Simple Efficient Extensible Mesh (SEE-Mesh) Proposal'. IEEE 802.11-05/0562r4. 2006

23. Sheu M., Kuo T., Jou T.S., Li J.R., Livet C., Tomici J., Zuniga J.C., Rudolf M., Roy V., Shyy D.J., Bhandaru N., Hares S., Aboul-Magd O., Sun S., So T., Fedyk D., Hiertz G.R., Zang Y., Stibor L., Max S., Junge T., 'IEEE TGs Wi-mesh Alliance, 802.11 TGs MAC Enhancement Proposal'. IEEE 802.11-05/0575r4. 2005

24. Baiamonte V., Casetti C., Chiasserini C.F., 'Distributed-Queue Access for Wireless Ad Hoc Networks'. IEEE VTC; 2005. pp. 1499–1503

25. Mahani A., Naderi M., Casetti C., Chiasserini C.F., 'Enhancing Channel Utilization in Mesh Networks'. *Proceeding of IEEE Military Communication Conference*; Florida, USA, 2007. pp. 1–7

26. Mahani A., Naderi M., Casetti C., Chiasserini C.F., 'MAC-Layer Channel Utilization Enhancement for Wireless Mesh Networks'. *IET Communication*. 2009; 3(5): 1–14

27. Mahani A., Rashvand H.F., Teymouri E., Naderi M., Abolhassani B., 'Wireless Mesh Networks Channel Reservation: Modeling and Delay Analysis'. *IET Communication*. 2009; 3(5): 772–783

28. Wang Q., Leng S., Zhang Y., Fu H., 'A QoS Supported Multi-channel MAC for Vehicular Ad Hoc Networks'. *Proceeding of IEEE Vehicular Technology Conference (VTC)*; San Francisco, USA, 2011. pp. 1–5

29. Leng S., Fu H., Wang Q., Zhang Y., 'Medium Access Control in Vehicular Ad Hoc Networks'. *Proceeding of IEEE Wireless Communications and Mobile Computing*; Leipzig, Germany, 2009. pp. 769–812

30. Wang Q., Leng S., Fu H., Zhang Y., 'An Enhanced Multi-channel MAC for the IEEE 1609.4 based Vehicular Ad Hoc Networks'. *Proceeding of IEEE INFOCOM Workshops*; San Diego, USA, 2010. pp. 1–2

31. Duc V., Nguyen K., Van L.P., 'Joint MAC and Routing protocol for OFDMA-based Ad Hoc Networks'. *Proceeding of IEEE 4th International Conference on Communication and Electronic (ICCE)*; Singapore, 2012. pp. 97–102

32. Chhetri A., Nguyen H., Scalosub G., Zheng R., 'On Quality of Monitoring for Multi-channel Wireless Infrastructure Networks'. *Proceeding of ACM Mobile Ad Hoc Networking and Computing*; Chicago, Illinois, USA, 2010. pp. 111–120

33. Arora P., Szepesvari C., Zheng R., 'Sequential Learning for Optimal Monitoring of Multi-channel Wireless Networks'. *Proceeding of IEEE INFOCOM*; Shanghai, China, 2011. pp. 1152–1160

34. Shin D.H., Bagchi S., Wang C.C., 'Distributed Online Channel Assignment Toward Optimal Monitoring in Multi-channel Wireless Network'. *Proceeding of IEEE INFOCOM*; Orlando, Fl, USA, 2012. pp. 2626–2630

35. Saeed S., Jumari K., Ismail M., Al-hemyari A., 'Challenges and Solutions of QoS Provisioning for Real Time Traffic in Mobile Ad Hoc Networks'. International Conference on Computer and Information Science (ICCIS); 2012. pp. 765–770

36. Yu X., Navaratnam P., Moessner K., 'Performance Analysis of Distributed Resource Reservation in IEEE 802.11e-based Wireless Networks'. *IET Communications*. 2012; 6(11): 1447–1455

Chapter 14*

Energy efficient local forwarding schemes

Wei Feng[a], Lin Zhang[b] and Jaafar M. H. Elmirghani[c]

Abstract

Geographic routing (GR) algorithms are attractive in ad hoc wireless networks owing to their efficiency, scalability and, in particular, energy efficiency. In this chapter, based on the fundamental GR algorithms, two energy efficient local forwarding schemes are proposed in a two-dimensional ad hoc wireless network. In the optimal range forward (ORF) algorithm, the optimal transmission ranges are utilized to reduce the energy consumption of the network. Furthermore, an optimal forward with energy balance (OFEB) algorithm is proposed to balance the residual energy of each node and to prolong the network lifetime. The authors compare the proposed algorithms with the existing GR algorithms, such as the most forward within radius and the nearest forward progress algorithms. The network lifetime, the network throughput, the number of packets successfully received by the destination and the average energy cost of each successfully received packet, resulting from all the algorithms mentioned above, are compared based on different node densities. It is shown that the performance of the OFEB algorithm is significantly better than the others.

14.1 Introduction

Due to their flexible structure, ad hoc wireless concepts have been widely used in different wireless sensor network applications. With complex application scenarios like battlefields and emergency relief scenarios (fire, flood or earthquake locations), it is costly or sometimes infeasible to replace or recharge the batteries of nodes. Therefore, energy limitations are among the critical constraints in ad hoc

*H. F. Rashvand and H.-C. Chao (Eds.), *Dynamic Ad Hoc Networks*, The IET Book Publishing Department, 2013, ISBN 978-1-84919-647-5, eISBN 978-1-84919-648-2
[a]Institute of Information Security, CCID, Beijing, China
[b]Department of Electronic Engineering, Tsinghua University, Beijing, China
[c]Electronic and Electrical Engineering, University of Leeds, Leeds, UK and Electrical and Computer Engineering Department, King Abdulaziz University, KSA

wireless network development. With the development of modern processing technology, nodes like sensors or smart laptops in ad hoc networks have become smaller than ever before, which limits the size of the nodes' batteries. However, the latter have shown less improvement in comparison to other computing devices such as CPU or memory. Furthermore, reported by some analysts, information communication technology accounts for 2−2.5% of the global carbon emissions, which is equal to the global aviation industry [1]. To this end, energy efficiency is important in wireless sensor networks to reduce energy consumption and to prolong the network lifetime.

The lifetime of ad hoc networks has real impact on the quality of communication, service discovery, quality of provisioned services (QoS) and network reliability. The network lifetime is defined as the time duration before (1) the first node dies [2], (2) a pre-defined fraction of active nodes' power drops below a threshold [3] or (3) the time until the aggregate delivery rate drops below a threshold [4].

To reduce the energy consumption of ad hoc networks, there are three main methods that can be applied. First, putting as many as possible nodes into a sleeping state to save energy. The energy consumption of each node varies according to its communication state: transmitting, receiving, listening or sleeping. In Reference 5, the authors conducted some measurements on the energy levels consumed during the different nodes' communication states. Consequently, the ratios between the listening, receiving and transmitting states are described as 1:1.05:1.4. Note that the energy consumed for listening or observing the radio environment is not negligible and a node consumes the least energy when it is in the sleeping state, thus putting (as many as possible) idle nodes (which do not transmit, receive or forward data) into the sleeping state will save energy.

Second, variable node transmission range can be applied to reduce the network energy consumption. Multi-hop communication (MHC) is broadly used in ad hoc wireless networks, and, in multi-hop communication, the total energy consumed for end-to-end communication increases as a function of both the number of relaying nodes and the energy consumption in each individual hop. The latter is mainly determined by the transmission distance (d). Moreover, the energy consumed in each individual hop increases in a nonlinear fashion with transmission distance according to d^n, where n is the propagation loss factor, usually $2 < n < 4$. Therefore, if the hop number is small (while the transmission distance is large), the energy consumed for single transmission increases nonlinearly with transmission distance. Alternately, for the same overall end-to-end distance, if the hop distance is small, the energy consumption will be dominated by the electronic energy cost in the transceivers and therefore the total energy increases almost linearly as a function of the hop number, where the hop number is large. Therefore, there is a trade-off between hop number and the transmission range of each hop in MHC to obtain the optimal energy efficiency.

Third, topology management or routing protocols can be used to achieve energy efficient performance. In this chapter, local forwarding schemes are considered to achieve energy saving, and geographic routing (GR) is the approach used in this chapter. GR or location/position-based routing for communication in ad hoc wireless networks has recently received increased attention, especially in the energy saving context [6, 7]. In GR, each node has knowledge of its own geographic information either via a Global Positioning System (GPS) or network localization algorithms, and broadcasts its location information to other nodes periodically. The next relay node is selected only based on the location of the source node, its neighbours and its ultimate destination, which is contained in the data packet.

The remainder of this chapter is organized as follows. In Section 14.2, related work is introduced and discussed. In Section 14.3, the energy consumption model is introduced, then the range of relay nodes locations that results in energy-efficiency is derived. The optimal transmission range is derived in terms of the propagation loss factor. The energy consumption of a multi-hop ad hoc wireless network is computed based on both optimal transmission range and direct transmission. The trade-off between energy consumption and delay time is analysed. In Section 14.4, energy efficient geographic local forwarding scheme is introduced and analysed, ORF and OFEB. In Section 14.5, the simulation results are introduced and analysed. In Section 14.6, recent work related to this chapter and further developments are introduced. In Section 14.7, a conclusion is drawn to this chapter.

14.2 Related work

Many mechanisms have been proposed to save energy in wireless communication systems. Since the power consumed in the listening state is less than power consumed in the transmitting and receiving states, but significantly greater than that in the sleeping state, energy efficiency is achieved if as many as possible nodes are put into sleeping state. Based on the fundamental work of IEEE 802.11 Power Save Mechanism (PSM) [8], the works of References 9–13 analyse the energy efficiency issue and other parameters. The work in Reference 9 proposed a routing protocol based on PSM to reduce the energy consumption and the transmission delay. In References 10 and 11 there is a discussion of how to sleep and wake the nodes by a packet-driven mechanism, which saved about 60 per cent of energy compared to the normal PSM. In Reference 12 a multi-frequency wake-up mechanism is proposed, where the nodes utilize different sleeping durations, while Reference 13 proposed a traffic shaping protocol to improve the performance of normal PSM, where the sleeping state is prolonged by shaping the unexpected traffic packets (only few packets during a nearly empty duration) to another transmission duration. The work in Reference 13 showed that about 83 per cent energy can be saved by using the traffic shaping protocol.

Transmission range adjustment as another energy saving approach has been the focus of numerous studies. Algorithms are proposed either for the general topology control purpose [14, 15] or for special tasks [16, 17], e.g. routing, data gathering and broadcasting. The objective of energy saving is usually achieved by computing the best transmission range based on the geographic information and the energy model. The authors in Reference 18 propose a quantitative analysis model for the optimal transmission range problem in this category. They use throughput and throughput per unit energy as the optimization criteria and conclude that the optimal transmission power is determined by the network load, the number of nodes and the network size. All nodes are active in their networks, and sleeping of nodes is not considered as an option for energy saving.

The works of References 19 and 20 studied the optimization of radio transmission range in wireless networks. In Reference 19, the optimal transmission range that maximizes the expected packet progress in the desired direction was determined for different transmission protocols in a multi-hop packet radio network with randomly distributed terminals. The optimal transmission ranges were expressed in terms of the number of terminals in range. It was found that the optimal transmission radius for slotted ALOHA without capture capability covers on an average eight nearest neighbours in the direction of the packet's final destination. The study's aim was to improve the system throughput by limiting the transmission interference in a wireless network with heavy traffic load. It was found in Reference 21 that a higher throughput could be obtained by transmitting packets to the nearest neighbour in the forward direction. In Reference 22, the authors evaluated the optimum transmission ranges in a packet radio network in the presence of signal fading and shadowing. A distributed position-based self-reconfigurable network protocol that minimizes energy consumption was proposed in Reference 20. It was shown in Reference 20 that the proposed protocol can stay close to the minimum energy solution when it is applied to mobile networks.

The optimization of transmission range as a system design issue was investigated in Reference 23. Considering the nodes without power control capability, the authors argued that the optimal transmission range should be set at the system design stage. Specifically, they showed that the optimal one-hop transmission progressive distance is independent of the physical network topology, the number of transmission sources and the total transmission distance. A similar assumption was made in Reference 24; they investigated the problem of selecting an energy efficient transmission power to minimize global energy consumption for ad hoc networks. They concluded that the average neighbourhood size is a useful parameter in finding the optimal balance point. The authors in Reference 25 studied the optimal transmission radius that minimizes the settling time for flooding in large-scale sensor networks. In the paper, the settling time was evaluated as the time when all the nodes in the network have forwarded the flooded packet. Regional contention and contention delay were then analysed.

The PSM and transmission range mechanism can be utilized together to achieve energy efficiency. In Reference 26 the authors proposed a linear network (where the nodes are distributed along a line) and, based on geographic adaptive fidelity (GAF) topology management, analysed both equal and adjustable grid model. A relationship between optimal transmission range and network traffic is derived in an equal-grid model. The work in Reference 27 uses clustering mechanisms to discuss energy saving in rectangular wireless networks. A relationship between optimal transmission range and traffic is derived based on a static traffic scenario. However, it only considered the static traffic scenario, so the result is not suitable for the VANET and MANET dynamic traffic scenarios.

References 28 and 29 analyse the energy distribution and propose a routing mechanism based on the location of nodes in linear wireless sensor networks. Note that the network traffic is determined by the location of nodes in the model of these papers; therefore, the nature of the work of References 28 and 29 is based on the relationship between the network traffic and transmission radio range. The results show that the energy consumption can be balanced and that the bottleneck associated with the network lifetime can be relaxed.

The balance of energy consumption is another parameter that can be pursued to prolong the network lifetime. The energy-proportional principle (EPP) is one of the algorithms than can achieve a balance in traffic load. It originates from the energy-proportional routing principle [30, 31]. In Reference 32, the authors proposed an energy efficient dynamic source routing algorithm based on load balance. In the model of this chapter, the energy balance is jointly utilized with optimal transmission range in the forwarding scheme algorithm to find the optimal next relay node.

14.3 Energy consumption model

The energy consumed by ad hoc wireless network nodes is the sum of the energy consumed for transmitting, receiving and listening. Considering a transmission from a transmitter to a receiver, where the distance between them is R, the received signal power can be expressed as [33]:

$$p_r(R) = \frac{p_t G_t G_r \lambda^2}{(4\pi)^2 R^n \text{Loss}} \tag{14.1}$$

where G_t and G_r are respectively the gains of the transmitter and receiver. The carrier wavelength is λ and Loss represents any additional losses in the transmission, n is the propagation loss factor, which is typically between 2 and 4. Thus, with $G_t = G_r = 1$, and Loss $= 1$, the received signal power can be calculated. Furthermore, to be successfully received by the receiver, the received signal power must be above a certain threshold power (p_{thr}). Therefore, the signal power at the transmitter must be above $\frac{p_{\text{thr}}(4\pi)^2 R^n}{\lambda^2}$. Assuming one signal represents one bit of data, the energy consumed for transmitting and receiving are respectively:

$$\begin{aligned} E_t &= (e_e + e_a R^n)P \\ E_r &= e_e P \end{aligned} \tag{14.2}$$

where, e_e is the *energy/bit* consumed in the transmitter electronics and $e_a = \frac{p_{\text{thr}}(4\pi)^2}{\lambda^2}$, which can be considered as the *energy/bit* consumed in the transmitter RF amplifier.

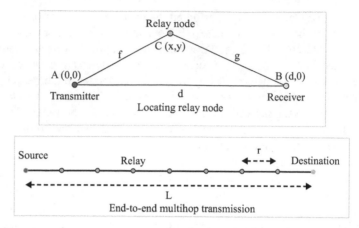

Figure 14.1   Locating the relay node and end-to-end multi-hop transmission

Based on References 27 and 34, the typical value of e_e is $e_e = 3.32 \times 10^{-7}$ J/bit. Given $p_{thr} = 8 \times 10^{-15} w$ and with a carrier frequency $f = 2.4 \times 10^9$ Hz, which is an unlicensed frequency band and one of the most popular in radio-based networking, e_a is computed as: $e_a \approx 8 \times 10^{-11}$ J/bit/m^n.

14.3.1   Relay node location

Considering the simple model shown in Figure 14.1, node A, located at $(0, 0)$, is the transmitter and node B, located at $(d, 0)$, is the receiver. As shown in Figure 14.1, the relay node is set to be node C at location (x, y), where the distance between A and C is f, and the distance between B and C is g. To achieve energy efficiency, the energy consumption when the relay node is involved must be smaller than the energy consumption without the relay node, introducing the coordinates of each node, leading to:

$$f^n + g^n < d^n - \frac{2e_e}{e_a}$$

$$[x^2 + y^2]^{\frac{n}{2}} + [(d-x)^2 + y^2]^{\frac{n}{2}} < d^n - \frac{2e_e}{e_a} \tag{14.3}$$

which defines the effective energy efficient zone of locations of the relay node. The energy saved (E_s) per packet by using the relay node is calculated as:

$$E_s = \left\{ e_a \left[d^n - (x^2 + y^2)^{\frac{n}{2}} - [(d-x)^2 + y^2]^{\frac{n}{2}} \right] - 2e_e \right\} P \tag{14.4}$$

where P is the data packet transmitted from transmitter (A) to receiver (B). Given $P = 1$ bit and $d = 200$ m, the relationship between the energy saved by utilizing the relay node and the location of the relay node is shown in Figure 14.2, for $n = 2$ and $n = 4$. In Figure 14.2, the energy saved increases when the relay node moves to the

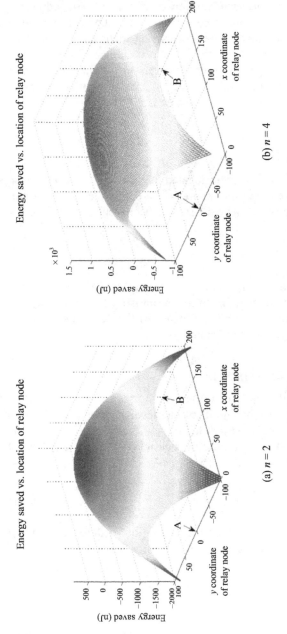

Figure 14.2 Energy saved versus location of relay node

middle between the transmitter and the receiver (100, 0). By comparing these two figures, the energy saved when $n=4$ is much more than the case when $n=2$.

According to the energy consumption model (14.2), the energy consumption is much more sensitive to the transmission range when $n=4$, compared to $n=2$: much more energy will be consumed when the node transmission range increases for large n. It should be noted that energy saving includes both positive and negative values, which respectively mean less and more energy consumption compared to the energy consumption of direct transmission from the transmitter to the receiver. Specifically, for the case of $n=2$, the zone of positive values, in which the energy is saved, can be derived from (14.3) as follows:

$$\left(x-\frac{d}{2}\right)^2 + y^2 < \frac{d^2}{4} - \frac{e_e}{e_a} \tag{14.5}$$

Thus, the relay node must be located in a sphere to achieve energy saving performance and the centre of the sphere is $(d/2, 0)$. To meet the condition in (14.5), $\frac{d^2}{4} - \frac{e_e}{e_a} > 0$ must be satisfied, which can be solved resulting in:

$$d \geq 2\sqrt{\frac{e_e}{e_a}} \tag{14.6}$$

This means that the energy consumption with a relay node does not achieve energy saving when the distance between the transmitter and the receiver is smaller than 128.4 m in this case, which is a function of the transceiver design parameters (e_e and e_a) and propagation coefficient.

14.3.2   *Optimal transmission range*

For an end-to-end multi-hop transmission, as shown in Figure 14.1, the data packet is forwarded from the source node to the destination node, where the distance separating them is L. Assuming that the range of each hop is r, the number of hops is $m = \frac{L}{r}$. Based on the energy consumption model mentioned above, the energy consumption of the end-to-end transmission is:

$$E_t = \frac{L}{r} \times [(2e_e + e_a r^n)P] \tag{14.7}$$

To compute the minimum energy consumption, with respect to the grid length, r, $\partial E_t/\partial r = 0$. Thus the optimal transmission range is:

$$r^* = \sqrt[n]{\frac{2e_e}{(n-1)e_a}} \tag{14.8}$$

With specific transceiver parameters, (14.8) shows that the optimal transmission radio range relates only to the propagation loss factor (n). The optimal transmission range decreases when the propagation loss factor (n) increases. As

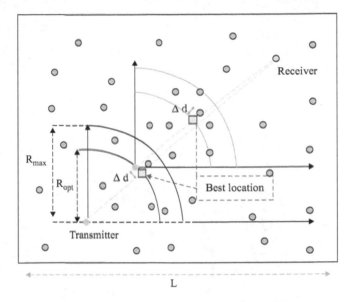

Figure 14.3   Forwarding scheme

mentioned, there is a trade-off between the energy consumed in each hop and the number of hops. Based on (14.7), when the number of hops (m) is large, the transmission range of each hop (r) becomes small, and here the fixed energy consumption for each hop dominates the energy consumption. When the number of hops is small, the transmission range of each hop becomes large, and the energy consumed in the transmitter amplifier of each hop increases rapidly and dominates the energy consumption. When n is large, the energy consumed in the transmitter amplifier becomes relatively more important than the fixed energy consumption, and vice versa. Specifically, the optimal transmission range is 90.1 m when $n = 2$, with the transmitter and receiver parameters assumed.

14.4   Energy efficient local forwarding schemes

Based on the optimal transmission range, two energy efficient GR algorithms for 2-D ad hoc wireless networks are proposed in this chapter: the optimal range forward (ORF) algorithm and the optimal forward with energy balance (OFEB) algorithm. The related parameters are depicted in Figure 14.3. To compare with the traditional GR algorithms, the Most Forward within Radius (MFR) algorithm and the Nearest Forward Progress (NFP), which are listed as flowcharts in Figure 14.4, the flowcharts of both ORF and OFEB, are depicted in Figure 14.5. For each current source node, the distance to the destination node (d_{CD}) is compared to the threshold distance that is determined by (14.6) in order to determine whether a relay node is required or if the data packet can be transmitted to the destination node directly. MFR selects as the next hop node the node nearest to the maximum range allowed in the system.

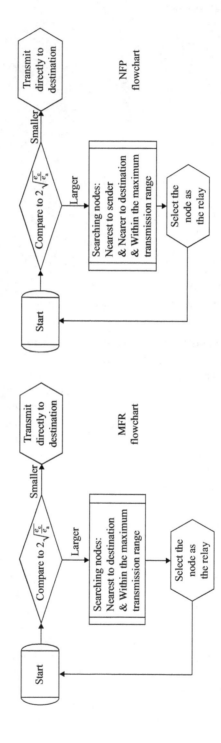

Figure 14.4 Flowcharts of MFR and NFP

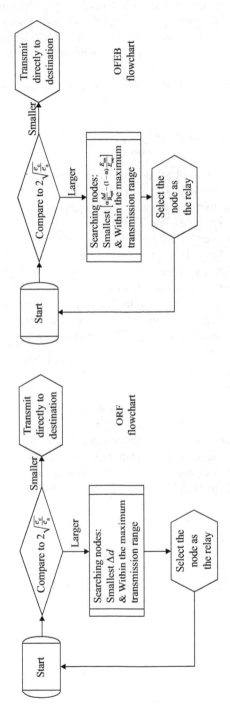

Figure 14.5   Flowcharts of ORF and OFEB

NFP selects the node nearest to the sender. Therefore, both algorithms do not make use of the optimal range that minimizes the energy consumption as derived in this chapter. ORF algorithm selects as the next hop the node nearest to the optimal transmission range (best location as shown in Figure 14.3, determined by the optimal transmission range) within the maximum allowed range and therefore minimizes the energy consumption. OFEB algorithm selects the next hop node as the node (within the maximum transmission range) that minimizes (14.9).

$$f(E_{res}, \Delta d) = \alpha \frac{\Delta d}{R_{opt}} - (1 - \alpha) \frac{E_{res}}{E_{cap}} \tag{14.9}$$

This is a node that uses the best combination of energy reserves and needs the minimum energy to be reached. The weight factor α determines the relative significance placed on these two requirements, and bigger α indicates more preference of throughput to energy balance. Therefore, OFEB is superior in concept and performance as will be seen. In (14.9), Δd is the distance between the neighbour nodes and the best location and E_{res} is the residual energy of the neighbours. Intuitively, without considering the energy balance, some nodes may be frequently selected as the relay nodes, and their energy may be drained out very soon compared to other nodes. Since E_{res} and Δd use different units, they are normalized as shown in (14.9). E_{res} is normalized with respect to the default energy capacity of each node (E_{cap}); Δd is normalized with respect to the optimal transmission range.

14.5 Simulation results

Simulation is carried out in a 2-D ad hoc network model, as shown in Figure 14.3, where N_n nodes are randomly distributed in the area. R_{max} is the maximum transmission range of each node. R_{opt}, which determines the best location of the next hop node, is the optimal transmission range computed based on (14.8) ($R_{opt} = 90.1$ m for $n = 2$). Δd is the distance between the best location and the neighbour node. In the network, the location information (coordinates) of each node is obtained by using GPS and is shared with its neighbours through periodic broadcasting. The location information of the source and the destination nodes is included in the transmitted packet. Therefore, in the forwarding scheme of each relay node, the next hop node can be selected according to the local geographic information and the location of the destination node. Using geographic routing, the simulation of a 2-D ad hoc wireless network (Figure 14.3) is carried out; the parameters used in the simulation are listed in Table 14.1. Furthermore, to facilitate comparison between the different GR

Table 14.1 Parameters of simulation

Propagation factor (n)	2	Node energy capacity (E_{cap})	0.001 J
Number of nodes (N)	50–500	Normalized simulation time (t)	10^6 s
Network length	500 m	Optimal transmission range (R_{opt})	90.1 m
		Maximum transmission range (R_{max})	250 m

algorithms, the source and destination nodes in each algorithm are fixed to (0, 0) and (L, L) respectively, and the other nodes are randomly deployed. By running the simulation 1,000 times, the average network lifetime and number of successfully received packets are determined.

14.5.1 Comparison of network lifetime and received packets in different GR algorithms

In this chapter the network lifetime is defined as the time duration until no source to destination connection is possible. In order to compare different GR algorithms, the ratios of the network lifetime and received packets are compared in Table 14.2, and the results show that the network lifetime of the NFP algorithm is the longest among all algorithms and the performance of the MFR is the worst.

Since the neighbour node that is closest to the final destination will be selected as the next hop node in MFR, the energy consumed for each hop in MFR is more than the other algorithms. Therefore, the network lifetime performance of MFR is the worst. Note that, even though the network lifetime of NFP is the longest, the number of packets successfully received by the destination is much smaller than the other algorithms. As has been explained the neighbour nodes closest to the current source node will be selected as the next hop node in NFP, and this requires more hops and more energy consumption.

In simulation, the average number of hops used by the transmission between the source and the destination nodes is 5.7 in MFR and 51.4 in NFP (for the others, see Table 14.2). This shows that the NFP algorithm uses too many hops for one successful transmission and the performance of NFP is limited even though its network lifetime is better than the others. Therefore, the network lifetime should not be the only parameter used to evaluate the performance of the algorithms. The number of packets successfully received by the destination is evaluated to compare the network performance as well. The ratio of successfully received packets show that the OFEB algorithm with $\alpha = 0.1$ has the best performance, and that the performance of NFP is the worst. For the MFR algorithm, the minimum number of hops between the source and the destination nodes is the criterion used in selecting the next hop node and the energy consumption is not considered. For NFP, the energy consumption of each hop is optimized while the number of hops between the source and the destination nodes and the network energy consumption are not

Table 14.2   Comparison of network performance in different GR algorithms

Number of nodes	NFP	MFR	ORF	OFEB ($\alpha = 0.9$)	0.7	0.5	0.3	0.1
			Network lifetime					
500	1	0.21	0.53	0.53	0.55	0.56	0.64	0.89
			Number of received packets					
500	0.31	0.60	0.80	0.80	0.82	0.86	0.89	1
			Average number of hops					
500	51.4	5.7	10.6	10.7	10.8	10.3	11.5	14.2

considered. Therefore, the number of packets received by the destination and the fraction of surviving nodes are the slowest among all GR algorithms. For ORF, the optimal transmission range is considered to reduce the network energy consumption. Therefore, the number of packets received by the destination and the fraction of surviving nodes are between those of MFR and NFP algorithms. For OFEB, not only the optimal transmission range but also the balance of node residual energy are considered to reduce the network energy consumption and prolong the network lifetime, and different weights (α and $1 - \alpha$) are considered. The results show that, compared with the ORF algorithm, the network lifetime has been significantly prolonged by considering the node residual energy balance in the OFEB algorithm, and the number of received packets increases too. Note that the ORF algorithm can be considered as a special case of OFEB, when the weight factor is $\alpha = 1$. Note that, with increasing weight factor, the time duration before the first node dies is significantly extended. The reason is that nodes with higher remaining energy will be selected as the next hop node, and therefore the loss of the first node is delayed.

14.5.2   Impact of node density on different GR algorithms

The simulation results show that, with increase in the number of nodes, the fraction of surviving nodes approaches 58 per cent when the number of nodes is more than 100. The impact of node density when using NFP shows similar trends to that of MFR, but the improvement in received packets is lower than that of MFR with increasing number of nodes. Furthermore, the fraction of surviving nodes in NFP decreases when the number of nodes increases, which means more nodes drained out. The reason is that the forwarding algorithm in NFP only considers the distance between the neighbour nodes to the current source node if the neighbour nodes are closer to the final destination, and this involves more nodes in the transmission. By comparison, it is clear that the ORF algorithm is better than MFR in terms of both network lifetime and number of received packets, and the fraction of surviving nodes approaches 52 per cent when the number of nodes is large. Regarding the network lifetime and received packets when the OFEB algorithm is utilized with different values of the weight factor (α), the results show that the performance of OFEB is better than all the other algorithms, and the performance improves when the weight factor becomes smaller.

14.5.3   Comparison of nodes' energy status in different GR algorithms

It is noted that the fractions of surviving nodes are different when there are no connections in different GR algorithms. Figures 14.6 and 14.7 show the 500-node energy status based on different GR algorithms when the network dies. In all figures, the source node is located at (0, 0), the destination node is located at (500, 500), and the locations of all the other nodes are fixed in different algorithms, and they have been classified into three types: unused nodes as represented by asterisk (*), used nodes as represented by triangle ($\triangle$) and dead nodes as represented by circle (o). In MFR, the proportion of unused nodes is very high compared to the other algorithms,

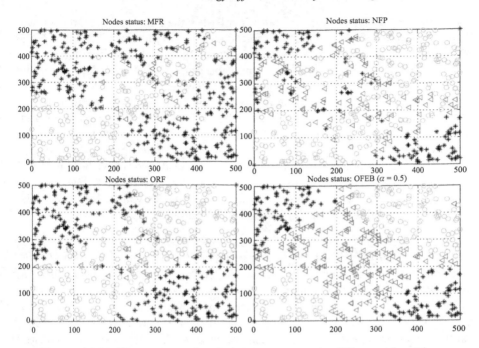

Figure 14.6   Comparison of nodes' energy status in different algorithms

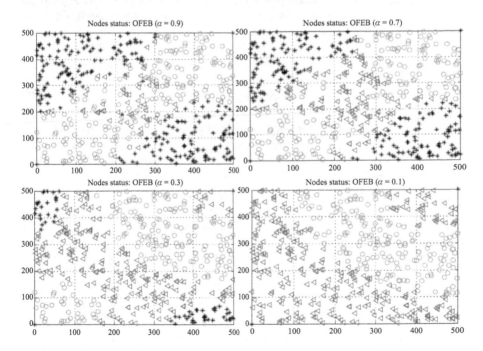

Figure 14.7   Comparison of nodes' energy status in OFEB

which means that the number of nodes involved in the transmission is much lower than the others. Also, the proportion of used nodes is very low in MFR. In ORF, the proportion of unused nodes is lower than that of MFR and the proportion of used nodes is comparable to that of MFR. In NFP, the proportion of unused nodes is quite low and the proportion of used nodes is much higher than that of MFR and NFP. By comparison, more nodes have been involved in the transmission between the source and the destination nodes in NFP. However, NFP uses too many hops in each transmission and the performance of NFP is not good even though a large proportion of nodes have been involved in the transmission. In OFEB, the proportion of unused nodes increases when the weight factor decreases, and all nodes have been involved in the transmission when the weight factor is 0.1. The results show that, by considering the balance of node residual energy, more nodes will be involved in the transmission and the network performance can improve.

14.5.4   Comparison of other parameters in different GR algorithms

In addition to the network lifetime and received packets, there are some other parameters worthy of being analysed, such as the average energy consumption for each received packet and the network throughput (bits per second). In Figure 14.8, the network lifetime, the number of received packets, the average energy consumption for each received packet and the network throughput are all compared based on different node densities in different GR algorithms. The number of received packets increases when the node density increases in all GR algorithms. The OFEB ($\alpha = 0.1$) algorithm has the best performance and the performance of NFP is the worst. The network lifetime increases when the node density increases in all GR algorithms, and NFP has the best performance and MFR has the worst performance. As we have mentioned, the network lifetime should be considered with the number of received packets to evaluate the performance of the algorithms. The energy consumed for each successfully received packet is lowest in the OFEB algorithm with large weight factor ($\alpha > 0.5$, ORF is a special case of $\alpha = 1$). In NFP, the energy consumed for each successfully received packet increases when the node density increases (whereas it decreases in the other algorithms when the node density increases). The reason is that based on the forwarding scheme used in NFP, when the node density is high, more hops are used for the end-to-end transmission between the source and the destination nodes; therefore, the energy consumed for one received packet increases. In MFR, the energy per packet decreases when the node density increases during the period of low node density, and it remains unchanged when the node density is high. In ORF, the energy per packet decreases as the node density increases, and the curve of energy per packet in OFEB ($\alpha = 0.5$, $\alpha = 0.7$ and $\alpha = 0.9$) has a similar trend to that of ORF (OFEB $\alpha = 1$). This shows that when the weight factor in OFEB is large, the energy consumed for one received packet decreases when the node density increases. In OFEB ($\alpha = 0.3$), the energy per packet is slightly smaller than that of MFR and larger than that of OFEB ($\alpha > 0.5$). The energy per packet in ORF has a similar trend to that of MFR, and the energy per packet remains unchanged when the node density is high.

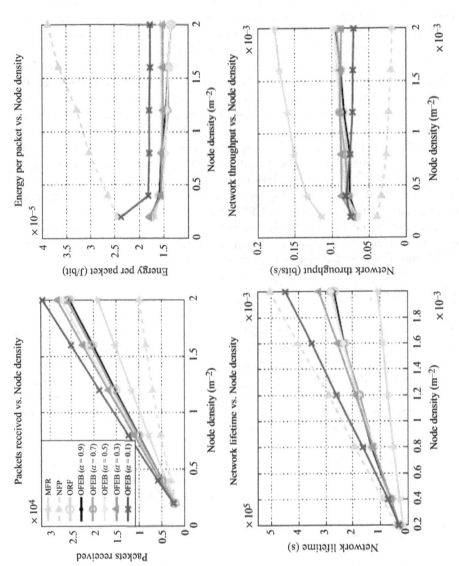

Figure 14.8 Comparison of all simulation results

In OFEB ($\alpha = 0.1$), the energy per packet is smaller than that of NFP but larger than the others, and the energy per packet remains unchanged when the node density is high. Note that, when the number of nodes is 50 in the network (node density is 2×10^{-4} m^2), the energy per packet of FEB ($\alpha = 0.1$) is equivalent to that of the NFP and much larger than that of the other algorithms. As a result, when the node density is low, the optimal transmission range has higher impact on the energy consumption. For network throughput, MFR and NFP respectively have the best and the worst performances. In MFR, the network throughput is much larger than that of the others since the most forward node is selected to be the next hop node in the MFR forwarding scheme. Also, the network throughput increases when the node density increases in MFR. In NFP, the network throughput is much smaller than that of the others. Here the nearest node to the current source node is selected to be the next hop node; therefore, it takes much longer time to forward the data packet to the destination node. The higher the node density the longer the time taken, thus the network throughput decreases when the node density increases in NFP. In ORF, the optimal transmission range is the metric to select the next hop node. Therefore, the network throughput is between MFR and NFP, and it increases when the node density increases. In OFEB, the network throughput increases when the node density increases in the low-density case. In the high node density case, the network throughput decreases when the weight factor is low ($\alpha = 0.1$ and $\alpha = 0.3$) but increases for high weight factor ($\alpha = 0.5$, $\alpha = 0.7$ and $\alpha = 0.9$).

14.6   Further development

With the development of wireless networks, more and more interest is being placed on geographic routing (GR) and energy efficiency due to the limit of energy capacity per node. The work of References 35 and 36 considers energy efficiency when utilizing GR algorithms. In Reference 35, an energy efficient multicast algorithm was proposed in mobile ad hoc networks, and energy efficient local forwarding schemes were proposed in Reference 36. In future work, the ORF and OFEB algorithms will be examined in this context to determine more interesting applications. First, the assumption of collecting information via GPS can be extended, and location aware algorithms can be combined into the forwarding scheme. Second, the ad hoc networks can be made into mobile ones, and more random parameters can be taken into account. Third, a test bed can be structured to verify the forwarding schemes.

14.7   Conclusion

In this chapter, energy efficient geographic local forwarding schemes, ORF and OFEB, were proposed to prolong the network lifetime and improve other network performance metrics. The results were compared to the existing GR algorithms including MFR and NFP. ORF scheme selects the next hop node as the node nearest to the optimal transmission range (within the maximum range) and therefore minimizes the energy consumption. OFEB scheme selects the next hop node as the node that minimizes the value of $\alpha \frac{\Delta d}{R_{opt}} - (1 - \alpha) \frac{E_{res}}{E_{cap}}$. This is a node that has the best combination of energy reserves and needs the minimum energy to be reached. The weight factor α determines the relative significance placed on these two requirements. The simulation results show that the OFEB algorithm has the best performance in which the network lifetime, the network throughput, the number of received packets and the energy consumed for each received packet have all been compared. This chapter is edited based on the authors' previous work [37].

References

1. Hodges R., White W., 'Go green in ICT', technique report, *GreenTech News*, 2008
2. Bao L., Garcia-Luna-Aceves J. J., 'Topology management in ad hoc networks', *Proceedings of the 4th ACM International Symposium on Mobile Ad Hoc Networking and Computing*, ACM New York, NY, USA, pp. 129–140, June 2003
3. Xu Y., Heidemann J., Estrin D., 'Geography-informed energy conservation for ad hoc routing', *Proceedings of the ACMMobil'01*, ACM New York, NY, USA, pp. 70–84, July 2001
4. Chen B. J., Jamieson K., Balakrishnan H., Morris R., 'Span: an energy-efficient coordination algorithm for topology maintenance in ad hoc wireless networks', *Wireless Networks*, vol. 8, pp. 85–96, September 2002
5. Stemm M., Katz R. H., 'Measuring and reducing energy consumption of network interfaces in hand-held devices,' *IEICE Transactions on Communications*, vol. E80-B(8), no. 8, pp. 1125–1131, 1997
6. Mauve M., Widmer J., Hartenstein H., 'A survey on position-based routing in mobile ad hoc networks', *IEEE Network*, vol. 15, pp. 30–39, 2001
7. Stojmenovic I., 'Position-based routing in ad hoc networks', *IEEE Communications Magazine*, vol. 40, pp. 2–8, July 2002
8. 802.11, 'Wireless lan medium access control(mac) and physical layer(phy) specifications', IEEE standard organisation, June 1999
9. Zhou Y., Tan Y. E., Laurenson D. I., McLaughlin S., 'Impact of power saving mac scheme on ad hoc network routing protocol', *Proceedings of the Vehicular Technology Conference. VTC 2005-Spring. 2005 IEEE 61st*, IEEE, Stockholm, Sweden, vol. 4, pp. 2463–2467, May 2005
10. Li N., Wang H., Zheng S., 'An energy-saving scheme for wireless lans', *Proceedings of the International Conference on Communication Technology*, IEEE, Beijing, China, pp. 1242–1245, April 2003
11. Li N., Xu Y., Xie S., 'A power-saving protocol for ad hoc networks', *Proceedings of the IEEE International Conference on Wireless Communications, Network and Mobile Computing*, IEEE, Wuhan, China, pp. 808–811, September 2005
12. Miller M. J., Vaidya N. H., 'Ad hoc routing for multilevel power save protocols', *Ad Hoc Networks*, vol. 6, pp. 210–225, April 2008

13. Chandra A. V. S., 'Application-specific network management for energy-aware streaming of popular multimedia formats', *Proceedings of the Usenix Annual Technical Conference*, USENIX Association Berkeley, CA, USA, pp. 329–342, 2002

14. Rodoplu V., Meng T. H., 'Minimum energy mobile wireless networks', *Proceedings of the IEEE International Conference on Communications, ICC 98*, vol. 3, IEEE, Atlanta, USA, pp. 1633–1639, June 1998

15. Li N., Hou J. C., Sha L., 'Design and analysis of an mst-based topology control algorithm', *Proceedings of the IEEE INFOCOM 2003*, IEEE, San Franscisco, USA, pp. 1702–1712, March 2003

16. Chang J. H., Tassiulas L., 'Energy conserving routing in wireless ad-hoc networks', *Proceedings of the IEEE INFOCOM 2000*, IEEE, Tel Aviv, Israel, pp. 22–31, March 2000

17. Banerjee S., Misra A., 'Minimum energy paths for reliable communication in multi-hop wireless networks', *Proceedings of the MobiHoc*, ACM New York, NY, USA, pp. 146–156, 2002

18. Park S. J., Sivakumar R., 'Quantitative analysis of transmission power control in wireless ad-hoc networks', *Proceedings of the International Workshop on Ad Hoc Networking (IWAHN)*, IEEE Computer Society Washington, DC, USA, pp. 56–61, August 2002

19. Takagi H., Kleinrock L., 'Optimal transmission ranges for randomly distributed packet radio terminals', *IEEE Transactions on Communications*, vol. COM-32, pp. 246–257, March 1984

20. Rodoplu V., Meng T. H., 'Minimum energy mobile wireless networks', *IEEE Journal on Selective Areas Communications*, vol. 17, pp. 1333–1344, August 1999

21. Hou T. C., Li V. O. K., 'Transmission range control inmultihop packet radio networks', *IEEE Transactions on Communications*, vol. COM-34, pp. 38–44, January 1986

22. Zorzi M., Pupolin S., 'Optimum transmission ranges in multihop packet radio networks in the presence of fading', *IEEE Transactions on Communications*, vol. 43, pp. 2201–2205, July 1995

23. Chen P., ODea B., Callaway E., 'Energy efficient system design with optimum transmission range for wireless ad hoc networks', *Proceedings of the IEEE ICC*, IEEE, New York, USA, pp. 945–952, 2002

24. Chen Y., Sirer E. G., Wicker S. B., 'On selection of optimal transmission power for ad hoc networks', *Proceedings of the 36th Hawaii International Conference on System Sciences.*, IEEE Computer Society Washington, DC, USA, pp. 300–309, 2003

25. Zuniga M., Krishnamachari B., 'Optimal transmission radius for flooding in large scale sensor networks', *Proceedings of the 23rd International Conference on Distributed Computing Systems Workshops*, Kluwer Academic Publishers Hingham, MA, pp. 697–702, 2003

26. Gao Q., Blow K. J., Holding D. J., Marshall I. W., Peng X. H., 'Radio range adjustment for energy efficient wireless sensor network', *Ad hoc Networks*,

Elsevier Science Publishers B. V. Amsterdam, The Netherlands, The Netherlands, vol. 4, pp. 75–82, January 2006

27. Yin B., Hongchi S., Shang Y., 'Analysis of energy consumption in clustered wireless sensor networks', *Proceedings of the 2nd International Symposium on Wireless Pervasive Computing,* IEEE, San Juan, Puerto Rico, pp. 102–114, February 2007

28. Gokturk M. S., Ercetin O., Gurbuz O., 'Energy distribution control in wireless sensor networks through range optimization', *Proceedings of the IEEE International Symposium on Personal, Indoor and Mobile Radio Communications (PIMRC)*, Cannes, French, pp. 34–38, 2008

29. Ercetin O., 'Distance-based routing for balanced energy consumption in sensor networks', *Proceedings of the Globecom 2008*, IEEE, New Orleans, LA, USA, pp. 302–311, 2008

30. Chen C. L., Lee K. R., 'An energy-proportional routing algorithm for lifetime extension of clustering-based wireless sensor networks', *Journal of Pervasive Computing*, vol. 3, pp. 304–321, 2006

31. Chen C. L., Lee K. R., 'An energy-proportional routing algorithm for lifetime extension of clustering-based wireless sensor networks', *Proceedings of the 2nd Workshop on Wireless, Ad Hoc, and Sensor Networks*, IEEE, Lisbon, Portugal, pp. 99–101, 2006

32. Talooki V., Marques H., Rodriguez J., Gua H., Blanco N., Campos L., 'An energy efficient flat routing protocol for wireless ad hoc networks', *Proceedings of the 19th International Conference on Computer Communications and Networks (ICCCN)*, IEEE, Zurich, Switzerland, pp. 1–6, 2010

33. Shankar P. M., *Introduction to wireless systems*. Wiley, USA, John Wiley & Sons, August 2001

34. Heinzelman W. R., Balakrishnan A. C. H., 'Energy-efficient communication protocol for wireless microsensor networks', *Proceedings of HICSS'00*, IEEE Computer Society Washington, DC, USA, vol. 2, pp. 4–7, January 2000

35. Xiang X., Wang X., Yang Y., 'Supporting efficient and scalable multicasting over mobile ad hoc network', *IEEE Transactions on Mobile Computings*, vol. 10, April 2011

36. Wang Y., Li X. Y., Song W., Huang M., Dahlberg T., 'Energy-efficient localized routing in random multihop wireless networksk', *IEEE Transactions on Parallel and Distributed Systems*, vol. 22, August 2011

37. Feng W., Zhang L., Elmirghani J., 'Energy saving geographic routing in ad-hoc wireless networks', *IET Communications*, vol. 6, January 2012

Chapter 15*

Dynamic spectrum sharing between cooperative relay and ad hoc networks: towards real-time optimal control

Yin Sun[a], Xiaofeng Zhong[b], Tsung-Hui Chang[c],
Shidong Zhou[b], Jing Wang[b] and Chong-Yung Chi[d]

Abstract

Spectrum sharing is an important technique to improve the spectrum efficiency of dynamic ad hoc networks. However, since the BUSY/IDLE state of the ad hoc traffic could vary quickly, it is difficult to reduce the traffic collisions between coexisting networks. This chapter investigates a spectrum-sharing scenario, where a cooperative relay network intends to access the spectral band of a dynamic ad hoc network without making too many collisions with the ad hoc traffic. Adopting a binary continuous-time Markov chain (CTMC) traffic model to characterise and predict the ad hoc traffic, the spectrum access design of the cooperative relay network is formulated as a non-convex optimisation problem. We simplify this spectrum access design problem as a convex optimisation problem, which allows us to obtain a low-complexity optimal spectrum access strategy. Moreover, owing to the dynamic nature of the ad hoc traffic, the optimal spectrum access strategy needs to be attained within a short time and under practical limitations. To this end, we generalise the spectrum access design to an ergodic setting and propose an online spectrum access strategy. This online spectrum access strategy is able to achieve the optimal ergodic performance with negligible control delay, moderate signalling overhead and little computational capability requirement for the user equipment.

*H. F. Rashvand and H.-C. Chao (Editors), *Dynamic Ad Hoc Networks*, The IET Book Publishing Department, 2013, ISBN 978-1-84919-647-5, eISBN 978-1-84919-648-2
[a]Department of Electrical and Computer Engineering, the Ohio State University, Columbus, OH 43210
[b]State Key Laboratory on Microwave and Digital Communications, Tsinghua National Laboratory for Information Science and Technology, and Department of Electronic Engineering, Tsinghua University, Beijing, China
[c]Department of Electronic and Computer Engineering, National Taiwan University of Science and Technology, Taipei, Taiwan
[d]Institute of Communications Engineering, and Department of Electrical Engineering, National Tsing Hua University, Hsinchu, Taiwan

Therefore, this strategy is appealing for practical implementations. Simulation examples are presented to demonstrate the efficiency of the proposed strategy.

15.1   Introduction

In recent years, spectrum sharing between heterogeneous wireless networks has been recognised as a crucial technology for improving spectrum efficiency and network capacity. There are two major models for spectrum sharing presently, namely the open sharing model and the hierarchical access model [1, 2]. In the open sharing model, each network has equal right to access the same spectral band, e.g. the unlicensed band, and there is no strict constraint on the interference level from one network to its neighbours. In the hierarchical access model that consists of a primary network and a secondary network, the secondary network, i.e. cognitive radio, dynamically accesses the spectrum provided that the primary users' transmission is almost not affected [1]. In either model, the inter-network interference make spectrum sharing a challenging task especially when the interference signal varies dynamically.

To address this interference issue, media access control (MAC)-layer spectrum access strategies have been proposed [3–6] for the hierarchical access model. While these works focus on MAC-layer spectrum access, there have been works focusing on physical-layer resource allocation of secondary networks, where strict constraints are imposed to limit the induced interference to the primary users; see Reference 7 for an overview. For the open sharing model, joint optimisation of MAC-layer spectrum access and physical-layer power allocation was studied in Reference 8, where the spectrum sharing between an uplink orthogonal frequency-division multiplexing (OFDM) system and an ad hoc network was considered. These spectrum sharing studies usually assume a quasi-static environment and rely heavily on optimisation techniques to derive the optimal trade-off between throughput enhancement and interference mitigation. Therefore, these optimisation techniques can yield promising performance only if the network environment varies slowly.

In practice, however, there are many spectrum-sharing scenarios where the network environment changes quickly. Under such circumstances, it is crucial that the network controller is able to solve the spectrum access design problem in real time. One important class of such spectrum-sharing scenarios is the coexistence of the considered dynamic ad hoc network and some other networks, e.g. the coexistence of Wi-Fi (IEEE 802.11) and WiMAX (IEEE 802.16) over unlicensed spectral bands [9], the coexistence of mobile ad hoc network and cellular network [10], and, in the domain of military communications, the coexistence of local ad hoc networks, such as sensor networks and tactical mobile ad hoc networks, and the broadband tactical backbone network [11]. In these scenarios, the existing spectrum access optimisation techniques may encounter the following implementation issues: First, real-time optimisation can be computationally quite demanding for realistic wireless networks [10]. Most of the handheld user equipment, however, have very limited computational capability. Second, spectrum sensing and channel estimation are usually performed at spatially separate nodes, which requires information exchange between these nodes before solving the optimisation problem. The computation and information exchange procedure may result in a significant control delay (or reaction time delay), which makes the derived spectrum access strategy out of date. Finally, the amount of information exchange between these nodes should not be too large. Therefore, *the spectrum access strategies with good performance, small control delay, moderate signalling overhead and little computational capability requirement for the user equipment are of great importance.*

In this chapter, we consider a spectrum-sharing scenario between a dynamic ad hoc network and an uplink broadband cooperative relay network (CRN), as illustrated in Figure 15.1. The CRN intends to access the spectral band of the dynamic ad hoc network without generating too many collisions with the ad hoc traffic. The CRN is composed of a source node (e.g. a handheld user equipment), a relay node and a distant destination node (e.g. a base station). The CRN adopts a two-phase transmission protocol for each time frame: in the first phase, the source broadcasts an information message to the relay and destination; in the second phase, the relay employs a broadband decode-and-forward (DF) strategy to forward the message. The source transmits a new message to the destination in the second phase as well. In order to communicate with the distant destination, the source and relay transmit signals with peak powers, which, however, will induce strong interference to nearby ad hoc links operating over the same spectral band. The transmitters in the ad hoc network, e.g. wireless sensor nodes, have relatively low transmission powers due to their short communication ranges, and thus their interference to the relay and

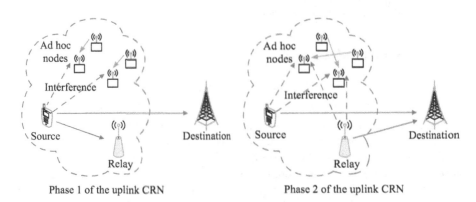

Phase 1 of the uplink CRN   Phase 2 of the uplink CRN

Figure 15.1   *System model. In Phase 1 (left plot), the source node broadcasts information to the relay and destination, and the transmitted signal interferes with the nearby ad hoc links; in Phase 2 (right plot), the source and relay transmit signals to the destination simultaneously and both transmitted signals interfere with the ad hoc links*

destination can be treated as noise. Such an asymmetrical interference scenario is known as the 'near-far effect' [12].

In order to design a spectrum access strategy fulfilling the desired features described above, we will present the following material in this chapter:

1.   Adopting a binary continuous-time Markov chain (CTMC) traffic model to describe the ad hoc traffic behaviour, we characterise the average traffic collision time between the ad hoc network and the CRN by means of traffic prediction. We formulate a spectrum access design problem that jointly optimises the power allocation and spectrum access actions of the CRN such that the average traffic collision time is minimised, while maintaining a desired throughput for the CRN.
2.   The formulated spectrum sharing problem is a difficult non-convex optimisation problem. To handle this problem efficiently, we first analyse the structure properties of the optimal spectrum access actions. Using these properties, we reformulate the spectrum access design problem as a convex optimisation problem, which allows us to obtain a low-complexity optimal spectrum access strategy based on Lagrangian dual optimisation.
3.   We then generalise this optimal spectrum access strategy to an ergodic problem setting and present an online spectrum access strategy.[1] This online spectrum access strategy is able to achieve optimal ergodic performance with negligible control delay, moderate signalling overhead and meanwhile has little computational capability requirement for the user equipment.

For ease of later use, let us define the following notations: The probability of event A is denoted by $\Pr\{A\}$, and the probability of event A conditioned on event B is denoted by $\Pr\{A|B\}$. $\mathbb{E}_\omega\{X\}$ represents expectation of X over random variable ω. The projections of x on the sets $[0, \infty)$ and $[0, y]$ are denoted by $[x]^+ = \max\{x, 0\}$ and $[x]_0^y = \min\{\max\{x, 0\}, y\}$ respectively.

15.2   System model

15.2.1   Cooperative relay network model

We assume that the CRN employs a broadband multi-carrier air interface, where signals are transmitted over N spectral channels, denoted by $\mathcal{N} = \{1, 2, \ldots, N\}$. The term 'channel' here can be either a frequency sub-band or a group of consecutive subcarriers in OFDM systems [1]. The ad hoc links operate in M non-overlapped frequency bands, denoted by $\mathcal{M} = \{1, \ldots, M\}$. We assume that the bandwidth of the ad hoc band is larger than that of the CRN channels. Moreover, the mth ad hoc band overlaps with a subset of consecutive CRN channels $\mathcal{N}_m \subset N$, where the subsets $\mathcal{N}_m$ satisfy that $\cup_{m=1}^M \mathcal{N}_m = \mathcal{N}$ and $\mathcal{N}_p \cap \mathcal{N}_q = \varnothing$ for $p \neq q$.

---

[1] This online spectrum access strategy is different from the ergodic spectrum access strategy in [13] and [14].

The CRN transmissions are organised in a frame-by-frame manner, where each frame has a fixed duration T_f. The time durations of Phase 1 and Phase 2 are set to αT_f and $(1 - \alpha)T_f$, respectively, where $\alpha \in (\delta, 1)$. At the start of each frame, the source node performs spectrum sensing to detect the BUSY/IDLE state of each ad hoc band. After spectrum sensing, the CRN may require some time to process the sensing result and determine its transmission action, which results in a control delay between spectrum sensing and CRN transmission. Since the ad hoc traffic varies dynamically, this control delay may cause additional traffic collision between the CRN and ad hoc networks. Therefore, we explicitly take into account this control delay in our spectrum sharing design. We assume that the control delay is δT_f with $\delta \in [0, 1)$. One major contribution of this chapter is *to obtain the optimal transmission action of the CRN with negligible control delay*; see Section 15.4 for more details.

We assume that the source and relay nodes can switch on and off their transmissions freely over each channel. Let $\mathbb{I}_n^{(1)} \subseteq [\delta T_f, \alpha T_f]$ denote the time set in Phase 1 when the source node transmits over the nth channel, and $\mathbb{I}_n^{(2)} \subseteq [\alpha T_f, T_f]$ denote the time set in Phase 2 when the source and relay nodes transmit over the nth channel, for $n = 1, \ldots, N$. As illustrated in Fig. 2 of Reference 14, $\mathbb{I}_n^{(1)}$ and $\mathbb{I}_n^{(2)}$ each may be a union of several disjoint transmission time intervals. Note that the source node cannot transmit during $[0, \delta T_f]$, owing to the aforementioned control delay. For convenience, let us define

$$\theta_n^{(1)} = \frac{\int_{\mathbb{I}_n^{(1)}} 1 dt}{T_f}, \theta_n^{(2)} = \frac{\int_{\mathbb{I}_n^{(1)}} 1 dt}{T_f}, \tag{15.1}$$

which represent the fractions of the CRN transmission time in Phase 1 and Phase 2 of each frame respectively.

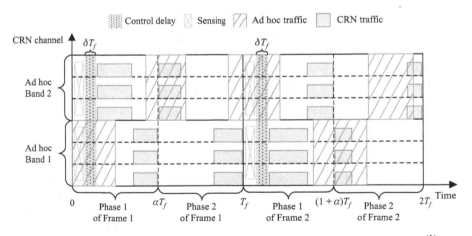

Figure 15.2   *An example illustrating the optimal spectrum access actions $\mathbb{I}_n^{(1)}$ and $\mathbb{I}_n^{(2)}$. The sensing outcomes of Frame 1 are $x_1 = 1$ and $x_2 = 0$, and the sensing outcomes of Frame 2 are $x_1 = 0$ and $x_2 = 1$*

We assume that the wireless channels of source-relay, source-destination and relay-destination links are block-fading, which means that the channel coefficients remain static within each frame, and can change from one frame to another. Let $h_n^{i,j}$ denote the frequency response of channel n between transmitter i and receiver j, where $i \in \{s, r\}$ and $j \in \{r, d\}$ $(i \neq j)$, in which s, r, d stand for the source node, relay node and destination node respectively. The interference plus noise at the relay and destination nodes are modelled as independent, zero mean, circularly symmetric complex Gaussian random variables, with N_n^r and N_n^d denoting the respective peak power spectral densities (PSD) over the nth channel (i.e. the weak interference from the ad hoc network to the CRN is treated as noise). Hence, the quality of the wireless links can be characterised by the normalised channel power gains $g_n^{s,r} \triangleq |h_n^{s,r}|^2 / N_n^r W$, $g_n^{s,d} \triangleq |h_n^{s,d}|^2 / N_n^d W$ and $g_n^{r,d} \triangleq |h_n^{r,d}|^2 / N_n^d W$, where W is the bandwidth of each channel. For broadband DF CRN with N parallel channels, it has been shown that the following rate is achievable [15, Eq. (45)]

$$
R_{CRN} = W \min \left\{ \sum_{n=1}^{N} \left[\theta_n^{(1)} \log_2 \left(1 + \frac{P_{s,n}^{(1)} \max\{g_n^{s,r}, g_n^{s,d}\}}{\theta_n^{(1)}} \right) + \theta_n^{(2)} \log_2 \left(1 + \frac{P_{s,n}^{(2)} g_n^{s,d}}{\theta_n^{(2)}} \right) \right], \right.
$$

$$
\left. \sum_{n=1}^{N} \left[\theta_n^{(1)} \log_2 \left(1 + \frac{P_{s,n}^{(1)} g_n^{s,d}}{\theta_n^{(1)}} \right) + \theta_n^{(2)} \log_2 \left(1 + \frac{P_{s,n}^{(2)} g_n^{s,d} + P_{r,n} g_n^{r,d}}{\theta_n^{(2)}} \right) \right] \right\},
$$

$$
(15.2)
$$

where $P_{s,n}^{(1)}$ and $P_{s,n}^{(2)}$ denote the transmission powers of the source over channel n in Phase 1 and Phase 2 respectively, and $P_{r,n}$ is the transmission power of the relay over channel n in Phase 2. The achievable rate R_{CRN} in (15.2) is a concave function of the transmission power and time variables [16].

15.2.2   Ad hoc traffic prediction and interference metric

The ad hoc traffic over the mth band is modelled as an independent, stationary binary CTMC $X_m(t)$, where $X_m(t) = 1$ $(X_m(t) = 0)$ represents a BUSY (IDLE) state at time t. The holding periods of both BUSY and IDLE states are exponentially distributed with rate parameters λ and μ respectively. The probability transition matrix of the CTMC traffic model of band m is given by [17, p. 391]:

$$
P(t) = \frac{1}{\lambda + \mu} \begin{bmatrix} \mu + \lambda e^{-(\lambda+\mu)t} & \lambda - \lambda e^{-(\lambda+\mu)t} \\ \mu - \mu e^{-(\lambda+\mu)t} & \lambda + \mu e^{-(\lambda+\mu)t} \end{bmatrix},
$$

$$
(15.3)
$$

where the element in the ith row and jth column of $P(t)$ stands for the transition probability $\Pr\{X_m(t + \tau) = j - 1 | X_m(\tau) = i - 1\}$ for $i, j \in \{1, 2\}$. This CTMC traffic model has been used in many theoretical spectrum sharing studies and verified by hardware tests; see References 3–6 and 8. In practice, the parameters λ and μ can be estimated by monitoring the ad hoc traffic in idle frames of the CRN [4].

We utilise the average traffic collision time between the CRN and the ad hoc network as the metric of interference experienced by the ad hoc links. Since the ad hoc nodes are near the source and relay nodes, the ad hoc links would suffer from communication errors, whenever the ad hoc transmission happens to collide with the CRN traffic. Let $x_m \in \{0, 1\}$ denote the sensing outcome for the mth ad hoc band, i.e. $X_m(0) = x_m$. Given x_m, one can predict the average traffic collision time based on the CTMC traffic model in (15.3). Specifically, the total traffic collision time summed over all the ad hoc bands is given by

$$
I = \sum_{m=1}^{M} \left[\int \bigcup_{n \in \mathcal{N}_m} \mathbb{I}_n^{(1)} \Pr\{X_m(t) = 1 | X_m(0) = x_m\} dt \right.
$$

$$
\left. + \int \bigcup_{n \in \mathcal{N}_m} \mathbb{I}_n^{(2)} \Pr\{X_m(t) = 1 | X_m(0) = x_m\} dt \right]. \tag{15.4}
$$

where $\bigcup_{n \in \mathcal{N}_m} \mathbb{I}_n^{(i)}$ reflects the fact that, in the strong interference scenario, the ad hoc transmission in the mth band is disrupted, even when the CRN transmits in one channel of $\mathcal{N}_m$ only.

15.3 Frame-level spectrum sharing: optimal design

The goal of the CRN is to optimise the source and relay's transmission powers $P_{s,n}^{(1)}$, $P_{s,n}^{(2)}$ and $P_{r,n}$, and the spectrum access actions characterised by $\mathbb{I}_n^{(1)}$ and $\mathbb{I}_n^{(2)}$, such that the total traffic collision time experienced by the ad hoc network I is minimised, while the uplink throughput of the CRN R_{CRN} is no smaller than $R_{\min}$. This spectrum sharing design problem is formulated as the following optimisation problem:

$$
(\text{P}) \quad \min_{P_{s,n}^{(1)}, P_{s,n}^{(2)}, P_{r,n}, \mathbb{I}_n^{(1)}, \mathbb{I}_n^{(2)}} \frac{I}{T_f} \tag{15.5a}
$$

$$
\text{s.t.} \quad R_{CRN} \geq R_{\min}, \tag{15.5b}
$$

$$
\sum_{n=1}^{N} \left[P_{s,n}^{(1)} + P_{s,n}^{(2)} \right] \leq P_{\max}^s, \tag{15.5c}
$$

$$
\sum_{n=1}^{N} P_{r,n} \leq P_{\max}^r, \tag{15.5d}
$$

$$
P_{s,n}^{(1)}, P_{s,n}^{(2)}, P_{r,n} \geq 0, n = 1, \ldots, N, \tag{15.5e}
$$

$$
\mathbb{I}_n^{(1)} \subseteq [\delta T_f, \alpha T_f], \mathbb{I}_n^{(2)} \subseteq [\alpha T_f, T_f], n = 1, \ldots, N, \tag{15.5f}
$$

$$
\int_{\mathbb{I}_n^{(1)}} 1 \, dt = \theta_n^{(1)} T_f, \int_{\mathbb{I}_n^{(2)}} 1 \, dt = \theta_n^{(2)} T_f, n = 1, \ldots, N, \tag{15.5g}
$$

where R_{CRN} is defined in (15.2), I is defined in (15.4), (15.5g) follows from (15.1), $P_{\max}^s$ and $P_{\max}^r$ in (15.5c) and (15.5d) denote the power constraints at the source and relay nodes, respectively.

Problem (P) is difficult to solve because the optimisation is over any possible spectrum access actions characterised by $\mathbb{I}_n^{(1)}$ and $\mathbb{I}_n^{(2)}$ satisfying (15.5f). In particular, Problem (P) is a non-convex optimisation problem. Fortunately, the optimal spectrum access actions $\mathbb{I}_n^{(1)}$ and $\mathbb{I}_n^{(2)}$ have a very nice structure, which can be utilised to reformulate Problem (P) as a convex optimisation problem, as shown below.

15.3.1   Convex reformulation of Problem (P)

The optimal spectrum access actions $\mathbb{I}_n^{(1)}$ and $\mathbb{I}_n^{(2)}$ satisfy the following two principles [14, Lemma 1]:

1. *In both Phase 1 and Phase 2, the source and relay nodes should transmit as soon (late) as possible if the sensing outcome is IDLE (BUSY).*
2. *The CRN should have identical spectrum access strategy for the channels overlapping with the same ad hoc band; that is, $\mathbb{I}_p^{(i)} = \mathbb{I}_q^{(i)}$ for all $p, q \in \mathcal{N}_m$, where $m \in \mathcal{M}$ and $i \in \{1, 2\}$.*

An example that illustrates these principles is provided in Figure 15.2.

Let $\hat{\theta}_m^{(i)}$ denote the fraction of transmission time over the channels $\mathcal{N}_m$ in phase i. Using these two principles, the interference metric in (15.4) can be simplified as

$$I = \sum_{m=1}^{M} \left[\phi_{(1)}\left(\hat{\theta}; x_m\right) + \phi_{(2)}\left(\hat{\theta}; x_m\right) \right], \tag{15.6}$$

where the functions $\phi_{(1)}\left(\hat{\theta}; x_m\right)$ and $\phi_{(2)}\left(\hat{\theta}; x_m\right)$ are defined by

$$
\begin{aligned}
\phi_{(1)}(\theta; x_m = 0) &= \int_{[\delta T_f, (\delta + \theta)T_f]} \Pr(X_m(t) = 1 | X_m(0) = 0)dt \\
&= \frac{\lambda}{\lambda + \mu} \left\{ \theta + \frac{1}{(\lambda + \mu)T_f} e^{-(\lambda + \mu)\delta T_f} \left[e^{-(\lambda + \mu)\theta T_f} - 1 \right] \right\} T_f,
\end{aligned} \tag{15.7}
$$

$$
\begin{aligned}
\phi_{(1)}(\theta; x_m = 1) &= \int_{[(\alpha - \theta)T_f, \alpha T_f]} \Pr(X_m(t) = 1 | X_m(0) = 1)dt \\
&= \frac{\lambda}{\lambda + \mu} \left\{ \theta + \frac{\mu}{\lambda} \frac{1}{(\lambda + \mu)T_f} e^{-(\lambda + \mu)\alpha T_f} \left[e^{(\lambda + \mu)\theta T_f} - 1 \right] \right\} T_f,
\end{aligned} \tag{15.8}
$$

for $\theta \in [0, \alpha - \delta]$, and

$$
\begin{aligned}
\phi_{(2)}(\theta; x_m = 0) &= \int_{[\alpha T_f, (\theta + \alpha)T_f]} \Pr(X_m(t) = 1 | X_m(0) = 0)dt \\
&= \frac{\lambda}{\lambda + \mu} \left\{ \theta + \frac{1}{(\lambda + \mu)T_f} e^{-(\lambda + \mu)\alpha T_f} \left[e^{-(\lambda + \mu)\theta T_f} - 1 \right] \right\} T_f,
\end{aligned} \tag{15.9}
$$

$$
\begin{aligned}
\phi_{(2)}(\theta; x_m = 1) &= \int_{[T_f - \theta T_f, T_f]} \Pr(X_m(t) = 1 | X_m(0) = 1)dt \\
&= \frac{\lambda}{\lambda + \mu} \left\{ \theta + \frac{\mu}{\lambda} \frac{1}{(\lambda + \mu)T_f} e^{-(\lambda + \mu)T_f} \left[e^{(\lambda + \mu)\theta T_f} - 1 \right] \right\} T_f,
\end{aligned} \tag{15.10}
$$

for $\theta \in [0, 1 - \alpha]$.

On the other hand, the constraint (15.5) of Problem (P) can be equivalently expressed as

$$R_1 \geq R_{\min}, R_2 \geq R_{\min}, \tag{15.11}$$

where

$$R_1 = W \sum_{m \in \mathcal{M}} \sum_{n \in \mathcal{N}_m} \left[\hat{\theta}_m^{(1)} \log_2 \left(1 + \frac{P_{s,n}^{(1)} \max\{g_n^{s,r}, g_n^{s,d}\}}{\hat{\theta}_m^{(1)}} \right) + \hat{\theta}_m^{(2)} \log_2 \left(1 + \frac{P_{s,n}^{(2)} g_n^{s,d}}{\hat{\theta}_m^{(2)}} \right) \right], \tag{15.12}$$

$$R_2 = W \sum_{m \in \mathcal{M}} \sum_{n \in \mathcal{N}_m} \left[\hat{\theta}_m^{(1)} \log_2 \left(1 + \frac{P_{s,n}^{(1)} g_n^{s,d}}{\hat{\theta}_m^{(1)}} \right) + \hat{\theta}_m^{(2)} \log_2 \left(1 + \frac{P_{s,n}^{(2)} g_n^{s,d} + P_{r,n} g_n^{r,d}}{\hat{\theta}_m^{(2)}} \right) \right]. \tag{15.13}$$

By (15.11) and (15.16), Problem (P) is equivalent to the following problem:

$$\min_{P_{s,n}^{(1)}, P_{s,n}^{(2)}, P_{r,n}, \hat{\theta}_m^{(1)}, \hat{\theta}_m^{(2)}} \frac{1}{T_f} \sum_{m=1}^{M} \left[\phi_{(1)} \left(\hat{\theta}_m^{(1)}; x_m \right) + \phi_{(2)} \left(\hat{\theta}_m^{(2)}; x_m \right) \right] \tag{15.14a}$$

$$\text{s.t.} \quad R_1 \geq R_{\min}, \tag{15.14b}$$

$$R_2 \geq R_{\min}, \tag{15.14c}$$

$$\sum_{n=1}^{N} \left[P_{s,n}^{(1)} + P_{s,n}^{(2)} \right] \leq P_{\max}^s, \tag{15.14d}$$

$$\sum_{n=1}^{N} P_{r,n} \leq P_{\max}^r, \tag{15.14e}$$

$$P_{s,n}^{(1)}, P_{s,n}^{(2)}, P_{r,n} \geq 0, n = 1, \ldots, N, \tag{15.14f}$$

$$0 \leq \hat{\theta}_m^{(1)} \leq \alpha - \delta, \quad 0 \leq \hat{\theta}_m^{(2)} \leq 1 - \alpha, \quad m = 1, \ldots, M, \tag{15.14g}$$

which is a convex optimisation problem. While problem (15.14) can be solved by interior-point methods, we present below a low-complexity Lagrangian dual optimisation solution.

15.3.2 Lagrangian dual optimisation solution for problem (15.14)

Suppose that problem (15.14) is strictly feasible. Then, according to the Slater's condition [16], the strong duality holds for (15.14). Hence, we can alternatively consider the following Lagrangian dual optimisation problem:

$$\max_{\zeta, \sigma, \varepsilon, \eta \geq 0} \left\{ \min_{(P_{s,n}^{(1)}, P_{s,n}^{(2)}, P_{r,n}, \hat{\theta}_m^{(1)}, \hat{\theta}_m^{(2)}) \in \mathcal{V}} L \right\}, \tag{15.15}$$

where $\mathcal{V} \triangleq \{(P_{s,n}^{(1)}, P_{s,n}^{(2)}, P_{r,n}, \hat{\theta}_m^{(1)}, \hat{\theta}_m^{(2)}) | 0 \le \hat{\theta}_m^{(1)} \le \alpha - \delta, \ 0 \le \hat{\theta}_m^{(2)} \le 1 - \alpha, P_{s,n}^{(1)},$
$P_{s,n}^{(2)}, P_{r,n} \ge 0, \ n \in \mathcal{N}, m \in \mathcal{M}\}$,

$$L = \frac{1}{T_f} \sum_{m=1}^{M} \left[\phi_{(1)}\left(\hat{\theta}_m^{(1)}; x_m\right) + \phi_{(2)}\left(\hat{\theta}_m^{(2)}; x_m\right) \right] + \frac{\zeta}{W}(R_{\min} - R_1) + \frac{\sigma}{W}(R_{\min} - R_2)$$
$$+ \varepsilon \left[\sum_{n=1}^{N}(P_{s,n}^{(1)} + P_{s,n}^{(2)}) - P_{\max}^s \right] + \eta \left[\sum_{n=1}^{N} P_{r,n} - P_{\max}^r \right],$$

(15.16)

is the partial Lagrangian [18] of (15.14); $\zeta \ge 0, \sigma \ge 0, \varepsilon \ge 0$ and $\eta \ge 0$ are the dual variables associated with the constraints (15.14b), (15.14c), (15.14d) and (15.14e), respectively. The key benefits of this method are as follows:

1. The inner minimisation problem of (15.15) has closed-form solutions, which are easy to compute.
2. The outer maximisation problem of (15.15) only has four variables, and thus is easy to solve.

We first provide the closed-form solutions of the inner minimisation problem of (15.15).

If $P_{s,n}^{(1)} > 0$, the optimal ratio $\frac{P_{s,n}^{(1)}}{\hat{\theta}_m^{(1)}}$ is given by the positive root x of the following quadratic equation:

$$\frac{\zeta \max\{g_n^{s,r}, g_n^{s,d}\}}{1 + \max\{g_n^{s,r}, g_n^{s,d}\}x} + \frac{\sigma g_n^{s,d}}{1 + g_n^{s,d}x} = \varepsilon \ln 2.$$

(15.17)

If (15.17) has no positive root, then $\frac{P_{s,n}^{(1)}}{\hat{\theta}_m^{(1)}} = 0$.

If $P_{r,n} > 0$, the optimal $\frac{P_{s,n}^{(2)}}{\hat{\theta}_m^{(2)}}$ and $\frac{P_{r,n}}{\hat{\theta}_m^{(2)}}$ are determined by

$$\frac{P_{s,n}^{(2)}}{\hat{\theta}_m^{(2)}} = \left[\frac{\zeta}{(\varepsilon - \eta g_n^{s,d}/g_n^{r,d}) \ln 2} - \frac{1}{g_n^{s,d}} \right]^+,$$

(15.18)

$$\frac{P_{r,n}}{\hat{\theta}_m^{(2)}} = \frac{\sigma}{\eta \ln 2} - \frac{1}{g_n^{r,d}} - \frac{g_n^{s,d}}{g_n^{r,d}} \frac{P_{s,n}^{(2)}}{\hat{\theta}_m^{(2)}}.$$

(15.19)

Instead, if $P_{r,n} = 0$, the optimal $\frac{P_{s,n}^{(2)}}{\hat{\theta}_m^{(2)}}$ and $\frac{P_{r,n}}{\hat{\theta}_m^{(2)}}$ are given by

$$\frac{P_{s,n}^{(2)}}{\hat{\theta}_m^{(2)}} = \left[\frac{\zeta + \sigma}{\varepsilon \ln 2} - \frac{1}{g_n^{s,d}} \right]^+,$$

(15.20)

$$\frac{P_{r,n}}{\hat{\theta}_m^{(2)}} = 0.$$

(15.21)

The optimal values of $\hat{\theta}_m^{(1)}$ and $\hat{\theta}_m^{(2)}$ are provided as follows:
If $x_m = 0$, we have[2]

$$
\hat{\theta}_m^{(1)} = \left[-\frac{1}{(\lambda + \mu)T_f} \ln\left\{ 1 - \frac{\lambda + \mu}{\lambda} \sum_{n \in \mathcal{N}_m} \left[\sigma f\left(g_n^{s,d} \frac{P_{s,n}^{(1)}}{\hat{\theta}_m^{(1)}} \right) \right.\right.\right.
$$
$$
\left.\left.\left. + \zeta f\left(\max\{g_n^{s,r}, g_n^{s,d}\} \frac{P_{s,n}^{(1)}}{\hat{\theta}_m^{(1)}} \right) \right] \right\} - \delta \right]_0^{a-\delta} ,
\tag{15.22}
$$

$$
\hat{\theta}_m^{(2)} = \left[-\frac{1}{(\lambda + \mu)T_f} \ln\left\{ 1 - \frac{\lambda + \mu}{\lambda} \sum_{n \in \mathcal{N}_m} \left[\zeta f\left(g_n^{s,d} \frac{P_{s,n}^{(2)}}{\hat{\theta}_m^{(2)}} \right) \right.\right.\right.
$$
$$
\left.\left.\left. + \sigma f\left(g_n^{s,d} \frac{P_{s,n}^{(2)}}{\hat{\theta}_m^{(2)}} + g_n^{r,d} \frac{P_{r,n}}{\hat{\theta}_m^{(2)}} \right) \right] \right\} - \alpha \right]_0^{1-\alpha} ,
\tag{15.23}
$$

where $f(x) \triangleq \log_2(1+x) - \dfrac{x}{(1+x)\ln 2}$.

If $x_m = 1$, we have

$$
\hat{\theta}_m^{(1)} = \left[\alpha + \frac{1}{(\lambda + \mu)T_f} \ln\left\{ \frac{\lambda + \mu}{\mu} \sum_{n \in \mathcal{N}_m} \left[\sigma f\left(g_n^{s,d} \frac{P_{s,n}^{(1)}}{\hat{\theta}_m^{(1)}} \right) \right.\right.\right.
$$
$$
\left.\left.\left. + \zeta f\left(\max\{g_n^{s,r}, g_n^{s,d}\} \frac{P_{s,n}^{(1)}}{\hat{\theta}_m^{(1)}} \right) \right] - \frac{\lambda}{\mu} \right\} \right]_0^{a-\delta} ,
\tag{15.24}
$$

$$
\hat{\theta}_m^{(2)} = \left[1 + \frac{1}{(\lambda + \mu)T_f} \ln\left\{ \frac{\lambda + \mu}{\mu} \sum_{n \in \mathcal{N}_m} \left[\zeta f\left(g_n^{s,d} \frac{P_{s,n}^{(2)}}{\hat{\theta}_m^{(2)}} \right) \right.\right.\right.
$$
$$
\left.\left.\left. + \sigma f\left(g_n^{s,d} \frac{P_{s,n}^{(2)}}{\hat{\theta}_m^{(2)}} + g_n^{r,d} \frac{P_{r,n}}{\hat{\theta}_m^{(2)}} \right) \right] - \frac{\lambda}{\mu} \right\} \right]_0^{1-\alpha} .
\tag{15.25}
$$

By substituting (15.33)–(15.36) into (15.28)–(15.32), the optimal $P_{s,n}^{(1)}, P_{s,n}^{(2)}, P_{r,n}$ can then be obtained.

The outer maximisation problem of (15.15) can be solved by the subgradient method [19]. Let $\nu \triangleq (\zeta, \sigma, \varepsilon, \eta)^T$ denote the dual variable. At the kth iteration, the subgradient method updates ν by

$$
\nu_{k+1} = [\nu_k + s_k \boldsymbol{h}(\nu_k)]^+ ,
\tag{15.26}
$$

---

[2] For the notational simplicity in (15.22)–(15.25), we have extended the definition of the natural logarithm $\ln(x)$ to that with $\ln(x) = -\infty$ for $x \in (-\infty, 0]$.

where s_k is the step size of the kth iteration, and $\boldsymbol{h}(v_k)$ is the subgradient of the dual function, which is given by Reference 20:

$$\boldsymbol{h}(\boldsymbol{n}_k) = \begin{bmatrix} (R_{\min} - R_1^\star)/W \\ (R_{\min} - R_2^\star)/W \\ \sum_{n=1}^{N}\left(P_{s,n}^{(1)\star} + P_{s,n}^{(2)\star}\right) - P_{\max}^s \\ \sum_{n=1}^{N}P_{r,n}^\star - P_{\max}^r \end{bmatrix}, \tag{15.27}$$

where $P_{s,n}^{(1)\star}$, $P_{s,n}^{(2)\star}$ and $P_{r,n}^\star$ are the optimal solution of the inner minimisation problem (15.15) at iteration k, and $R_1^\star$ and $R_2^\star$ are the corresponding rate values in (15.12) and (15.13) respectively. It has been shown that the subgradient updates in (15.26) converge to the optimal dual point $v^\star$ as $k \to \infty$, provided that the step size s_k is chosen according to a diminishing step size rule [19].

The direction of the subgradient update may happen to be nearly orthogonal with the direction towards the optimal dual variable, which results in a slow convergence speed; see Fig. 2 of Reference 21 for an illustration. An alternative two-level dual optimisation method was provided in Reference 21, which can improve the convergence speed. One may also scale the dual variable to modify the update direction. Some other acceleration techniques are available in References 20, 22 and 23, which are helpful to resolve this problem.

15.4   Ergodic spectrum sharing: practical online design

The spectrum access strategy introduced in the previous section is suitable for environments where the channel condition and ad hoc traffic change slowly. For example, if the CRN obtains the channel condition and sensing results in Frame 1, it can utilise them in Frame 2 to compute the optimal transmission action and then execute the transmission action in Frame 3. As long as the channel condition and sensing results in Frame 1 and Frame 3 remain similar, this strategy should exhibit a reasonable performance.

However, when the ad hoc traffic state changes quickly, the performance of the optimal spectrum access strategy can be poor. Therefore, it is essential that the network controller is able to solve the spectrum access design problem in real time. To this end, one possible approach is to generalise the optimal spectrum access strategy to an ergodic setting, and, based on it, design an online spectrum access strategy. Our online spectrum access strategy comes up with optimal ergodic performance, negligible control delay, moderate signalling overhead and little computation capability requirement for the user equipment, thereby appealing for practical implementations.

A side benefit of this ergodic setting is that it allows one more spectrum sensing at the beginning of Phase 2 to improve the accuracy of traffic prediction. This, however, cannot be exploited in the frame-level setting, because Problem (P) must be solved before this additional sensing in Phase 2 is carried out.

15.4.1 Problem formulation

Suppose that both the source and relay nodes perform one extra spectrum sensing at the beginning of Phase 2. The sensing outcome for the mth ad hoc band is denoted as $X_m(\alpha T_f) = y_m \in \{0, 1\}$ with $m = 1, \ldots, M$. This additional sensing outcome can be utilised to reduce traffic collision time, at the cost of an additional control delay in Phase 2, as shown in Figure 15.3. For notational simplicity, the duration of this additional control delay is also assumed to be δT_f.[3]

Let us define the network state information (NSI) as

$$\omega \triangleq \{g_n^{s,d}, g_n^{s,r}, g_n^{r,d}, x_m, y_m, \ n \in \mathcal{N}, m \in \mathcal{M}\},$$

which includes the channel fading gains and sensing results in both phases. In the ergodic setting, the NSI ω varies across different frames. We assume that the NSI is stationary and ergodic over time, and the stochastic distribution of the NSI is not available at the network controller.

The principles of the optimal spectrum access actions in Section 15.3.1 still hold in the ergodic setting, which are illustrated in Figure 15.3. According to Lemma 2 in Reference 14, the average traffic collision time for the ergodic setting is given by

$$I = \mathbb{E}_w \left\{ \sum_{m=1}^{M} \left[\phi_{(1)} \left(\hat{\theta}_m^{(1)}(\omega); x_m \right) + \hat{\phi}_{(2)} \left(\hat{\theta}_m^{(2)}(\omega); y_m \right) \right] \right\}, \tag{15.28}$$

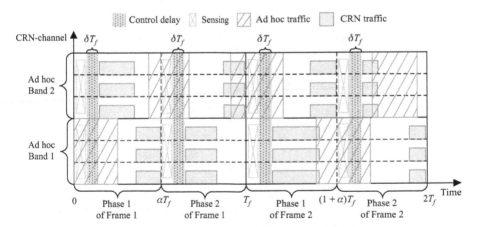

Figure 15.3   Time-frequency transmission structure for the ergodic setting. Here the sensing outcomes of Frame 1 are $x_1 = 1$, $x_2 = 0$, $y_1 = 0$ and $y_2 = 1$, and the sensing outcomes of Frame 2 are $x_1 = 0$, $x_2 = 1$, $y_1 = 1$ and $y_2 = 0$

---

[3] After a careful design of the computation and information exchange procedure, this additional control delay turns out to be negligible, as shown in Section 15.4.2.

where $\phi_{(1)}(\theta, x_m)$ has been defined in (15.7) and (15.8), and $\hat{\phi}_{(2)}(\theta, y_m)$ is defined by

$$\hat{\phi}_{(2)}(\theta; y_m = 0) = \int_{[(a+\delta)T_f,(\theta+a+\delta)T_f]} \Pr(X_m(t) = 1 | X_m(aT_f) = 0)dt$$

$$= \frac{\lambda}{\lambda+\mu}\left\{\theta + \frac{e^{-(\lambda+\mu)\delta T_f}}{(\lambda+\mu)T_f}\left[e^{-(\lambda+\mu)\theta T_f} - 1\right]\right\}T_f, \tag{15.29}$$

$$\hat{\phi}_{(2)}(\theta; y_m = 1) = \int_{[T_f - \theta T_f, T_f]} \Pr(X_m(t) = 1 | X_m(aT_f) = 1)dt$$

$$= \frac{\lambda}{\lambda+\mu}\left\{\theta + \frac{\mu}{\lambda}\frac{e^{-(\lambda+\mu)(1-a)T_f}}{(\lambda+\mu)T_f}\left[e^{(\lambda+\mu)\theta T_f} - 1\right]\right\}T_f, \tag{15.30}$$

where $\theta \in [0, 1 - a]$. Note from (15.28) that, in contrast to (15.6), the collision time in Phase 2 now depends on the sensing outcome y_m.

The achievable average rate of the multi-carrier CRN can be shown to be

$$R_{CRN} = \min\{R_1, R_2\}, \tag{15.31}$$

where

$$R_1 = W\sum_{m\in M}\sum_{n\in N_m} \mathbb{E}_w\left[\hat{\theta}_m^{(1)}(\omega)\log_2\left(1 + \frac{P_{s,n}^{(1)}(\omega)\max\{g_n^{s,r}, g_n^{s,d}\}}{\hat{\theta}_m^{(1)}(\omega)}\right)\right.$$

$$\left. + \hat{\theta}_m^{(2)}(\omega)\log_2\left(1 + \frac{P_{s,n}^{(2)}(\omega)g_n^{s,d}}{\hat{\theta}_m^{(2)}(\omega)}\right)\right], \tag{15.32}$$

$$R_2 = W\sum_{m\in M}\sum_{n\in N_m} \mathbb{E}_w\left[\hat{\theta}_m^{(1)}(\omega)\log_2\left(1 + \frac{P_{s,n}^{(1)}(\omega)g_n^{s,d}}{\hat{\theta}_m^{(1)}(\omega)}\right)\right.$$

$$\left. + \hat{\theta}_m^{(2)}(\omega)\log_2\left(1 + \frac{P_{s,n}^{(2)}(\omega)g_n^{s,d} + P_{r,n}(\omega)g_n^{r,d}}{\hat{\theta}_m^{(2)}(\omega)}\right)\right], \tag{15.33}$$

and $P_{s,n}^{(1)}(\omega), P_{s,n}^{(2)}(\omega), P_{r,n}(\omega)$ are the transmission powers for a given NSI ω.

It follows from (15.28) and (15.31) that the ergodic spectrum access design is formulated as the following problem:

$$\min_{P_{s,n}^{(1)}(\omega),P_{s,n}^{(2)}(\omega),P_{r,n}(\omega),\hat{\theta}_m^{(1)}(\omega),\hat{\theta}_m^{(2)}(\omega)} \mathbb{E}_w\left\{\sum_{m=1}^{M}\left[\phi_{(1)}\left(\hat{\theta}_m^{(1)}(\omega); x_m\right) + \hat{\phi}_{(2)}\left(\hat{\theta}_m^{(2)}(\omega); y_m\right)\right]\right\}, \tag{15.34a}$$

$$\text{s.t.} \qquad R_1 \geq R_{\min}, R_2 \geq R_{\min}, \tag{15.34b}$$

$$\mathbb{E}_\mathbf{w}\left\{\sum_{n=1}^{N}\left[P_{s,n}^{(1)}(\omega)+P_{s,n}^{(2)}(\omega)\right]\right\}\leq\bar{P}_{max}^{s}, \tag{15.34c}$$

$$\mathbb{E}_\mathbf{w}\left\{\sum_{n=1}^{N}P_{r,n}(\omega)\right\}\leq\bar{P}_{max}^{r}, \tag{15.34d}$$

$$P_{s,n}^{(1)}(\omega),P_{s,n}^{(2)}(\omega),P_{r,n}(\omega)\geq 0,\; n=1,\ldots,N, \tag{15.34e}$$

$$0\leq\hat{\theta}_m^{(1)}(\omega)\leq\alpha-\delta,\;\; 0\leq\hat{\theta}_m^{(2)}(\omega)\leq 1-\alpha-\delta,\; m=1,\ldots,M. \tag{15.34f}$$

15.4.2 Online spectrum access strategy

We now present an online solution to Problem (15.34) based on the Lagrangian dual optimisation method. The Lagrangian and the dual problem associated with (15.34) are provided in Reference 14. Let us define $\omega_\ell \triangleq \{g_n^{s,r}(\ell),g_n^{s,d}(\ell),g_n^{r,d}(\ell),x_m(\ell),y_m(\ell),\, n\in\mathcal{N},m\in\mathcal{M}\}$ as the NSI of Frame ℓ and define $\nu_\ell \triangleq (\zeta_\ell,\sigma_\ell,\varepsilon_\ell,\eta_\ell)^T$ as the dual variable of Frame ℓ. In Frame ℓ, our online spectrum access strategy is composed of two steps: First, we compute the primal solution $(P_{s,n}^{(1)}(\omega_\ell),P_{s,n}^{(2)}(\omega_\ell),P_{r,n}(\omega_\ell),\hat{\theta}_m^{(1)}(\omega_\ell),\hat{\theta}_m^{(2)}(\omega_\ell))$ according to the current NSI ω_ℓ and the dual variables ν_ℓ, then we update the dual variables ν_ℓ by a stochatic subgradient method.

15.4.2.1 Online primal solution update

In slow fading propagation environments, the base station is able to acquire the channel gain $\{g_n^{s,r}(\ell),g_n^{s,d}(\ell),g_n^{r,d}(\ell)\}_{n=1}^{N}$ through channel prediction before Frame ℓ starts, if the wireless channels vary slowly across the frames [24]. Given the channel gain $\{g_n^{s,r}(\ell),g_n^{s,d}(\ell),g_n^{r,d}(\ell)\}$, the base station computes the ratios $\frac{P_{s,n}^{(1)\star}(\omega_\ell)}{\hat{\theta}_m^{(1)\star}(\omega_\ell)}$, $\frac{P_{s,n}^{(2)\star}(\omega_\ell)}{\hat{\theta}_m^{(2)\star}(\omega_\ell)}$ and $\frac{P_{r,n}^{\star}(\omega_\ell)}{\hat{\theta}_m^{(2)\star}(\omega_\ell)}$ according to (15.17)–(15.21) in Frame $\ell-1$. The base station also computes the two possible values of $\hat{\theta}_m^{(1)\star}(\omega_\ell)$ in (15.22) and (15.24) for both of the sensing outcomes $x_m(\ell)=1$ and $x_m(\ell)=0$, and the two possible values of $\hat{\theta}_m^{(2)\star}(\omega_\ell)$ in (50) and (51) of [14] for both $y_m(\ell)=0$ and $y_m(\ell)=1$ in Frame $\ell-1$. Then, the base station sends these results back to the source and relay nodes before the spectrum sensing of Frame ℓ. In Frame ℓ, the source and relay nodes perform spectrum sensing, and then simply select the values of $\hat{\theta}_m^{(1)\star}(\omega_\ell)$ and $\hat{\theta}_m^{(2)\star}(\omega_\ell)$ according to the sensing outcomes $x_m(\ell)$ and $y_m(\ell)$ respectively.

15.4.2.2 Online dual variable update

After the primal solution is obtained, the base station updates the dual variable ν_ℓ by a stochastic subgradient method [25, 26] i.e.

$$\nu_{\ell+1}=\left[\nu_\ell+s_\ell\hat{h}(\nu_\ell,\omega_\ell)\right]^+, \tag{15.35}$$

where $\hat{h}(\nu_\ell, \omega_\ell)$ is a stochastic subgradient of the dual function, determined by

$$
\hat{h}(\nu_\ell, \omega_\ell) = \begin{bmatrix} \left[R_{\min} - R_1^\star(\omega_\ell)\right]/W \\ \left[R_{\min} - R_2^\star(\omega_\ell)\right]/W \\ \sum_{n=1}^{N}\left[P_{s,n}^{(1)\star}(\omega_\ell) + P_{s,n}^{(2)\star}(\omega_\ell)\right] - P_{\max}^s \\ \sum_{n=1}^{N} P_{r,n}^\star(\omega_\ell) - P_{\max}^r \end{bmatrix},
\tag{15.36}
$$

in which $R_1^\star(\omega_\ell)$ and $R_2^\star(\omega_\ell)$ are the corresponding rate values in Frame ℓ, defined by

$$
R_1^\star(\omega_\ell) = W \sum_{m \in M} \sum_{n \in N_m} \left[\hat{\theta}_m^{(1)\star}(\omega_\ell)\log_2\left(1 + \frac{P_{s,n}^{(1)\star}(\omega_\ell)\max\{g_n^{s,r}, g_n^{s,d}\}}{\hat{\theta}_m^{(1)\star}(\omega_\ell)}\right)\right.
$$
$$
\left. + \hat{\theta}_m^{(2)\star}(\omega_\ell)\log_2\left(1 + \frac{P_{s,n}^{(2)\star}(\omega_\ell)g_n^{s,d}}{\hat{\theta}_m^{(2)\star}(\omega_\ell)}\right)\right],
$$

$$
R_2^\star(\omega_\ell) = W \sum_{m \in M} \sum_{n \in N_m} \left[\hat{\theta}_m^{(1)\star}(\omega_\ell)\log_2\left(1 + \frac{P_{s,n}^{(1)\star}(\omega_\ell)g_n^{s,d}}{\hat{\theta}_m^{(1)\star}(\omega_\ell)}\right)\right.
$$
$$
\left. + \hat{\theta}_m^{(2)\star}(\omega_\ell)\log_2\left(1 + \frac{P_{s,n}^{(2)\star}(\omega_\ell)g_n^{s,d} + P_{r,n}^\star(\omega_\ell)g_n^{r,d}}{\hat{\theta}_m^{(2)\star}(\omega_\ell)}\right)\right].
$$

This online dual optimisation method is different from offline dual optimisation method proposed in References 13 and 14.

If the step sizes s_ℓ satisfy

$$
s_\ell \geq 0, \sum_{l=1}^{\infty} s_\ell^2 < \infty, \sum_{l=1}^{\infty} s_\ell = \infty,
\tag{15.37}
$$

the stochastic subgradient updates in (15.35) converge to the optimal dual solution [25, 26].

15.4.2.3   Merits of our online spectrum access strategy

The proposed online spectrum access strategy has the following merits: First, the transmission actions are optimal in the ergodic sense. Second, all the computations are carried out at the base station. The source and relay nodes with low computational capability only need to conduct simple selection operations. Third, the transmission actions of the source and relay nodes are determined right after spectrum sensing, which means that the control delay (or reaction time delay) is negligible, i.e. $\delta = 0$. Fourth, in each frame, the destination node needs to send $3N + 2M$ parameters to the source and relay nodes, including the ratios $\frac{P_{s,n}^{(1)\star}(\omega_\ell)}{\hat{\theta}_m^{(1)\star}(\omega_\ell)}$,

$\frac{P_{s,n}^{(2)\star}(\omega_\ell)}{\hat{\theta}_m^{(2)\star}(\omega_\ell)}$ and $\frac{P_{r,n}^{\star}(\omega_\ell)}{\hat{\theta}_m^{(2)\star}(\omega_\ell)}$, as well as the transmission time $\hat{\theta}_m^{(1)\star}(\omega_\ell)$ and $\hat{\theta}_m^{(2)\star}(\omega_\ell)$. On the other hand, the traditional CRN without spectrum sharing needs to feedback the power allocation results $\frac{P_{s,n}^{(1)\star}(\omega_\ell)}{\hat{\theta}_m^{(1)\star}(\omega_\ell)}$, $\frac{P_{s,n}^{(2)\star}(\omega_\ell)}{\hat{\theta}_m^{(2)\star}(\omega_\ell)}$ and $\frac{P_{r,n^\star}(\omega_\ell)}{\hat{\theta}_m^{(2)\star}(\omega_\ell)}$, but not the transmission time $\hat{\theta}_m^{(1)\star}(\omega_\ell)$ and $\hat{\theta}_m^{(2)\star}(\omega_\ell)$. Hence, the signalling overhead of traditional CRN is $3N$. Since the number of ad hoc bands M is smaller than the number of CRN channels N, the signalling overhead of this procedure is only slightly larger than that of traditional CRN without spectrum sharing. Fifth, this online spectrum access strategy does not require stochastic distribution information of the NSI ω. Finally, the transmission parameters of the CRN in Phase 1 is determined solely by $x_m(\ell)$ but not $y_m(\ell)$ in the ergodic setting. Hence, the primal solution to the ergodic transmission control problem can be computed in a causal manner. We note that in order to exploit $y_m(\ell)$ optimally in the frame-level spectrum access design problem (P), one needs to formulate a dynamic programming, which will significantly complicate the problem.

In summary, our online spectrum access strategy is able to achieve optimal ergodic performance, negligible control delay and moderate signalling overhead, and meanwhile has little computational capability requirement for the user equipment.

15.4.3 *Queueing process at the relay node*

In order to achieve the average rate $\bar{R}_{CRN}$, the relay node needs to queue up its received data from the source node, and forward the message to the destination node dynamically according to the channel condition in Phase 2 of each frame [15, 27]. In order to make sure that the data queue of the relay node is stable, its average arrival rate should be kept no larger than its average departure rate, which is not difficult to achieve.

An important benefit of the queuing process at the relay node is that when the sensing outcome of Phase 2 is BUSY, the relay node can reduce its transmission rate (the departure rate of the queue) and wait for better transmission opportunity. If there is no queue at the relay node, the relay node cannot adjust its transmission data rate according to the sensing outcome of Phase 2, which leads to more traffic collisions between the two networks.

In practice, sensing error may occur at the source and relay nodes, which means that the BUSY (IDLE) ad hoc traffic state is mistakenly detected as IDLE (BUSY). In this case, the source and relay nodes may transmit in different time intervals, leading to extra collisions to the ad hoc traffic. We note that sensing error does not affect the throughput of the CRN. The destination node first decodes the message from the relay node, and then decodes the source's message, by means of sequential interference cancelation decoding [15]. Therefore, the destination node is still able to decode the messages sent from the source and relay nodes. However, the sensing error may result in additional traffic collisions, which was considered in Reference 14.

15.5   Simulation results

Some simulation results are presented in this subsection to demonstrate the effectiveness of the proposed ergodic CRN spectrum access strategy. The number of channels is 16 ($N = 16$) and the number of ad hoc bands is 4 ($M = 4$). Each ad hoc band overlaps with four consecutive CRN channels, and the four ad hoc bands do not overlap with each other. The time fraction parameter in each frame α is set to 0.5.

The channel coefficients $h_n^{i,j}$ (where $i \in \{s, r\}$ and $j \in \{r, d\}$, $i \neq j$) are modelled as independent and identically distributed Rayleigh fading with zero mean and unity variance. We assume that the relay node is located right in the middle between the source node and the destination node. The large-scale path loss factor of all the wireless links is set to 4. Suppose that the signal-to-interference-plus-noise ratio (SINR) of the source-destination link is set to $P_{max}^s \mathbb{E}\{|h_n^{s,d}|^2\}/(NWN_n^d) = 5$ dB. Assume that $N_n^r = N_n^d$ and $P_{max}^s = P_{max}^r$. Then, the SINRs of both the source-relay and relay-destination links are equal to $P_{max}^s \mathbb{E}\{|h_n^{s,r}|^2\}/(NWN_n^r) = P_{max}^r \mathbb{E}\{|h_n^{r,d}|^2\}/(NWN_n^d) = 17$ dB according to the path-loss factor. The simulation results are obtained by averaging over 500 realisations of NSI (averaging over 500 frames). According to our online spectrum access strategy in Section 15.4.2, the computation and signalling delay is negligible, which means that $\delta \approx 0$ is attained.

Figure 15.4(a) shows the simulation results of normalised long-term average collision time ($\bar{I}/T_f$) versus required long-term average uplink spectrum efficiency $\bar{R}_{min}/(NW)$, for $\lambda T_f = \mu T_f = 1$ for all $m = 1, \ldots, M$. To compare with the proposed ergodic spectrum sharing strategy, we also perform the same simulations with its relay-free and sensing-free counterparts. The performance of the ergodic spectrum sharing strategy using only Phase 1 spectrum sensing is also presented. We can observe from Figure 15.4(a) that the proposed strategy outperforms both the relay-free strategy and the sensing-free strategy. Moreover, the proposed strategy with spectrum sensing in two phases performs better than with only Phase 1 spectrum sensing.

To further examine how the behaviour of the ad hoc traffic affects the performance of the proposed strategy, we define a parameter, called *the relative variation rate of the ad hoc traffic state* or *the relative sensing period of the CRN*, as

$$\varsigma \triangleq \frac{T_f}{\dfrac{1}{\lambda} + \dfrac{1}{\mu}}. \tag{15.38}$$

A small value of ς (that corresponds to small values of λ and μ) implies that the on-off state of the ad hoc traffic changes slowly in each CRN frame. However, the ad hoc traffic state would change many times in each CRN frame if ς is large (that corresponds to large values of λ and μ). Figure 15.4(b)–(d) show the simulation results of normalised average collision time ($\bar{I}/T_f$) versus relative variation rate ς for $\lambda = \mu$ and various values of $\bar{R}_{min}/(NW)$. Since the interference metric of sensing-free strategy is determined by the ratio λ/μ, but not how fast the ad hoc

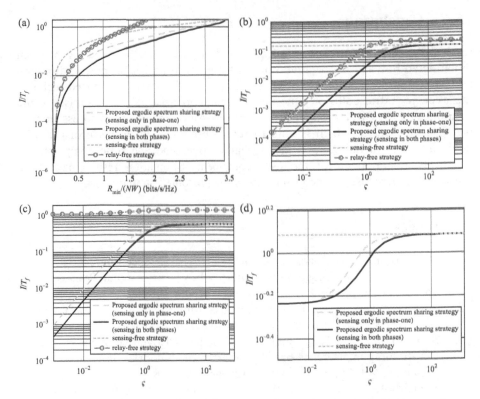

Figure 15.4 Simulation results of the proposed ergodic transmission control strategy of the CRN. (a) Normalised long-term average collision time ($\bar{I}/T_f$) versus required long-term average uplink spectrum efficiency $\bar{R}_{min}/(NW)$; (b)–(d) $\bar{I}/T_f$ versus ς for $\lambda = \mu$ and various values of $\bar{R}_{min}/(NW)$

traffic varies, the normalised average collision time of the sensing-free strategy is constant versus ς. From Figure 15.4(b), one can observe that the proposed strategy performs best. However, the performance gaps between the proposed strategy and the relay-free and sensing-free strategies decrease with ς, because the ad hoc traffic is more difficult to predict for large ς. For very large values of ς, the proposed strategy has similar performance as the sensing-free strategy. Therefore, spectrum sensing provides no further benefit in this case.

We can also see from Figure 15.4(b) and (c) that the performance of the relay-free strategy seriously degrades as $\bar{R}_{min}/(NW)$ increases from 0.6 bits/s/Hz to 1.7 bits/s/Hz. The performance degradation of the relay-free strategy is much worse than that of the proposed strategy because the CRN is capable of supporting higher uplink throughput than the relay-free strategy. In Figure 15.4(d), the results of the relay-free strategy are not shown because this strategy is not feasible in supporting $\bar{R}_{min}/(NW) = 2.8$ bits/s/Hz.

15.6 Conclusion

In this chapter, we have provided an introduction to spectrum sharing between dynamic ad hoc and cooperative relay networks. Physical-layer power allocation and MAC-layer spectrum access of the CRN have been jointly optimised such that the average traffic collision time between the two networks is minimised while guaranteeing the CRN throughput requirement. An online spectrum access strategy has been presented, which is able to realise optimal ergodic performance with negligible control delay, moderate signalling overhead and little computational capability requirement for the user equipment. Simulation results have been presented to demonstrate the efficiency of the presented strategy.

References

1. Q. Zhao and B. M. Sadler, 'A survey of dynamic spectrum access: Signal processing, networking, and regulatory policy', *IEEE Signal Process. Mag.*, vol. 24, no. 5, pp. 79–89, May 2007
2. J. Peha, 'Sharing spectrum through spectrum policy reform and cognitive radio', *Proc. IEEE*, vol. 97, no. 4, pp. 708–719, April 2009
3. S. Geirhofer, L. Tong, and B. M. Sadler, 'Cognitive medium access: Constraining interference based on experimental models', *IEEE J. Sel. Areas Commun.*, vol. 26, no. 1, pp. 95–105, January 2008
4. S. Geirhofer, L. Tong, and B. M. Sadler, 'Dynamic spectrum access in the time domain: Modeling and exploiting whitespace', *IEEE Commun. Mag.*, vol. 45, no. 5, pp. 66–72, May 2007
5. S. Geirhofer, J. Z. Sun, L. Tong, and B. M. Sadler, 'Cognitive frequency hopping based on interference prediction: Theory and experimental results', *ACM SIGMOBILE Mob. Comput. and Commun. Rev.*, vol. 13, no. 2, pp. 49–61, April 2009
6. X. Li, Q. C. Zhao, X. Guan, and L. Tong, 'Optimal cognitive access of Markovian channels under tight collision constraints', *IEEE J. Sel. Areas Commun.*, vol. 29, no. 4, pp. 746–756, April 2011
7. R. Zhang, Y.-C. Liang, and S. Cui, 'Dynamic resource allocation in cognitive radio networks', *IEEE Signal Process. Mag.*, vol. 27, no. 3, pp. 102–114, May 2010
8. S. Geirhofer, L. Tong, and B. M. Sadler, 'A sensing-based cognitive coexistence method for interfering infrastructure and ad-hoc systems', *Wirel. Commun. Mob. Comput.*, vol. 10, no. 1, pp. 16–30, January 2010
9. B. H. Walke, S. Mangold, and L. Berlemann, *IEEE 802 Wireless Systems: Protocols, Multi-Hop Mesh/Relaying, Performance and Spectrum Coexistence*. Hoboken, NJ: Wiley, 2006
10. K. Huang, V. Lau, and Y. Chen, 'Spectrum sharing between cellular and mobile ad hoc networks: Transmission-capacity trade-off', *IEEE J. Sel. Areas Commun.*, vol. 27, no. 7, pp. 1256–1267, September 2009

11. J. Mölsâ, J. Karsikas, A. Kârkkâinen, R. Kettunen, and P. Huttunen, 'Field test results and use scenarios for a WiMAX based Finnish broadband tactical backbone network', *Proceedings of IEEE MILCOM 2010*, San Jose, CA, October 31–November 3, 2010, pp. 2357–2362

12. V. Chandrasekhar, J. G. Andrews, and A. Gatherer, 'Femtocell networks: A survey', *IEEE Commun. Mag.*, vol. 46, no. 9, pp. 59–67, September 2008

13. Y. Sun, X. Zhong, Y. Li, S. Zhou, and X. Xu, 'Spectrum sharing between cooperative relay and ad-hoc networks: Dynamic transmissions under computation and signaling limitations', *Proceedings of IEEE ICC 2011*, Kyoto, Japan, June 2011

14. Y. Sun, X. Zhong, T.-H. Chang, S. Zhou, J. Wang, and C.-Y. Chi, 'Real-time optimal spectrum sharing between cooperative relay and ad-hoc networks', *IEEE Trans. Signal Process.*, vol. 60, pp. 1971–1985, 2012

15. A. Høst-Madsen and J. Zhang, 'Capacity bounds and power allocation for wireless relay channels', *IEEE Trans. Inf. Theory*, vol. 51, no. 6, pp. 2020–2040, June 2005

16. S. Boyd and L. Vandenberghe, *Convex Optimization*. Cambridge, UK: Cambridge University Press, 2004

17. S. I. Resnick, *Adventures in Stochastic Processes*. Boston, MA: Birkhâuser, 1992

18. M. Chiang, S. Low, A. Calderbank, and J. Doyle, 'Layering as optimization decomposition: A mathematical theory of network architectures', *Proc. IEEE*, vol. 95, no. 1, pp. 255–312, January 2007

19. S. Boyd, L. Xiao, and A. Mutapcic, 'Lecture notes of ee392o: Subgradient methods', Stanford University, 2003 [Online]. Available: http://www.stanford.edu/class/ee392o

20. D. P. Bertsekas, *Nonlinear Programming*, 2nd ed. Belmont, MA: Athena Scientific, 1999

21. Y. Sun, Y. Li, X. Zhong, S. Zhou, and X. Xu, 'Resource allocation for the cognitive coexistence of ad-hoc and cooperative relay networks', *Proceedings of IEEE ICC 2010*, Kempton, South Africa, May 2010

22. M. Bazaraa, H. Sherali, and C. Shetty, *Nonlinear Programming: Theory and Algorithms*, 3rd edn. Hoboken, NJ: Wiley-Interscience, 2006

23. N. Z. Shor, *Minimization Methods for Non-Differentiable Functions*. New York, NY: Springer-Verlag, 1985

24. Y. Zhang, S. Liu, Y. Rui, S. Zhou, and J. Wang, 'Channel prediction assisted by radio propagation environments information', *Proceedings of IEEE ICCSC*, Shanghai, China, Februry 2008, pp. 733–736

25. S. Boyd and A. Mutapcic, 'Lecture notes of ee364b: Stochastic subgradient methods', Stanford University, 2008 [Online]. Available: http://www.stanford.edu/class/ee364b

26. K. Marti, *Stochastic Optimization Methods*. Springer, Berlin, 2005

27. J. Tang and X. Zhang, 'Cross-layer resource allocation over wireless relay networks for quality of service provisioning', *IEEE J. Sel. Areas Commun.*, vol. 25, no. 5, pp. 645–656, May 2007

Part IV

Applications and uses of ad hoc networking

Chapter 16*

Quality of service for multimedia applications in mobile ad hoc networks

G. Varaprasad[a]

Abstract

Ad hoc network is a wireless network without having fixed equipment/components. Here, the mobile device functions as an endpoint as well as intermediate point. The intermediate points (devices) are used to forward the message if the two wireless mobile nodes are not within their transmission range. Current communication system is playing an important role to allocate the resources for the multimedia applications. This chapter discusses the various algorithms for the mobile wireless ad hoc networks, which is an efficient method to allocate the resources for the sensitive applications using the weighted fair queue system. This method is very important during the period of network congestion. This system allocates sufficient bandwidth and provides quality of service to the end-users. This chapter also talks about the quality of services at various layers of open system interconnection model. Adaptation schemes provide different levels of service to different classes of traffic. Some of the quality of service schemes propose that the class of traffic should be modified as a result of events occurring in the network. The quality of service driven resource management architecture is used to serve as a system-wide framework within which resource management decisions can be performed in a coordinated fashion. The resource allocation scheme for multimedia applications using mobile agent is used to allocate the resources in the mobile ad hoc network. In addition to that it allocates the resources for hand-off applications and new applications.

16.1 Introduction

Mobile ad hoc Network (MANET) is a multi-hop wireless network, where all nodes cooperatively maintain the connectivity without a centralized system [1]. In

*H. F. Rashvand and H.-C. Chao (Eds.), *Dynamic Ad Hoc Networks*, The IET Book Publishing Department, 2013, ISBN 978-1-84919-647-5, eISBN 978-1-84919-648-2
[a]Department of Computer Science and Engineering, BMS College of Engineering, Bangalore, Karnataka, India

MANET, each node functions as a host as well as router. The node routes the data packets to other nodes. In MANET, it uses portable devices such as PDAs and laptops. These devices have different access patterns. In MANET, different routing protocols use different metrics to route the data packets. The metrics are delay, link-quality, path-length, link-stability, location-stability and power [2]. Presently, the multimedia application has become one of the most promising services. The multimedia applications are keenly interested for stable networks to make Quality of Service (QoS) [3]. The effective utilization of bandwidth for multimedia applications with QoS is certainly one of the major challenges in future generation of networks. The transmission of sensitive applications requires more amount of bandwidth from the server. A large number of data packets are required by many nodes to proceed with the destination. It increases the communication overhead as well as delay. In order to reduce the communication overhead and delay, the system coordinates the various states and provides communication system in a stable manner. The service-differentiation enables the categorization of the traffic into a set of classes to which the network nodes provide priority-based treatment. The service-differentiation can be absolute or relative in nature. The relative differentiation is preferred in the MANETs given that the random node mobility, bandwidth and energy constrained operation. The unpredictable behaviour of radio channels requires a cost-effective solution. In addition, absolute differentiation requires sophisticated admission control and resource reservation mechanisms, which are difficult to achieve in high dynamic MANET. A relative differentiation mechanism supports a small number of the service classes which are simple in terms of implementation, deployment and manageability.

16.2 Characteristics of mobile ad hoc networks

The MANET has characteristics that can be divided into the following sections [4–7].

16.2.1 Unstructured network

The MANET is an unstructured network, where there is no central administration. Each node can communicate with every other. Hence, it becomes difficult to detect and manage the faults. In MANET, mobile nodes can move randomly. The use of this dynamic topology results in route changes, frequent network partitions and possibly packet losses. The MANETs are well suited for use in positions, where resource is not available/deployable. It is not a cost-effective system for communications. One of many potential utilizations of MANET is in some business situations, where two-way computing might be more significant in external office environment than inside. Another characteristic is the unpredictable capacity of bandwidth. In MANET, the wireless links are bandwidth-constrained. Moreover, since wireless links have lower capacity than the wired links, traffic congestion is typical rather than atypical. However, as a MANET is often an extension of a fixed network, the same services and demands must be accommodated where these demands will increase as multimedia computing become more mainstreams.

16.2.2 Distributed system

The MANET uses distributed operation for security, routing and host configuration. The decentralized nature of a MANET requires that any routing protocol should execute in a distributed fashion. It needs an effective distributed management solution in which it can handle the various tasks such as emergency and rescue operations. It can be able to tackle some of the other components of a management system such as resource management, privacy management and key management. Another characteristic is dynamic network. In MANET, the node can freely move from one location to another location and the node mobility lends to unpredictable network topology. These nodes can join or leave the network anytime, making the network topology dynamic in nature.

16.2.3 Mobile host

In MANET, each node acts as a host as well as a router to route the data packets from the source node to destination node. That is autonomous in behaviour and a packet can travel from the source to the destination either directly or through some set of intermediate nodes. Another characteristic is multiple-hop relay. The communication between the nodes is performed by direct connection or through multiple-hop relays. Another characteristic is power constraint. The power conservation is crucial in mobile wireless systems, since these nodes typically operated with limited power, which dictate whether a network is operational or not. In general, the mobile device needs power for three scenarios such as transmission time, receiving time and idle time; so the power constrain is one of major factors in MANETs.

16.2.4 Limited transmission range

The limited radio band results in reduced data rates as compared to the wireless networks. Hence, optimal usage of bandwidth is necessary by keeping low overhead as much as possible. The optimal reception range of a wireless transceiver cannot be represented by a fixed number. Rather, the factors that condition this value change constantly in any practical wireless environments. Different fading methods, some of which are frequency-dependent, have been extensively discussed and the resulting propagation models that can be used for modelling have been developed for different network operational conditions, such as terrain shape, atmospheric conditions and man-made obstacles. Another issue that determines the reception range is the transmission power. Large transmission power can significantly increase the power drainage and reduce the battery lifetime of the node.

Another characteristic is that wireless links are time varying. The MANET environment has to overcome certain issues of limitation and inefficiency. There are transmission impediments like fading, path loss, blockage and interference that add to the susceptible behaviour of wireless channels. The reliability of wireless transmission is resisted by different factors. Another characteristic is network partition. The network partition mostly affects the transitional nodes, and the performance of network will be going down. High mobility nodes need transitional nodes to route the data packets. These transitional nodes will act as critical nodes and the performance of system depends on the critical nodes.

16.2.5 Limited security

Mobile networks are more vulnerable to physical security threats such as eaves-dropping and jamming attacks. The common concerns in MANETs include the access control. There is a need of a method for restricting the access of foreign hosts into the network, which requires the use of a proper authentication method. Moreover, the communication between the insider hosts in the network must be protected from the attacks on confidentiality. If the link-layer does not support a valid encryption scheme, such a scheme must be involved in the network layer also. The group membership is noted in all of the mentioned multicast protocols, but they do not suggest any specific access control or authorization policies. In MANETs, Denial of Service (DOS) attacks must also be mitigated to ensure availability in the network. In MANETs, the malicious nodes may offer a non-existing multi-hop service to redirect traffic incorrectly and cause network congestion if the host is allowed to access the network/resource.

16.3 Applications of mobile ad hoc networks

The interest in MANETs has increased rapidly in recent years because it supports mobility and freedom in the networks. The data packets can be exchanged without wire and access points. Nowadays systems and phone makers implement ad hoc tools to their products. Table 16.1 gives an overview of current and expected appliances of MANETs [8].

16.3.1 Military purpose

It is perhaps deplorable that MANETs were first considered to use in the military. Imagine, a large number of soldiers spread out in a large battlefield and they have to communicate with others. Installing a telephone network in the battlefield or equip each soldier with cable is out of issue. An alternative is to provide each soldier in the battlefield with a transmitter that can reach all other soldiers in the battlefield at all times. The MANET is very well suited for this case. However, the transmitter has a smaller transmission range than the transmitter so that each soldier can only reach a few other soldiers. However, the transmitter is designed so that they can relay messages over single hop or multiple hops. These soldiers would form a network. This kind of network is obviously more robust, harder to intercept and suitable for military communications [8].

16.3.2 Rescue operations

Imagine the condition after a tremor when the communication does not work anymore. An exchange of the unstructured network has to be installed as soon as possible to support rescue operation [9]. It is clear that the installed network has to be simple to configure, easy to set up and maintain. It has to adjust to a dynamic

Table 16.1   Various applications of a typical MANET

Applications	Possible scenarios/services
Tactical networks	• Military communication and operations • Automated battlefields
Emergency services	• Search and rescue operations • Disaster recovery • Replacement of fixed network in case of environmental disasters • Policing and firefighting • Supporting doctors and nurses in hospitals
Commercial and civilian	• E-commerce: Electronic payments anytime and anywhere environments • Business: Dynamic database access, mobile offices • Vehicular services: Road or accident guidance, transmission of road and weather conditions, taxi cab network, inter-vehicle networks • Sports stadiums, trade fairs, shopping malls • Networks of visitors at airports
Home and enterprise	• Home/office wireless networking • Conferences, meeting rooms • Personal area networks • Networks at construction sites
Education	• Universities and campus settings • Virtual classrooms • Ad hoc communications during meetings or lectures
Entertainment	• Multi-user games • Wireless P2P networking • Outdoor Internet access • Robotic pets • Theme parks
Sensor networks	• Home applications: Smart sensors and actuators embedded in consumer electronics • Body area networks • Data tracking of environmental conditions, animal movements, chemical/biological detection
Context aware services	• Follow-on services, call-forwarding, mobile workspace • Information services: Location specific services, time dependent services • Infotainment: Tourist information
Coverage extension	• Extending cellular network access • Linking up with the Internet, intranets etc.

topology in order to support changes in numbers and density of nodes. The MANETs can be set up easily and quickly. The communication on unstructured network in the immediate area of disaster or emergency may be unusable, unavailable or completely destroyed. When emergency responders first arrive in the disaster area, it is critical for them to be able to communicate with other. The communications make it possible for the team members to coordinate the relief operations with other. Since communication on unstructured network is often unavailable, first responders need to be able to establish connectivity immediately. It is well suited for such applications to create connectivity rapidly with limited human effort.

16.3.3   Personal area network and bluetooth

The plan of personal area network is to create a localized network crowded by the network nodes that are closely connected with a single person. Bluetooth is a wireless local network and has small coverage transmission range. It does not need equipment/components or cable to connect end devices.

16.4   Issues in QoS for mobile ad hoc networks

In MANET, nodes are connected through the wireless links that are more prone to errors as compared to wired links. There are problems such as hidden terminal and multipath fading. As opposed to the wired network, there are no separate routers. Generally, mobile nodes are equipped with omnidirectional antennas and therefore transmission of a node is heard by nodes in its vicinity. It causes one more issue – nodes need to coordinate among themselves for transmissions through the shared media. In other words, a node cannot make a decision on it alone about the time of the beginning of a transmission, because the media might be occupied by another node in its vicinity. Therefore, the time taken in waiting for the transmission depends upon the neighbouring nodes contending for the media. In case of wired networks, there is no such issue as the media is not shared. Due to media contention, it is difficult to provide any hard guarantees about the end-to-end delays. Another issue in case of MANETs is that the resources of participating nodes are limited. Therefore, a routing protocol requires extensive computations, and communications may not be a good choice. It should provide QoS and light weight as far as possible and is able to utilize resources in an efficient manner.

16.4.1   QoS metrics

A flow of packets from the source to destination is done either unicast or multicast with QoS. The associated QoS should be best-effort service. A fundamental requirement of QoS is a measurable performance metric. Various QoS metrics are used to evaluate the network performance such as throughput, delay, packet delivery ratio, control overhead and hop count, bandwidth, packet loss rate, packet jitter and stability of link.

Throughput: It is the ratio of number of data packets received (n_r) at time $t + \Delta t$ and number of data packets sent (n_s) at time Δt. Δt is the time taken to send the data packet from the source to destination [10, 11].

$$Throughput = \left(\frac{n_r}{n_s}\right) bps$$

Delay: Delay is the difference between the time taken to receive a data packet $pt + \Delta t$ and time taken to send a data packet pt.

$$Delay = pt + \Delta t - pt$$

Hop count: It represents the total number of nodes a given piece of data packet passes through. Generally, more numbers of hops data packet traverse to reach destination, then greater transmission delay incurred.

Communication overhead: It is the ratio between the control data packets sent and delivery data packets. For analysis of communication overhead, the parameters request-to-send, clear-to-send and the acknowledgement are used. Here, the communication overhead is the ratio between the request-to-send and clear-to-send and acknowledgement.

$$Communication\ overhead = \frac{Request\ to\ send}{Clear\ to\ send}$$

Bandwidth: It presents the information carrying capacity of a node in networks. It is measured by bits per second. It refers to speed of bit transmission in a media or link. The bandwidth-related metrics are capacity, available bandwidth and bulk transfer capacity. The first two metrics are defined both for individual link and end-to-end paths, while the bulk transfer capacity is usually defined only for end-to-end path. The maximum possible bandwidth that a link or path can deliver is called capacity. The maximum-unused bandwidth at a link or path is called available bandwidth. Here, the available bandwidth is focused as QoS metric. The available bandwidth is the amount of bandwidth leftover after the cross-traffic. It can be determined by finding the time period for which the link is not utilized for transmitting data. Estimation of available bandwidth is difficult task in MANETs. Estimation of available bandwidth is as follows:

$$E - Available\ BW = BW\ physical - BW\ consumed$$

When the available bandwidth is estimated, the activities of the neighbours of nodes must be taken into account, since the wireless channel of a node is shared among the neighbouring nodes.

Packet loss: A packet loses due to transmission errors, no route, broken links, network congestions, etc. The effects of these causes are tightly associated with the node mobility, number of connections, traffic load, etc. Even building an approximate model to analytically evaluate packet loss is a difficult task. The packet loss problem is much more complicated in MANETs, because wireless links are subject to transmission errors and the network topology changes dynamically.

Packet jitter: It represents the relative delay between the successive packets arriving at destination. It is a measure of delay in variance. Ideally, jitter should be '0' and each packet must take equal time in travelling from the source to destination. This is not probable in practical environment due to various factors such as queuing delays and network congestions.

Link stability: It is given by its probability to persist for a certain time span, which is not necessarily linked with its probability to reach a very high age. It is to identify stable links in a MANET environment based on the analysis of link durations in several different mobility scenarios.

16.4.2 QoS support in mobile ad hoc networks

In MANET, it may not have more resource (components) or coordinators that determine which node has access to the shared media. Instead, the nodes must enter into contention for access to the media. This contention results in a large amount of collisions, which can result in lost of data or significant end-to-end delay [12]. In QoS scheme for MANETs, it is generally desirable that higher-priority traffic succeeds the contention over lower-priority traffic, and that a minimal amount of time is wasted on contention. Finally, it can be difficult to maintain service guarantees in a network if the nodes are mobile.

16.4.3 QoS in physical layer

With proliferation of wireless mobile nodes, wireless applications, especially wireless multimedia applications, are becoming increasingly dispensable for low-latency applications such as voice and video transmission of crucial missions on battlefields or rescue missions to time-sensitive interactions of multi-player games in daily entertainment. However, multimedia applications have stringent QoS requirements on data rates, delays and delay jitter, which pose major challenges in the wireless links, whose characteristics are unreliable, time-varying and fading [13, 14]. Therefore, it is essential to accurately characterize fading channel and time-varying capacity of the wireless link to facilitate QoS provisioning over MANETs. The physical-layer designers used signal-to-noise ratio (SNR) and bit error ratio (BER) to quantify the performance of MANETs. The MANET communication systems are designed to support constant-bit-rate voice traffic. Hence, queuing theory and queuing performance are not the concerns of physical-layer designers. To represent a different SNR or channel condition, Markov procedure is used to model characteristics of dynamics and statistics of the received SNR over fading channels. Here, each state represents different SNRs or channel conditions. In other words, the physical meaning of the channel state partitioning is to discretely categorize fading channel states according to the SNR, meaning that each partitioning represents a different probability of bit errors, together with state transition probability, which is used to predict the future condition of the channel. The SNR partitions to keep a received packet completely in one state and the following packets in the current state or neighbouring states become a critical issue of channel modelling.

Estimation of BER: Suppose we have a pair of nodes at distance D communicating using transmission signal power P over a wireless channel L with noise power P_{noise} through a medium with propagation constant ∞. The relationship between wireless channel BER and the received power P_{rcv} is a function of the modulation scheme employed. It considers non-coherent binary orthogonal phase shift keying (BPSK) where $P_{rcv} = P/D^8$ and the instantaneous channel BER is thus [15–17]:

$$BER(L) = \left(\frac{1}{2}\right)e^{-(p/D_\propto)1}/P_{noise}.$$

It computes the BER of multi-hop connections under an end-to-end retransmission scheme. The BER of a connection C, which traverses links $L_1, L_2, \ldots, L_k$ can then be computed as follows:

$$BER(C) = \prod_{i=1}^{k} BER(L_i)$$

In contrast, the network designers use data rate, delay bound, delay-bound violation probability, or packet loss ratio to quantify the performance of packet-based networking devices and networks. Since wired networks such as Internet are built on inherently reliable, low noise communication channels, the network designers are not interested in SNR, BER, communication theory and information theory as the physical-layer designers. With the emergence of broadband packet-based wireless networks and increasing demand of multimedia information on the Internet, wireless multimedia services are predicted to become widely deployed in the next decade. To support multimedia transmission over wireless channels, it is important to consider both the physical-layer QoS (SNR) and the networking-layer QoS (e.g. delay performance). Both the physical-layer bit errors and networking-layer buffer overflow can cause errors, which negatively affect the upper-layer multimedia applications.

16.4.4   QoS in data link and network layers

We describe the literature work reported on QoS at the MAC layer. The following major MAC layers for MANETs are Carrier Sense Multiple Access with Collision Avoidance (CSMA/CA), IEEE 802.11 and Time Division Multiple Access (TDMA). The CSMA model is one of the most widely used MAC layer in MANETs. Here, the nodes contend for the channel until the channel becomes free. The data packets that are marked real time have priority over non-real-time packets and a node that wishes to transmit real-time packet has a priority for access to the channel over the nodes that have non-real-time packets. A MAC protocol called sticky CSMA/CA provides implicit synchronization and real-time QoS in wireless mesh networks. In a MANET that is based on TDMA, the notion of bandwidth is related to free time slots available along a link for transmission. The number of free slots is decided by the neighbours' transmission/reception activities. Therefore, reservation of resource from the source to destination implies reservation of time slots that are free and are available for sending packets [18].

Some actions can be taken in the physical layer to improve QoS. In [27] Reference 27, an architecture is proposed which combines QoS reservation and scheduling at the MAC layer with Adaptive Modulation and Coding (AMC) at the physical layer. In AMC, the method for transmission varies when the link quality changes. For example, if the link quality degrades, then the physical layer may start transmitting using BPSK instead QAM-16. As a result, more time will be required to send the same amount of data, so the MAC layer must adjust its scheduling accordingly. Using this scheme, throughput performance closely matches the performance of the medial. When the link quality is good, it will take less amount of time to transmit QoS-guaranteed traffic as compared to link when quality is bad. At these times, there will be more resources available to transmit best-effort traffic. As a result, the total bandwidth is well utilized in the network. At the network layer the identified QoS requirements are call-blocking probabilities, call connection delays, packet congestion probabilities and packet loss rates. A method for call admission control that is based on multi-criterion reinforcement learning is used to maximize the average revenue of the network subject to call level as well as packet level QoS. This scheme can handle multiple QoS constraints. At the network layer, there is a service-differentiation scheduler that assigns different network resources to different classes. Several routing protocols are proposed in the literature work with a provision of QoS at the network layer. Their objectives differ due to their different requirements and strategies. In bandwidth-estimation-based routing, it finds a feasible route from the source to destination without taking into account current traffic in the network or specific requirements of an application. As a result, the network may become overloaded and the requirements of a real-time application that requires a support for QoS may not be met. Therefore, there seems a need to estimate the traffic in the network so that a feedback can be provided to the application in case when its requirements cannot be met. In interference aware routing, a QoS routing protocol that guarantees the bandwidth for MANETs with interference is considered. The protocol addresses the problem of ad hoc shortest widest path protocol. A routing protocol that is aware of the interference is renamed as interference-aware QoS routing. Here, several paths are probed using flow packets in a distributed fashion for meeting QoS. The paths that satisfy QoS are known as candidate paths. The best path is chosen by the destination node in terms of QoS among all paths. In position-based QoS routing, the geographical region is divided into squares of equal size and is called grid. Here, every vehicle possesses a digital map and knows its geographical position and the direction of its movement through Geographical Positioning System (GPS). The intermediate nodes remember the route till it is broken. In backbone-based QoS routing, it is aimed to satisfy bandwidth requirements of a flow from a given source to a destination. The protocol consists of three steps such as core extraction, link-state propagation and route computation. In the core extraction, a group of nodes are elected to form the core of the network in a dynamic and distributed fashion by using approximate algorithm for minimum dominating set. A core node is responsible for maintaining the local topology of the nodes in its domain and it also computes the routes for these nodes.

16.4.5 QoS in transport and application layers

The following metrics are used to evaluate QoS routing protocol performance [19].

Session acceptance/blocking ratio: The percentage of application data sessions (or transport layer connections) that are admitted into or rejected from the network. The value of this metric rejects both the effectiveness of the QoS protocols as well as conditions outside of their control such as link quality.

Session completion/dropping ratio: It represents the percentage of applications that were successfully (unsuccessfully) served after being admitted into the network. For example, if a VoIP session is accepted, then the session is completed properly by the users hanging up and not aborted due to route failure or any other error, and therefore that counts as a completed session.

16.5 QoS architecture for resource management

Three decision makers can participate in resource management system. They are the users/applications, resources and system. The goal of QoS-driven resource management architecture is to serve as a system-wide framework within which resource management decisions can be performed in a coordinated fashion. It believes that a proactive, system-wide entity, which we call the resource manager, must implement the system policies, coordinating the application, resource and system-level resource management decisions. The performance and objectives of the system is expressed in terms of application-level QoS, and a common definition of QoS should serve as the glue that unifies the various decision makers. Figure 16.1 shows the different models and their relationships to each other [20].

16.5.1 Application invocation model

The application invocation model holds the information that the user or the application on behalf of the user supplies when an application is invoked. It has a benefit function, which captures the user's QoS preferences for a given application. If the resource manager receives a request to perform an application, then the requestor

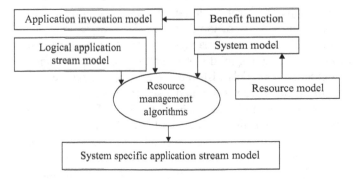

Figure 16.1 QoS architecture for resource management

supplies information on the basis of which the resource manager performs resource allocation and scheduling. The requestor supplies the desired values of the QoS parameters and information concerning the relative importance of these values in the terms of a benefit function. It has developed the benefit function to model an application's QoS requirements and preferences. The benefit function is a multi-dimensional graph specifying the benefit that the user receives, if the system provides a certain level of QoS. The system uses this information to provide QoS level that maximizes the application benefit. The benefit function is especially useful to facilitate a graceful degradation of the application QoS if the resource availability does not allow the system to provide the minimal QoS [21].

16.5.2   Logical application stream model

Logical Application Stream Model (LASM) captures an application's structure, resource requirements and relevant QoS parameters. It is independent of any system attributes or user requirements. Therefore, LASM may be used by multiple users, who want to invoke the same application with different QoS requirements. The application can be viewed as a set of algorithms that execute in a specific order that is defined during the design time. This order specifies the data flow within the application. It defines a single-layered model that is represented as a directed graph, where the vertices represent application components and the edges represent application flows and control data. From the perspective of the resource manager, each component indicates QoS transformation of the data, which flows through it. Associated with this transformation is the resource demand model, which describes the resource usage requirements of the component as a function of the QoS of the incoming data and the desired QoS of the outgoing data. The end-to-end QoS of the application is a composite of individual QoS transformations.

16.5.3   Resource model and system model

The resource model captures resource-specific information that is needed by the resource management algorithms. The resources represent the smallest grouping of hardware/software over which the resource manager has full control. It does not specify the precise granularity of the resources, because it allows the system designer flexibility to determine the level of granularity when QoS-driven resource management is executed. The purpose of the system model is to describe the outline of the system resources and to impose a management structure onto the system resources. A management structure is required that will allow for the definition of independent management domains. It models distributed systems by using hierarchical structure. The resources form the bottom layer and a set of resources monitored by a single resource management method forms a subsystem. A set of subsystems monitored by a single resource management method forms a higher-level subsystem and it is called parent subsystem. The parent subsystem sees all the resources and child subsystems within it as black boxes, whose internal composition is hidden. This hierarchical representation enables us to model heterogeneous systems running under different network protocols, operating systems and resource management methods.

16.5.4 Single layer model

In here a distributed application will view as a set of tasks executing in a specific order on a particular computing, storage, and communication resources. Algorithms running on computing resources, data transfer over communication resources and data transfer to and from storage resources all denoted tasks, using this view. It further denotes an atomic task as a Unit of Work (UoW). From the resource management perspective, each UoW within the application transforms the application QoS. This decomposition of an application into UoWs that transform data and QoS is a fundamental concept of application model. The UoWs are the smallest components of applications that are used for allocation and routing. The LASM captures application attributes at a logical or system-and user QoS-independent level. The structure of a single-layered LASM is represented using directed graph. Here, graph nodes correspond to Logical Units of Work (LUoW) and graph edges denoted Logical Edges (LE), dictating order in which LUoWs are executed. It will capture application QoS relationships using Logical Constraints (LC) set. The QoS parameters that must be allocated at the invocation by the user are declared in Logical Parameter (LP) set. The LASM is signified in aggregate as a tuple, LASM = (LUoW, LE, LC, LP). A simple example of LASM model is given in Figure 16.2. It describes a teleconference application. The video is captured and encoded using JPEG encoding transmitted over the network, decoded, synchronized with the audio and displayed. Similarly, the audio is captured, transmitted, synchronized and played.

16.5.5 Recursive model

This recursive LASM model further facilitates application restructuring and facilitates the modelling of large-scale applications. The structure of a recursive LASM is also represented using a directed graph. Graph nodes now correspond to Logical Services (LS). Each LS is recognized using Logical Realization of Service (LRoS), which is composed of either a set of child LS executing in a specific order or a single LUoW. The LUoWs are not decomposable. The structure of an LRoS is the same to that of an LASM, in that it is represented using the directed graph, where the graph nodes also correspond to LS and graph edges correspond to LE. An LRoS also has LC and LP sets. In addition, it has Import Data (ID) and Export Data (ED) sets to specify data sent from and to the LS to its LRoS. It is recursive because LS is realized by an LRoS,

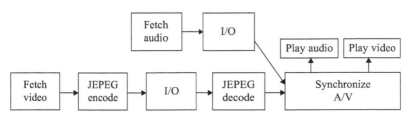

Figure 16.2   Single-layered logical application stream model for a teleconference application

which in turn is composed of a set of child LS, which in turn may each be realized by an LRoS. The recursion terminates when an LS is realized using LUoW.

16.6 Adaptation schemes

QoS-enabled networks provide different levels of service to different classes of traffic. Some QoS schemes propose that the class of traffic should be modified as a result of events occurring in the network.

16.6.1 Adaptive management

The network occurs, such as the admission of new clients or a degradation of link quality. In Reference 22, it is proposed to maintain the service level for high-priority traffic when these events occur by modifying the class of the traffic in response to the events. In this system, the traffic is divided into a number of priority classes where some classes get a greater fraction of the channel than others. The priority of traffic is specified, but not necessarily any other service guarantees. If a new client is added, then all other clients of the same class will receive a lower level of service. In order to receive the same level of service, some or all clients should raise their priority level. Whether the clients raise their priority level should depend on the application that is being used and the perceived QoS of the end-users. There is a limit to the amount of increased service a client can get by raising its priority class. In order to provide an acceptable level of service to all clients, simple admission control must be employed to block new clients if the media is fully loaded.

16.6.2 Dynamic class selection

The mainly distinguished problem with class adaptation is that it can create a position in which all clients are increasing their priority in a greedy way to the point where some or all of clients would not receive the desired level of service. An evaluation of this problem is presented in Reference 24. The flows will alter their class in response to past performance of that class. For example, if the desired throughput or delay was not met in the last slice of time, then the flow will increase its priority. The method is addressed as an extension to the IEEE 802.11e enhanced distributed coordination function (EDCF) that the priority increased by reducing the inter-frame spaces. The results show that this scheme outperforms EDCF in terms of throughput and delays in all cases except for ad hoc peer-to-peer communication with throughput lower bounds around 90 Kbps and up. A significant part of this analysis is a game theoretic evaluation, which shows that the clients can alter their class in a greedy way. All clients will still receive the desired service quality given there are sufficient network resources available.

16.7 Scheduling for multimedia for streaming

The scheduling model is important component in the provision of guaranteed QoS parameters. The design of scheduling algorithms for MANETs is a challenging one because of highly variable link error rates and dynamic nature. The schedulers are broadly classified as centralized and distributed schedulers. The distributed schedulers are suitable for MANETs [25, 26].

16.7.1 Static group-server scheduling

In the static group-server scheduling, a client schedules group-server instances at the time when it requests media content based on the current location, velocity and direction.

Let us consider a client i which requests a specific media data. First, server needs to be a single-hop peer of i as the first server starts streaming at time t_0. Thus, client i selects the best server instance, i.e. the peer with the largest value of $E_{ij} \forall j \in N_{to(i)}$.

Let us consider server is j_1 and client i schedules j_1 at time t_0. If the expected time duration is less than the required period, i.e. $E_{ij_1} < S/B$, then the client needs to find more server via multi-hops. It defines t_x as time when the link with j_x will break down. Since the link with j_1 is expected to break at time t_1, the client needs to find a server, which will provide a link at t_1. To achieve this, the client broadcasts queries within H hops. From information obtained by the queries, the client knows the set of available servers at time $t_1 - \delta t$. Here, δt is the required changing time denoted as $N_{t1} - \delta t(i)$. By measuring the link duration, the client finds the best server (j_2), which has the longest link duration starting from $t_1 - \delta t$. The client can change the server from j_1 to j_2 at $t_1 - \delta t$. If $t_2 \geq S/B$, then it can download whole media data from j_1 and j_2. Otherwise, it again finds a server until $t_k \geq S/B$. If the client cannot find group server $\{j_1, j_2, j_3, \dots, j_k\}$ to satisfy $t_k \geq S/B$, then the media streaming fails.

16.7.2 Dynamic group-server scheduling

In the dynamic group-server scheduling, the group-server scheduling is dynamically configured during the media streaming process. It improves the performance of the static case as it is comparatively easier to forecast near future link availability compared with the availability into the more distant future. In addition, a peer may move in a completely dissimilar route from what is expected. Therefore, the static scheduling scheme may not work well in highly mobile backgrounds. With dynamic group-server scheduling, a client i selects the first server j_1 among $N_{t0}(i)$ to download a media data starting from t_0. Client i periodically sends queries to the server to obtain its speed and way and update the expected link duration. The query interval is determined by a threshold. If the expected link duration of the server j_1 is less than the threshold, then the client tries to find a new server by broadcasting queries within H hops. By querying the server every interval, a client can change server before the link breaks. If the link with server j_1 will break at t_1, the client obtains the best server (j_2) among $N_{t1} - \delta t(i)$ peers. The client moves the server to download the media data at $t_1 - \delta t$ to keep the media streaming process continuous. The client repeats this approach until the whole file is downloaded. In case, no server can be found when the link disconnects, the media streaming will fail.

16.7.3   Waited fair queue scheduling

Waited fair queue (WFQ) scheduling provides a dynamic fair queue by dividing the resource based on the weight of traffic packets. It is a flow-based algorithm that simultaneously schedules interactive traffic to the front of a queue and reduces the response time. The WFQ model uses the traffic priority management system and sorts dynamically the traffic into messages that makes conversation. The WFQ model breaks up the flow of the packets within a conversation to ensure that the bandwidth is shared fairly among all users. The packets are transmitted in a timely way. The WFQ model differs from the round-robin method in that each class may receive a differential amount of service at any point of time. First, the model serves the queue with the lower weight. It functions as a work-conserving queue model and provides QoS for the end-users. The model reserves the bandwidth/resource for a particular client. It also provides a minimum guaranteed bandwidth/resource for every class. The remaining bandwidth will be divided proportionally to the reserved classes. The high-priority classes can be defined to have higher priority services for allocation of the bandwidth and resources. The probabilistic performance depends on the admission control algorithm. It is particularly important during the period of the network congestion. Under the WFQ model at any point in time, the class 'i' packets is transmitted with $W_i/(SW_j)$.

$$F(i,k,t) = Max\{F(i,k-1,t), R(t) + P(i,k,t)\}$$

Here, $P(i,k,t)$ is a size of packet and k is a packet number in the ith connection. $R(t)$ is a round number for $(k-1)$th packet. In the WFQ model, ith connection is revised by using $P(i,k,t)/\phi(i)$, instead of $P(i,k,t)$, where $\phi(i)$ is a factor for ith connection as follows:

$$F(i,k,t) = Max\{F(i,k-1,t), R(t) + P(i,k,t)/\phi(t)\}$$

The WFQ model ensures the service-differentiation over the multiple QoS among all classes at a network component (node). Hence, the problem is to develop scheduling (bandwidth allocation) and buffering management policies that each node can use to serve the multiple classes in order to satisfy the QoS. The system constraints such as maximum available buffer size, time-varying, link capacity are used to measure the system performance. The bandwidth allocation can be viewed as an optimization problem performed in a distributed way. The WFQ model classifies the packets into different queues based on the source-destination pair, source-destination ports, socket number and type of service value. The arrival rate of the packet is classified and has been kept in the queue. It uses the weight factor to determine the order of the queues that is emptied. The scheduler serves the packets in a circular manner (class 1, class 2, class 3 and so on) as shown in Figure 16.3.

The WFQ model is used to provide output packet scheduling services such as absolute priority queuing, minimum rate guarantee, shaping and bonding group dynamic bandwidth sharing on the network component. It is analysing the behaviour of WFQ model properly. This is the most multi-class feedback control scheme proposed for the computing servers to the date performance guarantees by logically allocating a separate fraction of the server bottleneck resource to every class of traffic.

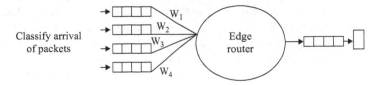

Figure 16.3 Weighted fair queue model

16.8   Support for multimedia applications

The real-time multimedia communication between the peers is described by imposing QoS constraints on the underlying networks. Examples of such constraints are minimum bandwidth, maximum delay and jitter requirements. In the Internet, increase in the file-sharing peer-to-peer traffic was not accompanied with a similar growth in terms of peer-to-peer multimedia traffic due to a lack of global QoS support from the network itself. In MANETs, all nodes must be constantly adapting to varying link quality towards neighbours and also to change in network topology. In such a situation, it is extremely hard to achieve guaranteed communication between the peers [23]. The situation becomes even more difficulty, if some of the sources generate more traffic with QoS requirements.

16.8.1   Support for jitter-constrained applications

It is coupled with jitter bandwidth measurement events, measuring jitter after bandwidth probing ends and only when necessary [25]. The source node must send packets with the size, IP TOS field value and data rate chosen by the application for 250 ms [26]. The receiving end, aware of the source packet-sending rate by explicit notification, calculates the mean and standard deviation values for jitter and returns them to the source. These measurements are only performed if the application's traffic is blocked, and they are performed only after delay and bandwidth probes, if both tests return a positive case. In case, the traffic from the application is already flowing through the network, there is no need to send jitter probes. In that situation, the destination can measure the jitter of the actual traffic received and send back to the source, since all applications are bounded with jitter requirements such as bandwidth and delay. It will use the first echo reply packet of delay measurement probe to carry the information from the destination to source. It avoids further probing if we find that the jitter requirements are not being met. Once traffic is admitted, the source will obtain statistics relative to delay and jitter every 1.5 s. Independent of the scheme used to measure jitter, once the source receives jitter statistics it will assess compliance with the maximum value requested by the application since jitter follows a normal distribution with a mean value of zero, about 95 per cent of the cases.

16.8.2   Support for delay-constrained applications

The method used to measure delay as part of distributed admission control mechanism is similar to the measurements made by a ping command divided by two round-trip times. Relative to ping command, the main difference in distributed admission control mechanism is that a new echo request packet when sent immediately after receiving an echo reply packet will reduce as much as possible the time used to perform measurements. The echo reply packet should have the same length and the same IP TOS field as that of echo request. The value of IP TOS in delay probes is the same and is requested by the application. The delay probes are grouped with bandwidth probes except when traffic is accepted and starts flowing. In those positions, it will send delay probes twice more often than bandwidth probes every 1.5 s on average instead of every 3 s, since it allows assessing the state of the path more frequently with just a little additional overhead. According to the previous analysis, it requires at least three consecutive round-trip times to obtain a consistent value. We start with four successive rounds of ping/pong delay probes to assess the end-to-end delay. The value of the first round is dropped since it is used as a warm-up round to trigger routing and find end-to-end bidirectional paths if necessary. The results from the remaining three rounds are averaged and stored. During the end-to-end probing process, any of the probe packets is lost, then the end-to-end path is considered to be broken and the traffic is blocked thereby concluding that round of probing. If it successfully finishes the delay probing tasks, then it proceeds to assess available bandwidth following the strategy defined in the previous section.

16.8.3   Support for bandwidth-constrained applications

The support for bandwidth-constrained applications is achieved with the periodic end-to-end measurements of available bandwidth using probes. It always configures bandwidth probes so that probe packets are mapped to the video MAC access category independent of the type of service registered by the application. We can avoid higher priority connection that causes the degradation of ongoing connection with low priority, if both connections are generated by the same user. Therefore, sharing the same node proposes a probabilistic strategy to reach a bandwidth-related verdict according to probe measurements. It will reduce the number of probes required to take a decision to a value as low as two probes. Such a fast decision occurs often in those situations where it becomes quickly evident that the available bandwidth is either much higher or much lower than the requested one. The maximum number of probes allowed per cycle is set to five, if after sending five probes still no decision can be reached. We maintain the previous path state. If a connection is waiting for admission, then it will remain blocked and if it is active it will remain active. Such criteria increase the stability of the system. In terms of applications with bandwidth constraints requesting distributed admission control mechanism services, their traffic are only accepted if a positive verdict is reached based on the bandwidth measurements. Since MANETs are environment prone to frequent packet losses, both the source and destination must accommodate to this event. Relative to distributed-admission control mechanism agent at the source, it keeps a timer to be able to react in case a probe reply is never received. This timer is set to go off 500 ms after sending the probe. If no probe reply is received, causing the timer to be triggered, or in the case that the probing process is completed successfully, the source will schedule a new probing cycle after 3.5 s and 500 ms of jitter to avoid possible negative effects due to probe synchronization. This value was carefully chosen taking into account the typical topology change rates and intends to offer a balance between the performance drops caused by poor reaction times.

16.9   Resource allocation scheme for multimedia applications using mobile agent

The resource allocation scheme for multimedia applications using mobile agent is used to allocate the resources in the MANET. In addition to that, it allocates the resources for hand-off applications as well as new applications.

16.9.1   Network graph

A graph $G = (N,L)$ is finite non-empty set of nodes and links. N consists of nodes $\{A,B,C,D,E,F,G,H,S\}$, L consists of links $\{(A,G,S), (G,S,H,C), (B,H,S), (H,B,D), (S, C,E,F)\}$ as shown in Figure 16.4. The network model is represented by adjacency matrix and is defined as:

$$Z_{ij} = \begin{cases} 1 & \text{if } (i,j) \; \varepsilon \; L \\ 0 & \text{Otherwise.} \end{cases}$$

$$b = \left(\sum_{k=1}^{y} pusize/(at_{k+1} - at_k) \right)/y \tag{16.1}$$

$$d = \left(\sum_{k=1}^{y} (at_{k+1} - st_k) \right)/y \tag{16.2}$$

$$d/dy = \left(\sum_{k=1}^{y} (at_{k+1} - at_k) - (at_{k+2} - at_{k+1}) \right)/y \tag{16.3}$$

$$l = plost/y \tag{16.4}$$

Equations (16.1)–(16.4) are boundary parameters for bandwidth, end-to-end delay and rate of change in delay with respect to d and presentation units loss.

16.9.2   Mobile agent

The mobile agent paradigm is considered as one of the mobile computing models. The mobile agent architecture is shown in Figure 16.5. It dynamically reallocates the resource by tracing mobile node. Aglets are created through proxy using getAgletContext() and createAglet() commands. The proxy provides the location for Aglet via proxy using its current location (local or remote). The mobile agent migrates from one node to other to discover the resources for a given

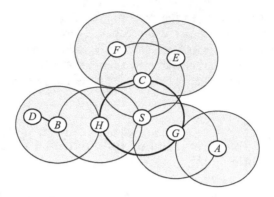

Figure 16.4   Network model

source-destination pair. The agent marks the visited nodes along with resource information to visited list. It exchanges information through the local agents for further usage.

```
Agletcontext ac=getAgletContext();
AgletProxy Proxy=ac.createAglet(null, "AnAglet", null);
URL destination=new URL("atp://localhost:5000/");
AgletContext ac=getAgletContext();
AgletProxy proxy=ac.create(null, "AnAglet", null);
proxy=proxy.dispatch(destination);
proxy=ac.retractAglet(destination,proxy.getAgletID());
proxy.dispose();
```

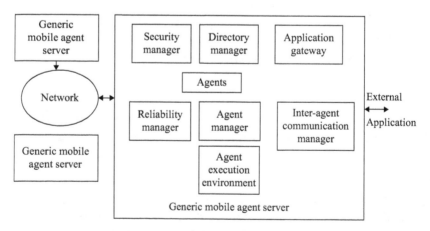

Figure 16.5   Mobile agent architecture

16.9.3   Manager agent and database

The mobile agent is an independent platform and is executed in a heterogeneous network. The communication and co-operation of other agents are used for achieving their goals. The mobile agent updates its information while interacting with others. The inter-agent communication has been done through the remote procedure calls and sends the information about the resource to the database. The mobile agent resides in the database and is mainly used to find the alternate path and captures resources. The manager agent holds bandwidth reservation for an application. The database contains the information of connected links and the bandwidth capacity of each link. The agent uses the database and passes information to others. The affected multimedia applications are transmitted over the alternate paths.

16.10   Conclusion

To support multimedia applications, it is desirable that the wireless communication has a provision of QoS. However, the provision of QoS in the MANET is a challenging task. This chapter presents a review of the current research related to the provision of QoS in the MANET environment. It examines issues and challenges involved in providing QoS in the MANETs. It has also discussed methods of QoS provisioning at different levels including those at the levels of routing, MAC and cross-layer. It has presented schemes for admission control and scheduling that are proposed in the literature for the provision of QoS. The resource allocation scheme for multimedia applications using mobile agent is used to allocate the resources in the MANET. In addition to that it allocates the resources for hands-off applications and new applications. This chapter has discussed a recursive logical application stream model that can be used by a resource manager to structure each end-to-end application, allocate resources to each application and schedule these applications on these resources; later when the system state changes, the resource manager can use this model to dynamically reallocate, reschedule and restructure these applications. The chapter has also discussed two group-server scheduling schemes, static group-server scheduling and dynamic group-server scheduling, for continuous media streaming among mobile ad hoc peers. Here, a client downloads the multimedia content from group server instances, which allows the user to continuously stream media content even if the link with the current server instance breaks up. Finally, it can be difficult to maintain service guarantees in a network if the nodes are mobile. The WFQ model breaks up the flow of the packets within a conversation to ensure that the bandwidth is shared fairly among all users. The packets are transmitted in a timely way. The WFQ model differs from the round-robin method in that each class may receive a differential amount of service at any point of time.

References

1. Varaprasad G. 'Efficient power aware routing algorithm for mobile adhoc networks'. *ACM Wireless Communications and Mobile Computing* (Special Issue on Recent Advancement in Wireless Ad Hoc and Sensor Networks). 2012;12(1):1–6
2. Bheemalingaiah M., Naidu M. M., Rao S. D., Varaprasad G. 'Power-aware node-disjoint multipath source routing with low overhead in mobile ad hoc network'. *International Journal of Mobile Network Design and Innovation* (Special Issue on Mobile Ad-Hoc Networking). 2009;3(1):33–45
3. Varaprasad G., Wahidabanu R. S. D. 'Quality of service model for multimedia applications in a mobile ad hoc network'. *IEEE Potentials*. 2011;30 (2):44–47
4. http://epubs.glyndwr.ac.uk/cair/29/
5. Chlamtaca I., Contib M., Liuc J. N. J. 'Mobile ad hoc networking: Imperatives and challenges'. *Ad Hoc Networks*. 2003;1:63, 64
6. Kumar M., Mishra R. 'An overview of manet:history, challenges and applications'. *Indian Journal of Computer Science and Engineering*. 2012;3 (1):121–125
7. http://www.eexploria.com/manet-mobile-ad-hoc-network-characteristics-and-features/
8. Hoebeke J., Moerman I., Dhoedt B., Demeester P. 'An overview of mobile ad hoc networks: applications and challenges'. *Journal of the Communications Network*. 2004;3:60–66
9. http://www.antd.nist.gov/wahn_mahn.shtml
10. Sivaraman R., Dhulipala S. V. R., Sowbhagya L., Prabha V. B. 'Comparative analysis of QoS metrics in mobile ad hoc network environment'. *International Journal of Recent Trends in Engineering*, 2009;2(4):68–70
11. Hanzo-II L., Tafazolli R. 'A survey of QoS routing solutions for mobile ad hoc networks'. *IEEE Comm. Surveys and Tutorials*. 2007;9(2):50–70
12. www.cse.wustl.edu/~jain/cse574-06/ftp/wireless_qos.pdf
13. Liao R., Tu W., Excell S. P., Grout V. 'QoS analysis models for wireless networks'. *Proceedings of Collaborative Research Symposium on Security, E-Learning, Internet and Networking;* Darmstadt, Germany, 2009. pp. 181–190
14. http://www.wu.ece.ufl.edu/projects/EffectiveCapacity/EC.html
15. Brahim G., Al-Fuqaha A., Guizani M., Khan B. 'A model for cooperative mobility and budgeted QoS in MANETs with heterogeneous autonomy requirements'. *Proceedings of IEEE GLOBECOM;* New Orleans, USA, November 2008. pp. 1–5
16. Loyka S., Gagnon F. 'Performance analysis of the v-blast algorithm: An analytical approach'. *IEEE Transactions on Wireless Communications*. 2004;3(4):1326–1337
17. Nosratinia A., Hunter T. E., Hedayat A. 'Cooperative communication in wireless networks'. *IEEE Communication Magazine*. 2004;42(10):74–80

18. www.citeseerx.ist.psu.edu/viewdoc/download?doi=10.1.1.174
19. Suri P. K., Maan S. 'Towards evaluation of effect of dos attacks on jitter in mobile ad-hoc networks carrying packet telephony'. *International Journal of Computer Science and Telecommunications.* 2011;2(4):31–34
20. Chatterjee S., Sydir J., Sabata B., Lawrence T. 'Modeling applications for adaptive QoS-based resource management'. *Proceedings of HASE*; Menlo Park, USA, August 1997. pp. 194–201
21. Sydir J.J., Chatterjee S., Sabata B. 'Providing end-to-end QoS assurances in CORBA-based system'. *Proceedings of ISORC;* Menlo Park, USA, April 1998. pp. 53–61
22. Hakima C., Anelise M. 'Adaptive QoS management for IEEE 802.11 future wireless ISPS'. *Wireless Networks.* 2004;10(4):413–421
23. Wang K., Ramanathan P. 'QoS assurances through class selection and proportional differentiation in wireless networks'. *IEEE Journal on Selected Areas in Communications.* 2005;23(3):573–584
24. Calafate C. T., Cano J. C., Manzoni P., Malumbres M. P. 'A QoS architecture for MANETs supporting real-time peer-to-peer multimedia applications'. *Proceedings of IEEE International Symposium on Multimedia;* Irvine, USA, December 2005. pp.193–200
25. Calafate C. T., Manzoni P., Malumbres M. P. 'Supporting soft real-time services in MANETs using distributed admission control and IEEE 802.11e technology'. *Proceedings of IEEE Symposium on Computers and Communications*; La Manga del Mar Menor, Spain, June 2005. pp.217–222
26. Sakai K., Ku W., Zimmermann R. 'Group-server scheduling for continuous multimedia streaming in MANETs'. *Proceedings of IEEE International Symposium on Multimedia;* San Diego, December 2009. pp.400–405
27. Liu Q., Zhou S., Giannakis G. B. 'Cross-layer scheduling with prescribed QoS guarantees in adaptive wireless networks'. *IEEE Journal on Selected Areas in Communications.* 2005;23(5):1056–1066

Chapter 17*

Road traffic management: traffic controllers, mobility and VANET

Hossein Ghaffarian[a], Mahmood Fathy[a] and Mohsen Soryani[a]

Abstract

With a long history, traffic controllers have great impact in our lives. In this chapter, we review five critical components in controlling traffic. We show that how different elements of these components can affect the traffic systems. Also, we present a quick review on mobility models, from communication engineers' and traffic engineers' perspectives. We show how these views are different from each other's. Intelligent transportation system (ITS) and its presence in the traffic controllers are the next topic of this chapter. Architecture of macroscopic and microscopic traffic controllers is explained too. Finally, we review the current issues in collaboration between VANET and traffic controllers before the conclusion of the chapter. The reviewed issues are deploying VANET infrastructures and using VANET-based P2P networks in traffic information systems.

17.1 Introduction

Traffic systems and traffic light controllers are inseparable parts of our daily life. Looking into the history indicates that the use of the traffic controller devices certainly began before the dawn of recorded history [1]. Milestones, a form of the traffic controller devices to show directions to travellers, are the first devices used by the ancient Roman road builders. The first signal lights were used 2,600 years ago as a guide returning fishermen to their tribes. The history of the modern traffic controllers started in the late nineteenth century at railroads. At the beginning of the twentieth century, Britain has started to use the first generation of the current traffic lights. They were semaphores with colour disks [2]. At the end of 1920s, the first traffic

*H. F. Rashvand and H.-C. Chao (Eds.), *Dynamic Ad Hoc Networks*, The IET Book Publishing Department, 2013, ISBN 978-1-84919-647-5, eISBN 978-1-84919-648-2
[a]The Hardware Group, School of Computer Engineering, Iran University of Science and Technology, Narmak, Tehran, Iran.

controllers in the current shape and format were introduced in England. After that, the traffic lights became public and were established all around the world.

Traffic system and its characteristics are the main elements affecting mobility of vehicles. As shown in Figure 17.1, in a typical city and its traffic system, there are road users, different types of roads, vehicles, intersections and signalling. All of these components interact with each other. The road users and the vehicles must obey traffic rules. The traffic rules are applied for safety and convenience of the road users and drivers. The rules are assigned based on the characteristics of the road, the intersections, the road users and the vehicles. They come to reality by using different types of the road signs and the signalling systems. And finally, all of these are just for better life.

Vehicular ad hoc Network (VANET) is a subdivision of ad hoc networks. In these networks, nodes of the network are vehicles. Although the vehicles can run in different geographical locations, their movement is restricted by the traffic rules and the road characteristics. While they can move very fast in the highways, their speed reduced significantly by law in residential regions.

Different elements can disturb VANET. Using VANETs, the vehicles can communicate *Vehicle to Vehicle* (V2V) along a road. Environmental obstacles, such as buildings, can stop this communication. Another affecting element is intersection. Suppose that two vehicles i and j drive on a road in the same direction. Also, they are equipped with VANET equipment. If these vehicles stand in the communication range of each other, they can make a V2V VANET (Figure 17.2(a)). Now suppose that the vehicle i passes a junction, but j could not. After a while,

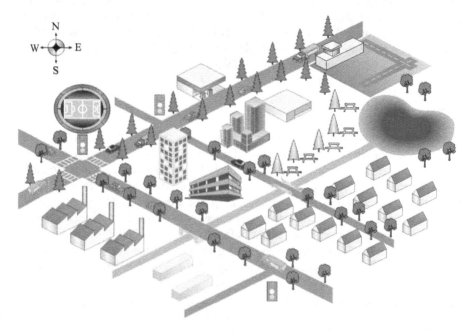

Figure 17.1   A typical city and its traffic system

(a)

(b)

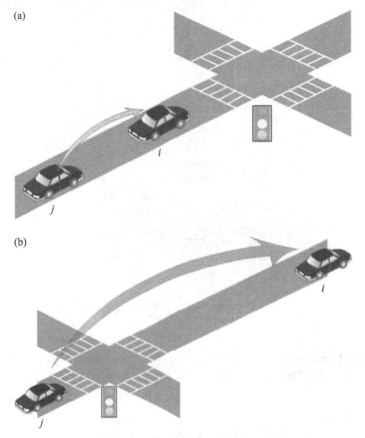

Figure 17.2   The effect of intersection on VANET

it is possible that i and j might not be in the communication range of each other. Therefore, their link is broken (Figure 17.2(b)).

In this chapter, we are looking to investigate the mutual effects of the traffic systems, especially intersections and VANET. To do this, first we present an overview on components of the traffic system and their characteristics. Mobility is affected by the traffic signs and controllers. We talk about this effect too. Also, we review that how this effect is presented in current mobility models. After all of these, a classification of the traffic control systems is prepared. The impact of VANET on the traffic management is discussed as follows. And at the end, we talk about the current issues in this area.

17.2   Components of traffic system and their characteristics

To understand how the traffic system affects mobility, it is important to understand how the various elements of a traffic system interact. There are five critical

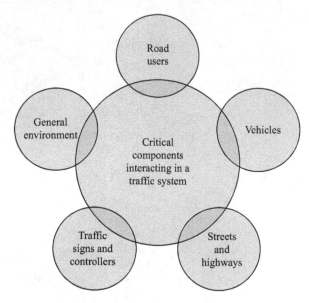

Figure 17.3   Critical components that interact in a traffic system

components that interact in a traffic system [3]: road users, vehicles, streets and highways, traffic signs and controllers and general environment (Figure 17.3).

17.2.1   Road users

Different characteristics of human can influence on driving. The main category of the road users is drivers. Key task in the traffic engineering is preparing enough information for the drivers to induce safe and proper responses. Among the different characteristics of drivers, visual acuity factors and reaction process are the main. However, other human abilities, like hearing, and characteristics of the vehicle and the road are important in safety too. The other category of the road users is pedestrian. Age and psychology status of the pedestrians, their personalities and how much they obey the rules are key factors in their mobility. Alcohol and drugs have great impact on the road users' capabilities too. The impact of these items on safety is different in various societies. Therefore, individual social investigations are necessary in each society.

17.2.2   Vehicles

Hundreds of millions of vehicles in the world induce enough interest in engineers to think about safety. Different types of the vehicles have different size, weight and operating characteristics. Their main characters in safety are engine capabilities for acceleration, turning characteristics and passive and active safety systems. These characteristics affect manoeuvre capabilities of the vehicles.

17.2.3   Streets and highways

Accessibility and mobility are two services provided by the roads. Traffic engineers should design specific roads to provide good accessibilities and load balancing in different zones, which tend to movement and mobility. To do this, roadway systems are classified into four categories [3]. Limited access facilities, such as freeway, have no direct access to abutting lands. Arterials permit some limited access to neighbouring lands. Local streets are designed to provide full access to abutting lands. The last category is collector that is between arterials and local streets. The local streets are divided into rural and urban streets. Subcategories of urban roads are residential, commercial and industrial. Drivers follow their trip in these categories and subcategories. While their movement is free in the first category, it is too restricted in the local streets. The main considerations in the road design are forecast demand volumes, patterns of development, topography, natural barriers, surface conditions, drainage patterns and economic and environmental and social considerations [3].

Curves in the roads affect the mobility too. In Reference 4, authors simulate a 2000 metre road, where there is a curve in the middle of this road. They use *Freeway* mobility model [5]. The vehicles must reduce their speed to the minimum allowable speed near the curve. The average density of the vehicles along the road is drawn in Figure 17.4. As shown in this figure, the traffic intensity around the curve is rapidly increased.

17.2.4   Traffic signs and controllers

The traffic signs and controllers are the main elements for speed reduction along the travel path. Using the traffic signs, the drivers have to drive with predefined

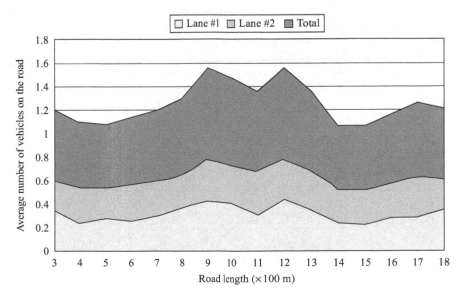

Figure 17.4   The effect of curve on the mobility [4]

limitations. For example, they cannot stop at specific places, e.g. at bus stops or near the junctions, or they should tune their speeds on different types of roads. The traffic light controllers affect the mobility too. While vehicles are free to pass the junctions during green light intervals, their movement is limited in the yellow light intervals. The movement is forbidden in the red light intervals. For safe stopping before the junctions, width of the junction and clearing the back end of the vehicle past the far intersection line are important in the light timing [3].

17.2.5 *General environment*

General environment, like weather conditions, lighting, density of developments and local policies, play key roles in the traffic management. Although most of the time these factors are considered qualitatively, the quantitative information is available to assist judgement in some situations. This happens because it is difficult to assess this information in any situation [3]. An example of such quantitative system is presented in Reference 6. Authors have combined intelligent transportation system (ITS) traffic data with archived weather data of I-4 region in Central Florida. By this, they have developed a crash prediction model for rainy weather in that area.

17.3 **Mobility models**

Modelling is a well-known tool to analyse different systems. By developing the traffic controllers, the first mobility models were introduced during the 1930s–1950s [7]. Researches show that, by adding the number of vehicles, performance of the traffic controllers is reduced 35–40 per cent [8]. In the traffic engineering, there are several proposed models for the mobility. Here, we first review the mobility models proposed by VANET researchers. Then we investigate the proposed models by the traffic engineers. Although most of the models in the first category are proposed to track the behaviour of the vehicles in an area, in the second category, we just review the proposed models for the traffic modelling at the intersections.

Vehicular mobility models are divided into two categories: *microscopic* and *macroscopic* [9]. In microscopic mobility models, the vehicles are considered as distinct entities. In this category, characters like position, length of the vehicle, velocity, acceleration, power engine and so on are key elements to model the behaviour of the vehicle. In macroscopic category, the overall behaviour of the traffic is looked in a bigger area. Parameters like speed boundaries, average speed, flow rate and density of the vehicles are considered in these models.

To generate realistic patterns of motions for the vehicles, following blocks should be considered in a mobility model [7]:

- Accurate and realistic topological maps consisting of different types of the roads, the intersections and their related limitations
- Obstacles on the roads
- Attraction and repulsion points in different regions, especially start and destination points of a trip

- The vehicle characteristics as discussed in Section 17.2.2
- Path of a trip
- Smooth and not sharp acceleration or deceleration
- Human driving patterns in the roads and the intersections, during breaking and over taking and traffic jams
- Management and control of the intersections
- Time pattern of trips in different days
- External influences such as temporal working areas or accident influence on mobility

While looking at the above list, we can find a strong relation between these blocks and five critical components of a traffic system, which is discussed in the previous section.

There are different surveys on mobility models. The survey in Reference 9 is an extensive and complete reference in this area. Readers can find different traffic models along with deep discussion on their properties in that paper. In Reference 10, authors focus on mobility models in ad hoc networks. Some of the reviewed models, such as *City Section* [11] and *Reference Point Group* (RPG) mobility model [12], are used in VANET. Another survey in this area is Reference 13. This survey, as a book chapter, is based on Reference 5. Authors try to introduce more categories in the models while keeping generality of a book chapter. Therefore, they directly talk about details of different mobility models. A good survey and taxonomy in mobility models for VANET are presented in Reference 7. Authors of this paper prepare a deep discussion on the necessities of mobility models and pros and cons of different category of the models. A brief and almost complete review for mobility models in VANET world is presented by Fiore [14]. This report presents many of the common mobility models of VANET in different categories.

By reviewing those surveys and models, it can be seen that the effects of the critical components of the traffic system, especially the intersections, are not modelled. For example, in the stochastic models group, in the *City Section* and *Manhattan* [5] mobility models, the vehicles pass the intersections without any limitations. They move over each other. There is no intersection in freeways and *Freeway* mobility model. In the RPG, followers just follow the group leader. *Real Track* mobility model [15] is derived from *Virtual Track* model [16]. In this model the whole map of the area is presented as a graph of switches and edges. Switches present intersections, and roads are presented by edges. The vehicles follow the RPG model along the edges. In the switches, they use *Random Waypoint* mobility model [17] to select the next switch. However, this model never validate against real data.

The traffic engineers go in a different way in modelling. One of the key models for the intersection traffic is proposed by Makigami *et al.* [18]. They present a 3D model. These dimensions are time, position and total number of the vehicles. Baras *et al.* [19] and Mirchandani and Zou [20] present different Markov models for the intersection modelling. Baras *et al.* have modelled queues of urban traffic. The model proposed by Mirchandani Zou is used to adopt timing of the traffic lights in an intersection. List and Cetin [21] use petri net to model the traffic controllers. *Car following* models [22] are considered as the main traffic engineering reference models. The goal of these models is avoiding any contact with the leading vehicle. For this reason, these models use set of rules. These models use time continuous models in their modelling. In Reference 23, these models are classified into five categories: *GHR, psycho-physical, linear, cellular automata* and *fuzzy logic*.

By comparing the proposed models by the communication engineers and the traffic engineers, it can be seen that their view to mobility is far different. Although focusing to the traffic flow models is common between both of them, it can be seen that the details of the critical components of the traffic systems and movement are not important in the communications as much as the traffic engineering.

For more clarity, let's have a look to the mobility simulation in famous network simulators. A deep discussion in this area is prepared in Reference 7. Authors of this paper investigate 26 different mobility model generators in detail. Also, they talk about more than 15 different network simulators. By reviewing the network simulators, it can be seen that even the well-known network simulators, such as NS-2 [24], OPNET [25], OMNet++ [26] and Qualnet [27], do not support embedded traffic movement generators. According to Reference 7, there are only a few network simulators that have embedded mobility generator. GrooveSim/GrooveNet [28], MoVes [29], AutoMesh [30] and NCTUns [31] fall in this category.

In the case of safety, a tight collaboration between network simulator and traffic generator is necessary. While traffic engineers focus on the detail of traffic movement and safety, it seems current network simulators cannot provide a realistic platform in this area. Due to coarse-grained network simulation part, traffic safety applications still have no chance for entering into the area of network simulators [7].

17.4   ITS and controlling traffic

Intelligent transportation system (ITS) refers to the application of modern telecommunications technology to the operation and control of the transportation systems [3]. In the 1990s, the common isolated traffic controllers have failed to control traffic efficiently. To cover this, ITS has been proposed. The used architecture for this consists of three parts: intelligent traffic controllers, communication infrastructures and *Traffic Control Centre* (TCC). In this architecture, the communication platforms transfer raw information of the traffic, gathered by the traffic controllers, to the processing systems in the TCC. After processing, they return the processed information to the intelligent traffic controllers. Using this architecture, the whole traffic system can work better than the previous one.

In addition, by adding wireless communication equipment to the vehicles, the vehicles can collaborate with this architecture. To support the vehicles, different wireless technology, such as satellites, cellular phones, WiMAX, *Long-Term Evaluation* (LTE) and mode of vehicle to infrastructure of VANET, can be used. Among these technologies, the cellular phones and VANET receive more attractions. The infrastructure of the cellular phones is widely installed all around the world. Therefore, no additional cost for infrastructure is needed. Because of long delay in the cellular networks, delay tolerant applications such as traffic management can be served on them. But they are not recommended for safety applications. VANET can answer to the needs of this type of applications.

To investigate the effects of ITS, we divide the traffic controllers into two groups: macroscopic and microscopic. In the former, we review some proposed ITS systems to control a big area. In the latter, we focus on the use of ITS in the traffic controllers in the isolated intersections.

17.4.1 Macroscopic controllers

The macroscopic controllers control wide areas in cities. They try to improve traffic movements in these areas. To do this, parameters like density of the vehicles and average speed of them are investigated. The detailed information of each vehicle is not necessary in these systems. As shown in Figure 17.5, the overall architecture of the macroscopic control systems consists of distributed agents and the controllers, the communication network and the TCC.

TRANSYT is an example of macroscopic controllers which have been installed in England. It controls the scheduling of traffic lights in a city. The big problem of this system is the required time to find the optimized scheduling. To overcome this problem, SCOOT is proposed [32]. SCOOT stands for *Split, Cycle and Offset Optimization Technique*. However, success of such controllers depends on the good work of the agents.

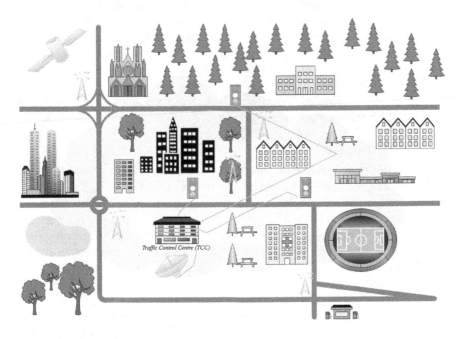

Figure 17.5 The macroscopic traffic controller covers large areas in cities

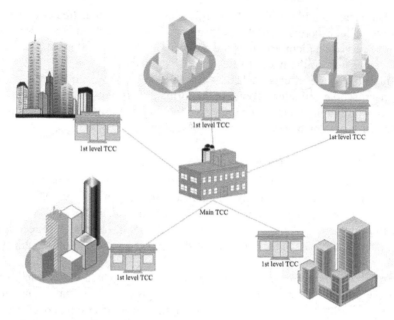

Figure 17.6   Hierarchical architecture of macroscopic TCC

The major problem in the macroscopic systems is the volume of information. By increasing the size of the under control area, the number of vehicles in the area is increased. Gathering and processing large amount of data are costly and time-consuming process. Hierarchical architecture is the answer. The gathered data is processed in small areas and then the processed information is sent to the upper level. By this, unnecessary information is removed in the first steps of processing locally. Figure 17.6 shows an example of such a hierarchical architecture. As an example, in Reference 33, a Fuzzy-Neural controller is proposed. Each level consists of isolated controllers. The proposed controller can re-learn Fuzzy rules in different levels.

17.4.2   Microscopic controllers

Although the macroscopic controllers can work well by gathering the information of the whole area, the cost of communication and processing is high. The economic plans may reject the installation of them in small cities and rural areas. The microscopic controllers are installed in an isolated mode in small areas like inter-sections, i.e. the intersection which is shown in Figure 17.7. They work locally. They try to improve traffic individually. Improving traffic movement in isolated intersections increases overall performance of a network of intersections [34]. However, it is possible to send some information from individual controllers to the other controllers or the central offices.

In the microscopic controllers, parameters of each vehicle are investigated individually. Also, the distances are low and time is restricted. Therefore, these controllers need real-time and accurate information. Different sensor types installed

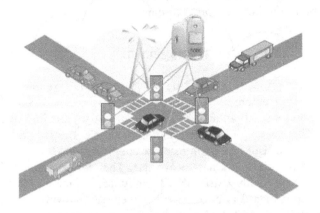

Figure 17.7   Microscopic TCC

in the road sides, like optical diodes, and embedded wireless equipment installed in the vehicles, like VANET, form the agents of this architecture. Wireless networks, like IEEE 802.11 family, form the main infrastructures of the communication networks. The controller is installed in the intersections, near the traffic lights. The installed controller in the intersection tries to reduce waiting time and stops in the intersection. To do this, having knowledge about the average length of vehicles, size of the area of the intersection and the average speed of the vehicles in the intersection is important. Adding some facilities for different types of the vehicles, like ambulances or police cars, can make more complexity in the controller.

In References 35–37, authors propose a multi-agent-based controller for the intersections. Their idea is based on a reservation area, called patch. To avoid collision, new movement of the vehicles in the patch must be guaranteed first. For this guaranty, according to the current and future information of the position of the vehicles in the intersection area, the traffic controller calculates the next position of the vehicle. This concept is followed in Reference 38. In Reference 34, a signalling scheduling algorithm for the isolated intersections is proposed. The proposed approach, namely *Longest Queue First–Maximal Weight Matching* (LQF–MWM), is based on the well-known switching algorithms, MWM and LQF, in computer networks [39]. The LQF tries to serve the longest queues first and the MWM tries to achieve the maximum weight of transferred packets. Instead of the packets, in Reference 34 the vehicles are passed across the intersection.

Simple intelligent ILP-based traffic controller (SI^{2}BTC) is introduced by Ghaffarian *et al.* [40]. In this controller, authors propose to gather information of vehicles using VANET. The heart of the proposed approach is an ILP optimizer. To ensure about safety, they modify proposed safe driving idea in Reference 41. The SI^{2}BTC tries to replace the traffic lights by VANET infrastructures completely. However, the authors do not extend their model to multi-lane intersections. Authors of Reference 42 use VANET to gather traffic information arriving to an intersection. Based on this data, a central controller adopts green light time such that waiting time in the intersection is minimized.

17.5   VANET and traffic management

As mentioned in the previous section, the wireless networks are the first option for communication infrastructure of the traffic systems. In the macroscopic controllers, each vehicle produces small amount of data in time. Also, this information can be non-real-time. Therefore, long-range long-delay wireless networks, i.e. cellular networks, are selected. But in the microscopic controllers, real-time information is mandatory. Also, the used data has local value. Therefore, low-range high-speed wireless networks, especially IEEE 802.11 family, are the main option.

IEEE 802.11p standard is developed to cover requirements of VANET. The standard can provide at least 3 Mbps speed. In the standard, the communication channel is divided into 100 ms time slots. Each time slot is divided into two 50 ms sub-slots: central *Control Channel* and six *Service Channels*. Safety messages can be transmitted in CCH intervals with default frequency of 10 Hz. Frequency of safety packet is important. In Reference 43, authors investigate the effect of frequency of packet generation and number of equipped vehicles to VANET tools in accident prevention.

From economic view, adding VANET to the traffic controllers is acceptable. Recent studies [44] show that VANET can boost the capacity of the roads by as much as staggering 273 per cent. They focus on that how number of VANET-enabled vehicles can make effect on this boost. By adding equipment of VANET to the microscopic traffic controllers, as supposed in Reference 40, we do not need to install the agents in the road sides. However, those agents can be used to confirm received data to make better decisions. In addition, to reduce the implementation cost of VANET, it can be connected to the Internet. By this, value-added services, like e-shopping, ecommerce, online games and weather forecast, can be run in VANET platforms.

If VANET wants to play a role in the traffic control systems, it must connect to the infrastructures. Therefore, we first talk about VANET infrastructure deployments and then we investigate how P2P VANET can be used in traffic information systems.

17.5.1   VANET infrastructure deployment

Deployment of infrastructures of VANET is a real challenge. The upper bound of direct communication range of VANET is 1,000 m. Different obstacles in the surrounding environment restrict the direct communications between nodes of VANET. Therefore, the installation cost of infrastructures is high and we can't cover a large area with too many VANET infrastructures. Low market penetration is another restriction factor in deployment. To review the proposed deployment strategies, we divide them into two categories: bottom-up deployments and top-down deployments.

In bottom-up deployment strategies, the researchers try to find the best placement for antennas, without any consideration about the applications. One of the primary works in this area is proposed in References 45 and 46. The basic of these strategies is that if we deploy infrastructures in the intersections, the maximum number of vehicles in the range of antennas can be achieved. Therefore, they select the intersections with highest waiting time as deployment points. This strategy is followed in Reference 47. In Reference 48, a deployment strategy for multi-operator infrastructure planning is proposed. This idea uses game theory with values of infrastructure capacity, interference and vehicle flows as inputs. The focus of the proposed ideas in References 49–52 is improving connectivity between vehicles to improve performance of VANET. Deployment based on connectivity and power saving in antennas is proposed in Reference 53. In none of these papers, the authors don't focus on specific applications and their requirements. They just focus on information propagation, especially in single hop communications.

Todays, top-down service-oriented network design methodologies, i.e. *Cisco Service Oriented Network Architecture*, take into consideration. Similar strategies can be found in VANET. As an example, in Reference 54, a cooperative scheduling strategy for download is proposed. The basic of this strategy is based on the prediction of future travel path of the vehicle and information on deployment of antennas along the roads. As second category of deployment strategies, we focus on the deployment of VANET infrastructures based on application requirements.

In Reference 55, authors prepare analytical calculations to minimize the average number of hops between vehicles and infrastructures and satisfy quality of service for real-time services like VoIP and video streams. Other analytical approaches for antenna placement are presented in References 56 and 57. Their main focus is on finding the best deployment to satisfy delay boundaries. Security issues are important in networks. In Reference 58, authors propose two algorithms to find the best placement for minimum number of antennas in a large area. Their goal is updating security certificates before their expirations.

Infrastructure planning for traffic safety and management is other interesting application. More integration between VANET and traffic management systems will provide more attractions for infrastructure planning. In Reference 4, the authors focus on safety issues in the curved roads. Their proposed strategy tries to maximize covered area using k antennas. Their goal is minimizing the delay of transmission of safety packets in the curved roads. Roadside placement for data gathering in a traffic information system is discussed in Reference 59. To reduce the necessary bandwidth, the proposed approach uses data aggregation in a hierarchical manner. This approach is good for the hierarchical TCCs. In Reference 60, authors propose a new approach for deployment based on mobility pattern. In this work, first, a mobility graph is prepared to capture mobility pattern of vehicles in an area. Then a deployment strategy is proposed such that a desired meeting probability is satisfied.

Finding best deployment points in large areas is costly and time consuming. If we have n possible installation points and k antennas, the search area has $n \times (n-1) \times \ldots \times (n-k+2) \times (n-k+1)$ different search patterns. Therefore, we can see that in different proposed strategies, greedy [45, 46], heuristic [52] and evolutionary [4, 47, 59] approaches are used.

17.5.2   VANET, P2P and traffic information systems

New challenges in urban traffics force the necessity of a permanent improvement in the efficiency of the traffic information systems. This objective covers different aspects of the traffic systems, from monitoring, control and management of the traffic to providing different information for the road users. Highly dynamic nature of the traffic, increasing demands for the traffic information between the road users and sophisticated traffic management systems, all depend on the real-time traffic data. As mentioned in the Section 17.5.1, infrastructure VANET is useful in this area.

Although the current traffic systems work in client-server modes, *Peer to Peer* (P2P) VANET is a new introducing approach for using in the traffic systems. Centralized and client-server approaches suffer from bottleneck and even single point of failure in the server side. P2P networks work cooperatively in a distributed manner. Also, they are highly scalable. Therefore, they are good option to overcome issues of centralized systems. In a P2P network, nodes create an *overlay network*, a logical application layer graph. In overlay, each node has up to 10 neighbours. Using different approaches, like *Distributed Hash Table* (DHT), P2P networks can store and retrieve the traffic information efficiently.

The traffic information has strong correlation, especially to the geographical information. Therefore, in classical DHTs, there are several key relating to each other. Finding these relations can help to improve the efficiency of the store and retrieval applications. Therefore, the key problems in VANET-based P2P traffic systems are deploying the overlay and enhancing search mechanism in store and retrieving application to respond to the queries with different key values.

The overlay construction approaches can be divided into three categories: designing the overlay on vehicles, designing the overlay on infrastructures and hybrid approach. In the first approach, each vehicle, as a peer, is responsible to act as part of the P2P system to make the overlay network. The vehicle is responsible to cover one part of the road, namely zone. All joining and leaving in the zone is managed by the responsible node. Because of highly dynamic nature of the mobility of the vehicles, if the zone depends on the current position of the vehicle, the overall P2P system fails soon. Therefore, the zone is geographical position free. The movement of the vehicle does not affect the responsible node(s)/peer(s) of each zone. However, this strategy is not efficient. The availability of the responsible is a real challenge in this approach. This can happen because of the distance between the responsible and its zone or setting off the responsible. Figure 17.8 shows a typical VANET-based P2P traffic information system. The zones are depicted as transparent clouds and the overlay is shown as circles above the map of the roads. Logical links between the responsible peers are presented as dashed lines. Authors of References 61 and 62 propose P2P traffic information systems from this category.

The second approach is planning the overlay on the infrastructure. Using this approach, the responsible (an antenna in this case) always serves to the nearest

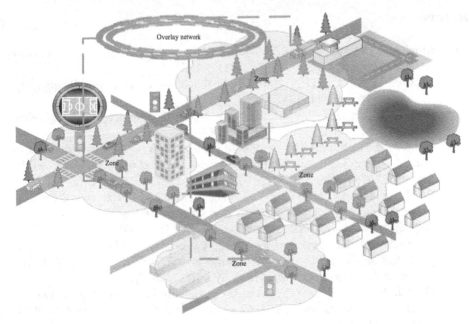

Figure 17.8   A typical VANET-based P2P structure in a traffic information system

zone. Also, we can use more processing power in stationary stations rather than mobile stations. However, as discussed in Section 17.5.1, deployment of infra-structures is costly. Therefore, it seems in the large areas using hybrid approaches is the best answer. Because of this, we can divide the area into k subareas, where k is the number of antennas. Then each subarea can be divided into some zones; each zone has its responsibility. Using this strategy, we have a multi-tier P2P network. Examples of hybrid P2P overlay networks for traffic information systems are pre-sented in References 63 and 64.

17.6   Conclusion

In this chapter, we have reviewed the traffic management and its five critical components. Also, we have prepared an overview on mobility models from VANET researchers and traffic engineers' perspectives respectively. Next, we have discussed about the ITS and its effect on the traffic controllers. We have divided the controllers into two groups: macroscopic and microscopic. We have tried to show the overall architecture of each group. At the end, we return to VANET and show that how we can use VANET in the traffic management systems. By using infrastructure VANET connected to the Internet, we can get more services to the users and reduce the installation costs. Finally, we have reviewed on VANET infrastructure deployment strategies and the P2P traffic information systems.

References

1. Mueller E. A., 'Aspects of the history of traffic signals'. *IEEE Transactions on Vehicular Technology.* 1970; 19(1):6–17
2. Breckenridge F. C., 'Fifty years of signal lighting'. *Illuminating Engineering Society;* 1958. pp. 311–17
3. Roess R. P., Prassas E. S., McShane W. R., *Traffic Engineering,* 3rd ed. New Jersey, USA: Pearson Prentice Hall, 2004
4. Ghaffarian H., Soryani M., Fathy M., 'Planning VANET infrastructures to improve safety awareness in curved roads'. *Journal of Zhejiang University Science C (Computers & Electronics).* 2012; 13(12):918–28
5. Bai F., Sadagopan N., Helmy A., 'The IMPORTANT framework for analyzing the impact of mobility on performance of RouTing protocols for Adhoc NeTworks'. *Ad Hoc Networks.* 2003; 1(4):383–403
6. Abdel-Aty M. A., Pemmmanaboina R., 'Calibrating a real-time traffic crash-prediction model using archived weather and ITS traffic data'. *IEEE Transaction on Intelligent Transportation Systems.* 2006; 7(2):167–74
7. Harri J., Filali F., Bonnet C., 'Mobility models for vehicular ad hoc networks: A survey and taxonomy'. *IEEE Communications Surveys & Tutorials.* 2009; 11(4):19–41
8. Hong Y. S., Jin H., Park C. H. K., 'New electrosensitive traffic light using fuzzy neural network'. *IEEE Transaction on Fuzzy Systems.* 1999; 7(6):759–67
9. Helbing D., 'Traffic and related self-driven many-particles systems'. *Reviews of Modern Physics.* 2001; 73(4):1067–141
10. Camp T., Boleng J., Davies V., 'A survey of mobility models for ad hoc network research'. *Wireless Communications and Mobile Computing.* 2002; 2(5):483–502
11. Davies V., 'Evaluating mobility models within an ad hoc network', Master's thesis, Colorado School of Mines, Colorado, 2000
12. Hong X., Gerla M., Pei G., Chiang C. C., 'A group mobility model for ad hoc wireless networks'. *2nd ACM International Workshop on Modeling, Analysis and Simulation of Wireless and Mobile Systems;* 1999. pp. 53–60
13. Bai F., Helmy A., 'Chapter 1: A survey of mobility models in wireless adhoc networks'. In *Wireless Ad hoc and Sensor Networks;* Kluwer Academic Publisher, 2004
14. Fiore M., 'Mobility models in inter-vehicle communications literature'. Politecnico di Torino, 2007
15. Zhou B., Xu K., Gerla M., 'Group and swarm mobility models for ad hoc network scenarios using virtual tracks'. *Military Communications Conference;* 2004. pp. 289–94
16. Nandan A., Tewari S., Das S., Gerla M., Kleinrock L., 'Adtorrent: Delivering location cognizant advertisements to car networks'. *Third Annual Conference on Wireless On-demand Network Systems and Services;* 2006. pp. 203–12

17. Johnson D. B., 'The dynamic source routing protocol for mobile ad hoc networks'. draft-ietf-manet-dsr-09.txt, 2003

18. Makigami Y., Newell G. F., Rothery R., 'Three-dimensional representation of traffic flow'. *Transportation Science*. 1971; 5(3):302–13

19. Baras J. S., Levine W. S., Lin T. L., 'Discrete time point processes in urban traffic queue estimation'. *IEEE Transaction on Automatic Control*. 1979; 24 (1):12–27

20. Mirchandani P. B., Zou N., 'Queuing models for analysis of traffic adaptive signal control'. *IEEE Transaction on Intelligent Transportation Systems*. 2007; 8(1):50–59

21. List G. F., Cetin M., 'Modeling traffic signal control using petri nets'. *IEEE Transactions on Intelligent Transportation Systems*. 2004; 5(3):177–87

22. Panwai S., Dia H., 'Comparative evaluation of microscopic car following behavior'. *IEEE Transaction on Intelligent Transportation Systems*. 2005; 6(3):314–25

23. Brackstone M., McDonald M., 'Car-following: A historical review'. *Transportation Research Part F: Traffic Psychology and Behaviour*. 1999; 2(4): 181–96

24. The Network Simulator – ns-2. [Online]. www.isi.edu/nsnam/ns/

25. OPNET. [Online]. www.opnet.com

26. OMNeT++ Network Simulation Framework. [Online]. www.omnet pp.org

27. QualNet - SCALABLE Network Technologies. [Online]. www.scalable-networks.com/content/products/qualnet

28. GrooveNet Hybrid-Network Simulator for Vehicular Networks. [Online]. http://mlab.seas.upenn.edu/groovenet/

29. MOVES (Motor Vehicle Emission Simulator). [Online]. www.epa.gov/otaq/models/moves/index.htm

30. Vuyyuru R., Oguchi K., 'Vehicle-to-vehicle ad hoc communication protocol evaluation using realistic simulation framework'. *Fourth Annual Conference on Wireless on Demand Network Systems and Services*; 2007. pp. 100–06

31. NCTUns 6.0 Network Simulator and Emulato. [Online]. http://nsl.csie.nctu.edu.tw/nctuns.html

32. Robertson D. I., Bretherton R. D., 'Optimizing networks of traffic signals in real time – The SCOOT method'. *IEEE Transaction on Vehicular Technology*. 1991; 40(1):11–15

33. Choy M. C., Srinivasan D., Cheu R. L., 'Cooperative, hybrid agent architecture for real-time traffic signal control'. *IEEE Transactions On Systems, Man, And Cybernetics—Part A: Systems And Humans*. 2003; 33(5):597–607

34. Wunderlich R., Liu C., Elhanany I., Urbanik T., 'A novel signal-scheduling algorithm with quality of service provisioning for an isolated intersection'. *IEEE Transaction on Intelligent Transportation Systems*. 2008; 9(3): 536–47

35. Dresner K., Stone P., 'Multiagent traffic management: A reservation-based intersection control mechanism'. *3rd International Joint Conference on Autonomous Agents and Multiagent Systems*; New York, USA. 2004. pp. 530–37

36. Dresner K., Stone P., 'Multiagent traffic management: An improved intersection control mechanism'. *4th International Joint Conference on Autonomous Agents and Multiagent Systems*; Utrecht, The Netherlands. 2005. pp. 471–77

37. Dresner K., Stone P., 'A multiagent approach to autonomous intersection management'. *Journal of Artificial Intelligence Research*. 2008; 31(1):591–656

38. Mehani O., Fortelle A. de L., 'Trajectory planning in a crossroads for a fleet of driverless vehicles'. *11th International Conference on Computer Aided Systems Theory*; Las Palmas de Gran Canaria, Spain. 2007

39. McKeown N., Mekkittikul A., Anantharam V., Walrand J., 'Achieving 100% throughput in an input-queued switch'. *IEEE Transaction on Communication*. 1999; 47(8):1260–69

40. Ghaffarian H., Fathy M., Soryani M., 'Vehicular ad hoc networks enabled traffic controller for removing traffic lights in isolated intersections based on integer linear programming'. *IET Intelligent Transport Systems*. 2012; 6(2): 115–23

41. Li L., Wang F. Y., Kim H., 'Cooperative driving and lane changing at blind crossings'. *IEEE Intelligent Symposium*; Las Vegas, Nevada, USA. 2005. pp. 435–40

42. Chang H. J., Park G. T., 'A study on traffic signal control at signalized intersections in vehicular ad hoc networks'. *Ad Hoc Networks*, Elsevier, 2012, http://dx.doi.org/10.1016/j.adhoc.2012.02.013

43. Busson A., Lambert A., Gruyer D., Gingras D., 'Analysis of intervehicle communication to reduce road crashes'. *IEEE Transactions on Vehicular Technology*. 2011; 60(9):4487–96

44. Tientrakool P., Ho Y. C., Maxemchuk N. F., 'Highway capacity benefits from using vehicle-to-vehicle communication and sensors for collision avoidance'. *IEEE Vehicular Technology Conference*; 2011. pp. 1–5

45. Cruces O. T., Fiore M., Casetti C., Chiasserini C.-F., Ordinas J. M. B., 'A max coverage formulation for information dissemination in vehicular networks'. *IEEE International Conference on Wireless and Mobile Computing, Networking and Communications*; Marrakech, Morocco. 2009

46. Cruces O. T., Fiore M., Casetti C., Chiasserini C.-F., Ordinas J. M. B., 'Planning roadside infrastructure for information dissemination in intelligent transportation systems'. *Elsevier Computer Communications*. 2010; 33(4):432–42

47. Cavalcante E. S., Aquino A. L. L., Pappa G. L., Loureiro A. A. F., 'Roadside unit deployment for information dissemination in a VANET: An evolutionary approach'. *Proceedings of the Fourteenth International Conference on Genetic and Evolutionary Computation Conference Companion*; ACM, New York, NY, USA, 2012. pp. 27–34

48. Filippini I., Malandrino F., Dan G., Cesana M., Casetti C., Marsh I., 'Non-cooperative RSU deployment in vehicular networks'. *9th Annual Conference on Wireless on-demand Network Systems and Services*; 2012. pp. 79–82

49. Kchiche A., Kamoun F., 'Access-points deployment for vehicular networks based on group centrality'. *3rd International Conference on New Technologies, Mobility and Security*; Cairo, Egypt, 2009. pp. 1–6

50. Kchiche A., Kamoun F., 'Centrality-based access-points deployment for vehicular networks'. *IEEE 17th International Conference on Telecommunications*; 2010. pp. 700–06

51. Reis A. B., Sargento S., Tonguz O. K., 'On the performance of sparse vehicular networks with road side units'. *IEEE 73rd Vehicular Technology Conference*; 2011. pp. 1–5

52. Aslam B., Amjad F., Zou C. C., 'Optimal roadside units placement in urban areas for vehicular networks'. *IEEE Symposium on Computers and Communications*; 2012. pp. 423–29

53. Manoharan R., Sivakumar T., 'Optimizing the power utilization of road side units in vehicular ad hoc network'. *International Journal of Computer Applications*. 2011; 32(7):41–45

54. Fiore M., Ordinas J. M. B., 'Cooperative download in urban vehicular networks'. *IEEE Mobile Ad-hoc and Sensor Systems*; Macau, China, 2009

55. Li P., Huang X., Fang Y., Lin P., 'Optimal placement of gateways in vehicular networks'. *IEEE Transactions on Vehicular Technology*. 2007; 56(6):3421–30

56. Agarwal A., Little T. D. C., 'Access point placement in vehicular networking'. *First International Conference on Wireless Access in Vehicular Environments*. Troy, MI, 2008. pp. 1–14

57. Abdrabou A., Zhuang W., 'Probabilistic delay control and road side unit placement for vehicular ad hoc networks with disrupted connectivity'. *IEEE Journal on Selected Areas in Communications*. 2011; 29(1):129–39

58. Wang S. W., Chang M. Y., 'Roadside units allocation algorithms for certificate update in VANET environments'. *17th Asia-Pacific Conference on Communications*; 2011. pp. 472–77

59. Lochert C., Scheuermann B., Wewetzer C., Luebke A., Mauve M., 'Data aggregation and roadside unit placement for a vanet traffic information system'. *Proceedings of the Fifth ACM International Workshop on Vehicular Inter-NETworking*; ACM, 2008. pp. 58–65

60. Xiong Y., Ma J., Wang W., Niu J., 'Optimal roadside gateway deployment for VANETs'. *Przeglad Elektrotechniczny (Electrical Review)*. 2012; 1(1): 273–76

61. Ybicki R. J., Pesch B., Mauve M., Scheuermann B., 'Supporting cooperative traffic information systems through street-graph-based peer-to-peer networks'. *17th GI/ITG Conference on Communication in Distributed Systems*; 2011. pp. 121–32

62. Rybicki J., Scheuermann B., Mauve M., 'Peer-to-peer data structures for cooperative traffic information systems'. *Pervasive and Mobile Computing*. 2012; 8(2):194–209

63. Tsao S. L., Cheng C. M., 'Design and evaluation of a two-tier peer-to-peer traffic information system'. *IEEE Communications Magazine*. 2011; 49(5): 165–72

64. Lu K., Cheng C. M., Tsao S. L., 'An adaptive routing algorithm for two-tier traffic information system'. *IEEE Consumer Communications and Networking Conference*; 2012. pp. 311–15

Chapter 18*

EMPIRE – Energy efficient trust-aware routing for wireless sensor networks

A. R. Naseer[a]

Abstract

The problem of providing energy efficient trust-aware routing arises due to easy exposure to insecure conditions and highly constrained nature of wireless sensor networks (WSNs). The reputation system-based solutions reported in the literature require the nodes to be in promiscuous mode to monitor continuously its environment to detect misbehaviour events which is considered to be a costly operation for WSN nodes due to their limited resources. In this chapter, a reputation system-based technique using efficient monitoring approach called Efficient Monitoring Procedure In Reputation System (EMPIRE) for trust-aware routing in WSNs is presented. EMPIRE provides a probabilistic distributed monitoring methodology that reduces the nodal monitoring activities, while keeping the performance of the system, from the behaviour and trust awareness perspective, at a desirable level. Simulation results of the reputation system show that reducing monitoring activities with EMPIRE does not have a significant impact on system performance in terms of security.

18.1 Introduction

The field of wireless sensor networks (WSNs) comes into the picture in the continuously and rapidly evolving area of wireless communication as a very hot area of research in all its aspects. WSN is a multi-hop network that is actually a special kind of mobile ad hoc network which is usually composed of a large number of spatially distributed autonomous sensor nodes to monitor cooperatively physical and environmental conditions and report events. In other words, every sensor node in the WSN has the capability to read the sensed data, assist each other in

H. F. Rashvand and H.-C. Chao (Eds.), Dynamic Ad Hoc Networks, The IET Book Publishing Department, 2013, ISBN 978-1-84919-647-5, eISBN 978-1-84919-648-2
[a]Dept. of Computer Science & Engineering, Jyothishmathi Institute of Technology & Science (JITS), also affiliated to Jawaharlal Nehru Technological University – JNTU, Hyderabad, India

forwarding the data to base stations or a sink node through multi-hop routing and sometimes perform in-network processing depending on the application being considered. In general, it is assumed that sensors will be equipped with non-rechargeable batteries and will be unattended after deployment. Since long-term operation requirement of sensor nodes with limited battery energy impose a design bottleneck for sensor networks, the sensor network protocols have to be designed to operate under minimum resource utilization. Security solutions for sensor networks have to be designed taking into consideration the limited computational power, limited memory and limited battery life of sensor nodes. Furthermore, WSN is gaining popularity due to the fact that it provides feasible and economical solutions to many of the most challenging problems in a wide variety of applications ranged from military, health care, traffic monitoring, pollution monitoring, weather monitoring, wildlife tracking to remote sensing. This has fuelled extensive research to address the critical issues of providing security, intrusion detection, high-availability and survivability of the sensor network.

At the routing layer, sensor networks are susceptible to attacks that are related to the node behaviour [1]. The most familiar attacks are non-forwarding attacks in which a compromised node will drop packets it receives instead of forwarding them. For example, a compromised or malicious node may refuse to forward all or part of the received traffic towards the destination thereby issuing a black-hole or grey-hole attack exhibiting selfish behaviour. Such attacks cannot be detected or avoided by identity checking mechanisms. In order to defend against these attacks, behaviour trust-based approach borrowed from human societies has to be implemented. In this trust-aware routing, nodes establish trust relationships between each other and base their routing decisions not only on geographical or pure routing information, but also on their trust that their neighbours will sincerely cooperate. Therefore, the best practice to obtain a trust-aware routing is by implementing reputation systems. A reputation system is a type of cooperative filtering algorithm which attempts to determine ratings for a collection of entities that belong to the same community. In the context of MANET and WSN, the reputation of a node is the amount of trust the other nodes grant to it regarding its cooperation and participation in forwarding packets. Hence, each node keeps track of each other's reputation according to the behaviour it observes, and the reputation information that may be exchanged between nodes to help each other to infer the accurate values. Any reputation system in this context should, generally, exhibit three main functions – monitoring, rating and response. Monitoring function is responsible for observing the activities of the nodes of its interest set, e.g. the set of its neighbours. Based on the node's own observation, other nodes' observations that are exchanged among themselves and the history of the observed node, a node will rate other nodes in its interest set. Once a node builds knowledge on others' reputations, it should be able to decide about different possible reactions it can take, like avoiding bad nodes or even punishing them.

The most expensive part in terms of resource usage for WSN is monitoring. That is because it requires a node to track the events occurring around it by overhearing packet transmissions, which consume lots of energy. Moreover, the computations and allocations of such events may consume a considerable amount of processing power and memory space, which are also important to conserve in WSN. As a result, a node has to monitor the behaviour of its neighbours in an efficient manner that can provide a better possible way of resource conservation, while being able to reach to a good conclusion about the neighbours' behaviours so that it will take a proper action based on what it has observed. Thus, an efficient monitoring mechanism should guarantee a satisfactory level of capturing neighbourhood activities while minimizing power consumption, memory usage, processing activities, communication overhead etc. In this chapter, we present a reputation system-based solution for trust-aware routing that implements a new monitoring strategy called Efficient Monitoring Procedure in Reputation System (EMPIRE) [2].

The rest of the chapter is organized as follows. In Section 18.2, we present briefly some specific discussions on secure routing requirements, highlighting the importance of trust-aware routing to mitigate node misbehaviours in WSN. In Section 18.3, our proposed reputation system, Sensor Node Attached Reputation Evaluator (SNARE) [3, 4], is presented with a brief description on our proposed rating approach for reputation systems called Cautious Rating for Trust-Enabled Routing (CRATER) [5] and our proposed enhanced protocol called Geographic Energy and Trust-Aware Routing (GETAR) [4] that aims to provide a secure packet delivery service guarantee by incorporating the trust awareness concept into the routing decision. In Section 18.4, we present a detailed description of EMPIRE algorithm with the main objective of providing good monitoring operation that satisfies the security requirements, while using the least possible nodal monitoring activity (NMA). In Section 18.5, we show reputation system performance evaluation with the main focus on the impact of EMPIRE in simulation results. This will be followed by discussion on some of the important related work and further developments in the area of reputation system-based trust-aware routing for WSN in Section 18.6.

18.2   Secure routing

Secure routing [1] in WSN is important for both securing obtained information as well as protecting the network performance from degradation and network resources from unreasonable consumption. Most WSN applications carry and deliver very critical and secret information (e.g. military and health applications). A WSN network infected by malicious nodes can alter or inject incorrect information, misroute packets, analyse data or do not forward packets to their destination. Thus, having a secure routing protocol or framework can protect data exchange, secure information delivery, maintain and protect the value of the communicated information. Since WSN lacks an infrastructure, nodes depend on the cooperation among each other to route their packets. Thus, a router in WSN is simply any node that offers a routing service and should be selected such that it will be the most secure choice to route the packet. To come up with a proper routing decision, we need to understand first what security goals we are targeting. Security problems in WSN at the network layer can be related to router identity or router behaviour. These two issues highlight two main tasks to be considered when we are designing a secure routing solution – Securing Packet Content and Securing Packet Delivery. The first task of securing packet content is concerned with identity-related security problems. The goal of this task is to assure that the packet is not accessed by unauthorized nodes as it travels from the source to the destination. Securing packet content is obtained usually based on the idea of identity trust in which a routing decision is made after verifying that the selected node is authorized and has an acceptable identity according to certain criteria. This is achieved in literature by using crypto-based systems. However, any solution must obey WSN constraints of processing capacity, memory limits and energy consumption.

The second task of securing packet delivery deals mainly with behaviour-related security problems. Its objective is to guarantee that any packet transmitted will be ultimately received at the target destination. Thus, a misbehaving router node should not be able to drop a packet, misroute a packet or deny the ability of routing of other nodes by denial of service attacks. This task can be interpreted in terms of a security service called data availability. If a node A is authorized to get information from another node B, then node A should acquire this information at any time and without unreasonable delay. There are different approaches to achieve this second task. In this case also, the designer should be aware of the suitability of the solution with WSN tight constraints such as energy scarcity. In this work, we are proposing a solution for securing packet delivery task with an account for energy efficiency. Our solution is based on the concept of behaviour trust where nodes should trust the behaviour of another node in order to select it as a router. This approach is well known in literature as trust-aware routing. Trust can be defined as 'the quantified belief by a trustor with respect to the competence, honesty, security and dependability of a trustee within a specified context' [7]. Reputation is defined as 'the global perception about the entity's behaviour norms based on the trust that other entities hold in the entity' [8]. Reputation is the opinion of one person about the other, of one Internet buyer about an Internet seller, and one WSN node about another. Trust is a derivation of the reputation of an entity. Based on a reputation, a level of trust is bestowed upon an entity. The reputation itself has been built over time based on that entity's history of behaviour, and may be reflecting a positive or negative assessment. In trust-aware routing protocol, a node incorporates in the routing decision its opinion about the behaviour of a candidate router. This opinion is quantified and called the trust metric. Trust metric should reflect how much a router is expected to behave, e.g. forward a packet when it receives it from a previous node. Obtaining the trust metric is a problem by itself since it requires several operational tasks on observing nodes behaviour, exchanging nodes' experience and opinions as well as modelling the acquired observations and exchanged knowledge to reflect nodes' trust values. A system that provides these tasks to ultimately output a 'rating' or a trust value on nodes is called a reputation system.

In the context of WSN, trust is the confidence of one node on another node that it will perform the given task as expected with full cooperation without any deviation. To evaluate the trustworthiness of its neighbours, a node not only monitors their behaviour, e.g., through direct observations also known as First-Hand Information (FHI), but may also communicate with other nodes to exchange their opinions, e.g., through indirect observations also known as Second-Hand Information (SHI). The methods for obtaining trust information and defining each node's trustworthiness are referred to as trust models. In WSN routing approaches, reputation system-based trust models borrowed from social networks have been proposed to combat misbehaviours. A trust model is mostly used not only for higher layer decisions such as routing and data aggregation, but also for cluster head election and for key distribution. The goal of the trust model is to improve security thereby increasing the throughput, the lifetime and the resilience of a WSN.

18.3   Reputation system for trust-aware routing

This section describes our proposed reputation system named as *Sensor Node Attached Reputation Evaluator* (SNARE) system. SNARE is a collection of protocols and algorithms that interacts directly with the network layer. The system consists of three main components: monitoring component – EMPIRE, rating component – CRATER and response component – GETAR.

The monitoring component, EMPIRE, observes packet forwarding events. A monitoring node will not be in a continuous monitoring mode of operation, rather it will monitor the neighbourhood periodically and probabilistically to save resources. When a misbehaving event is detected, it is counted and stored until an update time, T_{update} or T_{ON} is due, then a report is sent to the rating component. The rating component of a reputation system is a very critical part since it is responsible for providing the reputation of nodes. The rating component, CRATER, evaluates the amount of risk an observed node would provide for routing operation. The risk value is a quantity that represents the previous misbehaving activities of a malicious node. This value is used as an expectation for how much risk would be suffered by selecting that malicious node as a router. This risk value is computed based on three rating factors FHI, SHI and idle No-activity behaviour period (NBP) during which a node is not doing any activity. The FHI is achieved by the direct observation done by the node of concern. Risk values are updated based on the FHI every time a new misbehaviour report is received from the monitoring component. Moreover, if an observed node shows an idle behaviour during a certain period, its risk value is reduced. A monitor also updates the risk values of its neighbours by SHI received periodically from some announcers. The new contribution in CRATER is its mathematical approach that is used to rate nodes based on cautious assumptions in which a node is very cautious in dealing with other's information.

After a node monitors its neighbourhood using EMPIRE and rates them based on CRATER, the node should make the proper response that leads to a proper routing decision. In this work, we adopt the defensive approach where malicious nodes are simply avoided without any further actions against them. For that, we are proposing a new routing protocol that aims to provide a secure packet delivery service guarantee by incorporating the trust awareness concept into the routing decision. Our proposed protocol is called GETAR [5] that is an enhanced version of the Geographic and Energy Aware Routing (GEAR) [6] protocol. GEAR is basically a geographic routing protocol in which the next hop is selected based on two metrics: the distance between the next hop and the destination and the remaining energy level the next hop owns. The new contribution in GETAR adds a third metric in the next-hop selection process, i.e. the risk value of a node $r_{i,j}$ that is computed by the rating component, CRATER as the trust metric to account for trust awareness and which is also considered to be a routing resource. The risk value $r_{i,j}$, is a quantity that reflects, to some extent, the expectation that a node j will not forward the packet received from node i, assuming non-forwarding attack. The risk value metrics, along with distance and energy metrics, are used to compute a learned cost function for each neighbour. The concerned node, then, makes the routing decision by selecting the neighbour of the lowest cost.

The cost function that will be used to select the best router is as follows:

$$t(j, R) = \beta(r_{i,j}) + (1 - \beta)[\alpha d(j, R) + (1 - \alpha)e(j, R)] \tag{18.1}$$

where $t(j, R)$ is the *trust-aware* cost of using the node j by node i as a router to the destination R. $r_{i,j}$ is the *risk value* that node i so far knows about node j, $d(j, R)$ is the normalized distance from j to R (the distance from j to R divided by the distance from the farthest neighbour of i to R), $e(j, R)$ is the so far normalized consumed energy at node j which is announced periodically every T_{update}, α is a tuneable parameter $\in [0, 1]$ to give more preference to distance or energy, $[\alpha d(j, R) + (1 - \alpha) e(j, R)]$ is the GEAR component of the routing decision and β is a tuneable parameter $\in [0, 1]$ to give more or less preference to trust as opposed to other resources. If we are concerned about trust more than other resources, β should be close to 1. When β equals 1, the trust-aware cost will consider only the trust part of (18.1) and the next hop will be the most trusted one. Setting β to zero, however, turns the protocol to pure GEAR without any security considerations from the routing protocol perspective.

In order to understand how our system works and how simulations have been carried out, it is essential to formally identify the general assumptions on system requirements and boundaries. We will look at system assumptions from WSN, communication and security perspectives.

Network model: In this work, we consider a static WSN with nodes deployed randomly or in a grid topology inside a square area. It is assumed that the nodes communicate via bidirectional links so that they can monitor each other. Moreover, all nodes have equivalent power transmission capabilities, i.e. all have equivalent transmission range. It is also assumed that the consumed power during the simulation time does not impact the transmission range of nodes. The transmission and reception power are set to 1 W, whereas the processing power is considered to be 1 mW per transmission, reception or monitoring operation. RF channel is assumed to be ideal and collision free.

Communication model: The system adopts a general communication model in which each node in the system can initiate a routing operation. Thus, any node can be a source. Moreover, any node can be a destination for that node. The selection of the source-destination pair is done randomly. The reason of adopting this model is to study a very general case and not limiting our scope to particular scenarios.

Attack model: The system assumes always-suspicious nodes. This means that a node cannot be fully trusted. Every node is assumed to have a minimum risk value that can be encountered if that node is used as a router. The system assumes collusion-free attacks. The system treats only one type of behaviour-related attacks, i.e. non-forwarding attack. In this attack, when a malicious node receives a packet to forward, it drops this packet with a certain probability that will represent its actual risk value. The system assumes honesty in treating information exchange about nodes' energy levels or risk values. Honesty can be accounted for in the rating component.

18.4   Efficient monitoring procedure in reputation system

In this section, we describe our new monitoring strategy called EMPIRE [3] to solve the problem of efficient monitoring in WSN. The monitoring efficiency here is realized by the association between the NMA and various performance measures. NMA is determined by the frequency of monitoring actions that a node takes to collect direct observation information. Reducing the frequency of monitoring, i.e. reducing NMA, will affect the quantity and the quality of the obtained information that in turn will affect the performance measures. However, on the other hand, this reduction implies a saving in node's resources such as power, processing and memory. EMPIRE provides a probabilistic approach to reduce monitoring activities per node while maintaining the abilities to detect attacks at a satisfying level.

18.4.1   EMPIRE approach
18.4.1.1   Algorithm description
In EMPIRE approach, every sensor node is alternating between two NMA states, i.e. ON state and OFF state. A node that is in ON state is a node that performs monitoring activities such as overhearing packets, checking the headers for validation and storing packets to validate events. On the other hand, an OFF node is a node that does not do any monitoring activity. Notice that ON and OFF states are associated with the NMA. Thus, an OFF node may still receive, send and process data not related to monitoring issues. As explained earlier, the objectives of this procedure are realized through the frequency of NMA. Since nodes alternate between ON and OFF states, reducing NMA is determined by how much a node will stay in each of these states. Thus, when a node stays longer in ON state, its NMA will increase and when it stays longer in OFF state, NMA will decrease.

EMPIRE algorithm is summarized in Figure 18.1. The basic phenomenon of EMPIRE is to allow each node to enter a certain state probabilistically, stay there for a deterministic duration and then, at the end of that duration, it probabilistically leaves its state to the other one or stay for another epoch. The procedure implements

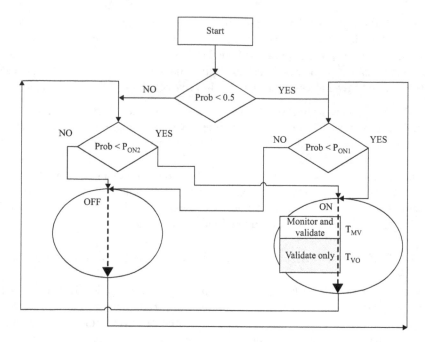

Figure 18.1   EMPIRE algorithm block diagram

this concept as follows. During the lifetime of a node, it encounters continuous monitoring cycles of length T. Each cycle is divided into two parts, $T1$ and $T2$ that can be of equal or different lengths. At the beginning of $T1$, each node will enter the ON state with probability P_{ON1} and stays there for $T1$, or enters an OFF state with probability $(1 - P_{ON1})$ and stays there for $T1$. Similarly, at the start of $T2$, the node can be in ON state with a different probability of P_{ON2} and stays there for $T2$ or it can be in OFF state with probability $(1 - P_{ON2})$ and stays there for $T2$. The purpose of partitioning the monitoring cycles into two parts is to have more randomized operation of the procedure hoping that it will provide more coverage of the WSN in terms of monitoring. Thus, the cycle can be further divided into more than two parts to have more random operation. However, in our work, we focus on the case of two parts. Moreover, each node can start its monitoring cycle with $T1$ or $T2$ with probability of 0.5. This way, more randomness is induced in the EMPIRE operation.

18.4.1.2   Non-forwarding attack detection

During an ON state, $T1$ or $T2$ is divided into two sub-periods, i.e. monitoring and validation period (T_{MV}) and validation only period (T_{VO}). In T_{MV}, a node will accept to monitor new packet transmission as well as validating old packets. However, in T_{VO}, it will only validate old packets. The validation mechanism is applied for the detection of non-forwarding attacks.

In T_{MV}, a node will perform the following:

- Record each overheard packet transmission.
- Search for a match for that packet in a monitoring queue.
- If a match is found, delete the packet from the monitoring queue. A match here corresponds to a match in source ID, destination ID and previous hop ID.
- If the match is not found, then if the next hop node in the packet is a neighbour, i.e. it can be monitored, add the recorded packet as a new entry to the monitoring queue; otherwise, ignore the packet.

During T_{VO}

- Record each overheard packet transmission.
- Search for a match for that packet in the monitoring queue.
- If a match is found, delete the packet from the monitoring queue; otherwise, ignore the recorded packet.

T_{VO} length should be designed such that if a packet is received as a new entry in the monitoring queue at the end of T_{MV}, the packet can be validated during T_{VO}. Finally, during an OFF state, a node will not record any packet transmission.

18.4.2   EMPIRE validation

EMPIRE aims to reduce NMA thereby guaranteeing savings in resource consumption. However, reducing NMA will affect the monitoring operation. Thus, we provide some validation tests to investigate the effect of changing NMA on the quantity and quality of the monitoring operation.

18.4.2.1   Simulation objectives and performance measures

To achieve a good monitoring operation, EMPIRE should meet the following requirements:

1. Quantitative requirements
   Percentage of ON nodes: This metric refers to the percentage of the average number of nodes in ON state at any instant of time that should be enough as per security level requirements. The higher the percentage is, the better monitoring results we expect. This is because more nodes will be in ON state and will be able to collect direct observations of their neighbours.
   Percentage of non-monitored neighbours per OFF node: This metric shows how many neighbouring nodes of an OFF node should not be monitored by other nodes in the network. If every node in the system continuously monitors its neighbours, this metric becomes zero. This means there are no OFF nodes as all nodes monitored by some nodes. As this figure increases, the monitoring operation becomes worse since some malicious activities will be missed.
2. Qualitative requirements
   If a node reduces its NMA, it should maintain the same ability to distinguish between malicious and non-malicious neighbours. For this purpose, we define a new metric called average Misbehavers Detection Metric (MDM). This metric

is used to measure the ability of a node to differentiate between malicious and non-malicious nodes. This metric is computed by the following steps:

(i) A node will sort its neighbours whose count equals n, in a list; call it the actual list (AL), in descending order based on their actual classification in terms of malicious behaviour or good behaviour. Thus, all malicious nodes will occupy the top positions of the actual list.

(ii) Then, the node will sort its neighbours in another list; call it the monitoring list (ML), in descending order based on the number of monitored misbehaviour events per neighbour.

(iii) Then, we calculate the difference between the position of the malicious node, i, in the actual list $POS_{i,AL}$ and its position in the monitoring list $POS_{i,ML}$.

(iv) To get the average difference, we sum the differences between the actual and monitoring positions of all malicious neighbours and divide that by their count.

So, *MDM* per node is calculated mathematically as:

$$MDM = \begin{cases} \dfrac{\sum\limits_{i=1}^{m}(POS_{i,ML} - POS_{i,AL})}{m} & ; m > 0 \\ 0 ; m = 0 \end{cases} \qquad (18.2)$$

where i represents a malicious neighbour and m is the number of malicious neighbours.

The best case is when $MDM = 0$; i.e. either a node has no malicious neighbours or it detects all malicious neighbours correctly that they are ranked as expected by the actual list. The worst case is when the node has only one malicious neighbour and it is observed mistakenly to have the least misbehaviour among all other neighbour nodes of total count of n. Thus, it will be ranked at the last position in the monitoring list and *MDM* will be equal to $(n - 1)$. Thus, our figure should be analysed within a scale from 0 to $n - 1$.

With this metric, EMPIRE should prove two points. First, the obtained value of *MDM* is small. Second, changing NMA will not affect the obtained value of *MDM* so that we are still able to distinguish between good and bad neighbours. This is because *MDM* should maintain the relativity of the misbehaviour events among all neighbours regardless of the frequency of monitoring.

18.4.2.2   Simulation setup, results and analysis

In all our simulation tests, we are studying the impact of changing NMA on the performance measures. Table 18.1 summarizes the simulation parameters used in our validation tests.

Figure 18.2 shows the impact of increasing P_{ON1} and P_{ON2} per node on the total number of ON nodes at any time. The results are for 100 nodes randomly deployed with 15 units transmission range. We can see that as NMA increases, i.e. as P_{ON1} and P_{ON2} increase, the percentage of ON nodes also increases. Although

Table 18.1   Summary of simulation parameters for EMPIRE validation

Parameter	Value	Parameter	Value
Network size	50, 100, 200, 300 nodes	Communication discipline	Random source to random destination
Network dimensions	Square area with an edge of length equal to $10\left(\sqrt{(number\_of\_nodes)}-1\right)$	Simulation platform	Event driven simulation using Java programming language
Transmission range	15, 25 units	Simulation time	200 s
Deployment	Random	$T_1 = T_2$	5 s
Malicious nodes	50% of the total population, randomly distributed	Routing protocol	GEAR
Attack type	Non-forwarding attack with probability of dropping equals 1	P_{ON1} and P_{ON2}	All nodes exhibit the same values of P_{ON1} and P_{ON2}, i.e. these two parameters are considered as network parameters in this work

the results seem trivial and predictable, there are some interesting conclusions that can be extracted regarding the choice of P_{ON1} and P_{ON2}. Assume that the operator is interested in having 90 per cent ON nodes. Then, there are two possible choices: choice $1 = (P_{ON1} = 0.9, P_{ON2} = 0.9)$ and choice $2 = (P_{ON1} = 0.1, P_{ON2} = 1)$. However, choice 1 is more resource consuming than choice 2. This is because each node in choice 1 will be in ON state for an average of 90 per cent of the simulation time, whereas in choice 2, it will be ON for around 55 per cent of simulation time. As a result, going for the second choice is better than choice 1, even though both provide the same average number of ON nodes. It has been found from simulation study that *MDM* is independent of NMA since it maintains its value between 0 and 1 for different flavours of P_{ON1} and P_{ON2}. This small value of *MDM* indicates that EMPIRE does not deviate very much from the actual ranking of malicious nodes and it can successfully distinguish among most of the malicious and non-malicious nodes. This means that EMPIRE can be trusted to provide the same ability to distinguish among different nodes irrespective of nodal monitoring activities. Thus, EMPIRE can reduce NMA 'safely' to meet resource constraints requirements.

Since EMPIRE has an independent operation of distributed nature, it should be scalable. That is, the number of nodes in the network does not affect the quantity or quality of the monitoring operation. It is evident from the simulation study with $P_{ON2} = 1$ for random deployment with different network sizes of 50, 100, 200 and

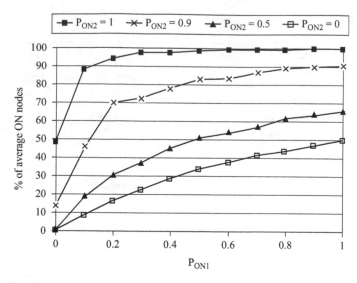

Figure 18.2   Percentage of average number of ON nodes for various NMA

300 nodes that the percentage of average number of ON nodes remain almost the same for different network sizes. This figure agrees with the scalability feature expected. Similar simulation studies also indicate that the percentage of average number of nodes of non-monitored neighbours per OFF node for different populations and the average MDM figure per ON node for different populations remain almost the same. We can notice from these studies that EMPIRE is not very much affected by increasing or decreasing the number of nodes in the system. Further, it is apparent from simulation studies that the network deployment and neighbourhood size have transparent effect on the performance measures. This is actually obvious since the percentage of ON nodes, and MDM should be independent of the deployment or neighbourhood size. However, the number of non-monitored nodes per OFF node must be affected by these conditions. Generally, as the neighbourhood size increases we should expect that the number of non-monitored nodes will decrease, because an ON node will cover more neighbours. Figure 18.3 shows this conclusion very clearly as the percentage of non-monitored nodes per OFF node in the case of 25 units transmission range is much less than the case of 15 units.

18.5   Performance evaluation of reputation system adopting EMPIRE

In this part of the work, our simulation tests are set to study the impact of adopting EMPIRE as a monitoring procedure on the performance of the reputation system. This will be done by studying some performance metrics under the effect of changing the NMA of each node as determined by variations in P_{ON1} and P_{ON2}.

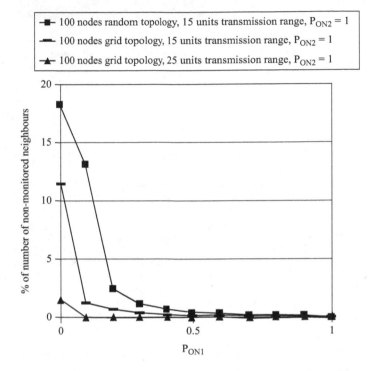

Figure 18.3   Percentage of average number of non-monitored neighbours per OFF node for different transmission ranges

The objective of this study is to analyse system trade-offs among security and processing energy as well as examining how our trust-aware routing will improve system security. Simulation settings and parameters are provided in Table 18.2.

Delivery ratio is defined as the ratio of the number of packets delivered successfully to their destinations to the total number of generated packets. We performed simulation studies to examine delivery ratio versus routing trust-awareness parameter, β, for different NMA situations with various percentages of attackers. It has been noticed that when $P_{ON1} = P_{ON2} = 0$, the delivery ratio does not improve as β increases and remains the same for all values of β. On the other hand, when NMA increases by increasing P_{ON1} and P_{ON2}, the delivery ratio of the system generally improves as β increases. This is because the monitoring operation takes effect in discovering malicious nodes and rating them appropriately by the rating component. Figure 18.4 shows delivery ratio versus β with three attackers' percentages, i.e. 10%, 30% and 50% under $P_{ON1} = P_{ON2} = 1$. It is trivial to conclude that as the attackers' percentage increases in the system, the delivery ratio degrades. However, the purpose of this simulation is to show how much improvement is expected by being exposed to less number of attackers under the lights of various values of β. Two important observations can be noticed in Figure 18.4. First, the impact of β on delivery ratio starts to appear significantly after $\beta = 0.4$, which is beyond the value

Table 18.2   Simulation parameters for repuation system evaluation

Parameter	Value	Parameter	Value
Number of nodes	100 nodes	Queuing model	M/M/1
Network dimensions	Square of 90 units × 90 units	Simulation platform	Event-driven simulation using Java programming language
Transmission range	15 units	Simulation duration	1,000 s
Network deployment	Random topology	Retransmission timeout	Explicit retransmission request
Power consumption	1 W per reception, 1W per sending, 1 mW per processing operation	Retransmission trials	Unlimited
Mean arrival rate	1 pps	Update strategy	Periodic, every 5 s
Mean service rate	500 pps	α	0.5 (GEAR parameter)
Outsider attackers' deployment	Random	Communication discipline	Random source to random destination
Escaping void	Using GEAR part and then distance	Void failure: max number of hops	100
% of attackers	50%	Attackers deployment	Random
f_{max}	10		

1/3 that provides equal preference for all factors in the routing cost function with $\alpha = 0.5$. This implies that any good design of the system should consider β values greater than 1/3, irrespective of the attackers' percentage. Second, the delivery ratio improves significantly by reducing the percentage of attackers in the system. For example, at $\beta = 0.9$, the delivery ratio improves from 0.49 to 0.9. Since WSN can be dynamically redeployed, one trick can be used here is to decrease the number of attacker by deploying more 'fresh' nodes. This guarantees that better nodes will exist in the vicinity of other nodes and they will be more qualified to be routers as opposed to the malicious ones.

Cooperative total consumed power per node per packet is defined as the amount of power (transmission, retransmission, reception, processing and monitoring) that each node consumes on average for any packet generated in the system, whether it is successfully delivered or not and whether the node has really cooperated in any related operation for that particular packet or not. In Figure 18.5, the cooperative total consumed power per node per packet is shown. Since the routing operation is cooperative in WSN, we assume in this figure each node will pay a power penalty for each packet generated. Thus, higher values of this figure indicate higher routing activities. Here, we can observe that except for the case where the system is off-monitoring, i.e. NMA values are ($P_{ON1} = P_{ON2} = 0$), the figure indicates that the cooperative total consumed power increases as NMA increases and as β increases. The reason is that when NMA increases, more

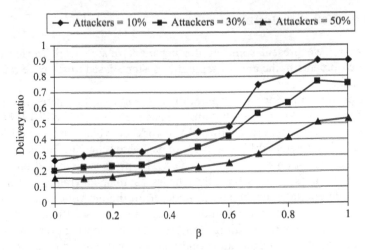

Figure 18.4   Delivery ratio with various percentages of attackers

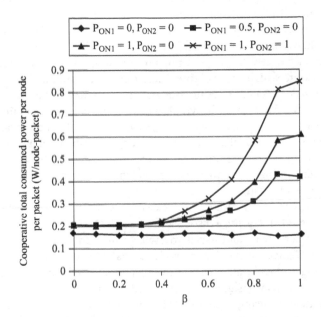

Figure 18.5   Cooperative power per node per packet

monitoring activities are induced. Also, due to the increase in path length to detour malicious nodes, more nodes will be incorporated in packet delivery. As a result, a good design should select an optimum value of β that meets certain delivery ratio at the lowest possible values of NMA that maintains this delivery ratio and guarantees less power consumption.

18.6 Further developments

In this section, we present some of the important related work carried out and further developments in the area of reputation system-based trust-aware routing for ad hoc networks.

An important reference for reputation systems in ad hoc networks is Cooperation Of Nodes – Fairness In Dynamic ad hoc Networks (CONFIDANT) [9]. It is a reputation-based secure routing framework in which nodes monitor their neighbourhood and detect different kinds of misbehaviour. The nodes use the SHI from others as a resource of rating as well. The protocol is based on Bayesian estimation that aims to classify other nodes as misbehaving or normal. The observing node excludes misbehaving nodes from the network as a response, by both avoiding them for routing and denying them cooperation. The protocol assumes a Dynamic Source Routing (DSR) operational routing protocol and lacks a provision on WSN constraints and conditions as it is designed for general ad hoc networks.

Another famous reputation mechanism in literature is Collaborative Reputation Mechanism to Enforce Node Cooperation in Mobile ad hoc Networks (CORE) protocol [10]. It is a complete reputation mechanism that differentiates between subjective reputations or observations, indirect reputation which includes only the positive reports by others (SHI), and functional reputation, also referred to as task-specific behaviour, which are weighted according to a combined reputation value that is used to make decisions about cooperation or gradual isolation of a node. The system assumes a DSR routing in which nodes can be requesters or providers. The rating is measured by comparing the expected result with the actually obtained result upon a request. In CORE, members have to contribute on a continuing basis (thereby enforcing node cooperation) to remain trusted or they will find their reputation deteriorating until they are excluded. CORE does not provide for a second-chance mechanism.

The closest work in literature that tackles WSN specifically is Reputation-based Framework for High Integrity Sensor Networks (RFSN) [11] where nodes maintain reputation for other nodes and use it to evaluate their trustworthiness. The authors focused on an abstract view that provides a scalable, diverse and a generalized approach hoping to tackle all types of misbehaviours resulting from malicious and faulty nodes. They also designed a system within this framework and employed a Bayesian formulation, using a beta distribution model for reputation representation. RFSN integrates tools from statistics and decision theory into a distributed and scalable framework. The monitoring mechanism uses a normal watchdog mechanism that assumes a promiscuous mode operation for every node. This is not suitable for the WSN conditions in terms of energy scarcity as discussed earlier.

A reputation-based scheme called Distributed Reputation-based Beacon Trust System (DRBTS) is proposed in Reference 12 for excluding malicious beacon nodes that provide false location information. It is a distributed security protocol aimed at providing a method by which beacon nodes can monitor each other and provide information so that sensor nodes can choose who to trust, based on a quorum voting approach. In order to trust a beacon node's information, a sensor must get votes for its trustworthiness from at least half of their common neighbours.

An approach to tackle selfishness in ad hoc networks called Observation-based Cooperation Enforcement in ad hoc Networks (OCEAN) [13] is proposed to disallow any SHI exchanges. A node makes routing decisions based solely on direct observations of its neighbouring nodes' interactions with it. Once the rating of a node falls below a certain threshold, the node is added to the faulty list comprising all misbehaving nodes. In order to tackle selfish behaviour, the authors introduce a simple packet forwarding economy scheme, relying again only on direct observations of interactions with neighbours. Due to the usage of only FHI, OCEAN is more resilient to spreading rumours.

A protocol called Trust Index Based Fault Tolerance for Arbitrary Data Faults in Sensor Networks (TIBFIT) to diagnose and mask arbitrary node failures in an event-driven WSN is proposed in Reference 14. The goal of the proposed TIBFIT protocol involves event detection and location determination in the presence of faulty sensor nodes, coupled with diagnosis and isolation of faulty or malicious nodes. In this system model, sensor nodes are organized into clusters with rotating cluster heads or data sinks. The nodes, including the cluster head, can fail in an arbitrary manner generating missed event reports, false reports, or wrong location reports. To determine the location of the event, the data sink must aggregate all reports from nodes within the detection radius. In this approach, a new parameter called *trust index* for this aggregation is introduced. Each node is assigned a trust index to indicate its track record in reporting past events correctly. The cluster head analyses the event reports using the trust index and makes event decisions.

In Reference 15, authors have proposed Parameterized and Localized trust management Scheme (PLUS) for WSN. The authors adopt a localized distributed approach and trust is calculated based on either direct observations or indirect observations. In Reference 16, the authors propose Locally Aware Reputation System (LARS) to mitigate misbehaviour and enforce cooperation. Each node only keeps the reputation values of all its one-hop neighbours. The reputation values are updated on the basis of direct observations of the node's neighbours. If the reputation value of a node drops below an untrustworthy threshold, then it is considered misbehaving by the specific evaluator node. In such a case, the evaluator node will notify its neighbours about misbehaviour. The misbehaving node is not excluded from the network forever. After a time-out period, it is accepted, but with the reputation value unchanged it would have to be built its reputation by good cooperation.

To secure multi-hop routing in WSN against intruders exploiting the replay of routing information, a Trust-Aware Routing Framework (TARF) for WSNs is proposed in Reference 17. This approach identifies malicious nodes that misuse 'stolen' identities to misdirect packets by their low trustworthiness, thus helping nodes circumvent those attackers in their routing paths. It incorporates the trustworthiness of nodes into routing decisions and allows a node to circumvent an adversary misdirecting considerable traffic with a forged identity attained through replaying. A resilient trust model, SensorTrust, with a focus on data integrity for hierarchical WSN is proposed in Reference 18. In this model, the aggregator maintains trust estimations for children nodes by integrating their long-term reputation and short-term risk and taking into consideration both communication robustness and data integrity. Since a node can behave maliciously regarding either wireless communication or data management, trustworthiness is evaluated from two aspects: communication robustness and data integrity. This model employs the Gaussian model to rate data integrity in a fine-grained style, and a flexible update protocol to adapt to different applications.

Dirichlet reputation system with moving window mechanism is proposed in Reference 19 to address the problem of node misbehaviours in wireless *ad hoc* networks. Dirichlet reputation model based on Bayesian inference theory evaluates reliability of each node in terms of packet delivery. It provides a way to predict and select a reliable path through combination of first-hand observation and second-hand reputation reports. The moving window mechanism is used to make the system adaptive to behaviour change of wireless nodes.

A trust and energy-aware routing protocol Ambient Trust Sensor Routing (ATSR) is proposed in Reference 20 which adopts the geographical routing principle to cope with large network dimensions and relies on a distributed trust management system for the detection of malicious nodes. Both direct and indirect trust information is taken into account to evaluate the trustworthiness of each neighbour thereby avoiding malicious nodes which perform routing attacks as well as attacks threatening the reputation exchange process (e.g. bad-mouthing and conflicting behaviour attacks). Similar to our work, in this proposed scheme, routing decisions are based on a weighted routing cost function which incorporates trust, energy and location attributes thereby taking into account the remaining energy of each neighbour, thus allowing for better load balancing and network lifetime extension.

Various trust models, trust evaluation metrics and trust management schemes have been reported in the literature. Current research on the trust management mechanisms of WSN has mainly focused on nodes' trust evaluation to enhance the security and robustness. Although some existing approaches have played greater roles in improving security of other ad hoc networks, trust management in WSN still remains a challenging field. The problem of assessing a reputation based on observed data is a statistical problem. Some trust models make use of this observation and introduce probabilistic modelling that uses a Bayesian updating scheme known as the beta reputation system [21] for assessing and updating the nodes reputations. The use of the beta distribution is due to the binary form of the events considered. For example, RFSN [11] uses a probability model in the form of a reputation system to summarize the observed information (FHI) and share the values of the parameters of the probability distributions as SHI. This shared information is soft data, requiring a proper way to incorporate it with the observed data into the trust model. Both these sources of information (FHI and SHI) are handled differently in the combining step by different trust models. RFSN uses Dempster–Shafer (DS) belief theory model, solving it using the concept of belief discounting, and doing a reverse mapping from belief theory to continuous probability. In Reference 22, a new Bayesian fusion algorithm to combine more than one trust component – data trust and communication trust – to infer the overall trust between nodes is proposed. As an extension to this work, authors proposed Recursive Bayesian Approach to Trust Management in Wireless Sensor Network (RBTMWSN) [23] by introducing a new trust model and a Gaussian reputation system (GRSSN) for WSNs based on a sensed continuous data. In this work, Bayesian probabilistic approach based on the work done in modelling expert opinion for mixing SHI from neighbouring nodes with directly observed information is proposed. In Reference 24, authors proposed a Node Behavioural Strategies Banding Belief Theory of the Trust Evaluation (NBBTE) algorithm. In this approach, at first, each node establishes the direct and indirect trust values of neighbour nodes by comprehensively considering various trust factors such as packet receive, send, strictness, delivery, consistency and availability, and combining these factors together with network security grade, correlation of context time and rewards degree. Next, fuzzy set theory is used to decide the trustworthiness levels in accordance with the fuzzy subset grade of membership functions. Based on the levels of trustworthiness, the basic confidence function of DS evidence theory is accordingly formed. Finally, using the revised Dempster rules of combination, the integrated trust value of a node is obtained by integrating its trustworthiness of multiple neighbour nodes.

The common and well-known reputation systems assume the operation of continuous mode watchdog. In this approach, each node continuously overhears the transmission of the next node. When the attack is detected, the observing node informs the source of the concerned path. Since the attacks are continuously monitored, the granularity of this mechanism is pretty much detailed than our approach. However, in EMPIRE, the continuous watchdog is, in fact, a special case that is achieved when the node monitoring activity (NMA) is the highest. Moreover, the evaluation of the monitoring efficiency is usually implicitly measured through the performance of the reputation system in all the reported work in the literature. In this work, we studied the issue of independent evaluation for monitoring component as a separate module as well as the impact of adopting EMPIRE as a monitoring procedure on the performance of the reputation system. As a future work, EMPIRE can be modified to work in deterministic manner according to MAC layer scheduling. For example, if a non-promiscuous mode of operation in MAC is adopted where nodes go to sleep and awake phases, nodes can perform monitoring only during awake phases. The selection of P_{ON1} and P_{ON2} requires a mapping between the security requirements of the network and the performance figures presented in this work. For example, a network operator should be able to tell what the minimum required percentage of ON neighbours is. This task is, in fact, very difficult for a new network deployment. However, if the network is already implemented, such figures can be experimentally specified and the NMA would be adjusted accordingly.

Considering the related work reported in the literature, it can be stated that the approaches and schemes proposed in related research literature are based on quite different assumptions, while the trust and reputation framework considered varies significantly in many aspects. Some of the aspects in which these reported approaches differ are computation of trust and reputation considering only FHI or both first-hand and SHI, propagation of SHI considering only positive, negative or both types of recommendation, degree of propagation, adopted model for reputation value computation, dishonest SHI provisioning, identification of misbehaving nodes, actions taken, node re-integration in the system, etc. The proposed reputation systems use several debatable heuristics for the key steps of reputation updates and integration. Some systems maintain a statistical representation of the reputation by borrowing tools from the realms of game theory. These systems attempt to counter selfish routing misbehaviour of nodes by enforcing nodes to cooperate with each other. More recent reputation systems proposed in the domain of ad hoc and sensor networks, formulate the problem in the realm of Bayesian analytics rather than game theory. Resource constraints in WSN node require energy efficient and energy aware schemes on all layers of the protocol stack to increase the lifetime of the network. The traditional layered networking approach has several drawbacks from WSN perspective – improvements in performance and energy efficiency are possible if significant amount of information is passed across protocol layers thereby improving network lifetime. There exists some research on cross-layer interactions and design in developing new communication protocols considering interactions among physical (PHY), medium access control (MAC), routing (network) and transport layers. Recent research in this direction reveals that cross-layer integration and design techniques result in significant improvement in terms of energy conservation. However, there is still much to be gained by reconsidering the protocol functions of network layers in a unified way so as to provide a single communication module for efficient communication in WSN. In other words, the cross-layer approach emerged recently still necessitates a unified cross-layer communication protocol for efficient and reliable event communication that considers transport, routing, and medium access functionalities with physical layer effects for WSN.

18.7 Conclusion

With the ever-increasing demand for deploying WSN to tackle many of the most challenging problems in a wide variety of critical applications, it has become highly essential to conserve energy of nodes and secure the network for longer lifetime of the network. In this direction, we proposed in this chapter a reputation system-based trust-aware routing approach for WSN which employs energy efficient probabilistic and distributed monitoring methodology called EMPIRE. The main objective of EMPIRE is to conserve node resources by providing efficient monitoring operation that satisfies the security requirements, while using the least possible NMA. Simulation studies show that EMPIRE is scalable and independent of the network deployment or neighbourhood size and can satisfy various levels of monitoring requirements with different possible choices of NMA levels. Moreover, EMPIRE can differentiate between malicious and non-malicious nodes regardless of the choice of the NMA thereby maintaining security efficiency at the desired level.

References

1. Naseer A.R., Maarouf I.K., Ashraf M. 'Routing security in wireless sensor networks'. *Handbook of Research on Wireless Security*. Idea Group Reference, USA, 2008, ISBN: 13:9781599048994, pp. 582–616

2. Naseer A.R., Maarouf I.K., Baroudi U. 'Efficient monitoring approach for reputation system based trust-aware routing in wireless sensor networks'. *International Journal of IET Communications – Wireless Adhoc Networks*, May 2009, vol. 3 no. 5, pp. 846–858, ISSN 1751-8628

3. Maarouf I.K., Naseer A.R. 'SNARE: Sensor node attached reputation evaluator'. *Proceedings of the IEEE/ACM 2nd International CONEXT Conference*, December 4–7, 2006, Lisboa, Portugal

4. Maarouf I.K., Naseer A.R. 'WSNodeRater: An optimized reputation system framework for security aware energy efficient geographic routing in WSNs'. *Proceedings of ACS/IEEE International Conference on Computer Systems and Applications*, AICCSA '2007, May 13–16, 2007, Amman, Jordan

5. Maarouf I.K., Baroudi U., Naseer A.R. 'Cautious rating for trust-enabled routing in wireless sensor networks', *EURASIP International Journal on Wireless Communications and Networking*, vol. 2 Article ID 718318, 16 pp., ISSN: 1687-1472, 2010

6. Yu Y., Govindan R., Estrin D. 'Geographical and energy aware routing: A recursive data dissemination protocol for wireless sensor networks'. Technical Report, UCLA/CSD-TR-01-0023, May 2001

7. Grandison T., Sloman M. 'A survey of trust in internet applications'. *IEEE Communications Surveys & Tutorials*, vol. 3 no. 4, pp. 2–16, 2000

8. Resnick P., Zeckhauser R., Friedman E., Kuwabara 'Reputation systems: Facilitating trust in internet interactions'. *Communications of the ACM*, vol. 43, no. 12, pp. 45–48, 2000

9. Buchegger S., Le Boudec J.Y. 'Performance analysis of the CONFIDANT protocol: Cooperation of nodes – fairness in dynamic ad-hoc networks'. *Proceedings of the IEEE/ACM Symposium on Mobile Ad Hoc Networking and Computing*, Lausanne, Switzerland, June 2002

10. Michiardi P., Molva R. 'Core: A collaborative reputation mechanism to enforce node cooperation in mobile ad hoc networks'. *Communication and Multimedia Security 2002 Conference*, Portoroz, Slovenia, 26–27 September 2002

11. Ganeriwal S., Srivastava M. 'Reputation-based framework for high integrity sensor networks'. *Proceedings of the 2nd ACM Workshop on Security of Ad Hoc and Sensor Networks*, Washington DC, USA, pp. 66–77, October 2004

12. Srinivasan A., Teitelbaum J., Wu J. 'DRBTS: Distributed reputation based beacon trust system'. *2nd IEEE International Symposium on Dependable, Autonomic and Secure Computing (DASC'06)*, Indianapolis, USA, pp. 277–283, 2006

13. Bansal S., Baker M. 'Observation-based cooperation enforcement in ad hoc networks'. Technical Report, Stanford University, http://arxiv.org/pdf/cs/0307012, July 2003

14. Krasniewski M., Varadharajan P., Rabeler B., Bagchi S., Hu Y. 'TIBFIT: Trust index based fault tolerance for arbitrary data faults in sensor networks'. *Proceedings of the International Conference on Dependable Systems and Networks (DSN'05)*, Yokohama, Japan, June 2005

15. Yao Z., Kim D., Doh Y. 'PLUS: Parameterized and localized trust management scheme for sensor networks security'. *Proceedings of the 3rd International Conference on Mobile Ad-hoc and Sensor Systems*, pp. 437–446, Vancouver, Canada, October 2006

16. Hu J., Burmester M. 'LARS: A locally aware reputation system for mobile ad-hoc networks'. *Proceedings of the 44th Annual ACM Southeast Regional Conference*, pp. 119–123, Melbourne, 2006

17. Zhan G., Shi W., Deng J. 'TARF: A trust-aware routing framework for wireless sensor networks'. *Proceeding of the 7th European Conference on Wireless Sensor Networks (EWSN'10)*, pp. 65–80, Coimbra, Portugal, 2010

18. Zhan G., Shi W., Deng J. 'Sensortrust – a resilient trust model for WSNs'. *Proceedings of the 7th International Conference on Embedded Networked Sensor Systems (SenSys2009)*, 4–6, Berkeley, California - November 4–6, 2009

19. Yang Li, Cemerlic A., Cui X. 'A Dirichlet reputation system in reliable routing of wireless *ad hoc* network', *Security and Communication Networks*, Volume 3, Issue 2-3, pp. 250–260, March - June 2010, (first published online: 13 Jan 2010, DOI: 10.1002/sec.173)

20. Zahariadis T., Leligou H., Voliotis S., Maniatis S., Trakadas P., Karkazis P. 'A novel trust-aware geographical routing scheme for wireless sensor networks'. Springer Wireless Personal Communications, pp. 981–991, April 2012 [online]

21. Josang A., Ismail R. 'The beta reputation system'. *15th Bled Electronic Commerce Conference, e-Reality: Constructing the e-Economy*. Bled, Slovenia, June 2002

22. Momani M., Challa S., Aboura K. 'Modelling trust in wireless sensor networks from the sensor reliability prospective'. *International Joint Conferences on Computer, Information, and Systems Sciences, and Engineering (CIS2E 06)*, University of Bridgeport, USA, 2006

23. Momani M., Aboura K., Challa S. 'RBATMWSN: Recursive Bayesian approach to trust management in wireless sensor networks'. *The Third International Conference on Intelligent Sensors, Sensor Networks and Information*, Melbourne, Australia, 2007

24. Feng R., Xu X., Zhou X., Wan J. 'A trust evaluation algorithm for wireless sensor networks based on node behaviors and D-S evidence theory'. *Sensors 2011*, Vol. 11(2), pp. 1345–1360, 2011, (Published online 2011 January 25. doi: 10.3390/s110201345)

Chapter 19*

Bio-inspired scheduling schemes for wireless ad hoc sensor networks

Chi-Tsun Cheng[a], Chi K. Tse[a] and Francis C. M. Lau[a]

Abstract

Wireless sensor networks, a special type of wireless ad hoc networks, consist of large numbers of wireless sensor nodes. The idea of a wireless sensor network is to achieve the same sensing quality as a remote sensing system by utilizing a large number of wireless sensor nodes to perform close-range sensing. Wireless sensor nodes are compact communication devices that can virtually fit in anywhere. They are battery-powered devices that can greatly reduce deployment overheads due to wirings. To ensure a terrain of interest is fully covered, usually more than enough wireless sensor nodes are deployed to provide redundant sensing coverage. With a proper on-off scheduling scheme, the total energy consumption of a network can be reduced without introducing significant impacts to its target detection capabilities. In this chapter, two bio-inspired scheduling schemes are revisited. In both schemes, wireless sensor nodes can decide to operate in different operation modes dynamically. The decisions are made based on local information. Performances of a network can be fine-tuned by adjusting the behaviours of the nodes in their mode decisions.

19.1 Introduction

Wireless sensor networks (WSNs) inherit most characteristics from wireless ad hoc networks. Both kinds of networks require technical expertise from a variety of disciplines including signal processing, communications and circuit design. The main difference of WSNs from traditional sensing systems is the usage of wireless sensor nodes in a massive number to perform close-range sensing. Thanks to technologies advances, compact wireless sensor nodes can now be manufactured at low cost. Wireless sensor nodes are battery-powered communication devices that

*H. F. Rashvand and H.-C. Chao (Eds.), *Dynamic Ad Hoc Networks*, The IET Book Publishing Department, 2013, ISBN 978-1-84919-647-5, eISBN 978-1-84919-648-2
[a]Core E, 6/F, Department of Electronic and Information Engineering, The Hong Kong Polytechnic University, Hunghom, Kowloon, Hong Kong

are vulnerable to attacks and failures. Furthermore, they are compact and light enough to be deployed in an airborne fashion. To ensure an interested terrain can be fully covered, more than enough wireless sensor nodes are usually deployed to provide redundant sensing coverage.

For applications with rarely existing events or targets, maintaining a 100 per cent coverage of the sensing terrain all the time is, however, not necessary. The surplus sensing power can be traded-off for lower energy consumptions by employing an energy-aware on-off scheduling scheme [1, 2]. Scheduling schemes can be classified into three main categories, namely *random on-off, selective on-off* and *periodic on-off* [3] scheduling schemes. In a random on-off scheduling scheme, wireless sensor nodes are set active with a probability. Such probability controls the averaged number of active nodes in the network. The randomized effect in a random on-off scheduling scheme makes it capable of detecting random targets with short delays. However, the same effect also affects its performance in continuous tracking. In a selective on-off scheduling scheme, a sensing field is partitioned. Only a limited number of nodes is allowed to stay active in each partition. An active node will broadcast messages regularly to suppress its neighbours from being active. By putting a number of nodes into active mode all the time, a selective on-off scheduling scheme can maintain short detection delay and high tracking capability. The set of active nodes will, however, increase energy consumption of a network. In a periodic on-off scheduling scheme, the trade-off between energy consumption and target detection performance is controlled by adjusting duty-cycles of wireless sensor nodes.

In this chapter, two scheduling schemes based on social insect colonies are discussed. The schemes are kinds of adaptive periodic on-off scheduling scheme. In both schemes, wireless sensor nodes make mode-switching decisions dynamically based on exchanges of local information. The schemes are designed for detection applications with targets, which will rarely present. By adjusting duty-cycles of wireless sensor nodes adaptively, a balance can be maintained between energy consumption and target detection capability of a network. Performances of the scheduling schemes can be further fine-tuned towards either objective by adjusting some control parameters. The rest of this chapter is organized as follows. Section 19.2 reviews related scheduling schemes in WSNs. The two bio-inspired scheduling schemes are discussed in Sections 19.3 and 19.4, respectively. In Section 19.5, performances of the two bio-inspired scheduling schemes are evaluated based on computer simulations. Effects of the control parameters are further discussed in Section 19.6. Future developments of the scheduling schemes are elaborated in Section 19.7. Finally, Section 19.8 concludes the whole chapter.

19.2   Related work

Turau and Weyer's scheduling scheme [4] aims to distribute the transmission time slots dynamically among sensor nodes such that nodes with heavier loadings will have more time slots and avoid being the bottlenecks of a network. Hohlt *et al.* [5] proposed a scheduling scheme for data dissemination such that child nodes will be active only when they need to report to their parent nodes. Both schemes are focusing on energy saving in data collection processes while schemes discussed in this chapter are on reducing surplus-sensing power adaptively.

Decker *et al.* [6] noticed the resources competition among different sensing tasks on a wireless sensor node and developed a scheduler to tackle the problem. Their work is focused on scheduling within a node but not scheduling from the network point of view. Sensing performances are not their main concern. Chamberland and Veeravalli [7] investigated the relationships among sleeping duration, detection delay and energy consumption. Their work addressed a stationary sensing field while the schemes discussed in this chapter are designed to track moving targets.

Rago *et al.* [8] proposed to use a local likelihood ratio as an indicator for wireless sensor nodes to make transmit/no-transmit decisions, which can greatly reduce the amount of uninformative data from reaching the base station. Their work has pointed out the fact that for rare targets detection, it is wasteful to collect data from all wireless sensor nodes, as most nodes will return with uninformative data. Ye *et al.* [9] proposed an adaptive on-off scheduling scheme with randomized sleeping durations, namely PEAS. In PEAS, a node will turn into active mode if all its neighbours are sleeping or turn back to sleep mode if it has more than one neighbour in active mode. The objective of PEAS is to maximize network coverage and maintain network connectivity by waking up a minimum number of wireless sensor nodes. Maintaining high coverage at all time can, however, lead to high-energy consumption. Lu *et al.* [10] proposed another adaptive on-off scheduling scheme, namely Power-Efficient Scheduling Method (PESM). The idea of PESM is to divide the terrain into several sub-terrains. In each sub-terrain, only one wireless sensor node will stay active. An active sensor node will suppress other node in the same sub-terrain from being active.

Cerpa and Estrin [11] suggested that when network density is high enough, a relatively small portion of wireless sensor nodes would be enough to handle routing processes of a network. They proposed an adaptive routing scheme, namely ASCENT, where wireless sensor nodes will decide to get involved in the routing processes based on some local information. Nath and Gibbons proposed a similar idea called CKN, which transforms the scheduling problem into a connected *k*-neighbourhood problem [12]. Note that although the approaches taken by ASCENT and CKN are similar to the bio-inspired scheduling schemes discussed in this chapter, the objectives and outcomes are very different. In ASCENT and CKN, the main objective is to maintain network connectivity and reduce packet loss by utilizing a minimum number of wireless sensor nodes. In ASCENT, active nodes are mainly located along the path between the source node and the base station. In CKN, a relatively large amount of active nodes are required to maintain network connectivity.

19.3 Scheduling scheme for WSNs based on social insect colonies

In this section, the bio-inspired scheduling scheme proposed in Reference 13 will be revisited. In Section 19.3.1, biological phenomena which inspire the work will be discussed. Afterward, mechanisms of the scheduling scheme will be explained.

19.3.1   Biological phenomena

In ant colonies, individuals are assigned to different task groups to perform different tasks such as foraging, patrolling and midden work. Basically, the allocation of individuals among different tasks in ant colonies involves two mechanisms, namely (1) interactions among individuals from the same or different task groups and (2) task performance evaluations of individuals [14].

In ant colonies, the probability for an ant to carry out a task *A* rather than a task *B* depends on the ratio of the number of task *A* workers it has encountered recently to that of task *B* workers [15]. For an ant doing task *A*, a high encounter rate with other ants doing the same task will increase the probability for the ant to switch task. Initially when the number of foragers is small, the encounter rate for a midden worker to other midden workers is much higher than that to foragers. In this case, midden workers will have higher probabilities of switching into the foraging group. As the number of foragers increases, the encounter rate for a midden worker to a forager increases. It makes midden workers less willing to go foraging. Such feedback system controls the sizes of different task groups and makes ant colonies adaptive to environmental changes.

When food sites started to deplete, more foragers return to their nest without food. When they are examined by the others, they are regarded as unsuccessful foragers. Encountering with unsuccessful foragers will stop non-foraging workers from switching to foragers [16]. Unsuccessful foragers will become inactive and idle in the nest. This mechanism forms a negative feedback in controlling an oversized task group. A task group should shrink when its consumption outruns its contribution to the colonies.

19.3.2   Mechanisms

In the scheduling scheme proposed in Reference 13, a WSN is analogous to an ant colony with each wireless sensor node mimicking an ant. Different tasks in an ant colony are mapped to different operation modes of wireless sensor nodes. The interactions among ants are represented by the information exchange among wireless sensor nodes. Wireless sensor nodes will make mode-switching decisions by examining information obtained from their neighbours. The scheduling scheme is operating in a discrete time unit called *round*. A wireless sensor node is only allowed to switch its mode at the end of a round.

In Reference 13, a wireless sensor node can operate in *sleep mode*, *listen mode* or *active mode*. A node in sleep mode will put its transceiver, micro-controller unit (MCU) and sensor board into power saving mode. The energy consumption of a wireless sensor node in sleep mode is therefore the lowest among the three modes. A wireless sensor node in active mode will perform sensing and it may broadcast information to its neighbours. An active node will turn on its MCU and transceiver during data transactions, and turn on its MCU and sensor board while sensing. As all the major components are active, energy consumption of a wireless sensor node in active mode is the highest among the three modes. A wireless sensor node in listen mode will preserve energy by turning its sensor board into power saving mode, but its MCU and transceiver will operate in active mode to eavesdrop communications nearby.

To initialize the scheme, each wireless sensor node will be put into sleep mode for a random sleep duration t_S, which is upper bounded by the system maximum sleep time t_{S_max}. At the end of the sleep duration, a wireless sensor node will put itself into listen mode. A wireless sensor node in listen mode will monitor communications nearby. By listening to the channel, a node can collect *evaluation results* of its active neighbours. A wireless sensor node j operating in active mode will sense the surrounding environment. If an interested target is captured, node j will set its evaluation result $e_j = 1$ (successful) and broadcast the result to its neighbours. A successful node will remain active for another round. Otherwise, it will set $e_j = 0$ (failure) and switch to sleep mode in the next round. Nodes that switch from active mode to sleep mode will sleep for a random duration, which is again bounded by t_{S_max}.

A node in listen mode will count the number of neighbours with positive results (i.e. n_{sa}). Given n_{sa}, the probability for a node in listen mode to switch to active mode is

$$\text{Prob(Active)} = \begin{cases} 1, & n_{sa} \leq c_1 \\ (c_2 - n_{sa})/(c_2 - c_1), & c_1 < n_{sa} \leq c_2 \\ 0, & n_{sa} > c_2 \end{cases} \qquad (19.1)$$

Similarly, the probability for a node in listen mode to switch back to sleep mode is

$$\text{Prob(Sleep)} = \begin{cases} 0, & n_{sa} \leq c_1 \\ (n_{sa} - c_1)/(c_2 - c_1), & c_1 < n_{sa} \leq c_2 \\ 1, & n_{sa} > c_2 \end{cases} \qquad (19.2)$$

Here, c_i, where $i = 1,2$ are tuning parameters provided that $c_1 \leq c_2$. An illustration on (19.1) and (19.2) is shown in Figure 19.1. A flow diagram of the bio-inspired scheduling scheme is shown in Figure 19.2.

Rationale behind (19.1) and (19.2) is as follows. A low value of n_{sa} indicates a network is lacking of active sensing units. Therefore, nodes in listen mode should turn active and perform target detection. A system with surplus sensing power will have a high value of n_{sa}. Under such situation, nodes in listen mode should switch back to sleep mode to conserve energy.

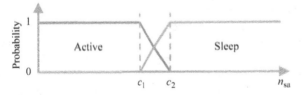

Figure 19.1   In a network with the scheduling scheme discussed in Section 19.3, the probabilities for a node in listen mode to switch to active or sleep modes

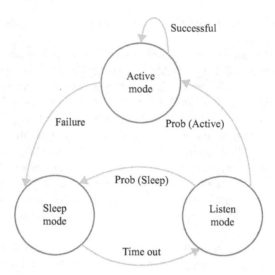

Figure 19.2   A flow diagram of the scheduling scheme discussed in Section 19.3

19.4   Scheduling scheme for wireless sensor networks with co-operative transmissions

In this section, an extended version of the scheduling scheme proposed in Section 19.3 is revisited [17]. The section will start with an example on a common drawback of typical on-off scheduling schemes. The example clearly shows the reasons for using the concepts of co-operative diversity in the extended version. Afterward, mechanisms of the extended scheduling scheme are discussed.

19.4.1   Co-operative diversity

This work is an extension to the scheduling scheme proposed in Section 19.3. In the scheme discussed in Section 19.3, wireless sensor nodes switch on and off depending on their neighbour's states. A common drawback of on-off scheduling schemes is that multi-hop communications are not always applicable as intermediate nodes are switching on and off from time to time [18]. To overcome such problem, a network can carry out data aggregation periodically by halting the scheduling scheme and turning on all the nodes. Such approach, however, limits a WSN to non-real-time applications.

Making wireless sensor nodes to communicate with the base station directly can be an option. In such a way, nodes with large separations from the base station will have to increase their transmission power in order to compensate losses due to fading and poor channel conditions. The RF power amplifier of a wireless sensor node may not be able to satisfy such a heavy demand. A high bit error rate at the receiver side can be resulted and retransmissions are required. The corresponding energy consumption can be huge and will drain the battery quickly [19]. The problem can be visualized with the following example.

Example 19.1 Suppose a wireless sensor node is equipped with a CC2420 transceiver [20] which uses O-QPSK modulation. The corresponding bit error rate (BER) is given by

$$\text{BER} = \frac{1}{2}\text{erfc}\left(\sqrt{\frac{E_b}{N_0}}\right) \tag{19.3}$$

Here, E_b is the energy per bit, N_0 is the noise spectral density, and erfc() is the complementary error function. From Reference 21, E_b/N_0 is expressed as

$$\frac{E_b}{N_0} = 7.6007 \times 10^{(E(P_{RX})+94)/10} \tag{19.4}$$

where $E(P_{RX})$ is the expected received power in dBm which is expressed as

$$E(P_{RX}) = P_{TX}(l) - \left(E(PL) + 10\log\left(\frac{d}{d_0}\right)^n\right) \tag{19.5}$$

Here, $P_{TX}(l)$ is the transmission power at the lth level, $E(PL)$ is the expected path loss in dB from a reference distance $d_0 = 1$ m, n is the path loss exponent and d is the communication distance. Furthermore, $E(PL)$ is expressed as

$$E(PL) = 10\log_{10}\left(\frac{(4\pi d_0)^2 L}{G_T G_R \lambda^2}\right) \tag{19.6}$$

where G_T and G_R are the transmitter and receiver antenna gains respectively, L is the system loss factor and λ is the wavelength. Consider a wireless sensor node which is trying to transmit a message of $a = 208$ bits to a base station. The node and the base station are separated by distance of d m. To ensure the base station can receive the message, the wireless sensor node will send the same message repeatedly using its maximum transmission power (i.e. $P_{TX}(8)$). The base station is equipped with a majority logic decoder that will start decoding once the first message is received. The decoding BERs at the base station side against the number of received packets are shown in Figure 19.3.

Example 19.1 shows that due to retransmissions, energy consumptions of nodes located remotely from a base station can be several times higher than their counterparts. Such phenomenon can lead to an uneven distribution of loading across a network and shorten its lifetime. The problem can be alleviated when utilizing co-operative diversity concepts. Besides the source node, a set of co-operative nodes can relay the same message to the base station repeatedly in an interleaved manner. The loadings due to retransmissions can therefore be distributed among a set of nodes. Unlike the co-operative mechanisms in References 22–25, the approach mentioned above only required nodes to be synchronized at the packet level.

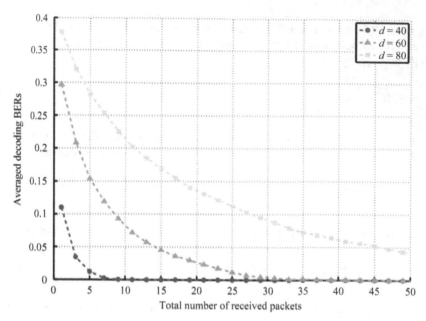

Figure 19.3   Averaged decoding BERs at the base station with different values of d, where $GT = GR = L = 1$, $n = 4$, and $\lambda \approx 0.125$

19.4.2   Mechanisms

In the extended scheduling scheme, a wireless sensor node is allowed to switch among four different operation modes, namely a sleep mode, a listen mode, an active mode and a co-operative mode. Similar to the scheme discussed in Section 19.3, the scheme is operated in a discrete time unit called *rounds*. A node can only switch its mode at the end of each round.

The scheme started by putting all sensor nodes into sleep mode with random sleeping durations t_S, which is upper bounded by t_{S_max}. A time-out event will trigger a sleeping node to switch into listen mode. A node in listen mode will monitor the communications nearby and collect evaluation results e_j from its neighbours [26]. In the extended version, nodes in both active and co-operative modes will broadcast their evaluation results to their neighbours. The content of an evaluation result indicates the successfulness of a node in its previous round.

A node in active mode will perform sensing. If a target can be detected, the node will classify itself as successful and broadcast a positive evaluation result to its neighbours. It will also try to report its sensing information to the base station. A successful active node will stay active for the next round. However, if no target is detected, an active node will switch to sleep mode in the next round. A node in co-operative mode will monitor the communications nearby. Whenever sensing information is captured, it will decode and forward the information to the base station. A node in co-operative mode will classify itself as successful if it can capture any sensing information from its active neighbours. A successful node in co-operative mode will broadcast a positive evaluation result to its neighbours. In contrast, an unsuccessful node will return to sleep mode.

A node in listen mode will count the number of neighbours with positive result n_{sa}. Given n_{sa}, the probability for a node in listen mode to switch to active mode is

$$\text{Prob(Active)} = \begin{cases} 1, & n_{sa} \leq c_3 \\ (c_4 - n_{sa})/(c_4 - c_3), & c_3 < n_{sa} \leq c_4 \\ 0, & n_{sa} > c_4 \end{cases} \qquad (19.7)$$

Similarly, the probability for a node in listen mode to switch to co-operative mode is

$$\text{Prob(Co - op)} = \begin{cases} 0, & n_{sa} \leq c_3 \\ (n_{sa} - c_3)/(c_4 - c_3), & c_3 < n_{sa} \leq c_4 \\ 1, & c_4 < n_{sa} \leq c_5 \\ (c_6 - n_{sa})/(c_6 - c_5), & c_5 < n_{sa} \leq c_6 \\ 0, & n_{sa} \leq c_6 \end{cases} \qquad (19.8)$$

Finally, the probability for a node in listen mode to switch back to sleep mode is

$$\text{Prob(Sleep)} = \begin{cases} 0, & n_{sa} \leq c_5 \\ (n_{sa} - c_5)/(c_6 - c_5), & c_5 < n_{sa} \leq c_6 \\ 1, & n_{sa} > c_6 \end{cases} \qquad (19.9)$$

Here, c_i, where $i = 3, \ldots, 6$ are tuning parameters provided that $c_3 \leq c_4 \leq c_5 \leq c_6$. An illustration on (19.7), (19.8) and (19.9) is shown in Figure 19.4. A flow diagram of the extended scheme is shown in Figure 19.5.

The rationale behind (19.7) and (19.9) is the same as in (19.1) and (19.2) respectively. Note that a moderate value of n_{sa} shows that the surrounding area is having enough sensing power. Adding extra active units will not provide significant improvement in target detection but increase energy consumption. Nodes in listen mode therefore switch into co-operative mode and help active nodes to relay their message to the base station through co-operative diversity. A high value of n_{sa} indicates the area is populated with successful nodes in active and co-operative modes. Under such situation, nodes in listen mode should reduce energy consumption by switching into sleep mode.

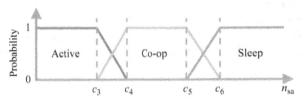

Figure 19.4   *In a network with the scheduling scheme discussed in Section 19.4, the probabilities for a node in listen mode to switch to active, cooperative, or sleep modes*

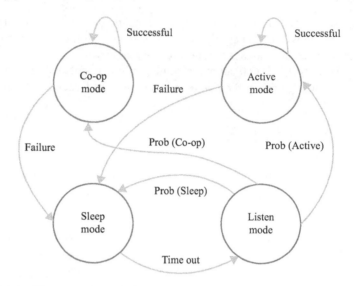

Figure 19.5   Flow diagram of the extended scheduling scheme discussed in Section 19.4

19.5   Simulation

The effects of the constants c_1 to c_6 to the performance of the scheduling schemes discussed in Sections 19.3 and 19.4 are evaluated using computer simulations. To ease the evaluation process, four performance indicators, namely target hit-rate (THR), detection delay (DD), energy consumption per successful detection (ECSD) and energy consumption distribution (ECD), are employed. Their definitions are shown as follows:

- THR is defined as the ratio of total time (in terms of rounds) that a target is detected by at least three nodes simultaneously to the total time that a target is moving within the sensing terrain.
- DD is defined as the time difference (in terms of rounds) between a target that enters the terrain and the time when it is first detected by at least three nodes simultaneously.
- ECSD is defined as the total energy consumption of the network divided by the time (in terms of rounds) a target is detected by at least three nodes simultaneously.
- ECD is defined as the standard deviations in the residual energy among nodes. It indicates how even the loading is distributed among the nodes.

The simulation settings and the simulation results are presented below.

19.5.1   Simulation settings

The simulations are conducted in Matlab. In each simulation, $N = [300,700]$ wireless sensor nodes are deployed randomly into a sensing field of $180 \times 180 \text{ m}^2$.

The base station is located at the centre of the terrain (i.e. (90,90) m). Each node is given an initial energy of 12420 J (i.e. $\approx$ 2 AA-size alkaline batteries). The base station is assumed to be an energy unlimited device and it can communicate with all the nodes within the sensing terrain. An interested target is moving across the terrain horizontally with a velocity of 3 m/round. The maximum sensing range of each sensor is 24 m. The energy model used in the simulation is given in Appendix A.

Simulations are conducted for different values of $t_{S\_max} = [8,16,24,32]$ to observe its relations with THR, DD, ECSD and ECD. In the original scheduling scheme, nodes are only allowed to switch among sleep mode, listen mode and active mode. Nodes in active mode will, therefore, send data to the base station by themselves. In the extended version, nodes in active mode will send data to the base station with their co-operative neighbours in an interleaved manner. In both schemes, the nodes will keep on sending their data until an acknowledgement is received from the base station [27]. Different combinations of c_1 to c_6 are used to study their effects on the performances of a scheduling scheme. Values of the constants used in both schemes are shown in Tables 19.1 and 19.2. The results presented in this chapter are the averaged values obtained from 100 independent simulations.

19.5.2   Simulation results

Simulation results are presented in Tables 19.3 and 19.4. In general, when t_{S_max} is increased, more nodes will be operated in sleep mode. Therefore, as t_{S_max} increases, THR decreases linearly at the same time (see Tables 19.3(a) and 19.4(a)). An increase in t_{S_max} will also lead to higher values of DD as the probability for a target to be detected by three nodes simultaneously is decreased. Again, t_{S_max} and DD are showing a linear relationship (see Tables 19.3(b) and 19.4(b)). Putting more nodes into sleep mode can reduce energy consumption of a network. However, putting more nodes into sleep mode will have negative impacts on target detection

Table 19.1   *Values of the constants c_1 and c_2*
              used in the scheduling scheme

Set	$\{c_1, c_2\}$
1-1	$\{0.5, 1.5\}$
1-2	$\{1.5, 2.5\}$

Table 19.2   *Values of the constants c_3 and c_6*
              used in the scheduling scheme

Set	$\{c_3, c_4, c_5, c_6\}$
2-1	$\{0.5, 1.5, 1.5, 2.5\}$
2-2	$\{0.5, 1.5, 2.5, 3.5\}$
2-3	$\{1.5, 2.5, 2.5, 3.5\}$

Table 19.3   Simulation results (THRs, DDs, ECSDs and ECDs) of networks with
           N = 300

(a) THRs

	t_{S_max}			
	8	16	24	32
Extended, Set 2-1	97.62	92.32	84.18	73.48
Extended, Set 2-2	96.90	92.32	84.69	77.52
Extended, Set 2-3	98.16	95.87	90.99	86.3
Original, Set 1-1	97.72	92.73	85.51	79.21
Original, Set 1-2	98.31	94.98	91.45	85.27

(b) DDs

	t_{S_max}			
	8	16	24	32
Extended, Set 2-1	0.685	1.712	2.450	3.965
Extended, Set 2-2	0.738	1.588	2.912	3.450
Extended, Set 2-3	0.708	1.312	2.308	2.885
Original, Set 1-1	0.719	1.738	2.981	3.212
Original, Set 1-2	0.658	1.746	2.381	2.935

(c) ECSDs

	t_{S_max}			
	8	16	24	32
Extended, Set 2-1	12.70	8.57	6.94	6.37
Extended, Set 2-2	12.74	8.53	6.90	6.05
Extended, Set 2-3	13.35	8.78	6.84	5.81
Original, Set 1-1	12.89	8.64	6.92	6.00
Original, Set 1-2	13.49	8.93	6.86	5.85

(d) ECDs

	t_{S_max}			
	8	16	24	32
Extended, Set 2-1	6.03	5.00	4.18	3.82
Extended, Set 2-2	5.90	5.04	4.29	3.83
Etended, Set 2-3	6.47	5.45	4.92	4.48
Original, Set 1-1	6.18	5.05	4.37	4.07
Original, Set 1-2	6.68	5.80	4.94	4.58

capabilities. Parameter t_{S_max} and ECSD are having an inverse relationship (see Tables 19.3(c) and 19.4(c)). The reduction in ECSD becomes less gradual as t_{S_max} increases. Large values of t_{S_max} put more nodes into sleep mode and thus yield lower values of ECD.

From the simulation results, it can be observed that with an appropriate combination of control constants (i.e. c_1 to c_6), networks with the extended scheduling scheme discussed in Section 19.4 can yield almost the same THRs, DDs, and ECSDs as networks with the original scheduling scheme discussed in Section 19.3. Nevertheless, with the introduction of the co-operative mode, the loading of nodes

Table 19.4   Simulation results (THRs, DDs, ECSDs and ECDs) of networks with N = 700

(a) THRs

	t_{S_max}			
	8	16	24	32
Extended, Set 2-1	99.73	99.09	98.50	97.34
Extended, Set 2-2	99.68	99.02	98.05	96.80
Extended, Set 2-3	99.70	99.07	98.64	97.34
Original, Set 1-1	99.64	99.05	97.95	97.11
Original, Set 1-2	99.66	99.05	98.45	97.55

(b) DDs

	t_{S_max}			
	8	16	24	32
Extended, Set 2-1	0.114	0.371	0.562	0.990
Extended, Set 2-2	0.133	0.410	0.781	1.190
Extended, Set 2-3	0.124	0.390	0.571	1.086
Original, Set 1-1	0.152	0.400	0.800	1.124
Original, Set 1-2	0.143	0.400	0.619	0.933

(c) ECSDs

	t_{S_max}			
	8	16	24	32
Extended, Set 2-1	28.91	18.47	13.72	11.13
Extended, Set 2-2	28.88	18.45	13.78	11.16
Extended, Set 2-3	30.41	19.53	14.47	11.75
Original, Set 1-1	29.37	18.63	13.85	11.17
Original, Set 1-2	30.71	19.66	14.60	11.82

(d) ECDs

	t_{S_max}			
	8	16	24	32
Extended, Set 2-1	4.74	3.97	3.51	3.11
Extended, Set 2-2	4.69	3.95	3.43	3.12
Extended, Set 2-3	5.40	4.30	3.90	3.66
Original, Set 1-1	4.76	4.15	3.63	3.31
Original, Set 1-2	5.43	4.31	4.06	3.83

in active mode can be partially off-loaded and thus yield better load distributions (see Tables 19.3(d) and 19.4(d)).

Since the sensing terrain is fixed, a higher value of N will increase the density of a network. As expected, networks with higher values of N can yield higher THRs and lower DDs. As the node density increases, information exchanges among nodes increase. Such extra overheads cause the ECSD to increase. Nevertheless, an increase in node density will increase the number of evaluation results received by nodes in listen mode. In the extended version, this will recruit more nodes into co-operative mode and yield lower values of ECDs.

19.6   Discussion

In the original version, constant c_1 controls the width of the ACTIVE fuzzy set. The same fuzzy set in the extended version is controlled by c_3. The wider the set, the more nodes in listen mode will switch to active mode. From the simulation results, it can be observed that in networks with a wider ACTIVE fuzzy set (sets 1-2 and 2-3), their corresponding ECSDs are higher than their counterparts. Furthermore, for those nodes operating in active mode, their energy consumptions will be relatively higher than those in other modes. A high number of nodes in active mode will increase ECDs. From Tables 19.3(d) and 19.4(d), it can be observed that networks with fuzzy sets 1-2 and 2-3 are having higher values of ECDs than the others. For networks with the fuzzy set 2-3, although some of the nodes are operating in co-op mode, the number of nodes in co-op mode is relatively small when compared with those in active mode. The nodes in co-op mode cannot distribute the workload of their neighbours in active mode in an effective way. Some of the nodes in co-op mode are overloaded by their active neighbours and further increase the ECD value of the network. Putting more nodes into active mode can, on the other hand, improve target detection capabilities of a network. From Tables 19.3(a) and (b), and 19.4(a) and (b), networks with fuzzy sets 1-2 and 2-3 are having high values of THRs and low values of DDs. Therefore, c_1 in the original version and c_3 in the extended version can be used to control trade-offs between energy consumption and target detection capability of a WSN.

The CO-OP fuzzy set exists only in the extended version. The width of the CO-OP fuzzy set is mainly controlled by constants c_4 and c_5. To obtain a low value of ECD, the number of nodes in the co-operative mode should be large enough, such that the transmission burdens can be distributed evenly. The ECD values of networks with the fuzzy set 2-2 are shown to be the lowest, when the CO-OP fuzzy set is much wider than that of the ACTIVE fuzzy set (see Tables 19.3(d) and 19.4(d)). As mentioned before, a narrow CO-OP fuzzy set will, on the other hand, introduce a more uneven distribution of energy consumption. The width of the CO-OP fuzzy does not show significant effects on THR and DD values as both values are mainly controlled by the number of nodes in active mode. By introducing the extra fuzzy set, networks with the extended scheduling scheme can always obtain lower values of ECD than those with the original scheduling scheme. Although the extra fuzzy set will put more nodes out of their sleep mode, nodes in co-op mode may be located closer to the Base Station (BS) than their neighbours in active mode. These co-op nodes can, therefore, have lower values of Packet Error Rate (PER) and help reducing the number of retransmissions required. From Tables 19.3(c) and 19.4(c), comparing with the original scheduling scheme, it can be observed that networks with the extended scheduling scheme can obtain the same or even lower values of ECSD at most of the time.

A low value of c_2 in the original version or a low value of c_6 in the extended version will shift the SLEEP fuzzy set to the left. That will cause more nodes in the listen mode to switch back to sleep mode. Networks with fuzzy sets 1-1 and 2-1 can yield low values of ECSDs. Note that c_6 of set 2-1 is higher than c_2 in set 1-1.

Therefore, in networks with fuzzy set 1-1, more nodes will be put into sleep mode. For networks with low densities, shifting the SLEEP fuzzy set to the left will reduce the detection capability of a network. On the other hand, for high-density networks, such practices can avoid having surplus sensing power. Furthermore, as t_{S_max} increases, having too many nodes in sleep mode can have negative effects on THR and DD values (see Tables 19.3(a) and(b), and 19.4(a) and (b) for $t_{S\_max} = 32$ rounds). Parameters c_2 and c_6 are desirable for high-density networks to control their ECSD.

19.7　Future developments

The scheduling schemes discussed in this chapter are trying to obtain reasonable trade-offs between energy consumption and target detection capability of a network. Wireless sensor nodes are co-operating with their neighbours to make their mode switching decisions. In fact, the scheduling issues during transmissions are not yet considered. For applications on target detection and tracking, wireless sensor nodes should obtain transmission schedules which can avoid collisions and interferences, while at the same time minimize the delay in a data collection process. In Reference 28, the authors of the scheduling schemes in References 13 and 26 proposed a delay-aware data collection network structure for WSNs. The idea of the proposed network structure organizes nodes into multiple layers, such that child nodes can communicate with their parent nodes in an interleaved manner. In Reference 28, two network formation algorithms are proposed. In such a project, data collected from different nodes are assumed to be 100 per cent fusible, such that multiple data packets can be fused into one using in-network data fusion algorithms. The idea was further analysed in Reference 29. In Reference 29, Cheng and Tse considered WSNs with rapid data collection processes. It is observed that consecutive data collection processes can be carried out by partial overlapping transmission schedules and adjusting clusters' sizes. In Reference 30, Cheng *et al.* considered scenarios when in-network data fusion does not yield any reduction in outgoing data sizes. A special network structure is designed such that the duration of a data collection process will not be greatly increased even when in-network data fusion is not applicable. All these delay-aware network structures can be incorporated with the scheduling schemes discussed in this chapter to enhance the detection and tracking capabilities of a WSN.

19.8　Conclusion

In this chapter, two bio-inspired scheduling schemes for WSNs are revisited and discussed. The early version of the bio-inspired scheduling scheme is capable of maintaining a balance between energy consumption and target detection capability of a network. The scheme can operate in a fully decentralized manner and is highly adaptive to changes in network densities. The scheme is a kind of adaptive periodic on-off scheduling scheme. In a network with an on-off scheduling scheme, multi-hop connections among wireless sensor nodes and a base station may not exist all the time.

High numbers of retransmissions are required for nodes, which are located remotely from base stations and thus introduce an uneven load distribution. In the extended version, concepts of co-operative diversity are introduced. Some nodes are dynamically assigned to operate in a co-operative mode. Their role is to off-load transmission burdens from their active neighbours by relaying data (of their active neighbours) to the base station in an interleaved manner. Both scheduling schemes can be further fine-tuned by adjusting some control parameters. Computer simulations were used to analyse the effects of the parameters to the performances of both scheduling schemes.

Appendix A

The energy model used in Section 19.5 is a modified version of the one proposed in References 26, 31 and 32. This model considers all the energy consumptions due to overheads and data processing. In general, a wireless sensor node can be regarded as a device of three major modules, namely the sensor module, the computation module and the communication module. Depending on the operating mode of a sensor node, each of these modules will consume different amount of energy. In an idling mode, a node will turn all its modules into power saving mode. The energy consumption of a node in the idling mode E_i is

$$E_i = \tau_i v_{cc}(i_{comm\_d} + i_{comp\_d} + i_{sen\_d}) \tag{A.1}$$

where τ_i is the duration of the idling mode and v_{cc} is the supply voltage. Here, i_{comm_d}, i_{comp_d} and i_{sen_d} are the current drawn by the communication, the computation and the sensor modules in their power down states respectively.

During a transmitting mode, a node will turn on its communication and computation modules. Suppose a data packet is α-bit long and the transceiver is operating at a data rate of β bit/s, a wireless sensor node will take $t_t = \alpha/\beta$ s to transmit a packet. Each node has a finite number of output power levels. As long as a desired signal-to-noise (SNR) ratio can be maintained at the receiving side, a node can conserve energy by reducing its transmission power [33]. The energy consumption of a node in the transmitting mode with its output power programmed to the hth level, i.e. $E_t(h)$, is expressed as

$$E_t(h) = E_{t\_OH}(h) + \tau_t v_{cc}(i_{comm\_t}(h) + i_{comp\_a} + i_{sen\_d}) \tag{A.2}$$

where $E_{t\_OH}(h)$ is the total overhead energy consumed by the communication and computation modules to switch between idle and active modes. Here, $i_{comm\_t}(h)$ is the current drawn by a communication module when it is transmitting with its output power programmed at the hth level and i_{comp_a} is the current drawn by a computation module when it is active.

On the other hand, the energy E_r consumed by a parent node to receive a data packet from one of its child nodes is expressed as

$$E_r = E_{r\_OH} + \tau_r v_{cc}(i_{comm\_r} + i_{comp\_a} + i_{sen\_d}) \tag{A.3}$$

where E_{r_OH} is the total overhead energy consumed by the communication and computation modules to switch between idle and active modes. Here, i_{comm_r} is the current drawn by a communication module while it is monitoring a communication channel. A parent node will take τ_p s to process data of a'–bit long, the corresponding energy consumption, i.e. E_p, is expressed as

$$E_p = E_{p\_OH} + \tau_p v_{cc}(i_{trx\_d} + i_{mcu\_a} + i_{sen\_d}) \tag{A.4}$$

where E_{p_OH} is the overhead energy consumed by the computation module to switch between idle and active modes. The parameters are selected based on a MICAz node [34], which consists of a CC2420 transceiver [20] and an ATmega128L microcontroller [35]. Values of the parameters are listed in Table A.1.

Table A.1   *Parameters used in the energy model*

Description	Parameter	Value
Data packet size	a	1024 (bits)
Data rate	β	250 (kbps)
Supply voltage	v_{cc}	3 (V)
Current drawn by the communication module (power down)	i_{comm_d}	2×10^{-5} (A)
Current drawn by the computation module (power down)	i_{comp_d}	3×10^{-7} (A)
Current drawn by the sensor module (power down)	i_{sen_d}	~0 (A)
Current drawn by the communication module (TX)	$i_{comm\_t}(1)$	8.5×10^{-6} (A)
	$i_{comm\_t}(2)$	9.9×10^{-6} (A)
	$i_{comm\_t}(3)$	11.2×10^{-6} (A)
	$i_{comm\_t}(4)$	12.5×10^{-6} (A)
	$i_{comm\_t}(5)$	13.9×10^{-6} (A)
	$i_{comm\_t}(6)$	15.2×10^{-6} (A)
	$i_{comm\_t}(7)$	16.5×10^{-6} (A)
	$i_{comm\_t}(8)$	17.4×10^{-6} (A)
Current drawn by the communication module (RX)	i_{comm_r}	18.8×10^{-6} (A)
Current drawn by the computation module (active)	i_{comp_a}	8×10^{-6} (A)
Overhead energy consumed by the comm. module (TX↔idle)	$E_{t\_OH}(1)$	0.293×10^{-4} (J)
	$E_{t\_OH}(2)$	0.297×10^{-4} (J)
	$E_{t\_OH}(3)$	0.301×10^{-4} (J)
	$E_{t\_OH}(4)$	0.304×10^{-4} (J)
	$E_{t\_OH}(5)$	0.308×10^{-4} (J)
	$E_{t\_OH}(6)$	0.312×10^{-4} (J)
	$E_{t\_OH}(7)$	0.316×10^{-4} (J)
	$E_{t\_OH}(8)$	0.319×10^{-4} (J)
Overhead energy consumed by the communication module (RX↔idle)	E_{r_OH}	0.3226×10^{-6}
Overhead energy consumed by the computation module (active↔idle)	E_{p_OH}	0.2605×10^{-6}
Time difference $\tau_r - \tau_t$	$\tau_r - \tau_t$	4.0 (ms)
Processing time	τ_p	6.5 (ms)

References

1. Farina A., Golino G., Capponi A., and Pilotto C. 'Surveillance by means of a random sensor network: A heterogeneous sensor approach'. *Proceedings of the 8th International Conference on Information Fusion*, (Fusion 2005); Rome, Italy, July 2005, vol.2, pp. 1086–1092
2. Benavoli A. and Chisci L. 'Towards optimal energy-quality tradeoff in tracking via sensor networks'. *Proceedings of the European Control Conference, (ECC '07)*; Kos, Greece, July 2007, pp. 1523–1529
3. Pattem S., Poduri S., and Krishnamachari B. 'Energy-quality tradeoffs for target tracking in wireless sensor networks'. *Proceedings of the 2nd International Conference on Information Processing in Sensor Networks, (IPSN'03)*; Palo Alto, CA, USA, April 2003, pp. 32–46
4. Turau V. and Weyer C. 'Scheduling transmission of bulk data in sensor networks using a dynamic TDMA protocol'. *Proceedings of the 2007 International Conference on Mobile Data Management*; Mannheim, Germany, May 2007, pp. 321–325
5. Hohlt B., Doherty L., and Brewer E. 'Flexible power scheduling for sensor networks'. *Proceedings of the 3rd International Symposium on Information Processing in Sensor Networks, 2004, (IPSN 2004)*; Berkeley, CA, USA, April 2004, pp. 205–214
6. Decker C., Riedel T., Peev E., and Beigl M. 'Adaptation of on-line scheduling strategies for sensor network platforms'. *Proceedings of the 2006 IEEE International Conference on Mobile Adhoc and Sensor Systems (MASS);* Vancouver, BC, Canada, October 2006, pp. 534–537
7. Chamberland J.F. and Veeravalli V. 'The art of sleeping in wireless sensing systems'. *Proceedings of the 2003 IEEE Workshop on Statistical Signal Processing*; St. Louis, MO, USA, September 2003, pp. 17–20
8. Rago C., Willett P., and Bar-Shalom Y. 'Censoring sensors: A low-communication-rate scheme for distributed detection', *IEEE Transactions on Aerospace and Electronic Systems*, April 1996, vol. 32 no. 2, pp. 554–568
9. Ye F., Zhong G., Lu S., and Zhang L. 'Geography-informed energy conservation for Ad-Hoc routing'. *Proceedings of the 10th IEEE International Conference Network Protocols (ICNP 2002)*, Paris, France, November 2002, pp. 2000–2001
10. Lu H.F., Chang Y.C., Hu H.H., and Chen J.L. 'Power-efficient scheduling method in sensor networks'. *Proceedings of the 2004 IEEE International Conference on Systems, Man and Cybernetics (SMC 2004)*; Taipei, Taiwan, October 2004, vol. 5 pp. 4705–4710
11. Cerpa A. and Estrin D. 'ASCENT: Adaptive self-configuring sensor networks topologies'. *IEEE Transactions on Mobile Computing*, July 2004, vol. 3(3), pp. 272–285
12. Nath S. and Gibbons P.B. 'Communicating via fireflies: Geographic routing on duty-cycled sensors'. *Proceedings of the 6th International Symposium of*

Information Processing in Sensor Networks (IPSN 2007); Cambridge, MA, USA, April 2007, pp. 440–449

13. Cheng C.T., Tse C.K., and Lau F.C.M. 'A scheduling scheme for wireless sensor networks based on social insect colonies'. *IET Communications*, May 2009, vol. 3(5), pp. 714 –722

14. Gordon D.M. 'The organization of work in social insect colonies'. *Nature*, March 1996, vol. 380(6570), pp. 121–124

15. Gordon D.M. and Mehdiabadi N.J. 'Encounter rate and task allocation in harvester ants'. *Behavioral Ecology and Sociobiology*, 1999, vol. 45 pp. 370–377

16. Gordon D.M. 'Behavioral flexibility and the foraging ecology of seed-eating ants'. *The American Naturalist*, 1991, vol. 138(2), pp. 379–411

17. Cheng C.T. and Leung H. 'A cooperative transmission protocol for wireless sensor networks with on-off scheduling schemes'. *Proceedings of the 14th International Conference on Information Fusion (FUSION 2011)*; Chicago, IL, USA, July 2011, pp. 1–7

18. Zahedi S., Srivastava M.B., Bisdikian C., and Kaplan L.M. 'Quality tradeoffs in object tracking with duty-cycled sensor networks'. *Proceedings of the IEEE 31st Real-Time Systems Symposium, (RTSS 2010)*; San Diego, CA, USA, November 2010, pp. 160–169

19. Alamouti S.M. 'A simple transmit diversity technique for wireless communications'. *IEEE Journal on Selected Areas in Communications*, 1998, vol. 16(8), pp. 1451–1458

20. CC2420 2.4 GHz IEEE 802.15.4/ZigBee-ready RF transceiver. Texas Instruments. [Online]. Available from http://focus.ti.com/ [Accessed January 2013]

21. Howitt I. and Wang J. 'Energy efficient power control policies for the low rate WPAN'. *Proceedings of the 1st Annual IEEE Communications Society Conference on Sensor and Ad-Hoc Communications and Networks, (SECON 2004)*; Santa Clara, CA, USA, October 2004, pp. 527–536

22. Laneman J.N., Tse D.N.C., and Wornell G.W. 'Cooperative diversity in wireless networks: efficient protocols and outage behavior'. *IEEE Transactions on Information Theory*, 2004, vol. 50(12), pp. 3062–3080

23. Li X., Chen M., and Liu W. 'Cooperative transmissions in wireless sensor networks with imperfect synchronization'. *Proceedings of the 38th Asilomar Conference on Signals, Systems & Computers*; Pacific Grove, CA, USA, November 2004, vol. 1 pp. 1281–1285

24. Hong Y.W. and Scaglione A. 'Energy-efficient broadcasting with cooperative transmissions in wireless sensor networks'. *IEEE Transactions on Wireless Communications*, 2006, vol. 5(10), pp. 2844–2855

25. Kailas A., Thanayankizil L.V., and Ingram M.A. 'A simple cooperative transmission protocol for energy-efficient broadcasting over multi-hop wireless networks'. *Computing Research Repository*, 2009, arXiv:0903.1675

26. Cheng C.T., Tse C.K., and Lau F.C.M. 'An energy-aware scheduling scheme for wireless sensor networks'. *IEEE Transactions on Vehicular Technology*, 2010, vol. 59(7), pp. 3427–3444

27. Sun D.C., Yi K.C., and Li X.H. 'A new space time cooperative diversity scheme based on simple feedback'. *Proceedings of the International Conference on Advanced Information Networking and Applications (AINA '09)*; Bradford, UK, May 2009, pp. 638–643

28. Cheng C.T., Tse C.K., and Lau F.C.M. 'A delay-aware data collection network structure for wireless sensor networks'. *IEEE Sensors Journal*, 2011, vol. 11(3), pp. 699–710

29. Cheng C.T. and Tse C.K. 'An analysis on the delay-aware data collection network structure using Pareto optimality'. *Proceedings of the 2012 International Conference on Cyber-Enabled Distributed Computing and Knowledge Discovery (CyberC 2012)*; Sanya, Hainan, China, October 2012, pp. 348–352

30. Cheng C.T., Leung H., and Maupin P. 'Delay-Aware Network Structure for Wireless Sensor Networks With In-Network Data Fusion'. *IEEE Sensors Journal*, 2013, vol. 13(5), pp. 1622–1631

31. Schmidt D., Krämer M., Kuhn T., and Wehn N. 'Energy modelling in sensor networks'. *Advances in Radio Science*, 2007, vol. 5 pp. 347–351

32. Karkvandi H.R., Pecht E., and Yadid-Pecht O. 'Effective lifetime-aware routing in wireless sensor networks'. *IEEE Sensors Journal*, 2011, vol. 11 (12), pp. 3359–3367

33. Wang Q., Hempstead M., and Yang W. 'A realistic power consumption model for wireless sensor network devices'. *Proceedings of the 2006 3rd Annual IEEE Communications Society on Sensor and Ad-Hoc Communications and Networks (SECON '06)*; Reston, VA, USA, September 2006, vol. 1 pp. 286–295

34. MICAz wireless measurement system. Crossbow Technology, Inc. [Online]. Available from http://www.xbow.com/ [Accessed January 2013]

35. ATmega128L 8-bit AVR microcontroller with 128K bytes in-system programmable flash. Atmel Corporation. [Online]. Available from http://www. atmel.com/ [Accessed January 2013]

Index

Printed in the USA
CPSIA information can be obtained
at www.ICGtesting.com
JSHW052345231024
R13776900001B/R137769PG72173JSX00001B/1

9 781849 196475